Recent Advances in Information Science and Technology

Recent Advances in Information Science and Technology

Nikos E. Mastorakis
(Editor)
Military Institutions of University Education
Hellenic Naval Academy, Greece

World Scientific
Singapore • New Jersey • London • Hong Kong

Published by

World Scientific Publishing Co. Pte. Ltd.

P O Box 128, Farrer Road, Singapore 912805

USA office: Suite 1B, 1060 Main Street, River Edge, NJ 07661

UK office: 57 Shelton Street, Covent Garden, London WC2H 9HE

British Library Cataloguing-in-Publication Data
A catalogue record for this book is available from the British Library.

RECENT ADVANCES IN INFORMATION SCIENCE AND TECHNOLOGY

ISBN 981-02-3657-3

This book is printed on acid-free paper.

Printed in Singapore by Uto-Print

To Maria

Preface

The revolution of information science and technology has swayed all the aspects of modern life. This book attempts to give a panoramic view of the most promising areas of modern computer science and engineering. Software engineering, computer languages, hardware engineering, VLSI design, computer networks, communications, Internet, signal processing, image processing, multidimensional systems, advanced numerical techniques are the main topics of this textbook.

This rich "anthology of papers" which compose this volume, contains the latest developments and reflects the experience of many eminent researchers working in different environments (universities, research centers and industry).

The book is divided into several parts

- *Software Engineering*. This part includes new trends and recent scientific results in software engineering, data structures, algorithms, knowledge based systems, VLSI design, computer languages, industrial computer applications etc.
- *Signal Processing*. In this part, modern topics in signal processing, identification, recognition, speech processing, detection etc. are presented.
- *Multi-Dimensional (m-D) Systems Theory and Applications*. At the beginning, this part contains some papers on research topics of *m*-D systems theory (one column format). Afterwards, other excellent research results in *m*-D systems theory are given. Finally, this Part finishes with some impressive applications of multidimensional systems mainly in signal processing
- *Communication Systems*. This Part covers modern topics of communication: Digital systems of communication, computer networks theory, ATM networks, optical networks, hybrid fiber coaxial networks, Internet, etc.
- *Modern Numerical Techniques and Related Topics*. This Part is devoted to some aspects of the computation science and technology.

I am grateful to all authors for the willingness with which responded to my invitation to present their recent research results as well as in many cases to give excellent surveys on the topics of their interest. I am sure that their efforts to provide high quality contributions will be appreciated by the electrical-electronics, telecommunication and computer engineers as well as by the applied mathematicians, physicists and other scientists.

I am also convinced that the book will be a source of knowledge and inspiration for all researchers and practitioners working or interested in the area of computer science and engineering.

I wish to thank Professor Emmanuel Skordalakis (National Technical University of Athens) for his various facilities that he provided me during the preparation of the book.

Finally, I also wish to thank my wife, Maria, for her patience and her understanding during the period of the editing of this textbook.

Nikos E. Mastorakis

CONTENTS

Preface vii

PART I: SOFTWARE ENGINEERING **1**

Developing Networked Courseware based on Software Engineering Practices 3
S. Retalis and E. Skordalakis

An Efficient Data Structure for Maintaining Future Events in a Discrete-Event Simulation System 11
M. Andreou and S. D. Nikolopoulos

LOGIDATA++: An Intelligent Object-Oriented Database Prototype 23
I. A. Letia and O. Pop

Computation of Reed-Muller Expansions from Incompletely Specified Boolean Functions 31
G. A. Khuwaja, A. N. Abu-Rezq and A. S. Tolba

Extending Knowledge-Based Support in Software Systems Development 36
V. C. Vescoukis, D. Anagnostopoulos and M. Nikolaidou

A Pattern Matching Algorithm 45
O. C. Dogaru

A Pedestrian Traffic Flow Simulation Study 49
D. Anagnostopoulos, V. C. Vescoukis and M. Nikolaidou

A Model for Organizing Software Configuration Management Repositories 55
J. Psaromiligos

Informatics Support to Change Management in a Deregulated Environment 63
Y. Markopoulos and A. T. Mandylas

Iterative Switching Networks 68
V. N. Kasyanov

Implementation of Real-Time Monitoring Software of
Brunnenhach P V Plant 73
A. Biasizzo, A. Žužek, F. Novak, P. Helm,
M. Bächler and M. Grottke

Logic-Automation Modeling in Engineering Systems and Computers 77
V. I. Levin

An Efficient VLSI Architecture for an Improved Three-Step
Search Algorithm 82
D.-L. Xu, C. Bailey and R. Sotudeh

Denotational Semantics of Evaluation Order in Expressions
with Side Effects 87
N. S. Papaspyrou

An Heuristic Method for Generating a Formal CSP + T
Model of a Real Time System 95
J. A. Pérez, R. Corchuelo and M. Toro

Parsing Invalid Inputs 101
R. Corchuelo and J. A. Pérez

Design Re-use and IP Cores: Practical Experience 108
L. Torres and E. Palm

AND/OR Graph Based Error Diagnosis in Multi-Valued Circuits 113
R. Dreschsler and A. Žužek

A Framework for Encapsulating Best Business Practices for
Electricity Supply Industry into Generic Patterns 117
C. Rolland, G. Grosz, P. Loucopoulos and S. Nurcan

An Agent Based Platform for a Service Provider 123
V. Carchiolo, M. Malgeri and G. Mangioni

The Specification of Geometrical Dynamic Behaviour in
Web Page Design 129
J. B-Cruz, L. Barbosa, L. Morgado, A. Reis,
J. Barroso, P. M-Pinto and P. Henriques

Address Translation in the PoP Border — A Mixed Model of Routing and IP Masquerading for Internet Access 136
A. Reis, A. Lopes, F. Rebelo, L. Santos, J. Luis, J. Barroso and J. B.-Cruz

Anycast as an Application Layer Service 141
M. Berzsenyi, H. Zhang and I. Vajk

Monotonicity Properties and Simple Bounds on the Mean Cycle Time in Acyclic Fork-Join Queuing Networks 147
N. K. Krivulin

Facilitating the Searching Methodologies in VLSI Circuit Design by Boundary Sampling 153
K. T. Chan and A. Wu

Techniques for the Hardware Implementation of Modular Multiplication 157
C.-D. Walter

Integrated Partitioning and Scheduling for Hardware/Software Co-design 162
H.-Q. Liu and D. F. Wong

MATLAB Programs for Simulating Multirate Systems 168
M. J. Er and N. E. Mastorakis

Integrated Reengineering: An Approach Towards Implementation of New Technologies 177
H. H. Liakos and D. I. Tseles

PART II: SIGNAL PROCESSING 181

Maximum Likelihood Estimation of the Instantaneous Optical Carrier Phase in Coherent Lightware Communications 183
A. Arvizu and F. J. Mendieta

The Analysis of Dynamics of a Complicated Systems State on Phase Portraits in Space of Eigenvectors 191
A. A. Boriskenvich, V. M. Demko, A. M. Krot and P. P. Tkachova

An Algorithm for Fast Polynomial Reduction in Digital Signal Processing Problems 195
A. M. Krot and H. B. Minervina

Multivariate Arx Model Identification and Control with Unknown Process Order 199
E. N. Demiris, S. D. Likothanassis and S. K. Katsikas

Low SNR Time Delay Estimation by Adaptive Postfiltering of Cross-Correlator Output Sequence 205
A. N. Dolia, V. V. Lukin and A. A. Zelensky

Autoregressive Hidden Markov Models for Isolated Words Recognition 211
E. I. Bovbel, P. P. Tkacheva and I. E. Kheidorov

Multiprocessor DSP System for Real-Time Digital Signal Processing Applications 215
N.-A. I. Livanos and E. Zigouris

Structure Selection of Semi-Linear Systems with Signal-Dependent Parameters 219
J.-Y. Dieulot and H. Baussart

Adaptive Event Recognition with the Use of Limited Training Data 225
G. Paliouras and D. S. Brée

A Novel Weighted Hough Transform for Robust Detection of Linear Formations 233
S. J. Perantonis, N. Vassilas, K. Seretis and Th. Tsenoglou

Comparison of Two Fuzzy Pixel-Clustering Algorithms: The Optimal Number of Clusters Approximation Issue 238
S. N. Raptis and S. G. Tzafestas

A Fuzzy Model for the Pitch Perception of Complex Tones 243
D. K. Fragoulis, C. N. Papaodysseus and J. N. Avaritsiotis

A Voice Scripting Language Interface of N-Arity for an OO Formant Synthesizer 247
D. V. Politis, L. A. Tsoukalas and P. Linardis

Identification of Discrete Input Nonlinear Systems for Digital Chaotic Signal Processing 251
A. M. Krot and M. A. Shcherbakov

PART III: MULTIDIMENSIONAL SYSTEMS THEORY AND APPLICATIONS **255**

On the Dynamic Motion of a Towed Array in the Ocean 257
N. V. Nikitakos, A. K. Leros and S. K. Katsikas

Equivalent Standard Systems for Singular Discrete-Time Systems with Delays 264
T. Kaczorek

Computation of the Vector Powers of Matrices which are Used in 2-Dimensional Systems 273
N. E. Mastorakis

Two-Dimensional Positive Systems: Minimal State Space Realization and Transfer Functions 282
G. Antoniou, A. Papis and A. Chilmaza

Primitivity of 2D Positive Systems 287
E. Fornasini

Reduced Order Two-Dimensional Adaptive State-Space Filters 293
T. Hinamoto, H. Manabe, A. Doi and M. Muneyasu

Multi-Dimensional Filters and Algorithms for Automative Real Time Detection and Classification of Railroad Sleepers in Video Images 297
J. Velten, A. Kummert and D. Maiwald

Stable Factorization of 2-D Filters Using a Constrained Optimization Algorithm 301
S. J. Perantonis, N. Ampazis and S. J. Varoufakis

A Method for Computing the 2-D Stability Margin Based on a New Stability Test for 2-D Systems 307
N. E. Mastorakis

Unsupervised Classification and Fusion of Multidimensional Slidescan Sonar Data 313
U. H.-Hoebing and D. Kraus

Transfer Function Models for Non Self-Adjoint Multidimensional Systems 317
R. Rabenstein

Efficient Implementation of Digital 3-D IIR Filters for Separation of Velocity Components in Data-Streams 321
G. Runze

PART IV: COMMUNICATION SYSTEMS 325

Capacity Related Reliability (CRR) as Topology Performance Measure Tool for ATM Transport Networks 327
K. Kyandoghere

The Design of Passive Optical Networks According to FSAN 333
G. A. Pikrammenos and J. D. Angelopoulos

An Alternative Method for Securing Privacy in PON and HFC Networks 339
J. Koulouris and A. Koulouris

On Hierarchically Organized Networks — An Algebraic Approach 345
A. Andreatos and P. Stefaneas

An Encryption Algorithm for Data Communication Security 350
M. Saeb and M. A. Baith

Bearing Estimation and Blind Source Separation 354
M. Frikel, V. Barroso, J. Gomes and S. Bourennane

New Horizons in Network Management 358
G. Bányász, G. Lucz, H. Charafl and I. Vajk

PART V: MODERN NUMERICAL TECHNIQUES AND RELATED TOPICS 365

Explicit A-Stable Runge-Kutta Methods for Some Linear Stiff-Equations 367
M. Nakashima

A Linear Matrix Inequality Approach to VSCS Design for Linear Systems with Mismatched Uncertainties 375
H. H. Choi

Solving Block-Structured Matrix Problems on RISC-Based Supercomputers 381
M. Parzycki, P. Yalamov and N. E. Mastorakis

Modelling and Simulation of Continuous Neural Networks for Constrained Optimization Problems 386
V. M. Mladenov and P. N. Proshkov

Modelling and Estimation of Synthetic Aperture Sonar Platform Motion 394
D. Kraus, F. M. Petey and J. Kalwa

A Generalized Bode Plot Construction 398
N. E. Mastorakis

Part 1

SOFTWARE ENGINEERING

Developing Networked Courseware Based on Software Engineering Practices

S. Retalis & E. Skordalakis

{retal,@softlab.ntua.gr, skordala@softlab.ntua.gr}

National Technical University of Athens
Department of Electrical and Computer Engineering
Division of Computer Science
Polytechnioupoli, 15780 Zografou, Athens, Greece.

Summary

The aim of the paper is to present a networked courseware development methodology for Open Learning Systems, entitled CADMOS. Networked courseware is educational software based on the Internet and the World Wide Web (WWW). Networked courseware development is not an easy task. A suitable methodology is needed which must be a function of the specific subject to be taught, the audience to be addressed to and the specific learning environment where learning takes place. CADMOS is such a methodology which is outcome of research in the area of Networked Open and Distance Learning. CADMOS intends to assure the quality of the networked courseware along with the completion of the developing task within predicted estimates of cost and scheduling. Principles from software engineering practices have been adopted as well as from specific instructional design approaches. The innovative aspects of CADMOS are its evolutionary development process model and its emphasis on the Object Oriented design methods. Test bed for the validation of CADMOS was a European partnership project called "An Experiment in Open and Distance Learning using New Technologies (EONT)" and other small scaled projects.

1. Introduction-Motivation

The phenomenal growth of the new information and communication technologies (ICTs), i.e. computer, telecommunication networks and hypermedia applications (especially the Internet and the World Wide Web), over the last years, coupled with the decrease in the cost of hardware, presents realistic and useful ways for supporting Open and Distance Learning. As a consequence, Networked Open and Distance Learning (NL) has emerged as a new educational paradigm which is based on ICTs [27]. Networked Open and Distance Learning [15, 26, 27] aims to:

- support open, flexible and learner-centred patterns of study;
- provide ways for learners to work collaboratively;
- encourage and facilitate human-human and human-computer interaction.

Like any other technology used in Open and Distance Learning, ICTs have advantages and disadvantages. Implementations that capitalise on the strengths of the technology and that circumvent or adjust for its limitations can be expected to be educationally effective [15]. However, educators often believe that it is sufficient to take a course syllabus and course material, transform them into electronic format and deliver it through the Internet [3].

On the contrary, learning material development for networked open and distance learning, that is networked courseware, is not an easy task. A methodology suitable for the specific subject to be taught, the audience to be addressed to as well as acceptable for a specific learning environment where learning takes place must be used. The term "networked courseware' means a set of digitised learning resources, especially designed and developed for instructional delivery via the Internet and the WWW. This set of learning resources (or else courseware components) includes [9]:

- *expositive documents*: There are typically viewed by a user without entailing any degree of involvement, other than navigation.
- *active documents*: these are multiple-choice questionnaires, simulations, auto-evaluation exercises, self-assessment material, etc.
- *interactive documents*: This refers to material produced by human-human communication. Such communication can be synchronous or asynchronous.

2. Courseware Development Approaches

In order to develop networked courseware, three options exist:

- to adopt/adapt a software development methodology. This is not the best option. Although courseware can be regarded as special type of software, its source code is limited (because of the use of authoring tools), quality metrics and quality assurance techniques are ill-defined. Contrary to software products, a lot of emphasis is given to select and specify learning objectives, pedagogical methods, learning activities, interface issues, etc., as well as to evaluate learning effectiveness for courseware development [6, 13, 21].
- to adopt/adapt a non-NL development methodology like the ones presented in [17]. This is a quite common strategy adopted by the networked courseware industry. However, industry has shifted

in the production of networked courseware driven by "technolove" mainly because ICTs are the cutting edge technologies and because of the features they contain instead of the learning they enable [40]. Such methodologies do not contain any specific analysis and design methods for the development of the interactive documents and so a lot of networked products are just textbooks in a hypermedia format.

to adopt a networked courseware development methodology. Up to our knowledge, no standard methodology exists, as yet. Research concerning the description, formalism, analysis and evaluation of the courseware development process has been conducted over the last years [9, 16, 18, 24, 32]. Most of them try to formalise some aspects of the construction process and provide supporting tools for it rather than to present a holistic view of the process.

The motivation and aim of our research work is to create a fine-grained methodology for developing networked courseware for Open Learning Systems, called CADMOS. Principles from software engineering practices have been adopted as well as instructional design approaches such as the fourth generation of instructional systems development, R. Gagne' definition of learning objectives as well as T. Shuell's learning functions. CADMOS is expected to give answers to problems encountered during the courseware development process. CADMOS includes functional (what), behavioural (how) and organisational (who and when) information useful to people involved in the development process, i.e. subject matter experts, users, analysts, designers, programmers, artists, evaluators, etc. CADMOS is more than an instructional design method; it is a system comprised by methods and tools following specific principles.

The innovative aspects of this work are its holistic perspective on most of the phases of the courseware development process, its evolutionary development process model and its emphasis on the Object Oriented design method of the networked courseware components.

The European partnership project called "An Experiment in Open and Distance Learning using the New Technologies" (EONT) [8, 29] was used as a case study and a test bed for CADMOS. Networked courseware was developed in the subject matter area of Software Engineering and it was embedded into a learning environment based on a HyperWave server [25]. More details about the project and the networked courseware developed can be found in [7, 20, 29].

The outline of rest of the paper is the following. In section 3, a presentation of the framework (adapted from software engineering [36]) which is the foundation of CADMOS is given. This framework provides an macroscopic view of CADMOS. In section 4, analysis of CADMOS will be made at a micro level. This means that detailed analysis of the activities, methods, tools and deliverables used at the various phases of the development process is given. Finally, in section 5, comments about CADMOS' usefulness and the future work plans are made.

3. CADMOS at a macro-level

Based on the software engineering practices [36], CADMOS can be abstractly described by the components framework shown in Figure 1.

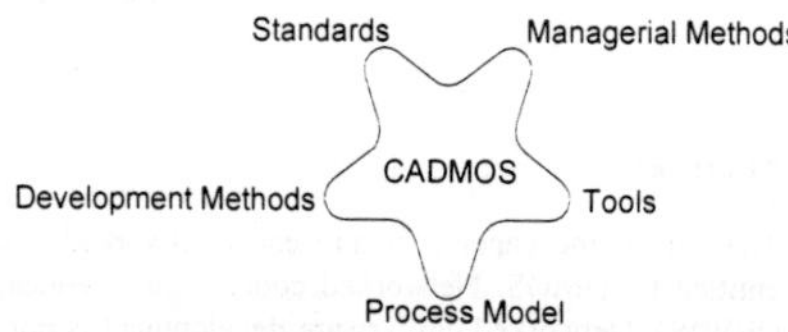

Figure 1. The components framework for describing CADMOS

The five boxes in Figure 1 are the components of the CADMOS. CADMOS' cornerstone is the Process Model (i.e. a life cycle model). The model describes the main phases which comprise the courseware development process and their sequence of implementation. Each phase is divided into activities. The development methods describe how the various activities are performed. The managerial methods describe how to control, steer and follow up the courseware development process as well as who will perform which activity. The tools support the individuals in their job to perform the various activities by automating some of their aspects. The standards give accepted solutions to recurring problems.

CADMOS should be viewed as a system of closely linked and interrelated components according to the systemic approach [2]. In fact, one of the bases of "its philosophy" is Aristotle's dictum which says that the whole is greater that the sum of the parts. If we only focus on the components themselves rather that on the way they form the methodology, the approach will be reductionist and the resultant methodology will be ambiguous. A holistic view of CADMOS which shows the relationship between the components is given in Table 1. The microscopic view of CADMOS which follows in section 3, will present the development activities and tools that support the development process. The sub-sections that follow present the three remainder components.

3.1 Process model

CADMOS is based on an evolutionary process model [36]. This model's purpose is to show abstractly what is to be done during the development phase and in what sequence. This model, shown in Figure 2, involves developing and delivering the courseware in an evolutionary fashion.

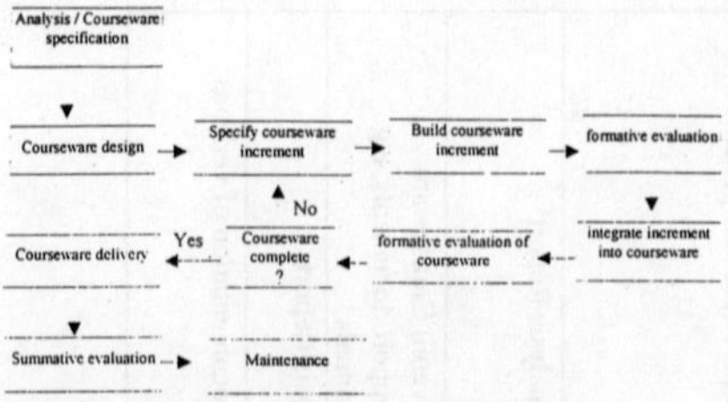

Figure 2. Evolutionary development process model

The use of the evolutionary development process model suggests that the networked courseware is divided into components, or increments, which cover part of the functionality of the overall courseware product and part of the overall requirements. The developer designs, builds, formatively evaluates and delivers the networked courseware, increment by increment. The learner's perception of the overall networked courseware end product is a moving target. As increments are being built and delivered, learners' and teachers' opinion regarding the value of the remaining increments may change. Features of them previously felt to be essential to the overall product may be deleted or new increments may be added to the list of increments to be incorporated into the overall product during some future development phase.

The advantage of this model is that the development process is very manageable and that it allows user feedback quite often during the process. Furthermore, this model allows the addition of courseware components that have not specified and included in the courseware design from the beginning. In fact, the evolutionary model does not distinguish between developing a product and enhancing (maintaining) it; enhancement is merely an additional increment built. Problems with this model can occur when the courseware architecture is not open which means that additional increments can not be easily incorporated into the overall courseware.

3.2 Managerial methods

The managerial methods describe how to control, steer and follow up the courseware development. Principles from software engineering have been adopted. The following pseudo-code is an attempt to present the iteration of the management activities:

- *Define constraints under which the project are to be carried out–constraints are: delivery time, budget, hardware and software resources, personnel, constraints by the learning environment (e.g. no use of synchronous interaction, complementarity of networked based instruction to classroom based one, etc.)*
- *Define standards to assess the development process*
- *Allocate tasks to personnel according to organisation model–examine the need of training*
- *Define project's milestones and deliverables*

According to the process model,

while development process has not been completed or cancelled:

- *perform activities*
- *review projects progress according to milestones*
- *evaluate / assess intermediate product and project's progress*

if (problem arises) then

- *initiate technical review*
- *re-negotiate project's constraints*
- *revise project's milestones and project plan*

endif

end loop

According to CADMOS, when developing networked courseware, the cost estimation technique used should be based on the one specified in [22] combined with on the experience of the working team (educated guess method) taking into consideration the various cost drivers of the project (e.g. human effort per development phase, prices of equipment, etc.). For project planning, *Bar charts* should be used which graphically illustrate the work plan and project over it the *milestones,* i.e. the crucial points where monitoring of the project progress should happen [10].

Furthermore, CADMOS proposed the use of the mixed-control team organisation method in case of multi-personal development team [41]. Finally, the main deliverable of those activities is the management plan which includes details of the project's objectives, the working schedule, the deliverables, the cost estimation, the resources, the allocation of tasks to personnel and so on, according to standards described in [10].

Phases	Activities	Methods	Tools	Deliverables
Analysis	– assess learning problems/needs – assess user/target population – determine ID competence of the developer/team – define constraints and restrictions imposed to the solution finding process – propose an ideal solution	– Situational Evaluation [39] – Guidelines by [31]	– statistical analysis	– Situational Evaluation – Ideal Solution
Courseware Design	– Development of architectural design – Courseware components specification – Interface design – Navigation design	– Use Cases	– Use Cases, UML – Entity-Relationship method – RMM [44]	– Utilisation Scenarios – Courseware architecture – Specifications of courseware components – Storyboard
Multimedia Design	– design of text – design of graphics – design of sound – design of animation – design of video	– compliance to technical standards		– Specifications of media
Multimedia Courseware Components Development	– preparation of texts – preparation of graphics – preparation of sound – preparation of animation – preparation of video	– Top-down method – Bottom up method	– Authoring tools – Graphical editors	– Courseware components
Formative evaluation	– pilot testing with real learners & teachers – analysis of feedback	– Post-test method [40]	– Questionnaires	– Analysis Report
Courseware Integration	– integration of the various elements into a whole		– Tools of learning environment (like WebCity, etc.)	– Overall Courseware – support documents, e.g. manuals
Summative evaluation	– pilot testing with real learners, tutors	– Pre- & post- test approach [8]	– Two questionnaires – statistical tools	Analysis Report
Maintenance	– maintenance for correction – maintenance for perfection – maintenance for adaptation			– Documentation of versions

Table 1. Phases, activities, methods, tools and deliverables in courseware development

3.3 Standards

The standards give accepted solutions to recurring problems. Research efforts are being made to construct well accepted standards for courseware development [1, 28]. However, no widely accepted standards, as is the case in software engineering, exist as yet. Thus, CADMOS has specified internal quality standards which are the following:

- *Usability*
  - *Usefulness: helps the learners to achieve their goals.*
  - *Ease of use: learners make few mistakes and achieve their goals in a few key presses of mouse movements.*
  - *Learnability: easy to learn to use.*
  - *Attitude: users like it.*
- *Aesthetics*
  - *Easy to assimilate the information on the screen.*
  - *Visually attractive (multimedia of good quality).*
  - *Interesting.*
- *Educational efficiency*
  - *Flexibility: allows the learners to navigate the material in a manner which suits them.*
  - *Allows for a variety of types of learning experience, using the full potential of the system.*
  - *Provides an integrated learning environment.*
- *Efficiency*
  - *A set of attributes that bear on the relationship between the level of performance of the educational courseware and the amount of resources used.*
- *Maintainability*
  - *A set of attributes that bear on the effort needed to make specified modifications.*

4. CADMOS at a micro level

In this section, description of the principles, methods, deliverable and tools used at each development phase is made.

4.1 Analysis phase

The scope of the analysis phase is the identification of a given instructional problem which the networked courseware will try to solve and the quantitative–ualitative awareness of the direct and indirect factors which affect the problem solution finding [39]. According to CADMOS networked courseware development should be regarded as a problem solving process.

During this phase, the instructional developer (or developing team) should:

- assess learning problems/needs
- assess user/target population
- determine the competence of the developer/team
- define constraints and restrictions imposed to the solution finding process
- propose an ideal solution

The ideal solution to the instructional problem emerges from *blending* four interrelated sets of learning elements: the syllabus (content), the learning objectives, the learning/pedagogical methods and the media. The ideal solution is illustrated graphically in Figure 3 and is the main product of this process.

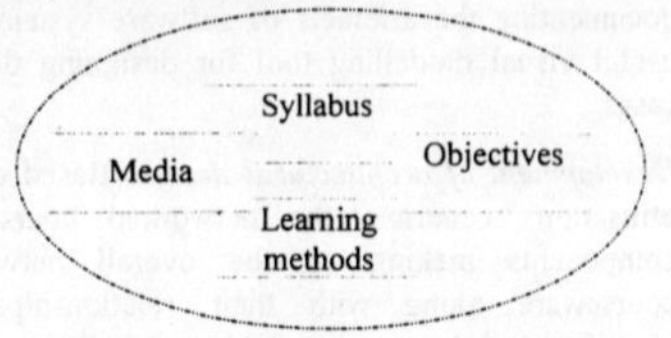

Figure 3. Structure of courseware

CADMOS suggests that the method and guidelines that should be followed for the qualitative and quantitative analysis of the direct and indirect factors which affect the problem solution are the ones clearly described at [39]. The deliverable of this phase is a situational evaluation document according to the template found in [39] with clear description of the ideal solution.

Moreover, there are a lot of debates on how to formally define the learning objectives and the learning methods. CADMOS follows the philosophy of Gagné, Briggs and Wager [11]. Furthermore, the learning methods commonly embedded into networked courseware are: exploratory method (free or guided) [19], case based (or story based) method [34], problem solving method [19] and collaborative method [15, 26].

4.2 Design phase

During the design phase, the networked courseware architecture will be created, based on the description of the ideal solution of the instructional problem. The networked courseware architecture is an abstract model, which denotes the way that of the ideal solution will be realised into an overall networked courseware product comprised by components (expositive, active and interactive documents). This model will clearly specify the interrelationships between the components and the assessment of risk involved for the development of each one of them.

The design activities are:

- *Design of utilisation scenarios*: An utilisation scenario is a written outline of the human-computer interactions and/or human-human interactions that will be supported and facilitated by the construction of the networked courseware with details about the actors (tutors, learners, computer system), their roles and the prospective learning outcomes. CADMOS believes in a change of the role of the teacher. A teacher should not only try to transfer her knowledge into the learners, but she should guide, facilitate, tutor, watch over the learner shoulder, partner him in the learning process. According to CADMOS philosophy, utilisation scenarios should be designed having as guidelines the Shuell's learning functions [35]. The method for specifying the utilisation scenarios is the "use cases" and the activity diagrams according to the Unified Modelling Language (UML) [http://www.rational.com/uml]. UML is a language for specifying, constructing and documenting the artefacts of software systems and useful visual modelling tool for designing the use cases.

- *Development of architectural design*: Based on the utilisation scenarios, the networked courseware components making up the overall networked courseware along with their relationships are identified and documented. Object Oriented methods must be followed to describe the architectural "blueprint". A networked courseware component could involve a set of classes and sub-classes with specific properties and behaviours.
- *Components specification*: for each component, a specification of the content, media, learning objectives and learning methods embedded in it is given. Moreover, the ways through which the user can navigate within each component as well as from one component to another are also specified.
- *Interface design*: for each component, its interface and layout are designed and documented into a storyboard as a screen layouts which include details about the media contained, the fonts, colour code, sounds, buttons layout, etc., as well as additional comments which must be taken into consideration by the graphic designers.

CADMOS focuses on the detailed open-ended design because success in the design phase guarantees that the actual implementation will go faster as well as the good quality of the overall courseware will be achieved.

4.3 Development

As already mentioned the courseware development should be done in an evolutionary way. Having a detailed courseware design, the manager allocates tasks to the members of the development team and the development is expected to progress according to a project's plan. CADMOS suggests two methods for the development of courseware components.

First, the top-down development method. By top-down, it is meant the method of working from a starting point which is the courseware design, proceeding the evolutionary development taking into consideration the user's feedback so that the end product is "finely tuned" according to the learners' needs and quality demands.

On the contrary, the bottom-up method is closely related with the notion of the re-usability of learning resources. The development team, having into mind the components' design specifications retrieves repositories of "units of learning material" (ULMs) to check whether they can be embedded into the courseware under development [12]. This method is cost and time effective if and only if the learning resources stored into repositories are well documented so as to easily locate the useful ones [18]. The issue of payment for copyrights should be seriously assessed before proceeding into adopting any of these learning resources.

4.4 Evaluation

Both **formative** and **summative** evaluation methods are suggested by CADMOS. **Formative** is used with the intention of improving the quality of the courseware while in the process of design and evolutionary development. Testing of courseware components during their development are made in order to identify areas where improvements are needed. Two questionnaires should be prepared for such purposes according to the guidelines by [40], the responses to which should be elicited by: a) tutors and subject matter experts and b) learners

Summative evaluation is being performed to check the courseware product upon the defined quality standards. The approach that is being followed is the "pre-test" and "post-test" one [4]. Two kinds of questionnaires are given to the learners. The first one concerns the "pre-test" which aims at identifying their expectations of the courseware and the learning environment. These questionnaires should be filled in during the first days of the courseware delivery and not later than the first week. The "post-test" questionnaire helps to deduce overall judgements and criticism on the courseware, the learning environment as well as course delivery mode. The completed questionnaires are being collected for statistical analysis, interpretation and report of the results.

CADMOS advocates that the effectiveness of networked courseware is conceptualised as being related to a multiple measurement index consisting of cognitive and attitudinal outcomes The evaluation study should be focused on the following criteria:

- *criterion of appropriateness*: the networked courseware is appropriate to the learner body for which it is intended.
- *criterion of engagement*: the learners find the networked courseware mode interesting, easy to follow, etc.
- *criterion of learner performance*: the learners have acquired some knowledge and increased their skills.

The data gathered are then analysed (using a variety of tools, like the PCM). On the one hand, sophisticated computer analysis can be carried out on complex quantitative data which leads to numerical calculations and pinpoints the trends of some figures. On the other hand, simple qualitative context analysis can be made which, of course, leads to different, but not necessarily invaluable, findings.

4.5 Maintenance

The activities during the maintenance phase are triggered by a set of change requests from users, developers or managers. Two different types of courseware maintenance can be identified [37]:

1. *Corrective maintenance* is concerned with fixing reported errors in the courseware. The activities for this type of maintenance are triggered after the summative evaluation of the courseware.
2. *Perfective maintenance* involves implementing new functional courseware requirements. These are generated by the users as their needs change.

No formal method has been followed for performing the activities of this phase because the use of the evolutionary development process model suggests that the maintenance is simply an enhancement of the networked courseware .

5. Discussion

In this paper, a networked courseware development methodology for Open Learning Systems, entitled CADMOS is presented which contains the main characteristics of software development methodologies based on systemic components framework and emphasises on the evolutionary development and the object oriented design. It aims at improving the effectiveness and the efficiency of the development process.

Methodologies for courseware development need specific foundation and experimental validation [6]. The first requirement has been fulfilled since the methodology follows specific software engineering techniques and instructional design principles which have been widely accepted by the research community. Furthermore, CADMOS is outcome of action research. Test bed for its validation and evaluation was the EONT project as well as two small scaled projects (3 man months development effort). The focus of CADMOS evaluation was given on whether it fulfils its objectives, i.e. it is used to developing good quality courseware and to assure the completion of the development process within specific limits in time, money and resources (a triple of constraints). The first evaluation results are encouraging [8] because the users have evaluated the overall quality of the networked courseware positively. CADMOS continues to evolve. We tend to believe that the required changes on its further formalism as well as its further experimental validation with other networked courseware development projects will lead us to a more fine grained methodology.

Acknowledgements

The project EONT is partially funded by the European Commission's SOCRATES Program. Its reference number is TM-OP-1995-1-GR-88(1/0).

References

1 Aviation Industry Computer Based Training Committee (1997). *Guidelines for CBT Courseware Interchange*, http://www.aicc.org/docs/AGRs/pgr007.rtf

2 D. Avison, G. Fitzgerald (1995). *Information Systems Development: Methodologies, Techniques and Tools*, McGraw-Hill.

3 J. Bourdeau, A. Bates (1996). Instructional Design for Distance Learning, Tutorial Notes within the *Fourth International Conference in Intelligent Tutoring Systems* (ITS'96), Montreal-Canada.

4 J. Calder (1995), *Programme Evaluation and Quality: A Comprehensive Guide to Setting up an Evaluation System*, Institute of Educational Technology, Open University, Kogan Page.

5 I. De Diana (1988). The EDUC system: Aspects of a methodology, development method, and instrumentation for tutorial CBL, *PhD thesis*, University of Twente, Netherlands.

6 I. De Diana, V. Schaik (1993). Courseware Engineering outlined: an Overview of some Research Issues, *Educational and Training Technology*, 30 (3).

7 S. Efraimidis, S. Retalis, E. Skordalakis (1997), Teaching Software Engineering through the Net, *Software Quality Engineering*, SQE'97, Udine, Italy, 4-7 May, 1997.

8 EONT Results Report (1997). *Deliverable 1, Socrates ODL project EONT GR-88*, National Technical University of Athens, Greece, http://hyperg.softlab.ntua.gr/EONT

9 E. Forte, M. Wentland, E. Duval (1997). The ARIADNE Project (Part 1): Knowledge Pools for Computer-based and Telematics-supported Classical, Open and Distance Education, *European Journal of Engineering Education*, 22 (1).

10 R. Freeman (1991). Quality assurance in learning materials production, *Open Learning*, 6 (3).

11 R. Gagné, L. Briggs, W. Wager (1994). *Principles of Instructional Design* (4th Ed.). Fort Worth, TX: HBJ College Publishers.

12 P. Goodyear (1994). Foundations for Courseware Engineering, In Automating Instructional Design, Development and Delivery, *Automating Instructional Design, Development and Delivery*, R. Tennyson (ed.), Berlin: Springer–Verlag.

13 P. Goodyear (1995). Infrastructure for courseware Engineering. *Automating Instructional Design: Computer-Based Development and Delivery Tools*, R. Tennyson & A. Barron (eds.), Berlin: Springer–Verlag.

14 M. Hamalainen (1996) A Model for Delivering Customezed On-Demand Education on the Internet, In A. Dumort & W. Paprotte, *The Road to the Information Society*, European Commission DG XIII, Lugembourg.

15 R. Hiltz (1995). *The Virtual Classroom Learning Without Limits via Computer Networks*, Ablex Publishing Corporation, U.S.A.

16 R. De Hoog, T. De Jong, F. De Vries (1993), Constraint driven instructional design: an escape from the waterfall model. Proceeding of *EARLI Conference*, Aix-en-Provence-France.

17 T. de Jong, L. Sart (1994). Design *and Production of Multimedia and Simulated-based Learning Material*, Kluwer Academic Publishers.

18 B. Kang and P. Goodyear (1996). Representations of Instructional Purpose in Courseware Requirements Engineering, *Computer Aided Learning and Instruction in Science and Engineering*, A. Diaz de Ilarraza Sanchez and I. Fernadez de Castro (eds.), Berlin: Springer–Verlag.

19 T. Khan and Y.J. Yip (1996). Pedagogical principles of case-based CAL, *Journal of Computer Assisted Learning*, 12 (3).

20 A. Koutoumanos, N. Papaspyrou, S. Retalis, H. Maurer, E. Skordalakis (1996), Towards a Novel Networked Learning Environment, *WebNet'96*, San Francisco, USA.

21 Al-Noor Ladhani (1996). Modelling and Using Performance Knowledge for Courseware Design, *PhD thesis*, University of Twente, Netherlands.

22 A. Thackaberry, J. Rada (1998). Estimation Metrics for Courseware Maintenance Effort, *Journal for Universal Computer Science*, Special Issue, 4 (3), April 1998.

23 I. Marshall, W. Samson, P. Dugard and G. Lund (1995). The Mythical Courseware Development to delivery time ratio, *Computer Education* 25 (3).

24 A. D. Marshall and S. Hurley (1996). The Design, Development and Evaluation of Hypermedia Courseware for World Wide Web, *Multimedia Tools and Applications*, 3 (5).

25 H. Maurer (1996). *Hyperwave: The Next Generation Web Solution*, Addison Wesley.

26 D. McConnell (1994). *Implementing Computer Supported Cooperative Learning*, Kogan Page.

27 Networked Open Learning (1997). *Course Material: Advance Learning Technology Programme*, University of Lancaster.

28 IEEE P1484 Working Group (1997). *Standards for Computer-Based Learning* http://www.manta.ieee.org/p1484.

29 N. Papaspyrou, A. Koutoumanos, H. Maurer, E. Skordalakis (1996). An Experiment in ODL using New Technologies, *WebNet'96*, San Francisco-USA.

30 X. Perrot (1995). Production des Hypermedias et des interactifs multimedias pour les musées, *Thése de doctorat*, Université Paris XIII.

31 D. Rowntree (1994). *Preparing Materials for Open, Distance and Flexible Learning: An Action Guide for Teachers and Trainers*, Open and Distance Learning Series, Kogan Page.

32 P. Van Schaik (1996). Methods for Courseware Development, *PhD thesis*, University of Twente, Netherlands.

33 D. Scheider (1994). The World Wide Web: A distributed hypermedia over the Internet, *Learntech'94*, Kalsruhe, Germany. htt p://tecfa.unige.ch/tecfa/tecfa-research/CMC/learntech94/learntec_1.html

34 R. C. Shank (1993). Learning via Multimedia Computers, *Communications of ACM*, 36 (5).

35 T.J. Shuell (1992). Designing instructional computing systems for meaningful learning. In M. Jones & P. Winne (Eds.), *Adaptive learning environments* (pp. 19-54), New York: Springer.

36 E. Skordalakis (1994). Software engineering teaching at NTUA, *First International Software Engineering in Higher Education*, G. King, C. Brebbia, M. Ross, G. Staples (Eds.), Computational Mechanics Publications.

37 I. Somerville (1995), *Software Engineering*, Addison Wesley,.

38 M. Spector (1994). Integrating Instructional Science, Learning Theory and Technology, *Automating Instructional Design, Development and Delivery*, R. Tennyson (ed.), NATO ASI Series, Berlin: Springer–Verlag.

39 R. Tennyson (1994). Knowledge Base for Automated Instructional System Development, *Automating Instructional Design, Development and Delivery*, R. Tennyson (ed.), NATO ASI Series, Berlin: Springer–Verlag.

40 M. Tessmer (1995). Formative Multimedia Evaluation, *Training Research Journal*, 1.

41 D. Yates and J. Cadle (1996). *Project Management for Information Systems*, Pittman Publishing, Second Edition.

42 Z. Zhiting (1996). Cross-Cultural Portability of Educational Software: A Communication-Oriented Approach, *PhD thesis*, University of Twente.

43 T. Isakowitz, Edward. A. Stohr, and P. Balasubramanian (1995). RMM: A Methodology for Structured Hypermedia Design, *Communications of the ACM*, August.

An Efficient Data Structure for Maintaining Future Events in a Discrete-Event Simulation System

Maria Andreou

Department of Computer Engineering and Informatics, University of Patras, GR-26500 Patras, Greece
email: mandreou@ceid.upatras.gr

Stavros D. Nikolopoulos

Department of Computer Science, University of Ioannina
P.O. Box 1186, GR-45110 Ioannina, Greece
email: stavros@cs.uoi.gr

Abstract — *This paper introduces an efficient data structure, the linked-heap structure, for maintaining future events in a general purpose discrete event simulation system. It combines the advantages of the linked-list and heap (static representation) structures providing a time / space efficient scheduling algorithm. To gain insight into the performance of the linked-heap scheduling algorithm and allow comparisons with the linked-list and heap algorithms, they are tested under a wide variety of conditions in an empirical / experimental way. For this purpose, a set of stochastic scheduling distributions are especially chosen to show the advantages and limitations of each algorithm. The processor time abstained with the linked-heap algorithm is relatively insensitive in the scheduling distributions or the number of events notices in the event set. Experimental results and comparisons point to the superiority of the linked-heap algorithm in respect of time performance and storage economy, and put strong emphasis upon the linked-heap as an important scheduling algorithm for practical use.*

Keywords: *Discrete-event simulation, event scheduling algorithms, data structures, heaps, time/space behaviour.*

1. Introduction

In a discrete-event simulation system based on the *next-event time-advance* approach, an event set algorithm performs the following three main operations: (a) schedule future events, (b) cause the events to occur on the proper simulation time, and (c) update the clock variable which represents time. In such a system, an event is a collection of actions which are considered as executed in specific time. The data structure used to maintain future events in the system is usually called *event set* or *event list* and the time at which events are scheduled to occur is called *event time* or *schedule time.*

In the simulation environment, events are generally kept in objects known as *event notices*. An event notice is represented by a record with two fields, say *t* and *a*, where *t* is the scheduled time for its occurrence, and *a* is the activity which is scheduled in time *t*. When the time *t* of a new event becomes known, it is scheduled, i.e., a event notice is created and it is inserted into the event set in a position ensuring that it occurs at the scheduled time *t*. On the other hand, when the *next-event* (i.e., the event with the minimum event time) occurs, it is removed from the event set, and the simulation clock is advanced to the time of the next-event. The responsibility for these operations is due to an algorithm which (i) scans the event set to determine the proper insertion position for the new event, (ii) removes the next-event from the event set, and (iii) advances the simulation clock to the time of the next-event. Such an algorithm which used to schedule events in a general purpose discrete event simulation system is known as an *event set algorithm* or *event scheduling algorithm*.

The above operations involved by an event scheduling algorithm, are the most frequent operations required by any discrete-event simulation system. It is obvious that, the scanning operation becomes quite expensive in "real-word" application of simulation where the number of schedule events in the event set becomes rather large. For "large" complex simulation systems which generate many events the execution time of an event scheduling algorithm is one of the most crucial factors of systems' performance. Although the factor memory is not so important for "small" systems, it becomes considerably more important as the number of event notices becomes large. It is therefore clear that the most important requires of an event scheduling algorithm are (i) speed of operation and (ii) storage economy.

There are two principal approaches to storing event notices in a computer system. Specifically, there are two principal approaches of internal representations for structures and their special varieties: *contiguous-memory* (or *static*) representations and *linked* (or *dynamic*) representations. The contiguous and linked representations of lists of event notices have several advantages and disadvantages for simulation modelling. Some of them are the following:

- In a contiguous representation, the event notices are stored in an array whose size is fixed and greater than or equal to the maximum length of the list of event notices to be represented. That is, contiguous representations have a predefined maximum size, whereas linked representations do not have this limitation.
- Contiguous representations are more efficient than linked representations, in bytes required per event notice, because the memory of pointers is not needed.
- Storage in contiguous memory is less attractive when the event notices have different lengths, because the *i*-th event notice cannot be found in constant time by simple arithmetic.
- Linked representations are more flexible than contiguous representations, because only the pointers need to be adjusted in order to insert or delete event notices, and because the maximum size of the set is bounded only by the total memory available in the system.
- Linked representation provides a general framework that allows one to store and manipulate many event sets simultaneously with ease, whereby event notices in deferent event sets may be processed in different way. This generality is one of the reasons for the use of linked representations by all major simulation languages.

Many researchers have been published work present both analytical and empirical results concerning the time/space performance of many event scheduling algorithms. They use different data structures for the simulation event sets, e.g., linear lists, special kinds of trees, time-indexed lists, two-level structures, etc., and different techniques for the operations performed by the scheduling algorithms; for example, see [3, 9, 16, 21].

In this paper we introduce an efficient data structure, the *linked-heap* structure, for the simulation event set which is based in part on linked-lists and in part on the notion of complete binary trees. Specifically, it combines the advantages of the linked representation of linear lists and the contiguous-memory representation of heaps, providing a time/space efficient scheduling algorithm.

To gain insight into the performance of the linked-heap and allow comparisons with both the linked-list and the heap scheduling algorithms, all the algorithms are coded and tested under a wide variety of conditions in an empirical/experimental way. The objective was to estimate the average complexity for each algorithm. For this purpose, we used a revised definition of complexity. That is, for a given configuration of event set and a given distribution providing the schedule time, we taken the processor time expended for the execution of the *Hold procedure* (or *Hold model*; see [17, 19]) as the complexity of the algorithm for that input. The Hold procedure combines the following operations:

(1) Determine the next-event, i.e., the event notice with the minimum schedule time.
(2) Create a new event notice with schedule time T, and insert it into event set; Insertion or Scheduling operation.
(3) Remove from the event set the event notice with the minimal event time; Removal operation.

Two main parameters affect the execution time of the above operations. They are (i) the schedule time T, and (ii) the size N of the event set. The parameter T, which is given by a stochastic distribution, determines how long an event will remain in the event set. Six stochastic distributions are especially chosen which are not only representative of typical simulation problems but also capable to show the advantages and limitations of each algorithm. All distributions have mean one and fall into three categories:

A. Unimodal continuous distributions
B. Bimodal continuous distributions
C. Discrete distributions

The parameter N defines the notion of the *small* and *large* event sets. In other words, it determines the size of the event set, i.e., the number of event notices in the set at any time. Tests were performed with values of N from 32 (small event set) to 1024 (large event set). This range is representative of actual simulations, and the behaviour for $N > 1024$ can be extrapolated from the results. The processor time obtained with the linked-heap algorithm is relatively insensitive to variations in the scheduling distributions (parameter *T*) or the number of event notices in the event set (parameter *N*). The linked-heap algorithm is much faster than the linked-list for event sets containing more than 32 event notices. Its time performance is comparable only with the heap algorithm, but the contiguous representation of the heap structure may waste space, since it uses a maximum amount of space independent of the number of event notices actually on the set at any time. On the other hand, the linked representation of the heap structure has a considerable space overhead. The results of this work shows that the linked-heap algorithm combines time performance, storage economy and simplicity of coding. As a consequence the linked-heap structure is well suited to incorporation in general purpose simulation languages [7, 8, 14, 18].

The paper is organized as follows: Section 2 presents the linked-list and the heap structure. Section 3 introduces the proposed linked-heap structure. Section 4 presents all the event scheduling algorithms tested, i.e., the linked-list, the heap (contiguous representation) and the linked-heap algorithms. Section 5 describes the Hold model and gives the conditions under which the algorithms were tested. Section 6 reports the experimental results and explain them, while Section 7 provides a comparison analysis of all the algorithms. Section 8 concludes the paper.

2. Structures for the Simulation Event Set

There are two approaches to storing event notices in a computer. In the *contiguous-allocation* approach, the even notices are put into physically adjacent storage locations, one notice after another. In the *linked-allocation* approach, each event notice contains its usual attributes and, in addition, pointers giving the local relationship of the notices to other notices in the event set.

In this section we present two data structures, the linked-list and heap structures, which are both suitable for the simulation event sets.

2.1 The Linked-List Structure

A straightforward way of grouping elements together is to place them in a "chain", with every element except the last having a unique successor and every element except the first having a unique predecessor. A *linked-list* is thus obtained; that is, a structure that imposes a strict ordering among its elements.

If those elements are records (event notices), the linked-list can be implemented by including as an attribute of each record a pointer to one (or both) of its immediate neighbours. One possibility is to have each record refer to its successor and predecessor; the results is the *doubly linked-list*. Now, given reference to the two ends, the list can be traversed in both directions; new elements can be inserted into, and old elements can be removed from, an arbitrary position without having to know their successors or predecessors. The appropriate manipulation of pointers for these operations can be found in any textbook of data structures; for example, see [15].

In some implementations the *circular doubly inked-list* is more convenient [15, 18]. It consists of (1) a doubly inked-list, and (2) a dummy node. The first and the last node of the doubly inked-list are successor and predecessor of the dummy node, respectively. A pointer, called *Header*, indicates the dummy node; any other node of this structure is reached through the Header.

2.2 The Heap Structure

Apart from the fact that tree structures arise quite naturally in many applications, trees are important because they lead to very efficient algorithms. A binary tree structure of special relevance to simulation is the *heap* [4, 10, 12, 15]. This is a complete binary tree where each node has associated with a real number.

Moreover, the number of a son is always greater (or smaller) than or equal to the parent. Thus the smallest number in a heap is at the root and largest one is at one of the leaves.

There are several ways other than the usual linked structures to represent complete binary trees, among which the contiguous-memory (or static) representation. We can represent heaps (complete binary trees) implicitly in an array without the use of pointers by simply putting the root at position 1 and the direct descendants of the node i at positions $2i$ and $2i+1$ [15, 18]. Specifically, a heap of N nodes is represented by an array $A[1..N]$, where the condition $A[i] \geq A[i \text{ div } 2]$ holds for any i, $2 \leq i \leq N$; *div* denoting integer division.

3. The Linked-Heap Structure

A major problem with the static representation of the heap structure is that it restricts discrete event simulation systems to handle a predefined number of event notices. That is, a maximum size decision must be made in advance. One natural way to avoid this restriction is to use pointer representation. Although, in principle, we can implement a heap as an explicit tree structure with parent and children pointers (dynamic representation), it is less efficient than the static one due to extra space used by the pointers.

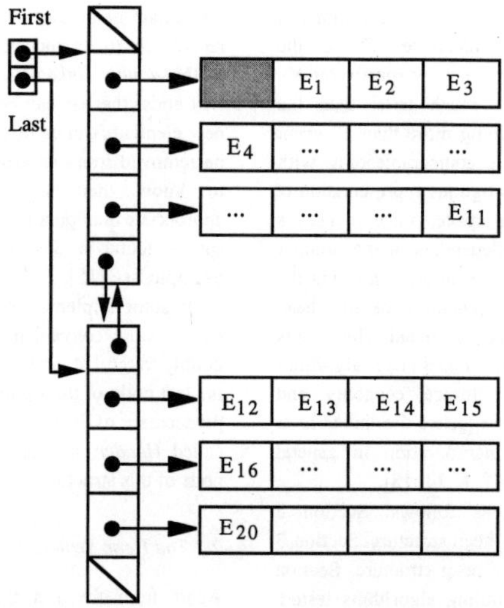

Fig. 1. A linked-heap structure; it consists of six blocks and a linked list of two arrays of pointers, and maintains twenty event notices.

We introduce a heap representation that overcame the static and dynamic drawbacks. It combines logarithmic behavior, space efficiency and simplicity, and thus, it can be efficiently used for the simulation event set. This structure is called *linked-heap*.

The linked-heap structure proposed here is based in part on the static representation of heap structure and in part on the linked-list structure. The structure consists of (1) a number of arrays of length h; these arrays are called *blocks*; (2) a linked list of arrays of pointers that indicate the blocks; (3) two pointers that give reference to the two ends of the linked list (see Fig. 1).

In this structure there are as many pointer as blocks. The kth pointer indicates the kth block, where $k \geq 0$. Each block, except the last, maintains h elements at positions 0, 1, 2, ..., h-1, and each array of pointers maintains q elements at positions 0, 1, ..., q-1. The ith position of the kth block is denoted by B[k, i], $0 \leq i \leq h$ and $k \geq 0$. The linked-heap of Fig. 1 consists of six blocks of length $h = 4$ and a linked list of two arrays of pointers, each of length $q = 3$.

Notice that the position B[0, 0] remains empty. The reson is that it makes the operations of finding the parent or a child of a node very easy (see the formulae which we prisent in the next paragraph).

There are several reasons why this static-dynamic representation is convenient:

1. The root r of the heap is always stored in the 1st position of the block 0.

2. If a node u ($u \neq r$) is stored in the ith position of the block k, then the parent $p(u)$ of u is stored in the following position:
   - Position (($i + kh$) *div* 2) *mod* h of the block (($i + kh$) *div* 2) *div* h.

3. If a node u ($u \neq r$) is stored in the ith position of the block k, then its children (if they exist) are stored in the following positions:
   - Left child is in position 2($i + kh$) *mod* h of the block 2($i + kh$) *div* h.
   - Right child is in position 2($i + kh$) *mod* h +1 of the block 2($i + kh$) *div* h.

4. In any case there are at most h-1 empty block positions.

The above formulas make it easy to implement algorithms that traverse a heap moving from a node to its parent or a child in various ways. It is worth noting that using linked-heaps we avoid predefining the size of the set.

4. Event Set Algorithms

The responsibility for deletion the notice with the minimum event time (next-notice) from the event set and insertion a new notice into event set is due to an event scheduling algorithm. Such an algorithm simply scans the event set to find (and remove) the next-notice and determine the proper insertion position for the new one. In this section we present the event scheduling algorithms that perform these operation on the data structures described above. Throughout the paper, the event notice with the minimum event time is referred to as *current notice*.

4.1 The Linked-List Algorithm

The linear circular doubly linked-list structure, with event notices ordered according to schedule times, is used by most current simulation systems. In our implementation event notices are ordered by increasing schedule times, i.e., the schedule time of an event notice is smaller than or equal to the successor and larger than or equal to the predecessor. Therefore, the current notice is always placed in known position; it is directly reached by a pointer which is called Header. It can be, thus, removed from the list in $O(1)$ time by changing the appropriate pointers. The scheduling (insertion) process is based on a normal, backward-directed list scanning method. That is, insertions are made by identifying the new event time and then linearly scanning the notices in the list for the proper insertion position of the new event. Thus, the complexity for the insertion operation is $O(N)$, where N is the number of event notices in the list. We point out that with the above scheduling process a FIFO ordering is maintained automatically.

4.2 The Heap Algorithm

In order to use the heap structure effectively, event notices are assigned to nodes of the heap so that the event time of a node is no later than that of its sons. Thus, using the static representation for the heap structure, the current notice is always located at A[1], where A is the array of length Nmax which maintains the heap elements, i.e., event notices. The algorithm works by first making the array A of notices into a heap and after an insertion or deletion operation traveling through the heap to re-establish the heap conditions.

For the insertion operation, the algorithm takes the current notice, which under the heap condition is placed in the root of the heap (see Section 2), and increases its event time, say t, by T (HOLD parameter). Then, create a new event notice with event time $t+T$, increases the size of the array by 1 and places the new event notice in A[N+1]. (Recall that N is the number of event notices in the array, where $N < N$max.) From there, it moves the new notice towards the root of the heap until it blocked by an event notice with an earlier or the same event time. For the deletion operation, the algorithm copy the notice of A[N+1] in A[1] and decreases the size of the array by 1. The event notice in A[1] is now moving back towards the leaves via the eldest son at each level until the heap condition is re-established.

The worst case behavior of a heap means the maximum number of comparisons between elements needed to adjust a heap. Thus, it is obvious that the worst case complexity of both insertion and deletion operations performed on a heap structure of size N is $O(\log N)$.

4.3 The Linked-Heap Algorithm

In Section 3, we introduced the linked-heap as an efficient structure for representing heaps. We now present the linked-heap event scheduling algorithm that performs the insertion and deletion operations. Initially, as with the static representation, event notices are assigned to nodes of the heap so that the event time of a node is no later than that of its sons. Then, the root of the heap is stored in B[0, 1], while the jth event notice (under level-by-level ordering) is stored in B[k, i], where $i = j \bmod h$ and $k = j \operatorname{div} h$. Recall that h denotes the length of the blocks of a linked-heap and B[i, j] denotes the jth position of the ith block, $0 \leq j \leq h$ and $k \geq 0$. Thus, the current notice is always located at B[0, 1] (see Fig. 1).

Let as consider the insertion and deletion operations. Suppose that there are N event notices in the linked-heap. Insertion take place by incrementing N and placing the new event notice in B[$(N+1) \operatorname{div} h$, $(N+1) \bmod h$] initially. From there it moves via its ancestor towards the root, i.e., B[0, 1], until blocked by a notice with an earlier or the same event time. For this movement the linked list of pointers is backward scanned, since the ancestor of a node is located in a different block.

Removing the current notice from B[0, 1] (it is always located at position 1 of the block 0), B[0, 1] is refilled from B[$N \operatorname{div} h$, $N \bmod h$] and N is decremented. The event notice in B[0, 1] now moves back towards the leaves via the earliest son at each level, until blocked by one with a late event time. For this movement the linked list of pointers is forward scanned to determine the pointer indicating the block which hold the earliest son.

As far as the complexity of the algorithm is concerned, it is easy to see that the worst-case complexity of both insertion and deletion operations are $O(\log N)$, where N is the size of the linked-heap.

Table I: Hold Time Distributions Tested

(A) Unimodal continuous
- (1) Negative exponential (mean 1).
- (2) Uniform distribution over the interval [0, 2].
- (3) Uniform distribution over the interval [0.9, 1.1].

(B) Bimodal continuous
- (4) 0.9 probability - uniform over the interval [0, S],
  0.1 probability - uniform over the interval [100S, 101S],
  where S is chosen to give the mixed distribution an average of unity.

(C) Discrete
- (5) T is constant with value of unity.
- (6) T is assigned the values 0, 1 or 2 with equal probabilities.

5. Testing the Algorithms

Closely coupled to the search for efficient scheduling algorithms is the problem of testing. We are interested in testing the proposed linked-heap scheduling algorithm, as well as the linked-list and heap algorithms, under a wide variety of conditions in an empirical/experimental way, in order to estimate their average time complexity. In this section we present the conditions under which all the algorithms were tested.

5.1. The HOLD Operation

The most frequent operations required by any discrete event simulation system are *deletion* of the current notice from the event set and *insertion* of a new notice into the event set. Following the research work performed to date [9, 10, 19, 21], we use the HOLD procedure which combines these two basic operations, to estimate the average time complexity of the algorithms.

The HOLD procedure first determines the event notice with the minimum event time t and removes it from the event set (deletion operation), then increases its event time t by T, where T is the random variate distributed according to some distributions, and reinsert it with the new value of event time $t+T$ into the event set (insertion operation). The difference between the new and old values of the event time is passed to the HOLD procedure as the parameter T. Throughout the paper the parameter T is referred to as *HOLD parameter* and the processor time (CPU time) for the execution of the HOLD procedure is referred to as *HOLD time*.

5.2 Test Conditions

One parameter which affects the execution time of the HOLD operation is the size N of the event set. We are interested in testing the performance of each algorithm using *small* and *large* event sets. Tests were performed for $N = 32, 64, 128, 256, 512$ and 1024. This range of sizes is representative for actual simulations and the behaviour of the algorithms for $N > 1024$ can be extrapolated for the results.

A crucial step in designing the tests lies in the selection of stochastic distribution which provides the event time T. The stochastic distribution used to determine how long an event notice will remain in the event set. Six distributions have been chosen as in [9, 10]. They differ widely in their characteristics and provide an efficient test for the good and bad points of the algorithms. All chosen distributions have mean 1 with different variances and fall into three categories; see Table I.

As the measure for estimating the average time complexity of the algorithms we have taken the processor time (CPU time) for the execution of the HOLD operation. In particular, for a given configuration of event set and a given hold time T, we have taken the processor time expended for the execution of HOLD(T) as the complexity of the algorithm for that input. Since the HOLD operation is affected by the size of the event set and the stochastic distribution, we have executed it with various combinations of event set sizes and distributions.

The algorithms were programmed in C and the test were performed using the XLC compiler on a IBM RS/6000 running under AIX version 3.2.5. The number of HOLD operations carried out was constant for all N and equal to 8000.

The sequence of operations in each test was as follows:

(i) Generate and insert N event notices into the event set. Initialize each event notice with event time generated from the chosen distribution F.

(ii) Before starting the time count, execute k HOLD operations with the same distribution F, where $k = 2N$.

(iii) Execute 8000 HOLD operations and count the total processor time (CPU time).

Operation (i) initializes the system. Operation (ii) is executed to permit the system to reach steady state. In analytical work, it is assumed that k is infinity. In practice, k is some small multiple of the size of the event set. In our case $k = 2N$. Operation (iii) yields a measure of the complexity of the tested algorithms.

The time required to generate the random numbers, perform the loops and call the HOLD procedure was subtracted from the running time so that the CPU times are comparable from one distribution to another. The random numbers generator used in all distributions in based on the Lehmer's congruential method [11] and is reported and tested by Downham and Roberts [5]. The generator is coded in such a way as not to give overflow on 32-bit computer.

5.3. Limitations Using the HOLD Model

Although the HOLD procedure combines the most frequent operations required by any discrete event simulation system (insertion and removal operations), there are some other operations that are often carried out on such a system. Most of these operations change some parameters which affect the performance of an event scheduling algorithm. For example, the *cancel* operation (delete an event from the event set, so that it will never be occurred), changes the size of the event set. Obviously, this operation does not affect the size of the event set in the case where the static representation approach is used.

Using the HOLD operation, it is clear that the size of the event set does not change (a deletion is followed by an insertion). This is not very realistic, since in real simulations the size of the event set varies dynamically. Furthermore, all event notices in the event set are scheduled with the same distribution. The effect of these assumptions was not tested in this work; this could be a topic for future study.

In this work, the tests were designed in such a way that the results provide a clear insight to the factors affected the performance of each event scheduling algorithm. Based on these results, we can determine whether or not a proposed algorithm is a suitable scheduling algorithm for practical use. Obviously, such an algorithm should be operate efficiently either with small or large sizes of the event set. Moreover, its time complexity should be insensitive to the stochastic distribution of event times.

It is important to point out that the HOLD procedure is just a model and, therefore, its operations differ significantly from the operations performed in a real simulation. However, since all the algorithms were tested under the same conditions, the comparative results are valid.

6. Presentation of the Results

Each of the algorithms was coded and run to collect evidence of performance under realistic conditions. The experimental results for each algorithm are represented in figures in the form of graphs of total CPU time against the size N of the event set. For all algorithms a logarithmic scale has been used in their graphs. The graphical results showing the time performance of the *linked-list*, *heap* and *linked-heap* algorithms are presented in Fig. 2. The real processor time (CPU time) taken by the algorithms are showed in Tables II, III and IV.

For the linked-list algorithm, the graph is a family of curve lines passing through a common point for small N. We observe that the variation of HOLD times with N, given by the slope of each line, increases as the variance of the scheduling distribution increases. Accordingly, its performance is best under Discrete distributions (FIFO distributions) and worst with the Bimodal distribution. We point out that the average complexity of the algorithm is nearly independent of N under the Discrete(1). Moreover, this distribution gives only slight improvement over the Uniform(0.0, 2.0). That is, the algorithm performs identically and exceedingly well with these two distributions.

The Heap algorithm provides the best time performance over all the event set algorithms tested. In all cases we observe the expected $O(\log N)$ time complexity (logarithmic behaviour) of this algorithm. An important point it should be stressed is that the variation of HOLD times with N, given by the slope of each line, increases as the variance of the scheduling distribution decreases. It was expected because the liked-list algorithm scans backwards the list for the insertion operation, i.e., from large to small event time, while the linked-heap algorithm scans forward the array for the removal operation, i.e., from small to large event time. We also observe that the time performance of this algorithm is almost the same with all the distributions. Specifically, it is best with both Discrete(0, 1, 2) and Discrete(1) distributions (FIFO distributions) as well as with Uniform(0.0, 2.0) and Uniform(0.9, 1.1) distributions, and worst with Exponential(1).

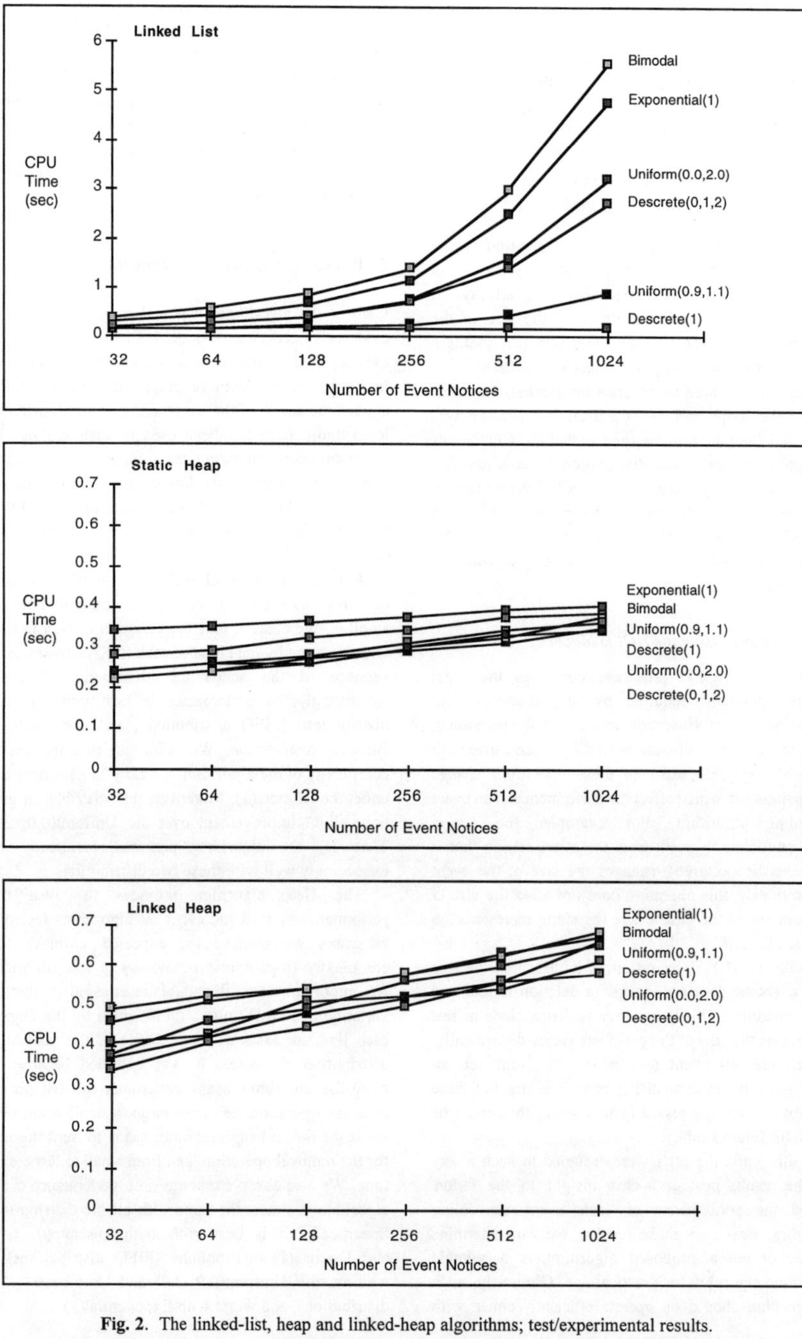

Fig. 2. The linked-list, heap and linked-heap algorithms; test/experimental results.

Table II: The Linked-list Algorithm; CPU Time

Size \ Distrib	EXPON	U(0.0, 2.0)	U(0.9, 1.1)	BIMODAL	DISCR(1)	DISCR(0, 1, 2)
N = 32	0.31	0.22	0.15	0.37	0.15	0.22
N = 128	0.64	0.40	0.19	0.84	0.16	0.40
N = 512	2.47	1.60	0.44	3.00	0.16	1.40
N = 1024	4.80	3.23	0.88	5.60	0.16	2.73

Table III: The Heap Algorithm; CPU Time

Size \ Distrib	EXPON	U(0.0, 2.0)	U(0.9, 1.1)	BIMODAL	DISCR(1)	DISCR(0, 1, 2)
N = 32	0.34	0.22	0.22	0.28	0.24	0.24
N = 128	0.36	0.27	0.26	0.32	0.28	0.26
N = 512	0.39	0.31	0.32	0.37	0.34	0.33
N = 1024	0.40	0.35	0.37	0.38	0.36	0.34

Table IV: The Linked-heap Algorithm; CPU Time

Size \ Distrib	EXPON	U(0.0, 2.0)	U(0.9, 1.1)	BIMODAL	DISCR(1)	DISCR(0, 1, 2)
N = 32	0.49	0.41	0.37	0.46	0.38	0.34
N = 128	0.54	0.51	0.48	0.54	0.49	0.45
N = 512	0.63	0.54	0.56	0.62	0.60	0.56
N = 1024	0.68	0.61	0.66	0.67	0.65	0.58

As far as the behaviour of the linked-heap algorithm is concerned, we observe that it performs very well with all the sizes and distributions. Specifically, it gave the expected $O(\log N)$ behaviour in all cases. As with the Heap algorithm, the variation of HOLD times with N given by the slope of each line, increases as the variance of the scheduling distribution decreases. It was an expected similarity since both algorithms use the same technique for the insertion and deletion operations.

It should be pointed out that the heap algorithm gives a slight improvement over the linked-heap algorithm. Its better behaviour is caused of the fact that it uses a static representation while the linked-heap uses a combination of static and dynamic representations.

The linked-heap algorithm was implemented having block size h = 32 and size of the arrays of pointers q = 32. Tests with others values of theses parameters is a topic for future work.

Although the graphical presentations of the results show the time performance of the algorithms tested clearly, we include here the real processor time (CPU time in *sec*) taken by the algorithms, for more clarity and accuracy. Tables II, III and IV correspond to the empirical mean complexity for the linked-list, heap and linked-heap algorithms, respectively. The rows correspond to the value of N and the columns to the choice of distribution delays.

7. Linked-List and Heap vs Linked-Heap

Comparing the linked-list with the heap structures, we can make the following remarks:

- For the linked-list structure consecutive event notices can be identified in $O(1)$, while for heaps in $O(N)$ (N denotes the number of notices in the set). Such operations are supported by some extant languages (see [7, 14]), but these are performed so infrequently that $O(N)$ time is acceptable.
- With the linked-list structure a FIFO or LIFO ordering is maintained automatically. The heap structure can also maintain these orderings; for this, a secondary compound key that contains the event creation time concatenated to the event time is necessary.
- The average complexity for the HOLD(T) operation is $O(N)$ for linked-lists, while the average and worst case complexity for the heap structure is $O(\log N)$. The experimental results presented in Fig. 2 confirm the linear and logarithmic behaviour of these structures. In addition, Fig. 3 points to the superiority of the heaps structures over the linked-list in respect of time performance.
- The implementation of heaps (static or static-dynamic) is based on index functions that replace pointers. As a consequence, to store event notices heaps require less of the memory needed for the linked-list structure (see Table V).

Take into consideration these remarks as well as the fact that the execution time is a critical factor in most situations, we are led to the conclusion that heaps are more efficient structures than linked-lists for the simulation event set.

The array representation (static representation) of heaps uses array indexing, which is often faster than pointer representation (dynamic representation). Moreover, it avoids the space overhead of pointers. All static representations have a predefined maximum size, whereas dynamic representations do not have this limitation. Hence, the static representation of a heap is preferred whenever we know the maximum possible size of the list of events in a simulation system; in all other situations, the dynamic representation is preferable.

The unknown amount of events that is stored and manipulated by a discrete event simulation system dictates clearly the use of a dynamic approach (not dynamic representation) for storing events in such a system.

The dynamic representation of the heap structure requires a large amount of memory locations. Furthermore, it has a time overhead associated with the pointer manipulation process. On the other hand, the static representation provides excellent time performance for both insertion and deletion operations, but it suffers for inability to maintain any amount of events. That is, the number of events in the system is bounded by Nmax, where Nmax is the predefined length of the array used to represent the heap. Additionally, extra space is reserved in the case where the number of events in the system is less that Nmax.

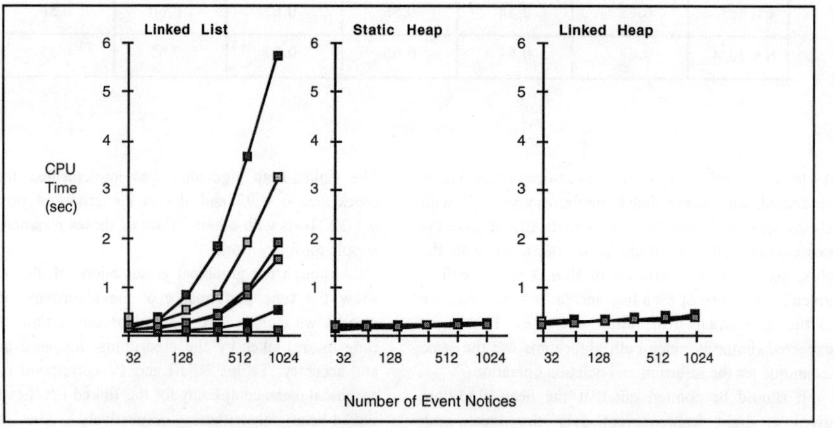

Fig. 3. Linked-list and heap vs linked-heap; test/experimental results.

We can overcame the above drawbacks adopting the linked-heap structure which incorporate both static and dynamic memory-allocation approaches. It provides very good (logarithmic) time performance, size flexibility and space economy. Moreover, the experimental results showed that its performance is relatively insensitive to variations in the scheduling distributions or the number of event notices in the event set. We realize that the heap (static representation) performs better that the linked-heap, but the deference is not noticeable.

Table V shows (depicted) the memory needed by each algorithm. For comparison reasons, we include in this table the memory needed by the dynamic representation of a heap. In this tabulation, *e* and *p* indicate the memory needed to store a data (event notice) and a pointer respectively. *N* is the number of events in the set and *N*max is the predefined maximum length of the array used to represent a heap (static representation).

Looking at table V, we observe that the linked-heap structure uses almost the same memory to storing the data (event notices) as the linked-list and heap (dynamic representation) structure. In the worst-case it uses only *h*-1 more data locations. We observe the waste of data space of the heap (static representation) in the case where *N* is much (smaller) (less) than *N*max.

Table V: Memory Needed By Each Algorithm

Structure	Data space	Pointer space
Linked-list	e N	2p N
Heap (static)	e Nmax	0
Heap (dynamic)	e N	3p N
Linked-heap	e $(N + h - i),\ 1 \leq i \leq h$	p $\lceil N / h^2 \rceil (2 + h)$

As far as the pointer space is concerned, it is clear that the static representation of the heap is out of competition since it uses no pointers. Comparing the remainder structures, we observe the superiority of the linked-heap in respect of storage economy. Specifically, for $h = 1.28$ it uses the same pointer space as linked-list and for $h = 1$ it uses the same pointer space as heap (dynamic representation). For all other cases it is by far the best. We note that, the pointer space of the linked-heap was evaluated with $h = q$. This also applied to the tests, i.e., $h = q = 32$.

The comparisons made in this section give evidence of using the linked-heap structure for the simulation event set.

8. Conclusions

The linked-heap structure presented in this paper could usefully replace the linked-list and heap (static or dynamic representation) structures in a general purpose discrete event simulation system. The processor time obtained with the linked-heap algorithm is relatively insensitive to variations in the scheduling distributions or the number of event notices in the event set. In general, it provides both time efficiency, size flexibility and space economy.

The results showed that the linked-list algorithm could easily be used in cases where the factor "speed" is no so important!!! We include here without any comment the last sentence of the Reeves' paper "... it may be thought scandalous if the simple linear linked-list remains in common use any longer" [20].

Recently, many articles have reported major improvements in execution time by implementing event scheduling algorithms other than the heap or the commonly used linked-list [1-3, 6-10, 13, 17, 19, 20, 21]. Some of them provide a constant insertion time independent of the number of event notices in the event set. Best performance is achieved with the indexed-list and the two-level scheduling algorithms [6, 18]. However, theses algorithms are unsuitable for a general purpose discrete event simulation system for several seasons (e.g., space consuming, setting parameters, etc.). For example, before the indexed-list can be used in a system, an adaptive mechanism must be devised to set some parameters (interval parameters) according to the operating conditions. The linked-heap algorithm does not have such limitations.

The results of this work prompts us to suggest the linked-heap as an efficient data structure for the simulation event set in a general purpose discrete event simulation system.

References

[1] J.H. Blackstone, G.L. Hogg and D.T. Phillips, "A Two-List Synchronization Procedure for Discrete Event Simulation", *Comm. of ACM*, Vol. 24, No. 12, pp. 825-829, 1981.

[2] R. Brown, "A Fast *O*(1) Priority Queue Implementation for the Simulation Event Set Problem", *Comm. of ACM*, Vol. 31, No. 12, pp. 1220-1227, 1988.

[3] J.C. Confort, "A Taxonomy and Analysis of Event Set Management Algorithms for Discrete Event Simulation", Proc. 12th Annual Simulation Symposium, pp. 115-146, 1979.

[4] E-E. Doberkat, "Inserting a New Element into a Heap", *BIT*, Vol. 21, pp. 255-269, 1981.

[5] D.Y. Downham and F.D.K. Roberts, "Multiplicative Congruential Pseudo-random Number Generators", *Comput. J*, Vol. 19, No. 1, pp. 74-77, 1975.

[6] J.O. Henriksen, "Event List Management - A Tutorial", Proc. 1983 Winter Simulation Conference, Washington, D.C., pp. 543-551, 1983.

[7] G.S. Fishman, *Concepts and Methods in Discrete Event Digital Simulation*, John Wiley & Sons, 1973.

[8] W.R. Franta, *The Process View of Simulation*, Elsevier North-Holland, New York, 1977.

[9] W.R. Franta, and K. Maly, "An Efficient Data Structure for the Simulation Event Set", *Comm. of ACM*, Vol. 20, No. 8, pp. 569-602, 1977.

[10] W.R. Franta, and K. Maly, "A Comparison of Heap and the TL Structure for the Simulation Event Set", *Comm. of ACM*, Vol. 21, No. 10, pp. 873-875, 1975.

[11] A.T. Fuller, "The Period of Pseudo-random Numbers Generated by Lehmer's Congruential Method", *The Computer Journal*, Vol. 19, No. 2, pp. 173-177, 1978.

[12] G.H. Gonnet, "Heaps Applied to Event Driven Mechanisms", *Comm. of ACM*, Vol. 19, No. 7, pp. 417-418, 1976.

[13] A. Jonassen and O-J. Dahl, "Analysis of an Algorithm for Priority Queue Administration", *BIT*, Vol. 15, pp. 409-422, 1975.

[14] A.M. Law and W.D. Kelton, *Simulation Modeling & Analysis*, McGraw-Hill, Inc., 1991.

[15] H.R. Lewis and L. Denenberg, *Data Structures & Algorithms*, Harpel Collins Publishers, New York, 1991.

[16] B.D. Lubachevsky, "Efficient Distributed Event-Driven Simulations of Multiple-Loop Networks", *Comm. of ACM*, Vol. 32, No. 1, pp. 111-123, 1989.

[17] W.M. McCormack and R.G. Sargent, "Analysis of Future Event Set Algorithms for Discrete Event Simulation", *Comm. of ACM*, Vol. 24, No. 12, pp. 801-812, 1981.

[18] I. Mitrani, *Simulation Techniques for Discrete Event Systems*, Cambridge University Press, 1982.

[19] S.D. Nikolopoulos and R. MacLeod, "An Experimental Analysis of Event Set Algorithms for Discrete Event Simulation", *Microprocessing and Microprogramming*, Vol. 36, No. 2, pp. 71-81, 1993.

[20] C.M. Reeves, "Complexity Analyses of Event Set Algorithms", *The Computer Journal*, Vol. 27, No. 1, pp. 72-79, 1984.

[21] J.G. Vaucher and P.A. Duval, "A Comparison of Simulation Event List Algorithms", *Comm. of ACM*, Vol. 18, No. 4, pp. 223-230, 1975.

LOGIDATA++: An Intelligent Object-Oriented Database Prototype

Ioan Alfred Letia and Ovidiu Pop
Department of Computer Science
Technical University of Cluj-Napoca
C. Daicoviciu 15, RO-3400 Cluj-Napoca, Romania
Ovidiu.Pop@cs.utcluj.ro

Abstract: An extended object-oriented data model LOGIDATA++ (derived from the LOGIDATA model) for object-oriented databases is proposed. Terminological reasoning with cycles has been applied for this extended data model. An objective SQL-type query language and a persistence mechanism for the LOGIDATA++ data model have been specified and implemented. Some of the advantages of using terminological reasoning for OO databases are illustrated by examples. The model seems to support rapid prototyping.

1 Introduction

It seems to be widely accepted that the OO model will gain in the end in Data Base Management Systems. Its competition, and motivation as well, come from the hierarchical and relational data models, which have a well defined semantics (particularly the relational model) and have contributed to sound DBMSs. The motivation for change lies in the limitations and disadvantages of traditional models. The necessity to reduce the cost of software projects through increased productivity in the analysis, design and implementation phases have caused an outbreak in the CASE market, several of these instruments using an OO approach. The lack of a unique OO data model leads to lack of finality for these tools: generation of OO code for an OO database model.

Our object oriented data model is an extension of LOGIDATA+ [2,4,5,6], derived from the model O_2 [12] and modified to allow the definition of cyclical relations between concepts [7]. The O_2 model has a sufficiently well defined semantics and has been implemented in the system O_2 developed by O_2 Technology. Moreover, this model turned out to be pretty appropriate for the terminological operations assumed by the reasoning mechanism.

Regarding the reasoning model, the terminological formalism (based on the organization of concepts in taxonomies) is quite natural for the domain of OO databases. Another decision that had to be taken was the well-known conflict between expressivity and determinism of concept languages, namely, any concept language that is sufficiently expressive is in the most general case intractable. The compromise and also the chosen solution is the most expressive, but decidable terminological language. The results communicated by the research groups from DFKI regarding ALCN and ALCR, sublanguages of ALCNR [10], that satisfy the requirement of determinism have been used by improving on two algorithms that determine subsumption by deciding the satisfiability of concepts.

As software engineering is clearly dominated by the object-oriented trend, the objective of our project was to study and try to find justifications for the application of a terminological formalism to the domain of OO databases. The goal was to specify and implement an OO database prototype on the basis of a general accepted architecture. The transfer of the terminological reasoning to the OO data model aimed to obtain solutions that could later allow further development of the project. The research reported here is a contribution to the specification/design of intelligent databases by applying a terminological formalism to OO databases.

2 SQLO Query Language

First generation OO databases have been criticized for not allowing declarative queries. The point of view that OO databases do not need query facilities is outdated. Moreover, the existence of an expressive and optimized query language is a quality feature of every OO database system [15].

Almost all OO database systems use optimization methods proposed for the relational data model. However, there are a few problems closely connected to the OO models that make the querying in OO databases more difficult than in relational databases: (i) *OO systems are type based systems*. Unlike relational systems, that operate on a single aggregate type (relation), OO systems create and handle an extended set of types. The result of applying operators of an OO algebra are, in general, sets (collections) of objects of (possibly) different types. Moreover, the same operators may be applied on semantically distinct collection types (e.g. sets, lists, bags), and this imposes additional requirements on the inference of types in order to correctly determine the resulting type. (ii) *encapsulation*. The optimization of queries in the relational model is dependent on the physical structure of data. In the OO case, data and procedure encapsulation raise the problem of access to data. In the LOGIDATA++ model, the access to data has been solved by treating the query processing as an application capable to "break" encapsulation, having as effect the direct access to data [9]. (iii) *complex objects and inheritance*. Objects have complex structures, where the state of an object is a reference to other objects. Accessing these objects is based on the optimization of path expressions. Also, as objects belong to types in inheritance hierarchies, the efficient access to objects raises another problem that distinguishes the OO domain from the processing of relational queries. (iv) *OO models*. Unlike the relational model, the OO database model lacks a unique definition model. Although there is an almost unanimous consensus over the features that an OO model should have, the concrete framework differs from one OO model to another. Therefore, processing queries may differ fundamentally, up to incompatibility in the limit.

OO database models incorporate elements and underlying mechanisms originating from relational models, complex object models or OO programming languages. Even though there is a lack of consensus regarding an overall definition of an OO database, features like complex structures, abstract data types, object identity, subtyping and late binding are unanimously considered as necessary ingredients.

The GemStone system [13], developed by Servio Logic, is a system based on Smalltalk for which the query language OPAL has been developed. OPAL is a complete language for defining and handling of data, in which a query is expressed in the general form *select : argument message*. The query can be applied to a set of objects, the function of the argument being to describe the selection condition. The module for data queries in the O_2 data model is based on a declarative query language [3], on an algebraic query language or a rule-based query language. The declarative language and algebra allow the use of both objects and values, the returned result being a value. The rule-based language is used exclusively to handle objects with identity. In Orion [11], the declarative language has been designed to allow queries on a single class or the descendants of this class in the hierarchy.

2.1 Design Criteria for SQLO

The SQLO (SQL Objective) has been designed as data query language in conformance with the LOGIDATA++ data model [14]. The following principles and/or hypotheses have been observed: (i) SQLO is not a complete query language. This hypothesis is a direct consequence of the fact that, being a version of SQL, SQLO inherits its incompleteness feature [8]. In compensation, SQLO allows an easy access to the objects in the database. (ii) SQLO allows a declarative access to objects. (iii) SQLO is based on the LOGIDATA++ data model. (iv) the formal semantics of SQLO is easy to define. (v) the syntax of the language is of SQL type. (vi) SQLO offers both high-level primitives that operate on sets of objects and low-level primitives that allow access to the values of object attributes. (vii) SQLO does not explicitly specify operators for updating (INSERT, DELETE, UPDATE), their function being performed by the operations defined on objects. (viii) SQLO can easily be optimized due to its declarative feature.

As an independent language, SQLO allows the query of objects through their names, that play the role of entry points in the database. As a language associated to LOGIDATA++, SQLO facilitates the query of data through expressions that may have atoms, complex structures, collections or literals. An SQLO query is a function that, applied on an entry, generates an object whose type is inferred on the basis of query operator.

2.2 Object Identity Reflected in SQLO

Object identity may lead to important decisions regarding the initial design of a data query language associated to an OO data model [1]. In an OO database model, an object has an identity independent of its state. The notion of object identity is formally similar to that of the key of a relation, in the sense of unique identification. The difference resides in the fact that the value of an object identifier, unlike that of a key, is inaccessible to the user, the values of an object identifier being handled by the system.. From the point of view of a data query language, object identity favours object sharing. In the case of data models with object identity, defining equality between objects plays an important role. Since the equality operator appears in predicates used to express queries, object identity manifests itself especially at generation of new objects through a query and in the case of an alternative definition of the notion of query equivalence.

2.3 Object Equality

Object equality in a query may refer to any definition of equality for the type of generic object (e.g. identity, equality or weak equality) or to equality operations defined for certain abstract data types. Any query language may allow the use of a variety of predicates, for example, from the operation

a.car = b.car,

the equality operator may be interpreted in several ways: (i) as identity between sets (i.e. a and b refer to the same set of cars), or (ii) as weak identity between sets (the sets of cars referred to by a and b contain exactly the same cars) or (iii) as sets with the same cardinality. Therefore, in the presence of object identity, the equality operator may be treated as a method.

2.4 Object Creation

A major decision for any data query language is linked to the existence or inexistence of a facility to create new objects by the query language. In principle, if the query language does not allow the creation of new objects, then queries do not allow the appearance of new relations between objects. On the other hand, if the query language allows the creation of identity objects, then it must have the necessary mechanisms to determine and handle new identities. As far as SQLO is concerned, the decision of not allowing the creation of new objects leads to the exclusion of operations like INSERT, DELETE or UPDATE. It has been considered that to implement such operators would be redundant, since the functions of such operators would be covered by the mechanisms or methods specified at TBox and/or ABox level. Moreover, the implementation of these operators would also cause complications for the maintenance of data integrity, since after each object creation the coherence verification mechanism should be invoked, which might significantly increase the processing time of some queries.

Therefore, the result of an SQLO query is an object with or without identity, where some objects are generated by the interpreter of the SQLO query language, and others derive directly from the database (ABox).

2.5 SQLO Grammar

In a reasonably flexible BNF, the grammar of SQLO may be expressed as follows:

query_program ::= {query_definition;}query
query_definition ::= **define** identifier **as** query
(a) Basic queries
query::= nil | true | false | integer | real | string
(b) Arithmetic
query::= query + query | query - query | query * query | query / query
query::= - query | query ***mod*** query | ***abs***(query)
(c) Comparison
query::= query = query | query != query | query >= query | query <= query
(d) Boolean expressions
query::= **not** query | query **and** query | query **or** query
(e) Database access operators
query::= query **dot** attribute_name | query **dot** relationship_name
dot::= **.** | →
(f) Collections
query::= **for all** identifier **in** query : query
query::= **exists** identifier **in** query :query
query::= query **in** query
query::= **select [distinct]** query
from: identifier **in** query {,identifier **in** query}
[where query]
query::= **sort** identifier **in** query **by** query {,query}
query::= **count**(query) | **sum**(query) | **min**(query) | **max**(query) | **avg**(query)

query::= **group** identifier **in** query
by (identifier : query {,identifier : query})
[with (identifier : query {,identifier : query})]

3 LOGIDATA++

LOGIDATA++ is an OO database prototype which serves for attaining the following goals: (i) all features of an OO database should be reflected by the system; (ii) terminological reasoning on concepts and values conforming to the LOGIDATA++ data model should be allowed by the system; (iii) specification and implementation of a data query language should be adequate for the data model used (SQLO language) and a persistence mechanism should be available.

3.1 TBox

The grammar for the TBox of LOGIDATA++ (Fig. 1) has been extended (relative to the original LOGIDATA+ model) as in fig. 1.
(i) A new basic type called **range** has been introduced, which from a semantic point of view facilitates the expression of constraints of type value domain on types of LOGIDATA++. (ii) An explicit conjunction between classes (denoted by **INTERSECT**) completes and augments the ways of declaring a new class in LOGIDATA++. (iii) The cardinality operator on sets of the general form **(integer, integer)** has the same semantics as the terminological operators for roles **atmost** and **atleast.** (iv) The keyword **PERSIST** allows to declare all objects of a class (and implicitly all objects of subsumed classes) as persistent.

3.2 Terminological Cycle Elimination

The elimination of terminological cycles uses a dependence graph (with vertices given by class names, and edges represented by "depends_on" relations) labelled by instantiation and finally validated. In general, a dependence graph is specified according to the definition:
Definition A dependence graph is a triple <N, A, r>, consisting of
(i) a set N of nodes;
(ii) a collection A of edges called (a-edges) denoted by <n_1, n_2, a>, where n_1 and n_2 are nodes, and a is an attribute name. Every a-edge is labelled by an attribute name.
(iii) a node r from N, called root node.

A node from a dependence graph is a pair <C, T>, where C is a set of concept names (node atoms) and a collection T of tuples called node r-edges. An r-edge is a tuple of the form <R,m,M,G>, where R is a role name, m and M are two positive integer values representing a minimum and a maximum, respectively, and G is a dependence graph recursively defined representing the node restriction graph.

Intuitively, a dependence graph is an oriented and labelled multigraph. The graph nodes correspond to the descriptions, and the edges to the restrictions imposed on roles or attributes.

3.3 ABox

Our ABox grammar preserves the structure of LOGIDATA+ [3,4]. ABox plays the role of container of all known values (atomic or complex) associated to concepts from TBox or, in other words, it represents the extension of the OO database. The validation of data from ABox is realized by the algorithm for coherence validation and data consistence invoked after hybrid reasoning. The (validated) values from ABox represent the entry data ("raw materials") for the instantiation process.

3.4 Hybrid Reasoning

Up to this moment, between the two basic components of the system (ABox and TBox) no apparent link has been established, each one having been treated and presented on its own with their own properties and mechanisms. Actually, all steps previous to hybrid reasoning are independent steps, with exactly the role to anticipate the moment in which the link between the intensional and extensional levels is performed. Hybrid reasoning is specific to the terminological formalism and represents the moment of "unification" between the terminological concepts and their values from ABox. From the point of view of the LOGIDATA++ system, hybrid reasoning is performed by constructing an intermediate file using input data from the files ABox and TBox using the grammar shown in figure 2. As can easily be noticed, hybrid reasoning consists in combining already obtained results, namely: (i) from TBox for each concept are extracted: (a) the set of all concepts subsumed by the current concept, (b) the set of concepts relative to which cyclic relations exist, and (c) the set of concepts referring the current concept; (ii) from the ABox values the expansion of concepts is performed, but without the actual values (which may be done after the instantiation of all concepts only), but with types or domains of admissible values only.

4. Persistence in LOGIDATA++

In LOGIDATA++ any object of a class may be declared persistent, by inclusion of the keyword **PERSIST** in the class declaration. Persistence in LOGIDATA++ is *orthogonal to the system of types*. As the definition and alocation of persistent objects is not different from the definition and alocation of temporary objects, persistence is *orthogonal with respect to object instantiation too*. In all files associated to object descriptions there is no difference between the definition of a temporary object and a persistent object. Also, there is no further distinction between objects regarding their manipulation. This model of persistence obeys the principle of *behavioural transparency*, in the sense that the user's only responsability is to decide upon persistent classes, the rest of the mechanism being transparent. *Persistence propagation* is by inheritance, meaning that any subclass of a persistent class will also be persistent.

4.1 Basic Architecture for Persistence

The main steps associated to the implementation of persistence are shown in figure 3. Some of the details of the persistence mechanism are the following. (i) *TBox traversal* aims to determine at least one class prefixed with the keyword **PERSIST**. (ii) *Persistance mechanism initialization* refers to the setting of some variables and structure fields to indicate the fact that a mechanism to coordinate persistence has been created at the level of the database associated to the TBox accessed in the previous step. (iii) *Persistence propagation* consists in the propagation (transparent to the user) of the persistence property to the level of all subsumed classes declared persistent in TBox. As already mentioned, there are two possible approaches to propagate persistence: by inheritance or by reference. The solution adopted in LOGIDATA++ was to propagate persistence by inheritance. (iv) *Persistence structure creation*: for each persistent class a structure is created for saving instance objects of that particular class. (v) *Persistence structure completion* corresponds to the step in which instance objects of a class become effectively persistent by copying/transfer on disc. (vi) Persistence *control structures setting* refers to the initialization of data structures that have the role to control the persistence mechanism (i.e. handling data in files). (vii) *Instantiation optimization* refers to the reduction of the time required by the reasoning algorithms to determine the instances of a class. The set of all instances may be obtained as a union of two sets: (a) a first set resulted from instantiation algorithms (possible and legal instances); (b) the set of all persistent instances for which the membership to a class has been previously deduced.

4.2 Persistence Example

In the example shown in figure 4 it is assumed that the user wishes to declare persistent all instances of type Employee and Branch. As a consequence, the file associated to the TBox modelling the company will have the classes Employee and Branch prefixed with the keyword PERSIST.

The persistence propagation may be seen in the file describing the *company* (figure 5) through the symbol "P" prefixing the types that have become persistent by inheritance. We can notice that the persistence declared for concepts Employee and Branch is transmitted to the concepts Secretary and Clerk, respectively Department and Office. For the six persistent classes from the previous example files will be created containing all the instances of these classes. On loading ABox, these files will be filled with objects.

The visualization of the files created by the persistence mechanism is a verification of the theoretical considerations discussed above.In table 1, the features associated to the persistence mechanism in several implementations of OO databases are presented. From the comparative analysis of these features we may conclude that the persistence mechanism in LOGIDATA++ is completely defined and it has all the facilities that the set of implementations considered have.

5 Conclusions

The specification and implementation of LOGIDATA++ extends its predecessor on several lines: (i) it extends the number of operators and the semantics of some operators in the OO definition language attached to the model; (ii) adds an object identity mechanism to the LOGIDATA++ model; (iii) adds a persistence mechanism to the LOGIDATA++ model; (iv) adds an OO SQL-type query language (SQLO) to the LOGIDATA++ data model.

Regarding the reasoning model adopted, it is our view that a terminological formalism (based on the organization of concepts in taxonomies) is suitable in a natural manner to the domain of OO databases. One fundamental problem that required a compromising position was the conflict between expressivity and determinism of concept (terminological) languages, namely, any concept language sufficiently expressive is in the most general case intractable. The compromise and at the same time the solution chosen consists in the most expressive, but still decidable terminological language. For the identification of such a language the results communicated by research groups from DFKI have been used. More exactly, the languages ALCN and ALCR, sublanguages of ALCNR, satisfy the requirement of determinism. Two improved algorithms have been developed for these languages to determine subsumption on the basis of satisfiability of concepts. The examples presented illustrate of the model. Future work will cover enterprise modelling at terminological level, as a way to achieve rapid prototyping through reuse of analysis knowledge.

References

[1] S. Abiteboul, P. Kanellakis - Object Identity as a Query Language Primitive, in SIGMOD Proc., ACM, 1989, pag 159-173.

[2] A. Artale - Introducing Taxonomic Reasoning in LOGIDATA+, in Lecture Notes in Computer Science, Springer 1993, P.Atzeni eds., pag. 85 - 104.

[3] F. Bancilhon - Object Database Systems : Functional Architecture, Proc. Object Technologies in Advanced Software, Kanazawa, Japan, 1993, pag. 163-175.

[4] D. Beneventano - Subsumption for complex object data models. Proc. of the Intl. Conf. on database Theory, Berlin, 1992.

[5] S. Bergamaschi - On Taxonomic Reasoning in Conceptual Design. ACM Transactions on Database Syst., Vol. 17, No. 3, Sept.1993, pag. 385-422.

[6] D. Beneventano, S.Bergamaschi et al. - Taxonomic reasoning with cycles in LOGIDATA+. Research report 1993.

[7] S. Bergamaschi, B.Nebel - Acquisition and validation of complex object database schemata supporting multiple inheritance. Technical report 1993.

[8] R.G.C. Cattell - The Object Database Standard : ODMG-93, Morgan Kaufmann Publishers, San Mateo, California, 1993, pag. 65-81.

[9] S. Cluet, C. Delobel - A general framework for the optimization of object-oriented queries. Proc. of ACM-SIGMOD Intl. Conference on Data Management, 1992, 383-392.

[10] B. Hollunder, W. Nutt - Subsumption algorithms for concept description languages, Proc. 9th ECAI' 90 Stockholm, 1990, pag. 348-353.

[11] W. Kim - A foundation for object-oriented databases, MCC Technical Report, 1988.

[12] C. Lecluse,P.Richard,F.Velez - O2, an Object-Oriented Data Model, in Building an Object-Oriented Database System, F. Bancilhon, C.Delobel, P.Kanellakis eds., Morgan Kaufman Publ, 1992, pag. 77-97.

[13] D. Maier, J. Stein - Development and Implementation of an Object-Oriented DBMS, in Research Directions in Object-Oriented Programming, MIT Press, 1987, pag.355-392

[14] O. Pop - Terminological reasoning in object-oriented databases, Ph.D. thesis, Technical University of Cluj-Napoca, Oct. 1996.

[15] M. Stonebraker et. al - Third Generation Data Base System Manifesto, ACM SIGMOD Record, Vol 19, No 3, pag. 31-44.

Persistence	EXODUS	ONTOS	ODE	O_2	LOGIDATA++
Language	E	C++	C++	O_2C	*C++*
Principle	syntactic	inheritance	syntactic	nominative	*syntactic*
Orthogonal./ types	DB-types	NO	YES	YES	*YES*
Orthogonal./ instances	"persistent" "in"	YES	"persistent" "pnew"	YES	*YES*
Root of persistence	instance collection	instance aggregate	class	instance	*class*
Propagation	structural	inheritance	NO	structural	*inheritance*
Behavioural persistence	YES	Hybrid	YES	YES	*YES*

Table 1

<declaration>	:= <type_declaration>|<class_declaration>
<type_declaration>	:= **TYPE**<type_id>=<constructor_type>
<class_declaration>	:= **PERSIST** <class_decl> | <class_decl>
<class_decl>	:= **CLASS**<class_id> (**ISA** <class_id>+) =<type_id> |
	CLASS<class_id>(**ISA**<class_id>+) = <constructor_type> |
	CLASS<class_id> =**INTERSECT**<class_id> <class_id>+]
<constructor_type>	:= <tuple_type> | <set_type> | <range>
<type>	:= <constructor_type> | <class_id> | <type_id> | <base_type>
<tuple_type>	:= **TUPLE**<tuple_component>+ **END**
<tuple_component>	:= <label> : <type>
<set_type>	:= **SET OF** <type> (integer,integer)
<range>	:= <integer_range> | <float_range>
<integer_range>	:= integer - integer
<float_range>	:= float - float
<base_type>	:= string | integer | float | range
<label>	:= <identifier>
<class_id>	:= <identifier>

Fig. 1 TBox grammar in LOGIDATA++

```
declaration          :=  T( class_name ) = class_declaration | class_relationship
class_declaration    := tuple_value | set_value
class_relationship   := K (class_name +)  D (class_name +) R (class_name +)
tuple_value          :=  [ tuple_component +]
set_value            := { '<' int int '>' , base_value }
tuple_component      := label : value_type
value_type           := tuple_value | set_value | base_value
base_value           :=  string | ' * ' string  | int | ' * ' int  |  real  |' * ' real | class_name | ' * '  ' < ' int int ' > '
class_name           :=  ' # ' identifier
label                := identifier

where:
    K(class_name+) denotes the set of concept names subsumed by the specified concept
    D(class_name+) denotes the set of  concept names refered by the specified concept
    R(nume_clasă+) denotes the set of concept names cyclicly refered by the specified concept
```

Fig.2 Grammar associated to hybrid reasoning

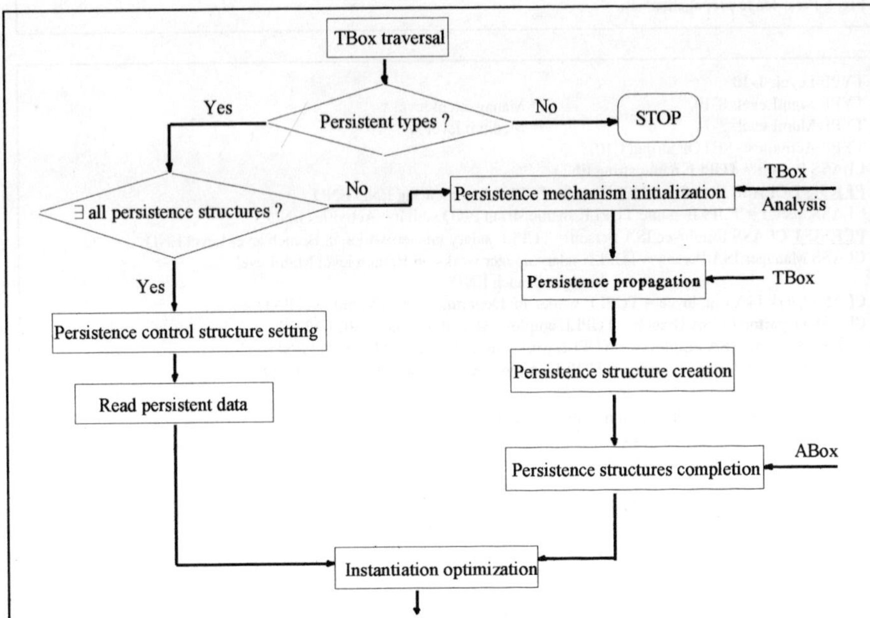

Fig. 3 Persistence mechanism

```
T(#Person)=[name:""] K(#Employee,#Manager) D() R()
PT(#Branch)=[name:[bname:""]] K(#Department,#Office) D() R()
T(#Sector)=[name:[sname:""], activity:{<1 10>,""}] K(#Office) D() R()
PT(#Employee)=[salary:1, works_in:#Branch, level:<1 10>, name:""] K(#Clerk,#Secretary)
            D(#Branch) R()
T(#Manager)=[salary:1, works_in:#Branch, level:<8 10>, head_of:#Branch, name:""] K()
            D(#Branch) R()
PT(#Clerk)=[works_in:#Department, level:<2 7>,salary:1, name:""] K() D() R(#Departament)
PT(#Department)=[employs:{<1 100>,#Clerk}, name:[bname:""]] K() D(#Clerk)R()
PT(#Secretary)=[works_in:#Office, level:<2 7>, salary:1, name:""] K() D() R(#Office)
PT(#Office)=[employs:{<1 10>,#Secretary}, name: [bname:"", sname:""],
            activity:{<1 10>,""}] K() D(#Secretary) R()
```

Fig. 5 Persistence propagation

```
TYPE Level=1-10
TYPE MgmLevel=8-10                  /* Management level */
TYPE MdmLevel=2-7                   /* Medium level */
TYPE Activities =SETOF string(1,10)
CLASS Person = TUPLE name:string END
PERSIST CLASS Branch = TUPLE  name:TUPLE bname:string END END
CLASS Sector = TUPLE name:TUPLE sname:string END activity: Activities END
PERSIST CLASS Employee ISA Person = TUPLE salary:integer works_in:Branch level:Level END
CLASS Manager ISA Person = TUPLE salary:integer works_in:Branch level:MgmLevel
                         head_of:Branch END
CLASS Clerk ISA Employee = TUPLE works_in: Department level:MdmLevel END
CLASS Department ISA Branch = TUPLE employs:SETOF Clerk(1,100) END
CLASS Secretary ISA Employee = TUPLE works_in: Office level:MdmLevel END
CLASS Office ISA Branch Sector = TUPLE employs:SETOF Secretary (1,10) END
```

Fig. 4 Class persistence declaration in the Company model TBox

Computation of Reed-Muller Expansions from Incompletely Specified Boolean Functions

G. A. Khuwaja, Ph.D., A.M.I.E.E.†
A. N. Abu-Rezq, Ph.D., M.I.E.E.E.
A. S. Tolba, Ph.D., M.I.E.E.E.
Digital Electronics Group
Department of Physics
University of Kuwait
Safat 13060, P O Box 5969, Kuwait
†email: khuwaja@kuc01.kuniv.edu.kw

Abstract

In this paper we investigate the possibility of exploiting incompletely specified Boolean functions for the purpose of minimizing Reed-Muller (R-M) forms. Various techniques for handling incompletely specified Boolean functions for the case of R-M domain are investigated. A computer algorithm for handling incompletely specified Boolean functions is presented. The computer results of functions are compared to those in the literature.

1 Introduction

It has long been conjectured that the realization of switching functions as mod-2 (Exclusive-OR) sum-of-products (ESOPs) is more economical than the conventional sum-of-products (SOPs) [1, 2]. However, the Reed-Muller (R-M) forms are not yet popular because of the lack of efficient algorithms for circuit design and function manipulations, and lack of convincing proof that its use really is more efficient than SOP representation [3]. And perhaps one reason for the low popularity of Ex-OR gates is that, in earlier technologies, such gates were expensive and much larger and slower than AND/NAND/OR/NOR blocks. This is no longer true with the present technologies [4, 5, 6].

The Reed-Muller (R-M) algebraic domain supports a large number of possible canonical forms. These have been arranged into a nested hierarchy of families which have increasing size and decreasing general structure [7]. The positive or zero-polarity R-M canonical form for n variables, in which every variable occurs in true (uncomplemented) form, is just a special case of a set of 2^n generalized fixed-polarity forms. These, in turn, are members of a larger family of 3^n Kronecker mixed-polarity forms in which some or all the variables can occur in both true and complemented form. Much larger families of pseudo- and quasi-Kronecker forms also exist which still retain some semblance of general structure and their coefficients can be deduced from an extended form of the normal truth vector. Beyond. these forms are an even larger number which retain very little general structure and are not easily derived in a simple systematic way. This implies that the minimum form of a given function could be found by searching through *all* the available canonical forms. However, this will not usually be a feasible proposition. If the number of canonical forms is restricted to be just the well-structured fixed or mixed polarity types. the search time may be reduced but the absolute minimum form cannot be guaranteed. An alternative approach, based on the more general problem of simplifying modulo-2 sum-of-products expressions. has been tackled, using a wide variety of techniques adapted from those employed for Boolean algebraic expressions, by a number of researchers [8. 9. 10]. Recently, it has been proved [11] that these two approaches are ultimately equivalent provided all the canonical forms are considered.

An incompletely specified Boolean function is characterized by the fact that one or more of the rows on its truth table have undefined output values. These undefined conditions manifest themselves as *don't-cares* or ϕ terms on the equivalent Karnaugh map and they can be utilized to simplify the synthesis of the function. This is achieved by adopting the values for these undefined terms and the particular values selected depends on values of the specified portion of the function. Thus, design methods catering for ϕ terms are function dependent and a simple strategy of electing to set all unspecified terms to zero or to one does not generally yield an optimum representation [12]. ϕ terms provide a degree of freedom to the process of logic minimization and synthesis. ϕ terms are usually encountered at a high level specification stage of the function, but are also generated at the intermediate stages of certain decomposition and optimization procedures [13]. Logic functions currently in use have of the order of a hundred inputs and as many outputs, many of the outputs being unspecified. The specification of ϕ terms to fixed logical values to achieve certain goals such as minimum area, etc, is a difficult problem often requiring exhaustive searches in the domain of all possible solutions [14].

In the case of classical Quine-McCluskey logic minimization procedure, the addition of ϕ terms does not introduce any extra complexity into the procedure for determining the minimal sums. Any ϕ terms that are present are treated as 1-terms in forming the prime implicants, with the exception that no prime implicants containing only ϕ terms are formed. No prime implicants are included in order to ensure that each ϕ term is contained in at least one prime implicant of the minimal sum [15]. This is quite obvious that ϕ terms are used to make the prime implicants as large as possible.

However, when an incompletely specified function is transformed to Reed-Muller (R-M) form the ϕ terms are transformed along with the specified terms and their effects are distributed over several terms of the new representation. Certain choices for the values of unspecified terms in the operational domain will lead to more economic function domain representations than others [12]. For most procedures currently in use, the minimality is measured as the number of product terms or the number of literals in the sum-of-product-expansion (SOPE) of the function. However, ϕ terms can also be assigned to meet other goals such as testability, if these can be formulated in terms of appropriate cost functions. Such requirements are often extremely difficult to formulate or too complex to evaluate. Hence, an alternate approach is to restrict the implementations to networks that are easily testable, such as, R-M networks [16].

In this paper we present a computer algorithm for handling incompletely specified switching functions. The method incorporates a transform scheme for incompletely specified Boolean functions based on the consistency of the successive coefficients which could be combined to give minimal R-M form. A combination of coefficients like 0011 or 1100 does not result in such a large reduction in the number of R-M product (π) terms 1001 or 0110 produces still less reduction while 1101 or 1011 is the worst case.

2 Background

In recent years, the interest in the design of logic circuits which use ExOR gates has increased. Functions realized by such circuits can have fewer gates. fewer connections, and take up less area when realized in VLSI circuits [17]. The promise of cheaper and easily testable implementations using ExOR and finite field circuits makes transform-based methods a viable alternative to standard synthesis approaches. However, the problem arises when we have an incompletely specified Boolean function or system. Little research has been done in covering the case of incompletely specified functions, where it is possible to minimize R-M forms by assigning suitable values for the unspecified points [6, 18].

Tran [10] described a graphical method for handling incompletely specified functions. By this, ϕ terms in a R-M coefficient map will not be determined until after grouping in the same way as in a conventional Karnaugh map where each ϕ term is determined after grouping the minterms or the maxterms which gives a minimal SOPs or POSs (product-of-sums). At first, all the *don't care* terms are denoted by ϕ and each can be assumed either 0 or 1. However. in constructing the R-M coefficient map of an incompletely specied function, some of the cells will have undetermined values which are the ExOR of more than one ϕ terms. This technique is useful only for small functions. Green [12] presented an exhaustive search. In this, the Boolean function is partitioned into specified (with all ϕ terms set to zero) and unspecified (with all specified terms set to zero) portions. Both portions are then transformed into the R-M coefficient forms separately. One of the possible combinations of ϕ terms is selected out of 2^m. here m is the number of ϕ terms. The resultant R-M form for the unspecified portion is then added to the specified R-M form, term by term, for this particular selection of the ϕ terms, and weight of the function is noted down. This process is repeated for the rest of possible combinations of ϕ terms. Varma and Trachtenberg [15] proposed a heuristic (approximate) to avoid the exhausitive search, by considering the unspecified points in the order of their perceived influence on the polynomial coefficients. McKenzie et al. [19] devised a branch and bound method that is capable of finding the optimal assignment of unspecified points.

3 Vector-Folding

This algorithm handles the incompletely specified Boolean functions in four passes:

Pass One:

1. Divide the incompletely specified Boolean vector **d** into an array of size $2^{n-2} \times 4$.

2. Get $(n-2)$ bit length binary number of the row number.

3. Find which rows can be combined by knowing the number of zeros present in the $(n-2)$ bit row number, e.g., a row numbered $(0)_{10}$ for $n = 6$ can be combined to rows numbered $(1, 2, 4, 8)_{10}$ because $(0)_{10} = (0000)_2$ has four zeros so it can be combined with $(0001)_2 = (1)_{10}$, $(0010)_2 = (2)_{10}$, $(0100)_2 = (4)_{10}$, and $(1000)_2 = (8)_{10}$ only. Likewise, a row numbered $(3)_{10} = (0011)_2$ can only be combined to $(0111)_2 = (7)_{10}$, and $(1011)_2 = (11)_{10}$.

4. Specify the ϕ terms of *all* the dependent rows (two rows are said to be dependent if they could be combined) consistently as follows:

   (a) Take any two rows which can be combined.

   (b) The two rows must have same specified coefficients. If not, go to step 5.

   (c) If one coefficient of the one row is ϕ term, then, replace it by the corresponding specified coefficient of the other row.

   (d) If both coefficients are ϕ terms then: if the ϕ term coefficient of the row is even (odd) then look for the next (previous) odd (even) number coefficients of both rows and if they are also either ϕ terms or zeros, replace all the four coefficients by zeros otherwise replace the one even (odd) coefficient by another even (odd) coefficient.

5. Repeat the step 4 for all 2^{n-2} rows.

Pass Two:

1. If two coefficients of a row are next to each other and first is even and second is odd, i.e., (0 and 1) or (2 and 3) and either both are ϕ terms or one of them is 0 and other is ϕ term then replace them by zeros.

2. Specify the individual row with consistency, i.e., 0101, 1010, 1111, and 0000.

3. Repeat the steps 1 and 2 for all 2^{n-2} rows.

Pass Three:

1. If there are still rows with ϕ terms and may be combined then:

   (a) Get the quaternary code of the rows by considering first even coefficient as the least significant and second odd coefficient as the most significant by setting ϕ terms equal to zeros and then ones, e.g.,
   row 0 = { ϕ 1 1 0 }
   case 1: $\phi = 0$; { ϕ[0] 1 1 0 } → { 1 ϕ[0] 0 1 } = { 2 1 }
   case 2: $\phi = 1$; { ϕ[1] 1 1 0 } → { 1 ϕ[1] 0 1 } = { 3 1 }
   row 1 = { 0 0 0 1 } → { 0 0 1 0 } = { 0 2 }

   (b) Select the two rows so that the sum (modulo-4) is the same, i.e., for the above case, row 0 = { 3 1 } = 3 mod-4 1 = $(2)_4$ and row 1 = { 0 2 } = 0 mod-4 2 = $(2)_4$. Hence set ϕ equal to one.

Pass Four:

1. Replace all the remaining ϕ terms, if any, by zeros.

For example, for $n = 3$ and an incompletely specified truth vector, BF = [ϕ 1 1 0 ϕ ϕ 0 1], the ϕ terms can be specified as follows;

Pass One: BF = ϕ 1 1 0
ϕ ϕ 0 1
Pass Two: BF = ϕ 1 1 0
0 0 0 1

Pass Three:
row 0: case 1: 0 1 1 0 = 2 mod-4 1 = $(3)_4$
case 2: 1 1 1 0 = 3 mod-4 1 = $(2)_4$
row 1: case 1 & 2: 0 0 0 1 = 0 mod-4 2 = $(2)_4$
Hence, the specified truth vector is given by.

BF = [1 1 1 0 0 0 0 1]

4 Experimental Results

A computer program is written in C++ by implementing the developed algorithm. As there are no benchmark results reported for the incompletely specified functions, the computer results obtained for a few selected functions [10, 12, 15] are given. The specified function is then simplified using the already developed technique [20]. Also, the average results obtained for a set of 100 randomly generated incompletely specified Boolean functions for a range of three to six variables are given in the Table 1. From

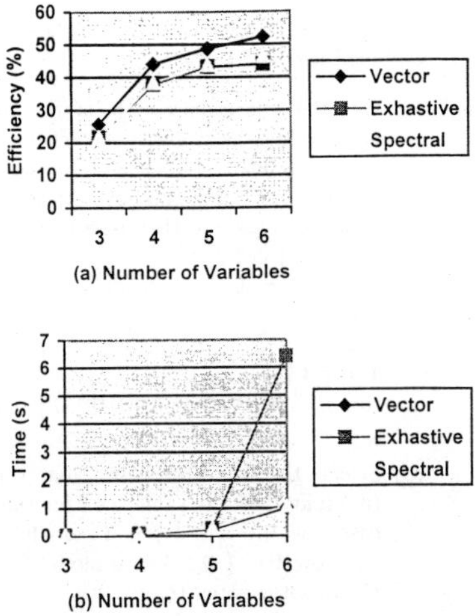

Figure 1: Pictorial illustration for various techniques (a) Efficiency (percentage reduction) vs variables, and (b) time vs variables.

the results, it can be seen that the overall performance of newly developed vector-folding technique is better than the existing techniques in both the reduction of weight (efficiency in percentage) for a given function and computer execution time. Although, from exhaustive search, the number of coefficients, i.e., the weight of R-M function vector is minimum, however, the final reduced R-M form is not necessarily minimum. Fig. 1 gives the pictorial illustration for various techniques.

	Vector-Folding		Exhastive		Spectral	
n	time	$\eta(\%)$	time	$\eta(\%)$	time	$\eta(\%)$
3	.031s	25.71	.034s	21.78	.036s	21.78
4	.076s	44.02	.084s	37.91	.084s	38.30
5	0.25s	48.67	.277s	43.18	.277s	43.81
6	1.02s	52.30	6.41s	43.85	1.09s	46.38

Table 1: Results, on average, for vector-folding, exhaustive-search, and spectral techniques.

1. This is an example from [10], $\sum m(0,3,5,6,9,10,15) + \sum d(4,13,14)$. The three possible given solutions are:
   $f(x_1x_2x_3x_4) = \sum m(0,3,5,6,9,10,14,15) = x_3 \oplus x_4 \oplus \acute{x}_1\acute{x}_2 \oplus x_1x_2x_4$
   $f(x_1x_2x_3x_4) = \sum m(0,3,5,6,9,10,13,15) = x_3 \oplus x_4 \oplus \acute{x}_1\acute{x}_2 \oplus x_1x_2x_3$
   $f(x_1x_2x_3x_4) = \sum m(0,3,5,6,9,10,13,14,15) = x_3 \oplus x_4 \oplus \acute{x}_1\acute{x}_2 \oplus x_1x_2x_3x_4$
   Our solution is: $f(x_4x_3x_2x_1) = \sum m(0,3,4,5,6,9,10,15) = \acute{x}_4 \oplus \acute{x}_3x_1 \oplus \acute{x}_3x_2 \oplus x_3x_2x_1$

2. This is an example from [12]. $\sum m(0,2,7,8,11,15) + \sum d(1,5,6,9,14)$. The given solution is:
   $f(x_4x_3x_2x_1) = \sum m(0,1,2,7,8,9,11,15) = \acute{x}_3 \oplus x_4\acute{x}_3x_2 \oplus x_2x_1$
   Our solution is: $f(x_4x_3x_2x_1) = \sum m(0,2,7,8,11,15) = \acute{x}_3\acute{x}_1 \oplus x_4\acute{x}_3x_2 \oplus x_3x_2x_1$

3. This is an example from [15]. $\sum m(1,2,7) + \sum d(0,4,5)$. The given solution is:
   $f(x_0x_1x_2) = \sum m(1,2,4,7) = x_0 \oplus x_1 \oplus x_2$
   Our solution is: $f(x_3x_2x_1) = \sum m(0,1,2,7) = x_2x_1 \oplus \acute{x}_3$

5 Conclusion

Various techniques for handling the incompletely specified Boolean functions for the case of R-M logic design have been investigated. Since, the optimum selection of ϕ terms for Boolean case is not the same as the optimum selection of ϕ terms for R-M form [12], alternate methods have to be developed to handle the incompletely specified Boolean functions. The map-folding technique [10] is useful, however, only for small number of variables. The exhaustive search technique [12], on the other hand, gives a better choice of selection of ϕ terms to give the minimum weight function vector. However, it has disadvantages of suffering from large computational complexity and the reduced R-M expansion is not necessarily an optimal one. The spectral technique [15] uses heuristic procedure for assigning ϕ terms. Finally, the developed computer algorithm for handling the incompletely specified Boolean functions gives either the same cost function or better, however, the computer execution time is very low. After handling the ϕ terms of Boolean function, the function can be simplified by adopting the developed truth-vector simplification technique [20].

References

[1] Mukhopadhyay, A. and Schmitz, G. : "Minimization of Ex-OR and logical equivalence switching circuits", IEEE Trans., 1970, C-19, pp 132-140.

[2] Robinson, P. and Yeh, C.H. : "Methods for modulo-2 minimization", IEEE Trans., 1982, C-31, pp 800-801.

[3] Saul, J., Eschermann, B., and Froessi, J. : "Two-level logic circuits using EXOR sums of products", IEE Proceedings-E. Vol. 140, No. 6,November 1993, pp 348-356.

[4] Tsai, C.C. and Marek-Sadowska, M. : "Minimization of fixed-polarity AND/XOR canonical networks", IEE Peoc. Comput. Digit. Tech.,Vol. 141, No. 6, November 1994, pp 369-374.

[5] Chattopadhyay, S., Roy, S., and Chaudhuri, P. : "Synthesis of highly testable fixed-polarity AND-XOR canonical networks - A genetic algorithm-based approach", IEEE Trans. Comput., Vol. 45, No. 4, April 1996, pp 487-490.

[6] Zeljko Zilic and Zvonko G. Vranesic: "A multiple-valued Reed-Muller transform for incompletely specified functions", IEEE Trans. Comput., Vol. 44, No. 8, August 1995, pp 1012 1020.

[7] Green, D.H. : "Families of Reed-Muller canonical forms", Int. J Electronics. 1991, Vol. 70, pp 259-280.

[8] Kantopoulos, S.V. : "Classification of Ex-OR structures in the minimization of logic functions", Int. J. Electron., 1980. Vol. 49, pp 115-129.

[9] Lofti, Z.M., Aoulad-Syad, D., and Tosser, A.J. : "Determination of the set of irredundant modulo-2 sum-of-products expression of a logic function", IEE Proc E, 1979, Vol. 2, pp 2-6.

[10] Tran, A : "Graphical method for the conversion of minterms to Reed-Muller coefficients and the minimization of ExOR switching functions", IEE Proc. E, 1987, Vol. 134, pp 93-99.

[11] Green, D.H. and Khuwaja, G.A. : "Simplification of switching functions expressed in Reed-Muller algebraic form", Computers and Digital Tech., IEE Proc. -E, 1992, Vol. 139, No. 6, pp 511-518.

[12] Green, D.H. : "Reed-Muller expansions of incompletely specified functions", IEE Proc. E. Vol. 134, No. 5, Sept. 1987, pp 228-236.

[13] Karpovsky, M.G. : "Finite Orthogonal Series in the Design of Digital Devices", *John Wiley and sons, New York, 1976.*

[14] McCluskey, E.J. : "Logic Design Principles: with emphasis on testable semi-custom circuits". *Prentice-Hall Int. Editions.*

[15] Varma, D. and Trachtenberg, E.A. : "Computation of Reed-Muller expansions of incompletely specified Boolean functions from reduced representations", IEE Proc. E, Vol. 138, No. 2, March 1991, pp 85-91.

[16] Reddy, S.M. : "Easily testable realizations for logic functions", IEEE Trans., 1972. C-21, pp 1183-1188.

[17] Ning Song and Marek A. Perkowski : "Minimization of exclusive sum-of-products expressions for multiple-valued input, incompletely specified functions", IEEE Trans. Computer-Aided Design of Integrated Circuits and Systems, Vol. 15. No. 4, April 1996, pp 385-395.

[18] Zakrevskij, A.D. and Zakrevski, L.A. : "Fast algorithm for minimizing Reed-Muller expansions of systems of incompletely specified MVL functions", 1997 IEEE, 0-8186-7910-7/97. pp 61-65.

[19] McKenzie, L., Almaini, A.E.A., Miller, J.F., and Thomson, P. : "Optimization of reed-Muller logic functions", Int. J. Electronics, Vol. 75, No. 3, Sept. 1993 pp 451-466.

[20] Khuwaja, G.A. and Siyal, M.Y. : "Computation of Reed-Muller expansions from Boolean functions", IEEE Singapore Int. Conf. on Signal Processing, Circuits and Systems, Vol. 1. July 1995. pp 284-287.

EXTENDING KNOWLEDGE-BASED SUPPORT IN SOFTWARE SYSTEMS DEVELOPMENT

Vassilios C. Vescoukis
V.Vescoukis@cs.ntua.gr

Dimosthenis Anagnostopoulos
dimosthe@di.uoa.gr

Maria Nikolaidou
mara@di.uoa.gr

Software Engineering Lab
National Technical University of Athens
Zografou 15780, Greece

Department of Informatics
University of Athens
Panepistimiopolis, Athens 15784, Greece

Abstract. *The development of software systems has always been a hard task to accomplish. Apart from the tracking of the development process itself, in order to have an clear image of what the development process is actually about, it is important to keep track of knowledge about the problem domain and the reasons behind the decisions taken during this process. Software development methods do not provide support for the latter, thus the research community began to explore the recording of reasoning in software evolution. Several data models have been presented, aiming to support developers by maintaining repositories of reasoning elements about the decisions taken during development; these repositories are part of special tools that can be classified as Software decision management systems. However, several problems still remain unresolved and today such tools are only used in experimental environments. PROFILE is a conceptual logic-based meta-model that integrates software process modelling with deliberation representation and decision factors, useful in the development of DSSs. It provides a Knowledge Base of decision rules about the whole life cycle of systems whose development involves a lot of decisions, and also can be used in capturing assumptions as real-world reasoning elements. The authors have used PROFILE to support not only the development of software systems, but also decisions taken during the design and development of Computer Network simulation systems. The basic elements of the model, together with experience from the disciplines in which it has been used so far, are presented in this paper.*

Keywords: meta-models, knowledge-based support for software engineering, knowledge-based systems development, logic-based models, reasoning.

1. Introduction

Software evolution is done according to models that propose a set of software engineering activities, methods and practices, needed to produce, enhance, repair, and maintain software [Humphrey89]. They define what actions should be performed and in what sequence, in order the desired software elements to be produced. Apart from the source code, these artifacts are known as "documentation". Documentation is the only practical tool for understanding a software system. It must, therefore, be as complete, understandable and easy-to-communicate, as possible. It is the real world that changes, which has an effect in software and these changes must be properly reflected in software documentation.

In this context, software documentation is the result of several problem-solving activities defined by software development methods. It is the answer to "*what*"- or "*how*"-type questions raised during software development. Experience shows that this kind of documentation is not equally well understood by all persons involved in, or related in any manner to software development. This is where the need for knowledge-based support appears. By introducing this need, a new dimension in software documentation is defined which supports the tracking of the reasons behind software development actions, which can make them more useful, conceivable and easy-to-communicate. However, little has been published about experience in using such tools and on practical results of the proposed approaches.

Our central thesis is that a wider perspective is needed in representing reasoning in software development. Supporting only the phases of design and requirements specification, can provide limited help. Reasoning needs to be supported through the whole software life cycle, in a flexible and customizable way. The development and maintenance of a Knowledge Base containing knowledge about problem-solving practice in software evolution as active reasoning elements has to be the core of new systems. Assumptions should be recorded at a global level so that their impact can be thoroughly understood. PROFILE is a logic-based conceptual meta-model aiming to provide a framework for reasoning support in software evolution. It enhances existing models by maintaining a Knowledge Base for software evolution, by providing support for the whole software life cycle, and by handling assumptions as global reasoning elements.

This paper is organized as follows: in section 2, we present a new logic-based conceptual meta-model, called PROFILE. An instance of PROFILE and a prototype Software Evolution Decision Support System implementing this instance is presented in section 3. Section 4 presents our experience, practical results and issues in using this system. In section 5 we discuss the related work. Finally, in section 5 we present some concluding remarks and directions for our future work.

2. Main Characteristics of PROFILE

Software life cycle representation. Software life is divided in discrete phases in which several actions take place. A software evolution model is a set of software engineering activities, methods and practices, needed to produce, enhance, repair, and maintain software [Humphrey89]. Such a model defines what actions should be performed and in what sequence. As these actions take place, software Artifacts are produced. Software evolution models do not define the same types of artifacts, or consider similar types of artifacts in an equivalent way. Reference to the software evolution model is necessary for a fine definition of Artifact. Hence, the software life cycle followed, should be a part of the model. Apart from a better definition of Artifact, this could be useful in classifying decisions, and in understanding the impact and the importance of decisions according to the evolution phase they have been made in.

Development knowledge representation. Developers use software metrics to define quality measures for the software applications they produce, and require produced software artifacts to comply to certain norms or constraints when evaluated using these measures. This is a global software development organization's policy that can justify decisions in a proper context, independently of the specific software application in the development of which such decisions take place. Another case of policy is that of specifying steps that should be taken in solving specific categories of problems. Such requirements can be considered as *decision factors*, because they provide guidance on what piece of information should be considered significant in a problem-solving activity in software evolution. Decision factors are therefore *active* deliberation elements and can be (a) constraints on evaluation, if metrics are well-defined, (b) logic rules, in the case of problem-solving steps, or (c) free-text containing general guidelines, if neither can be formulated. All three types of decision factors can be expressed as rules using predicate logic.

User-defined deliberation representation model. In a deliberation, it is not clear what the most useful information to keep is. The different semantic orientation of the models introduced so far, suggests that this information is not the same in all phases of software evolution. The argument that it can be different even among developers, has a standing basis, too. It is therefore required that any deliberation representation schema, not necessarily the same throughout the whole evolution, should become a part of the model under discussion.

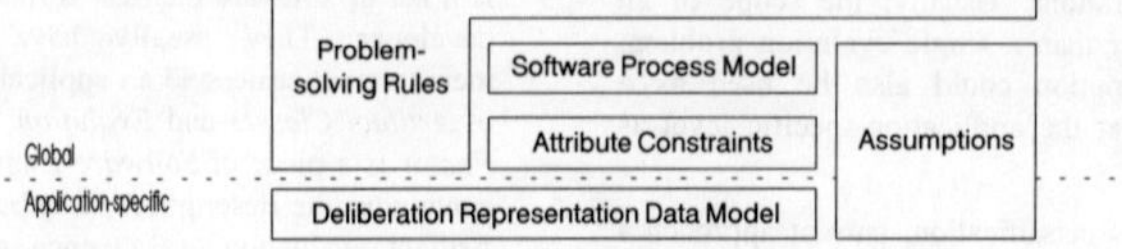

Figure 1. Levels of reasoning in software evolution.

Representation of assumptions in a proper context. Assumptions play an important role in software development [Lehman91]. In e-type applications [Lehman80], they can be considered as a bridge between the real world and software. Attaching assumptions in any software engineering artifact, provides a basis for better reasoning in software evolution by capturing important deliberation information in an appropriate context.

2.1. A hierarchy of reasoning in software evolution

We use a two-level hierarchy of reasoning elements in software evolution (Figure 1) which best fits our practical purposes, while maintaining simplicity.

The lower level is called *application-specific* and contains reasoning elements unique for every particular software application. Such information includes the deliberation elements during evolution problem-solving and is captured using a Deliberation Representation Data Model.

The higher level is called *global* and contains reasoning elements global to software development organizations, or at least, to specific problem-domains. In more detail, the global level contains the following elements:

- A rule base containing knowledge about the implementation of the process model and the practice followed by the developer during evolution problem solving.
- The software process model which defines the phases in software evolution, an analysis of each phase in a hierarchy of tasks, and the software artifacts produced in each task. If the

definition of the software process model is done at a highly-detailed level, the internal structure of the software artifacts, is also represented.

- The constraints that are applied on the evaluation of software artifacts using any measurable attributes.

Assumptions represent conditions or the real world and in particular of a software development environment and/or a problem domain. *Assumptions* are true for a period of time and deserve a special role as reasoning elements in deliberations. Usually, the scope of an assumption is wider than a single evolution problem; however, an assumption could also be used as a reasoning element at the application-specific level as shown in Figure 1.

With respect to this classification, current approaches to the problem provide reasoning support only at the application-specific level [Potts88][Lee90][Arango93], and only partially consider the notion of assumption [Ramesh92] as a reasoning element.

2.2. Description of PROFILE

2.2.1. Abstract data model

Figure 2 shows the main elements of a conceptual meta-model developed to satisfy the requirements presented above, called PROFILE (PROcess modelling and decision Factors In software deLiberation and Evolution). This is an abstract view of PROFILE; in the practical use of this model, several elements need to be replaced with detailed data models, so that a real implementable model instance can be obtained. We call this process "model instantiation".

Step 1. The first element to define is the software evolution model. This requires representation of phases and their sequence in software evolution. Such a definition can be made in any of three levels of detail as described in [Humphrey89]. In the most detailed level (called the Atomic level) a complete definition of Software *Artifact* classes, including their internal structure, is possible.

Step 2. Second, comes the representation of policies followed during software evolution. *Quality measures* is a set of software metrics, formal or not, used by a developer. They usually have a description, a measurement scale, and an applicability scope in terms of *Artifact Classes* and *Evolution Phases*. A *Decision Factor* is a piece of *Software Engineering Knowledge* containing the description of either a constraint upon Artifact evaluation, a sequence of actions taken in problem-solving, or a generic guideline expressed using natural language.

Step 3. A deliberation representation data model for capturing rationale at the *application-specific* level is the next element of the model to define. It can be the same throughout the whole evolution, or it can be different according to evolution phases. In the latter case, we have a complex three-dimensional model with reference to the software evolution model used. This implies a higher overhead in software evolution and should be carefully balanced with expressiveness and exploitation of collected information.

Using the *Quality Measures* we defined above, alternative solutions to software evolution problems are qualified by assigning values to attributes of Software

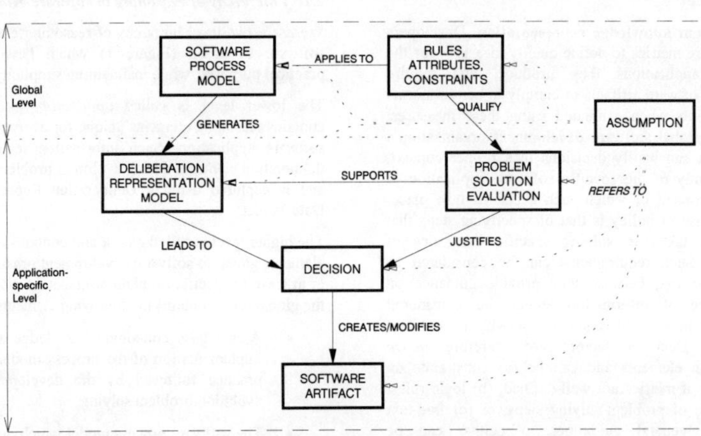

Figure 2. An abstract view of PROFILE.

Artifacts. This is a key in justifying decisions in software evolution. It is well known that software metrics have failed to provide objective measures of software characteristics, except maybe for program code, but metrics is all we have. Defining *Viewpoints* for supporting multiple qualifications made under different assumptions or by different persons, is a realistic solution to this.

The notion of *Assumption* in PROFILE is rather universal than part of the deliberation representation model (*global* vs. *application-specific* reasoning level). Assumptions can be attached to any entity of the model to represent a condition that is true within a time frame. Implementations are responsible for handling the temporal dimension of assumption validity, and determine what happens when an assumption is no longer valid.

A *Decision* is a trigger for the creation or modification of software Artifacts. Removal of Artifacts is a special case of modification. A complete definition of Decision depends upon the deliberation representation model that will be used, and can only be done within the context of an instance of PROFILE. A *Decision Signature* is a key notion in PROFILE and is defined as a set containing references to the context in which a Decision was made. We thus have:

$$DSig = \{ DPh, DF^*, Q^*, A^*, J, S^* \}$$

where *DPh* = design phase, *DF* = applicable decision Factors, *Q* = solutions qualification, *A* = standing assumptions, *J* = justification as captured in the deliberation representation model, *S* is the scope of the decision in terms of Artifacts or development steps, and the asterisk (*) denotes a set instead of a single element. *DPh*, and *J* are pointers to the corresponding entities of the software evolution and deliberation representation models, respectively. A *Decision* is *valid* as long as all the elements of its *Signature* are valid (true). *Decision Signatures* can be used in decision support by submitting queries about software evolution rationale to the system and will be further discussed in the sequence.

2.2.2. Implementation and use

In this section we present the actions that need to be taken in order to specify an implementable instance of PROFILE, we address some implementation issues and discuss a few aspects of using such an implementation in a real software development environment. From now on, such an implementation will be called a Software Evolution Decision Support System (SE-DSS). The data model that will be put in practical use in a SE-DSS highly depends upon the user characteristics; hence, such a system cannot be regarded as "one more CASE tool". The use of a SE-DSS implies a measurable overhead in the software process, however its necessity cannot be considered well understood by development teams: things can easily end up in a documentation-mess where the effort is clearly measurable, while the outcome is not. A developer should proceed in small steps, evaluating experience and using as much feedback as possible from those who actually do the "dirty job" in software development.

At first, the software development organization should specify its requirements from the use of such new elements in software documentation. Some organization-wide research has to be done in order to collect useful knowledge that will be embodied in the SE-DSS. Such information is the software life cycle model, the quality measures, the decision factors, and the application-specific elements of deliberation in software evolution that will be recorded. Determining the first two is the easy part of this work. Determining the decision factors is more or less equivalent to creating a special knowledge base by acquiring experts' knowledge on software evolution, which is not an easy thing to do. The initial set of decision factors will contain constraints about metrics and maybe a few guidelines expressed in natural language; as experience is gained, this set will contain fruitful knowledge on software development. It is apparent that a SE-DSS can be best implemented in an environment suitable for knowledge representation. Such a "standard" environment is Prolog, in which we have chosen to implement the prototype presented in this paper; frame-based environments such as ConceptBase [Jarke91] can also be used. In the following discussion we consider Prolog as the implementation environment.

The main functions of a SE-DSS are the maintenance of software evolution history and the relevant information extraction, the maintenance and handling of trigger events whenever certain conditions become true, the maintenance of the knowledge base, and the support of decisions by consulting this knowledge base and examining similar situations of the past.

3. An Instance of PROFILE

3.1. Architecture and services

Figure 3 shows an instance of PROFILE, described above. Based on this instance, we have developed a SE-DSS which has been used in supporting the development of software systems, as well as in the design of simulation systems.

A prototype SE-DSS system based on this model, has been implemented and we have been experimenting with it in the development of several applications. It is based on the MS Windows environment where a RDBMS and a Prolog implementation host a relational database and a rule base respectively. The data model shown in figure 3 is implemented in the RDBMS. Prolog queries implement most of its functions. The main user interface elements are a set of forms for data entry and a graphical browser for browsing through an evolution graph. A front-end user interface provides a working environment to users. The main services provided by this system can be categorised in development information management services and in reasoning support services.

chain-effects to the decisions in the justification of which this assumption is used. This situation is automatically managed by the system.

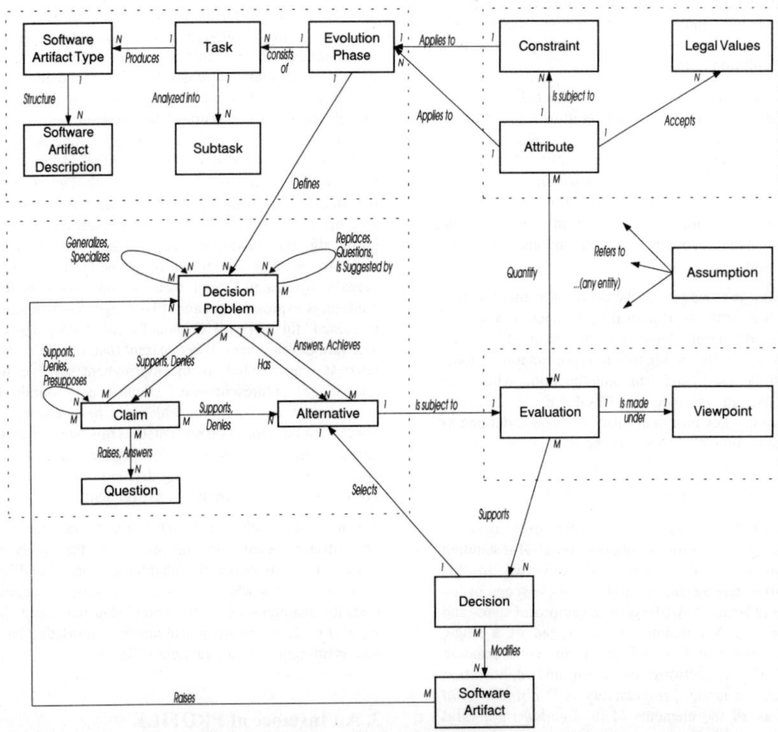

Figure 3. An instance of PROFILE.

Development information management

Software Process Model management. The user can describe the steps taken in software development at any required level of detail, as a basis for reasoning support during evolution. If this description is done at a high level of detail, the internal structure of software artifacts is also represented and managed. The current implementation of the system embodies the Waterfall life cycle model at the Atomic level of detail, which is the highest with reference to [Humphrey89].

Software Deliberation Representation model management. Several elements of the deliberation representation model (e.g. Viewpoints, Evaluation formulas) reflect the user's policy on evaluation of alternative solution to evolution problems, and therefore are user-defined.

Assumption management. The true state of an assumption is subject to change which results in a set of

Reasoning support

Evolution history tracking and playback. Recording of the evolution history is done using either the form-based interface, or the graphical editor. Playback is done using a customizable graphical browser that supports layers of information and can zoom into specific entities to display the required detail. The user decides which classes of entities and what details will be displayed at any time. Walking through the history graph is done using semantic guidance through Prolog queries - not by scrolling a graphical display.

Deliberation management at the application-specific level. Using the deliberation representation data model as a basis, the evolution problems, the alternative solutions and a set of arguments and mathematical evaluations of the alternatives, are stored and managed. Evaluation of alternatives can be made using multiple Viewpoints.

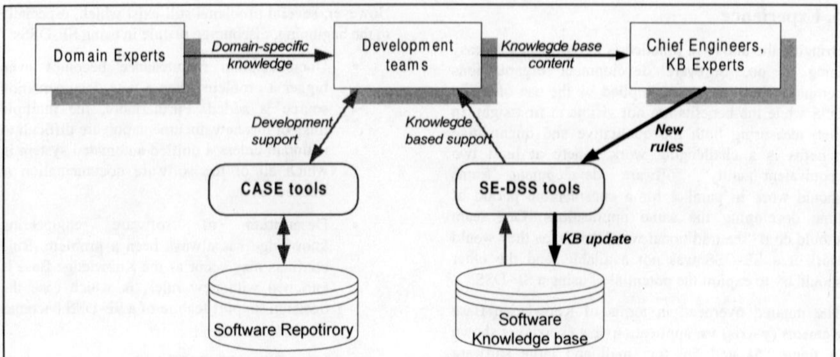

Figure 4. Use of a SE-DSS in a software development context.

What-if analysis based on Assumptions. Modifying current assumptions can affect the validity of decisions taken and change the status of the system. In many cases the system becomes unstable, since some issues cannot be resolved in the new context, and a new problem-solving activity has to take place. Such situations are common during maintenance, where changes in the real world can affect the validity of assumptions and make the system out-of-date, and can be explored using this feature. If some artifacts are modified during this procedure, references to the assumption that initiated the problem are automatically generated and attached to the deliberation information of these artifacts.

What-if analysis based on Viewpoints. A similar situation occurs when considering different evaluations of artifacts' quality measures. Depending on the set of decision factors applied, some issues cannot be resolved, which initiates a new problem-solving activity. This is a common situation when doing scenario analysis. The system provides support in such cases by generating alternative evolution graphs that correspond to Viewpoints and by marking unresolved issues. The original evolution graph is modified only when a scenario is accepted and the necessary references to the new viewpoint are automatically generated.

Decision support is provided through the notion of decision signature. A deliberation takes place in a certain context that is determined by the problem domain, the life cycle phase, the valid assumptions and the applicable decision factors. These elements, except for the problem domain, are part of the Decision Signature as defined earlier in this paper. We can therefore formulate a query to the knowledge base and extract information about "what has been decided in similar situations". The result of this query can be a long list that can be somehow shortened by running successive refinement queries. The real information obtained from this procedure depends on two factors: The first one is the use of Assumptions. Proper use of Assumptions can help in effectively characterizing situations and similarities between situations. The second one is the Decision Factors rule base. Every time a decision is taken, the user should consider if adding a new rule to the KB is possible. The system's behaviour in decision support is expected to improve as the KB accumulates knowledge about software development practice in the user's organization.

Synthesis library maintenance. A synthesis is a reusable collection of artifacts that share the same qualitative attributes and assumptions in the same functional domain. It can be a set of assumptions, of requirements, of design artifacts, of program elements, or of any type of entities that exist in the software life cycle. A synthesis is viable when all attributes and assumptions of its members are valid. The system provides support for maintaining synthesis libraries, for verifying synthesis viability and for performing what-if analysis of the viability of a synthesis in a similar way as in the previous cases.

3.2. Intended use

Figure 4 shows the use of such a DSS in a software development environment. *Chief software engineers* are responsible for the initialization of the system by defining the global characteristics of the software development organization, and an initial set of rules and constraints. *Software development teams* use the system for application-specific deliberation recording and support and provide chief software engineers with feedback regarding the development process itself, and the *domain experts* with feedback concerning the application domain. *Chief software engineers* and *domain experts* are responsible for formulating software practice knowledge and domain knowledge respectively, and for updating the knowledge base.

4. Experience

Bringing the above in practice is by no means an easy thing to do. Software development organizations complain about overhead implied by the use of a SE-DSS while the benefits are not visible at first sight. In fact, measuring both the qualitative and quantitative benefits is a challenging work, where at least two "equivalent-quality" software development teams should work in parallel for a considerable period of time developing the same applications. One team should do it "the traditional way" that is, as they would work if a SE-DSS was not available, and the other should try to exploit the potential of using a SE-DSS.

The implied overhead in terms of Knowledge Base elements (y-axis) vs. application size (x-axis) is shown in figures 5a and 5b, for small and large software applications respectively (scales are in thousands) and for the several data models we have been working with. It is obvious that the overhead is considerable and cannot be acceptable unless it is balanced with a significant improvement in the software process. Our experience after several discussions with software development teams who used the systems for a few weeks, indicates that such an improvement is focused in the following points:

- During software maintenance, where a better understanding of the software saves time and errors.
- During requirements specification where the reasons behind the answers to "why this"-type questions are documented.
- In situations where the development team changes and the new members need to understand a lot of things in limited time in order to become productive.
- In performing what-if analysis at any phase of development.
- In illustrating the software for educational purposes.

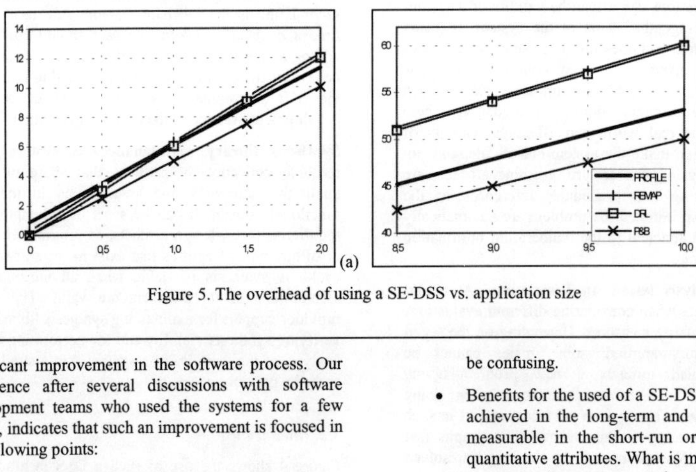

(a) (b)

Figure 5. The overhead of using a SE-DSS vs. application size

However, several problems still exist which, especially in the beginning, discourage people in using SE-DSSs:

- Documentation maintenance becomes even bigger a problem when a new documentation source is added. Furthermore, the multiple links of this new documentation are difficult to maintain unless a unified automated system in which all of the software documentation is tracked, exists.
- Description of software engineering knowledge has always been a problem. Rule conflicts may occur as the Knowledge Base is enriched with new rules, in which case the decision support feature of a SE-DSS becomes weaker.
- Integration with CASE tools is also a problem. CASE tools usually do not deliver what they promise, nor are they sufficiently used [Iiv96]. Adding a SE-DSS in such environments can be confusing.
- Benefits for the used of a SE-DSS can only be achieved in the long-term and are not well-measurable in the short-run or in terms of quantitative attributes. What is more important to expect, is a process and software quality improvement.

The development of **knowledge modules for each context or engineering discipline** where this schema is used has been made possible. We currently have created modules for the waterfall software life cycle model, for the development of technical constructions management software applications (domain-specific module) and for the development of network simulation systems (domain-specific module). We have also proposed a model for non-engineering disciplines, in particular for operational research and management [VVesc98].

5. Related Work

Potts & Bruns have presented a first approach in capturing deliberations in software design [Potts88]. The data model they proposed is a simple and easy-to-use one. A justification is a free-text description of the reasons for which a decision has been made. Their model cannot capture several arguments on the same issue neither the relations among them. The software development organization's practice (software evolution model) is not represented, and neither is the problem-solving policy using metrics, constraints and rules. Furthermore, their model is not supported by an integrated tool but instead one has to switch between a hypertext editor and a Prolog environment.

SYBIL is a decision management system [Lee90] implementing DRL (Decision Representation Language) that supports goals, alternatives, claims and relations among them, in software design deliberation. DRL provides better support for representing argumentation than P&B, and has some common qualitative semantic elements with the IBIS model (DRL's decision problem vs. IBIS's issue, alternative vs. position, claim vs. argument). However, IBIS and its implementations such as gIBIS [Conklin88] and IBE [Lease90] can be considered as generic systems for capturing deliberations in engineering disciplines and do not support explicit representation of goals, or the results of deliberations. Neither of these models supports knowledge acquisition and reuse, or domain characteristics representation. Approaches for domain-oriented design support have been presented by Fisher et al. [Fischer92] and Arango et al. [Arango93], [Arango93b] however, they are not integrated with deliberation representation schemes, which, we believe, should be done in the future.

REMAP [Ramesh92] is a conceptual model used to capture deliberations during requirements analysis that relates process knowledge to the objects that are created during the requirements engineering process which uses the IBIS model for capturing argumentation. REMAP is useful in capturing deliberations and knowledge when transforming requirements into design and enhances previous approaches by adding explicit representation of decisions, constraints and assumptions, and by introducing process knowledge components. REMAP does not support all phases of software evolution and the necessity for the development of a generic model for capturing and representing process knowledge across various phases of systems development is clearly pointed out by the authors.

The development of such a generic model is the main objective of our approach. The representation of the software process model at a highly detailed level (step hierarchy, products and product internal structure), the maintenance of a software evolution KB, and the ability to use a variable deliberation recording model, are the principal REMAP enhancements that PROFILE suggests. As a consequence, we handle constraints and assumptions in a different way. Constraints are regarded as special cases of decision factors, which are rule-based representations of evolution knowledge and are applicable to evolution phases instead of to decisions and design objects. Assumptions can be assigned to any entity instead of to arguments only, which allows a better understanding of their role in software development. In addition, we provide a set of mechanisms for decision support in software evolution.

Several other models for representing deliberations have been presented [Fischer92] [Dong91] [Rose91] [Toulmin84], but they are either less complete than REMAP, or have a different orientation such as group coordination or domain semantics capturing. Relevant studies also include [Rich92], [Oivo90].

6. Discussion

Reasoning is a new dimension in software documentation. Its necessity is not well understood by developers, and existing data models and tools that support reasoning, seem to be immature and not integrated with other tools used in software development. Although there is much discussion of this topic, a common terminology has not yet been agreed. Furthermore, little has been published about experience and so far, there is not any commercially available CASE tool that supports any of the models that have been presented.

Further research is needed in integrating deliberation representation models with existing methods and tools. A unified approach in using AI techniques in Software Engineering is also useful, especially in determining qualitative similarities among problem-solving contexts. These tasks cannot be accomplished unless enough experience from real software development environments has been gained.

We are currently conducting experiments on the topic of measuring the overhead as well as the long-term gain for developers when capturing deliberations in software evolution by using a SE-DSS. This will provide a basis for a classification of existing deliberation representation models according to a cost-benefit ratio. The development of an new version of our SE-DSS in a portable co-operative platform is our second action line.

The development of knowledge modules for several software life cycle models is the third action line of our research. The evolution of UML as a global modelling language has motivated us towards the refinement of our model for use in object-oriented software development using the Objectory method. Finally, we are conducting a series of experiments in commercial software development organizations to support both evaluation of our approach and to collect quantitative measurements. The outcome of these actions and the experience that will be gained is expected to be valuable and helpful for the continuation of this effort.

REFERENCES

[Arango93] Arango, Guillermo, and Eric Schoen, and Robert Pettengill, ***A Process for Consolidating and Reusing Design Knowledge***, Proceedings of the 15th International Conference on Software Engineering, IEEE Computer Society Press, pp. 231-242, 1993.

[Arango93b] Arango, G., and E. Shoen, R.Pettengill, and J.Hoskins, ***The Graft-Host Method for Design Evolution***, Proceedings of the 15th International Conference on Software Engineering, IEEE Computer Society Press, 1993.

[Conklin88] Conclin, j., and M.L.Begeman, ***gIBIS: A Hypertext Tool for Exploratory Policy Discussion***, Vol 6, No 4, pp. 303-331, 1988.

[Devanbu91] Devanbu, P., and R. Brachman, P. Selfridge, and B. Ballard, ***LaSSIE: A Knowledge-Based Software Information System***, Communications of the ACM, Vol 34, No 5, pp. 3549, May 1991.

[Dong91] Dong, Jinghuan, and Chris Wild, and Kurt Maly, ***A Software Development and Evolution Model Based on Decision-making***, Proceedings of the 3rd International Conference on Software Engineering and Knowledge Engineering, Knowledge Systems Inst., Skokie, IL, USA, pp. 9-14, 1991.

[Fischer92] Fischer, Gerhard, and A. Girgensohn, K. Nakakoji, and David Redmiles, ***Supporting Software Designers with Integrated Domain-Oriented Design Environments***, IEEE Transactions on Software Engineering, Vol 18, No 6, pp. 511-522, June 1992.

[Iiv96]Iivari, Juhani, ***Why Are CASE Tools Not Used?***, Communications of the ACM, Vol.39, No.10, October 1996.

[Jarke91] Jarke, M., ***Conceptbase 3.0 user manual***, Univ. Passau, Passau, Germany, Tech. Rep. MIP-9107, March 1991.

[Lease90] Lease, M., and M. Lively, and J. Leggett, ***Using an Issue-based hypertext system to capture the software life-cycle process***, Hypermedia, vol. 2, no. 1, 1990.

[Lee90] Lee, Jintae, ***SIBYL: A Qualitative Decision Management System***, Artificial Intelligence at MIT: Expanding Frontiers, Winston and Shellard, editors, MIT Press, Cambridge, MA, Vol 1, Ch. 5, 1990.

[Lee91] Lee, Jintae, ***Extending the Potts and Bruns Model for Recording Design Rationale***, Proceedings of the 13th International Conference on Software Engineering, IEEE Computer Society Press, pp. 114-125, 1991.

[Lehman91] Lehman, M.M., ***Software Engineering, the software process and their support***, IEE Software Engineering Journal, special issue on Software Environments and Factories, 6(5), pp. 243-258, September 1991

[Oivo90] Oivo, Markku, ***Knowledge-Based Support for Embedded Computer Software Analysis and Design***, Technical Research Centre of Finland, ISBN 951-38-3763-7, September 1990.

[Potts88] Potts, Collin, and Glenn Bruns, ***Recording the Reasons for Design Decisions***, Proceedings of the 10th International Conference on Software Engineering, IEEE Computer Society Press, pp. 418-427, 1988.

[Ramesh92] Ramesh, B., and V. Dhar, ***Supporting Systems Development by Capturing Deliberations During Requirements Engineering***, IEEE Transactions on Software Engineering, Vol 18, No 6, pp. 498-510, June 1992.

[Rose91] Rose, T., and M. Jarke, and M. Gocek, and M. Maltzahn, and H. Nissen, ***A decision based configuration process environment, Software Eng. J.***, vol. 6 no.5, pp. 332-346, 1991.

[Rich92] Rich, Charles, and Yishai A. Feldman, ***Seven Layers of Knowledge Representation and Reasoning in Support of Software Development***, IEEE Transactions on Software Engineering, Vol 18, No 6, pp. 451-469, June 1992.

[Vesc95] V.C.Vescoukis, ***Software Design Decisions***, proceedings of CAiSE 95 W3, Jyvaskyla, Finland, June 1995.

[Vesc96a] V.C.Vescoukis, ***Reasoning Support in Software Evolution***, Ph.D. Thesis, National Technical University of Athens, January 1996, Athens, Greece.

[Vesc96b] V.C.Vescoukis, N.Papaspyrou and E.Skordalakis, ***A logic-based framework for reasoning support in software evolution***, proceedings of CAiSE 96, Heraklion, Greece.

[Vesc98] V.C.Vescoukis, D.Anagnostopoulos, ***A generator of logic-based models for the design of operational decision support systems***, 12th Panhellenic conference of the Hellenic Society for Operational Research (submitted).

[Humphrey89] Humphrey, S. Watt, ***Managing the Software Process***, SEI, Addison-Wesley 1989, ISBN 0-201-18095-2.

A PATTERN MATCHING ALGORITHM

Octavian C. Dogaru
West University of Timişoara
Bd.V.Pârvan,nr.4,Timişoara,1900,Romania
E-mail:dogaru@info.uvt.ro

Abstract

In this paper a string search algorithn is presented. Its name is OD. The used method is one of forward search with shift to determine if a word p of m characters is or it is not in a string s of n characters $(0 < m \leq n)$. Theoretically the number of comparisons, to determine if p is or it is not in s, in the most unfavourable case, is $m(n-m+1)$.

1. Introduction

Pattern matching is the problem of finding an occurence of a *word* named and *pattern* $p[0..m-1]$ of characters in a *text* $s[0..n-1]$ of characters, where $0 < m \leq n$. We present an algorithm which finds the *first* occurence of p in s.

In [9] a straight string search algorithm is presented. We reffer to it as DIRECT algorithm. The core of DIRECT algorithm is following

```
i:=-1;
repeat
i:=i+1; j:=0;
while  (j<m)  and  (s[i+j]=p[j])  do
j:=j+1 repeat
until (j=m) or (i=n-m)
```

The term j=m in the terminating condition implies an existance of p in s and the term i=n-m implies the nonexistance of a match anywhere in the string. In analysis of this algorithm one shows it is very inefficient in the case where s is of the form $a^{n-1}b$ and p is of the form $a^{m-1}b$ where a and b are characters. In this case $n*m$ comparisons are necessary to find the match of p in s.

This problem is well studied because it is important in a number of informatics domains as data retrival, symbol manipulation and text editing. The best known algorithms for this problem are Knuth-Morris-Pratt algorithm[KMP] which necessitates $2n$-m+1 comparisons to determine that 'p is not in s' and Boyer-Moore algorithm[BM] which necessitates $7n$ comparisons by Knuth, $4n$ by R.Cole, to determine that 'p is not in s'. R.Cole and R.Hariharans [2] have presented an algorithm which makes $n(1+8/3/(m+1))$ comparisons to determine that p is or it is not in s. Their algorithm is intricated and it utilies the precompiling of p as KMP and BM algorithms and special methods to handle the words which have proper suffixes which are also prefixes. Such substrings are named presufs.

In the DIRECT method presented above one compares succesively p_0 with s_i, i=0,1,..,$n-m$. If there exists no match of p_0 with s_i, i=0,1, ...,$n-m$ then 'p is not in s' and the process is terminated. Now let s_i be the first occurence of p_0 in the substring $s_0, s_1, ..., s_{n-m}$. Then one compares respectively p_1 with $s_{i+1}, ..., p_{m-1}$ with s_{i+m-1}. If all p_j match with s_{i+j}, j=1,2,...,$m-1$ then 'p is in s' else the process continues. Therefore in a straight string search the scan always begins at the first pattern character p_0 after a mismatch.

The method that we propose differs from the above in that after a mismatch occurs the searching continues with the character of pattern which has produced the mismatch and not at the first pattern character.

2. Main result

Starting from the idea presented above we propose an algorithm of string search to find the *first* occurence of p in s which will contain the following principal steps.

1.One compares successively $p_0, p_1, ..., p_{m-1}$ with corresponding $s_0, s_1, ..., s_{m-1}$. If there exists all matches then 'p is in s'. This is the first occurence of p in s and the algorithm terminates.

2.If $p_0, p_1, ..., p_{j-1}$ respectively match with $s_0, s_1, ..., s_{j-1}$ then let p_j be the first character of the pattern p which produces a mismatch of s_j.

Now one searches the first occurence of p_j in the right part of s_j between s_{j+1} and s_{n-m+j}. If p_j is not in this substring then 'p is not in s' and the algorithm terminates else let s_i

be the first occurence of p_j in the substring $s_{j+1}, s_{j+2}, ..., s_{n-m+j}$. Now one verifies if the right part of p_j that is $p_{j+1}, p_{j+2}, ..., p_{m-1}$ match with the corresponding right part of s_i, that is $s_{i+1}, s_{i+2}, ..., s_{i-j+m-1}$. If yes then one tests if the left part of p_j that is $p_0, p_1, ..., p_{j-1}$ match with the corresponding left part of s_i, that is $s_{i-j}, s_{i-j+1}, ..., s_{i-1}$. If all matches then '$p$ is in s' and the algorithm terminates.

3.If left part of p_j does not match with the corresponding left part of s_i then the process of searching is resumed with the same j and i:=i+1.

4.If in the process of testing of the right parts of p_j and s_i there exists an index k, $j+1 \le k \le m$-1 for which $p_k \neq s_{i-j+k}$ then $p_j, p_{j+1}, ..., p_k$ will be shifted and the process of searching p_j will be resumed with the new index i:=i-j+k+1 and j:=k.

5.If i>n-m+j then 'p is not in s'.

Example. One wishes to verify if the word

```
Hooligan
```

exists in the string

```
Hoola girls like Hooligans.
Hooli
    ....ig
          ........Hooligan
```

Here p_j='i' is the first mismatch of *Hooligan* in the text with s_j='a' from *Hoola*. In this case according to the algorithm proposed above one compares p_j='i' with the characters from the right part of s_j='a'. The following occurence of 'i' from *Hooligan* is in the word *girls*. Now one compares the right part of 'i' from *Hooligan* with the right part of 'i' from *girls*. p_{j+1}='g' and s_{i+1}='r' produces a mismatch. Now the new p_j='g' from *Hooligan* is searched in the rest of string and an occurence is found in the substring *..Hooligans*. The new s_i is now 'g'. One compares the right part of s_i='g' in *Hooligans* with right part of p_j='g' from *Hooligan*. There exists a match. Then one compares the left part of p_j='g' from *Hooligan* with the left part of s_i='g' from *Hooligans*. There exists a match too. The word *Hooligan* occurs in the string.

In this example the string has n=26 characters and the word has m=8. There are necessary 29 comparisons to determine that the word is in the string.

Our complet algorithm is the procedure named OD(written in the SPARK algorithmic language described in [6], slight modified). It is the following.

```
procedure OD(p, s, m, n, f)
//find the first occurence of a word p(0:m-1) in a string s(0:n-1),0<m≤n.
The index j controles p, the index i controles s and the Boolean variable f returns true if 'p is in s' and false otherwise //
char p(0:m-1),s(0:n-1); integer i, j, k, m, n; Boolean f;
j:=0; f:=false
while (j < m) and (p(j)=s(j)) do
j:=j+1 repeat
if j=m then f:=true; return endif
//the character p(j) ≠ s(j)//
i:=j+1
while i≤ n − m + j do
  if p(j)≠ s(i) then i:=i+1; cycle
  endif
  // exist p(j) = s(i), compare right parts of p(j) and s(i)//
  k := j+1
  while (k < m) and (p(k)=s(i − j + k)
  do k := k+1 repeat
  if k = m then
  //right parts match, one compares left parts of p(j) and s(i)//
    k:=0
    while (k < j) and (p(k)=s(i-j+k)
    do k := k+1 repeat
    if (k = j) then //left parts match too//
      f:=true; return
      else
      //left parts do not match//
      i := i+1
    endif
  else //right parts do not match//
  i:=i-j+k+1; j:=k
  endif
repeat
return // i>n-m+j//
endOD.
```

We recall that the *cycle* statement in SPARK language, which appears in the above program, transfers the control to the next iteration.

Theorem 1. *The algorithm OD works correctly.*

Proof. To proof the correctness of the algorithm we shall develop a proof tableau. In this we shall insert a set of assertion between the statements of the program and begining from the preconditions one reaches to the postconditions. The justifications are based on the application of logical equivalences and rules of inference to the sequence of Pascal statements which are similar with this SPARK language statements[8]. Therefore we shall use

i)the *assignement rule of inference*

{ P(e) } v:=e { P(v) }

ii)the *conditional rule of inference*

a) { P ∧ B} s { Q }
P ∧¬ B ⇒ Q

{P} if B then s {Q}

b){P∧ B} s1 {Q}
{P∧¬ B} s2 {Q}

{P} if B then s1 else s2 {Q}

iii)the *loop rule of inference*

{ inv ∧ B } s { inv }

{ inv } while B do s { inv ∧¬ B }

where P,Q denote propositions, B-Boolean expression, inv-the invariant of the loop and s, s1, s2- are statements.

```
procedure OD(p, s, m, n, f)
char p(0 : m-1),s(0 : n-1);
integer i, j, k, m, n; Boolean f;
{ pre: input=p(0:m-1) ∧ s(0:n-1) ∧
m ≥ 1 ∧ n ≥ 1 ∧ ∀ j ∈{0,1,...,m-1}:p_j ∧
∀ i ∈{0,1,...,n-1}:s_i are characters
∧ output=∅}
j:=0; f:=false;
while (j<m) and (p(j) = s(j)) do
{inv: ∀h ∈ {0,1,...,j-1}:p_h = s_h ∧
0 ≤ j ≤ m ∧ f=false}
    j:=j+1
repeat
{(∀ h ∈ {0,1,...,m-1}: p_h = s_h ∧ j=m)
∨ (∀ h ∈{0,1,...,j-1}:p_h = s_h
∧ p_j ≠ s_j∧ 0 ≤ j < m ∧ f=false}
if j=m then f:=true
{j=m ∧∀ h ∈ {0,1,...,m-1}:p_h = s_h∧
f=true}
        return {output=f}
endif
{∃ j ∈ {0,1,...,m-1}:p_j ≠ s_j∧ f=false}
{i=j}
    i:=j+1
{i>j ∧ 0≤ j<m ∧ 0< i≤ n-m+j ∧ f=false}
while i ≤ n − m+j do
{inv: f=false ∧ 0 ≤ j < m}
    if p(j) ≠ s(i) then i:=i+1
{i ≤ n-m+j ∧ 0 ≤ j < m ∧
∀ h ∈ {j+1,...,i-1}:p_j ≠ s_h ∧ f=false}
                    cycle
    endif;
{∃ i ∈ {j+1,...,n-m+1}:p_j = s_i ∧
0≤ j ≤ m-1 ∧ f=false ∧
∀ h∈ {j+1,...,i-1}:p_j ≠ s_i}
    k:=j+1; //compare right parts//
{f=false ∧ k≤m }
    while (k<m) and (p(k)=s(i − j+k))
do
{inv:f=false ∧ k ≤ m ∧ ∀h ∈ {j+1,...,k-
1}:p_h = s_{i−j+h} ∧ i ≤ n-m+j}
        k:=k+1
    repeat
{f=false ∧ i ≤ n-m+j ∧ j ≤ m-1 ∧
∀h ∈ {j+1,...,m-1}:p_h = s_{i−j+h} ∧ k =
m}∨
{f=false ∧ i≤ n-m+j ∧ j ≤m-1 ∧
∃ h∈ {j+1,...,m-1}:p_h ≠ s_{i−j+h}}
    if k = m then //right parts match//
{∀ t ∈ {j+1,...,m-1}:p_t = s_{i−j+t}}
        k:=0; //one verifies left parts//
        while (k < j) and (p(k) = s(i −
j + k) do
{inv:f=false ∧∀ t ∈ {0,1,...,k-1}:p_t =
s_{i−j+t} ∧ 0 ≤k ≤ j}
            k := k + 1
        repeat
{(f=false ∧∀ t ∈{j+1,...,m-1}:p_t = s_{i−j+t}
∧∀ r ∈ {0,1,...,j-1}:p_r = s_{i−j+r}∧k=j)∨
(f=false ∧
∃ k ∈ {0,1,...,j-1}:p_k ≠ s_{i−j+k})}
        if k = j then f:=true
{f=true ∧∀ t ∈ {j+1,...,m-1}∧
∀t ∈ {0,1,...,j-1}:p_t = s_{i−j+t}} ≡
{true ∧∀ k ∈ {0,1,...,m-1}:p_k = s_{i−j+k}}
        return{output=f}
            else //left parts do not
match//
            i:=i+1
        endif
{f=false ∧∃h ∈ {0,1,...,j-1}:p_h ≠ s_{i−j+h}∧
i ≤n-m+j ∧0 ≤ j ≤ m}
            else //right parts do not
match//
{f=false ∧∃ k ∈ {j+1,...,m-1}:p_k ≠
s_{i−j+k}}
```

```
i:=i - j+k+1; j:=k
      endif
{f=false ∧i ≤n-m+j ∧0≤ j<m}
   repeat
{f=false ∧i> n-m+j ∧∃ j ∈ {0,1,...,m-
1}:p_j ≠ s_{n-m+j}}
 return{output=f}
endOD.
```

Theorem 2. *The maximum number of comparisons to determine that a pattern p is or it is not in a string s is, in the most unfavourable case, of* $m(n-m+1)$.

Proof. To determine the maximum number of comparisons, in the worst case, without loss of generality, we assume that the first character in p which produces a mismatch is $p_{m-1} \neq s_{m-1}$, that is the last character of p and $p_0 = s_0, p_1 = s_1, ..., p_{m-2} = s_{m-2}$. There are m comparisons. Now we assume that for $i=m, m+1, ..., n-1$, $p_{m-1} = s_i$ which are yet $n-m$ comparisons, the left neighbours of p_{m-1} match respectively with the left corresponding neighbours of s_i excepting $p_{m-2} \neq s_{i-1}$. These are $(m-1)(n-m)$ comparisons. In all there are $m+(n-m)+(m-1)(n-m) = m(n-m+1)$ comparisons. This is a bound of the algorithm.

The algorithm may be completed and slight modified to determine all occurences of the word p in the text s.

3. Profiling

We effected a comparison between the DIRECT algorithm presented at the biginning of the paper, the OD algorithm and the BM algorithm. The tests have been realized on texts having n of 1000,2000,3000,4000,5000,6000, 7000 characters and words of m characters where the values of m was 5,10,15,30,50,100. The *Table* contains in each column the average times of five tests for the same m and all n. The p's and s's have been entered randomly. We used a 386DTK PC and the time is calculated in hundredth of seconds.

If we denote by t_{DIRECT}, t_{OD} and t_{BM} the average time for the DIRECT algorithm, OD algorithm and BM algorithm respectively then, from the *Table*, one may observe that there exists the following relations

$$t_{OD} = 1.46 t_{BM}; t_{DIR} = 1.27 t_{OD}$$

From the same *Table* one can observe that, for small value of $m(m=5)$, as it is the case of searching, the average calculus time of OD algorithm is comparable with the average calculus time of BM algorithm.

Table

m	DIRECT	OD	BM
5	12.6	9.72	9.34
10	12.34	9.91	7.71
15	12.85	10.17	7.2
30	13.25	9.97	5.8
50	13.7	9.97	5.8
100	10.37	9.54	4.91

References

[1] R. S. Boyer, J. S. Moore, A fast string searching algorithm, *Comm ACM,* **20,** 10(1977), 762-772

[2] R. Cole, R. Hariharan, Tighter Bounds on The Exact Complexity of String Matching, *Procc.33rd Symp.on Foundation of Computer Sci.*,(1992), 600-609

[3] R. Cole, Tight Bounds on Complexity of the Boyer-Moore string matching algorithm, *SIAM J. Comput.*, **23**, 5(1994),1075-1091

[4] R. Cole, R. Hariharan, M. Paterson, U. Zwick, Tighter Lower Bounds on the exact Complexity of String Matching, *SIAM J. Comput.*, **34**,1(1995),30-45

[5] Z. Galil, A constant-Time Optimal Parallel String Matching Algorithm, *J. ACM*, **42**, 4(1995), 908-919

[6] E. Horowitz, S. Sahni, Foundamentals of Computer Algorithm, *Computer Science Press*(1983), 626 pp

[7] D. E. Knuth, J. H. Morris, V. R. Pratt, Fast pattern matching in string, *SIAM J. Comput.*, **6**, 2(1977), 323-349

[8] A. B. Tucker, W. J. Cupper, R. D. Garnick, Fundamentals of Computing, I, *McGraw-Hill, Inc*, 1992, 400 pp

[9] N. Wirth, Algorithm and Data Structures, *Prentice-Hall, N.J.* (1986), 288 pp

A Pedestrian Traffic Flow Simulation Study

D. Anagnostopoulos[1] **V. C. Vescoukis**[2] **M. Nikolaidou**[1]

[1] Dept. of Informatics
University of Athens
Panepistimiopolis, 15784
Athens, Greece
email: dimosthe@di.uoa.gr

[2] Software Engineering Lab
National Technical University of Athens
NTUA Campus, Zografou 15780
Athens, Greece
email: bxb@cs.ntua.gr

Abstract

The qualitative design of a pedestrian environment requires a basic understanding of related human characteristics and capabilities. Pedestrian traffic volumes and queuing relationships are already introduced to meet requirements in pedestrian environment design and level of service standards, determined on the basis of average pedestrian area, are used for modelling the significant entities in a pedestrian environment. Simulation modelling enables an in depth analysis of the domain under study under real conditions. A pedestrian traffic simulation study is presented, as conducted for an underground station during peak hours, aiming at extracting conclusions for the level of service provided to the passengers. Emphasis is given to the modelling principles of pedestrian flow and handling of the overall complexity encountered, along with the analysis of the results extracted.

1 Introduction

Transportation, whether by walking or by other means, has always been a significant determinant in the design of the city. Because the internal transportation of the cities of the past was based on the convenience of walking, these cities were characterised by more attention to the human qualities of design. The advent of machine transportation has changed this perspective, forcing man to an unbalanced competition for urban space.

The qualitative design of a pedestrian environment requires a basic understanding of related human characteristics and capabilities [1]. The physical dimensions of the body determine working widths of doorways and passageways and affect the practical capacity of moving stairs and walkways. Psychological preferences of avoiding body contact with others are a determinant of inter-person space in queues and other crowded pedestrian environments. Normal human locomotion involves many complex characteristics of balance, timing and even human sight, which are often taken for granted by all but the handicapped. Human locomotion exhibits different characteristics in level surfaces and on stairs, with the latter requiring much more attention to design because of safety and energy expenditure.

Humans value personal space. As they acquire status and wealth they select larger offices and homes. The pedestrian has his own personal space preferences, which are related to his sense of "territory" and body image. If freedom of choice exists, pedestrians will adopt personal spacing which avoids personal contact with others, except in special circumstances such as a crowded elevator, where this unwritten law may be temporarily suspended. It is therefore evident that the level of service provided to the pedestrian strongly depends on his personal space.

The concept of personal space is also used to express the inter-person separation, denoted as human buffer zone. This concept extends to many activities, as for motorists in the highway which establish a larger buffer zone, comprised of his mental image of the extremities of his vehicle, plus the amount of space required for safe stopping of the auto. Penetration of this zone by the cutting in of other motorists is strongly resented.

The space required for locomotion may be divided into a pacing zone, the area required for foot placement, and the sensory zone, the area required by the pedestrian for perception, evaluation and reaction. The length of the pacing zone is dependent on the age, sex, and physical condition of the pedestrian, and has been shown to have a direct linear relationship with speed [2].

The capabilities of human vision and distance judgement can have a significant impact on pedestrian activities. Pedestrians are able to keep track of the varying speeds and angles of incoming pedestrians through the use of vision and their own specialised mental computer and to accurately adjust their pace and speed to avoid collisions.

Walking is a uniquely human skill, one of man's invigorating exercises, stimulating the mind and the virtually every muscle of the body, while consuming very little energy. Stair climbing and descent is quite different from walking. Locomotion on stairs is necessarily more restricted because of safety considerations and the restrains imposed by the stair trend and riser configurations.

Pedestrian traffic flow simulation projects have been conducted for the purposes of large transportation projects, as the construction of airport and bus terminals as well as underground stations. A number of tools are operational in more than one domain, emphasising on specific requirements [3], [4]. Simulation enables an in depth analysis of the domain under study under real conditions in order to indicate potential errors or inefficiencies in the design of buildings and operations. Nevertheless, simulation modelling is not as widely applied as expected when designing building sections accommodating pedestrian traffic.

In the remainder of the paper, we emphasise on traffic and space characteristics used for modelling the most significant entities as walkways, entrances, stairs etc. Measures representing simple concepts of efficient pedestrian locomotion are introduced, along with an in depth discussion of the level of service concept. Level of service standards are determined for the above entities, each one characterised by specific values.

The pedestrian traffic simulation study presented in the following sections is conducted for a station of the underground. Selection of this particular station is due to its increased significance, size and complexity. The overall station description is given, along with an output analysis of the simulation results and some useful conclusions.

2 Traffic and Space Characteristics

There are many examples of poor, and even hazardous, human environments resulting from a lack of understanding of the traffic-flow relationships and space requirements of pedestrians. A number of authorities have been using maximum pedestrian capacity as a basis for design. Yet, analysis of pedestrian traffic flow on walkways and stairs have shown that capacity is reached when there is a dense crowding of pedestrians, causing restricted and uncomfortable locomotion. Insufficient consideration of human space requirements has resulted in inadequate design of many areas where pedestrians may be required to accumulate in large groups. In some instances, overcrowding of these areas has resulted in injury and loss of life.

To meet these inadequacies, pedestrian traffic volumes and queuing relationships are introduced [1] on the basis of average pedestrian area occupancy, providing easily understood measures for design. These are the following:

1. Flow volume: the number of traffic units passing a point in a unit of time, designated as P. It also can be expressed as passengers per foot width per minute (PDF).
2. Speed: locomotion speed, expressed in distance per unit of time, usually in feet per minute, designated as S
3. Density: the number of traffic units per unit of area. The reciprocal of density is also used to express the square feet of area per pedestrian and is designated as M, the pedestrian area module
4. Headway: the time and distance separation between traffic units
5. Queue: one or more traffic units waiting for service

The flow equation, the classic relationship of traffic design is the following:

Flow Volume = Average Speed x Average Density or, $P = S \times D$

Pedestrian volume, the number of persons passing a point in a time unit, is the most important walkway design parameter. A favourable environment is created if a walking section is sufficiently wide to allow for normal walking convenience and avoidance of conflicts during all the expected fluctuations in traffic demand. Free walking speed increases, as more area is available for locomotion.

Average pedestrian areas beyond 25 square feet per person were required before near normal, free flow walking speeds could be attained. Pedestrian traffic volume, on the other hand, is inversely proportional to pedestrian area occupancy. Flow volume increases as pedestrian volume decreases, until reaching a critical point where locomotion becomes so restricted due to lack of space, that flow volumes begin to decline. Many designers have been using this maximum flow volume, which occurs at or near at this critical pedestrian area occupancy, as a basis for design. This produces a limited walking section that restricts normal locomotion and is susceptible to intermittent interruptions and stoppages with normal fluctuations in traffic demand.

Entrances are walkway sections in which pedestrians are channelled into equal, door width traffic lanes. In addition to imposing restricted lateral spacing in the traffic stream, entrances may require the pedestrian to perform some time consuming function, such as opening a door or turnstile. Since pedestrians have different average time and distance separations in a traffic stream, depending on the flow volume, when a pedestrian opens a door, there must be a sufficient time headway separation between this one and the following pedestrian. Otherwise, a growing pedestrian queue will develop. As with walkway flow, doorway systems designed on or near maximum capacity and are likely to generate frequent queuing and offer poor level of service.

Locomotion on stairs is much more stylised and restricted than walking, because the dimensions of stairs themselves tend to determine many of the aspects of locomotion that the pedestrian may more freely choose on a level surface. The pacing distance is imposed by the length of the stair tread. The pacing rate may be freely adjusted, but because of greater energy requirements and concerns for safety, this is also limited.

2.1 Level of service standards

The Level of Service concept was first developed in the field of traffic engineering in recognition of the fact that capacity design was resulting in planned congestion. This concept provides a useful model for the design of pedestrian spaces. Pedestrian service standards are based on the freedom to select normal locomotion speed, the ability to pass slow-moving pedestrians and the relative ease of cross and reverse flow movements at various pedestrian traffic concentrations [1].

The various levels of service for walkways are determined on the basis of the walking speed, pedestrian spacing and the probability of conflict at traffic concentrations. The standards provide the means for determining the design quality of corridors, sidewalks and entranceways.

Walkway standards are operative within a definitive range of flow for which meaningful relationships have been observed. Beyond this range, pedestrian flow tends to be slightly erratic and less defined. This does not retract from the value of the standards, since they are still representative of a crowded situation. Six levels of service are defined for walkways, as described in the following:

1. Level of service A: Pedestrian area occupancy 35 square feet per person or greater, average flow volume 7 PFM, or less.
2. Level of service B: Pedestrian area occupancy 25-35 square feet per person, average flow volume 7-10 PFM.
3. Level of service C: Pedestrian area occupancy 15-25 square feet per person, average flow volume 10-15 PFM.
4. Level of service D: Pedestrian area occupancy 10-15 square feet per person, average flow volume 15-20 PFM.
5. Level of service E: Pedestrian area occupancy 5-10 square feet per person, average flow volume 20-25 PFM.
6. Level of service F: Pedestrian area occupancy 5 square feet per person or less, average flow volume variable, up to 25 PFM.

At walkway level of service F, all pedestrian walking speeds are extremely restricted and forward progress can only be made through shuffling. There would be frequent, unavoidable contact with other pedestrians, and reverse or crossing movements would be virtually impossible. This level of service is representative of a loss of control and a complete breakdown in traffic flow. Pedestrian areas below 5 square feet are more representative of a queuing rather than a traffic flow situation and this level of service is not recommended for walkway design.

The above levels of service are extensively referenced within this study, as the basis of the pedestrian moving mechanism.

3 Simulation Study

This paper emphasises on these issues on the basis of a pedestrian traffic simulation study, which was conducted for a station of the underground, serving as an interchange station between two lines. The simulation study aims at extracting conclusions for the level of service provided to the passengers using the station during morning peek hours as well indicating possible bottlenecks in passenger flow in peak hours or during peaks within peak hours.

3.1 Underground station description

This station serves as an interchange station for lines 1 and 2 and has 8 entrances/exits. The overall station consists of 4 distinct underground levels. The first underground level (L1) is the concourse level, the next one (L2) is the line 1 platform level, the third one (L3) is the transfer level for passengers moving between lines 1 and line 2 and the forth one (L4) is the level for line 2 platforms. The overall station is depicted in figure 1.

There is a single central platform for line 1 in L2. For line 2, on the other hand, there are two platforms in L4, one for each direction (northbound and southbound).

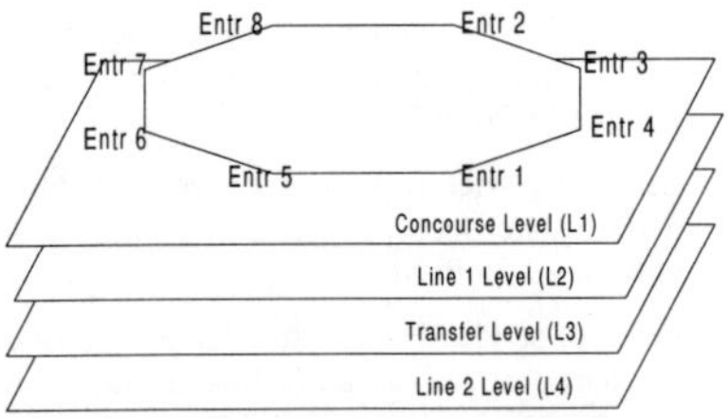

Figure 1: Abstract station design

The concourse level is considered to be of increased significance since most passenger flows either originate or exit through L1. Complexity of L1 is also increased since it is used not only from passengers of lines 1 and 2, but also from pedestrians only traversing the station without entering areas restricted for the two lines. In addition, several entities of the station operation are located there, along with the necessary equipment, as ticket issuing and cancelling devices. Special attention is thus given to the concourse level.

All data used to describe the station structure and operations are based on current measurements as well as long term predictions. Quantitative data for passengers moving in all possible entry point/destination combinations during morning peak hours are presented in figure 2. Most passengers originate from trains of lines 1 and 2, exiting the station from street, and very few ones move towards the opposite direction.

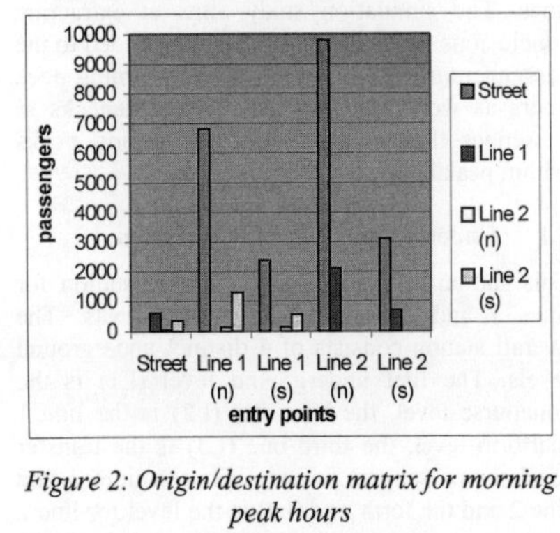

Figure 2: Origin/destination matrix for morning peak hours

3.2 Simulation modelling

To provide an in depth view of the overall station operation, all levels are divided into segments. Segmentation process is performed on the basis of certain criteria to ensure modelling efficiency. Among these, limits of each segment are defined in such a way that density as uniform as possible throughout the segment. It is easy to conclude an improved performance is obtained when the number of segments is increased.

Segmentation is considered as a standard modelling procedure for simulation tools studying the behaviour of passengers moving inside a station. In this case, the overall station was divided into 87 discrete segments, to provide an analytical view. This segmentation schema includes all walkways (corridors and open space), stairs and escalators.

Modelling of passenger flows in the station is performed according to the widely accepted level of service model, proposed by Fruin [1]. This includes the segmentation of all four levels space into segments in which pedestrians can develop a maximum speed determined upon the existing level of service. The level of service is constantly adjusted according to the current density of the segment.

For the overall station, it is possible to pre-determine the number of discrete routes from all possible origins to all possible destinations that passengers may choose. In handle and maintain the possible routes from all entry points to all destinations, depending on whether passengers enter the station from street or the trains, a routing table is constructed. This table acquires more than 1600 entries, corresponding to all possible routes, each entry maintaining information about the next segment that passengers must cross, along with the walking distance within that segment. The routing table is 3-dimensional and entries are specified through the entry point, final destination and current position. This schema ensures the efficient handling of all passenger movements within the station.

A number of assumptions were also used for standardising the behaviour that pedestrians exhibit. Main assumptions are the following:

- From all pedestrians entering the station from street, 80 percent use the underground lines 1 and 2 and 20 percent are only traversing the station.
- From all passengers entering the station from street, 70 percent acquire multiple journey tickets and thus not use ticket-issuing

services. The remaining 30 percent are obliged to do so.

- Passengers always use the same route from street to the trains, and vice versa, which is the shortest one.
- Pedestrians traversing the station never use the same entrance or the two neighbour entrances/exits as their exit point. Only the remaining 5 entrances/exits are therefore considered as possible options.

Discrete event simulation is used to represent passenger flows within the boundaries of the station. Primary entities of this modelling approach include passengers, segments (walkways, stairs and escalators), ticket issuing and cancelling machines and trains of both lines. Object oriented modelling is adopted purpose due to the representation capabilities provided by object orientation. Simulation models are implemented in Modsim II.

3.3 Simulation results

Experimentation with the simulation model was performed for the morning peak hours where most passengers enter the station from the trains and exit from the street. This scenario is reversed during the evening peak hours. The simulation experiment duration covers the two-hour duration of the morning peak hours, from 7.00am to 9.00am. The simulation results extracted can be used to indicate certain aspects of the station operation. These results refer to all possible routes from the trains to the street, and vice versa, as well as the pedestrians traversing the station without using the underground.

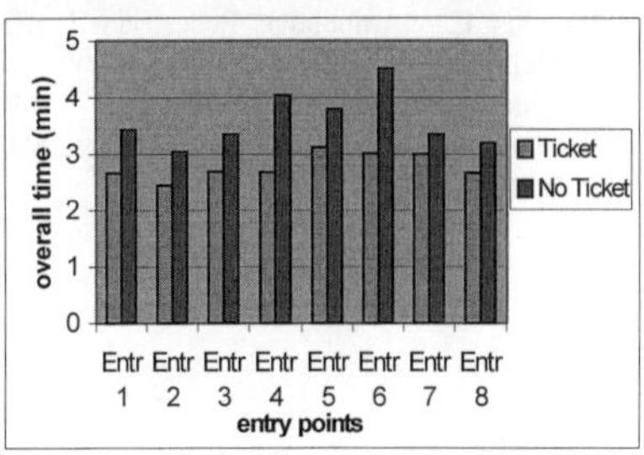

Figure 3: Average time for passengers heading to line 1

The results extracted emphasise on the following main issues: the number of passengers using a particular route, the overall time needed to reach the route destination and the level of service provided to the passengers. Average values are calculated for each case.

In figures 3 and 4, sample results are presented for passengers entering the station from all 8 street entrances during morning peak hours. Passengers are heading either to the single platform of line 1 or the platforms of line 2. A distinction is made between passengers that acquire multiple journey tickets and passengers that do not.

Total time is measured from the point where a passenger enters the station either from the street or the train until the time he exits through the trains or the street, respectively. As expected, the time required for passengers without a ticket is increased, since they have to purchase one. Nevertheless, the additional time seems to be acceptable (below 1.5 min).

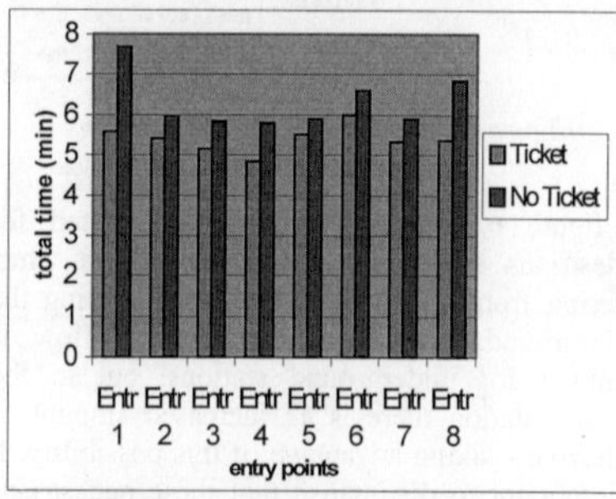

Figure 4: Average time for passengers heading to line 2 (n)

Simulation results for passengers heading towards the opposite direction, originating from trains of lines 1 and 2, from both northbound and southbound directions, and exiting from street, are presented in figure 5

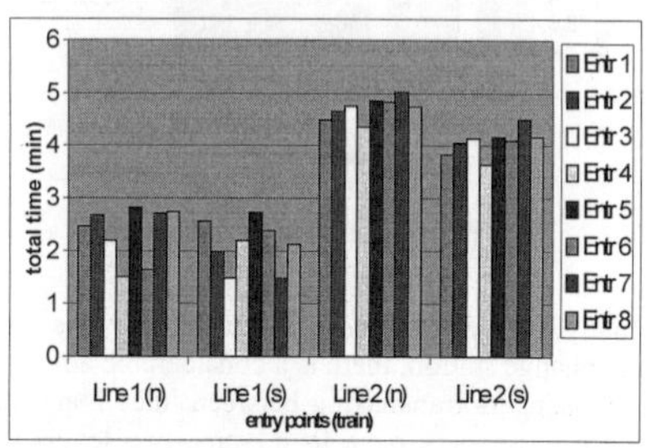

Figure 5: Average time for passengers heading to street exits

This figure is of increased significance, since the majority follows this direction. As expected, line 1 passengers reach considerably earlier their exit points than passengers from line 2, since they have to traverse only 2 levels. Different values in the time required for the 8 street entrances/exits is merely due to the station design.

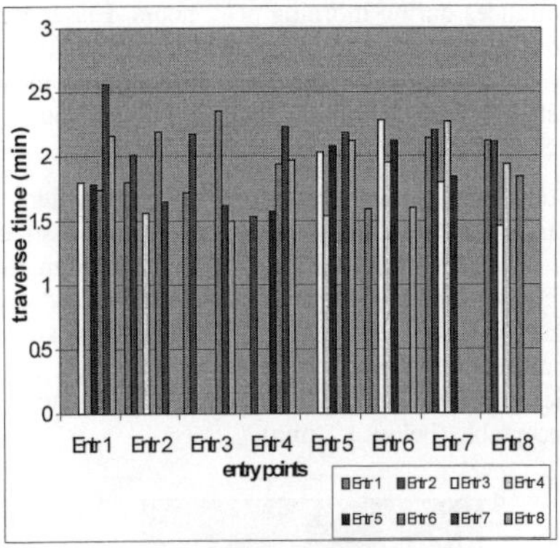

Figure 6: Average time for pedestrians traversing the station

In figure 6, average times are presented for pedestrians simply traversing the station when entering from all 8 entrances, without using the underground. This type of pedestrian flow is common for underground stations, but in the specific station there is an increased amount of pedestrians taking advantage of this possibility. It is important to distinguish that these pedestrians may as well choose to follow an alternative route on the ground level if the level of service provided is not acceptable.

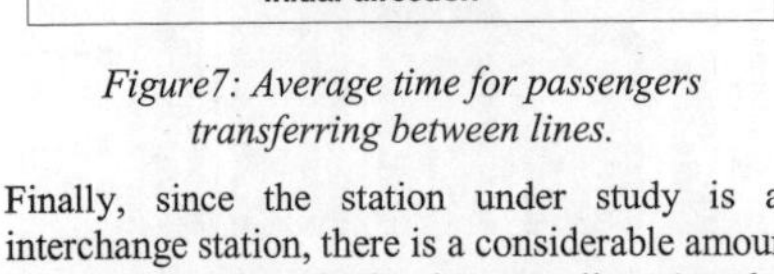

Figure7: Average time for passengers transferring between lines.

Finally, since the station under study is an interchange station, there is a considerable amount of passengers transferring between lines 1 and 2. These passengers have to traverse two levels to reach their destination. The overall time required is thus reduced as far as pedestrian locomotion is concerned, but it also involves the time waiting for the train. This is the reason for not observing a considerably reduced average time compared to the case where exiting station from the street. Simulation results for passengers transferring between trains of the two lines are presented in the following figure.

4 Conclusions

The measurements obtained indicate that the overall station operation appeared to be within acceptable limits. For specific routes, shorter times may have been expected. A limited number of segments of the concourse level also appeared to be especially crowded, thus providing an undesirable level of service.

Current work is oriented towards these specific segments to indicate the possible inadequacies and decisions that may be revised. Studying the station efficiency under an emergency evacuation scenario (emergency planning) is also scheduled for the near future.

5 References

1. Fruin J. John, "Pedestrian planning and design", 1974
2. Robert B. Noland "Pedestrian Travel Times and Motor Vehicle Traffic Signals", Traffic Control Devices, Visibility, and Evaluations, 1996.
3. Kosonen I, Davidsson F, "Evaluation and testing of SPOT and SOS-II control strategies using HUTSIM simulator", Seventh international IEE conference on road traffic control and monitoring, 1994
4. Karplus E., "Ambulans: Pedestrian Traffic Modeling: A Microcosmic View of Reconciliation of Competition and Cooperation",http://ucsub.colorado.edu/~karplus/ambulans.html, 1998

A Model for Organizing Software Configuration Management Repositories

J. Psaromiligos
Greek Atomic Energy Commission
P.O. BOX 60228, 153 10 Ag. Paraskevi
jpsaromi@eeae.nrcps.ariadne-t.gr

Abstract. This paper presents a model for organizing a software configuration management repository which is the core element of a unified configuration management model. Recently, there has been an increasing need for combining efforts in configuration management support with efforts in process modeling. The configuration management repository should represent the development and evolution of configurations so that various life cycles (procedures, policies, etc.) expressing an organization's specific needs could be supported, while at the same time it should ensure and maintain the consistency of the given configurations. Our model formalizes as well as integrates some concepts and activities of configuration development and configuration evolution, thus providing a strong framework for the development of smarter software tools.

1 Introduction

Software Configuration Management (SCM) is the discipline of managing the evolution of software systems both during the initial stages of development and during all stages of maintenance. SCM constitutes a key element to the software process and includes many activities that must be carried out consistently. Moreover, it involves many different individuals, such as customers, managers and software engineers, as well as many different software products. SCM has four coordinating functions [12,13]:

- Configuration identification: The definition of software components that will be under control, their baselines and how they will change.
- Configuration Control: The technical and administrative procedures in order to control the changes to components.
- Configuration Audit: The function that makes the current status of any software component visible to management.
- Configuration Status Accounting: The function that provides the development history of any software component by recording the activities of the previous SCM functions.

In addition to the above definition, Dart [6] suggests three more functions:

- Manufacture: The function that manages the construction and building of the software product in an optimal manner.
- Process management: The function that ensures the proper implementation of the organization's procedures, policies and life cycle model.
- Team work: The function that controls the work and interactions between multiple developers.

In large scale software, the management of these activities is an extremely difficult task, but essential to the effective and reliable evolution of such software. Computer assistance is of great importance, because large scale software has a long lifespan and its representation and evolution history are very complex. Moreover, it can help avoid the confusion caused by interaction among the different individuals, and thus improving productivity. Although several tools, largely satisfying many of the SCM functionality requirements, have emerged, [3,4,5,7,8,10,11,22,24,25, 26] there are still difficulties and problems arising from the lack of a unified CM model [9,8,26,5]. This paper describes a model for organizing a SCM repository, which is the core element of a unified CM model, towards this direction. The model supports the "CM Protocol" layer, which is the second layer of the three levels of CM services as reported in [9] and integrates the activities of software development process with the activities of software evolution process, thus providing a strong framework for the development of smarter software tools.

2 Development and evolution of configurations

Although there is an obvious relationship between the software development process [18] and the process of software evolution, the two are usually loosely coupled [1]. Both processes include an ordered set of steps that are controlled by the managers of the software project and are carried out by the software engineers. The development steps are of many different types depending on the life cycle model, the size of the software project as well as on the tools used in the development. The evolution steps result from change requests that are approved and scheduled by the management. It is obvious that knowledge of the different development steps, the order in which these steps have been applied, the inputs and outputs of the steps, the decisions taken at each step, etc., are all valuable for the management of software evolution and especially for effective scheduling of the evolution steps.

The development steps are related to each other producing software artifacts of many different types, such as management plans, specifications (requirements, design, test), source code, executable code, user's manuals, etc. Some of them are delivered to customers and called exported components. The others are intermediate components which are necessary for the construction of the deliverable components of the system. A software system is composed of the deliverable components as well as the various intermediate components. The completion of the development process leads to the production of a concrete version of the software system (i.e. a new system configuration).

The evolution steps implement changes to software components, but the software components are immutable. Thus, in order to implement a change to a software component, a second one embodying the changes is created, called new version of the first. In this way the evolution steps produce the versions of software components according to the requested changes. However, each evolution step is actually a new development step producing a new version of the altered component. Therefore, a change request affecting a specific set of components can be implemented by initiating the given development steps that have produced the affected components. For example, a change in a source code module can effects other modules that directly or indirectly use it as well as software components that are derived from it (e.g., object code modules). If a new development process starts in order to implement the previous change, only the steps that produced the affected components should be initiated. The given steps would produce a new version of each affected component. This process could result in the creation of a new system configuration (i.e. a new version of the whole software system). Also, there are evolution steps that are abandoned for many reasons, e.g. high implementation cost. In the rest of the paper the term "step" is used both for a development and an evolution step.

A step can be "manual" or "automatic". Manual steps are carried out manually by software engineers, while automatic steps are carried out automatically by software tools. The output of manual steps are software components, called "source", while the output of automatic steps are software components, called "derived". The tools used in the development are software components too, called "derivers".

Both the software components and the steps can be composite or atomic entities. A software component or a step is composite if its body can be viewed as a collection of related parts, and it is atomic if otherwise. The parts can be composite or atomic entities of many different types too. A composite part is composed of other composite or atomic parts and so on, leading to a tree structure between composite entities and their parts. An atomic part is undivided. As is seen, a software system has many parts of many different types and with many relations among them. In general, a system structure is extremely complex.

Software components have a significant rate of changes, and so they have many versions. Especially in large scale systems, software components are subject to numerous, and sometimes conflicting, changes during their lifetimes. Versions have unique identifiers. A version identifier is a double (variation-id, revision-id) where variation-id is a variation identifier and revision-id is a revision identifier. Variations represent independent lines of development and each one consists of an ordered sequence of revisions. Revisions result from changes the purpose of which is to fix bugs, to implement enhancements, and so forth. Each variation has a set of attributes, which are of primary interest to the designers. All variations of a component share a subset of these attributes, which characterize the component itself. Variations can be organized using a class-subclass hierarchy according to their sets of attributes [20]. Then, each revision will be an instance of exactly one variation class.

3 Modeling configurations as a three-dimensional space

The configuration management repository should represent the development and evolution of configurations so that various life cycles (procedures, policies, etc.) expressing the organizations' specific needs could be supported, while at the same time it should ensure and maintain the consistency of the given configurations. In this section we model the universe of configurations in a repository as a three-dimensional space. The first dimension represents the configuration development, the second dimension represents the configuration evolution and the third dimension represents the decomposition of a configuration (fig. 1).

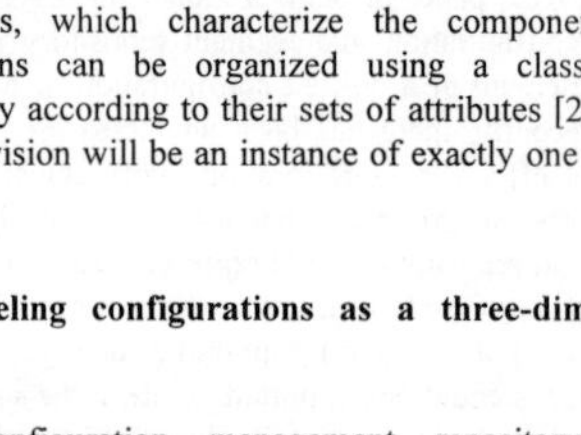

Figure 1. Configurations as a three-dimensional space.

The dimension of development represents the "development cycle" of each configuration. A "development cycle" (DC) is defined as the development process of a concrete configuration version. A DC includes steps and software components as well as states and state transitions that are needed for the production of the given configuration. Each step of a DC produces a single version of a software component. Both steps and components may have several levels of decomposition, which define new development (sub)cycles, i.e. one development (sub)cycle for each composite component. Some of the components are exported components, i.e. correspond to the deliverable parts of the system. Moreover, the model permits the abandonment of development cycles.

The dimension of evolution represents the evolution history of each configuration. The evolution history of each software component is the result of all the DCs that include versions of the given software component. These cycles are usually initiated according to change requests of the system. Such a cycle involves initiations of those steps that are needed for the implementation of the changes as well as new steps that introduce new components. For example, if there is a change request to a software component that represents the "software design", a new DC must start by initiating the "design step" (the step that has produced the "software design" component). The new "design step" produces the next version of the "software design" but it could cause initiations to other steps in order to implement changes to other software components that are affected by the change. Also, if a software component is shared among different software systems, a change in this object may initiate multiple DCs. In such cases a scope must be associated with each change request. Each DC must be within the scope of the change request in order to be initiated.

The dimension of decomposition represents the decomposition process related to each configuration. The term "decomposition process" refers to the development process of the composite entities of the configuration until all the elementary (atomic) entities of the system are created. This process reveals the structure of each configuration. The structure depends on the objects that are under configuration control and are included in the configuration as well as on the granularity level, i.e. the level at which the organization control changes. Composite steps produce composite components while atomic steps produce atomic components.

A more formal description of the above dimensions is given in the next paragraphs. The description takes the form of a graph model which is influenced by previous work as reported in [14,2,11] and consists of two parts: the "Instance Graph" (IG) and the "Type Graph" (TG). The IG represents instantiated configurations, i.e. snapshots of the evolution history of configurations at various points in time. The term instance is referred to the elements of the IG which are instances of concrete types. These types constitute the elements of the second part, the TG. The TG is a key element to the model because it generates the IG and it can be easily implemented by existing technology.

3.1 The instance graph

There are three basic elements involved in each dimension of the configurations' space that constitute the basic building blocks of the IG: components, steps and relations. The IG consists of nodes that represent software components (C nodes) and steps (S nodes), while the arcs of the graph represent three kinds of relations: (1) between components and steps, called "input relations" ($I \subseteq C\times S$) (2) between steps and components, called "output relations" ($O \subseteq S\times C$) and (3) between components, called "dependency relations" ($DR \subseteq C\times C$).

Each component represents a concrete version of some software object, it is an instance of a concrete type (component type) and it can represent a source, a derived or a deriver software object (tool). Steps are also instances of concrete types (step types representing the life cycle model of the organization), and they can be "manual" or "automatic".

Each component is the output of a unique step. There are no primitive components as are defined in [3,15] because the model represents the development process from the beginning and not after the development of the initial configuration (i.e. the first version). The previous definition can be expressed formally as follows:

$$\text{ALL}\ (s1\ s2{:}S,\ c{:}C{::}\ [s1,c] \in O\ \&\ [s2,c] \in O \Rightarrow s1=s2)$$

A source component is the output of a manual step, while a derived component is the output of an automatic step. Each step may have many inputs but only one if any output. Both inputs and outputs are versions of software objects, i.e. components. More specifically, the inputs of a step are components which directly affect the output component or affect the components that are part of the output (if it is composite). However, there may be steps with no output component.

$$\text{input}(s : S) = (c : C \mid [c,s] \in I)\ \&\ |\text{input}(s)| \geq 0$$
$$\text{output}(s : S) = (c : C \mid [s,c] \in O)\ \&\ |\text{output}(s)| \leq 1$$

Steps and components may be composite or atomic entities. Composite components and composite steps are abstract entities that represent collections of other (composite/atomic) software components or steps respectively and they are treated as a single entity. The components or the steps of the collection may include instances of the same or different (component/step) types. The "composition-list(c)" represents the set of components that are part of component c, while the "composition-list(s)" represents the same set for step s. Atomic components and steps can be defined according to their composition lists.

$$\text{atomic}(c{:}C) = \neg\text{EXISTS}(c'{:}C :: c' \in \text{composition-list}(c))$$
$$\text{atomic}(s{:}S) = \neg\text{EXISTS}(s'{:}S :: s' \in \text{composition-list}(s))$$

The output of a composite step is a composite component, while the output of an atomic step is an atomic component. The (sub)steps that are part of a composite step produce the components that are part of the composite component, which is the output of the corresponding composite step. These can be expressed formally as follows:

$$\text{ALL}(s1\ s2{:}S,\ c1\ c2{:}C :: c1 \in \text{output}(s1)\ \&\ c2 \in \text{output}(s_2)\ \&\ s2 \in \text{composition-list}(s_1) \Rightarrow c2 \in \text{composition-list}(c_1))$$

The above representation can capture steps and components which may be shared among different software systems.

Relations are the third element of the graph. The input (I) and output (O) relations define the dependencies among the components and steps of the IG. All the dependencies belong to the D+ relation, which is defined as the transitive closure of the D=(IUO) relation. According to D+ relation, a c1 component depends on a c2 component if [c2,c1] ∈ D+, and an s1 step depends on an s2 step if [s2,s1] ∈ D+. These dependencies are very important in software evolution because they can be used for impact analysis of changes to components and steps. For example, the set of steps affected by a change in a c component is defined as follows:

$$\text{affected-steps}(c{:}C) = (\, s{:}S \mid [c,s] \in D+ \,)$$

However, the D+ relation can not represent the various relationships among the components of the development process, while, by restricting the consequences of changes according to a specific set of relationships, it gives a more meaningful set of triggered steps. Moreover, the various tools used in the development could more effectively operate upon the objects of the repository if they make use of their own specific relationships.

We classify the relationships among the software components in three basic superclasses "uses", "derives" and "consists-of". The "uses" relationships represent the dependencies of source components induced from the manual steps of the development process and are defined between source components and general components (sometimes a source component may use a derived). The "derives" relationships represent the dependencies of derived components induced from the automatic steps of the development process and are defined between general components and derived components. The "consists-of" relationships represent the structure of a software system (system model) and are defined between composite components and the components that are included in their composition lists. These relationships define a hierarchy with nodes representing composite components and leaves representing atomic components. The "uses", "derives" and "consists-of" relationships may have many subclasses according to various types of software components involved in the development process. Each dependency relation of the IG is an instance of a specific relationship class.

Examples of "uses" relationships, as they are imposed by programming languages, are the “includes” relationship by C, the “with” and "separate-of" relationships by Ada, the “calls” relationship of a programming language and so forth. At a high granularity level we may define the following relationships between source code modules: "uses-a-data-type", "access-a-variable", "calls-a-procedure", "sends-a-message-to", etc. Relationships imposed by other types of components are: “design-uses-requirements”, “source-code-uses-design”, "test-case-uses-module-spec", and so forth. A typical "derives" relationship is the ".c-derives-.o" relationship between a source code file in C and the corresponding object code file. A typical "consists-of" relationship is the "system-composition" that corresponds with the system and the objects comprising it (system model in some configuration management systems).

3.2 Initiating development cycles

A DC is initiated as part of the development process during the initial stages of development or as part of one or more change requests to the system at any point of time during its life cycle. The first case corresponds with the development of the initial configuration while the second corresponds with the development of a new configuration. The evolution of a software system causes the initiation of many development cycles. Changes are inevitable both during a development cycle and after its completion, and they usually cause initiations of a subset of the development steps in order to be implemented. However, we can not arbitrarily initiate a step. This is necessary if we are to avoid inconsistencies and maintain some kind of stability in the implementation of changes. The change process is based on the notion of "baselines", i.e. the identification of specific reference points during the system life cycle which enforce stability. Stability emanates from the fact that no one can change a baseline without following the prespecified procedures and policies of the organization. This guarantees a common reference point (the baseline) if need be for baseline to change. A DC that is initiated by the change process includes a set of steps that result from the change implementation and it is based on a part of another development cycle.

We consider three parts of a development cycle: a "dynamic", a "controlled" and a "baselined" part. The dynamic part represents the development process itself as it is guided and controlled by the developers. This process takes place under the developers' workspaces which are outside the configuration repository. As the DC proceeds, software components from the developers' workspaces are put under configuration control. These components constitute the controlled part of the development cycle. This part needs management approval in order to be integrated into the configuration repository. The controlled components that have approval for integration constitute the baselined part of the DC. These components are part of the configuration repository and are represented by corresponding nodes and arcs of the IG. Each DC that is initiated by the change process is based on the baselined part of a previous DC. This is necessary for ensuring stability to the new development cycle.

Also, there are abandoned development cycles. Such a cycle has no output component as part of the configuration repository, but some of its substeps with the corresponding output components may be parts of the repository. This is the case when a development cycle is abandoned after the execution of several steps and so it may result in having an initial part of it baselined, e.g. a preliminary design. A development cycle may be part of another development cycle that represents the development of another system. This is the case when a software system is composed of independent subsystems. Then the development cycles of the latter become parts of the development cycle of the former.

3.3 Defining states for development cycles

In order to control the development cycles, i.e. the development of the configurations that are inserted into the repository, we associate states with each step of the cycle. Our goal here is to define a global set of states for management purposes. This approach can be refined so that states can capture the design decisions taken during the execution of a step as reported in [23]. This can be easily integrated in our model by refining the global states that we describe in this paragraph so that they can be (re)defined at the type level of each step. We define the following states of a step:

Opened: In this state the step is checked to determine that it satisfies some criteria before implementation starts, such as identification of the input components (including tools and input parameters when the step is automatic), determination of substeps (if the step is composite) and their priorities, determination of costs and of any other impact on the system.

Started: In this state the implementation of the step has started, the task has been assigned to the authorized person(s), there is a unique identifier for the output component (which, however, is not under configuration control yet) and the input components of the step have been copied in the private workspaces of the developers. Some steps may be implemented in parallel. For automatic steps, all of the input components must be available. When a composite step reaches the started state all of its substeps must be in the same state.

Controlled: In this state the step has produced the output component which is under configuration control, but not yet part of the configuration repository. Configuration control ensures that changes to the output component can not be implemented arbitrarily. However, in this state the component may be rolled back to the started state for several times. This situation arises when the component can not pass an integration test or it depends on other components that are not in the controlled state yet. When a composite step reaches the controlled state all of its substeps must be in the same state.

Baselined: In this state the step is stable, it is part of the configuration repository and is represented by the IG. Derived components may not physically be part of the repository for efficient space storage. The representation of an automatic step captures all the necessary information in order to (re)create the output component at any time. When a composite step reaches this state all of its substeps must be in the same state.

Abandoned: In this state the step has been canceled. There is no output component in the repository nor in the IG. The reasons that led to this state are stored for future reference. This state is the final state for all steps that were canceled by the management in the opened, started or controlled states.

The above states do not fully cover all of the phases that a specific step may go through in order to be completed. More specific substates which can be assigned to specific step types are needed. For example, there are separate substates for manual and automatic steps, substates for top level steps or composite steps in general, as well as single atomic steps. In a detailed implementation of our model this can be resolved by associating substates with the type level of each step.

The possible transitions of a step from one state to another are illustrated in the following figure 2.

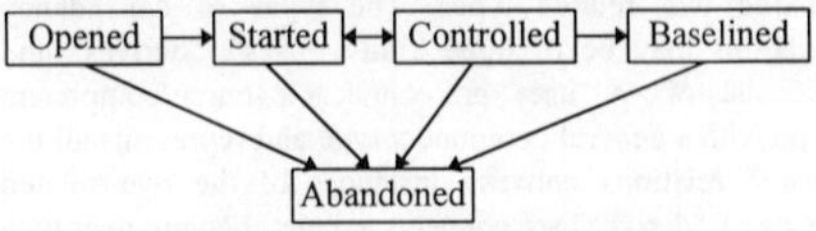

Figure 2. State transitions for steps.

Because of the composite steps, there must be, and there are some constraints on some state transitions - between them and their corresponding substeps - in order to ensure consistency in the development cycle. These constraints include the following:

1) When a composite step changes from the "opened state" to the "started state", all of its substeps make the same transition automatically.
2) A composite step changes automatically from the "started state" to the "controlled state" if all of its substeps make the same transition.
3) A composite step changes automatically from the "controlled state" to the "baselined state" if all of its substeps make the same transition.
4) When a composite step changes to the "abandoned state", all of its substeps make the same transition.

3.4 Evolution history of software components

The evolution history of a software component is included in the DCs that involve steps with output versions of the above object. Each version of a component has a unique identifier which is a triplet (object-id, variation-id, revision-id) where object-id is an identifier for the object, variation-id is an identifier for the variation and revision-id is an identifier for the revision. Thus, the evolution history of a c object is all components with identifiers (c, *, *), where asterisk means all.

Within a development cycle there may exist new software objects, new variations of an object, as well as versions which combine the features of several variations of an object (version merging [15,26]). The last case may be treated as a new variation or as the most recent revision of one of the existing variations of the given object.

4 The Type Graph

The TG represents the domain of all elements (components, steps and relations) included in the IG. The elements of the graph are types of three kinds: component types (source, derived and deriver), step types (manual and automatic) and relation types. The nodes represent component types (C^T nodes) and step types (S^T nodes). The arcs represent relation types (1) between types of components and steps, called "input relation types" ($I^T \subseteq C^T x S^T$) (2) between types of steps and components, called "output relation types" ($O^T \subseteq S^T x C^T$) (3) between types of components, called "dependency relation types" ($DR^T \subseteq C^T x C^T$). An input (output) arc represents all input (output) relations between instances of the two related types. The types of dependency relations may be of three kinds: "uses", "derives" and "consists-of". A "uses" arc connects a source component type with a general component type and represents all the "uses" relations between instances of the two related types. A "derives" arc connects a general component type with a derived component type and represents all the "derives" relations between instances of the two related types. Finally, a "consists-of" arc connects a composite component type with a general component type and represents all "consists-of" relations between instances of the two related types.

The definition of the TG should reflect the life cycle model of the organization, the granularity level of change control as well as the tools (derivers) used in the development. The life cycle model defines the types of top level steps and components - including the types of all the deliverables of the system - as well as the corresponding types of relations between them. Top level components are usually composite entities with several levels of decomposition. Each composite component type (generic configuration in some SCM systems) has a decomposition structure that is represented by corresponding "consists-of" arcs of the TG. The "consists-of" arcs with the same label represent the decomposition of the composite component type. The definition of a composite component type includes the definition of the analogous types of substeps for the development of the subcomponent types. The tools used in the development influence the TG, too. For example, the various programming languages define distinct types of automatic steps, derivers, source and derived components. The types of dependency relations between the components of different programming languages are also distinct. These kinds of relation types may become more complex if we wish to control changes at a level lower than that of "unit" [18].

4.1 The generation process

The IG evolves with time, and new versions of the graph are continuously generated. However, each new version of the IG may be created only by consistent extension, i.e. all previous graphs representing past states must be initial subgraphs of the current and must be subject to the same global labeling function. The generation process of each version includes the instantiation of the appropriate nodes and arcs of the TG. More specifically, the C^T and S^T nodes of the TG generate the C and S nodes of the IG respectively, while the I^T, O^T and DR^T arcs of the TG generate the I, O and DR arcs of the IG. The whole process is guided by the life cycle model of the organization and the corresponding change requests.

5 An example

Figure 5 shows the TG for a refinement of the Waterfall life cycle model. The type "Development__Cycle" represents the top level step of the model which is composed of the following step types:
-"Requirement Step": It generates the "Requirements".
-"Design Step": It generates the "Design".
-"Code Step": It generates the "Source Code".
-"Compile Step": It generates the "Object Code".
-"Link Step": It generates the "Executable Code".
The first three steps are regarded as manual and the last two as automatic, while the C programming language is used. Obviously, the above steps and components can be refined and decomposed into several levels of decomposition. For simplicity purposes our presentation regards the "Source Code" and "Object Code" components as well as the corresponding "Code Step" and "Compile Step" steps as composite entities.

A new DC starts by instantiating the top level step "Development_cycle". The new instance has a unique identifier and generates the first version of the system when its state becomes "closed". Because it is composite, all of its substeps must first be integrated. Thus, following the Waterfall life cycle model, instances of the step types "Requirement_Step", "Design_Step", "Code_Step", "Compile_Step" and "Link_Step" are generated until an instance of the "Executable_Code" type is generated. This fact changes the state of the top level step to "closed" state and an instance of the component type "System" is generated, i.e. the first version of the system (figure 4).

Lets now assume that there is an approved change request upon the "Design.V1.R1" component. If the new change must be deployed in the next version of the system, a new DC will be generated as a new instance of the "Development_cycle" step type. However, the new DC will not instantiate all the step types, but only the step types of the affected components (figure 4).

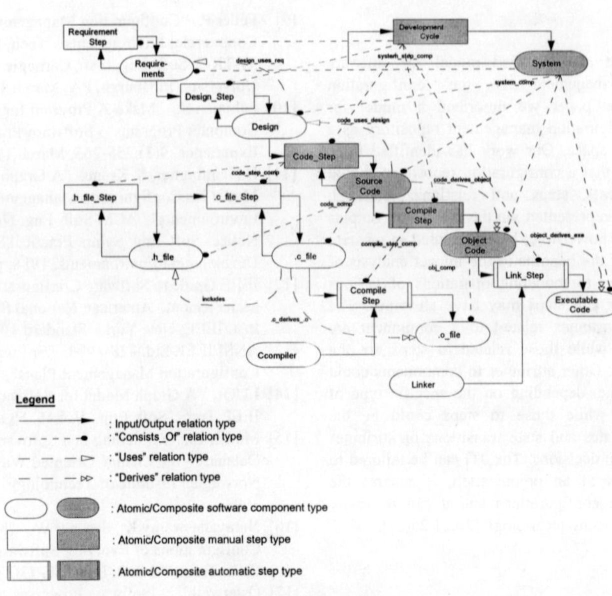

Figure 3. An example of a TG.

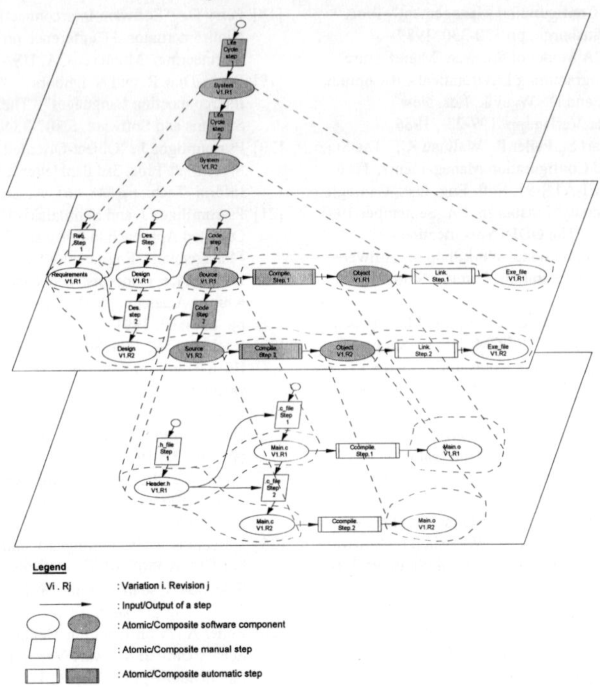

Figure 4. The IG representing only the relations "consists_of" between components.

6 Conclusion

The core element of a unified model for software configuration management is the configuration repository. In this paper we described a model for organizing a configuration management repository as a three dimensional space. Our work has identified three first class objects that a configuration repository should contain: components, steps and relations. Although relations could be represented via the inputs and outputs of steps, it is more powerful to be represented as separate objects because of the benefits to the impact analysis of changes as well as to modeling operations of various tools. Components and steps may have attributes. The minimal set of attributes related to a component are version attributes while those related to steps are the inputs and outputs. Other attributes to components could be type specific, i.e. depending on the specific type of each component, while those to steps could be the estimating cost, states and state transitions or attributes representing design decisions. The TG can be tailored to the specific needs of an organization, it ensures the consistency of the configurations and it can be easily implemented by existing technology [20,21,25,15].

References

[1] Y.Bernard and P. Lavency, "A Process-Oriented Approach to Configuration Management", Proc. 11th ICSE, Pittsburgh, pp.320-330, 1989.

[2] Borison E., "A Model of Software Manufacture", Advanced Programming Environments, R.Conradi, T. Didriksen, and D. Wanvik, Eds. New York:Springer-Verlag, pp. 197-22-, 1986.

[3] Brown A., Dart S., Feiler P., Wallnau K., "The State of Automated Configuration Management", Tech. Rep. CMU/SEI-ATR-91, Soft. Eng. Inst., Carnegie Mellon University, Pittsburgh, PA, September 1991.

[4] G.M. Clemm, "The ODIN Specification Language", International WorkShop on Software Version and Configuration Control, Stuttgart, FRG, January 1988.

[5] Conradi R., "Software Configuration Management", selected papers ICSE'97 SCM-7 WorkShop , Volume 1235 of Lecture Notes in Computer Science, Boston, MA, USA, May 1997, Springer-Verlang.

[6] Dart, Susan A., "Concepts in Configuration Management Systems", Third International Software Configuration Management WorkShop, ACM Press, June 1991.

[7] Estublier J., "Configuration Management:the notion and the tools", International WorkShop on Software Version and Configuration Control, Stuttgart, FRG, January 1988.

[8] Estublier J., Software Configuration Management:selected papers ICSE SCM-4 and SCM-5 WorkShops , Volume 1005 of Lecture Notes in Computer Science, Seattle Washington, October 1995, Springer-Verlang.

[9] Feiler P., "Configuration Management Models in Commercial Environments", Tech. Rep. CMU/SEI-91-TR-7, Soft. Eng. Inst., Carnegie Mellon University, Pittsburgh, PA, March 1991.

[10] Feldman S., "Make-A Program for Maintaining Computer Programs", Software-Practice and Experience, 9(3):255-265, March 1979.

[11] D.Heimbigner, S. Krane, "A Graph Transform Model for Configuration Management Environments", ACM Soft. Eng. Notes/SIGPLAN Notices Soft. Eng. Symp. Practical Soft. Development Environments, 1988, pp.216-225.

[12] IEEE Guide to Software Configuration Management, American National Standards Inst./IEEE, New York, Standard 1042-1987, 1988.

[13] ANSI/IEEE Std. 828-1990, "Software Configuration Management Plans", 1990.

[14] LUQI, "A Graph Model for Software Evolution", IEEE Trans. Soft. Eng., Vol.16, NO.8, Aug. 1990.

[15] Munch B., "Versioning in a Software Engineering Database - the Change Oriented Way", PhD Thesis, Norwegian Institute of Technology, September 1993.

[16] Narayanaswamy K., Scacchi W., "Maintaining Configurations of Evolving Software Systems", IEEE Trans. on Soft. Eng., SE-13(3), March 1987.

[17] Osterweil L., "Software Processes Are Software Too", 9th ICSE, 1987.

[18] Perry D., "Software Interconnection Models", Ninth Internatonal Conference on Software Engineering, Monterey CA, USA, March 1987.

[19] Prieto-Diaz R. and Neighbors J., "Module Interconnection Languages", The Journal of Systems and Software, 6:307-334, 1986.

[20] Psaromiligos J., "Object-Oriented Version Selection", Proc. 3rd PanHellenic Conference on Inform. Tech., pp.648-661, Athens, October 1991

[21] Psaromiligos J. and Skordalakis E., "An Object-Oriented Approach to Software Configuration Management", Engineering Systems with Intelligence, Concepts, Tools and Applications, Kluwer Academic Publishers edr. S. G. Tzafestas, pp. 555-563, 1991.

[22] Rochkind M., "The Source Code Control System", IEEE Trans. on Soft. Eng., SE-1(4):364-370, December 1975.

[23] Rose T., M. Jarke, "A Decision-Based Configuration Process Model", Proc. 12th ICSE, pp.316-325, 1990.

[24] Tichy W., "RCS-a system for version control", Software-Practice and Experience, 15(7):637-654, July 1986.

[25] Vescoukis V., Psaromiligos J. and Skordalakis E., "PBVSS:A Prolog-Based Software Version Selection System", Parallel & Distributed Computing In Eng. Systems, North Holland, 1992.

[26] Zeller A., "Configuration Management with Version Sets-A Unified Software Versioning Model and its Applications", PhD Thesis, Technischen Universitat Braunschweig, April 1997.

"Informatics support to change management in a deregulated environment."[1]

Yannis Markopoulos, European Programs Coordinator Singular Software S.A.
Alexandras Av. 158 & Koniari 45 Str
T.K. 114 71
Athens, Greece
JMARK@Singular.Singular.gr

Anastasios T. Mandylas, System Analyst, Singular Software S.A.
Alexandras Av. 158 & Koniari 45 Str
T.K. 114 71
Athens, Greece
TMAND@Singular.Singular.gr

1. Introduction

European Union driven by political, economical and social considerations has published a number of directives considering the deregulation of its Electricity Supply sector. The worldwide changes that have taken place the last years in this sector have drastically transformed the Electricity market to a demanding environment raising a need for more competitive companies.

In order to create a more competitive Electricity Supply Industry (ESI) it is primary necessary to examine and document all alternative restructuring scenarios and secondly to develop a consultancy tool providing all needed information in order to apply the company restructuring.

ELEKTRA is an ESPRIT[EU96] funded project aiming to meet the two aforementioned goals. The target group of the intended toolset are entrepreneurs of the energy domain who cope with companies' reorganisation and restructuring problem. Two ESI companies' departments are respectively examined: PPC's (Greece) Distribution Department and Vattenfall's (Sweden) Human Resources Department.

Restructuring in the ESI sector in not a straightforward task to address since a significant number of external influences have to harmoniously blend with internal market dynamics, constraints and tendencies. The degree of harmoniousness reached usually denote company's success and award of a market share.

To name but a few external factors which strongly influence ES business orientation and structure (especially within EU and the commercially attached countries) are[Mark98]:

- Deregulation directives (Directive 96/92/EC concerning common rules of the internal market in electricity adopted by the Council of ministers on 19 December 1996)
- The European Energy Charter (December 1991)
- The Energy Charter Treaty (December1994)
- The Transeuropean Energy Networks (February 1992)
- The IEA World Energy Model[Yaji97]

In order to avoid ad hoc and unstructured attempts to change, a methodological approach is adopted, namely the Enterprise Knowledge Development (EKD), which represents an integrated set of techniques and associated tools for the purpose of dealing with situations of change. More specifically, this approach defines the means, through its modelling components of describing current and future situations, by which an organisation could respond to change stimuli.

Due to the complexity of the addressed problem and the need to identify alternative change scenarios, an ESI tailored environment is implemented, namely ESI Toolset, aiming at supporting the aforementioned methodology and incorporating ESI related knowledge, practices, constraints and trends. The proposed essay aims to elaborate on the ESI Toolset structural specifications and functionality as a final product.

The aim of the toolset is to enable ESI companies to introduce their own organisation model and propose transition routes into future states, implicitly and explicitly imposed by market needs, taking advantage of all the related global ESI models and guidelines provided.

The platform chosen for implementing the environment and the architecture adopted constitutes an open environment aiming to assist expansion, communication with other ESI informatics systems and introduction of new models. Special attention has been placed on the user interaction who is able to interact with the ESI Toolset using a graphical user interface while he is able to observe company models through a wide range of alternative facets. Needless to mention that an integral part of the environment will be the training and guidance material thus enabling ESI experts to model respective enterprises and propose solutions for change.

---

[1] This research has been produced within the ESPRIT ELEKTRA project partially funded by DGIII

2. The ESI Toolset Architecture

2.1 ESI-ST Generic Architecture

The architectural structure of the ESI Toolset is demonstrated in the figure below[Mand98]:

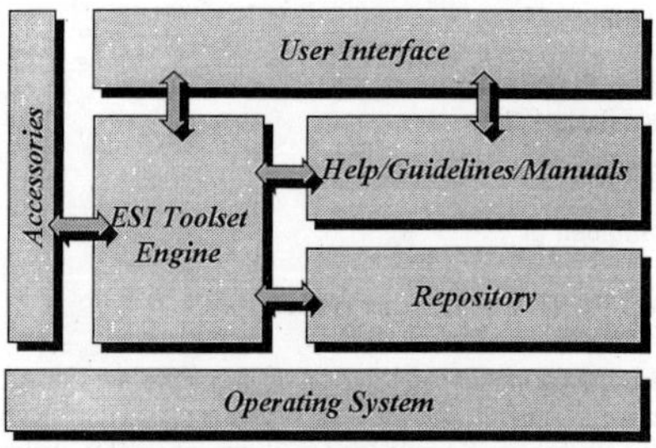

Figure 1. *ESI Toolset Architecture*

As illustrated in figure 1. the Toolset is composed by the following operational modules:

- *The User Interface,* which will serve as a common workplace for all functions supported by the Tool
- *The Help/Guidelines/Manuals Module,* implementing the documentation requirements and supporting the change management guidance and a context-sensitive help on EKD modeling application.
- *The Accessories Module,* supporting the exchange of data with other applications.
- *The ESI Toolset Engine,* supporting all functions defined by the implementation requirements such as, model integrity checking, ESI Knowledge management, change management support.
- *The ESI Toolset Repository,* supporting the storage and retrieval of all EKD and non-EKD entities.

2.2 ESI Toolset User Interface

The ESI Toolset interface is used for the user interaction with the Toolset. The functionality of the interface is divided into the two following subset of functions:

- The Data Manipulation Functions
- The Graphics Manipulation Functions

A more detailed description of the ESI Toolset User Interface functionality is provided in the forthcoming paragraph. In figure 2 the user interface is illustrated indicating its data and graphics manipulation functions.

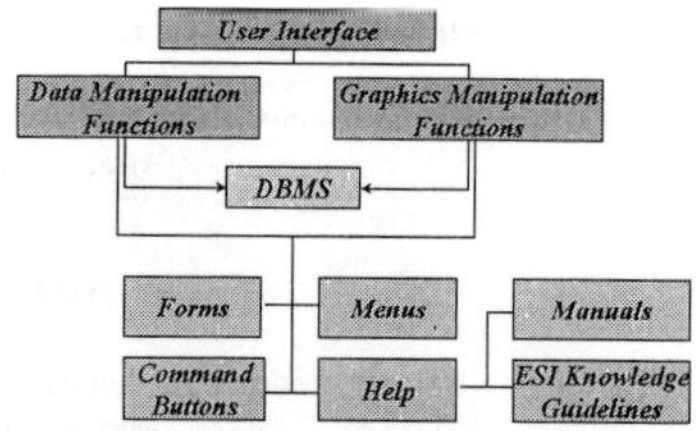

Figure 2. *ESI Toolset User Interface*

2.2.1 Data Manipulation Functions

The Data Manipulation Functions (DMF) aim to provide data access and insure the interface consistency across the sub-systems of the Toolset. Consequently, it is important to implement a robust yet flexible set of functions interfacing the Repository Management System (RMS) and supporting all its operations. The RMS will be extensively presented in another section of this document.

DMF imposes the existence of the following three groups of functions:

- *The Data Entry Functions*, supporting the data integrity checking in conformance to the prescribed models
- *The Data Export Functions,* supporting the data export to other systems and Tools such as MS-Office and data print outs.
- *The Data Retrieval,* supporting queries to the repository and reuse of data in conformance to predefined enterprise rules and functions.

2.2.2 Graphics Manipulation Functions

As already mentioned, all EKD graphical subviews supported by Tool will be accessed using the Graphics Manipulation Functions (GMF). Its main task is to provide the graphical representation of EKD models and support user friendly creation and retrieval of enterprise models. The GMF in collaboration with the DMF will accommodate the description of all enterprise entities in EKD terms. Using GMF, one will be able to introduce EKD notation (in a drag and drop mode) to the models.

GMF consists of the following three groups of functions:

- *The Graphics Creation Functions*, supporting the modeling nation constraints
- *The Graphics Export Functions,* supporting graphics export to other systems and Tools such as MS-Office and graphics print
- *The Graphics Retrieval Functions* (for the purpose of updated and maintaining existing models).

2.3 *Help and Guidelines Module*

The Toolset will provide all necessary EKD Modeling and Change Management guidelines. Either of the two guidelines are developed in the "Help" menu of the ESI Toolset User Interface. The first of these subsets describes extensively the EKD Modeling concepts and components while the second one describes the EKD methodological application on enterprises.

2.4 *Accessories Module*

Interfaces to external tools and accessories are provided by the ESI Toolset. The graphical representation of the enterprise models, the specific enterprise data and the change management reports may be exported to respective formats supported by MS-Windows. Graphics will be exported in Bitmap formats (.bmp) as well as in any other format supported by the graphical Toolbox. Texts will be exported in document (doc) formats.

2.5 *ESI Toolset Engine*

The ESI Toolset Engine is the core of the Toolset. Within this module all major functional requirements presented in the first chapter, are implemented. The Engine consists of the following subsystems:

- *The Tools and Accessories Interconnection Subsystem (TAIS*), supporting the Toolset interconnection with external Tools and accessories (see the "ESI Toolset User Interface" description).
- *The Change Management Subsystem (CMS),* composed by the transition procedures (e.g. between different market states) and the report generation functionality.
- *The Repository Management System (RMS),* supporting insertion, deletion and maintenance of the database entities.
- The ESI Toolset Engine architectural components and their interconnections are demonstrated in figure 3.

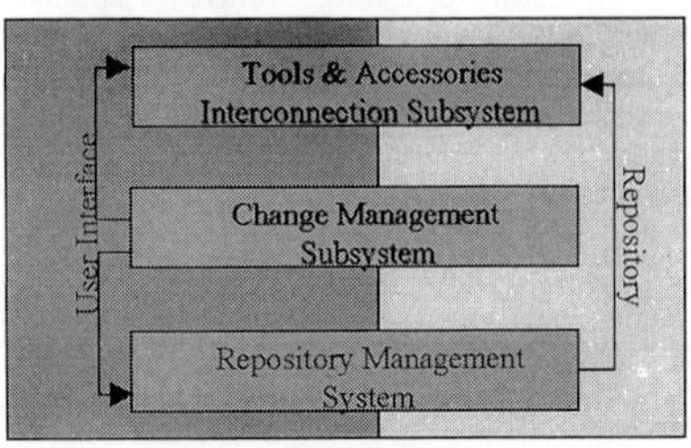

Figure 3. *ESI Toolset Engine Subsystems*

In the sequence there exists a detailed description of the aforementioned ESI Toolset Engine modules.

<u>*Tools and Accessories Interconnection Subsystem (TAIS)*</u>

TAIS links the repository to the user interface supporting export of reports. Export is achieved using the OLE protocol or using the "save as" utility (e.g. generating RTF files)

<u>*Change Management Subsystem (CMS)*</u>

CMS supports the following functionality:

- *Transition procedures.* These procedures implement the successive steps leading from the source state to the intended market state. The transition procedure is illustrated in figure 4.
- *Report generation procedures.* Transition reports are generated while specific user queries are accommodated.

<u>*Repository Management System (RMS)*</u>

RMS supports user operations on the database. In figure 5 the RMS architecture is demonstrated. We should note that the arrows indicate the internal communication of the RMS subsystems.

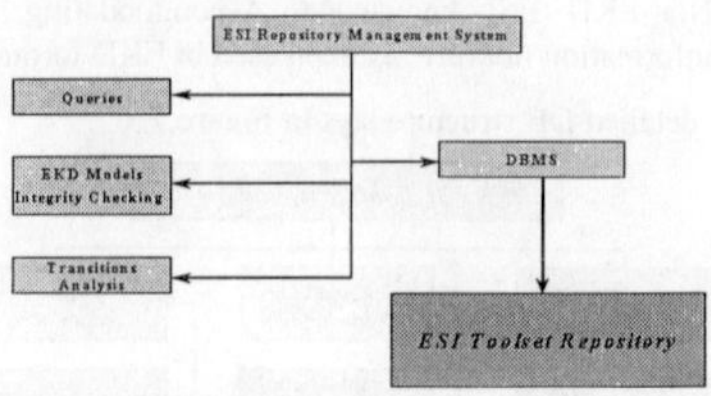

Figure 5. *RMS architecture*

Within RMS the following operations are implemented:

1. Insertion, retrieval and integrity check of EKD models and well as a query support mechanism.
2. The non-EKD Data Management (ESI specific data i.e. measurable indicators)

All these operations are applied on the repository as it is illustrated in figure 5. The repository functional structure is extensively described in the forthcoming section.

2.6 *ESI Toolset Repository*

The Toolset repository is structured in a way to support the predefined model categories and the respective change management procedures (figure 6):

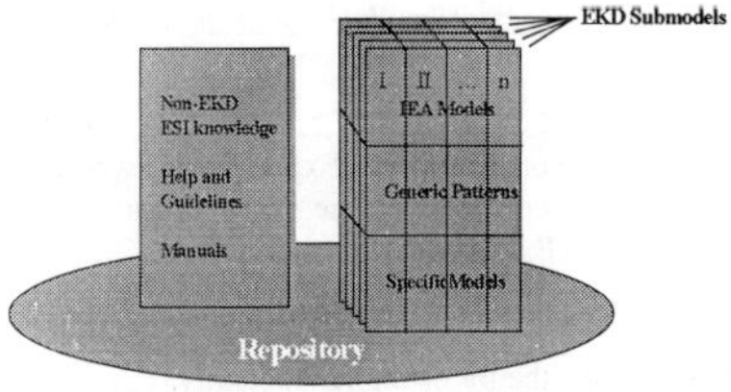

Figure 6. *ESI Toolset Repository*

The ESI Toolset Repository architecture comprises of succeeding components:

- IEA Models. In this level the various ESI market state models are described in conformance to EKD
- Generic Patterns. The generic pattern level describe generic ESI models and facilitates transition between market states
- Specific Models. In this level both organisational and functional structures of an ESI enterprise are described in EKD terms.
- Non-EKD ESI knowledge. Accommodating all information not directly expressed in EKD format.

The detailed DB structure lays in Figure 7.

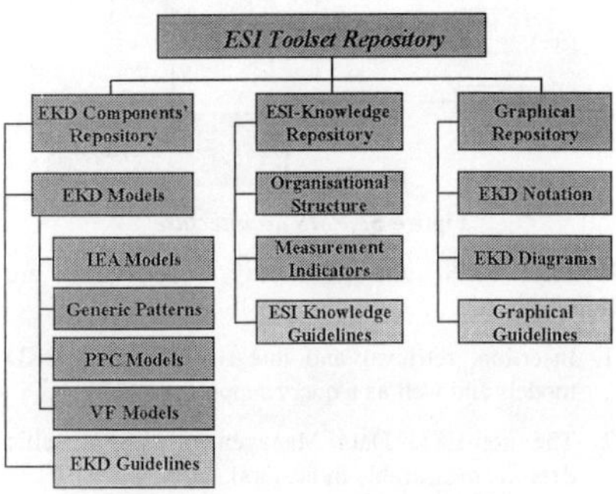

Figure 7. *ESI Toolset Repository structure.*

3. Test Cases and Modeling Support.

3.1 The Two Test Cases

The main aim of the ELEKTRA project to tailor and apply the EKD approach to change management problems within PPC and Vattenfall and to generalise best business practices in changing management for dissemination and application to other companies in the ESI sector.

The PPC case and the Vattenfall case together create a comprehensive understanding and exploration of the nature of change management in the Electricity Supply Industry sector in Europe with focus on the CEU Directives as well as the demands from the customer driven market forces.

By the different approaches in the Vattenfall and PPC application of the EKD method, the cases are complementary to each other:

1. Complementary examination of the EKD method applicability.

PPC has been modelling operational business processes. Vattenfall has been modelling strategic goal and problem descriptions. With different demands on tools and stakeholders. In the ESI change process a wide use of the method will be necessary.

2. Complementary aspects of the change process.

PPC focus the reconstructing of the organisation and Vattenfall focus the knowledge management. Two important ingredients to be successful in the new situation.

3.2 Modeling Support: The EKD Methodology

The EKD approach represents an integrated set of techniques and associated tools for the purpose of dealing with situations of change such as the transformation of business processes, the re-engineering of information systems, the transition of high-level requirements to systems supporting these requirements and so on. EKD represents the confluence of a number of interrelated methodological components. At the centre of the approach is the development of enterprise knowledge models pertaining to the situations being examined. The definition of such models is carried out using appropriate *modelling* techniques and tools. The modeling component of EKD is defined in terms of the concepts that constitute the approach and the notation that enables us to use these concepts.

The total set of EKD concepts constitutes what is termed the EKD metamodel. This defines the logical form of the enterprise knowledge. The metamodel includes information about the semantics of the enterprise knowledge; it identifies the enterprise entities their attributes and explicit relationships between them.

Although there is a single EKD metamodel, upon which any enterprise knowledge model will be, it is more convenient to consider different partitions according to the areas of concern. Each partition is organised according to the objectives of the logically coherent concepts that constitute the partition. These partitions, the metamodels, are designated in the table below:

EKD Metamodels	EKD Metamodels Description
Business Goal Metamodel	Describes the company's intentions of change and provides guidelines for the transition within the current and the intended state.
Enterprise Object & Concepts Metamodel	Describes the current structure of the company providing information about the interrelation of the enterprise components.
Business Processes Metamodel	Relates the functional structure of the enterprise with the change prospects linking all operations taking place within it.
Actor-Role Metamodel	Linking clustered operations with the operating authority.
Role-Activity Metamodel	Clustering lower level operations according to common enterprise tasks.
Enterprise Rules Metamodel	Constrains processes, activities and operations execution according to predefined enterprise rules.
Technical Component & Requirement Metamodel	Defines a set of high level requirements or goals, for the information system as a whole and supports the business goals and processes as defined in the Business Goals and Business Processes Metamodel.

4. Conclusions

The ESI Toolset is meant to become the link between theory and practice: a powerful and easy-to-use tool dedicated in the application of EKD methodology to real-life situations of the ESI sector.

As a result of the efforts that have been made towards the introduction of an enterprise reengineering theory in an IT system, and the respective requirements provided by the users, the ESI Toolset aims to incorporate a large amount of restructuring knowledge applicable in companies of the ESI sector.

The software analysis and development process suggested in this document embed all above mentioned research and implementation attempts as they accrued in an R&D project.

Following the requirements presented in a previous section, we could easily point out that an open system will finally be produced conformant to current software development standards. In addition, this environment will be easily deployable to every company of the ESI sector since it enables customisation, introduction of new market states, models and specifics of respective ESI knowledge.

The ESI Toolset, aims to incorporate a wide range of models conformant to the EKD methodology. Nevertheless, since the target audience is the changing ESI enterprise market, the introduction and handling of respective information was put up-front in our efforts to design the Toolset functionality and interface. In support to the produced architecture, great amount of research is under performance in order to:

- identify worldwide ESI related information and models applicable to enterprise restructuring
- generate transition roadmaps
- generate ESI enterprise modeling guidelines.

All aforementioned issues constitute current and future development of the ESI Toolset. Until the end of the project these will lead to the construction of an innovative IS Tool, consultative to any restructuring attempt of an ESI sector company.

5. References

[Mark98] Energy Market Analysis, Yannis Markopoulos, 1998

[EU96] "ELectrical Enterprise Knowledge *for* Transforming Applications", Project No:22927

[Dodo97] "Homer: Requirements for the ESI Toolset",.Dodopoulos,Y.Markopoulos,Y. Haralambidis, 1997

[Bube97] "Balder: Initial requirements Model for Vattenfall",J.Bubenko,A.Bergenheim,J. Stirna, 1997

[Louk97] "Athena: Initial Requirements Model for PPC", P.Loukopoulos, V.Kavakli,G.Grosz, 1997

[Mand98] "Ikarus: Design of the ESI Toolset", A.Mandylas, Y.Markopoulos, 1998

[Rola98] "Generic Patterns", C.Roland, G.Grosz, 1998

[Yaji97] "Deregulatory Reforms of the Electricity Supply Industry", Quorum Books, Westport, Connecticut,1997

Iterative switching networks *

V.N.Kasyanov
Institute of Informatics Systems
Siberian Division of the Russian Academy of Sciences
630090, Novosibirsk, Russia
E-mail: kvn@iis.nsk.su

Abstract

In the paper the construction of so called iterative networks is studied. This class contains rearrangeable N-inputs M-outputs networks carrying any n connections, where $n \leq m$, with roughly $2(N+M)\log(NM/(N+M))$ contacts if $m = \min(N, M)$ and with roughly $2(N+M)\log m$ contacts if $m < \min(N, M)$; these results are the best obtainable by the methods used.

1 Introduction

A switching (N, M, m)-networks, $m \leq \min\{N, M\}$, is a system for establishing simultaneous n paths, where $n \leq m$ from N terminals called inputs to other M terminals called outputs. The paths are established through single-pole single-throw switches called contacts. A contacts may be either "on" ("closed") or "off" ("open"). At any moment in time, at most m paths may be established simultaneously. Such a set of paths will be called a *state*. In any state of the (N, M, m)-network any input may be connected to at most one output and each output can be connected to at most one input.

Rearrangeable and nonblocking networks arise in a variety of communications contexts. Common examples include telephone systems and network architectures for parallel computers.

Rearrangeable (N, M, m)-networks can establish any set of s, $s \leq m$, connections from inputs to outputs. An additional request for connection in a state α, such that $|\alpha| < m$, however, may require a complete rearrangement of the state α. A request for disconnection, of course, presents no problems.

Nonblocking (N, M, m)-networks like rearrengeable (N, M, m)-networks, can establish any set of s, $s \leq m$, connections from inputs to outputs. In contrast, however, an additional request for connection can be satisfied without disturbing connections and irrespective of which state the history of connections and disconnections has left the network in.

A slightly weaker notion of nonblocking network called also a *strict-sense* nonbloking network is that of a *wide-sense* nonbloking network. A wide-sense nonbloking network does not make guarantee as a strict-sense one. A network is a wide-sense nonbloking network if there is an algorithm for establishing path in the network, one after another, so that after each path is established, it is still possible to connect any unused input to any unused output. Still weaker is the notion of rearrangeable network because a rearrangeable network is capable of realizing any m connections of inputs to outputs with node-disjoint paths provided that all the requests for connections to be made are known in advance.

A nonblocking or rearrangeable network is called a *generalized* network if it has the additional property that each input can be simultaneously connected to an arbitrary set of outputs, provided that every output is connected to just one input.

A network may be represented as a directed graph in which nodes represent terminals and edges represent switches (see Figure 1). Any desired connection of inputs and outputs corresponds to subgraph of the graph representing the network. This subgraph includes all edges (or contacts) in the on state. Input i is connected to output j if there is a path from i to j in the subgraph just described.

Nonblocking and rearrangeable (N, N, N)-networks (or simply N-networks) have a rich and lengthy history. See [13] for an excellent survey and [7] for more comprehensive description of previous results. In 1950, Shannon [14] proved that any rearrangeable or nonblocking N-network must have $\Omega(N \log N)$ contacts. Further work on lower bounds can be found in [2]. In 1953, Clos [6] constructed a strict-sense nonblocking network with $O(N^{1+1/j})$ contacts and depth j, for fixed j. (The degree of the nodes is not bounded.) Bounded-depth nonblocking networks have subsequently been studied extensively [7], [8], [9], [12]. In the early 1960s, Beizer [3] and Beneś [4] independently discovered bounded-degree rearrangeable N-network with depth $O(\log N)$ and size $O(N \log N)$, and Waksman [15] gave an elegant algorithm for determining how the nodes should be set in order to realize any particular permutation. Ofman [10] follows with a generalized rearrangeable N-network of size $O(n \log^2 N)$. The existence of a bounded-degree strict-sense nonblocking N-network with size $O(N \log N)$ and depth $O(\log N)$ was first proved by Bassalygo and Pinsker [2].

More recent work has focuses on the construction of generalized nonblocking networks [1], [7], [13]. A generalized rearrangeable N-network with $O(N \log N)$

*Supported in part by the Russian Foundation for Basic Research under grant 98-01-00748.

contacts and a generalized nonblocking N-network with $O(N\log^2 N)$ contacts were studied by Pippenger [13]. Arora, Leighton and Maggs [1] described a nonblocking N-network with $O(N \log N)$ bounded-degree nodes and an algorithm that can satisfy any request for connection or disconnection between an input and an output in $O(\log N)$ bit step, even if many requests are made at once.

For $N \neq M$ and $m = \min(N, M)$ nonblocking (N, M, m)-networks with $O(N\log^2(M+1))$ contacts were constructed by Ofman [11].

In the paper the construction of so called iterative networks is studied. This class contains rearrangeable N-inputs M-outputs networks carrying m connections with roughly $2(N+M)\log(NM/(N+M))$ contacts if $m = \min(N, M)$ and with roughly $2(N+M)\log m$ contacts if $m < \min(N, M)$; these results are the best obtainable by the methods used.

These networks may be more useful in the context of real systems, where a number of inputs can be unequal to a number of outputs and there are limitations on the number of connections which may be established simultaneously (e.g., it is unlikely that everyone on the the East Coast will call someone on the West Coast at the same time).

2 Iterative Networks

The networks that we use to obtain these results are constructed in much way that is described in [8]. We refer to these networks as *iterative* networks. The nonblocking networks of Beneś [5] and Ofman [10] are the most similar.

Any iterative networks G is either simple or compound. We start by describing the class V^0 of simple iterative networks being nonblocking networks.

The N-inputs M-outputs crossbar (or $N \times M$-crossbar) has a separate contact for connecting each input to each output.

A simple iterative (N, M, m)-network G, $G \in V^0$, is either an $N \times M$-crossbar, if $m = \min(N, M)$, or a network obtained from the $N \times m$ crossbar and the $m \times M$ crossbar by merging the output l of the first crossbar with the input l of the second one for all $1 \leq l \leq m$, if $m < \min(N, M)$.

Suppose for some integer $n > 0$ an iterative network $G_{n-1} \in V^{n-1}$ is constructed as $(N_{n-1}, M_{n-1}, m_{n-1})$-network. For any integer $k_n > 0$ the compound iterative (N_n, M_n, m_n)-network $G_n \in V^n$, where $k_n = N_n/N_{n-1} = M_n/M_{n-1} = m_n/m_{n-1}$, can be constructed from G_{n-1} used as an internal subnetwork. G_n is formed by gluing together k_n copies of G_{n-1} and $N_{n-1} + M_{n-1}$ copies of $k_n \times k_n$-crossbar in the way represented in Figure 3 (here internal subnetworks are denoted by $G^1_{n-1}, \ldots, G^{k_n}_{n-1}$). The compound iterative network G_n is formed by merging the output l of the input crossbar s with input s of the internal subnetwork l for all $1 \leq l \leq k_n$ and $1 \leq s \leq N_{n-1}$ and by merging the input t of the output crossbar r with input r of the internal subnetwork t for all $1 \leq t \leq k_n$ and $1 \leq r \leq M_{n-1}$.

We shall say that G_n has the construction coefficients $k_n, k_{n-1}, \ldots, k_1$ where $k_{n-1}, \ldots, k_1$ are the construction coefficients of subnetwork G_{n-1}.

Let L_n will denote size of G_n (or number of switches of G_n). It is easy to see that G_n consists of $L_n = (N+M)\sum_{i=1}^{n} k_i + NM(\prod_{i=1}^{n} k_i)^{-1}$ switches if $m = \min(N, M)$, and G_n consists of $L_n = (N+M)(\sum_{i=1}^{n} k_i + m(\prod_{i=1}^{n} k_i)^{-1})$ switches if $m < \min(N, M)$.

Theorem 1.

$$\min_{k_1,\ldots,k_n} L_n = \begin{cases} (n+1)(N+M)(\frac{NM}{N+M})^{\frac{1}{n+1}}, & \text{if } m = \\ \quad = \min(N, M), & \\ (n+1)(N+M)m^{\frac{1}{n+1}}, & \text{otherwise.} \end{cases}$$

and reached when

$$k_1 = \ldots = k_n = \begin{cases} (\frac{NM}{N+M})^{\frac{1}{n+1}}, & \text{if } m = \min(N, M), \\ m^{\frac{1}{n+1}}, & \text{if } m < \min(N, M). \end{cases}$$

Proof. It is sufficient to show that for any $a > 0$

$$F(a) = \min_{k_1,\ldots,k_n>0} \{\sum_{i=1}^{n} k_i + a(\prod_{i=1}^{n} k_i)^{-1}\} = (n+1)a^{\frac{1}{n+1}}$$

and reached when $k_1 = \ldots = k_n = a^{\frac{1}{n+1}}$.

Note that for any $a > 0$ the value $F(a)$ is equal to

$$\min_{k_1,\ldots,k_{n+1}>0} \{\sum_{i=1}^{n+1} k_i : \prod_{i=1}^{n+1} k_i = a\} = (n+1)a^{\frac{1}{n+1}}$$

and reached when $k_1 = \ldots = k_n = a^{\frac{1}{n+1}}$. But

$$\frac{1}{n+1}(\sum_{i=1}^{n+1} k_i) \geq (\prod_{i=1}^{n+1} k_i)^{\frac{1}{n+1}},$$

i.e. $F(a) \geq (n+1)a^{\frac{1}{n+1}}$.

From the other hand

$$F(a) \leq \sum_{i=1}^{n+1} a^{\frac{1}{n+1}} = (n+1)a^{\frac{1}{n+1}}.$$

□

Corollary 1. *If $m = \min(N, M)$ then*

$$\min_{k_1,\ldots,k_n>0} L_{n=\log\frac{NM}{N+M}-1} = 2(N+M)\log\frac{NM}{N+M}.$$

Corollary 2. *If $m < \min(N, M)$ then*

$$\min_{k_1,\ldots,k_n>0} L_{n=\log m-1} = 2(N+M)\log m.$$

3 Establishing Connections

Below we will consider a compound iterative (N', M', m')-network G' which is constructed from a rearrangeable (N, M, m)-network G with a coefficient k, i.e. $k = N'/N = M'/M = m'/m$. Let the inputs and outputs of G' be denoted by I' and U' corresponding. Inputs and outputs of the ith subnetwork G^i of G', where $1 \le i \le k$, will be denoted by I^i and U^i corresponding. Let $\bigcup_{1\le i\le k} I^i$ and $\bigcup_{1\le i\le k} U^i$ be denoted by $\tilde{I}$ and $\tilde{U}$. So, $| I' |= k \mid I \mid=\mid \tilde{I} \mid$ and $| U' |= k \mid U \mid=\mid \tilde{U} \mid$.

In order to describe the technique for reconfigurating G' the term of connection sequence will be considered.

Two nodes from $\tilde{I} \cup \tilde{U}$ will be called *equivalent* if either they are merging with the outputs of the same input crossbar or they are merging with the inputs of the same output crossbar.

Consider a state α of G'. We define a node to be *busy* in α if there is a path currently routing through it in α and *idle* otherwise.

Let Y be a set of all inputs and outputs of some subnetworks G^s and G^t of network G'.

A sequence of nodes from Y

$$(p_{i_1}, p_{i_2}, p_{i_3}, p_{i_4}, \ldots, p_{i_r}), r \ge 1,$$

is called a *connection sequence* in α under $\{s,t\}$ with initial node p_{i_1} and terminal node p_{i_r} (denoted by $[\alpha, p_{i_1}, s, t]$) if the following properties hold:

1) p_{i_1} and p_{i_r} are idle nodes,

2) p_{i_j} is a busy node for any j, $1 < j < r$,

3) p_{i_j} and $p_{i_{j+1}}$ are equivalent nodes for any odd j, $1 \le j < r$,

4) p_{i_j} is connected with $p_{i_{j+1}}$ for any even j, $1 < j < r$.

The connection sequence $x = [\alpha, p, s, t]$ is *trivial* one if its length (denote $| x |$) is equal to 2. A trivial connection sequence contains only idle nodes. Let a number of pairs of such busy nodes of a subnetworks G^l, $1 \le l \le k_n$, which are belong to x and connected in α be denoted by $n_l[x]$.

It is easy to see that the following properties hold.

Property 1. *Any connection sequence $(p_{i_1}, p_{i_2}, p_{i_3}, p_{i_4}, \ldots, p_{i_r})$, $r \ge 1$, consists of different nodes, i.e. for all k, r $p_{i_k} \ne p_{i_r}$ if $k \ne r$.*

Property 2. *For any state α and any s,t two connection sequences in α under $\{s,t\}$ either contain no the same node or consist of the same set of nodes.*

Property 3. *For any connection sequence x and any node $p \in Y$ if p is either connected with a node $q \in x$ or equivalent to a node $q \in x$ then $p \in x$.*

Property 4. *For any state α and any idle nodes p and q if eiter $p \in I^s$ and $q \in U^t$ or $p \in U^s$ and $q \in I^t$ then $q \notin [\alpha, p, s, t]$.*

Lemma 1. *For any connection sequence $x = [\alpha, p, s, t]$*

$$n_s[x] = \begin{cases} n_t[x] - 1, & \text{if } \mid x \mid = 0(mod\ 4), \\ n_t[x], & \text{otherwise.} \end{cases}$$

Proof. From Property 3 it follows that the following two properties hold:

1) the connection sequence x includes the same number of nodes of subnetworks G^s and G^t,

2) all busy nodes of the connection sequence x are decomposed onto pairs of connected nodes.

From the other hand, the connection sequence x insludes only two idle nodes: the initial node of x and the terminal node of x. By this, the initial node of x belongs to G^s always, and the terminal node belongs to G^s if and only if $| x |= 0(\text{mod } 4)$. □

Corollary 3. *If p and q are some idle nodes of subnetworks G^s and G^t corresponding and $| [\alpha, p, s, t] |= 0(mod\ 4)$ then $q \notin [\alpha, p, s, t]$.*

Lemma 2. *If for a state α number of connections established trough a subnetworks G^s is less than number of connections established trough a subnetworks G^t then there is such an idle output p of G^s that $| [\alpha, p, s, t] |= 0(mod\ 4)$.*

Proof. We will find such an idle output p of G^s that $| [\alpha, p, s, t] |= 0(\text{mod } 4)$.

Let A and B be the sets of all busy outputs of subnetworks G^s and G^t. By condition of Lemma we have that $| A |<| B |$.

So, there are equivalent outputs p and q of the subnetworks G^s and G^t such that $p \notin A$ and $q \in B$. Consider connection sequence $[\alpha, p, s, t]$. If $| [\alpha, p, s, t] |= 0(\text{mod } 4)$ then the needed output p is obtained.

Let $| [\alpha, p, s, t] | \ne 0(\text{mod } 4)$. Then the above considerations can be applied to sets $A' = A \setminus [\alpha, p, s, t]$ and $B' = B \setminus [\alpha, p, s, t]$, since $| A' |<| B' |$ by Property 5. From Property 2 it follows that in this case also by means of a finite steps the needed output p will be obtained. □

Let α be a state of G'. A *trace* of a path $P \in \alpha$ is the element $(p_1, p_2, p_3, p_4) \in I \times \tilde{I} \times \tilde{U} \times U$ in which every $p_i \in P$ is a busy node in the state $\{P\}$. The set of traces of all paths $P \in \alpha$ will be denoted by $TRACES(\alpha)$.

A state β is called *immediately reached* from a state α if there is such a communication sequence x in α that for all nodes p_1, p_2, p_3, p_4 $(p_1, p_2, p_3, p_4) \in TRACES(\beta)$ if and only if there is such $(q_1, q_2, q_3, q_4) \in TRACES(\alpha)$ that the following properties hold:

1) $p_1 = q_1$ and $p_4 = q_4$.

2) either $p_2 \notin x$, $q_2 \notin x$, $p_2 = q_2$ or $p_2 \in x$, $q_2 \in x$, p_2 and q_2 are equivalent nodes,

3) either $p_3 \notin x$, $q_3 \notin x$, $p_3 = q_3$ or $p_3 \in x$, $q_3 \in x$, p_3 and q_3 are equivalent nodes,

A state β is called *reached* from a state α if there is such a finite sequence $(\gamma_1 = \alpha, \gamma_2, \ldots, \gamma_r = \beta)$, $r \ge 1$, of states of G' that for any t, $1 < t \le r$, the state γ_t is immediately reached from the state γ_{t-1}.

Lemma 3. *For any state α and any input (or output) p of a subnework G^s, $1 \le s \le k$, if $| [\alpha, p, s, t] | \ne 0(mod\ 4)$ or $n_s < m$ then there is such a state β that β is reached from α by the communication sequence $[\alpha, p, s, t] \mid$ and*

$$n_t[\beta] = \begin{cases} n_t[\alpha] - 1, & \text{if } \mid [\alpha, p, s, t] \mid = 0(mod\ 4), \\ n_t[\alpha], & \text{otherwise.} \end{cases}$$

Proof. Lemma immediatly follows from the definition of iterative network construction, Lemma 2 and Property 3. □

Theorem 2. *G' is a rearrangeable network.*

Proof. Let α be such a state of G' that $|\alpha| < km = m'$, and let $(u,v) \in I \times U$ be a pair of idle terminals, i.e. u and v are unused in α.

Let the set of all subnetworks in which the input being adjancent with p is idle in α will be denoted by $N[\alpha]$. $m[\alpha]$ will denote the set of all such subnetworks G^r that $\alpha_r < m$ where α_r is a number of all paths in α currently routing through G^r. Let the set of all subnetworks in which the output being adjacent with q is idle in α will be denoted by $M[\alpha]$.

It is clear that if

$$N[\alpha] \cap M[\alpha] \cap m[\alpha] \neq \emptyset$$

then a connection of the input p with the output q can be established without rearrangement of current connections of α.

Let $N[\alpha] \cap M[\alpha] \cap m[\alpha] = \emptyset$. Thus, one of the following four cases arises:

1) $N[\alpha]$,$M[\alpha]$ and $m[\alpha]$ are mutually disjont,
2) $N[\alpha] \cap M[\alpha] \neq \emptyset$,
3) $N[\alpha] \cap m[\alpha] \neq \emptyset$,
4) $M[\alpha] \cap m[\alpha] \neq \emptyset$.

Since the case 4 is reduced to the case 3 by reorientation of network archs, in order to prove the theorem it is sufficient to consider the cases 1-3 and to show that for the each case there is such a state β being reached from α for which $N[\beta] \cap M[\beta] \cap m[\beta] \neq \emptyset$.

Case 1. For subnetworks $G^s \in m[\alpha]$ and $G^t \in M[\alpha]$ there is such an output p of G^s that $|[\alpha,p,s,t]| = 0(\text{mod } 4)$ by Lemma 2. From Lemma 3 it follows that there is such a state β that β is reached from α by the connection sequence $[\alpha,p,s,t]$ and $G^t \notin m[\beta]$. In addition, by Corollary 3 the idle output q of G^t being equivalent to p does not belong to $[\alpha,p,s,t]$ and so $G^t \notin M[\beta]$. Thus the state β is reached from α and $G^t \in m[\beta] \cap M[\beta]$, i.e. we have the case 4 for the state β being reached from α.

Case 2. From Property 4 follows that a consideration presented above and applied to subnetworks $G^s \in m[\alpha]$ and $G^t \in N[\alpha] \cap M[\alpha]$ can be used in order to obtain such a state β that β is reached from α and $N[\beta] \cap M[\beta] \cap m[\beta] \neq \emptyset$.

Case 3. Let $G^s \in m[\alpha] \cap N[\alpha]$, $G^t \in M[\alpha]$ and p be such an idle input of G^t which is adjacent to u. By Lemma 3 there is a state β being reached from α by the the connection sequence $[\alpha,p,s,t]$. Since the input q of G^t being adjacent to u is equivalent to p and so belongs to $[\alpha,p,s,t]$, we have that $G^t \in N[\beta]$. From the other hand, the idle output of G^t being adjacent to v does not belong to $[\alpha,p,s,t]$ by Property 4 and so $G^t \in N[\beta]$. Thus, by Lemma 3 follows that β is either a needed state if $|[\alpha,p,s,t]| = 0(\text{mod } 4)$ or β is such a state that $N[\beta] \cap M[\beta] \neq \emptyset$, i.e. we have the case 2 for the state β being reached from α, if $|[\alpha,p,s,t]| \neq 0(\text{mod } 4)$. □

Corollary 4. *To establish an additional connection of an idle input with an idle output in a state α, $|\alpha| < m$, it is sufficient to rearrange at most of $3m-1$ connections of α.*

Theorem 3. *If $k > 1$ and $m > 2$ then G' is not a wide-sense nonblocking network.*

Proof. Let $I(i,j)$ denote the input i of the input crossbar j and and $U(i,j)$ denote the output i of the output crossbar j for all $1 \leq i \leq k$ and $1 \leq j \leq m$.

Consider the following sequence of pairs input-output: $(I(1,1),U(1,1)),(I(2,1),U(2,1)),\ldots,(I(k-1,1), U(k-1,1)),(I(k,1),U(1,2)),(I(1,2),U(1,3)),(I(2,2), U(2,3)),\ldots,(I(k-1,1),U(k-1,3))$. It is clear that the length of the sequence is equal to $2k-1$, i.e. the length is less than km.

There are two following kinds of states for connection the pairs considered:

1) such a state α that there are a subnetwork which connects the input 1 with the output 2 and the input 2 with the output 3, a subnetwork which connects the input 1 with the output 1 and $k-2$ subnetworks in every one of which the input 1 with the output 1 and the input 2 with output 3 are connected,

2) such a state β that there are a subnetwork which connects the input 1 with the output 2 and $k-1$ subnetworks in every one of which the input 1 with the output 1 and the input 2 with output 3 are connected,

It is clear that for the first case without reconnection of the existing state α it is impossible to connect $I(k,2)$ with $U(k,1)$. For the second case without reconnection of the existing state β it is impossible to connect $I(k,2)$ with $U(2,2)$. □

References

[1] S.Arora, F.T.Leighton, and B.M.Maggs. Path selection in nonblocking network. SIAM J. Comput., 25 (1996), pp.600–625.

[2] L.A.Bassalygo, M.S.Pinsker. Complexity of optimal non-blocking switching systems without reconnections. Problems of Inform.Transmission, 9, 1 (1973), pp.84–87. (In Russian).

[3] V.E.Beizer. The analysis and synthesis of signal switching networks. In Proc. Symp. on Math. Theory of Automata, Brooklyn Polytechnic Institute, Brooklyn, NY, 1962, pp.563–576.

[4] V.E. Beneś. Optimal rearrangeable multistage connecting networks. Bell System Technical J., 43 (1964), pp.1641–1656.

[5] V.E. Beneś. Mathematical Theory of Connected Networks and Telephone Traffic. Academic Press, New York, 1965.

[6] C.Clos. A study of non-blocking switching networks, Bell System Technical J., 32 (1953), pp.406–424.

[7] P. Feldman. Wide-sense nonblocking networks. SIAM J. Discrete Math., 1 (1988), pp.158 –173.

[8] V.N. Kasyanov. On rearrangeability of switching networks. In Computational mathematics and programming, Computing Center, Novosibirsk, 1975, pp. 123–134. (In Russian).

[9] D.Nassimi and S.S.Ahni. Parallel permutation and sorting algorithms and a new generated connection network. J.Assoc.Comput.Math., 29 (1982), pp.642–667.

[10] Y.P.Ofman. An universal automation. Trans. Mascow. Soc., 14 (1965), pp.186–199. (In Russian).

[11] Y.P.Ofman. On parallel computer. Problems of Inform.Transmission, 4, 3 (1968), pp.58–61. (In Russian).

[12] N.Pippenger. On rearrangeable and nonblocking switching networks, J.Comput.System.Sci., 17 (1978), pp.145–162.

[13] N.Pippenger. Telephone switching networks. In Proc. Symposia in Applied Math., Vol.26, AMS, Providence, RI, 1982, pp.101–133.

[14] C.E.Shannon. Memory requirements in a telephone exchange. Bell System Technical J., 29 (1950), pp.343–349.

[15] A. Waksman. A permutation network. J. Assoc. Comput. Mach., 15 (1968), pp.159 – 163.

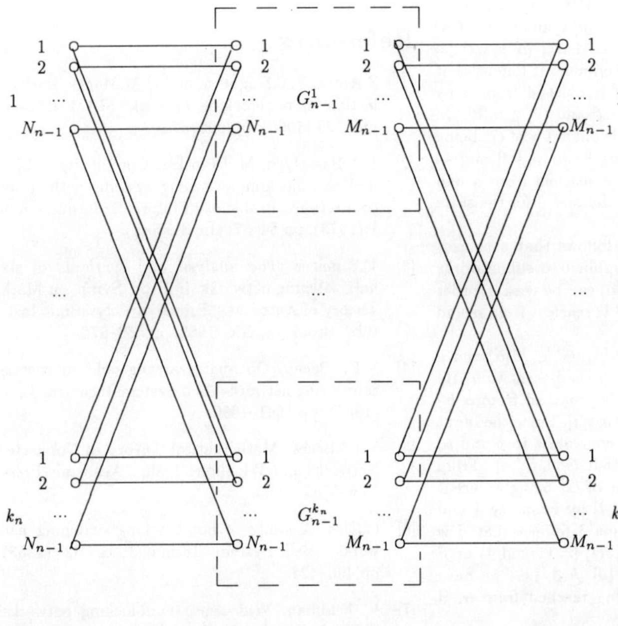

Figure 1: A compound iterative network G_n.

IMPLEMENTATION OF REAL-TIME MONITORING SOFTWARE OF BRUNNENBACH PV PLANT

Anton Biasizzo, Alenka Žužek, Franc Novak
Jožef Stefan Institute, Jamova 39, 1000 Ljubljana, Slovenia

Peter Helm, Manfred Bächler, Matthias Grottke
WIP, Renewable Energies Division, Sylvensteinstr.2, 81369 Munich, Germany

Abstract

The paper describes the implementation of real-time diagnostic monitoring of Brunnenbach photovoltaic plant. In the first part, general characteristics of Brunnenbach PV plant are shortly presented. Next, the implementation overview of the real-time monitoring software package is given. User interface consisting of a hierarchical screen structure is described. More details are given on some particular problems regarding DDE communication and LabVIEW programming.

1 Introduction

The Brunnenbach photovoltaic plant is the second realized project of 30 PV plants sponsored by the German Department of Research and Technology from 1987 to 1991, [1]. The photovoltaic stand-alone plant, built in 1989 by Isar-Amperwerke AG, supplies electricity to the agricultural site Brunnenbach located some 80 km south of Munich. During the plant operation, intensive measurements are taken for operational and scientifical purposes. Another objective is to test the components of the photovoltaic system in regular operation at the site providing more realistic data than under operation in laboratory conditions. Within the JOULE II project "Real-time plant diagnostics and management of dispersed PV and battery grid-connected systems in remote areas" performed by WIP, Renewable Energies Division, Munchen, the real-time monitoring system (RTMS) software of the Brunnenbach PV plant has been developed by Jožef Stefan Institute. The aim of the project was to develop an advanced monitoring system capable of performing on-line plant assessment and also to generate plant performance summary reports. In this way, time intensive off-line data analysis can be reduced. For this purpose, an in-depth user requirement specification of the RTMS [2] has been elaborated. The authors of this paper wish to pay tribute to the extensive expert knowledge of M.Imamura in the field of photovoltaic system technology as well as to his guidance which considerably contributed to the successful implementation of the RTMS software.

2 Brunnenbach PV plant description

The key features of the 10.4 kW PV plant Brunnenbach are summarized as follows:

PV Array	2 subarrays (10.4 kWp total, 170 Vdc nominal)
Subarray	4 strings, each 10 SM-144/18 modules in series
DC/DC Converter	12 kW with MPP tracking
Battery	108 cells, 500Ah, 216 Vdc, 108 kWh
Inverter 1	10 kVA, 3-phase
Inverter 2	3 kVA, 1-phase
Rectifier	10 kVA
Diesel	15 kVA
Loads	motors, heaters, milking machines cranes, household appliances, etc.

The solar arrays, divided in four separately mounted parts, have active area of 80 m^2 monocrystalline silicium cells. Their elevation angles can be manually adjusted (40^0 in summer, 70^0 in winter). DC/DC converter with maximum power point tracking capability modifies the current produced by the solar cells and provides a constant charge to the battery. Larger loads (e.g. milking machines, cranes, etc.) are powered from the battery via a 3-phase invertor which starts automatically once a load is applied. A small 1-phase invertor is used to supply power to small consumers (e.g. farmers household). If the battery voltage drops below 212 Vdc, back-up system (a diesel engine) is activated in order to provide power to the inverters. It can also charge the battery if surplus power is available. More details on Brunnenbach PV plant and its operation modes are available in [2], [3].

3 RTMS implementation overview

Brunnenbach PV Plant RTMS package performs monitoring and diagnostic procedures that provide

- quick-look and off-line analysis,
- identification of failed components or abnormal operation conditions,
- minimization of trouble-shooting efforts and maintenance work,

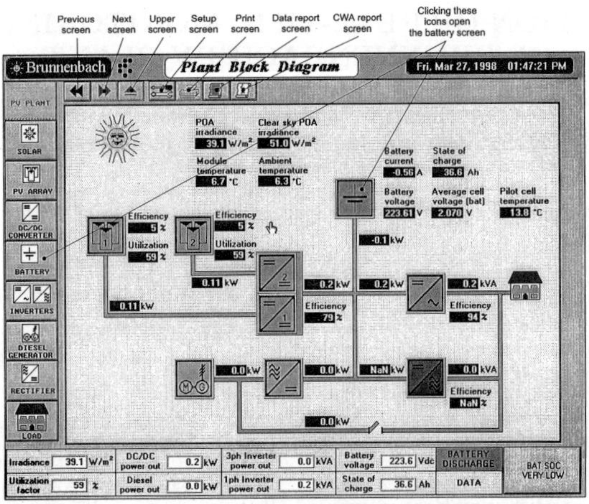

Figure 1: Plant Block Diagram

- prevention of key components damages,
- improvement of overall system performance and reliability.

The RTMS consists of:

- data acquisition; there are about 130 parameters acquired every 5 seconds.
- data calculation; around 120 parameters are calculated on the basis of the most recent data acquired. For each part of the PV plant diagnostic rules are performed which can generate cautions, warnings and alarms (CWA) messages. Also a plant performance summary of important data (including CWA messages) is generated to reduce off-site analysis effort.
- user interface: RTMS provides intelligent information displayed as digital values, meters, y-t graphs and buttons. The whole system is composed of 45 different screens, which the user(operator) can easily navigate through. The interface enables setting of the parameters that have to be given by the user.

3.1 User Interface

User Interface of the RTMS package consists of a hierarchical screen structure. On the top level, the basic RTMS data are displayed in the Plant Block Diagram screen, given in Figure 1. On the next level, solar irradiance on plane of array, utilization factor of entire array, DC/DC converter power output, Diesel generator power output, 3-phase and 1-phase inverter power output, battery voltage, and state-of-charge data are displayed. The level of details increases toward lower level screens.

Display manager module handles the apperance of the screens and the navigation through the screen structure. Since it is desirable to have several screens opened at the same time, each screen is displayed by a separate program. In this way, concurrent refreshing of multiple screens is accomplished.

3.1.1 Data screens

The title of the currently presented screen appears in the middle of the title bar. Current date and time are displayed at the right of the top line.

The following fundamental data are displayed at the bottom of the screen:

- Caution/Warning/Alarm(CWA) flag and button (dimmed if there is no CWA event)
- Data reception flag
- Battery status flag
- Basic plant data: solar irradiance on plane of array, utilization factor of entire array DC/DC converter power output, diesel generator power output, 3-phase inverter power output, 1-phase inverter power output, battery voltage and state-of-charge

For switching between screens, two groups of icons (i.e. buttons) are available on each screen. The first group (placed in a column on the left) represents the main parts of the PV Plant. Icons have pictorial and textual

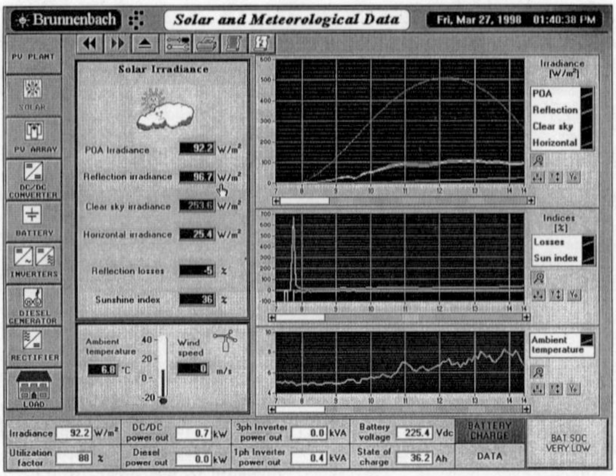

Figure 2: Solar and Meteorological Data

representations. The user can open the selected screen by clicking its icon. For example, by clicking the button SOLAR the screen with solar and meteorological data appears, as given in Figure 2.

On the top of the screen there is another group of buttons which allows the user to select a screen by tracing the path through the screens that have already been displayed. The button for the setup screen is also included in this group.

RTMS data are presented in the central part of the screen by digital, slide or rotary indicators. Operating status of PV Plant components is presented by a coloured icons and energized power lines.

The graphs are accompanied with scrolling and zooming option. The time scale is displayed in relative time (seconds) if the range of the time is within 2 hours, otherwise the hours are displayed.

3.1.2 Setup screens and reports

Setup screens and reports have the same title bar as data screens, displaying the name of the screen, current date and time.

The settings of parameters is realized using one or two-valued slide numeric controls. Each slide has a digital display.

Setup screens are also used for enabling/disabling of individual CWA criteria.

In order to reduce off-site analyses efforts, a plant performance summary on a monthly basis is automatically generated. The performance summary includes:

- plant monitoring system performance,
- solar and meteorological data,
- energy data and plant performance indices,
- a survey on CWA events.

3.2 Data acquisition and storing

The existing data acquisition system configuration in Brunnenbach PV Plant consists of Schlumberger Isolated Measurement Pod (IMP) system and RTM 3500 software, Version 3.10. DDE communication was used for data transfer between the RTM 3500 software and LabVIEW.

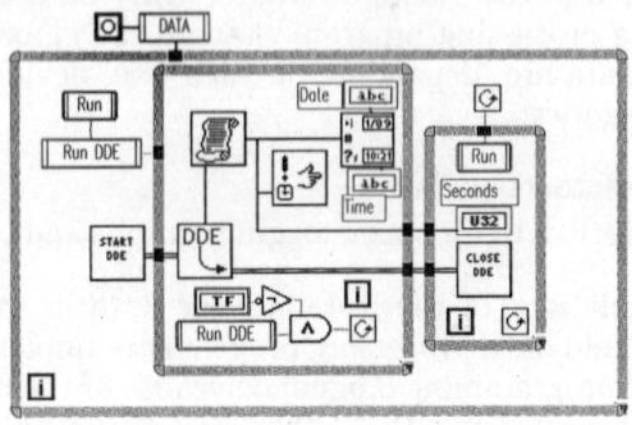

Figure 3: Data Acquisition and Processing Module

The data acquisition and data processing must be independent of the user interface. Thus the multitasking of the LabVIEW programs was used to implement data acquisition and data processing as a different process (*i.e. program*), which runs separatly from the user interface programs (*i.e. screens*).

The DDE communication is made by a cold DDE link. In the first version more efficient hot DDE link was implemented, but the RTM 3500 DDE server did not support it. LabVIEW module for data acquisition and processing of the acquired data is presented in Figure 3. It acquires new data from the RTM 3500 DDE server, process and store data in the global database. The screen processes fetch the data from the database

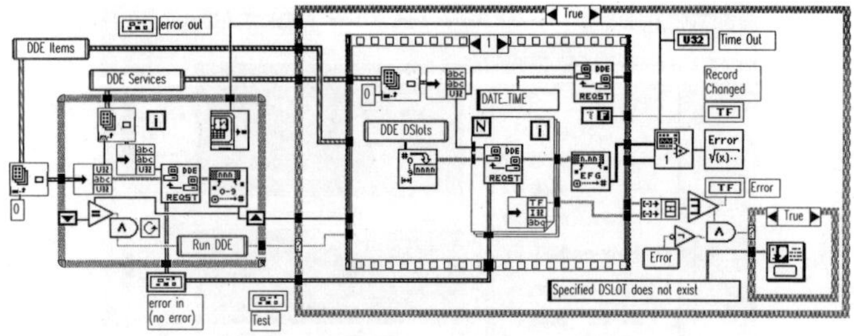

Figure 4: DDE Data Acquisition Procedure

and display them. The database is maintained by the LabVIEW environment by means of shared memory.

Since we use the cold link, the data acquisition was further devided into two phases:

- detection of the data change,
- acquisition of the whole set of data.

During the detection of the data change only one data slot is monitored (acquisition time). In this way DDE traffic does not become excessive. The acquisition procedure is presented in Figure 4.

The second part of the acquisition program deals with data processing. The actual data displayed on different screens are calculated from the acquired data and stored in the global database. Only data transfer and data processing program changes the global data. Global data are, depending on their use, devided into two categories:

- instantaneous data
- history data for alarm logging, graphs and reports.

All calculations of the instananeous data in the data transfer and data processing program are implemented in the C programming language because of the difficulties with presenting the if-then-else structures (a lot of nested if-then-else structures) and of the speed of computation.

Graph and report screens require data for monitored signals during some period. Since the recording of the monitored data to the disk file and retreiving from the file would be time consuming, all data have to be recorded in the random access memory. The management of the history data for monitored signals is handled by a seperate module written in the C programming language for two reasons:

- handling of large amounts of data in LabVIEW becomes unefficient in a complex application like RTMS of Brunnenbach PV Plant,
- functions for data processing implemented in C are executed faster.

Experiences have shown that the minimum data acquisition sampling time for the Brunnenbach RTMS system was approximately 1 second which justifies our decision to write the time critical parts of 12:47 amthe RTMS package in C.

4 Summary

The RTMS package has been developed with LabVIEW, Full Development System. The RTMS package also includes subroutines written in C/C++. The implementation is based on Watcom C/C++ Version 10.0. The executable RTMS package version installed in Brunnenbach has been created by means of LabVIEW Application Builder, following the instructions from the LabVIEW Application Builder Release Notes for Windows, Version 3.1. The package runs on a PC under Windows 3.1 or Windows95.

Acknowledgement

This work was performed under the JOULE II Programme, CEC Contract No. JOU2-CT92-0149, Supplementary Agreement ERB CIPD CT 930324.

References

[1] H.Stadtmüller, *Photovoltaic power supply of a remote agricultural site Brunnenbach - Independent from public grid*, Proc. 11th E.C.Photovoltaic Solar Energy Conference, Montreux, 12-16 October 1992, pp. 1567-1570.

[2] M.Bächler, M.S.Imamura, *Real-time monitoring system for Brunnenbach PV plant, Specification*, August 1994.

[3] *Real-time plant diagnostic and management of dispersed PV and battery grid-connected systems in remote areas*, semi-annual reports for the work performed under conctract No. JOU2-CT92-0149.

[4] M.S.Imamura, P.Helm, W.Palz, *Photovoltaic System Technology, A European Handbook*, CEC Solar Energy R&D Programme.

LOGIC-AUTOMATON MODELING IN ENGINEERING SYSTEMS AND COMPUTERS

Levin V. I.
Penza Technological Institute,
Russia, 440605, Penza, pr. Baidukova, 1[a]
e-mail: levin@vmis.pti.ac.ru

Key words: *continued logic, logical determinants, dynamical automaton, automaton model*

Summary

The main ideas of the dynamical automata' theory are considered. The application of this theory for the mathematical modeling in engineering, computers and systems is shown. Continued logic and logical determinants used for analytical modeling are described.

1. Introduction

Mathematical methods are used in science and technology - physics, chemistry, mechanics, computers and so on. However, in humanitarian and social sciences - economics, sociology, psychology, history and so on this application began lately. The mathematical methods which we use here are different, but most of then are connected with the theory of probability and mathematical statistics. But probabilistic approach has an obvious defect - it calls for statistics data' knowledge about studying system, which are absent in practice. That is why the determinist approach to the humanitarian and social systems' studying rouses interest. Here we only need determinate data about system.

We give an account of one such approach. This is the mathematical modeling of the humanitarian and social systems with the help of the theory of dynamical automata. In this theory we use Boolean algebra of logic, algebra of continued logic and logical determinants. The main quality of our method is its constructivity: mathematical modeling of any economical, social and so on system reduces to the standard operation of calculation of response of automaton model on given input processes.

2. The general information

The dynamical automaton without memory is the model in which input $x_i(t)$ and output $y_k(t)$ processes take place in continued time t and are connected by logic operators G_k in form [1]

$$y_k(t) = G_k[x_1(t),\dots,x_n(t)],\quad k = 1,\dots,m;\ x_i \in X,\ y_k \in Y, \tag{1}$$

Usually input X and output Y alphabets are binary, i.e. $X = Y = \{0,1\}$. Any dynamical automaton without memory builds with combinatorial scheme of logical elements, which are elementar automaton introduced type. Let input processes of element are given. Then the response on the element's output calls dynamical process in the element. The dynamical processes in all elements of the scheme form the dynamical process in the scheme. The problem of the evaluation of the dynamical automaton without memory is to evaluate dynamical, process in combinational scheme which accorded to this automaton. The evaluation is being made with the way of division this scheme on consecutive steps with depth of one element and consecutive substitution of ratios "input processes-output processes" [1, 2]. This ratios are expressed with the help of continued logic's operations: disjunction $\vee = \max$ and conjunction $\wedge = \min$, determinate on the set of the real numbers R [1-3]. The big set of ratios is given in [3]. As a result of the evaluation of dynamical automaton its output data are expressed through input processes with the help of the operations of disjunction and conjunction of continued logic.

At the dynamical automaton' evaluation which schemes have larger dimension we use canonization of input effects of the scheme on the base of the theorem 1 [3].

Theorem 1. Let $x_1(t),\dots,x_n(t)$, $x_i \in \{0,1\}$, are arbitrarily processes on n inputs of the combinational scheme which realizes the symmetrical Boolean function of inputs. Then this processes can be replaced with equivalent set of free impulses $1(a^r,b^r)$, $r = 1,\dots,M$, which are ordered linearly, i.e.

$a^1 \le \dots \le a^M$, $b^1 \le \dots \le b^M$. Here a^r - is the moment of r-th in order of the change $0 \to 1$ in the input processes, b^r - is the moment of r-th in order of the change $1 \to 0$ in this processes.

Theorem 1 give us possibility to divide time on the intervals. The constant number of free impulses effects. In every interval on scheme's inputs. Because of that there is a constant value on output. So for the evaluation of the output process $y(t)$ is enough to evaluate its value in any one point of every interval.

Process $y(t)$ is expressed with logical determinants $A^r = \left|a_{ij}\right|^r$, $B^r = \left|b_{ij}\right|^r$. Here a_{ij} is a moment of j-th in order of the change $0 \to 1$ on i-th input of scheme, b_{ij} is a moment of j-th in order of the change $1 \to 0$ on i-th input of scheme, r is rank of the determinant. Logical determinant $D^r = \left|d_{ij}\right|^r$ of the rank r calls the function $\{d_{ij}\} \to d^r$, which reflects the set $\{d_{ij}\}$ of elements into r-th in order element d^r. The determinant D^r is expressed through elements d_{ij} with the help of disjunction and conjunction of continued logic [3].

3. Automaton modeling in manufacturing

The dynamical automata without memory is a proper model for describing of many systems in technics, economics, sociology, psychology and so on functioning in continued time and having discrete state. Let's consider the manufacturing system as the first example. (Changes of the employment).

Let we have n enterprises with the number of workers at everyone N. Every enterprises can work or not work at any moment of time. In the first case all coworkers are considered as employed, in the second all of them are considered to be unemployed. We have m projects for creation of new working places. The realization of any projects creates on fixed time N quantity of working places, i.e. gives possibility to give job for all unemployed of one enterprise.

The mathematical model of employment's dynamics builds in such way. We describe given dynamics of i-th enterprise with binary process $x_i(t)$, $i = 1,\dots,n$ where $x_i = 1$ means job, and $x_i = 0$ means time wasted of the enterprises. We describe given dynamics of i-th project with binary process $y_i(t)$, $i = 1,\dots,m$ where $y_i = 1$ means realization, and $y_i = 0$ unrealization of the project. Let us describe the employment's dynamics in the system of enterprises with binary processes $z_i(t)$, $i = 0,\dots,n$ where $z_i = 1$ means that the result number of unemploys is equal iN, and $z_i = 0$ means that it is not equal iN. Let introduce symmetrical Boolean logical functions: $f_n^r(x_1,\dots,x_n)$ is the function of index r from n variable quantities $x_1,\dots,x_n$; $F_m^r(y_1,\dots,y_m)$ is the function of index r from m variable quantities $y_1,\dots,y_m$; $F_m^{\ge r}(y_1,\dots,y_m)$ is the function of index $\ge r$ from m variable quantities $y_1,\dots,y_m$. The function $f_n^r = 1$ if equally r arguments (it does not matter which one) are equal 1. F_m^r determinates in the same way. Function $F_m^r = 1$ if $\ge r$ arguments are equal 1. It is obvious that total number of unemploys determinates with the ratio of the number of those who become unemploys on the reason of closing enterprise and the number of those who get new working places. From here we get such expression of variable quantities z_i in disjunctive normal form of Boolean algebra of logic

$$z_0 = f_n^0 \vee f_n^1 F_m^{\ge 1} \vee f_n^2 F_m^{\ge 2} \vee \dots \vee$$
$$\vee f_n^n F_m^{\ge n}, \tag{2}$$
$$z_i = f_n^i F_m^0 \vee f_n^{i+1} F_m^1 \vee \dots \vee f_n^n F_m^{n-i},$$

$$F_m^{\ge r} = F_m^r \vee F_m^{r+1} \vee \dots \vee F_m^m. \tag{3}$$

The system of Boolean logic functions $z_i = z_i(x_1,\dots,x_n,y_1,\dots,y_m)$, $i = 0,\dots,n$, which are expressed with formulas (2), (3) and their arguments - processes $x_i(t)$, $y_i(t)$ are the abstract automaton model of employment's dynamics. Combinational scheme which realizes this automaton is a structural automaton model of employment's dynamics (fig. 1).

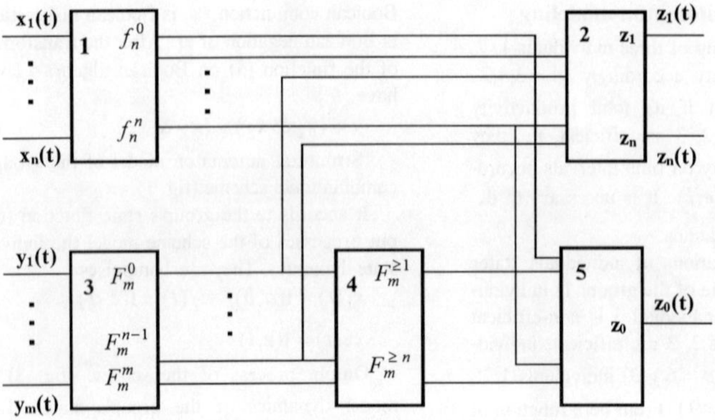

Fig. 1

The problem is evaluation of employment's dynamics of the system $z_i(t),\ i=0,\ldots,n$, if dynamics of enterprises states $x_i(t),\ i=1,\cdots,n$ and the dynamics of working places' creation $y_i(t),\ i=1,\cdots,m$, are given. This problem is being decided with evaluation of the processes $z_i(t)$ on the output of the combinational scheme-model (fig. 1). Input processes of the scheme $x_i(t)$ and $y_i(t)$ are given. Theory of dynamical automata is used for evaluation [3]. We can design the algorithms of employment's control if we know employment's dynamics.

4. Automaton modeling in group dynamics

Let's consider the social group from n individuals. Every individual can be in two states: efficient and non-efficient. The group can be in one of two states: efficient and non-efficient. Static model of the group - dependence of its state on the individuals' state in the same moment of time is given. It is necessary to determinate the group state's dynamics.

We describe the states dynamics of i-th individual with binary process $x_i(t),\ i=1,\ldots,n$. Here $x_i=1$ is efficiency and $x_i=0$ is non-efficiency of the individual. We describe the group state's dynamics with binary process $y(t)$, where $y(t)=1$ is efficiency, and $y(t)=0$ is non-efficiency of the group. The static model of the group is described with Boolean logic function of group's states

$$y=f(x_1,\ldots,x_n) \qquad (4)$$

Function (4) and its arguments - processes $x_i(t)$ are abstract automaton model of group state's dynamics. Combinational scheme, which realizes this automaton is structural automaton model of group states' dynamics (fig. 2).

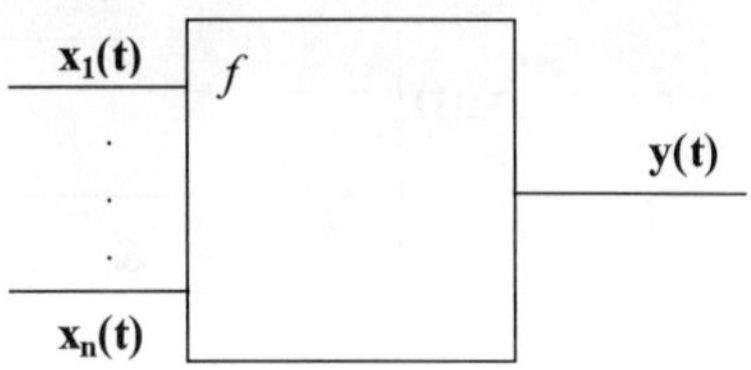

Fig. 2

The problem is evaluation of the process of group state's change $y(t)$, when the processes of individuals states' changes $x_1(t),\ldots,x_n(t)$ and the function of group's state (4) are known. The last one means evaluation of the processes $y(t)$ on the output of the combinational scheme-model (fig. 2), if input processes $x_1(t),\ldots,x_n(t)$ are known. Here we use the methods of dynamical automata' theory [3].

5. The example of automaton modeling

Let we have the group of three individuals 1, 2, 3 with their productivity accordingly $p = 3,4,2$. The group is efficient if its total productivity $p \geq 6$. Individuals 1, 2, 3 are efficient, i.e. they supply their productivity on time intervals accordingly (a,b), (c,d), (e,l). It is necessary to determine the group's dynamics.

We have 3 combinations of individuals states which give efficient state of the group: 1) individuals 1, 2 are efficient, individual 3 is non-efficient ($p = 7$); 2) individuals 2, 3 are efficient, individual 1 is non-efficient ($p = 6$); 3) individuals 1, 2, and 3 are efficient ($p = 9$). From here function of group's state (4) is

$$y = (x_1 \,\&\, x_2 \,\&\, \bar{x}_3) \vee (\bar{x}_1 \,\&\, x_2 \,\&\, x_3) \vee \vee (x_1 \,\&\, x_2 \,\&\, x_3) \quad (5)$$

Here $x_i = 1$ and $x_i = 0$ are efficiency and non-efficiency of the i-th individual, $y = 1$ and $y = 0$ are analogous states of the group, & is Boolean conjunction, $\vee$ is Boolean disjunction, $\bar{a}$ is Boolean negation of a. After the transformation of the function (5) on Boolean algebra's laws we have

$$y = (x_1 \,\&\, x_2) \vee (x_2 \,\&\, x_3) \quad (6)$$

Structural automaton model of the group is a combinational scheme (fig. 3).

It accords to the group's state function (6). Input processes of the scheme model the individuals state dynamics. They are 1-impulses

$$x_1(t) = 1(a,b), \;\; x_2(t) = 1(c,d), \;\; x_3(t) = 1(e,l) \quad (7)$$

Output process of the scheme (fig. 3) $y(t)$ model dynamics of the group's states. Let us evaluate this process. In accordance to theory of dynamical automata [1-3] we evaluate the process on the outputs of the first step.

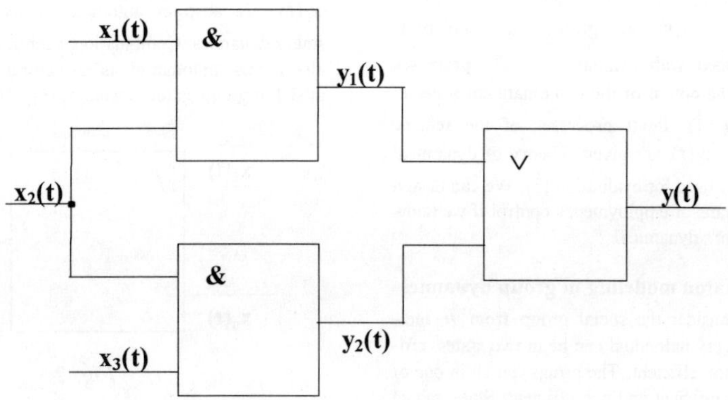

Fig. 3

$$y_1(t) = x_1(t) \,\&\, x_2(t) = 1[a \vee c, a \vee c \vee (b \wedge d)], y_2(t) = x_2(t) \,\&\, x_3(t) = = 1[c \vee e, c \vee e \vee (d \wedge l)].$$

Here and lower $\vee$ and $\wedge$ are disjunction and conjunction of continued logic. Then let's evaluate the process on the output of the second step

$$y(t) = y_1(t) \vee y_2(t) = 1[c \vee (a \wedge e), c \vee \vee (a \wedge e) \vee (a \wedge d \wedge l)]0(-,-)1[a \vee c \vee \vee e, a \vee c \vee e \vee (b \wedge d) \vee (d \wedge l)] \quad (8)$$

The process (8) has two 1-impulses, where $y = 1$, and one pause, where $y = 0$. So in common case there are two intervals of time where the group is efficient. They are shown in (8). In other time the group is non-efficient.

6. Conclusions.

The new mathematical model dynamical automaton is suggested. It gives the large possibility for analytical modeling of many applied systems. The problems of economical presentation, evaluation, analyses and syntheses of systems are being decided on this base according examples from engineering, systems, computers and so on are in [5-12]

References

1. Levin V.I. Introduction to dynamical theory of finite automaton, Zinatne, Riga, 1975 (in Russian).
2. Levin V.I. Dynamics of logical devices and systems, Energija, Moskow, 1980 (in Russian).
3. Levin V.I. Theory of dynamical automaton, Penza techn. university Publ. House, Penza, 1995 (in Russian).
4. Pospelov D. A. Logical methods of schemes analysis and synthesis, Energija, Moskow, 1978 (in Russian).
5. Levin V.I. Theory of automaton and complex systems modeling, Penza techn. university Publ. House, Penza, 1995 (in Russian).
6. Levin V.I. Mathematical modeling of social and economical processes (automaton and logical methods and models), Penza techn. university Publ. House, Penza, 1997 (in Russian).
7. I AllRussian conference "Continuous logic and its application in engineering, economics and sociology", Proceedings, V.I. Levin ed., Penza, 1994 (in Russian).
8. International conference "Continuous-logical methods and models in sciences, engineering and economics", Proceedings, V.I. Levin ed., Penza, 1995 (in Russian).
9. Mathematical methods and computers in economics (International conference) Proceedings, V.I. Levin ed., Penza, 1996 (in Russian).
10. Continuous logic in engineering, economics and sociology (International conference) Proceedings, V.I. Levin ed., Penza, 1996 (in Russian).
11. II International Conference "Mathematical methods and computers in economics", (International conference) Proceedings, V.I. Levin ed., Penza, 1997 (in Russian).
12. AllRussian conference "Continuous logic in informatic, economics and sociology", Proceedings, V.I. Levin ed., Penza, 1997 (in Russian)

AN EFFICIENT VLSI ARCHITECTURE FOR AN IMPROVED THREE-STEP SEARCH ALGORITHM

Donglai Xu, Chris Bailey and Reza Sotudeh
Computer Architecture Research Unit, School of Science and Technology
University of Teesside, Borough Road, Middlesbrough, TS1 3BA, UK
D.Xu@Tees.ac.uk

Abstract: In this paper, we present a simple and efficient VLSI architecture for an improved three-step search (ITSS) algorithm that is superior to the existing three-step search (TSS) algorithm in all cases and also to the recently proposed new three-step search (NTSS) algorithm when used for low bit-rate video coding, as with the H.261 standard. Based on a VLSI tree processor and an FPGA addressing circuit, the proposed architecture can successfully implement the ITSS algorithm on silicon with the minimum number of gates. Because of the flexibility of the architecture, it can also be extended to implement other three-step search algorithms.

1. Introduction

It is well known that motion estimation algorithms play an important role in video sequence compression. Many fast block-matching algorithms for motion estimation have been proposed because of their lower computation overhead than that of full-search block-matching algorithm, such as the existing three-step search (TSS) algorithm [1] and the recently proposed new three-step search (NTSS) algorithm [2]. Recent studies show that the motion vector distribution of a real world image sequence within the search window is highly centre-biased. Based on this fact, we propose an improved version of the well-known TSS method, the ITSS algorithm [3], specifically aiming towards low bit-rate video coding applications. The ITSS has much better performance and faster speed than the original, and compared to the NTSS, its performance is better when applied to our target applications, such as videophone applications, and its speed is faster as well, without any direct or hidden costs.

Compared to TSS, the ITSS uses the same number of checking points in each step, but a different search pattern. This leads to better performance of ITSS while maintaining the same data flow of TSS. That means the architecture for TSS can also be used for ITSS. Many VLSI architectures [4], [5] have been proposed for TSS. However, these architectures either have low throughput, or high hardware cost, or little flexibility. To avoid these drawbacks and to implement the proposed ITSS algorithm on silicon with the minimum number of gates, a low-latency and high-throughput parallel pipeline computing architecture, based on a VLSI tree processor and an FPGA addressing circuit, is presented. Owing to its simple and modular properties, the tree processor is suitable for VLSI implementation, and because of the use of FPGA to implement addressing and control circuits, the architecture is flexible enough to implement different three step search algorithms. Furthermore, the tree processor can be decomposed into sub-trees to reduce hardware cost and pin count. Memory interleaving and pipeline interleaving are also employed to enhance memory bandwidth and to raise pipeline utilisation to 100%.

In the next section, we will describe the ITSS algorithm. In section 3, we will present the computing architecture for ITSS. A sample design for videophone application will be discussed in section 4. Finally, the conclusion will be given in section 5.

2. ITSS Algorithm

The experimental results in [2] have shown that the block motion field of real world image sequences is usually gentle, smooth, and varies slowly. It results in a centre-biased global minimum motion vector distribution instead of a uniform distribution. This is particularly true in low bit-rate video applications, including videophone and video conferencing, where fast and complex movements are involved rarely. For most video sequences, there are nearly 80% blocks that can be regarded as stationary or quasi-stationary blocks and most of the motion vectors are enclosed in the central 5×5 area. For such a distribution, we have developed the ITSS algorithm which uses a centre-biased checking point search pattern adapted to the centre-biased motion vector distribution, hence its performance is expected to be far better than that of TSS which uses a uniformly distributed checking point search pattern. Additionally, the ITSS employs a smaller number of search points than TSS to speed up block matching.

The details of the algorithm are given in the example described below.

Following earlier block matching techniques, our example takes a block size of 16×16 pixels and a maximum search range of ±7 pixels in both horizontal and vertical directions. The mean absolute error (MAE) is used as an appropriate estimate of the block distortion measure (BDM). For a given (x,y), the MAE between $block(m,n)$ of the current frame and $block(m+x,n+y)$ of the previous (reference) frame is defined as:

$$MAE_{(m,n)}(x,y)=\frac{1}{256}\sum_{i=0}^{15}\sum_{j=0}^{15}\left|f_k(m+i,n+j)-f_{k-1}(m+x+i,n+y+j)\right|$$

where $f_k(i,j)$ and $f_{k-1}(i,j)$ are the pixel intensities at position (i,j) of the current frame k and the previous frame $k-1$ respectively, and the $block(m,n)$ is the block with its upper left corner at position (m,n) of a frame. The first step of the algorithm employs a centre-biased search pattern with nine checking points on a 5×5 window instead of the 9×9 window with TSS. The centre of the search window is then shifted to the point with minimum BDM. The search window size of the next two steps depends on the location of the minimum. If the minimum lies at the centre of the search window, the search will go to the final step (step 3) with a 3×3 search window. Otherwise, the search window size is maintained at 5×5 for step 2. In the final step, the search window is reduced to 3×3 and the search stops at this small search window. The three search steps of ITSS can be summarised as follows:

Step1: The minimum BDM point is found from a nine-checking-points pattern on a 5×5 window located at the centre of the 15×15 searching area as shown in Figure 1(a). If the minimum BDM point is found to coincide with the centre of the search window, then go to step 3 else go to step 2.

Step 2: The search window size is maintained at 5×5 with a search pattern chosen after considering the two alternatives:

a) If the previous minimum BDM point is located at one of the corners of the previous search window, then five additional checking points are considered. An example is shown in Figure 1(b) where black circles and grey circles represent additional and previously evaluated pixels respectively.
b) If the previous minimum BDM point is located at the middle of any horizontal or vertical edge of the previous search window, then three additional checking points are considered. An example is shown in Figure 1(c) where black circles and grey circles represent additional and previously evaluated pixels respectively.

Step 3: The search window is reduced to 3×3 around the minimum BDM point found in step 2 as shown in Figure 1(d) and the direction of the overall motion vector is taken to be the minimum BDM point among these nine search points, of which eight are new.

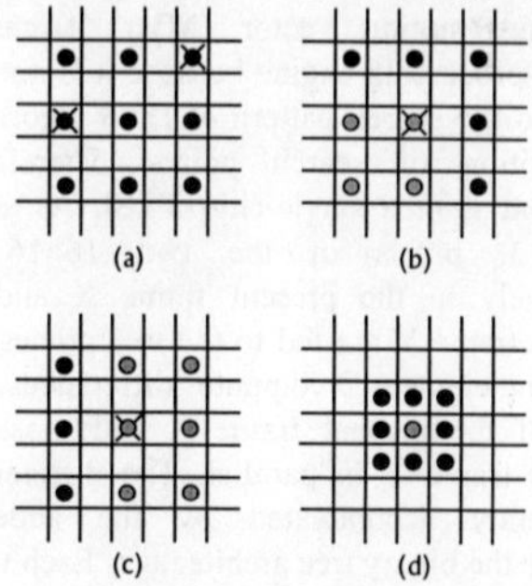

Fig.1. Search Pattern of ITSS Algorithm. (a) First step centred on centre pixel; (b) Second step centred on a corner pixel; (c) Second step centred on a middle pixel; (d) Third step

Because there are some overlapping check points on the 5×5 search window in the second step of ITSS, the total number of checking points will vary from a minimum of (9+8)=17, when step 2 can be skipped, to (9+5+8)=22 in the worst case which is three block matches less than TSS, eleven block matches less than NTSS.

3. Proposed Architecture

The system architecture of ITSS, which consists of memory subsystem, tree processor, and address generation circuit, is described in Figure 2.

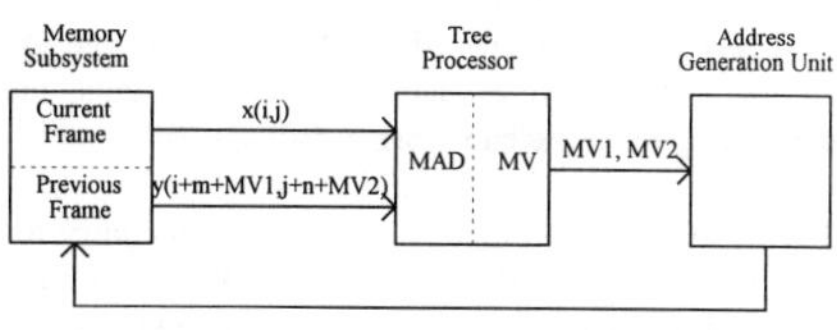

Fig.2. Block Diagram of System Architecture for ITSS Algorithm

The memory subsystem stores the current and previous video frames by which the tree processor is provided with input data. To enhance memory bandwidth, the memory system adopts multiple memory modules, such as an N×N module array, to apply memory interleaving for simultaneous accesses. In addition, the memory system is divided into multi-banks and multi-ports in order that the memory cycle time can afford the huge partitions of pixels in a matching block to be interleaved.

The tree processor, with the major computation overhead in this architecture, computes MAE and determines motion vector (MV). It can be a modular-processing engine because it is not directly related to the search pattern of ITSS algorithm and the position of search points. Therefore, we implement it in a single-chip VLSI. As shown in Figure 3, pixels of the two 16×16 blocks respectively in the present frame X and in the previous frame Y are fed to the tree processor. The processing element D computes differences between pixels of the present frame X and those of the previous frame Y in parallel. The differences are concurrently accumulated by the adders that comprise the binary tree architecture. Each tree level can be viewed as a parallel pipeline stage; not only does this reduce the computational data path length (tree height) but also prevents the data from skewing in the course of doing the parallel computations. However, extensive pipelining always leads to lost resources if computed results are not ready when are needed, thus resulting in hazards. In the pipelined computation of ITSS, during its three-step operations, the current step must complete its computation before the next step begins; therefore, it will lead to lost resources because the computed results of the current step are not ready when they are needed by the next step. To avoid performance degradation caused by these hazards, pipeline interleaving is employed. The main approach is to interleave the execution of adjacent block-matching tasks in a pipeline, that is the current task and the task next to it. They can be jointly processed without any interference because they are independent of each other. In other words, when a step of the current task awaits data, a step of the next task can be processed in advance to fill out the empty machine cycles caused by delays; thus, the computing machine can work at full speed.

The address generation unit will address memory for computing MAE and motion vector. It controls the search pattern of the ITSS algorithm and assigns search points by selecting the proper block address and pixel address within the block. By changing the design of this component, different hierarchical search algorithms could be implemented in this architecture. Therefore, FPGA implementation is used, to provide future flexibility.

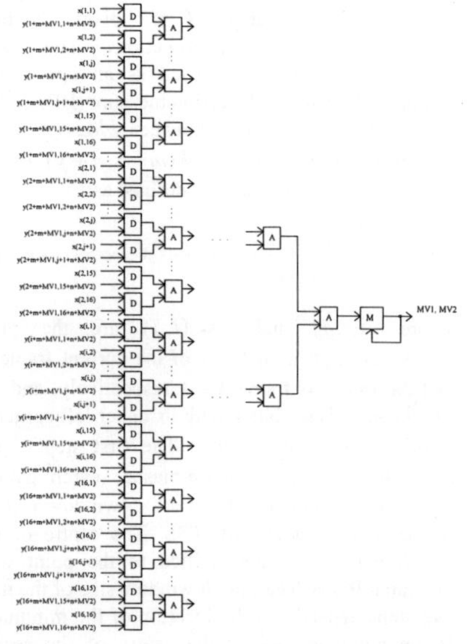

Fig.3. Tree Architecture Processor for MAE and MV Computing

4. Application Design

In VLSI implementation of the tree processor for specific applications, it is not always necessary to implement the whole tree architecture on a single chip because the area-speed product is always taken as the most important consideration. To reduce hardware cost, the tree architecture can be cut into sub-trees. Figure 4 illustrates the tree-cut technique. In this illustration, the full tree is folded to be a 1/2-cut sub-tree. Similarly, the other sub-tree configurations can be obtained in the same manner. With the employment of memory interleaving, whenever the tree is folded into a sub-tree, the required number of memory modules is also cut in half, and the phenomenon of independent pixel distribution will still occur. Therefore, the mullet-bank memory system with memory interleaving can also be applied to the sub-tree architecture.

In the following, we consider the hardware implementation of the tree architecture (N=16) for a videophone application. Suppose dynamic random access memories (DRAM's) with 200ns access time

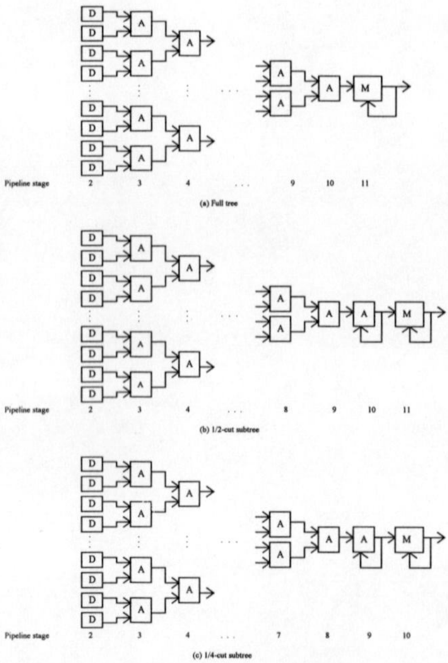

Fig.4. Illustration of Tree-Cut Technique for Block Size 16×16

are used to implement the memory system and the time to latch a pixel from a memory module is simulated to be about 50ns. If a 1/C-cut sub-tree architecture and a B-bank memory system are adopted, then we have the following constraint:

$$\frac{200ns \times B}{(256\text{memory modules})\,/\,C} \geq 50ns;$$

and thus C×B ≥ 64

Thus the 1/C-cut sub-tree architecture must connect with a memory system of at least 64/C memory banks to allow simultaneous accesses. On the other hand, the period time for each pipeline stage is also constrained by memory cycle time and is 200ns. For videophone application (288×352 frame size, 16×16 block size, and 10Hz frame rate), the throughput required by the processing system is

$$\frac{352 \times 288}{16 \times 16} \times 10 = 3.96\text{k block/second},$$

so that 252.5 us is allowed for each vector. With a 1/C-cut sub-tree, the number of time cycles required to compute a motion vector is 27×C. Thus, the sub-tree architecture for the application is constrained by:

200ns×(27×C time cycles for 1/C-cut sub-tree)≤252.5us;

and thus C ≤ 46.76

Consequently, the 1/32-cut (C=32) sub-tree architecture with two memory bands (B=2) for this videophone application is optimal in speed or hardware cost for the realisation of ITSS algorithm.

The real throughput rate depends on the clock rate applied to it. For the above application, the clock cycles required to estimate a motion vector is 27×C=864. Suppose a clock rate of E MHz is applied to the sub-tree processor. Then, in order to estimate motion vector in real time for the application, there should be the following constraints:

$$\frac{E \times 10^6}{864} \geq 3.96 \times 10^3 \;;\; \text{then } E \geq 3.42 \text{ MHz}$$

This means that the minimum clock rate to do real-time block matching is 3.42 MHz. The single chip 1/32-cut sub-tree is currently synthesised and simulated in a 0.7um CMOS standard cell technology, requiring about 5000 equivalent gates.

5. Conclusions

In this paper, we describe a simple and efficient architecture for implementation of the novel ITSS algorithm. In this architecture, simple and modular tree structures facilitate VLSI implementation, the FPGA designs for addressing and control circuits improve the flexibility of the system, and memory interleaving and pipeline interleaving enhance the overall system computing performance. Furthermore, the tree-cut technique is introduced to reduce the hardware cost of the tree processor; but still allowing real-time processing requirements to be met in the sub-tree architecture for specific applications. Finally, a videophone application is considered and its speed and hardware cost trade-offs are evaluated to find out an optimal VLSI implementation.

References

1. Koga T., Iinuma K., Hirano A. and Ishiguro T. Motion-compensated interframe coding for video conferencing, Proceedings of National

Telecommunication Conference, pp. G5.3.1-G5.3.5, New Orleans, LA, USA (November 1981).

2. Li R., Zeng B. and Liou M.L. A new three-step search algorithm for fast block motion estimation, IEEE Transactions on Circuits and System for Video Technology **4,** 438-442 (1994).
3. Booth W., Noras J.M. and Xu D. A novel fast three-step search algorithm for block-matching motion estimation, Lecture Notes in Computer Science **1325,** 623-630 (1998).
4. He Z., Liou M.L., Chan P.C.H. and Li R. An efficient VLSI architecture for new three-step search algorithm, Proceedings of the 1995 IEEE 38th Midwest Symposium on Circuits and Systems, pp. 1228-1231, USA (August 1995).
5. Gupta G. and Chakrabarti C. Architectures for hierarchical and other block matching algorithms, IEEE Transactions on Circuits and Systems for Video Technology **5,** 477-489 (1995).

Denotational Semantics of Evaluation Order in Expressions with Side Effects

Nikolaos S. Papaspyrou
(nickie@softlab.ntua.gr)

National Technical University of Athens
Department of Electrical and Computer Engineering
Division of Computer Science, Software Engineering Laboratory
Polytechnioupoli, 15780 Zografou, Athens, Greece.
Tel. +30-1-7722486, Fax. +30-1-7722519

Abstract

The presence of side effects in even a very simple language of expressions gives rise to a number of semantic questions. The issue of evaluation order becomes a crucial one and, unless a strict order is enforced, the language becomes non-deterministic. In this paper we study the semantics of such a language under a variety of possible evaluation strategies, from simpler to more complex, concluding with unspecified evaluation order, unspecified order of side effects and the mechanism of sequence points that is particular to the ANSI C programming language. In doing so, we adopt the denotational semantics approach and use monads to improve modularity and to reduce the number of changes required for each transition. The result is a better understanding of different evaluation strategies, possibly leading to non-determinism in the presence of side effects, and a unified way of specifying their semantics. Furthermore, a significant step is achieved towards a correct denotational semantics for ANSI C.

1 Introduction

Expressions play a very important role in the vast majority of programming languages. In many languages expressions are *pure*, i.e. their evaluation depends on but may not alter the program state. For such "ideal" languages several theories exist that can be used to prove properties of programs, starting from Hoare's work on axiomatic semantics in the late '60s. Since then, many theoretical treatments of formal semantics have preferred to study languages with pure and deterministic expressions, because their semantics is relatively simple and elegant. By introducing *side effects* in expressions, the semantics becomes significantly more complex. At the same time, several issues arise, related to the *evaluation order*, i.e. the order in which the subparts of an expression are evaluated. If the evaluation order is not strictly defined, the presence of side effects in expressions is a source of non-deterministic behaviour.

The formal semantics of pure expressions can most of the times be easily specified in operational [Henn90], denotational [Stoy77] or axiomatic form [Dijk76]. The introduction of side-effects implies serious complications in the axiomatic semantics but only small ones in the other two forms. Non-determinism caused by unspecified evaluation order can usually be expressed more easily in operational semantics than in denotational semantics. However, both approaches are possible and in this paper the denotational approach is used.

One of the most important drawbacks of classic denotational semantics is its lack of modularity. Small changes in a language's definition often imply a complete rewrite of its formal semantics. The use of category theory and monads [Mogg90] has been proposed as a remedy and has become quite popular in the denotational semantics community. Monad notation is used in this paper and it is demonstrated that, as a result, the semantics is significantly improved in terms of modularity and elegance.

This paper aims at investigating various evaluation strategies for expressions that may generate side effects and providing a unified way of describing their formal semantics. For this reason, a simple strict and impure expression language is studied under various different evaluation strategies, starting from simple left-to-right evaluation and moving on to more complex ones. The language is slightly extended in the process to allow constructs specific to the studied strategies.

The last evaluation strategy that is considered deserves special mention; execution interleaving is allowed and both the order of expression evaluation and the order in which side effects take place are unspecified. The introduction of sequence points and a few additional restrictions makes the example language a subset of the core of the ANSI C programming language. The proposed semantics that develops naturally is sufficient to model this subset correctly and is on its own a significant result. It should be mentioned that the present research was motivated by problems encountered in a bigger project, aiming at a complete denotational semantics for ANSI C.

The structure of this paper is as follows. Section 2 defines the example language and briefly discusses semantic issues related to evaluation order. In Section 3 a denotational semantics is gradually built for four different evaluation strategies. Section 4 shows how our work relates to the literature and Section 5 concludes with some final remarks and directions for future work.

2 Evaluation order

Consider a simple strict expression language with side effects, that will be called ELSE hereafter. The abstract syntax of ELSE is given below. It will be slightly extended in Sections 3.3 and 3.4.

$$E : \mathbf{Expr} ::= n \mid I \mid I\texttt{=}E \mid E_1\texttt{+}E_2 \mid \texttt{-}E \mid E_1\texttt{,}E_2$$

The language features a single data type (integer), constants, variables, an assignment operator, a binary operator (integer addition), a unary operator (integer negation) and a juxtaposition operator (comma). The informal semantics of ELSE expressions is certainly familiar to most readers. The value of I=E is the value of E and the value of E_1 , E_2 is the value of E_2.

Apart from the comma operator, which always evaluates its left operand before its right operand, evaluation order of ELSE expressions is left unspecified, for the time being, and various possibilities will be considered in the sequel. It should be clear, however, that this renders the evaluation of ELSE expressions ambiguous, since different evaluation strategies may lead to different results. As an example, consider the simple expression `x=0, x+(x=1)` [1] whose evaluation may result in 1 or 2, depending on whether the (implicit) dereferencing of x will take place before or after the assignment. It should also be clear that different evaluation orders are only possible in the presence of operator +, since evaluation order is specified for the comma operator and trivially defined for all other constructs.

3 Semantics of ELSE

The denotational semantics of ELSE is given in an abstract form, using monads to improve modularity and elegance of notation. Comprehensive introductions to monads and their use in denotational semantics can be found in [Mogg90, Wadl92, Lian95]. In brief, a monad is a tuple $\langle \mathsf{M}, \mathsf{unit}_\mathsf{M}, *_\mathsf{M}\rangle$, where M is a domain constructor, $\mathsf{unit}_\mathsf{M} : A \to \mathsf{M}(A)$ and $\cdot *_\mathsf{M} \cdot : \mathsf{M}(A) \times (A \to \mathsf{M}(B)) \to \mathsf{M}(B)$ are polymorphic functions for arbitrary domains A and B, satisfying three monad laws.[2] By using different monads, it is possible to derive different flavours of ELSE's denotational semantics without having to change the semantic equations each time.

The flat domain of integer numbers $\mathbf{N}$ is used to denote the values of ELSE's only data type.[3] Bottom element represent abnormal values, mainly run-time errors since non-termination is not possible in ELSE. Domains constructed by monad M denote *computations*, e.g. the domain $\mathsf{M}(\mathbf{N})$ denotes computations returning values from $\mathbf{N}$. The definition of M depends on our notion of computation and it is evident that, in the case of ELSE, computations may read and modify values of variables, i.e. the *state*. The result of $\mathsf{unit}_\mathsf{M}\ v$ is a computation returning v and the result of $m *_\mathsf{M} f$ is the combined computation of m returning v, followed by computation $f\ v$. Evaluation order is thus implicitly specified when using $*_\mathsf{M}$, since the result of the first computation is needed before the second computation can begin.

Before we can proceed to the semantics of ELSE, we have to define the notion of state. Abstractly, the state can be defined as a domain $\mathbf{S}$ together with the following operations,

$$\begin{aligned} s_\circ &: \mathbf{S} \\ \mathsf{get} &: \mathbf{Ide} \to \mathbf{S} \to \mathbf{N} \\ \mathsf{put} &: \mathbf{Ide} \to \mathbf{N} \to \mathbf{S} \to \mathbf{S} \end{aligned}$$

where $s_\circ$ represents an empty state, i.e. a state where all variables have undefined values, $\mathsf{get}\ I\ s$ reads the value of I in state s, and $\mathsf{put}\ I\ n\ s$ modifies state s by making the value of I equal to n. A simple implementation of state is given below.[4]

$$\begin{aligned} \mathbf{S} &= \mathbf{Ide} \to \mathbf{N} \oplus \mathbf{U} \\ s_\circ &= \lambda I.\ \mathbf{inr}\ \mathbf{u} \\ \mathsf{get} &= \lambda I.\ \lambda s.\ [\mathsf{id}, \bot]\ (s\ I) \\ \mathsf{put} &= \lambda I.\ \lambda n.\ \lambda s.\ s[I \mapsto \mathbf{inl}\ n] \end{aligned}$$

The semantic function $[\![\cdot]\!]$ maps an expression E to its denotation $[\![E]\!]$. Denotations of expressions are computations, and since there is only one data type in ELSE, it suffices to take $\mathsf{M}(\mathbf{N})$ as the domain of denotations. The semantic equations for all ELSE constructs are given below,

$$\begin{aligned} [\![n]\!] &= \mathsf{unit}_\mathsf{M}\ n \\ [\![I]\!] &= \mathsf{state} *_\mathsf{M} (\lambda s.\ \mathsf{unit}_\mathsf{M}\ (\mathsf{get}\ I\ s)) \\ [\![I\texttt{=}E]\!] &= [\![E]\!] *_\mathsf{M} (\lambda n.\ \mathsf{update}\ (\mathsf{put}\ I\ n) *_\mathsf{M} \\ &\qquad (\lambda s.\ \mathsf{unit}_\mathsf{M}\ n)) \\ [\![E_1\texttt{+}E_2]\!] &= ([\![E_1]\!] \bowtie [\![E_2]\!]) *_\mathsf{M} \\ &\qquad (\lambda \langle n_1, n_2\rangle.\ \mathsf{unit}_\mathsf{M}\ (n_1 + n_2)) \\ [\![\texttt{-}E]\!] &= [\![E]\!] *_\mathsf{M} (\lambda n.\ \mathsf{unit}_\mathsf{M}\ (-n)) \\ [\![E_1\texttt{,}E_2]\!] &= [\![E_1]\!] *_\mathsf{M} (\lambda n.\ [\![E_2]\!]) \end{aligned}$$

where, apart from the details of M's implementation, we have yet to define operator $\bowtie$ and functions $\mathsf{update} : (\mathbf{S} \to \mathbf{S}) \to \mathsf{M}(\mathbf{S})$ and $\mathsf{state} : \mathsf{M}(\mathbf{S})$. The last two, as in [Lian95], are used as an interface between computations and the state. The implementation of update depends on monad M and the result of $\mathsf{update}\ f$ is a computation that modifies the state by applying function f and returns the previous state (before the modification). On the other hand, state simply represents a computation returning the present state and can be defined as follows.

$$\mathsf{state} = \mathsf{update}\ \mathsf{id}$$

Operator $\cdot \bowtie \cdot : \mathsf{M}(A) \times \mathsf{M}(B) \to \mathsf{M}(A \times B)$ is very important in this paper. It "combines" two independent computations into a single one. If $m_a : \mathsf{M}(A)$ and m_b :

[1] In all examples we adopt the same operator precedence and associativity as in C and use parentheses to group expressions. All these details are hidden in the abstract syntax.

[2] This description, although naïve, is sufficient for the purpose of this paper. The notation used is similar to the one used in [Wadl92], with the exception of the bind operator, which is denoted here as $*$.

[3] The choice of the mathematical space used for domains is not very important for such a small language. Pointed cpo's are a reasonable option. The domain notation used in this paper is the same as in [Moss90].

[4] $\mathbf{U}$ is the two-point domain $\{\bot, \mathbf{u}\}$ with $\bot \sqsubseteq \mathbf{u}$. It is used to express values that are not important unless they are abnormal. Also, the function update operator $f[x \mapsto y]$ is strict in all its arguments.

$\mathsf{M}(B)$ are two computations returning values $v_a : A$ and $v_b : B$, then $m_a \bowtie m_b$ is the combined computation returning the pair of values $\langle v_a, v_b \rangle$. The implementation of $\bowtie$ generally depends on the implementation of M and, as is evident from the semantic equations, specifies the order in which expressions are evaluated. The following sections discuss several implementations of $\bowtie$ reflecting various possible evaluation strategies for ELSE. Monad M is carefully defined each time to support the desired evaluation order semantics.

3.1 Left-to-right evaluation

A very simple, common and natural evaluation order is *left-to-right.*[5] In the case of ELSE, left-to-right evaluation specifies that the left operand of + is evaluated completely before the right operand. This is reflected in the following definition of operator $\bowtie$.

$$m_1 \bowtie m_2 = \\ m_1 *_{\mathsf{M}} (\lambda v_1 .\, m_2 *_{\mathsf{M}} (\lambda v_2 .\, \mathsf{unit}_{\mathsf{M}} \langle v_1, v_2 \rangle))$$

Before we can have a complete semantics for ELSE, it is necessary to define an appropriate monad M. In this section, we choose a direct semantics approach, making use of an additional monad P as a provision for the following sections. Definitions of M and update are straightforward.

$$\begin{aligned} \mathsf{M}(T) &= \mathbf{S} \to \mathsf{P}(T \times \mathbf{S}) \\ \mathsf{unit}_{\mathsf{M}} &= \lambda v .\, \lambda s .\, \mathsf{unit}_{\mathsf{P}} \langle v, s \rangle \\ m *_{\mathsf{M}} f &= \lambda s .\, m\, s *_{\mathsf{P}} (\lambda \langle v', s' \rangle .\, f\, v'\, s') \\ \mathsf{update} &= \lambda f .\, \lambda s .\, \mathsf{unit}_{\mathsf{P}} \langle s, f\, s \rangle \end{aligned}$$

For the purpose of this section, the identity monad is a reasonable choice for P, ending up with the conventional direct semantics for ELSE.

$$\begin{aligned} \mathsf{P}(T) &= T \\ \mathsf{unit}_{\mathsf{P}} &= \mathsf{id} \\ p *_{\mathsf{P}} f &= f\, p \end{aligned}$$

Left-to-right evaluation evidently produces unambiguous results. As an example, let us consider again the expression `x=0, x+(x=1)`, whose denotation is given below. The result of its evaluation is the value 1 and the final state is identical to the initial one, except that x has the value 1.

$$[\![\texttt{x=0, x+(x=1)}]\!] = \lambda s .\, \langle 1, s[\texttt{x} \mapsto 1] \rangle$$

3.2 Non-deterministic choice

We continue by considering evaluation strategies that allow for ambiguity in expression evaluation. In this case, it is necessary to replace P by a monad supporting multiple results. An obvious choice is the *powerdomain* monad, that is defined below using an appropriate powerdomain constructor such as Plotkin's convex powerdomain [Plot76]. Multiple results are constructed with the polymorphic operator $\cdot \uplus_{\mathsf{P}} \cdot : \mathsf{P}(A) \times \mathsf{P}(A) \to \mathsf{P}(A)$.

$$\begin{aligned} \mathsf{P}(T) &= T^{\natural} \\ \mathsf{unit}_{\mathsf{P}} &= \lambda v .\, \{\!| v |\!\} \\ p *_{\mathsf{P}} f &= \mathsf{ext}^{\natural}\, f\, p \\ p_1 \uplus_{\mathsf{P}} p_2 &= p_1 \uplus^{\natural} p_2 \end{aligned}$$

In the above $\{\!|\cdot|\!\} : A \to A^{\natural}$, $\mathsf{ext}^{\natural} : (A \to B^{\natural}) \to A^{\natural} \to B^{\natural}$ and $\cdot \uplus^{\natural} \cdot : A^{\natural} \times A^{\natural} \to A^{\natural}$ are standard operators of the convex powerdomain.

A simple evaluation strategy that allows for ambiguous results is the *non-deterministic choice*. According to this, operands may be evaluated in any order but the evaluation of each one is performed individually and no interleaving is possible. In the case of ELSE, non-deterministic choice specifies that the operands of + may be evaluated left-to-right or right-to-left but, in any case, evaluation of one of them will have been completed before evaluation of the other starts.

In order to formally specify non-deterministic choice in our semantic model, it suffices to redefine operator $\bowtie$ and include right-to-left evaluation as well. We do this by introducing a new polymorphic operator $\cdot \parallel \cdot : \mathsf{M}(A) \times \mathsf{M}(A) \to \mathsf{M}(A)$, which represents non-deterministic choice in computations and whose implementation depends on monad M. Given two computations $m_1 : \mathsf{M}(A)$ and $m_2 : \mathsf{M}(A)$, the set of possible results for computation $m_1 \parallel m_2 : \mathsf{M}(A)$ is the union of the sets of all possible results for both m_1 and m_2.[6]

$$m_1 \parallel m_2 = \lambda s .\, m_1\, s \uplus_{\mathsf{P}} m_2\, s$$

$$\begin{aligned} m_1 \bowtie m_2 = \\ & m_1 *_{\mathsf{M}} (\lambda v_1 .\, m_2 *_{\mathsf{M}} (\lambda v_2 .\, \mathsf{unit}_{\mathsf{M}} \langle v_1, v_2 \rangle)) \parallel \\ & m_2 *_{\mathsf{M}} (\lambda v_2 .\, m_1 *_{\mathsf{M}} (\lambda v_1 .\, \mathsf{unit}_{\mathsf{M}} \langle v_1, v_2 \rangle)) \end{aligned}$$

It may be interesting to notice that, by defining $m_1 \parallel m_2 = m_1$, non-deterministic choice degenerates into left-to-right evaluation.

In this evaluation strategy, `x=0, x+(x=1)` may produce 1 or 2 and `x=0, x+(x=1, x=2, 0)` may produce 0 or 2, as shown below.

$$[\![\texttt{x=0, x+(x=1)}]\!] = \\ \lambda s .\, \{\!| \langle 1, s[\texttt{x} \mapsto 1] \rangle, \langle 2, s[\texttt{x} \mapsto 1] \rangle |\!\}$$

$$[\![\texttt{x=0, x+(x=1, x=2, 0)}]\!] = \\ \lambda s .\, \{\!| \langle 0, s[\texttt{x} \mapsto 2] \rangle, \langle 2, s[\texttt{x} \mapsto 2] \rangle |\!\}$$

3.3 Interleaving

The notion of execution *interleaving* is a well known one in the theory of concurrency. An interleaved evaluation of an expression consists of an arbitrary merging of the *atomic steps* that constitute the evaluation of its subparts. In the case of ELSE it is natural to consider side effects, i.e. read and write accesses to the state, as the only kind of atomic steps. Furthermore, it is often useful to disable interleaving and evaluate an arbitrary expression in a single atomic step. To achieve this, we introduce a new construct in ELSE.

$$\begin{aligned} E : \mathbf{Expr} ::= &\; n \mid I \mid I\texttt{=}E \mid E_1\texttt{+}E_2 \mid \texttt{-}E \\ \mid &\; E_1\texttt{,}E_2 \mid \texttt{<}E\texttt{>} \end{aligned}$$

[5] Left-to-right evaluation is used by many programming languages, such as Standard ML and Java.

[6] Operator $\parallel$ would be useful on its own in a hypothetical extension of ELSE that would support non-determinism explicitly, e.g. in expressions of the form $E_1 ? E_2$.

Expression <*E*> is equivalent to E with the only difference that the former is evaluated in a single atomic step, and therefore no interleaving is permitted during its evaluation. The semantics of the newly introduced construct may be expressed using a new function exhaust : $\mathsf{M}(A) \to \mathsf{M}(A)$, that transforms a computation consisting of several steps to an equivalent one consisting of a single step.

$$[\![<E>]\!] = \mathsf{exhaust}\ [\![E]\!]$$

In the non-interleaving semantics of the previous sections, expressions <*E*> and E are equivalent and it suffices to take exhaust = id.

In order to formally specify interleaving in our semantics, it is necessary to modify the domain of denotations. We define monad M as follows, implementing thus a tree-like *branching semantics*. We retain the powerdomain monad P from the previous section.

$$\begin{aligned}
\mathsf{M}(T) &= T \oplus (\mathbf{S} \to \mathsf{P}(\mathsf{M}(T) \times \mathbf{S})) \\
\mathsf{unit}_{\mathsf{M}} &= \mathbf{inl} \\
m *_{\mathsf{M}} f &= \mathbf{fix}\,(\lambda g.\,[\,f, \lambda r.\,\mathbf{inr}\,(\lambda s.\,r\,s *_{\mathsf{P}} \\
&\qquad (\lambda \langle m', s' \rangle.\,\mathsf{unit}_{\mathsf{P}}\,\langle g\,m', s' \rangle))\,])\;m \\
\mathsf{update} &= \lambda f.\,\mathbf{inr}\,(\lambda s.\,\mathsf{unit}_{\mathsf{P}}\,\langle \mathbf{inl}\,s, f\,s \rangle) \\
\mathsf{exhaust} &= \mathbf{fix}\,(\lambda g.\,[\,\mathbf{inl}, \lambda r.\,\mathbf{inr}\,(\lambda s.\,r\,s *_{\mathsf{P}} \\
&\qquad (\lambda \langle m', s' \rangle.\,[\,\lambda v'.\,\mathsf{unit}_{\mathsf{P}}\,\langle \mathbf{inl}\,v', s' \rangle, \\
&\qquad \lambda r'.\,r'\,s'\,]\,(g\,m')))\,])
\end{aligned}$$

In this semantics, the denotation of an expression is either a computed value or a function mapping the current state to a set of possible intermediate results, that may be produced after a single atomic step is performed. Each such result consists of the denotation of a partially computed expression and a new state. Such denotations are called *resumptions* and are frequently used in specifying the semantics of concurrency [Moss90, dBak96]. The resumption semantics that we use in this section is derived from the direct semantics of section 3.1.

We should emphasize here that expressions whose value is constant and does not depend on the state are considered as already computed and are denoted by elements of the left summand of $\mathsf{M}(T)$. In contrast to that, expressions whose computation requires one or more atomic steps to be performed and whose value depends on the state are denoted by elements of the right summand of $\mathsf{M}(T)$.

Operator $\|$ can be easily defined for the new semantics.[7] We notice again that by taking $m_1 \parallel m_2 = m_1$ interleaving degenerates into left-to-right evaluation.

$$\begin{aligned}
m_1 \parallel m_2 &= \mathbf{inr}\,(\lambda s.\,\mathbf{let}\;f = [\,\lambda v.\,\mathsf{unit}_{\mathsf{P}}\,\langle \mathbf{inl}\,v, s \rangle, \\
&\qquad \lambda r.\,r\,s\,]\;\mathbf{in}\;f\,m_1 \uplus_{\mathsf{P}} f\,m_2)
\end{aligned}$$

The definition of operator $\bowtie$ becomes more elegant by the introduction of the following two functions.

$$\begin{aligned}
\mathsf{analyze} &: \mathsf{M}(A) \to (A \to B) \times B \to B \\
\mathsf{analyze} &= \lambda m.\,\lambda \langle f, z \rangle.\,[\,f, \lambda r.\,z\,]\;m \\
\mathsf{apply} &: \mathsf{M}(A) \to (\mathsf{M}(A) \to \mathsf{M}(B)) \to \mathsf{M}(B) \\
\mathsf{apply} &= \lambda m.\,\lambda f.\,[\,f \circ \mathbf{inl}, \lambda r.\,\mathbf{inr}\,(\lambda s.\,r\,s *_{\mathsf{P}} \\
&\qquad (\lambda \langle m', s' \rangle.\,\mathsf{unit}_{\mathsf{P}}\,\langle f\,m', s' \rangle))\,]\;m
\end{aligned}$$

Function analyze can be used to distinguish between a computation that has been completed and one that requires atomic steps to be performed. Function apply performs the first atomic step of the computation specified by its first argument, if this is possible, and applies its second argument to the partial results. By using these two functions, operator $\bowtie$ can be defined as follows.

$$\begin{aligned}
m_1 \bowtie m_2 = {} & \mathbf{fix}\,(\lambda g.\,\lambda \langle m_1, m_2 \rangle. \\
& \mathsf{analyze}\;m_1\;\langle \lambda v_1.\,m_2 *_{\mathsf{M}} (\lambda v_2.\,\mathsf{unit}_{\mathsf{M}}\,\langle v_1, v_2 \rangle), \\
& \mathsf{analyze}\;m_2\;\langle \lambda v_2.\,m_1 *_{\mathsf{M}} (\lambda v_1.\,\mathsf{unit}_{\mathsf{M}}\,\langle v_1, v_2 \rangle), \\
& \mathsf{apply}\;m_1\;(\lambda m_1'.\,g\,\langle m_1', m_2 \rangle) \parallel \\
& \quad \mathsf{apply}\;m_2\;(\lambda m_2'.\,g\,\langle m_1, m_2' \rangle)\rangle\rangle)\;\langle m_1, m_2 \rangle
\end{aligned}$$

When both computations of m_1 and m_2 require atomic steps to be performed, operator $\bowtie$ must choose between performing an atomic step from m_1 or m_2.

Returning to our example `x=0, x+(x=1)`, resumption semantics produces 1 or 2 as possible results, exactly as non-deterministic choice. However, expression `x=0, x+(x=1, x=2, 0)` may now produce the result 1, in addition to the possible results 0 and 2 of non-deterministic choice, in case the (implicit) dereferencing of `x` is interleaved between atomic steps `x=1` and `x=2`. The denotations of both examples in equational and schematic form are shown in Figure 1. Their exhausted versions are also shown, so that the results of their (uninterrupted) evaluation can be examined.

3.4 Sequence points

A language that does not fully specify evaluation order and, at the same time, allows evaluation of expressions to produce side effects is an inherently ambiguous language.[8] However, for a programming language to be useful, ambiguities in program execution should be avoided as much as possible. In this section we focus on the ANSI C programming language which features the combination of characteristics mentioned before. In order to disallow undesired ambiguities, the C standard introduces restrictions imposed on expression evaluation. An attempt to define the semantics of these restrictions is made in this section.

The C standard is very careful not to overspecify, in order to allow for reasonable optimizations in implementations of the language. Such optimizations may see fit to postpone a side effect and, for instance, store a variable's value in a register instead of its appointed location in memory.

> At certain specified points in the execution sequence called *sequence points*, all side effects of previous evaluations shall be complete and

[7] However, our resumption semantics forces us to introduce an atomic step for the non-deterministic choice between two computed values. This could be avoided by using the more complicated monad $\mathsf{M}(T) = \mathsf{P}(T) \oplus (\mathbf{S} \to \mathsf{P}(\mathsf{M}(T) \times \mathbf{S}))$.

[8] Several programming languages, such as ALGOL 60, Pascal, C/C++ and Scheme, prefer not to impose a specific evaluation order on implementors.

Expression: `x=0, x+(x=1)`

$$
\begin{array}{l}
[\![\texttt{x=0, x+(x=1)}]\!] = \mathbf{inr}\,(\lambda\, s.\,\{\!|\\
\quad \langle \mathbf{inr}\,(\lambda\, s_1.\,\{\!|\\
\qquad \langle \mathbf{inr}\,(\lambda\, s_{11}.\,\{\!|\langle \mathbf{inl}\,(s_1\,\mathrm{x}+1), s_{11}[\mathrm{x}\mapsto 1]\rangle|\!\}), s_1\rangle,\\
\qquad \langle \mathbf{inr}\,(\lambda\, s_{12}.\,\{\!|\langle \mathbf{inl}\,(s_{12}\,\mathrm{x}+1), s_{12}\rangle|\!\}), s_1[\mathrm{x}\mapsto 1]\rangle\\
\quad |\!\}), s[\mathrm{x}\mapsto 0]\rangle\\
|\!\})
\end{array}
$$

$$
\begin{array}{l}
\mathsf{exhaust}\,[\![\texttt{x=0, x+(x=1)}]\!] = \mathbf{inr}\,(\lambda\, s.\,\{\!|\\
\quad \langle \mathbf{inl}\,1, s[\mathrm{x}\mapsto 1]\rangle,\\
\quad \langle \mathbf{inl}\,2, s[\mathrm{x}\mapsto 1]\rangle\\
|\!\})
\end{array}
$$

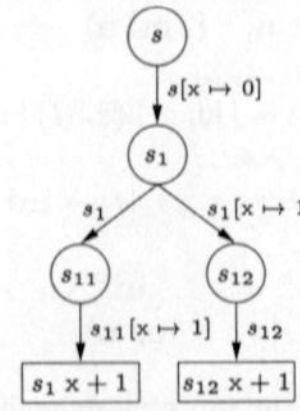

Expression: `x=0, x+(x=1, x=2, 0)`

$$
\begin{array}{l}
[\![\texttt{x=0, x+(x=1, x=2, 0)}]\!] = \mathbf{inr}\,(\lambda\, s.\,\{\!|\\
\quad \langle \mathbf{inr}\,(\lambda\, s_1.\,\{\!|\\
\qquad \langle \mathbf{inr}\,(\lambda\, s_{11}.\,\{\!|\\
\qquad\quad \langle \mathbf{inr}\,(\lambda\, s_{111}.\,\{\!|\langle \mathbf{inl}\,(s_1\,\mathrm{x}), s_{111}[\mathrm{x}\mapsto 2]\rangle|\!\}), s_{11}[\mathrm{x}\mapsto 1]\rangle\\
\qquad |\!\}), s_1\rangle,\\
\qquad \langle \mathbf{inr}\,(\lambda\, s_{12}.\,\{\!|\\
\qquad\quad \langle \mathbf{inr}\,(\lambda\, s_{121}.\,\{\!|\langle \mathbf{inl}\,(s_{12}\,\mathrm{x}), s_{121}[\mathrm{x}\mapsto 2]\rangle|\!\}), s_{12}\rangle,\\
\qquad\quad \langle \mathbf{inr}\,(\lambda\, s_{122}.\,\{\!|\langle \mathbf{inl}\,(s_{122}\,\mathrm{x}), s_{122}\rangle|\!\}), s_{12}[\mathrm{x}\mapsto 2]\rangle\\
\qquad |\!\}), s_1[\mathrm{x}\mapsto 1]\rangle\\
\quad |\!\}), s[\mathrm{x}\mapsto 0]\rangle\\
|\!\})
\end{array}
$$

$$
\begin{array}{l}
\mathsf{exhaust}\,[\![\texttt{x=0, x+(x=1, x=2, 0)}]\!] = \mathbf{inr}\,(\lambda\, s.\,\{\!|\\
\quad \langle \mathbf{inl}\,0, s[\mathrm{x}\mapsto 2]\rangle,\\
\quad \langle \mathbf{inl}\,1, s[\mathrm{x}\mapsto 2]\rangle,\\
\quad \langle \mathbf{inl}\,2, s[\mathrm{x}\mapsto 2]\rangle\\
|\!\})
\end{array}
$$

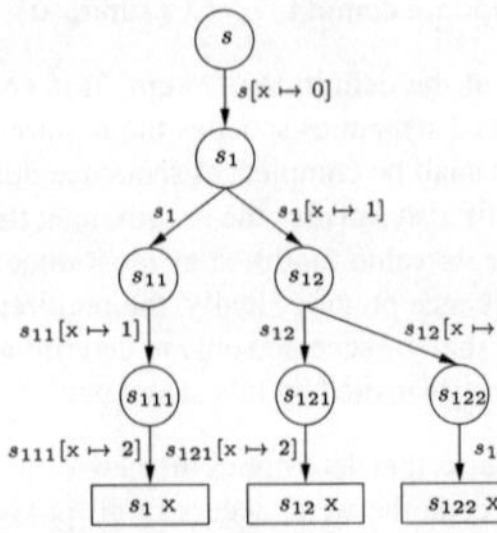

Figure 1: Two examples of interleaving semantics.

no side effects of subsequent evaluations shall have taken place. [ANSI90, §5.1.2.3]

Sequence points are the standard's guarantee that all side effects will eventually take place properly and that optimizations will not affect normal execution. Additional restrictions are imposed to disallow excessively ambiguous expressions.

> Between the previous and next sequence point an object shall have its stored value modified at most once by the evaluation of an expression. Furthermore, the prior value shall be accessed only to determine the value to be stored. [ANSI90, §6.3]

The first restriction disallows expressions such as `(x=1)+(x=2)`. The second is careful enough to disallow `x+(x=1)` but not `x=x+1`. We should notice however that these restrictions do not completely eliminate ambiguity in C expressions. Function calls are always surrounded by sequence points and do not allow interleaving in their execution. Therefore, an expression such as `f()+g()` does not violate the sequence point restrictions and is ambiguous when both `f()` and `g()` produce side effects, since the order in which they will be called is not specified by the standard.

In order to study the semantics of ANSI C's mechanism of sequence points, we modify our example language. We first change the semantics of the comma operator, by enforcing a sequence point between the (left-to-right) evaluation of the two operands. We also add a unary operator #, which enforces two sequence points: one just before and one just after the evaluation of its operand. Although ELSE still does not feature functions, an expression of the form <#E> is a reasonably equivalent to a call to a C function with no arguments.

$$
\begin{array}{rcl}
E : \mathbf{Expr} & ::= & n \mid I \mid I\texttt{=}E \mid E_1\texttt{+}E_2 \mid \texttt{-}E\\
& \mid & E_1\texttt{,}E_2 \mid \texttt{<}E\texttt{>} \mid \texttt{\#}E
\end{array}
$$

The required changes in the semantics of ELSE are given by the following equations, where $\mathsf{seqpt} : \mathsf{M}(\mathbf{U})$ represents a computation that enforces a sequence point.

$$
\begin{array}{rcl}
[\![E_1\texttt{,}E_2]\!] & = & [\![E_1]\!] \ast_{\mathsf{M}} (\lambda\, n.\ \mathsf{seqpt} \ast_{\mathsf{M}} (\lambda\, u.\ [\![E_2]\!]))\\
[\![\texttt{\#}E]\!] & = & \mathsf{seqpt} \ast_{\mathsf{M}} (\lambda\, u_1.\ [\![E]\!] \ast_{\mathsf{M}}\\
& & \qquad (\lambda\, n.\ \mathsf{seqpt} \ast_{\mathsf{M}} (\lambda\, u_2.\ \mathsf{unit}_{\mathsf{M}}\, n)))
\end{array}
$$

By taking $\mathsf{seqpt} = \mathsf{unit}_{\mathsf{M}}\ \mathbf{u}$, the semantics of this section degenerates into that of the previous section.

To distinguish between a side effect that has taken place and one that has not, it is necessary to change the definition of state. By taking into account the additional restrictions imposed by the mechanism of sequence points, it is possible to define $\mathbf{S}$ as a pair of two functions, the first representing the memory and the second representing the pending side effects. Knowing that at most one writing to each memory location takes place between two successive sequence points and that no reading takes place after the writing, we may specify that all side effects actually take place at the following sequence point by a call to function $\mathsf{commit} : \mathbf{S} \rightarrow \mathbf{S}$. The new definition of $\mathbf{S}$ is given below.

$$
\begin{array}{lcl}
\mathbf{S} & = & (\mathbf{Ide} \to \mathbf{N} \oplus \mathbf{U}) \times (\mathbf{Ide} \to \mathbf{N} \oplus \mathbf{U}) \\
s_\circ & = & \langle \lambda I.\, \mathbf{inr\ u}, \lambda I.\, \mathbf{inl\ u} \rangle \\
\mathsf{get} & = & \lambda I.\, \lambda \langle s_n, s_x \rangle. \\
 & & \quad [\, \bot, \lambda u.\, [\, \mathsf{id}, \bot\,]\, (s_n\ I)\,]\, (s_x\ I) \\
\mathsf{put} & = & \lambda I.\, \lambda n.\, \lambda s. \\
 & & \quad [\, \bot, \lambda u.\, \langle s_n, s_x[I \mapsto \mathbf{inl}\ n] \rangle\,]\, (s_x\ I) \\
\mathsf{commit} & = & \lambda \langle s_n, s_x \rangle. \\
 & & \quad \mathbf{let}\ s'_n = \lambda I.\, [\, \mathbf{inl}, \lambda u.\, s_n\ I\,]\, (s_x\ I) \\
 & & \quad \mathbf{in}\ \langle s'_n, \lambda I.\, \mathbf{inr\ u} \rangle
\end{array}
$$

Implementations of get and put guarantee that no reading or writing is permitted if a side effect for the same variable is pending. Subsequently, we can define seqpt as follows.

$$\mathsf{seqpt} \ = \ \mathsf{update\ commit} *_{\mathsf{M}} (\lambda s.\ \mathsf{unit}_{\mathsf{M}}\ \mathbf{u})$$

By looking at the definition of seqpt, it is easy to see that the proposed semantics satisfies the requirement that all side effects shall be complete at sequence points. The definition of put also satisfies the requirement that an object shall have its value modified at most once between successive sequence points. Finally, the requirement that the prior value shall be accessed only to determine the new value is indirectly satisfied by this semantics:

- A read access that determines the new value will certainly precede the write access in all possible evaluation orders. It is therefore always allowed by the definition of get.

- A read access that does not determine the new value is only allowed by the definition of get if it precedes the write access in the evaluation order. But it can be easily proved that there exists an evaluation order in which this is not true and, for this particular evaluation order, the definition of get produces an error. This error will propagate in the denotation of the expression and, therefore, if we rule out expressions containing errors as possible results, our semantics satisfies the requirement.

Of course, it is possible to define a semantics satisfying this last requirement directly, by defining **S** in such a way as to keep track of performed read accesses.

As an example, we consider again the expression `x=0, x+(x=1)`. The semantics shown in Figure 2 is similar to the one in Figure 1 with the exception of the extra commit step.[9] In the exhausted version, we can see that the result 2 has been replaced by an error, since read access s_{112} x is performed on state $s_{11}[\mathrm{x} \mapsto 1]$, without an intermediate sequence point.

4 Related work

Research in the field of expression languages, side effects and evaluation order spans a wide area of interest. Among the earliest related publications we should mention the work of Boehm [Boeh82] and Kowaltowski [Kowa77] on the axiomatic semantics of expression languages with side effects. Both avoid the pitfall of evaluation order by assuming left-to-right evaluation. The work of Filinski [Fili96] focuses on the introduction of various kinds of effects in functional languages, using appropriate monads for state and continuations, but does not address the issue of evaluation order semantics. Evaluation order analysis in lazy functional languages is dealt with in the work of Draghicescu and Purushothaman [Drag90] and Bloss [Blos94]. Both do not define a semantics of execution for different evaluation strategies and are primarily interested in optimizations and the destructive update problem.

The semantics of many popular programming languages has been formally specified in literature, at least partially. Unspecified evaluation order is modeled mostly using permutation oracles or appropriate transition systems. Often the issue is excluded from the formal description and a convenient assumption is made. To the best of our knowledge, techniques as the one used in this paper have not been used for this purpose in relation with "real-world" programming languages.

Significant research has been conducted recently concerning semantic aspects of the C programming language, mainly because of the language's popularity and its wide applications. In what seems to be the earliest formal approach, Sethi addresses the semantics of pre-ANSI C, using the denotational approach and assuming left-to-right evaluation of expressions [Seth80]. In the work of Gurevich and Huggins [Gure93] a formal semantics for C is given in the form of evolving algebra. The semantics of evaluation order is based on the assumptions that no interleaving is possible in expression evaluation (i.e. non-deterministic choice as described in Section 3.2 is used) and that side effects take place as they are generated. Both assumptions do not agree with the ANSI standard. A higher-level axiomatic semantics is proposed by Black and Windley [Blac96], which removes side effects from expressions and treats them as separate statements. In the work of Cook and Subramanian [Cook94b] a semantics for C is developed in the theorem prover Nqthm. It employs an oracle for determining evaluation order and order of side-effects, but this is not really used since the authors consider a subset of C with pure expressions. Cook et al. have also developed a denotational semantics for C based on temporal logic [Cook94a]. Although left-to-right evaluation is assumed in this work, the authors suggest how this can be remedied. However, it is not clear whether the suggestion allows for interleaving and there is no treatment of sequence points. To the best of our knowledge, the only semantics of ANSI C that correctly models unspecified order of evaluation, side effects and sequence points is defined in the work of Norrish [Norr97] in the form of operational semantics with small-step reductions. No similar denotational approach is known to us.

5 Conclusion and future work

This paper was mainly concerned with exploring the semantics of evaluation order in strict expression languages with side effects. The semantics of the example language ELSE was developed under various different evaluation strategies in a unified way, based on monad notation which

[9] To reduce complexity in the figure, we keep the old notation instead of the newly defined state operations get and put.

Expression: `x=0, x+(x=1)`

$$
\begin{array}{l}
[\![\texttt{x=0, x+(x=1)}]\!] = \mathbf{inr}\,(\lambda\, s.\, \lbag \\
\quad \langle \mathbf{inr}\,(\lambda\, s_1.\, \lbag \\
\qquad \langle \mathbf{inr}\,(\lambda\, s_{11}.\, \lbag \\
\qquad\quad \langle \mathbf{inr}\,(\lambda\, s_{111}.\, \lbag \langle \mathbf{inl}\,(s_{11}\,\mathsf{x}+1), s_{111}[\mathsf{x} \mapsto 1]\rangle \rbag), s_{11}\rangle, \\
\qquad\quad \langle \mathbf{inr}\,(\lambda\, s_{112}.\, \lbag \langle \mathbf{inl}\,(s_{112}\,\mathsf{x}+1), s_{112}\rangle \rbag), s_{11}[\mathsf{x} \mapsto 1]\rangle \\
\qquad \rbag), \mathsf{commit}\; s_1\rangle \\
\quad \rbag), s[\mathsf{x} \mapsto 0]\rangle \\
\rbag)
\end{array}
$$

$$
\begin{array}{l}
\mathsf{exhaust}\; [\![\texttt{x=0, x+(x=1)}]\!] = \mathbf{inr}\,(\lambda\, s.\, \lbag \\
\quad \langle \mathbf{inl}\; 1, s[\mathsf{x} \mapsto 1]\rangle, \\
\quad \langle \bot, s[\mathsf{x} \mapsto 1]\rangle \\
\rbag)
\end{array}
$$

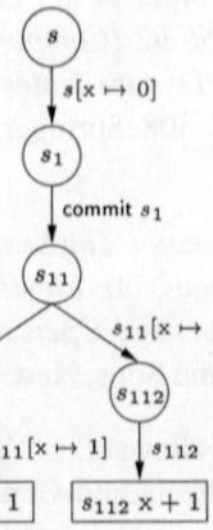

Figure 2: Interleaving semantics with sequence points.

improves the modularity and elegance of the result. The final version of ELSE is a significant subset of the language of C expressions and its semantics has been successfully modelled, including unspecified evaluation order, order of side effects and the mechanism of sequence points. This is a valuable result that opens the road towards a complete denotational description of ANSI C. Although ELSE is not capable of non-termination, the semantics is powerful enough to model it. Variable aliasing can be included by separating environment and state and the direct semantics in the definition of monad M can be easily replaced by continuations, which will be needed in a complete formal treatment of C. It is also easy to extend operator $\bowtie$ to for any number of operands.

Future work will have to proceed on several fronts. On the one hand it would be interesting to relate the denotational semantics described in this paper to operational semantics for the same languages, by equations of the form $\mathcal{O} = \mathsf{abs}\ \mathcal{D}$, and study the issue of full abstraction in the style of [dBak96]. This will be rather complicated, primarily because of monad notation, but we believe that it is possible although we still lack a firm proof. On the other hand, the replacement of domains with functor categories in the foundations of our model should be considered. In this way, a possible worlds semantics of evaluation order will be feasible, which can subsequently be used as a basis for the abstract treatment of local variables. Finally, this work is part of an ongoing bigger project, aiming at the development of a denotational semantics for the complete ANSI C language, in which the resumption semantics of Section 3.4 will have a prominent role.

References

[ANSI90] American National Standards Institute, New York, NY, *ANSI/ISO 9899-1990, American National Standard for Programming Languages: C*, 1990, Revision and redesignation of ANSI X3.159-1989.

[Blac96] P. E. Black and P. J. Windley, "Inference Rules for Programming Languages with Side Effects in Expressions", in *Proceedings of the 9th International Conference on Theorem Proving in Higher Order Logics (TPHOLs'96)*, pp. 51–60, Turku, Finland, 26–30 August 1996, Springer Verlag.

[Blos94] A. Bloss, "Path Analysis and the Optimization of Nonstrict Functional Languages", *ACM Transactions on Programming Languages and Systems*, vol. 16, no. 3, pp. 328–369, May 1994.

[Boeh82] H. J. Boehm, "A Logic for Expressions with Side Effects", in *Proceedings of the ACM Symposium on Principles of Programming Languages*, pp. 268–280, 1982.

[Cook94a] J. Cook, E. Cohen and T. Redmond, "A Formal Denotational Semantics for C", Technical Report 409D, Trusted Information Systems, September 1994.

[Cook94b] J. Cook and S. Subramanian, "A Formal Semantics for C in Nqthm", Technical Report 517D, Trusted Information Systems, October 1994.

[dBak96] J. de Bakker and E. de Vink, *Control Flow Semantics*, Foundations of Computing Series, MIT Press, Cambridge, MA, 1996.

[Dijk76] E. W. Dijkstra, *A Discipline of Programming*, Prentice Hall, Englewood Cliffs, NJ, 1976.

[Drag90] M. Draghicescu and S. Purushothaman, "A Compositional Analysis of Evaluation-Order and its Application", in *Conference Record of the ACM Symposium on Lisp and Functional Programming*, pp. 242–250, Nice, France, 1990.

[Fili96] A. Filinski, *Controlling Effects*, Ph.D. thesis, Carnegie Mellon University, School of Computer Science, May 1996, Also as Technical Report CMU-CS-96-119.

[Gure93] Y. Gurevich and J. K. Huggins, "The Semantics of the C Programming Language", in E. Börger et al., editors, *Selected Papers from CSL'92 (Computer Science Logic)*, vol. 702 of *Lecture Notes in Computer Science*, pp. 274–308, Springer Verlag, New York, NY, 1993.

[Henn90] M. Hennessy, *The Semantics of Programming Languages: An Elementary Introduction Using Structural Operational Semantics*, John Wiley and Sons, New York, NY, 1990.

[Kowa77] T. Kowaltowski, "Axiomatic Approach to Side Effects and General Jumps", *Acta Informatica*, vol. 7, pp. 357–360, 1977.

[Lian95] S. Liang, P. Hudak and M. Jones, "Monad Transformers and Modular Interpreters", in *Conference Record of the 22nd ACM SIGPLAN-SIGACT Symposium on Principles of Programming Languages (POPL'95)*, San Francisco, CA, January 1995.

[Mogg90] E. Moggi, "An Abstract View of Programming Languages", Technical Report ECS-LFCS-90-113, University of Edinburgh, Laboratory for Foundations of Computer Science, 1990.

[Moss90] P. D. Mosses, "Denotational Semantics", in J. van Leeuwen, editor, *Handbook of Theoretical Computer Science*, vol. B, chapter 11, pp. 577–631, Elsevier Science Publishers B.V., 1990.

[Norr97] M. Norrish, "An Abstract Dynamic Semantics for C", Technical Report TR-421, University of Cambridge, Computer Laboratory, May 1997.

[Plot76] G. D. Plotkin, "A Powerdomain Construction", *SIAM Journal on Computing*, vol. 5, pp. 452–487, 1976.

[Seth80] R. Sethi, "A Case Study in Specifying the Semantics of a Programming Language", in *Proceedings of the 7th Annual ACM Symposium on Principles of Programming Languages*, pp. 117–130, January 1980.

[Stoy77] J. E. Stoy, *Denotational Semantics: The Scott-Strachey Approach to Programming Language Theory*, MIT Press, Cambridge, MA, 1977.

[Wadl92] P. Wadler, "The Essence of Functional Programming", in *Proceedings of the 19th Annual Symposium on Principles of Programming Languages (POPL'92)*, January 1992.

An Heuristic Method for Generating a Formal CSP+T Model of a Real Time System

José A. Pérez Rafael Corchuelo Miguel Toro

Dpto. de Lenguajes y Sistemas Informáticos
Universidad de Sevilla
Avd. Reina Mercedes s/n
Tel. (95)455.65.22
e-mail: (jperez, corchu, mtoro)@lsi.us.es

Abstract

In this paper, we introduce an algorithmic method for building a formal model for a real time system in an early phase of the system development. This method takes the system structured design charts and timing constraints, and by application of a number of rules, generates a model expressed in CSP+T language, a timed variant of the well-known CSP language. The system design is supossed to be expressed in Ward/Mellor or other similar structured design method for real-time systems.

Keywords: Real-Time, CSP, CSP+T, Structured Design, Formal Methods

1.- Introduction

At present, a considerable effort is being taken in order to formalize Real Time Systems (RTS from now on) design process, as well as to develop formal specification methods for such systems.

With respect to design methods there are several groups: the first one includes the Structured Analysis Methods for Real Time (SA/RT), derived from DeMarco's Structured Analysis [1]. Among these, perhaps the best known and most widely accepted for being the SA/RT's forerunner would be the Ward/Mellor's method [2]; in this method, data transformations are the same as in Structured Analysis, and a new type of transformations -control transformations- is added in order to express control activities in the system, which are modeled as State Transition Diagrams. Another similar SA/RT widely accepted is the Boeing/Hatley method [3], which emphasizes hierarchical data and functional decomposition. A third approach, ESML (Extended System Modeling Language) tries to merge both former methods. Other methodologies in this group are DARTS (Design Approach for Real Time Systems)[4] and DARTS/DA (DARTS for Distributed Applications) [5]. The latter is a variation which takes into account the possibility of distributed processing; in both cases, they start with a data flow model using Structured Analysis, and emphasizes in RTS's decomposition in concurrent tasks and their interfaces definition.

Another interesting group is that of Object-Oriented Methodologies. A good representative of this group is ROOM (Real-Time Object Oriented Modeling) [6].

The research effort taken on formal specifying methods for RTS is also very important. Some of these efforts are directed towards temporal logic, widely used in reactive systems [7]. Some of these logics are TLA (Temporal Logic of Actions) [8], TPTL (Timed Propositional Temporal Logic)[9], RTTL (Real-Time Temporal Logic)[10], just to mention some of the most important ones.

Another group is composed of algebraic languages extensions, being the most popular ones Hoare's CSP (Communicating Sequential Processes)[11], Milner's CCS (Calculus for Communicating Systems)[12], and LOTOS [13]. As a CSP derivative we should mention Timed CSP [14]. It was originally proposed by Reed and Roscoe in 1986, and then succesively extended by other authors (Steve Schneider built an operational semantics for Timed CSP in 1.995. CSP+T [16], a simpler approach and less powerful approach is also found in this group. Due to its simplicity, this is the method we have chosen in this paper. About CCS derivatives there is a large set of works, some of them contributed by the same authors who worked on CSP. A very recent example of this can be found in [17], [18] and [19].

Special treatment deserves the use of finite state machines for specifying, modeling and later validation trough simulation of RTS. Petri Nets (PN) have been widely used for this purpose; an example of PN application for validation can be found in [20].

During a STR development process, there is a conceptual design phase. Once the system has been defined, a system formal specification is built and used as the basis for later implementation of the system. As much design as implementation can be performed by the use of any of the former methodologies, and development of the formal model from the design would be performed in a more or less formal manner. In this paper, we show an heuristic-based method for building a CSP+T model from a Ward/Mellor design plus its timing constraints (expressed in natural language). For brief, the method is introduced trough an AC motor control example. The full method explanation can be obtained from the authors via e-mail.

Before introducing the example, some CSP+T notions are presented. We shall not comment CSP or the Ward/Mellor's method, because they are supposed to be widely known.

2.- The CSP+T Language

CSP+T syntax is a superset of the basic untimed deterministic subset of CSP language presented by Hoare [13] in 1985. The main changes to untimed CSP are:

a) A new event, $\bigstar$, is introduced both into the algebra and traces model to denote process instantiation. Every process definition system must be instantiated before it can execute. This event is unique since it must be associated with a unique global time, and represents the global time when the system of processes may start at. For example, let us consider a process which can only engage in an *a* event. Such process would be modeled in untimed CSP as

$$P=a \rightarrow STOP$$

In CSP+T, this process must be instantiated before it can execute. If the timed version of *P*, *P'*, is instantiated at time 1, *P'* would be given as:

$$P'=\bigstar \rightarrow a \rightarrow STOP$$

and its temporized traces set would be

$$\{<>,\ <1.\bigstar>,\ <1.\bigstar, s.a>\}$$

where $s \in [1,\infty)$. Note that event *a* can only occur once within the $[1,\infty)$ interval for an execution of *P'*.

The times in the traces model are absolute (global) but in the algebra model shall usually be relative to events.

b) A new event operator $\bowtie$ is introduced, which is used in conjunction with a variable to record the time when an event occurs at. So if we write

$$ev \bowtie var$$

it means that the time when event *ev* is observed at the process execution is recorded in variable *var*.

This time is taken from the set of positive real numbers, with successive event times in a monotonic nondecreasing sequence. A number of successive events in a single process trace having the same time is allowed. So, if we have a process *P* defined as

$$P=1.\bigstar \rightarrow a \bowtie var \rightarrow STOP$$

then the variable *var* holds the global time when the event *a* occurs, and it shall always be verified that $var \geq 1$ (Note the possibiliy of equality).

Variables associated with the operator $\bowtie$ are called *marker variables* and their scope is restricted to strict sequential processes. This means that they cannot be shared through parallel process compositions.

c) Every event has an associated time interval, called enabling interval. Such interval represents the time period when the event is available to the process and its environment. The process behaves as STOP if it can not engage in any alternative event after the actual event 'expiration'. Enabling intervals are continuous and if a marker variable is referenced the time is considered as absolute. Otherwise (there is no maker variable) the interval is considered relative to the preceding event.

Let us assume that *P* is a process which can only engage in an event *a* which can only occur from 1 to 2 time units since the process instantiation, and stores in the maker variable *var* the time when the event occurs at. Such process specification is

$$P=0.\bigstar \rightarrow [1,2]a \bowtie var \rightarrow STOP$$

then, after this process execution it shall be verified that $1 \leq var \leq 2$.

If no enabling interval is specified for a given event, the default interval $[0,\infty]$ is assumed.

d) Only deterministic processes can be described using CSP+T.

3 From Ward/Mellor to CSP+T

We shall build a CSP+T model for a Ward/Mellor design. We shall restrict this design as a hierarchy of charts composed of:

- Data and Control Transformations
- Data and Control Stores
- Control Flows
- Continuous and Discrete Data Flows.
- State Transition Diagrams (STD's).

3.1 An overview of the modeling method

Our modeling process needs a Ward/Mellor design which consists of a transformation charts hierarchy, where the top level chart is the System Context Diagram. Every transformation process appearing in it shall be exploded as a new transformation chart, as a state transition diagram or as a data transformation specification.

In order to obtain a CSP+T system model, we are going to associate every entity in the charts to some CSP+T processes. So, we shall write a CSP+T process for every:

- Data transformation process (DTP from now on)
- Control transformation process (CTP from now on)
- Data store (DS from now on)
- Control store (CS from now on)
- Continuous data flow

Consequently, control flow shall be modeled as CSP events, and data flow shall be modeled as CSP channels.

Roughly speaking, the method we shall follow is a bottom-up algorithm, and its main steps are:

1st) Prepare the charts for their transformation. Perhaps it shall be necessary to rename some entities to avoid name conflicts when building the CSP+T model.

2nd) Build the model for the CTP's and DTP's in the lowest level, in other words, those which do not explode as a new chart.

3rd) Take the other charts in ascendant hierarchical order, and build the model for every entity within them.

4th) Once every entity within a chart is modeled, build the whole chart model. If such chart represents a CPT or a DPT in the upper hierarchy level, apply to its chart the third step, integrating this way in a bottom-up way the system CSP+T model.

5th) Hierarchical integration process ends when the last model built is the system context diagram -top level-.

3.2 Data types

In a Ward/Mellor transformation chart, data is modeled flowing between transformation processes and data stores. Every datum is an instance of a more general concept, named data type. When building the CSP+T model, data flows throuhgt communication channels and is stored in variables. In CSP, no explicit data type specification is given. This is an open door where data type specification is left for algebraic techniques. In general, we shall assume that every data type is algebraically specifiable, using an algebraic language such as ACT-ONE [21]. Type specifications shall be omitted in our example.

3.3 An overview of the system

The system we are modeling is an AC motor control. This is a subsystem of a device that forces a fixed programmable air flow through a thin paper filter.

The open loop motor control is achieved by feeding it with controlled 220V 50Hz AC. This control is issued by 'cutting' the AC sinusoid using an electrical device called 'triac' (see Fig. 1). To achieve this, we need to perfectly synchronize with the 50Hz input voltage zero-crosses; when this occurs, the triac automatically cuts, and no current flows through it. If the triac was excited after a given number of milliseconds, it would sature and the current would pass through it until the 50Hz voltage crosses zero again. Controlling the time between zero-cross and triac excitation, we can make the motor run faster o slower (the longer the time, the slower the motor runs). The relationship between time and motor R.P.M. is well known and does not matter for our example.

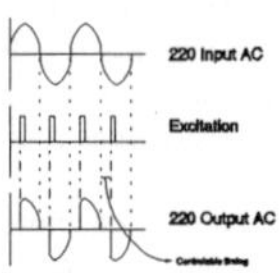

Fig. 1

Closed loop control is achieved by periodically reading the actual flow value through a flow sensor, and then computing a new reference value for the open loop control as a digital P.I.D. calculus between the old reference and the actual flow. Details about P.I.D. computation are omitted.

Furthermore the motor control, the system must perform some security tasks:

•If the circuitry which synchronizes the system with 50Hz input voltage fails, the system has to raise an exception to report this event, and the motor has to be immediately stopped.

•If the triac overheats (it is provided with a small temperature sensor) it may shortcircuit and make the motor run at full speed. This kind of AC motor is designed to run under controlled AC, and feeding them with 220 AC directly may damage them in a few seconds. So if overheating is detected, the motor has to be immediately stopped and an exception must be raised.

So the system context diagram is:

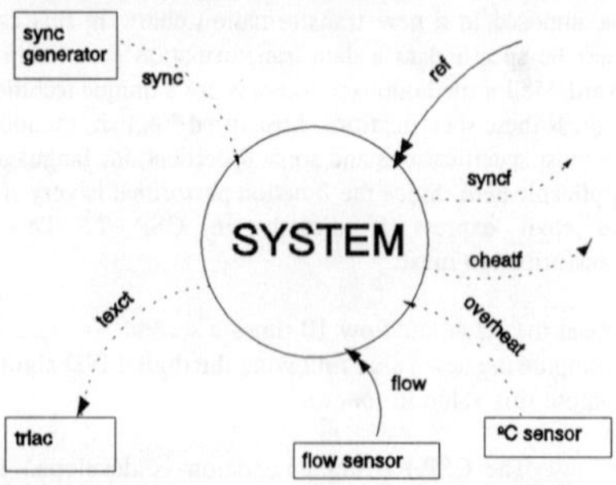

Fig. 2

The *sync* control flow is generated by a specialized circuitry to report the system every time a zero-cross is observed at 220V. The *texct* control flow has to be generated by the system every time the triac has to be excited. The air flow sensor produces a continuous data flow *flow* available at any time, and the triac temperature sensor produces a control flow *overheat* when the critical temperature is reached. The continuous input flow *ref* indicates the system the desired air flow value. In order to prevent anomalous situations, *syncf* indicates failure in synchronization, and *oheatf* indicates failure due to overheat.

At a lower level, this system may be decomposed into two separated processes (Fig. 3), one which performs the open loop control as described above, and another one which computes the timing for the open loop control, following the digital P.I.D. algorithm.

timeval is designed as a continuous data flow instead of discrete in order to decouple the open loop control process from the PID computation process. If both processes would have to synchronize when reading timeval, the frequency at which *timeval* is produced would be dependent on the

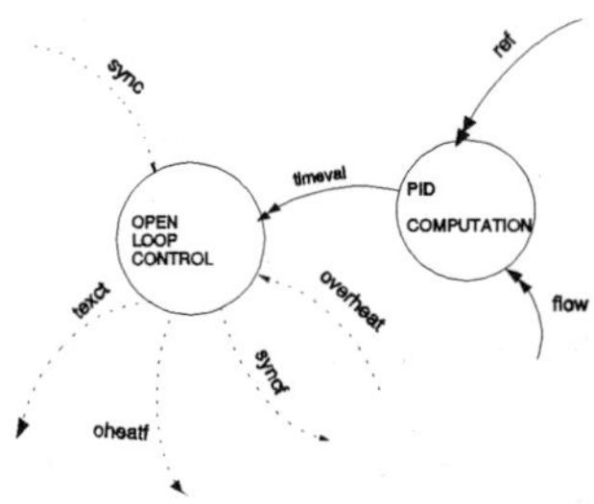

Fig. 3

frequency at what 'open loop control' reads it. Making this flow continuous, both subsystems are independent.

The data transformation 'PID computation', is not decomposed in a new transformation chart. In this case, it must be specified as a data transformation specification. In Ward/Mellor methodology, there is not a unique technique to express these specifications. Structured English, pseudocode, pre/post specifications and some specifications languages are applicable here. Since the function performed is very simple, we shall express it directly in CSP+T. This data transformation must:

•Read the actual air flow 10 times a second.
•compute the new value following the digital PID algorithm.
•output this value in *timeval*.

The CSP+T implementation is developed in the following section.

The 'open loop control' process may be decomposed again into two independent transformations:

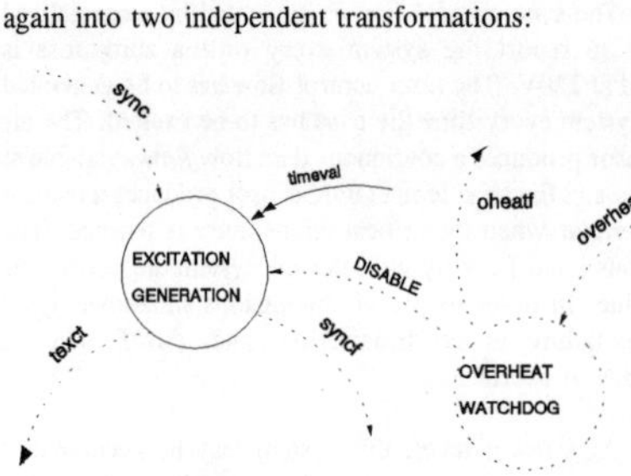

Fig. 4

The transformation 'excitation generation' performs the *texct* generation from the *sync* control flow and the *timeval* data flow, and other transformation 'overheat watchdog' monitorises temperature, disabling immediately the *texct* generation if temperature goes over the critical value (*overheat*). The transformation 'excitation generation' performs a control transformation. But, since it receives a continuous data flow, it is formally represented as a data transformation.

The transformations 'excitation generation' and 'overheat watchdog' are also lowest level transformations. This means that they do not explode into another transformation chart. 'overheat watchdog' shall be specified as a transition state diagram; and given that 'excitation generation', performs a control function, it shall be specified also this way, although it is a data transformation.

'overheat watchdog' does not usually do anything, except when overheat is reported. Then, timing restrictions apply: it has to activate *oheatf* and disable the excitation generation within 1 second. The transition state diagram (without time constraints) is:

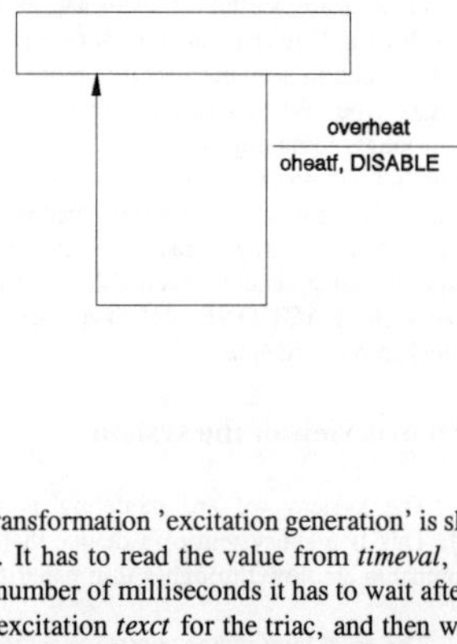

Fig. 5

The transformation 'excitation generation' is slightly more complex. It has to read the value from *timeval*, which represents the number of milliseconds it has to wait after *sync* to produce an excitation *texct* for the triac, and then wait for a *sync*. If a complete semicycle time of a 50Hz is spent and a sync is not accepted, this means that synchronization is lost. Then *syncf* has to be activated and the process has to be terminated. Otherwise, if *sync* is activated in time, it must wait the number of milliseconds read from *timeval* before to activate, and restart then getting a new *timeval* value. Severe timing restrictions apply here:

•Maximum error allowed in *texct* activation is ± 0.1 ms.
•Maximum time separation between two *sync*s is 11 ms (a half 50 Hz period plus 1ms error margin).

In the following illustration, we represent this as a transition state diagram with time constraints expressed in an informal manner.

3.4 Building the CSP+T model

Since we are following a bottom-up methodology, we shall begin by building the model for the lowest-level hierarchy charts. They are the state transition diagrams for

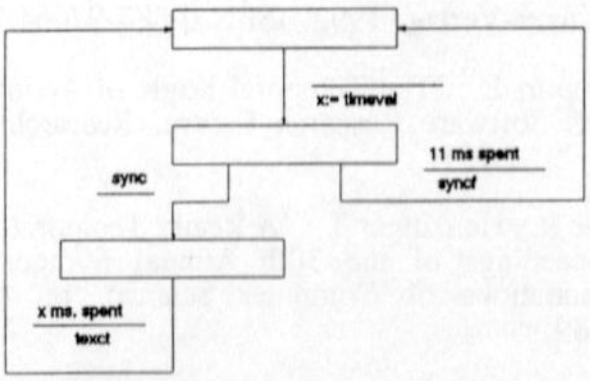

Fig. 6

'overheat watchdog' and for 'excitation generation', and the transformation specification for 'PID generation'.

Roughly speaking, the method for deriving a CSP+T model from a state transition diagram consists of associating a process to every state and events to every condition and action the following way:

Let us assume the transitions are 4-tuples (q_i, c, a, q_j), where q_i is the initial state, q_j is the target state, c is a condition and a is an action. If the time when an action or condition occurs is taken as a reference for a time constraint, we shall name that action/condition a *marker action/condition*. If the occurrence time of an action or condition is restricted to a time interval relative to another action/condition, we shall name it a *restricted action/condition*. The building rules are:

- for every transition (q_i, c, a, q_j), write a CSP+T process
$$Q_i = c \rightarrow (a \rightarrow Q_j)$$
- for every transition (q_i, λ, a, q_j) -c is null-, write a CSP+T process
$$Q_i = a \rightarrow Q_j$$
- for every transition (q_i, c, λ, q_j) -a is null-, write a CSP+T process
$$Q_i = c \rightarrow Q_j$$
- if c and/or a are *marker events*, add the marker variables mc and/or ma at Q_i definition and replace c and/or a with $a \bowtie ma$, $c \bowtie mc$.
- if c and/or a are events restricted to an interval $I(r)$, where $I(r)$ is an interval which depends on a maker variable mr that holds the time at which marker event r occurred, replace in Q_i and/or a with $I(r).c$, $I(r).a$.
- Once all processes generated by rules above have been written, rewrite them in a way such that for every process $Q_i = e_1 \rightarrow (e_2 \rightarrow Q_j)$ or $Q_i = e \rightarrow Q_j$, such that there are more than one definition for Q_j: $Q_j = e_m \rightarrow \theta_m$ … $Q_j = e_n \rightarrow \theta_n$, Q_i looks like
$$Q_i = e \rightarrow (e_m \rightarrow \theta_m \mid \ldots \mid e_n \rightarrow \theta_n).$$

This guarantees that there exist one only process $Q_0 = \theta$, where Q_0 is the process associated to the diagram initial state.

With these rules application, the process 'overheat watchdog' would be modeled as (all units in milliseconds):

$$Q_0 = overheat \bowtie ot \rightarrow (oheat \rightarrow (I_0(ot).disable \rightarrow Q_0))$$

where the $I_O(x)$ interval is defined (see temporal restrictions) as

$I_O(ot) = [ot, ot+1000]$ so we can write
$OW = Q_0$

The other chart modeled as a state transition diagram is that of 'excitation generation'. Its description would be constructed as:

$$Q_1 = timeval?x \rightarrow Q_2$$
$$Q_2 = I_1(t).sync \bowtie t \rightarrow Q_3$$
$$Q_2 = I_2(t).syncf \rightarrow Q_1$$
$$Q_3 = I_3(t,x).texct \rightarrow Q_1$$

The $I_1(t)$, $I_2(t)$ and $I_3(t,x)$ intervals are defined as:

$I_1(t) = [t, t+11]$
$I_2(t) =]t+11, \infty)$
$I_3(t,x) = [t+x-0.1, t+x+0.1]$ (0.1 = allowable error margin)

Since we have written two process definitions for Q2, we shall rewrite it as $Q_2 = I_1(t).sync \bowtie t \rightarrow Q_3 [] I_2(t).syncf \rightarrow Q_1$

Because 'excitation generation' may be disabled, we model disabling through CSP interrupt operator. In order to model disabling, we write an auxiliary process:

$DIS = disable \rightarrow STOP$ and, since there is a variable which needs initialization, we add a fictitious *inic* event and write EG as:

$$EG = (inic \bowtie t \rightarrow Q_0)\hat{}DIS$$

Since we already have written the model for both transformations which integrate the chart for 'open loop control', we can obtain the model for 'open loop control' now. The integration rule consists of making the integrating processes parallel composition, hiding within them all events not appearing in their interface (internal events). Because EG has an internal event (fictitious event *inic*, we write (see its functionallity in section 3.3):

$$OLC = OW \mid\mid EG \setminus \{inic\}$$

and now we have the model for 'open loop control'.

Following hierarchical increasing order, we have to model 'PID computation'. This is the data transformation we decided to model directly in CSP+T. To hide PID calculation complexity, we shall abstract it as a function call to *pid(valref, valflow)* which computes the new control value. The definition would be:

$$PID = inic \bowtie t \rightarrow Q_4$$
$$Q_4 = I4(t).flow?valflow \bowtie t \rightarrow Q_5$$
$$Q_5 = ref?valref \rightarrow (timeval!pid(valref, varflow) \rightarrow Q_4)$$

Now we have modeled 'open loop control' and 'PID computation'. But, since *timeval* is a continuous flow, we need to write a synchronization process to model it. This is a process:

$SYNC_0$= timeval?x→Q_5
Q_5= timeval?x→Q_5 | timeval!x→Q_5

we force a first read event to avoid output a garbage value upon a first *timeval!x*.

Now, we can integrate 'system', hiding the internal events:
SYSTEM= OLC\{disable} || PID\{inic} || $SYNC_0$

and since SYSTEM is the top level transformation, the complete model of the system is a process:

ALL=SYSTEM\{timeval}

It is not necessary to write synchronization processes for *flow* or *ref* use because we are at top hierarchy level, so we do not need to integrate this chart (this is the system context schema). If this chart were integrated as part of a bigger system, the integration process would continue recursively.

4 Conclusions

An heuristic-based method has been exposed using a sample system for building a CSP+T model from a structured design. This modeling process is far still from automatical generation, but for small systems it helps in finding a general design refinement. The full method is available from the authors on request.

Future work consists of using timed petri nets for model verification, and translating these results into object oriented methodologies.

Bibliography

[1] DeMarco T.: 'Structured Analysis and System Specification' Englewood Cliffs, N.J. Prentice Hall, 1978.

[2] Ward P.T., Mellor S.J.: 'Structured Development for Real-Time Systems' Jourdon Press Computing Series, 1985.

[3] Hatley D., Pirbhai I.: 'Strategies for Real-Time System Specification' New York, Dorset House, 1988.

[4] Gomaa H.: 'Software Development of Real-Time Systems' Communications of the ACM 29, 1986.

[5] Gomaa H.: 'A Software Design Method for Distributed Real-time Applications' The Journal of Systems and Soft. 9, pp 81-94 1989.

[6] Selic B., Gullekson G., Ward P.T.: 'Real-Time Object-Oriented Modeling' Wiley Prof. Comp. 1994. ISBN 0-471-59917-4.

[7] Manna Z., Pnueli A.: 'The Temporal Logic of Reactive and Concurrent Systems' Springer-Verlag, 1992. ISBN 0-387-97664-7

[8] Lamport L.: 'The Temporal Logic of Actions'. DEC Software Research Centre. Research Report Nº 79. 1.991.

[9] Alur R., Henzinger T.: 'A Really Temporal Logic'. Proceedings of the 30th Annual Symposium of Foundations of Computer Science, pp 164-169 1.989.

[10] Ostroff J.S.: 'A Framework for Teal-Time Discrete Event Control'. IEEE Transactions on Automatic Control, Vol. 35, Nº 4, April pp 386-397 1.990.

[11] Hoare C.A.R.: 'Communicating Sequential Processes'. Prentice Hall, 1985 ISBN 0-13-153271-5 1.985.

[12] Milner R.: 'A Calculus of Communicating Systems'. Springer-Verlag LNCS 92 1.980.

[13] ISO-8807: 'Lotos: A Formal Descritpion Technique based on The Temporal Ordering of Observational Behaviour' International Standards Organization 1988.

[14] Reed G., Roscoe A.: 'A timed model for Communicating Sequential Processes'. Automata, Languages and Programming, 13th International Colloquium Proceedings. Lecture Notes in Computer Science, vol. 226 Springer-Verlag, New York 1986.

[15] Scheider S.A.: 'An Operational Semantics For Timed CSP'. Inf. & Comp., 116(2) 1995.

[16] Zic J. J.: 'CSP+T: A formalism for Describing Real-Time Systems'. Ph. D. Thesis. Basser Dept. of Computer Science, Univ. of Sydney. 1.991.

[17] Fidge C., Zic J.: 'A Simple, Expressive Real-Time CCS'. Technical Report 94-27, Software Verification Research Centre, Department of Computer Science, The University of Queensland, December 1994.

[18] Fidge C., Zic J.: 'An expressive real-time CCS'. Second Australasian Conference on Parallel and Real-Time Systems (PART '95), Fremantle, September 28-29, 1995.

[19] Zic J., Fidge C.: 'A notion of refinement in CCS'. Proceedings of the Fourth Australasian Refinement Workshop (arw'95), April 1995, University of New South Wales, Sydney.

[20] Bucci G., Vicario E.: 'Compositional Validation of Time-Crtical Systems Using Communicatings Time Petri Nets'. IEEE Transactions on Software Engineering, Vol. 21, Nº 12. December 1.995.

[21] H. Ehrig and B. Mahr: Fundamentals of Algebraic Specification I Springer Verlag, 1985

Parsing Invalid Inputs

Rafael Corchuelo and José A. Pérez
Dep. de Lenguajes y Sistemas Informáticos
Facultad de Informática y Estadística, Universidad de Sevilla
Avda. de la Reina Mercedes s/n, 41.012, Sevilla (Spain)
Tel/Fax: +34 5 4 557139, e-mail: corchu@lsi.us.es

Abstract

This paper is devoted to explain an error–repair algorithm for the class of LR(k) parsers which require $k \leq 1$ symbols of lookahead. It locally inserts, deletes or shifts tokens at the positions where errors are detected, thus modifying the right context in order to resume parsing on valid piece of input. This method improves over the most popular ones because it does not require the user to provide additional information about repairing, it does not require precalculation of big, auxiliary tables, and it can be easily incorporated into existing LR parser generators.

Keywords: Compilers, LR(k) parsers ($k \leq 1$), automatic method, error repair, PCYACC[1].

1 Introduction

Parsing methods became quite systematic after the development of a formal theory on context–free grammars. Since then, many efficient techniques for parsing such grammars have been developed, and many of them have been used in compilers. However, in practice, the most successful are the LL(1) method, either recursive–descent or table–driven, and the LALR(1) method used by yacc and bison, two widely-used parser generators.

However, compilers are more often confronted with syntactically–invalid programs than with correct ones. Therefore, translators have to implement a strategy for dealing with such inputs, and they have been usually classified into two groups:

1. Error recovery. These techniques detect errors and their effect on a local piece of input, isolate them and resume parsing on the next valid part of the input, i.e., they tend to ignore invalid pieces of input. They have been paid much attention [ABBS83, Gra87, Gro90], but we are in no doubt that the most popular is the error production method by Aho and Ullman [AU72].

2. Error repair. This is a form of error recovery which modifies the input stream in order to make it syntactically valid. Usual modifications include deletion or insertion of symbols at the positions where errors are detected. These techniques have also been paid much attention [FL88, Dai94], and, in general, they are much more difficult to implement than simple recovery.

   Sometimes, the terms error recovery and error repair are confusing, especially to novice, but they designate quite different concepts: the goal of error recovery is to allow the parser to continue analysing the input for further errors, whereas the goal of error repair is to change the input stream so that it becomes syntactically valid.

In general, error–handling methods can be further classified into local or global. A local method recovers by manipulating the input on the right of errors, and a global method manipulates the whole input stream. Algorithms for global recovery [AP72, Kra80, AB81] were paid much attention over the last two decades, but they are usually based on Early's algorithm [Ear70] for general context–free parsing. Therefore, they are not practical because they require $O(n^3)$ time and $O(n^2)$ space. Other techniques involving the left context have been outlined, but none of them is practical. The main reason is that the left context represents information concerning a piece of input which has been already parsed and is no longer available for examination. In addition, if we take into account semantic actions, the problem becomes much more hard and difficult because in such cases changing the left context might require the algorithm to be able to revoke much of the processing already done (syntax tree constructions, symbol table manipulations, object code emitted, and so on.)

Another problem is that of repair validation. Algorithms usually produce repairs which correct the input stream and guarantee the parser to accept it, but another error could occur on the next input symbol, thus leading to an undesirable avalanche of errors. Ideally, a compiler ought to recover so thoroughly that it would generate exactly one message

[1] PCYACC is a software product of Abraxas Software.

per error and would not generate further messages due to that error. These avalanches ought to be avoided by taking care to produce adequate repairs.

This paper presents an error–repair method for the class of LR(k) parsers which require $k \leq 1$ symbols of lookahead. The paper is organised as follows: a short introduction to LR parsing is provided in section 2, section 3 presents our algorithm formally, section 4 discusses its main handicaps and shows several improvements which turn it into a practical tool, section 5 shows our yacc–based implementation and provides some experimental results. Finally, section 6 compares our proposal with other well-known techniques.

2 The LR–parsing method

In this section, we sketch the main concepts about grammars and LR parsers[2] we need to introduce our algorithm. [HU79] is a classical book on these topics.

A context–free grammar, or CFG for short, describes the syntax of a language. They are denoted by means of tuples of the form (N, T, S, P) where N denotes a set of nonterminals, T a set of terminals, S the starting symbol of the grammar, and P a set of context–free productions. The set $N \cup T$ is usually referred to as the vocabulary of the grammar. For example, $G_E = (\{E\}, \{n, +, (,)\}, E, \{E ::= n, E ::= E+n, E ::= (E)\})$ describes a very simple expression language we shall use through the following sections.

The LR–parsing method is a technique for deciding whether an input string of terminal symbols belongs to the language a CFG describes or not. This method scans the input stream from left to right in a bottom–up manner. It starts in a state where no input symbol has been analysed, and attempts to get back to the starting symbol by finding a sequence of symbols which constitute the right hand side of a production. If such a sequence is found, it is replaced with the symbol on the left hand side of that production. For example, the sequence of steps in recognising the input string $(n + n)$ is $(E + n)$, (E), and E. In spite of the fact that this method cannot deal with the whole set of CFGs, it is widely used because it is particularly suited to parsing usual programming languages, it can detect errors as soon as it is possible, and many efficient implementations are in widespread use.

The LR parsing method is formally defined by means of a deterministic transition relation $\rightarrow_{LR}$ on configurations of the form (S, I) where S denotes a stack and I is an input stream followed by the end-marker \$. S maintains stacked pairs of the form sq where s is a symbol of the vocabulary or \$, and q denotes the state the parser enters on scanning an input symbol. $\rightarrow_{LR}$ is a general relation which has to be customised for a particular grammar by means of an action function f and a go to function g whose signatures follow:

$$f : Q \times T \cup \{\$\} \rightarrow A$$
$$g : Q \times N \rightarrow Q$$

Here, $Q = \{q_0, q_1, \ldots, q_k\}$ denotes a set of parsing states and A is a set of actions, namely:

- *shift* q. This means that a pair of the form tq (where t is the current input symbol) needs to be stacked and the input pointer advanced.
- *reduce* $A ::= \alpha$. This means that $|\alpha|$ pairs need to be popped off the stack. The state q_t which appears then at the top and A are used to determine the pair we need to push in order to continue parsing. This pair is of the form Aq, where $q = g(q_t, A)$.
- *accept*. This means that the input has just been accepted.
- *error*. This means that a conflicting symbol has just been detected.

Several methods for obtaining these functions have been developed and implemented successfully. LR(0), SLR(1), LR(1) or LALR(1) are a few examples.

Given these functions, $\rightarrow_{LR}$ is formally defined by means of the following transition system *à la* Plotkin [Plo81]:

1. Shift rule (LR1):

$$\frac{f(q_m, t_1) = shift\ q}{([s_0 q_0 \ldots s_m q_m], [t_1 t_2 \ldots t_n]) \rightarrow_{LR} \rightarrow_{LR} ([s_0 q_0 \ldots s_m q_m t_1 q], [t_2 \ldots t_n])}$$

2. Reduce rule (LR2):

$$\frac{f(q_m, t_1) = reduce\ A ::= \alpha \wedge \wedge r = |\alpha| \wedge g(q_{m-r}, A) = q}{([s_0 q_0 \ldots s_m q_m], [t_1 t_2 \ldots t_n]) \rightarrow_{LR} \rightarrow_{LR} ([s_0 q_0 \ldots s_{m-r} q_{m-r} A q], [t_1 t_2 \ldots t_n])}$$

A configuration $([s_0 q_0 \ldots s_m q_m], [t_1 t_2 \ldots t_n])$ is said to be accepting if and only if $f(q_m, t_1) = accept$, it is said to be rejecting if and only if $f(q_m, t_1) = error$, and intermediate in other cases. An input stream I is said to be accepted if starting at configuration $([\$q_0], I)$ we can reach an accepting configuration by repeated application of $\rightarrow_{LR}$. If we can reach a rejecting configuration, it is obviously said to be rejected.

[2]Hereafter, LR refers to LR(k), $k \leq 1$.

For instance, table 1 shows the LALR(1) action and go to functions for grammar G_E[3]. Blank entries represent errors or undefined situations. Repeated application of $\rightarrow_{LR}$ to the initial configuration $([\$q_0], [(n+n)\$])$ yields the configurations shown in table 2.

	n	$+$	(	)	\$	E
q_0	$s\ q_2$		$s\ q_3$			q_1
q_1		$s\ q_4$			*accept*	
q_2		$r\ r1$		$r\ r1$	$r\ r1$	
q_3	$s\ q_2$		$s\ q_3$			q_5
q_4	$s\ q_6$					
q_5		$s\ q_4$		$s\ q_7$		
q_6		$r\ r2$		$r\ r2$	$r\ r2$	
q_7		$r\ r3$		$r\ r3$	$r\ r3$	

$r1 = E ::= n \quad r2 = E ::= E + n$
$r3 = E ::= (E)$

Table 1: Action and go to functions for G_E.

Stack	Input	Rule/Action
$\$q_0$	$(n+n)\$$	LR1/$s\ q_3$
$\$q_0(q_3$	$n+n)\$$	LR1/$s\ q_2$
$\$q_0(q_3nq_2$	$+n)\$$	LR2/$r\ r1$
$\$q_0(q_3Eq_5$	$+n)\$$	LR1/$s\ q_4$
$\$q_0(q_3Eq_5+q_4$	$n)\$$	LR1/$s\ q_6$
$\$q_0(q_3Eq_5+q_4nq_6$	$)\$$	LR2/$r\ r2$
$\$q_0(q_3Eq_5$	$)\$$	LR1/$s\ q_7$
$\$q_0(q_3Eq_5)q_7$	\$	LR2/$r\ r3$
$\$q_0Eq_1$	\$	-/*accept*

Table 2: Application of $\rightarrow_{LR}$ to $(n+n)\$$.

3 Our algorithm

Our concept of repair has been adapted from that proposed by Mauney [Mau83]: a repair is a sequence of insertions, deletions or shifts (with a final insertion or deletion) such that after applying it to an input stream, parsing can either continue for at least N tokens or accepts it. Our definition differs in that we take into account the possibility of incorporating input symbols into the repair. We also validate repairs, thus preventing avalanches of errors. In practice, setting $N = 3$ has been found to produce good results.

Our algorithm works on rejecting configurations, and it is formally defined as a new transition rule:

3. Repairing rule (LR3):

$$\frac{(S,I) \text{ is rejecting} \wedge R \text{ is a repair} \wedge \\ \wedge (S,I,[]) \rightarrow^*_{ER} (S',I',R)}{(S,I) \rightarrow_{LR} (S',I')}$$

This rule relies on a new transition relation, $\rightarrow_{ER}$, which shall be referred to as the error repairing transition. It works on configurations of the form (S,I,R) where R is a sequence of insertions, deletions or shifts. For example, if $R = [ins\ t, shf, del]$ is a repair, it means that we need to insert t, shift the current input symbol, and delete the next input symbol to repair the input stream.

Let $([s_0q_0 \dots s_mq_m], [t_1t_2 \dots t_n])$ be a configuration. $\rightarrow_{ER}$ behaves the following way:

1. It searches the action function for those symbols $t \neq \$$ such that $f(q_m, t) \neq error$ and creates new configurations where t is in front of t_1.

2. It also produces a new configuration where t_1 has been deleted.

3. And, if applied to an intermediate configuration, it also produces a new configuration by applying $\rightarrow_{LR}$ to it, i.e., it parses the remaining input symbols until a new error is found, an accepting configuration is reached or N symbols have been parsed.

This way[4], $\rightarrow^*_{ER}$ explores all of the possible configurations we can reach by inserting, deleting or shifting symbols. Therefore, it eventually finds a repairing configuration (S',I',R) such that parsing can continue normally on (S',I'). This configuration is guaranteed to exists because, in the worst case, we can delete the remaining input tokens and then insert suitable symbols to complete the input stream.

A formal definition for $\rightarrow_{ER}$, where $S = [s_0q_0 \dots s_mq_m]$, $I = [t_1t_2 \dots t_j \dots t_n]$, $t_n = \$$, and $R = [r_1, r_2, \dots, r_k]$, follows:

1. Insertion rule (ER1):

$$\frac{f(q_m,t_0) \neq error \wedge t_0 \neq \$ \wedge \\ \wedge (S,[t_0t_1t_2 \dots t_j \dots t_n]) \rightarrow^*_{LR} (S',I)}{(S,I,R) \rightarrow_{ER} (S',I,[r_1,r_2,\dots,r_k, ins\ t_0])}$$

2. Deletion rule (ER2):

$$\frac{n \geq 2}{(S,I,R) \rightarrow_{ER} (S,[t_2 \dots t_n],[r_1,r_2,\dots,r_k,del])}$$

3. Forward move rule (ER3):

[3]Due to space limitations, we have abbreviated *shift* to s and *reduce* to r.

[4]$\rightarrow^*_{ER}$, denotes the Kleene closure of $\rightarrow_{ER}$, i.e., its application zero, one or more times to a configuration.

$$\frac{(S,I) \rightarrow^{*}_{LR} (S',I') \wedge \\ (j = N \vee 0 < j < N \wedge f(q_r, t_{j+1}) \in F)}{(S,I,R) \rightarrow_{ER} (S',I',R')}$$

where

$$\begin{array}{lcl} F & = & \{accept, error\} \\ S' & = & [s_0 q_0 \dots s_r q_r] \\ I' & = & [t_{j+1} \dots t_n] \\ R' & = & [r_1, r_2, \dots, r_k, \underbrace{shf, \dots, shf}_{j}] \end{array}$$

In order to illustrate how our algorithm works, we shall confront it with the input string[5] $(n_1 n_2 \$$. Repeated application of $\rightarrow_{LR}$ to the initial configuration $([\$q_0], [(n_1 n_2 \$])$ yields $([\$q_0(q_3], [n_1 n_2 \$])$, $([\$q_0(q_3 n_1 q_2], [n_2 \$])$ and now an error is detected. So a new configuration of the form $([\$q_0(q_3 n_1 q_2], [n_2 \$], [])$ is built and the error rules ER1 and ER2 can be applied. They produce three new configurations:

$$\begin{array}{l} C_1 = ([\$q_0(q_3 E q_5 + q_4], [n_2 \$], [ins\ +]) \\ C_2 = ([\$q_0(q_3 E q_5) q_7], [n_2 \$], [ins\ )]) \\ C_3 = ([\$q_0(q_3 n_1 q_2], [\$], [del]) \end{array}$$

Now, we can inspect configuration C_1 and apply rule ER3[6]. This leads us to configuration $C_4 = ([\$q_0(q_3 E q_5], [\$], [ins\ +, shf])$. Here a new error is detected at state q_5, so ER1 is now the only applicable rule and it produces two new configurations:

$$\begin{array}{l} C_5 = ([\$q_0(q_3 E q_5) q_7], [\$], [ins\ +, shf, ins\ )]) \\ C_6 = ([\$q_0(q_3 E q_5 + q_4], [\$], [ins\ +, shf, ins\ +]) \end{array}$$

Now we can apply rule ER3 to C_5 so that we reach the repairing configuration $C_7 = ([\$q_0 E q_1], [\$], [ins\ +, shf, ins\ )])$. Therefore, inserting a +, shifting n_2, and then inserting a) is a repair for the incorrect input string $(n_1 n_2 \$$, and it transforms it into $(n_1 + n_2)\$$.

However, there are infinitely many other repairs. For instance, starting at configuration C_2, we can also reach a repair which transforms the erroneous input into $(n_1) + n_2 \$$, and starting at C_3 we can transform the input into $(n_1)\$$. Nevertheless, other repairs are also possible. For instance, starting at configuration C_6, we can transform our input into $(n_1 + n_2 + \dots + n_k)\$$ for an arbitrarily large k.

4 Problems and solutions

Unfortunately, the algorithm we presented in last section suffers from several problems, namely:

1. Several repairs might be possible because of the nondeterminism embodied in the definition of $\rightarrow_{ER}$. Deleting the remaining input and inserting adequate symbols is always a repair, but it should be avoided, just like repairs which involve too much modification of the input stream if another requiring less modification is possible.

2. $\rightarrow_{ER}$ generates an infinite set of configurations if the underlying language is infinite. So, before finding a suitable repair, a huge search space might be unsuccessfully explored, resulting in a waste of user and computer time. In addition, if we do not use an adequate search procedure, it might loop while traversing an infinite branch. For example, when state q_5 is on top of the stack, inserting a + and then an n is always possible, and it would produce an infinite set of configurations.

3. There is no upper limit to the number of insertions, deletions or shifts a configuration may need to became repaired.

Fortunately, they are all solvable in an efficient way. As for the first and second problems, several authors [AB81, FL88] proposed a method called least–cost recovery which associates a cost with each operation on the input stream. So each repair has an associated cost which can be used to select among several repairs and to prune the search space. If this method is used, then the least–cost repair is always chosen and the first repair $\rightarrow_{ER}$ finds can be used to prune configurations with a higher cost, i.e., a configuration is explored if and only if its cost is smaller than that of the best configuration we have found. But finding out these costs is a difficult task where intuition and experimentation are the most powerful tools we can use, and a good algorithm may became quite poor for a particular language if our choice of costs is not good enough. Therefore, we decided to use a simpler heuristic: we select that configuration which results in the smallest number of changes in the input stream. If there are several possibilities, then we let the user favour those with a greater number of insertions or deletions, and if there are still several possibilities, one of them is arbitrarily selected. Of course, if you have good costs for your grammar, you can use them.

Preventing infinite branches is easy if we traverse the search space in a breadth-first manner. However, we have not still introduced an upper limit to the number of insertions, deletions or shifts, and some errors could take an arbitrary large time to become repaired. For example, repairing an input of the form $((\cdots((n\$$ could take our computer for longer and longer periods of time as the number of mismatched parentheses increases. In practice, limiting the repairing process to a portion of the input of size S, limiting the number of insertions to N_i and the

[5] The symbol n has been indexed for the sake of clarity.

[6] Obviously, ER1 and ER2 are also applicable in this situation. However, for the sake of simplicity, we shall incorporate some intuition into our search. Later we shall present some heuristics to speed up the search process.

number of deletions to N_d (where S, N_i and N_d are constants), are good ideas. In our experiments, setting $S = 10$, $N_i = 4$ and $N_d = 3$ produced good repairs.

However, if we introduce these limits, our algorithm is no more guaranteed to find a repair because there might not be a repair of the input involving 4 insertions and 3 deletions in a fixed-sized region of 10 tokens. In that cases, reverting to an efficient secondary recovery mechanism is a good idea, and we have selected panic mode [Hol90]. This method consist of scanning down the stack until a state accepting the offending symbol is found or the stack is emptied. In the former case, parsing resumes, and in the latter the stack is restored, the offending symbol is deleted and the procedure applied again to the resulting configuration. If the input stream is emptied, then the procedure bails out, but this situation is not likely to arise in practice.

Finally, another improvement which reduces significantly the size of the search space consists of not examining for further insertions those configurations where the last operation is a deletion. For example, if state q_5 is on top of the stack and n is the current input symbol, deleting n and then inserting + or) results in the same configurations as inserting + or) and then deleting n. This way, we avoid duplication of effort in many usual cases.

5 Our implementation

We have incorporated our algorithm into PCYACC [Lan89], a widely available, efficient implementation of Johnson's yacc. We have not modified PCYACC at all, but the skeleton it uses to produce a parser. PCYACC is used to generate the LALR(1) tables we need to implement the action function and the go to function, and the skeleton we have written implements the transition relations $\rightarrow_{LR}$ and $\rightarrow_{ER}$ in a very portable way. The configurations have been implemented as abstract data types, thus allowing for easy, efficient manipulation of stacks and input streams without a significant slowdown of parsing. Of course, a hard-coded implementation would be possible and it would be more efficient, but we keep insisting that wasting a few milliseconds in calling a routine or checking an assertion, is not a real waste of time. The benefits of using abstract data types to develop programs are clear.

Although our method can be used to build parsers with error handling for any language which can be described by a yacc specification, we have concentrated performance evaluation on the programming language Pascal. There are two major reasons for this choice: firstly, the primary aim of our work is to improve error handling in practice, and the language we use to teach our students compilers is a Pascal clone, so we have a lot of syntactically-invalid programs they submit for compilation; secondly, many authors have used the Ripley/Druseikis [RD78] database of Pascal programs to evaluate the quality of their repairs, so comparisons of our scheme with others is possible for Pascal. Using the Ripley/Druseikis suite, more than 85% of repairs were very good, with only a 5% judged poor in terms of what we would have done to correct the error. The collection contains 197 errors, and the parser was reverted to panic mode only in one situation. We think that this percentage is quite acceptable for practical purposes.

The algorithm is also very efficient, in both space and time. In order to test it, we used the Ripley/Druseikis collection of 126 erroneous Pascal programs. The experiments we present were conducted using PCYACC on a 200Mhz Pentium computer, and we limited the amount of available data memory to 64 Kbytes. The parser never ran out of memory, thus proving that it does not produce a significant memory overhead. Of course, results on a particular computer are not conclusive, but they prove that our algorithm is good enough to be used in practical applications.

Figure 1 summarises the time our algorithm took to recover from 197 errors in the Ripley/Druseikis collection. As shown, more than 80% of errors were repaired in less than 0.1 seconds. Our pruning techniques were also proved very adequate, as shown in figure 2.

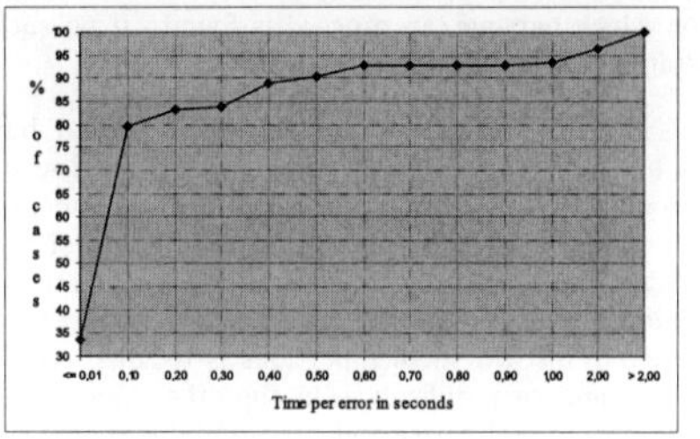

Figure 1: Time to recover from individual errors.

6 Related work

In this section, we compare our algorithm with other well-known methods. Comparisons are brief and hardly justice to the creativity and hard work of their authors. Our purpose is to give the reader a view of

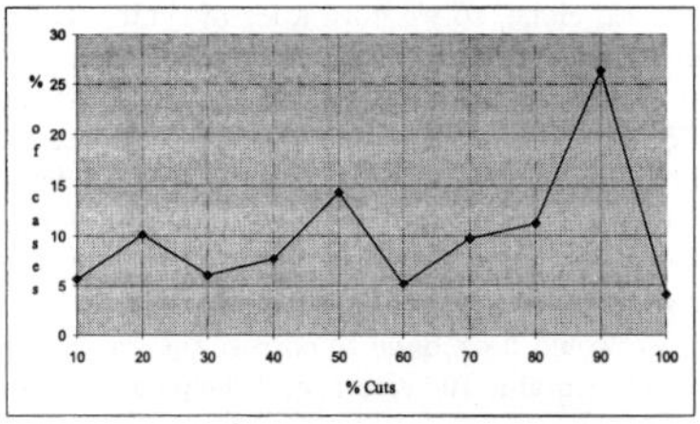

Figure 2: Prunning performance.

the spectrum of possibilities that are available, their strengths and weakness. A more general survey on these methods can be found in [Dai91].

6.1 The error production method

The error production method available in yacc was one of the very first error–recovery techniques [AU72]. It requires the user to decide what major nonterminals shall have error recovery associated with them. Usually, nonterminals representing expressions, statements, routines or declarations are selected. The user then has to add error productions of the form $A ::= \alpha\, error\, \beta$ to the grammar. They are treated as ordinary productions while producing parsing tables, but when the parser detects an error it treats the states containing error productions in a special way. It pops symbols off its stack until such a state is found, shifts the fictitious token *error*, and starts discarding input symbols until one on which parsing can proceed is found. If no such state is found, the parser bails out.

Maybe, this is the most widely–used method, but it has an important drawback: writing good error productions is a difficult task which requires in-depth knowledge of the LR–parsing procedure and of the underlying automaton. In general, this method tends to discard big portions of the input, and tuning it in order to discard smaller portions is tedious, error–prone and very difficult. On the other hand, it is efficient, in both space and time, and does not slowdown parsing of valid input programs.

6.2 Fischer and LeBlanc's method

Fischer and LeBlanc introduced a method [FL88] based upon continuation strings, i.e., strings whose concatenation to the parsed input forms a sentence of the language being parsed. When an error is detected, the method generates a set of continuation strings and selects a prefix of one of them to be inserted in front of the remaining input. Afterwards, some input symbols are deleted in order to restart parsing. The authors use a cost criterion to choose the best combination of insertions and deletions, and they validate repairs before issuing them.

This method is almost automatic, in the sense that it only requires the user to provide insert/delete costs. With careful tuning of costs and validation, the algorithm produces quite good repairs, and is not too much expensive. However, it has two major drawbacks: (1) it needs to precalculate and store a continuation action table and cost vectors used to compute continuations, and these tables can be large for typical programming languages; (2) it also requires modification of our parser generator in order to calculate these tables.

6.3 Dain's method

In [Dai94], Dain proposed a method for error recovery using minimum distance between two strings as a criterion for choosing a repair. It can be used in parsers which possess the correct prefix property, i.e., parsers such that when an error is detected, the parsed input is a prefix of some sentence of the language. The idea behind the method consist of generating a set of prefixes of continuation strings for the input already parsed, and to choose from it a string whose minimum distance from a prefix of the remaining input is minimum over the set. The continuation is used to replace part of the remaining input. Similarity between two strings is based on the number of operations we need to transform the former into the latter.

Dain generates the set of continuation strings by sequential exploration of the valid transitions at the state where an error is detected. The method requires more and more memory and time as the length of the continuation prefixes is required to be greater. Unfortunately, the whole search space has to be explored and no validation of the repairs is done. According to [Dai94], generating continuation prefixes of length 6, 7 or greater becomes unpractical because the algorithm takes long times to recover with this parameter.

The algorithm is very easy to use, but, unfortunately, it produces repairs which can lead the parser to avalanches of errors, and may consume a lot of memory and take long time to recover.

7 Conclusions

A new algorithm for error repair in a class of LR parsers has been presented and defined formally. It improves over existing ones in that it does not require the user to provide additional information (except insert/delete costs, if used), it does not require precalculation of auxiliary tables, it uses input symbols to complete repairs, and it does not require modification of existing LR parser generators.

Several improvements in the basic algorithm which result in a significantly better repairing speed have been discussed, and a yacc–based implementation and several practical results have been presented, as well. However, in practice, certain errors might require long time to become repaired, and some limits to the amount of repairing have been imposed. The algorithm is then no more guaranteed to find a repair, and it has to revert to panic mode in such cases.

In the future, we are going to incorporate it into bison, which stores parsing tables in a format which is not compatible with PCYACC. Furthermore, we would like to find an analytical model of its complexity.

References

[AB81] S. O. Anderson and R. C. Backhouse. Locally least-cost error recovery in Early's algorithm. *ACM Transactions on Programming Languages and Systems*, 3(3):318–347, July 1.981.

[ABBS83] S.O. Anderson, R.C. Backhouse, E.H. Bugge, and C.P. Stirling. An assessment of locally least-cost error recovery. *The Computer Journal*, 26(1):15–24, February 1.983.

[AJ74] A.V. Aho and S.C. Johnson. LR parsing. *ACM Computing Surveys*, 6(2):99–124, June 1.974.

[AP72] A.V. Aho and T.G. Peterson. A minimal distance error correction parser for context free languages. In *SIAM J. Computing'72*, pages 305–312, 1.972.

[AU72] A.V. Aho and J.D. Ullman. *The Theory of Parsing, Translation and Compiling*. Prentice Hall, Englewood Cliffs, New Jersey, 1.972.

[Dai91] J.A. Dain. Syntax error handling in language translation systems. Technical Report CS-RR-188, Department of Computer Science, University of Warwick, Coventry, UK, June 1.991.

[Dai94] J. A. Dain. A practical minimum distance method for syntax error handling. *Computer Languages*, 20(4):239–252, November 1.994.

[Ear70] J. Early. An efficient context–free parsing algorithm. *Communications of the ACM*, 13:94–102, 1.970.

[FL88] C.N. Fischer and R.J. LeBlanc. *Crafting a Compiler*. Benjamin/Cummings Series in Computer Science. The Benjamin/Cummings Publishing Company, Menlo Park, California, 1.988.

[Gra87] R.W. Gray. Automatic error recovery in a fast parser. In USENIX Association, editor, *Proceedings of the Summer 1987 USENIX Conference*, pages 337–346, Berkeley, CA, USA, July 1.987. USENIX.

[Gro90] J. Grosch. Efficient and comfortable error recovery in recursive descent parsers. *Structured Programming*, 11(3):129–140, 1.990.

[Hol90] A.I. Holub. *Compiler Design in C*. Prentice Hall, Englewood Cliffs, New Jersey, 1.990.

[HU79] J.E. Hopcroft and J.D. Ullman. *Introduction to Automata Theory, Languages, and Computation*. Addison–Wesley, 1.979.

[Kra80] T. Krawczyk. Error correction by mutational grammars. *Information Processing Letters*, 11(1):9–15, August 1.980.

[Lan89] Alex Lane. Generating parsers with PCYACC. *Dr. Dobb's Journal of Software Tools*, 14(6):76–77, 79, 81, 110–112, June 1.989.

[Mau83] J. Mauney. *Least–Cost Syntactic Error Repair Using Extended Right Context*. PhD thesis, University of Wisconsin-Madison, 1.983.

[Plo81] G.D. Plotkin. A structural approach to operational semantics. Technical Report DAIMI FN–19, Computer Science Department, Aarthus University, 1.981.

[RD78] G.D. Ripley and F.C. Druseikis. A statistical analysis of syntax errors. *Computer Languages*, 3(4):227–240, 1.978.

Design Re-use and IP Cores : Practical Experience

By L. TORRES[(1)] and E. PALM[(2)]

[(2)]ATMEL ES2,
Design Technology Department
Z.I. Rousset
13 106 Rousset - FRANCE
Tel: (33) 4.42.53.60.00, Fax: (33) 4.42.53.63.23, Email : epalm@es2.fr

[(1)] LIRMM-UMII
Université de Montpellier II : Sciences et Techniques du Languedoc
UMR C5506 CNRS - 161 Rue Ada 34392 Montpellier Cedex 5 FRANCE
Tel: (33) 4.67.41.85.67, Fax: (33) 4.67.41.85 .00, Email : torres@lirmm.fr

Abstract:
The top down design flow is changing, design re-use and re-usable cores provided by specific suppliers allow reducing the design cycle, but new design constraints appear and must be defined. The aim is to present different approaches for circuit design, and to define applied terms and definitions in "modern" design flow methodology.

1 – Introduction

The design re-use and IP cores concept is becoming increasingly present in the top down design flow and this changes the way for the electronic engineers works. The impact on time-to-market can be considerable, but to make it happen, new design methodologies and flows must be developed [1,2]. CAD tools must change in response to this issue. The development of parameterized procedure for synthesis and for verification environment must be considered in the future design flow [3,4,5].
Our experiences in the field of HDL supercell libraries show the difficulty to obtain the assessment of the quality of microprocessor cores and peripherals.
The purpose is to formalize the requirements and to deliver macrocells or cores with regard to the fulfillment of these requirements.
The section 2 reminds the technology and design flow evolution and the reasons to use macrocell cores. Section 3 describes different implementation styles, and constraints brought by them. Section 4 defines the quality requirements for macrocell acceptance and describes a checklist of deliverables. In section 5, two examples of qualification and porting flow of IP cores are presented.

2 - Technology and design flow evolution

The rapid advance in VLSI technology and the increase of computation time required for recent application infer large chip densities and high clock frequencies. The reason of this explosion is explained by the submicronic technology evolution. The last year, a ratio of two in speed and four in density was won, as well for standard CMOS technologies as for non-volatile memory technologies. The figure 1 summarizes this evolution.

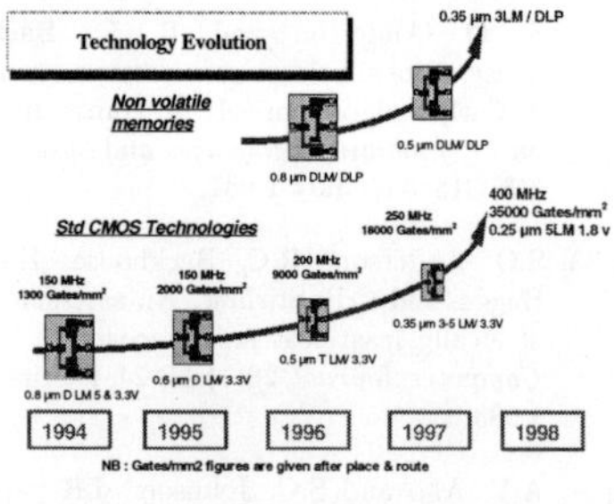

Figure 1: Standard CMOS and non-volatile technology evolution

One typical example is the advance in mobile phone applications, where the design cycle between two generations of mobile phone decreases. Due to the high density, one mobile phone system on chip solution is now possible.
To increase main parameters such as density, performance, cost and time to market, macrocells or cores are now the solution adopted by the main IC vendors. This implies a critical change in the design flow methodology and CAD tools use. A global design flow is presented in figure 2.

The design flow is moving to a higher level of abstraction, concept such as co-simulation, co-synthesis and co-design are more and more used and applied, and become an industrial reality.
Around this vocabulary re-usable cores seem to be the right way to go toward the system on chip and

[1] *This work is funded by EC (ESPRIT #20724)-TOMI : Tools for the OMI. Partners: LEDA,TI+D, TGI and UPM*

to implement the interface between the system specification and the final physical level. Moreover, software parts could be developed in concurrence with the hardware, with the ability to use CAD tool efficiently.

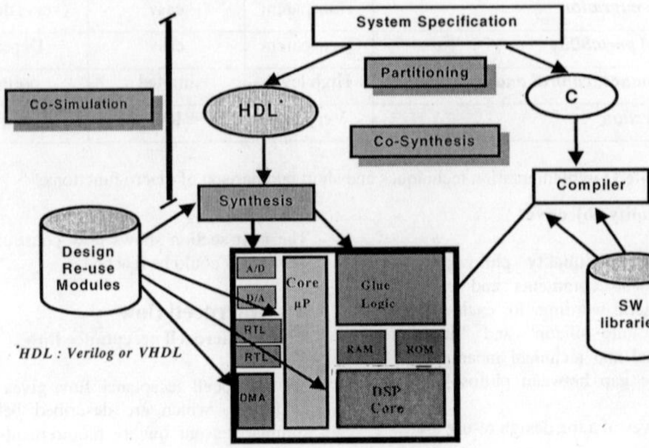

Figure 2: Global design flow

3 - Introduction to Macro or Supercells or core implementation techniques.

Macro- or Supercells or cores are pre-designed circuits that perform specific, high level functions, most of which implement a formal or a de facto markets standard VLSI function. Whereas macrocells, supercells or cores are qualitatively the same, the latter name is usually reserved for more complex programmable functions. A key advantage of pre-designed supercells is their re-usability and the resulting saving of time [6].

RTL core
An RTL description, ready for synthesis, fixes architectural and detailed functional choices but may not yet really be considered as an « implementation ». Nevertheless, in a design methodology where high level and low level design work is carried out by different groups of people it is more than worthwhile considering this case.
Indeed, the RTL description can be released to the ASIC designer who may directly synthesize for the target process, putting his own optimization criteria and constraints (speed, area, and power).

Firm core:
The most frequent implementation technique of supercells is as a schematic or structural HDL description with functional calls to elements of one or several libraries of pre-characterized cells (standard cells, data path, megacells, analog parts). Netlist or gate-level verified by logic simulation is the normal choice of implementation. For complex cores in this format, a physical placement information is given by floorplanning steps to improve the pre-layout estimated timing accuracy.

Hard core
On the other side, complex logic functions may be implemented as fixed layouts, using various design techniques such as full-custom, symbolic layout with compaction [7], data-path or other layout compilation, some standard cell routing or, most often, some kind of combination of these.
All model types, starting with C or compiled- or uncompiled HDL behavioral models, going through RTL to structural models may be envisaged.

3.1 Short comparison

The most relevant advantages and drawbacks of the implementation techniques are listed in table 1.
As opposed to hardcells, firm core implementations often may have specific simulation models, without timing parameters for layout. Nevertheless, as a requirement of re-usable supercells is to guarantee the behavior of a standard function, some of these elements can or must be attached to the macrocell. This leads then to implementation variants with various degrees of control of placement and routing. At the highest degree of control corresponds a pre-placed and routed implementation with corresponding post-layout timings; this is equivalent to the hard block implementation described above, with possible variants on the simulation model.

Criteria	RTLcore	Firm core	Hard core
Flexibility	Very high	High	Very low
Process migration	Transparent	easy	(very) difficult
Cad tool portability	Transparent	easy	Depends
Performance, control and optimization	High level	limited	optimal
IP protection	Very low	low	high

Table 1: implementation techniques and short comparison of macro functions

3.2 General quality objectives

Quality objectives and quality philosophy are described below. The comments and examples attached to the general wording, for each category "modeling", "flow into silicon" and "flow into test", give an actual and technical meaning to it, thus narrowing the gap between philosophy and reality.
The quality objectives of a the design re-use are:

Structured availability on macrocells.
All view items for of the supercell are present for each step design, in a documented and understandable manner to the user.

Predictable design effort and performance.
Pre-layout timing model as close possible to post-layout ones, the number of Place & Route iteration is well estimated, test aspects are treated early and coverage is achieved.

Safety implementation methodology.
The flow into silicon is secure and silicon will work according to simulation, the model is sufficiently sophisticated to flag abnormal situations, provided test vectors are safely adapted to the embedded cell use.

Efficiently use.
Meaning that the timing simulation is acceptable, the design flow is productive and test vectors are minimizing test time.

Flexible methodology must be proposed.
It is usable in different simulation environments, it allows for a variety of floorplan implementation according to specific needs, the predefined test vectors can be adapted easily to a variety of cell uses.

Easy of use of the proposed cores.
User can concentrate on the actual design problems.

Generic and re-usable views and flows must be developed.
Re-usability also implies portability between processes and between different design tools. Standard implementations of models will thus be preferred. Naming restrictions may have to be set up for compliance with VHDL, Verilog, various platforms, PC etc.

Maintenance and support of the supercell offer must be provided.

Intellectual Property Right (IPR),
Last, but not least, must be protected for all present parties to protect their development and their Intellectual Property Right (IPR), the original IP provider, the intermediate provider, i.e. the foundry and the end user.

The next section shows how constraints discussed previously could be reached.

4 – Macrocell flow

4.1 Macrocell acceptance flow

The macrocell acceptance flow gives the main steps to follow, which are described below. Figure 3 summarizes our quality requirements for incoming macrocell acceptance.

<u>Common deliverables:</u>

Independently of the macrocell style used, the main information expected from the supplier and necessary for good understanding is the following :

• Documentation: short and full datasheet must be provided describing the functionality, the hierarchy of the design, the pinout description, if applicable a reference to the official standard specification (IEEE, ISO, or others). Detailed information such as accurate timing, critical path, test methodology, electrical specifications are also required although not always supplied.

• Another part of the common deliverable is the quality assessment of the macrocell functionality by the supplier. The different points to check are:
- external audit if possible,
- internal cross check is made,
- testbenches covering all the functionality of the macrocell,
- the references customer,
- test chip (in FPGA or ASIC).

ATMEL ES2 has always had the responsibility of providing high quality, well-integrated and well-documented macrocell core. To obtain this quality, the different items listed before strengthen the assessment of the macrocell.

The internal cross check is a reference often required, but the level of confiance is lower than for the external audit. The access to a customer references list allows determining the experience of others ASIC designers with the macrocell database.
Test chip or/and emulation board confirms the functionality of the macrocell in a real environment.

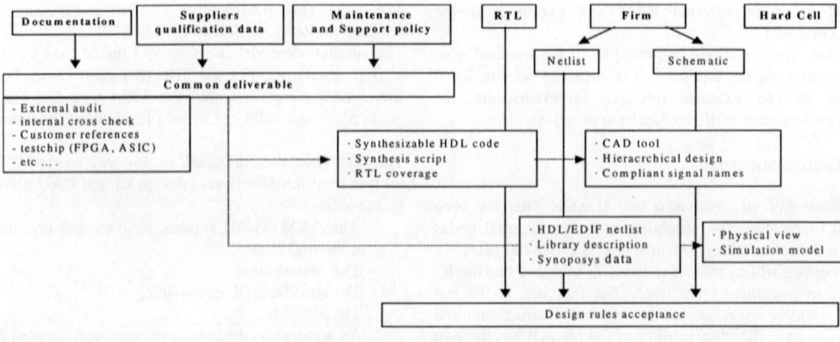

Figure 3: Design acceptance flow

A good coverage of the RTL testbenches assumes that no redundant code (in facto no redundant hardware) is present and that all the code is fully tested (statement coverage, branch and condition coverage, path coverage, variable trace coverage). This allows post-synthesis verification

• One further important item is the maintenance and the support procedure, which must be flexible and yet well defined and efficient.

All these references are needed to evaluate the HDL quality of a Supercell before supplier selection.

Firmcore flow:

In this case, in addition to the common deliverables, the hierarchical HDL or/and EDIF netlist is needed based on generic primitives. If the gate level netlist uses generic primitives, the supplier must provide the description of the library, the Synopsys library files and Synopsys scripts for retargetting.
For schematic database, we accept only Firmcores using ATMEL ES2 cells library. Most of the CAD tools are available (Cadence, Viewlogic, Mentor Graphics ... so on), but a hierarchical design documentation is required and the instance and signal names must be clearly defined and compliant with HDL language rules (Verilog/VHDL).

RTL flow:

Hierarchical HDL (VHDL/Verilog), fully synthesizable RTL code for Synopsys tool, with synthesis script and functional testbenches with highest possible coverage of RTL code.

Hard cells flow:

The physical view (layout) must be in GDS2. Transistor schematic or/and netlist for LVS (Layout Versus Schematic). With the physical view, a simulation model is required which is a functional model with accurate delay and constraints timings constraints files (SDF file):

- RTL model
- or/and a HDL behavioral model,
- C Model linked with simulators (Verilog, VHDL) with accurate SDF file.

The HDL behavioral model is preferred.

Design rules acceptance:

The goal is to determine if basic design recommendations are well respected. Any design rules violations must be explained and documented. For example it is checked if the supercell gate level netlist is a fully synchronous design, if the clock and reset bufferisations are well respected, if there are no combinational problems (no delay line, no floating bus, no tree-states ... etc).

5 – Example of validation work

The goal here is to analyze and assessment of quality of microprocessors cores from the point of view of VHDL modeling and flow into manufacturing. We are going to present two examples to show basic problems encountered: one is an 8-bit microcontroler firm core, the second is the ARM7TDMI core.

5.1 Validation on the 8032 8-bit microcontroller firmcore

The original version of the 8-bits microntroler was a HDL gate level netlist in 0.8 µm CMOS technology. To translate it to CMOS 0.5 µm TLM a retargetting through synthesis approach has been preferred, which allowed also performing optimisation trials. An optimisation run has been performed to suppress all the last problems of overload. In this way the synthesis tool (Synopys) changed only a few gate strengths and inserted buffers as necessary.

Testbenches quality:

To further assess the quality of the 8-bit microcontroler implementation, a specific set of assembler code has been used in functional gate-level simulation. This set of assembler code exercises all the instructions of the microcontroller code (more than 110 instructions). The assembler program is compiled with a cross-assembler software. Through simulation the hexadecimal code is

loaded in to an external RAM and executed by the microcontroller.
This new simulation will become part of the standard non-regression suite for this core. The idea can be developed further to use external reference programs, for the functional validation of macrocells appropriate.

Fault coverage analysis:

To obtain 98% of coverage a tree of XOR gates has been added to increase the testability of a few internal nodes (that were not testable). The area cost is about 200 gates.
The numbers of test vectors is about 73 000, and two modes of the microcontroler are used. The first one is the test mode, which exercises some internal instructions and allows to have the observability of the internal bus through the parallel port (primary input), the second one is the use of functional vectors, which allows also to validate the speed performance.

Place & Route analysis:

The Place & Route has been made with Cell3 (Cadence). To decrease clock skew, we used the clock tree synthesizer option of Cell3. The testchip was realized, tested and characterized on silicon to validate the qualification methodology describes in previous section. Figure 4 shows the testchip layout and the features.

The main steps of the porting flow in a CAD environment has been shown, from the basic netlist to the testchip validation. The described flow demonstrates the necessary effort to consider before to deliver or to use a qualified firmcore.

The full database of the 8032, ready to be deliver is composed of:

- The full and short datasheet,
- An application note describing some specific technical point,
- The 8032 CAD library,
- The testchip library,
- The Vectors file in tabular format,
- Release notes and history version.

This database is fully completed, checked and could be released to the end user.

Features :
- *Frequency : 40 Mhz*
- *Area : about 1 mm² (core)*
- *Number of transistors : 50 000*
- *Internal data bus : 8 bits*
- *Inputs/Ouputs : 44 pins*
- *Package : PQFP 44*
- *Technology CMOS 0.5µm TLM*

Figure 4: Testchip layout and features

5.2 Validation on ARM7TDMI Hard core

In this example only the main steps of the porting flow are described.

The ARM7Thumb hardcell is a 32-bits architectures RISC microcontroller core, deliver by ARM [9].
The simulation model is a C-model linked into Verilog or VHDL simulators. For the SDF (Standard Delay Format) file, a back-annotation onto the ARM's models has been put in place and validated by on silicon characterisation.

The final flow was validated, in this way an ARM7TDMI kit was built inside different design kit and CAD platforms that contains:

- The ARM7TDMI symbol, abstract and layout (only for internal use)
- The vectors files,
- The specific HDL executable,
- The SDF file,
- An application describing the technical detailed flow.

In this way, this database is fully completed, checked and could be released to end users in different CMOS processes.

6 – Conclusion

An overview of design re-use core constraints, methodology and design rules were presented in this paper. For the application of system on chip it is especially important that the behavior of library elements in a design system (possibly at customer site) and on silicon is highly predictable and that industry compatible, embedded supercells behave as the market standard product or the corresponding reference product.
The design re-use core confronts us with new challenges: ASIC or systems on a chip must be designed with quality criteria to guarantee an easy and quick integration. The qualification of the supercell or core is an essential issue, since there is a guarantee attached to the supercell for design compliance. For this reason the supercell methodology presented show us the main design rules to respect for system on chip success.

Bibliography

[1] "VSI alliance, Architecture document", version1, 1998, obtained on the web site: http://www.vsi.org.
[2] D. Gajski, F. Vahid, S. Narayan, J. Goy : "Specification and Design of Embedded Systems", Edition Prentic&Hall, 1994.
[3] T. Riesgo, Y. Torroja, E. De La Torre, J. Ulcida: "Quality Estimation of Test Vectors and Functional Validation Based on Fault and Error Models", DATE'98 Conference, pp 955-957, Paris, February 1998.
[4] S.Olcoz, L.Ayuda, I.Izaguirre, O. Penalba : "VHDL Team Work, organization units and workspace management", DATE'98 Conference, pp 297-301, Paris, February 1998.
[5] P.Camposano : "Design Planning for 0.25µm and beyond", Third Annual Synopsys European Symposium, Aachen, October 1997.
[6] B. Behnam, G. Saucier : " IP Catalog : The catalyst of worlwide IP business", IWLA'97, pp 53-59, Grenoble, December 1997.
[7] F. Moraes, R. Reis, L. Torres, M. Robert, D. Auvergne : "Pre-layout performance prediction for automatic macrocell synthesis", IEEE ISCA'96 Conference, Atlanta, May 1996.
[8] L.Torres, E. Palm : "Quality Requirement for Incoming Macrocell Acceptance" - Specification AG8 - II02 A, ATMEL ES2 internal Report.
[9] ARM company, Web site http://www.arm.uk

AND/OR Graph Based Error Diagnosis in Multi-Valued Circuits

Rolf Drechsler
Institute of Computer Science
Albert-Ludwigs-University
79110 Freiburg im Breisgau, Germany
email: drechsle@informatik.uni-freiburg.de

Alenka Žužek
Computer Systems Department
Jožef Stefan Institute
Jamova 39, 1111 Ljubljana, Slovenia
email: alenka.zuzek@ijs.si

Abstract

In this paper we present a model for diagnosis of errors in Sequential Multi-Valued Logic Networks (SMVLN). The method allows not only to detect errors in an implementation, but also identifies the fault location. In contrast to many previously presented approaches this model does not consider a specific implementation. Instead the model assumes tests based on the transition behavior of the corresponding MVL Finite State Machine (FSM) on the functional level.

We present a method for constructing a minimal cost test based on AND/OR graphs using tests with MV outcomes. The model enables encoding over two-valued circuits as well as consideration of SMVLNs. The new approach provides efficient solution even for large MVL FSMs with up to 50000 states. Experimental results for randomly generated FSMs are given that demonstrate the efficiency of our approach.

1 Introduction

Several circuit design methods for *Multi-Valued Logic* (MVL) have been proposed in the past few years [3, 6]. These new approaches raise hope in solving problems such as pin limitations and interconnection difficulties in VLSI design. But beside the synthesis step several tools are needed for supporting the designer. Nowadays, circuit design is becoming more and more complex. Thus, the error probability also increases. Since time-to-market aspects are increasingly important it is desirable to detect errors as early as possible, since this reduces the production costs. For this, several verification approaches have been suggested (see e.g. [9]). Recently, also first methods for *MVL Networks* (MVLNs) have been discussed [4]. Furthermore, it is desirable to not only detect an error, but also to diagnose it, i.e. nowadays VLSI CAD tools should support features for error detection *and* correction.

Diagnostic algorithms presented for Boolean networks so far work mainly on the gate level and thus the result is fixed to one specific design (see e.g. [12]). These approaches have the drawback that for each implementation of the function the error diagnosis has to be performed again, e.g. after resynthesis.

In this paper we consider *Sequential MVLNs* (SMVLN), i.e. MVLNs with memory elements, on a higher level of abstraction. We model a SMVLN as a *Finite State Machine* (FSM) and describe the behavior by transition relations. Only few approaches for diagnosis for sequential circuits have been proposed so far, but the algorithms work on the gate level description (see [5]). In contrast, we consider the problem of diagnosing faults on the functional level.

Recently, a new diagnosis model has been introduced in [5] that allows to model binary sequential circuits as FSM purely on the functional level. In this paper we show that this model can be extended to MVL: Given a FSM description of a SMVLN we assume with a given probability that the system is "in error", i.e. the FSM is currently in a wrong state. (Notice that the approach can be applied to the reset state, but also to each state during normal operation.) By applying test vectors it can be checked whether this assumption was correct. If a faulty state is identified it is not only determined that a fault occurred, also the faulty transition is identified. The test vectors can be derived analogously to some classical approaches to test pattern generation for sequential circuits [2].

Obviously, a critical point for the model is the construction of a "cheap" test, i.e. a test of minimal length. Due to the probablistic assumption we often have to check several different states. Thus, it is desirable to have a test sequence that checks the more likely faults first. We give an algorithm for identifying a test sequence of minimal length based on AND/OR graphs with MV outcomes. AND/OR graphs are mainly used in the area of artificial intelligence, but have recently been proposed for CAD problems [8]. In our approach we do not only use the underlying structure, but also make use of the efficient search algorithms known from artificial intelligence (see e.g. [7, 11]).

Thus, algorithms developed for sequential diagnosis on the system level [1] can be applied in the model described here. We give experimental results to demonstrate the efficiency of our approach. We randomly generate FSMs and determine a minimal test with respect to our model. In contrast to the two-valued approach, where FSMs with only 1000 states could be handled, our multi-valued approach can work with FSMs with up to 50000 states.

2 Sequential MVL Networks

In this section we introduce sequential multi-valued logic networks.

We start with the combinational case: In general, a *Multi-Valued Logic Network* (MVLN) can be modeled as a directed acyclic graph $C = (V, E)$ with some additional properties: Each vertex $v \in V$ is labeled with the name of a basic cell or with the name of a *Primary Input* (PI) or *Primary Output* (PO). The collection of basic cells available is given by a fixed library. This library contains MIN-, MAX-[1], INV- and LITERAL-gates. Of course, basic cells with arbitrary complexity, especially with an arbitrary number of inputs, are possible. There is an edge (u,v) in E from vertex u to v, iff an output pin of the cell associated to u is connected to an input pin of the cell associated to v. This means that edges contain additional information to specify the pins of the source and sink node they are connected to. Vertices have exactly one incoming edge per input pin. Nodes labeled as PI (PO) have no incoming (outcoming) edges.

To simulate the circuit, each PI may assume values from a given totally ordered finite set $P = \{0, \ldots, k-1\}$ where k denotes the number of elements of the logic. The complement (INV-gate) of a signal x is defined as $\overline{x} = (k-1) - x$. A LITERAL-gate (a,b) $(a, b \in P, 0 \leq a \leq b < k)$ has one input and one output[2]. For a given input x the behavior of such a gate is defined by:

$$f(x) = \begin{cases} k-1 & : \quad a \leq x \leq b \\ 0 & : \quad \text{otherwise} \end{cases}$$

It can then be proven that the set of gates defined above is functionally complete [10].

In a second step, we add memory elements that allow the storage of values from P. The corresponding inputs and outputs of these elements are denoted as *Secondary Inputs* (SIs) and *Secondary Outputs* (SOs) of the circuit. By adding these elements to the MVLNs as defined above we obtain *Sequential MVLNs* (SMVLNs). The resulting behavior can easily be modeled as a multi-valued FSM (analogously to the binary case).

We briefly review the main notations, that are important for the understanding in the following:

Definition 1 A finite state machine M is defined as a quintuple $M = (I, O, S, \delta, \lambda)$, where I is the input set, O is the output set and S is the set of states, $\delta : S \times I \rightarrow S$ is the next state function, and $\lambda : S \times I \rightarrow O$ is the output function.

Since we consider a gate level realization of the FSM, we have $I = P^n$, $O = P^l$ and $S = P^m$. n denotes the number of primary inputs, l denotes the number of primary outputs and m denotes the number of memory elements. The functions δ and λ are computed by a MVLN. We use the standard identification of SMVLNs and FSMs in the following, i.e. δ describes the next state behavior and λ gives the output values.

In the following we do not distinguish between a SMVLN and its corresponding FSM.

3 Diagnostic Model

In this section we describe the diagnostic model to handle SMVLN. The model is generalization of the model recently introduced in [5] for two-valued circuits. (Notice that the generalization is not trivial and the use of MVL allows the handling of much larger problem instances.) To simplify the understanding we first briefly describe the main idea:

In normal operation the SMVLN should be initialized (by a reset signal or a reset sequence). Then starting from the initial state s_0 dependent on the inputs of the circuit the FSM goes to different states.

If everything is operating correctly so far lets assume that the system is in state s_i after e steps. We now assume with some probability that the system might be in a different state, say s_j. For one given state s_i and one state s_j it is easy to compute a sequence of input assignments such that the correctness is verified evaluating test outcomes.

In the following we do not only consider one state s_j. Instead we consider a set of states s_l $(l \in \{0, \ldots, m\})$ that are the present state in the case of an error. For each state there exist tests that check whether this fault might be possible. Furthermore, for each state a different probability might be considered since depending on the correct state other parts in the FSM may be effected, e.g. as a result of state encoding.

Beside the definition of the model we want to consider in the following the problem of finding an optimal test sequence, i.e. for all assumed errors the cheapest (=shortest) test sequence should be obtained that uniquely identifies a faulty state. In the rest of this section we define our model more formally.

3.1 Model Definition

Let $M = (I, O, S, \delta, \lambda)$ be a FSM as defined above. (Notice that the FSM can be considered over Boolean values or multiple values.) Similarly to the basic model from [5] we have:

- The set of states $S = \{s_0, s_1, .., s_m\}$, where s_j denotes the *fault-free* state and s_i $(0 \leq i \leq m)$ denotes one of m potential faulty states of the system; $p = \{p_0, .., p_m\}$ is the set of *a priori* probabilities of the system being in state s_i. $T = \{t_1, .., t_n\}$ is a finite set of available test vectors and $c = \{c_1, .., c_n\}$ is the set of test costs measured in terms of length of the test e.g. determined by a test pattern generator.

The model for the general FSM is extended by:

- The set of possible outcomes of all tests T is $R = \{r_1, .., r_L\}$. (If the outcomes are used as an encoding over k-value logic, the maximal number of different outcomes is k^l, where l is the number of outputs.) The test matrix is $D = [d_{ij}]$, where d_{ij} is the outcome from set R of test t_j if the FSM is in the state s_i. (It is possible to extend the model to include test unreliabilities [1], that can interpret *Don't Cares*.)

Based on these definitions the identification of an efficient test can be formulated as follows:

Find a test sequence of minimal average cost that is able to isolate each state using the test set T.

A test sequence that unambiguously identifies each state exists iff no two rows of the test matrix are identical and furthermore the number of tests (in the case of L-ary tests) is $n > log_L(m+1)$.

[1] In the binary case Min- and MAX-gates correspond to AND- and OR-gates, respectively.

[2] These LITERAL-gates are also called *window literals.*

4 Construction of Optimal Test by AND/OR Graphs

In this section we give an algorithm for the solution of the test sequencing problem described above based on MV AND/OR graphs. For the exact and heuristic solution we use algorithms from artificial intelligence.

The algorithms have been implemented for MV AND/OR graphs in a sequential diagnosis system for diagnosis on the system level (see also [1]). The user can choose among different algorithms that compute the diagnostic decision trees. These algorithms require different amounts of time and space and provide different solution quality.

It is well known that the construction of the optimal decision tree is an NP-hard problem, therefore for large SMVLNs it is necessary to explore heuristic approaches for guiding the AND/OR graph search. The existing solution approaches can mainly be categorized into two different groups:

Heuristic algorithms: A class of sub-optimal algorithms provides a trade-off between optimality and computational complexity. They perform a local step-by-step optimization using problem-domain knowledge. The diagnostic tool described in this paper offers two such algorithms: *separation heuristic* and *information heuristic* [7].

Exact algorithms: Also the exact approaches use problem-domain knowledge in the form of a *Heuristic Evaluation Function* (HEF), to avoid enumerating the entire set of potential solution trees. The HEF is an easily computable heuristic estimate $h(x)$ of the optimal cost-to-go, from any node of ambiguity subset to the goal nodes of zero ambiguity.

The implementation of the optimal AND/OR graph search techniques in [1] corresponds to algorithm AO^* [11] with extension of multi-outcome tests. The algorithm AO^* is an ordered best-first search algorithm; it expands only the node of the search graph that offers the most promising way on the basis of two heuristics: (i) Huffman code-based heuristics (HEF_1) and (ii) entropy-based heuristics (HEF_2). Using these, AO^* is guaranteed to find an optimal solution. (For detalis see [11].) Experiments for randomly generated FSM in [5] showed that HEF_2 is poor in comparison to HEF_1. The latter requires fewer nodes and backtracks to compute the optimal diagnostic tree. For this, we restrict ourselves to HEF_1 for our experimental studies in the following.

The resulting test sequence can be described by a MV AND/OR decision tree, with OR nodes containing current candidate system states, and by AND nodes denoting tests for partitioning the set of candidate system states. The leaves correspond to the individual failure state with no ambiguity, and the average length of the tree represents the expected test cost.

Before we have a closer look at larger examples we explain the MV AND/OR graph construction for a small SMVLN in detail:

Example 1 We consider a randomly generated FSM over 8-valued logic $P = \{0, .., 7\}$. We assume a set of eight states. A set of five tests is available for checking the FSM. For simplicity all test lengths equal one and

System states	Tests t_1	t_2	t_3	t_4	t_5	Probabilities p_i
s_0	0	0	0	0	0	0.343
s_1	5	1	2	7	2	0.088
s_2	0	7	5	3	6	0.071
s_3	1	6	4	4	2	0.095
s_4	2	0	5	7	1	0.105
s_5	6	2	7	1	7	0.119
s_6	3	2	7	1	5	0.084
s_7	0	6	0	7	6	0.095

Table 1: Test matrix and fault probabilities

the output set $O = P^1$. Thus, we have eight different outcome for given tests. The *a priori* probabilities of the FSM being in one of the states along with the test matrix is given in Table 1. In the test matrix of dimension 8×5 each test is represented by an outcome column vector. E.g. test t_5 will have outcome 6 if the system is in the state s_2 or s_6.

The optimal solution for the problem from Table 1 is obtained by applying the algorithm AO^* using HEF_1. The resulting minimal length J^* is given by: $J^* = [p_3 + p_1] \cdot (c_5 + c_1) + [p_7 + p_2] \cdot (c_5 + c_2) + [p_0 + p_4 + p_6 + p_5] \cdot c_5 = 1.349$.

When the diagnostic tree is used, first test t_5 is applied. If the result is 1, the system is in s_4.

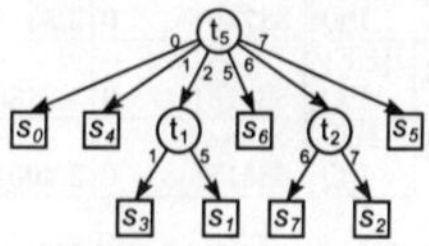

Figure 1: Optimal diagnostic tree for Example 1

5 Experimental Results

In this section we present experimental results for randomly generated FSMs. Similar as in [5], the test problems were generated using a uniform distribution. For simplicity all tests have cost one. (A different choice of these values gives similar results.) For all examples the number of tests was chosen around 4× the minimal number of tests required (see Section 3.1). All experiments have been carried out on an *HP 9000-J210* workstation with *CPU PA-7200* and 160 MByte of main memory. (All runtimes are given in CPU seconds, minutes and hours.)

In [5] the experiments showed that exact algorithms using Boolean values can be reasonably applied only for small examples up to 100 states. We showed that the number of backtracks along with the number of generated nodes measures the quality of heuristic evaluation function used by the exact algorithms. The experiments reflected that (HEF_2) is poor in comparison to (HEF_1). Using heuristic algorithms we were able to consider FSMs with up to 1000 states.

In the following we study the behavior of the heuristic algorithm and exact algorithm, with respect to runtime and space complexity.

States	Out-comes	Algo-rithm	Nodes gen.	Back-tracks	Cost	CPU time
100	16	HEF_1	124	220	2.14	0.4
		PQ	136	0	2.38	0.1
250	16	HEF_1	616	84	2.4423	2.9
		PQ	358	0	2.7735	0.5
500	16	HEF_1	1025	297	2.4520	9.1
		PQ	697	0	2.7380	1.0
750	16	HEF_1	2057	112	2.8966	15.5
		PQ	1115	0	3.2705	1.9
1000	32	HEF_1	2400	1144	2.4921	21.4
		PQ	1351	0	2.7314	3.6
2500	32	HEF_1	7090	225	2.8698	1 : 48.1
		PQ	3585	0	3.1517	13.1
5000	32	HEF_1	12791	512	2.9812	4 : 47.9
		PQ	6971	0	3.3819	25.6
7500	32	HEF_1	32546	2938	3.0090	16 : 39.1
		PQ	10119	0	3.4385	40.4
10000	64	HEF_1	30877	512	2.8787	20 : 57.2
		PQ	13831	0	3.0752	1 : 54.9
15000	64	HEF_1	41330	513	2.9574	31 : 57.4
		PQ	20384	0	3.1929	2 : 58.4
20000	64	HEF_1	52784	577	2.9838	1 : 03 : 00.3
		PQ	26717	0	3.2704	4 : 51.6
25000	64	HEF_1	55775	549	2.9838	1 : 16 : 23.5
		PQ	32476	0	3.2824	5 : 00.4
30000	64	HEF_1	–	–	–	–
		PQ	38749	0	3.3317	6 : 43.9
40000	64	HEF_1	–	–	–	–
		PQ	50478	0	3.3480	11 : 10.3
50000	64	HEF_1	–	–	–	–
		PQ	63313	0	3.4004	21 : 13.7

Table 2: Performance of exact and heuristic algorithm

The results are shown in Table 2. A "-" symbolizes that the algorithm run out of space computing the complete diagnostic tree. We applied two different search algorithms presented in the previous section for each example. PQ and HEF_1 denote the information-heuristic algorithm and AO^* with Huffman code-based heuristics, respectively. The second column shows the maximal number of different outcomes of tests. The fourth column displays the number of nodes generated by the search algorithms. This directly reflects the space requirements of the two methods. As can be seen the heuristic algorithm uses around a factor of two less memory. Therefore it was possible to apply the heuristic method for FSMs with up to 50000 states for chosen number of outcomes, while AO^* with HEF_1 run out of space for FSMs larger than 25000 states.

The number of backtracks is given in the next column. The process of backtracking is performed only by exact algorithms and the consequences is also reflected in runtimes given in the last column. Note that the heuristic method took much less time to compute a solution. But the difference measured in the quality of the result of both methods is evident: The average cost of diagnostic tree computed by heuristic algorithm exceeded the outcome of the optimal average cost obtained by exact algorithms up to 15%. (The difference even increases if the examples are generated with larger number of tests.)

The diagnostic modeling presented in this paper with additional concept of multi-valued logic is considerably more profitable than two-valued, because the algorithms efficiently use maximal diagnostic resolution given by each test. Due to this, in comparison to the two-valued approach from [5], we can handle more realistic SMVLNs with a large number of states with respect to time and space complexity.

6 Conclusions

We presented a model for error diagnosis in sequential multi-valued logic networks modeled as FSMs. The model introduced in [5] has been extended by multi-valued outcomes tests. We used an AND/OR graph based method to determine a test with minimal cost by solving the test sequencing problem. Based on the MV encoding much larger problem instances could be handled, i.e. our experiments showed that over MV encodings solutions for FSMs with up to 50000 states can be computed, while the two-valued approach failed for more than 1000 states.

References

[1] A. Biasizzo, A. Žužek, and F. Novak. Sequential diagnosis tool. Proc. *Int'l Work. on Sys.Test & Diagnosis*,pp. 3–12, 1998.

[2] X. Chen and M. Bushnell. *Efficient Branch and Bound Search with Application to Computer Aided Design.* Kluwer Academic Publisher, 1996.

[3] K.W. Current and M.E. Hurlsten. A bi-directional current-mode cmos multiple-valued logic memory circuit. Proc. *Int'l Symp. on multi-valued Logic*, pp. 196–202, 1991.

[4] R. Drechsler. Verification of multi-valued logic networks. Proc. *Int'l Symp. on multi-valued Logic*, pp. 10–15, 1996.

[5] R. Drechsler and A. Žužek. Efficient functional diagnosis for synchronous sequential circuits based on AND/OR graphs. Proc. *Int'l Symposium on IC Technologies, Systems and Applications*, pp. 312–315, 1997.

[6] D. Etiemble. On the performance of multivalued integrated circuits: Past, present and future. Proc. *Int'l Symp. on multi-valued Logic*, pp. 156–164, 1992.

[7] E.J. Kletsky. An application of the information theory approach to failure diagnosis. *IRE Trans. on Reliability and Quality Control*, 9:29–39, 1960.

[8] R. Drechsler W. Kunz, D. Stoffel, and A. Žužek. Decision diagrams and AND/OR graphs for design automation problems. Proc. *International Conference on Information, Communication & Signal Processing*, pp. 246–250, 1997.

[9] K.L. McMillan. *Symbolic Model Checking.* Kluwer Academic Publisher, 1993.

[10] J.C. Muzio and T.C. Wesselkamper. *Multiple-Valued Switching Theory.* Adam Hilger, Bristol and Boston, 1986.

[11] K.R. Pattipati and M.G. Alexandridis. Application of heuristic search and information theory to sequential fault diagnosis. *IEEE Trans. on Systems, Man, and Cybernetics*, 20:872–887, 1990.

[12] A. Wahba and D. Borrione. A method for automatic design error location and correction in combinational logic circuits. *Jour. of Electronic Testing: Theory and Applications*, 8:113–127, 1996.

A FRAMEWORK FOR ENCAPSULATING BEST BUSINESS PRACTICES FOR ELECTRICITY SUPPLY INDUSTRY INTO GENERIC PATTERNS

C. Rolland*, G. Grosz*, P. Loucopoulos, S. Nurcan***

* Centre de Recherche en Informatique
Université Paris 1 - Panthéon - Sorbonne
90, rue de Tolbiac 75013 Paris, France
{rolland, grosz, nurcan}@univ-paris1.fr

** Department of Computation, UMIST
P.O. Box 88, Manchester M601QD, U.K.
pl@sna.co.umist.ac.uk

Abstract *: This work presents a Web based tool implementing a framework that is being used to fulfil one of the main objectives of the ESPRIT project ELEKTRA[1] : the discovery of the generalised patterns of change management for re-using them in similar settings in other electricity companies. The term 'pattern' refers to knowledge that may be repeatable from one situation to another, and shareable by different users. The issues of defining (a) the structure of a knowledge repository of good business practices for managing change in organisations and (b) a Web based tool for providing a means for retrieving and accessing this knowledge are developed in this paper. The tool allows to introduce, in a company involved in a change management, a common repository of reusable knowledge easily accessible and customisable by the stakeholders.*

Keywords *: Generic Pattern, Reuse Process, Change process, WWW*

1. Introduction

Recent years have witnessed an increasing interest in the use of patterns within the software development community and in particular by those advocating object-oriented approaches and re-use (Coad, 1992), (Beck, 1997), (Buschmann, *et al* 1996), (Coplien, Schmidt, 1995), (Gamma *et al*, 1994), (Vlissides *et al*, 1996), (Hay, 1996), (Fowler, 1997), (Rolland, Plihon, 1996), (Harmsen *et al*, 1994). These efforts have in common their attempt to exploit knowledge about *best practice* in some domain. Best practice knowledge is constructed in 'patterns' that are subsequently used as the starting point in the domain activities. Different studies have shown that it seems possible that generic knowledge can be exhibited for the modelling of change in the *Electricity Supply Industry* (ESI) sector, e.g. (Yajima,1997).

In ELEKTRA, we propose to describe the reusable knowledge encapsulated in patterns in terms of the EKD (Enterprise Knowledge Development) methodology concepts (i.e. enterprise goals, enterprise processes etc.). EKD is an approach that provides a systematic and controlled way of analysing, understanding, developing and documenting an enterprise and its components by using Enterprise Modelling (Loucopoulos *et al*, 1997), (Bubenko et al. 1997), (Rolland *et al*, 1997a), (Rolland et al, 1997b), (Rolland *et al*, 1998a). In the context of this project, the patterns will be specific to the ESI sector and will not be applicable to any other sector. The framework however, for organising these patterns, is independent of any application and could potentially be used in other domains. The rationale is that all concepts defined and used within this framework are based on the EKD method which is totally domain independent.

An important aspect of the ELEKTRA project concerns the dissemination of best business practices within the ESI sector companies. To this end, we encapsulate the knowledge describing the best business practices within a pattern repository and propose a tool called 'Electronic Guide Book' that allows to retrieve and access this knowledge over the Web. The 'Electronic Guide Book' can either be used in a standalone manner or in connection with other tools supporting the change management. In the latter case, the 'Electronic Guide Book' can be seen as an on-line powerful and intelligent help that can be activated by an EKD engineer at any time while using other change management support tools. In the former case, the 'Electronic Guide Book', that indeed can be used through the Internet, acts as an hypertext encyclopaedia that allows any EKD engineer to gain knowledge on the change management, as well as on the way these knowledge shall be re-used.

Section 2 discusses the notion of a pattern, proposes a pattern template and the corresponding HTML representation. Section 3 describes the structure of the pattern repository allowing an easy navigation and retrieval of patterns and illustrates the HTML representation of the indexing hierarchy used in the pattern repository. Section 4 describes the process of retrieving generic patterns through HTML hyper-links navigation and presents the 'Electronic Guide Book' through a scenario of use.

2. The notion of a pattern and its HTML representation

There are three key ideas concerning patterns that can be found in the literature (Coad *et al*, 1996), (Alexander *et al*, 1977), (Alexander, 1979), (Gamma *et al*, 1994). First is the fact that a pattern relates a *problem* to a *solution* to this problem. The second point draws our attention to the fact that what is important in pattern identification is not so much to recognise the commonalties among candidate elements but to identify the discriminant criteria. Finally, the genericity may be at different levels: (i) A pattern can be used for different applications in a specific domain repeatable in different organisations/settings (application independent but

[1] This work is partially supported by the ESPRIT project ELEKTRA (N°22927) funded the by the EC in the Framework IV programme.

domain specific). Example: generic patterns for ESI sector ; (ii) A pattern can be used in different domains (domain independent pattern). Example: generic patterns for goal refinement. For the pattern to be generic and reusable, the pattern structure should be able to state (a) that a given problem exists within a stated range of applications and (b) that in the given context, a given solution solves the given problem.

2.1. The pattern template

The pattern 'template' is a predetermined structure according to which the generic knowledge has to be represented. Clearly, there is a need to make a difference between the *reusable knowledge* contained in a pattern and its *description*. The former is represented using an EKD model fragment in our framework. We call it the *body* of the pattern. The latter, namely *descriptor*, aims to describe the context in which the body of the pattern can be reused (situation) and the problem it can resolve (usage intention). Therefore, a pattern is completely defined with its descriptor and its body (see figure 1).

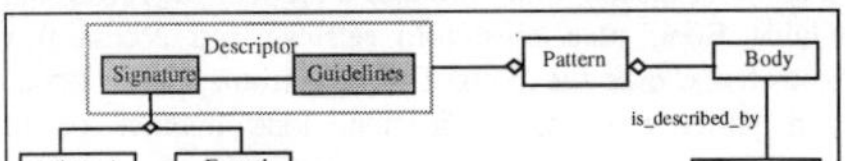

Figure 1 - The pattern template

2.1.1. The body

We propose a refinement of the conceptual modelling approach by using the EKD concepts to describe the body of a pattern (Loucopoulos *et al*, 1997). The structuring framework for the generic patterns is domain independent, the only dependency being in its use of EKD descriptions. Figure 8 shows the body of a pattern describing dependencies between roles involved in the electricity consumption measurement.

2.1.2. The descriptor

Our proposal is to have a pattern descriptor defined as an aggregation of a signature and guidelines (figure 1). The former describes in which situation and for which problem it is relevant to reuse the body of the pattern whereas the latter are recommendations on the way the body of a pattern can be reused. A *signature* aims at describing the characteristics of a pattern, when it can be used, why, etc.. It has a formal part and an informal part as shown in figure 1. As we will develop in sections 3 and 4, *formal signatures* are used in the reuse process in order to retrieve patterns which are appropriate for a given situation having a given usage intention in mind. Some additional requirements for describing patterns are encapsulated in the *informal signature*. We have chosen to combine a *faceted approach* with a *contextual approach* (Grosz *et al.*,1997) to describe the *formal signature* which is therefore composed of a *situation* part -the context- and a *usage intention* part -the problem.

- The *situation* precisely describes the applicability conditions which must hold for reusing the generic pattern. It comprises two facets :
  - The *type*: the type of the pattern (Actor/Role, Role/Activity, Object, Rule, Goal, Change process patterns) (see section 2.2).
  - The *domain*: it describes the activity domain for which the pattern is applicable to (Customer servicing, restructuring, etc.).
- The *usage intention* expresses the goal to be achieved by the use of the generic pattern. It has two facets:
  - A *verb* (invoice, change, ...), and
  - A *set of parameters* described as a set of sub-facets: source, target and manner. Each parameter plays a different role with respect to the verb, some of them having sub-types (e.g. target has two sub types : object and result).
  - The *target* designates what is affected by the usage intention. We distinguish two types of targets: objects and results. As opposed to *objects*, the *results* are affected by the usage intention. They do not exist prior to the usage intention.
    Measure $_{\text{verb}}$ *(electricity consumption)* $_{\text{result}}$
  - The *source* identifies the origin of what is affected by the usage intention.
    Measure $_{\text{verb}}$ *(electricity consumption)* $_{\text{result}}$ *(from meter reading)* $_{\text{source}}$
  - The *manner* parameter is used to express in which way the usage intention is achieved.
    Measure $_{\text{verb}}$ *(electricity consumption)* $_{\text{result}}$ *(from meter reading)* $_{\text{source}}$ *(automatically)* $_{\text{manner}}$

2.2. Pattern typology

2.2.1. Product patterns

Since we have chosen to represent the bodies of patterns as EKD models fragments, we adopted the EKD typology of models for patterns. Therefore, the body of a pattern can be either a goal pattern represented with the EKD goal model concepts or a business process pattern represented with the EKD business process model concepts. A business process pattern is specialised in turn into actor/role pattern, role/activity pattern, object pattern and rule pattern. All these patterns describe ESI structural models and are referred to as *product patterns.* However, EKD addresses both the description of the business processes (and their associated goals) and the description of the change process itself. The former leads to product patterns whereas the latter introduces the needs for another type of pattern called, *change process patterns.*

2.2.2. Change process patterns

Our proposal is to use an extended goal model as a means to represent the body of generic change process fragments. Following the semantics of an EKD goal graph, a change process pattern is represented as a goal hierarchy using the AND, OR and AND/OR connectors. In order not to confuse between company business goals and the company change goals, we decide to rename for the latter the concept of 'goal' as 'change intention'. The leaves of this goal hierarchy are called operationalisable change intentions which correspond to intentions that do not require any further decomposition, it means that their realisation can be expressed in terms of one or several product patterns (i.e. a set of EKD models).

2.3. The HTML representation of a pattern

Figure 8 shows an example of an HTML page representing a pattern with respect to our pattern template. The body of the pattern which is an actor-role model is designed in such a way that, according to our belief, it is applicable to all ESI organisations dealing with the problem of measuring electricity consumption.

3. The pattern repository structure and its HTML representation

Composed patterns are meaningful. The first possibility is to define a pattern as an aggregation of other patterns, i.e. to compose complex patterns using more elementary patterns. The drawback of this solution is that it hinders a flexible reuse process. A more flexible solution consists of (i) keeping patterns at the knowledge level in the repository, and (ii) expressing their possible composition through an indexing hierarchy (meta-knowledge) level. This is the option that we propose (Rolland *et al.*, 1998b).

3.1. Relationships among patterns and their formal signatures

Since a formal signature is intentional, the proposal is to express the relationships among patterns using intention connectors. We identify three types of connectors, AND, OR (exclusive OR) and AND/OR (inclusive OR). This way of expressing the possible combinations of patterns leads to a hierarchical representation of the domain knowledge which is intentional as it is expressed with domain goals (i.e. usage intentions of formal signatures). Our belief is that this representation eases the retrieval of relevant patterns for a given situation having a given usage intention in mind.

3.2. Repository organisation

The repository of the ESI patterns is composed of : (i) the patterns part (defined at the knowledge level), and (ii) the indexing hierarchy part (defined at the meta-knowledge level). The patterns part represents the ESI knowledge for a single problem. The descriptor of the pattern is an expression of the problem whereas the body is the reusable solution provided to this problem. The indexing hierarchy part describes this knowledge in terms of the ESI domain goals (usage intentions) that can be fulfilled by reusing the patterns with the corresponding applicability situations. The hierarchical organisation of the pattern formal signatures helps structuring the problem in intentional terms that are (or should be) easily understood by the domain experts because they describes their context of work and their problem.

In figure 2, the top level usage intentions figures out what is the overall objective of the ELEKTRA project, namely to 'Manage change in the ESI sector' and tells us that there are two problems in managing the change which are supported by pattern based solutions in the repository: 'Understand ESI models' and 'Manage the change process'. While browsing through the indexing hierarchy associated to the former usage intention, the possible paths lead to a set of product patterns, whereas while browsing through the hierarchy associated to the latter, the possible paths lead to change process patterns. The leaves of these change process patterns make explicit references to product patterns.

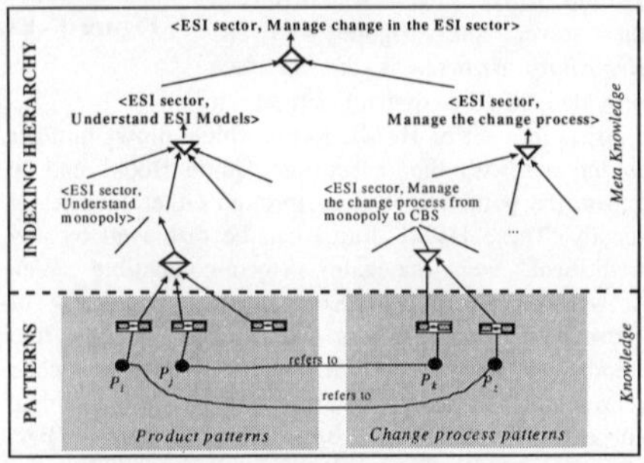

Figure 2 - The pattern repository structure

3.3. The HTML representation of the pattern repository

Figure 3 shows examples of two HTML pages representing respectively an AND-ed node (background window) and an AND/OR-ed node (foreground window) in the indexing hierarchy.

4. The 'Electronic Guide Book' for retrieving patterns

As illustrated in figure 4, the process of reusing a generic pattern is a three steps process which consists of : (1) the retrieval and selection of the generic patterns from the repository of generic patterns, (2) the storage of the selected generic patterns in the work space, and (3) the customisation/expansion/refinement of the generic pattern. The 'Electronic Guide Book' that is described in this section handles the first step of this process and proposes browsing and querying facilities tailored to the pattern repository.

4.1. The architecture of the 'Electronic Guide Book'

Our approach emphasises the integration of Web based and hypertext based technologies for facilitating the reuse of generic knowledge. The hypertext technology helps users by streamlining access to and providing rich navigational features around related information, thereby increasing user comprehension of information and its context (Bieber, 1995). Used in the context of reuse, hypertext facilities permit to access to generic knowledge in a simple manner, providing different levels of details, allowing to combine textual descriptions along with graphical ones. The Web based technology offers accessibility, portability and eases the distribution. There are many potential approaches for integrating Web servers with knowledge bases. Our approach uses conjointly traditional CGI, applets and client scripting written as Visual basic scripts and Java scripts.

The 'Electronic Guide Book' is composed of two inter-related modules: the *Repository Browser* which runs at the client site and *Pattern Search Engine* which runs at the server site (figure 4). The *Repository Browser* is the interface provided to the domain expert, it consists in a set of HTML forms which allows him/her to interact with the 'Electronic Guide Book' and to access the pattern repository through either Internet or locally. These HTML forms can be displayed by any traditional web navigator (form-compatible Web browser), such as Microsoft Internet Explorer® or Netscape®, among others. We embed, directly into Repository Browser HTML forms, VBScript® code represented as standard ASCII text. VBscript is a simple subset of Microsoft Visual Basic for Applications (VBA) (Brophy, 1996). This code runs entirely within the Repository Browser at the client site and aims at helping CGI applications by pre-processing user's actions and information entered through the HTML forms. Some client-side applications, for instance a graph browser written in the Java language, are downloaded through the network from the Web server. The *Patterns Search Engine* is composed of a Web server, a set of CGI applications, and the pattern. repository. It runs at the server site. The Web server is responsible for all exchanges between the client(s) and CGI applications (arrows labelled 1.1 and 1.2 in figure 4) that run on the server. It receives request from client(s) in the form of formal signatures elements and sends the resulting Web pages that are generated "on the fly" from the pattern repository (arrows labelled 1.1 and 1.6 in figure 4). We chose to use the software called "Website ®" for the development of our Web server. Website ® provides a fully graphical "property sheet" administration tool that makes web server construction and configuration very easy to use, it also offers an integrated toolkit for developing CGI applications using Visual Basic. The Web Browser and Server communicate each other by using the Hypertext Transfer Protocol (HTTP). The interactions between the pattern repository and the Web server are handled by a set of Common Gateway Interface (CGI) applications. The CGI applications are organised in two modules: the Dynamic Form Processing module and the Query module. The first one transforms repository output data, embeds them into HTML forms (arrows labelled 1.4 and 1.5 in figure 4) and returns them to the Web Server. The second module manages all queries that emanate from the domain expert. This module interacts directly with the pattern repository by transforming users queries into SQL queries (see arrows 1.2 and 1.3 in fig. 4). The pattern repository is implemented with Microsoft Access ® RDBMS. It is structured according to the formalism presented in section 2. Thank to the multimedia ability of Microsoft Access, images are directly stored into the database.

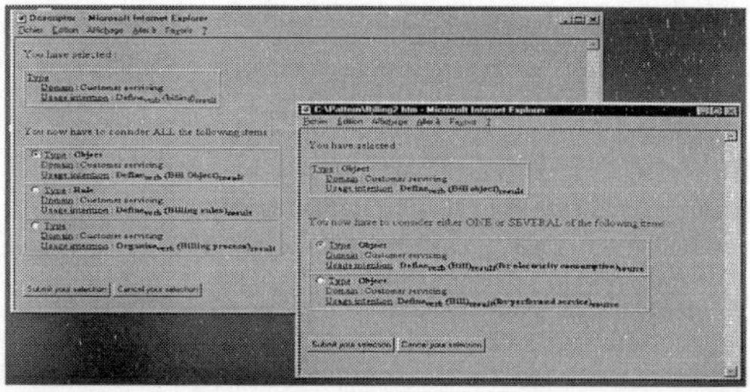

Figure 3 - Examples of HTML pages representing the indexing hierarchy

4.2. Using the 'Electronic Guide Book'

We shall now detail the different windows that the domain expert goes through while using the 'Electronic Guide Book'. For the sake of readability, the presentation follows an imaginary scenario of use. The background window of figure 5 presents the home page of the 'Electronic Guide Book'. The main suggestion is

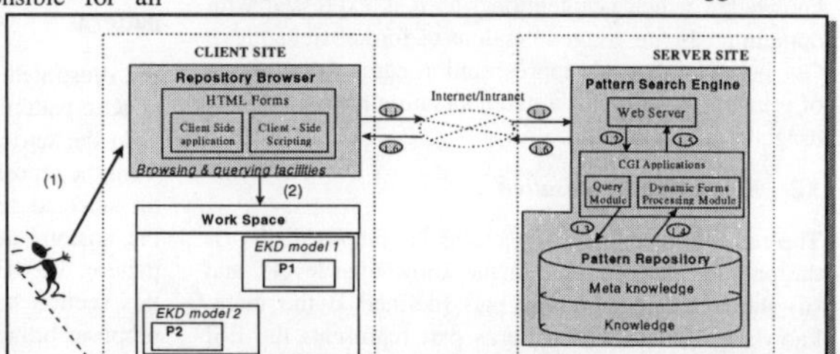

Figure 4 - Global Architecture of the 'Electronic Guide Book'

to get the list of domain for which generic patterns have been defined within the repository. After the domain expert had clicked on the button, a query is sent to the Patterns Search Engine to retrieve the list of domains for which patterns have been defined. The result is sent to the Repository Browser which displays the foreground window of figure 5. The domain expert has now to select the one he/she has interest in. Then, as shown in the background window of figure 6, two options for querying or browsing the pattern repository are proposed. Assume the domain expert selects the query facility,

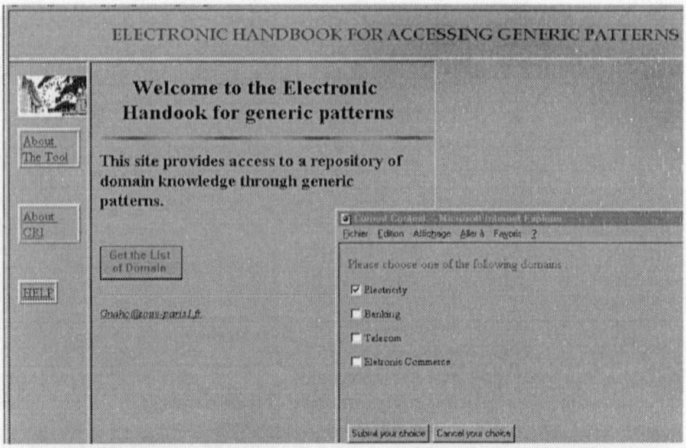

Figure 5 - The home page of the 'Electronic Guide Book'

he/she is now asked to fill a form based on the formal signature structure. For each field, a list of possible values is accessible. Selecting an item from this list guarantees the conformity of the values towards those stored in the repository. The domain expert fills the properties he/she knows the value of. For instance, he/she may fill the property 'domain' = '*customer servicing*' and describe partially its usage intention, '*Measure*$_{\text{verb}}$ (*electricity consumption*)$_{\text{result}}$. After the form has been submitted (click on the 'submit your choice' button), the Pattern Search Engine searches within the repository for the formal signatures that match the properties that were given. The search through the indexing hierarchy is performed in a top-down manner. In order to minimise the number of retrieved formal signatures for the sake of guiding the domain expert, the search engine only retrieves the most general formal signatures that match the query. The foreground window of figure 6 displays the resulting list of formal signatures. All elements that complete the initial elements of the query are displayed in bold. The domain expert is asked to select one of these retrieved formal signatures. Based on his/her selection, the Pattern Search Engine continues to descend the indexing hierarchy to retrieve more specialised formal signatures that refine the selected one as shown in the background window of figure 7. In our example, two are matching. Because these two are alternative, the domain expert is asked to select one of them. Assume, he/she selects the first one. The next steps consist in descending the hierarchy until product or change process patterns are found. The next step, shown in the foreground window of figure 7, leads the Pattern Search Engine to reach leaves of the hierarchy.

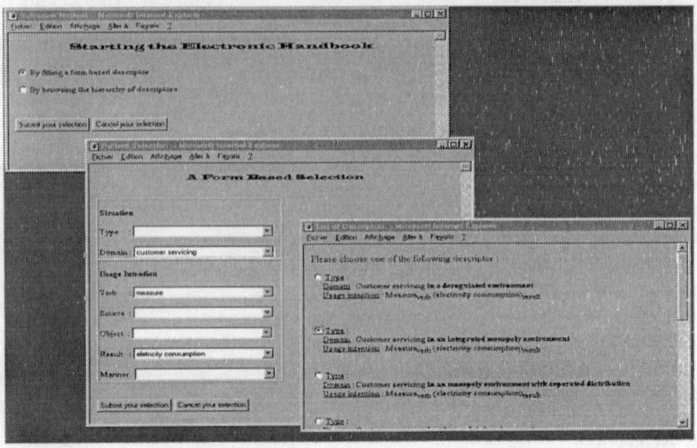

Figure 6 - Submitted query and associated matching formal signatures

Assume the domain expert selects the first item of the list, the associated product pattern is then displayed as shown in figure 8 with all its components (i.e. formal signature, informal signature, guidelines and body). The domain expert has the ability to display the example(s) associated to this pattern in a different window. If this pattern satisfies his/her expectations, he/she can download the body of the pattern into his current work space. At this point, he/she can choose to stop the retrieval because he/she found what he/she was looking for. Otherwise, he/she has the possibility of continuing the retrieval thanks to the 'what to do next' button. Clicking on this button will lead the tool to propose the pending options that were listed for this query. In our example, this would first lead the tool to suggest the study of the 'object' product pattern (the second item in the foreground window of fig. 7).

5. Conclusion

A critical factor in being able to share best business practice (including best practice for system development) is the appropriate reuse of existing 'chunks' of best practice. Patterns provide the mechanism for achieving this. The generic patterns will have to be built by empirical observation and tested on a range of examples within case studies. Prior to discovering patterns however in these case studies, there is a need to establish the framework for maintaining and using the knowledge pertinent to the patterns. This paper has attempted to provide first a framework for defining generic patterns for the Electricity Supply Industry (ESI) sector and second the associated 'Electronic Guide Book'. For engineers involved in change management, the 'Electronic Guide Book' represents an opportunity of reusing already tested generic knowledge in similar settings, by customising them with respect to the particularities of the studied organisation. Both the patterns framework and the tool are independent of any application and could potentially be used in other domains. The 'Electronic Guide Book' is built over the web and provides a uniform interface across platforms that allows domain experts, working in incompatible environment, to share generic knowledge. Moreover, the web environment provides a medium for an easy distribution and use of the 'Electronic Guide Book'. Studying the feedback from the users should lead to validate and complete the pattern repository.

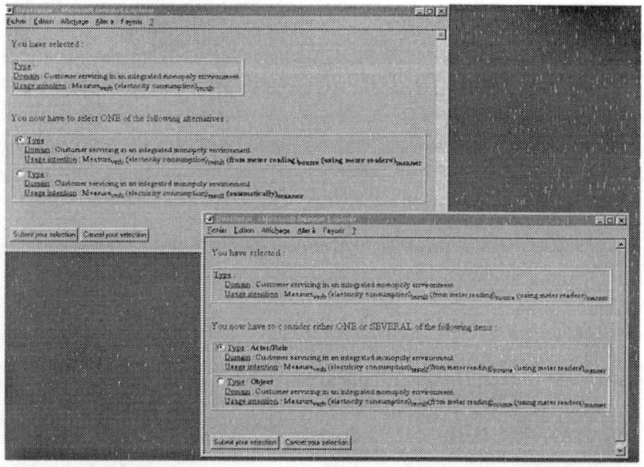

Figure 7 - Descending the hierarchy of formal signatures

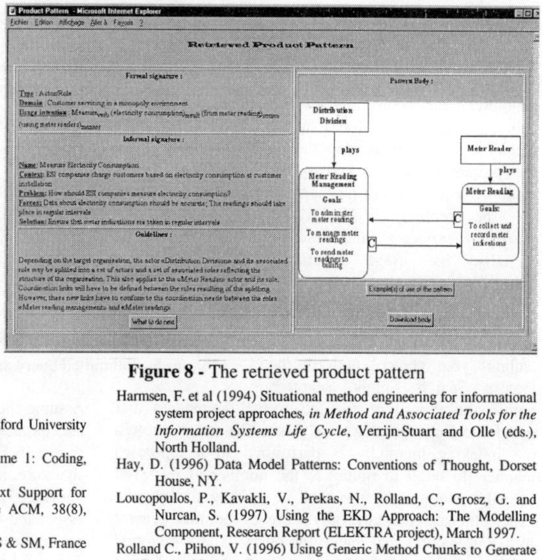

Figure 8 - The retrieved product pattern

6. References

Alexander, C., Ishikawa, S., Silverstein, M., Jacobson, M., Fiksdahl-King, I. and Angel, S. (1977) A Pattern Language, Oxford University Press, New York.

Alexander, C. (1979) The Timeless Way of Building, Oxford University Press, NY.

Beck, K. (1997) Smalltalk Best Practice Patterns. Volume 1: Coding, Prentice Hall, Englewood Cliffs, NJ.

Bieber, M. and Kacmar, C. (1995) Designing Hypertext Support for Computational Applications, Communication of the ACM, 38(8), 1995, 99 - 107.

Brophy, K., Koets, T., (1996) Le programmeur VBScript S & SM, France 1996.

Bubenko, J., Strina, J. (1997) EKD User Guide, research report, ELEKTRA project.

Buschmann, F., Meunier, R., Rohnert, H., Sommerland, P. and Stal, M. (1996) Pattern-Oriented Software Architecture - A System of Patterns, John Wiley.

Coad, P. (1992) Object-Oriented Patterns, in *Communications of the ACM*, Vol. 35, No. 9, 152-159.

Coad, P. et al. (1996) Object Models - Strategies Patterns and Applications, Yourdon Press Computing Series.

Coplien, J.O. and Schmidt, D.O. (1995) (ed.) Pattern Languages of Program Design, Addison-Wesley, Reading, MA.

Fowler, M. (1997) Analysis Patterns: Reusable Object Models, Addison-Wesley.

Gamma, E., Helm, R., Johnson, R. and Vlissides, J. (1994) Design Patterns: Elements of Reusable Object-Oriented Software, Addison-Wesley, MA.

Grosz, G., Rolland, C., Schwer, S., Souveyet, S., Plihon, V., Si-said, S., Ben Achour, C., Gnaho,C. (1997) Modelling and Engineering the Requirements Engineering Process: An Overview of the NATURE Approach, in *Requirements Engineering Journal*, (2), 115-131.

Harmsen, F. et al (1994) Situational method engineering for informational system project approaches, *in Method and Associated Tools for the Information Systems Life Cycle*, Verrijn-Stuart and Olle (eds.), North Holland.

Hay, D. (1996) Data Model Patterns: Conventions of Thought, Dorset House, NY.

Loucopoulos, P., Kavakli, V., Prekas, N., Rolland, C., Grosz, G. and Nurcan, S. (1997) Using the EKD Approach: The Modelling Component, Research Report (ELEKTRA project), March 1997.

Rolland C., Plihon, V. (1996) Using Generic Method Chunks to Generate Process Models Fragments, in *ICRE'96*, Colorado-Spring, USA, April 1996.

Rolland, C., Nurcan, S. and Grosz, G. (1997a) Guiding the participative design process, in *Association for Information Systems, Americas Conference on Information Systems*, Indianapolis, Indiana, 15-17 Aug. 1997, USA, 922-924.

Rolland, C., Nurcan, S. and Grosz, G. (1997b) A way of working for change processes, in *International research Symposium: Effective Organisations*, Sept. 4-5, 1997, Dorset, UK.

Rolland, C., Nurcan, S. and Grosz, G. (1998a) A unified framework for modelling co-operative design processes and co-operative business processes, in *the 31st Annual Hawaii International Conference on System Sciences*, Big Island, Hawaii, USA, 6-9 January 1998.

Rolland, C., Grosz, G., Loucopoulos, P., Nurcan, S. (1998b) The patterns model, Intermediary Research Report, (ELEKTRA Project), January 1998.

Vlissides, J.M., Coplien, J.O. and Kerth, N.L. (1996) (ed.) Pattern Languages of Program Design 2, Addison-Wesley.

Yajima, M.(1997) Deregulatory reforms of the Electricity Supply Industry, Quorum Books.

An Agent Based Platform for a Service Provider *

Vincenza Carchiolo, Michele Malgeri, Giuseppe Mangioni
Istituto di Informatica e telecomunicazioni - Universita' di Catania
Viale Andrea Doria, 6 - I95125 Catania (Italy)
E-mail {car, mm, gmangion} @ iit.unict.it

Abstract

This paper presents an approach based on mobile agents for the implementation of a platform for an Internet service provider. The aim of the approach is to implement a service provider that can provide services that are reliable, low-cost and flexible. One of the main features is to make it possible to serve clients who do not have particular hardware characteristics and do not need special software to access the service they require, but are only equipped with an engine for network access.

1 Introduction

A problem that has emerged in the last few years is the need to access network services available, in Internet, in such a way as to exploit the resources provided by servers. There are two requirements in this scenario: one the one hand, it is necessary to have something which is able to provide these services, i.e. a service provider, and on the other it is necessary to define the features a client has to possess in order to request certain services and the modality (payment, authentication, etc.) with which the service provider provides them. An ideal service provider has to be reliable, fault-tolerant, and powerful enough to meet a client's requests with an acceptable level of performance. An ideal client should be general-purpose; he does not have to possess special software for certain kinds of service, but just needs an engine which will allow him access to service provider. The approach normally followed in implementing a service provider is to have a single host, possibly with some mirror hosts (to ensure a certain degree of fault tolerance), which provides all the services. An alternative is to have several hosts, each providing a single service. The main problems in this sort of scheme are linked to a waste of resources (the mirror host is normally not active), the dynamic reconfigurability of the system, and data consistency maintenance. In this paper we present a solution for implementation of a service provider based on a distributed architecture which offers a high degree of fault tolerance and dynamic reconfigurability. The system has been developed following the mobile agents paradigms. The idea of a distributed service provider is an attractive one because functions can be split between several hosts. In our case, the architecture is a LAN of heterogeneous, non-dedicated hosts, so as to maximise reuse of existing resources. It also allows us to optimise the workload distribution, as the services are distributed. Mobile agent technology, as discussed in [1] [2], possesses particularly interesting features for the development of an open system for the provision of services in an electronic market. To implement the system we chose an approach based on MOLE [3], a mobile agent platform implemented in Java [4] which guarantees a hardware-independent system and thus one that is easily reconfigurable and portable. All the services by the system are built on an infrastructure based on a distributed database which ensures data consistency and availability thanks to well-known database management techniques. Section 2 of the paper describes the architecture of the system in greater detail. Section 3 introduces mobile agent technology and its potential, highlighting the features of the MOLE environment. Section 4 gives details of the server and the main features of the client and discusses the policy used in managing the server. The final section draws conclusions on the use of this platform.

2 Service Provider Platform

A service provider is a host that provides a set of clients with a certain number of remote services. As mentioned previously, it is extremely important for a service provider to be highly reliable. To achieve

*Work carried out under the financial support of the Ministero dell'Universita' e della Ricerca Scientifica e Tecnologica (MURST) in the framework of the Project *"Design Methodologies and Tools of High Performance Systems for Distributed Applications"*.

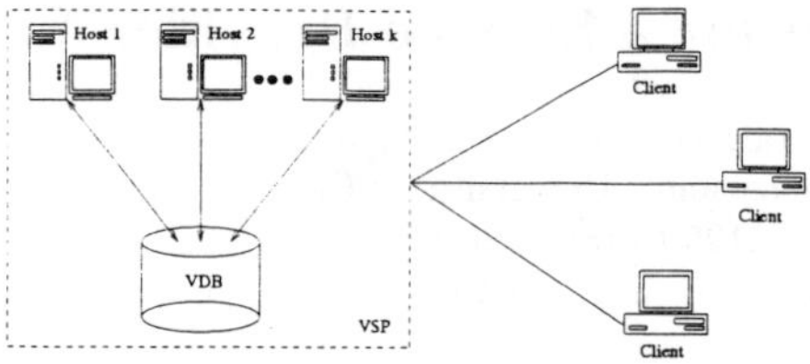

Figure 1: Logical structure of the VSP

this, we have designed a platform based on use of a pool of heterogeneous hosts, each of which provides some of the services required. One of the main problems we had to solve, is that a client requiring a service has to be able to know which host can currently provide it. A very attractive solution, especially in view of the fact that no restriction has been made on the kind of the service the server provides or the features of the client, would be to show the client a single virtual server to whom he can apply to request a service. A Virtual Service Provider (VSP) is a set of heterogeneous hosts connected by an Intranet. The set can be modified by eliminating a host, for example if it is no longer connected, or adding a new one that can supply further services. As said previously, consistency of the data distributed over the hosts in the VSP is guaranteed by a distributed database (called a Virtual Database - VDB), which contains the data to manage both the VSP or the services the VSP offers. This information, contained in the VDB, includes a list of the hosts making up the VSP at any one time and the services they can offer. Fig. 1 shows the logical structure of the VSP.
To manage the addressing of the set of hosts, which the client sees as a single entity, we used multicast addressing, thus assigning all the hosts a single group address. Therefore, a client requesting a service sends his request to the group without necessarily knowing how many hosts there are, or where they are located, and who actual provides the service: this information may change from one call to another. It is necessary that same service is provided by several hosts belonging to the VSP in order to service to be reliable. The use of an agent-based system developed in Java, allows users not only to access services for which they have a provider, but also to obtain client software (for either a new or an updated version of the service) directly from the server, in the form of an agent or a Java class. Fig. 2 shows the real mechanism whereby a generic client accesses a node. A client requiring a service can obtain it by connecting up with the virtual address of the VSP. The search for available services and the type of access are managed in the same way as any of the services available.

3 Mobile Agent Technology

3.1 General features

Mobile agents are active objects that have a behaviour, a state and a location. An agent can be seen as a set of data, a code and an execution context that can migrate through a network during execution. Mobile agents are autonomous because once called they decide autonomously where to migrate to and what code to execute. This behaviour is implicitly defined by the agent code [5]. An agent reacts to stimuli from the outside environment and can be persistent in the sense that its execution can be interrupted and the data stored so as to be re-used when the agent wakes up again, even in a different location. The use of a mobile code is extremely important as it offers the following facilities:

- software distribution on demand;
- management of asynchronous tasks;
- reduction in communication costs.

There are several code mobility modes:

1. *Remote Execution and Code on Demand*: the agent is transferred before execution of the associated code so both code and data are transferred. This scheme is followed by Tacoma [6], whereas the Code on Demand scheme is used to manage Java Applets [4].

2. *Weak Migration*: only code + state of data are transferred. This is the scheme used by Aglets and Mole.

3. *Strong Migration*: code + data + state of execution are transferred. This scheme is the most

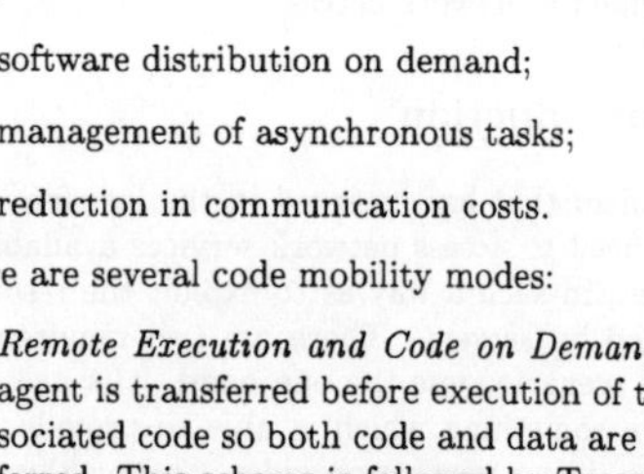

Figure 2: Accessing mechanism

complete one and is used for AgentTcl [5], Telescript [7] and Odissey [8].

In reality the Remote Execution and Code on Demand schemes do not allow mobile agents to be managed as well as the weak and strong migration schemes do. Choice between the latter, which have the same power of expression, depends on implementation features.

3.2 Mole

In this section we will give a brief description of the features of MOLE. A complete introduction can be found in [3]. As mentioned above, an agent-based system is a set of abstract locations, each to provide certain services. An agent is an active entity and in the MOLE model it is a multithread entity whose state and code can be transferred when agent migration is requested. MOLE is based on the weak migration mode, as Remote Execution and Code on Demand do not possess either flexibility or simplicity. Strong migration was not chosen because it would require modification of the Java Virtual Machine. Each agent is identified by a global name generated by the system when it is created. The location where agent has been created can be derived from location name and it is independent from current one, this implies that the agent identifier is location independent. Migration is implemented using a part of the Java Remote Method Invocation package. After an agent want to migrate all the threads belonging to it are suspended, all pending messages are delivered and, at last, the agent is serialised. The serialised version of the agent is sent to destination location where it is reinstantiated, if some Java classes are not locally available they are requested to source location or to a code server. Two kind of agents are present into MOLE: system and user agent. The former is able to perform any action on the local system whereas the latter cannot.

4 Implementation of the Provider

The VSP is implemented by executing a MOLE engine on each host, which provides an environment for agent execution (both system agent and user agent). As an engine can manage several locations on the same machine, each VSP host makes one or more locations available. At each location there are some system agents that can access the system's resources without causing any security problems as they are immobile and can only be run by the manager of the location involved. Fig. 3 shows the architecture of the server. It is made up of a VDB and a set of agents: a Token Agent, an agent for each of the services of the VSP provides (SA_i), a Ring Manager agent and a Service Manager agent.

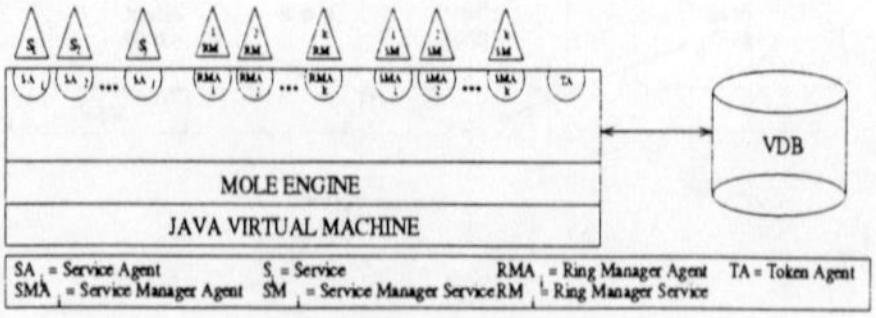

Figure 3: VSP architecture

At each location there are service agents for the services available at that location. The VSP has a Virtual Location (VL) which is made up of all the locations in the various nodes making up the VSP. Fig. 4 shows the structure of a VL with three locations, LA, LB and LC (which can be on a single host or on two or three different hosts) which allows access to three services, S1, S2 and S3. Services S1 is available at locations LA and LB, services S2 at locations LB and LC and service S3 at locations LA and LC. So at location LA there will be the service agents SA1 and SA3, at location LB the service agents SA1 and SA3, and at location LC the service agents SA2 and SA3. The services provided by a location can include both services for management of the VSP and user-oriented services. A location can provide more than one service and a service can be provided by several locations.

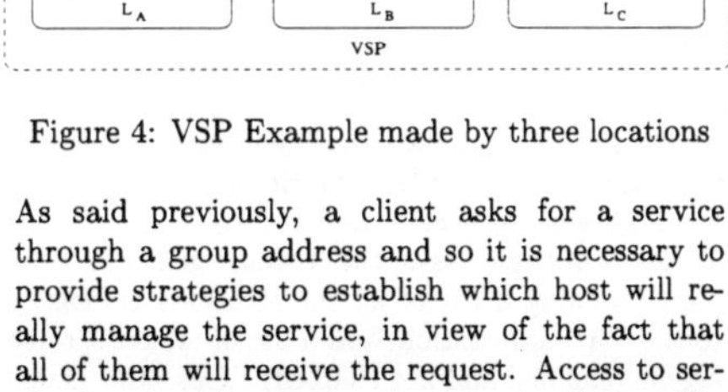

Figure 4: VSP Example made by three locations

As said previously, a client asks for a service through a group address and so it is necessary to provide strategies to establish which host will really manage the service, in view of the fact that all of them will receive the request. Access to service is gained by means of an agent which, unlike the service agents which are stationary, exploits the mobility features of MOLE agents and is received by all the hosts making up the VSP, as shown in

Fig. 5.

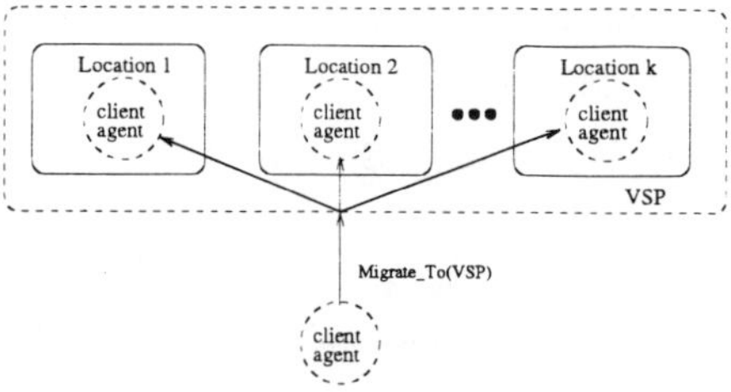

Figure 5: Agent mechanism

A service request comprises two phases:

1. a request for acquisition of the software needed to manage the service required (if not already present);

2. access to the service.

4.1 Policy for choosing the service agent which is to provide the service

As the Client Agent accessing the service actually reaches all the VSP locations, it has to be decided which of the hosts will actually provide the service. This problem is solved by creating a logical ring managed by a mobile agent called Token Agent, whose task it is to guarantee that only one location at a time is enabled to provide the service. The Token Agent, which migrates to all the hosts in the logical ring, has to enable a service agent at a location, guaranteeing that no other service agent at another location is enabled for the same service. A client agent that wants to access a service (e.g. S1) therefore migrates to all the locations in the VL but is discarded by:

- locations that are unable to provide the service (i.e. LC);

- locations whose service agent has not been enabled by the Token Agent (i.e. LB).

After completing its task the client agent returns to the source location, called the Home Location, with the results of the service (see Fig. 6).
To perform these tasks, the Token Agent has a table containing a list of all the locations belonging to the Virtual Location, and a list of all the service agents (enabled and not enabled). This table is updated with the information the Token Agent picks up while migrating from one location to another. Each location has a service called Ring Service, with a relative agent called a Ring Manager. The Ring

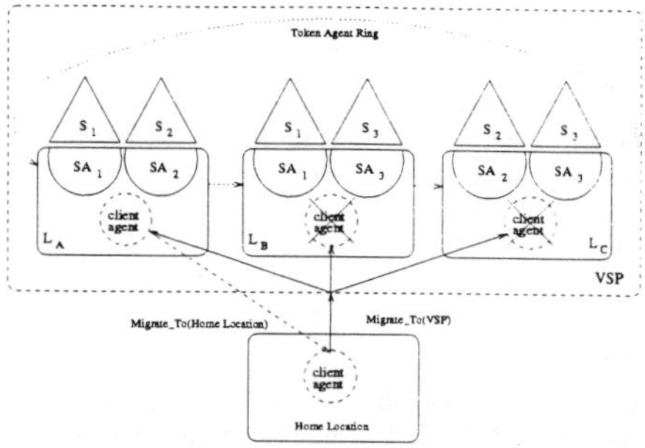

Figure 6: Client agent path

Manager has the task of managing the logical ring, guaranteeing that there is always an active Token Agent and that there is only one. Each location can be in one of the following states (see Fig. 7):

1. ***non-active***: a location that does not belong to the ring;

2. *ready*: a location that does not belong to the ring but possesses the necessary features to be able to become an active location and has asked to be inserted;

3. *active*: a location that belongs to the ring;

4. *faulty*: a location that has been temporarily removed from the ring due to malfunctioning;

5. *stopped*: a location that belongs to the ring but has asked to be eliminated.

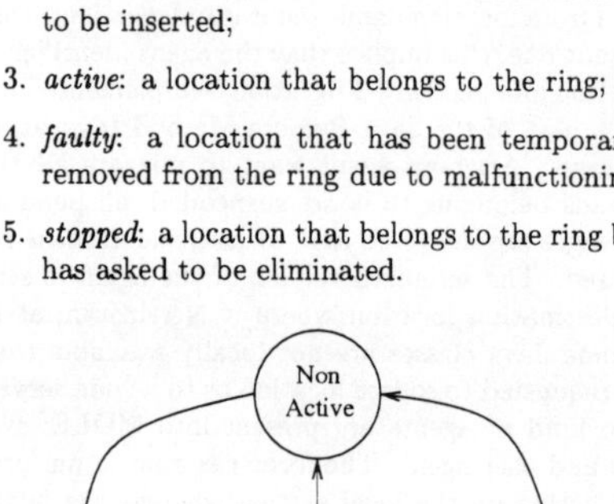

Figure 7: States of a location

Transitions between one state and another are managed by the Ring Manager in collaboration with the

Token Agent. The service manager has the following functions:

1. initialising the ring;
2. inserting a new location;
3. elimination of a location from the ring;
4. management of token loss due to malfunctioning.

In performing these operations it has to guarantee that there is only one Token Agent. To manage the ring it is necessary to set two time-outs, T_{ins} and T_{lost}: an agent can be considered lost if it has not been received by T_{lost}. T_{lost} depends on various factors such as:

1. the number of hosts in the VSP;
2. the traffic on the Intranet on which the VSP is implemented.

These values are highly dynamic, so the value of T_{lost} has to be modified whenever the structure of the VSP changes. The Token Agent is generated during initialisation of the logical ring. It possesses a table containing the unicast addresses of the locations, the services they offer and the enabled locations. During normal functioning of the VSP the Token Agent migrates from one location to another collecting specific information about the hosts (load, response time, resources, etc.) and the traffic on the network. On the basis of this information, following a pre-estabilished strategy, the Token Agent establishes which services each of the hosts is to provide. This balances the workload between the various hosts making up the VSP. To guarantee restoration of the ring following the loss of a Token Agent, the latter creates a copy of itself (called a Ghost Token Agent) on each location it passes through, one of these agents will be awakened after T_{lost} fires. Finally, the Token Agent calculates the optimal time-outs value to manage the VSP, updating them when necessary.

4.2 Insertion and deletion of a location

A location in a non -active state can ask to be inserted in the ring at any time. This operation in managed by the local Ring Manager, which creates a Ring Agent, whose task is to request insertion of the new location (ready state). The location that has created a Ring Agent waits for it to return until the time-out T_{ins} fires. If it receives no reply, it tries again up to a maximum of N attempts. If the ring agent returns, the location becomes active; otherwise it assumes that it is the only active location and creates a logical ring made up of itself alone. As insertion of a new location changes the structure of the network, it is necessary to modify the time-out T_{lost}. This is done by the Token Agent: whenever it arrives at a location with the enabled Ring Manager, it calculates the new time-out value on the basis of the number of locations in the ring. After having updated the tome-out value, the Token Agent does a complete round of the ring updating the time-outs. The aim of this is to prevent the insertion of a new location from making the Token Agent appear to be lost. If, in fact, locations were always inserted immediately, the Token Agent might take longer than expected to do its round, the causing the oldest time-out to expire: this would make it seem that the Token Agent was lost.
A similar procedure is followed when a host is eliminated. In this case, as a consequence of a request to be eliminated, an active location passes to the *stopped* state and then the *non-active* state.

4.3 Initialisation of the ring

Initialisation of the logical ring is a special case of the addition of new locations.
As said above, insertion of a new location is managed by a Ring Agent which is sent by each location when it is activated.
Initialisation occurs when the ring agent is sent N times without returning. In this case the location creates a Token Agent and generates a logical ring containing the location alone.

4.4 Token loss and multiple tokens

A Token Agent can be lost when it tries to migrate to a location that is stopped due to a fault or because its possessor is faulty and takes the agent with it. In this case the Token Agent has to be regenerated trying to lose as little information as possible. It is therefore not possible to re/initialise the ring as all the information would be lost. The solution is to make the Token Agent leave a copy of itself, called a Ghost Token Agent, on each host.
The problem that arises is how to choose the Ghost Token Agent to replace the lost Token Agent.
The enabled Ring Manager activates a time/out equal to T_{lost}, the value of which is calculated by the Token Agent on the basis of the current VSP configuration. If the location at which the Ring Manager is active does not receive the Token Agent by a time T_{lost}, the Ring Manager considers the Token Agent to be lost and restores the logical ring and the Token Agent. This operation consists of the following actions:

2. The creation of some Explorer Agents whose task is to migrate to all of the host in the VSP in order to see which of them are really functioning. Hosts whose Explorer Agent do not return are considered to be faulty.

2. Activation of the local Ghost Token Agent which takes on the functions of the Token Agent. Before the activation of the Ghost Token Agent, the Ring Manager updates the table of the awakening Ghost Token Agent on the basis of the results obtained by the Explorer Agents.

If the faulty host is the one on which the active Ring Manager resides, re-activation of the ring will be managed by the host which follows it in the logical ring.
Re-insertion of faulty hosts is managed by the Ring Manager, which periodically tries to send Explorer Agents to them.
This procedure for the restoration of a Token Agent may cause regeneration of a Token Agent even when it is not actually lost. If, for instance, a network fault temporarily isolates one or more locations, after the time-out expires a new Token Agent is generated, thus causing the presence of two Token Agent and two logical rings.
In fig. 8 Token Agent 1 rotates between locations L1 and L2 and considers L3 and L4 to be faulty, whereas Token Agent 2 rotates between locations L3 and L4 and considers L1 and L2 to be faulty.

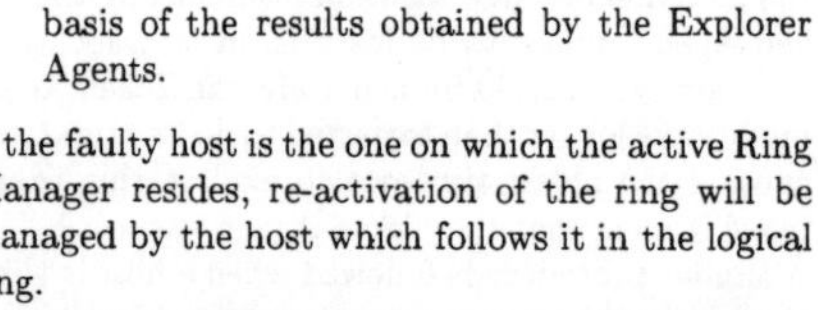

Figure 8: Multiple tokens

Afterwards, when the network is restored, it will be necessary to merge the two rings. This is achieved by the active Ring Managers by means of Explorer Agents.

5 Conclusions

This paper has presented a service provider based on a distributed mobile agent architecture. It has been implemented using MOLE, which is based on JAVA. These choices allow us to guarantee total independence of the hardware and operating system hosting the service provider.
The decision to use distributed architecture allows us to avoid the well/known problems linked to monolitic providers. In addition, it makes it possible to exploit the resources existing in a LAN and therefore to offer continuos, reliable services at low cost.
Similar approach can be found in Odissey [8] and Atomas [9].
The platform described has been implemented and tested on four hosts, moreover the E-mail service, completely based on mobile agents, has been implemented on this platform.

References

[1] B. Libermann, F. Griffel, M. Merz, and W. Lamerdof. Java-Based Mobile Agents - How to Migrate, Persist, and Interact on Electronic Service Markets. In *Proceedings of MA97 Workshop*, Berlin, 1997. Springer LNCS.

[2] T. Megadanz, K. Rotherlem, and S. Kruse. Intelligent Agents: an Emerging Technology for Next Generation Telecommunications. In *Proceedings of IEEE Infocom*, San Francisco, 1996.

[3] M. Strasser, J. Baumann, and F. Hohl. MOLE - a Java Based Mobile Agent System. In *Proceedings of Workshop ECOOP*, 1996.

[4] The java WEB pages. URL: http://www.javasoft.com.

[5] R. S. Gray. AgentTCL: A Transportable Agent System. In *Proceedings of CIKM - Workshop on Intelligent Information Agent*, 1995.

[6] D. Johansen, R. van Renesse, and F. B. Schneder. An Introduction to TACOMA Distributed System Version 1.0. Technical Report 95-23, University of Tromso, 1995.

[7] General Magic Inc. The telescript language reference. URL: http://www.genmagic.com/telescript/TDE/TDEDOCS_HTML/telescript.html.

[8] General Magic Inc. Odyssey web site - URL: http://www.genmagic.com/agents.

[9] M. Strasser, J. Baumann, F. Hohl, N. Radouniklis, K. Rothermel, and M. Schwehm. ATOMAS - A Transaction Oriented Open Multi Agent system annual report. Technical Report 97-14, Fakultat Informatik, University of Stuttgart, 1997.

The specification of geometrical dynamic behaviour in Web page design

José **Bulas-Cruz** (*), Luís **Barbosa** (*), Leonel **Morgado** (*), Arsénio **Reis** (*), João **Barroso**(*), Pedro **Melo-Pinto** (*) e Pedro **Henriques** (**)

(*) Projecto GeIRA, Universidade de Trás-os-Montes e Alto Douro
Apt. 202, 5001 Vila Real Codex, Portugal, Tel (059) 320356 Fax (059) 32048 email:jcruz@utad.pt

(**) Projecto GeIRA, Universidade do Minho
Campus de Gualtar, 4710 Braga, Portugal, Tel (053) 604140 Fax (053) 612251

Abstract

The development of a large number of Web pages, under the GeIRA project, requires co-operation between designers and Web page developers. A mixed team is usually the best option: designers and Web-page developers working together. This may produce a synergetic effect, using the best of both worlds. However, all the information regarding behaviour, related with the variable dimensions of a page, is absent from a traditional design, which relies on fixed dimensions. This results in problems for the implementation team, that should be detected and corrected at an earlier stage.

This paper presents a model for the description of the dynamical behaviour of Web pages. This approach minimises the occurrence of errors, saving time and resources in the development process. The model lays a common ground between designers and computer experts, allowing for the development of tools that support the site development process. These tools will speed up the development process, ensure greater quality, and introduce an element of clarification of the design specifications.

A specification language and a layout tool are being developed under this model. The layout tool will provide a designer with the means to graphically implement several page elements, and at the same time see how these elements are positioned in the page for different page dimensions.

Overall, the improved communication between designers and developers results in a Web-site creation process that is more efficient, flexible and economical.

1 Introduction

Several organisations in Northern Portugal, namely those related to archaeology, museums, libraries/archives, and universities/research organisations, are joining efforts to promote their activities using interactive and multimedia technologies. The GeIRA project (URL: http://www.geira.pt/) aims the support and integration of these activities, and includes a multidisciplinary research team. The research team integrates designers, multimedia technicians and computer experts.

The development of Web sites that wish to draw the interest of the Internet community requires an attractive design. Traditional designers, while highly skilled on conventional technologies (printed media), lack the technical expertise to efficiently implement their designs as Web pages and to maintain and manage the graphical aspects of a Web site. Increasingly complex database and geographical information-driven Web sites emphasise this aspect.

In view of the fact that the design team faces a set of different problems from those that the implementation team has to deal with, the GeIRA project adopted a pipeline organisation, as illustrated by Figure 1. This organisation enables co-operation between the designers and the site developers, providing as well an extra degree of autonomy for each group (the specific decisions of each group are less affected by the others).

An alternative organisation is proposed by the *Cnet* online magazine [GORMAN 1997]. Their solution is based on allocation of a job to a team of two persons:

a designer and a computer expert. This solution requires design and development to work concurrently in the same Web page, which is not one of the options available to our teams. This solution seems to be generally well suited for small projects. But it is our belief that it is difficult to adopt in an environment where professionals must share their time through several distinct projects, due to the permanent assignment of two resources to one task.

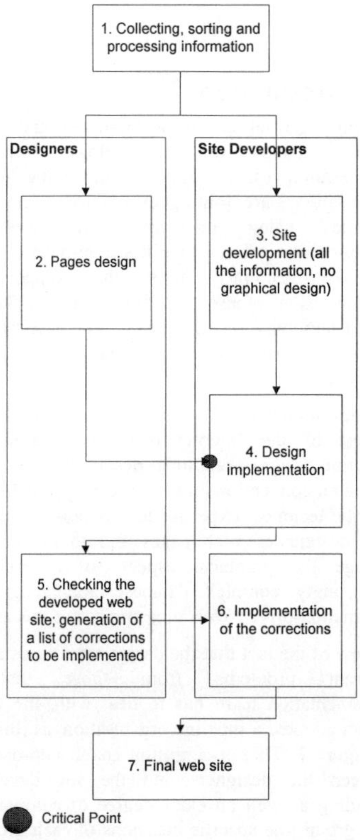

Figure 1: Web-site development pipeline

The proposed solution for the GeIRA project enables the design to be relatively independent from the information sources, leading to a higher flexibility in the sequence of tasks that have to be completed. This pipeline organisation can be used for individual pages or smaller sections of a Web site, as well as for the complete project of a large Web site. This scalability is well adapted to the nature of the GeIRA project.

A closer look at Figure 1 shows the various tasks, by stages. The iterative process is repeated until a solution is reached. The output of stage 1 is a site specification for use by the developers and the designers. Depending on the available resources, such output can be one single document or two separate ones, one emphasising the graphical aspects and the other focusing on the organisation of information.

At stages 2 and 3, both teams are working without formal communication and they can share their time and effort by the various projects underway. The output of stage 2 is a graphical design specification, while the output of stage 3 is a working Web site, without graphic design concerns.

At stage 4, the graphical design devised by the designers is applied to the Web site.

At stage 5, the designers check the resulting Web site, searching for possible design misunderstandings and faulty graphical elements.

Stage 6 is the clean-up phase. Any errors detected at stage 5, such as unreadable portions of text, are corrected at this stage. The final Web site is then ready at stage 7.

The circle in Figure 1 marks the point where formal communication between the designers and the developers first takes place. Improving communication support at this stage results in a smaller list of corrections as the output of stage 5. Since the communication is clearer, the probability of corrections being so serious as to impact the overall site structure is considerably diminished. This results in a faster and easier Web site development cycle.

The paper is organized as follows. Next section describes the proposed model and presents the model organization in an object oriented methodology. Section 3 is concerned with the support tools under development, namely a descriptive language and a layout tool. Finally, section .4 presents the conclusions.

2 Support for dynamic behaviour in the design phase

2.1 The conceptual Web page model

In order to clarify the interface between designers and developers, a conceptual Web page model has been devised, providing the design team with the means to specify the design of the page. This includes a specification for given page dimensions (the most common approach) and, having this design as a starting point, the specification of the dynamic behaviour of the page, i.e., how should objects change their position as the dimensions vary.

Since the positioning of an element in a Web page, when the viewing window changes dimensions, depends only on the current dimensions of the Web browser's viewing window, there are no other events or changing conditions to address. Therefore, the model is purely descriptive, i.e., it must define positioning rules for the Web page's elements.

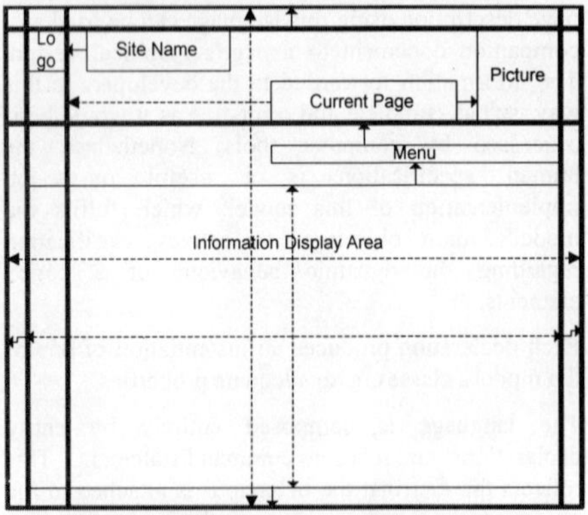

Figure 2: Specifying the geometrical dynamic behaviour of a Web page

The basic idea is that given a starting element arrangement (static description), the designers need to specify the distances between the several page elements and between those elements and the borders of the page. These distances can be seen as fixed *links* (*wires*) whose length does not change with the dimensions of the viewing window; or as variable *links* (*springs*) whose length depends on the current viewing window dimensions.

In order to allow the designer to specify alignments, the concept of a *ruler* was incorporated in the model. A *ruler* is an invisible object, which can be used to define the position of other objects. This idea is similar to the traditional *ruler* in graphic design, being therefore intuitive for design professionals.

Figure 2 illustrates these concepts. Solid lines represent fixed-length *links* (*wires*); dashed lines represent variable-length *links* (*springs*). The thicker lines are *rulers*. Looking at the figure, it is easy to see that "Logo", "Site Name" and "Picture" are top-aligned. Some other conclusions, however, can only be drawn from a scheme of this kind: for instance, it can be seen that "Current Page" can move left, if the page width diminishes, but only as far as to reach the right border of "Logo". This kind of dynamic constraint involves the entire page structure, and its assessment is very important in avoiding major page restructuring later on. Another example is the *link* between "Picture" and "Current Page", indicating that the distance between these two elements is fixed (does not change with the dimensions of the page).

2.2 Model description

The model represents the result of an object-oriented analysis process [BOOCH 1994; COX 1986; MEYER 1988; WEGNER 1990; WIRSF-BROCK 1989]. The positioning of the elements of a generic Web page, and its dynamic behaviour, are modelled using the OMT methodology proposed by Rumbaugh et al [RUMBAUGH 1991].

Under the proposed model, a Web page is a set of elements connected by *links* that can have fixed or variable length. The variable *links* allow for the dynamic behaviour of the page elements.

There are displayable elements called *bricks*, reference elements called *rulers* and *links*. *Brick* and *ruler* objects are connected by *links*, and are called *fabrics*. Each *fabric* is associated with two *link* objects, which represent its width and height attributes.

A *brick* can represent any visible page element, i. e., an image, a text block or an undefined area to be clarified on a later development phase. The *bricks* can be laid out on a page with the aid of placement *rulers*, which are non-visible objects with no other purpose beyond acting as references for *brick* placement.

Rulers and *bricks* are connected by means of *links*, which are (just like the *rulers*) non-visible objects which act as references for *brick* placement. A *link* can have fixed or variable length. For clarity, the adopted analogy for those two types of *links* is one of *wires* and *springs*, respectively.

A page has at least four *rulers*, one representing each border. But there is no upper limit to the number of *rulers* present on a page. It contains also at least two *springs*, which determine the page dimensions: one between the top and bottom borders, another between the left and right borders.

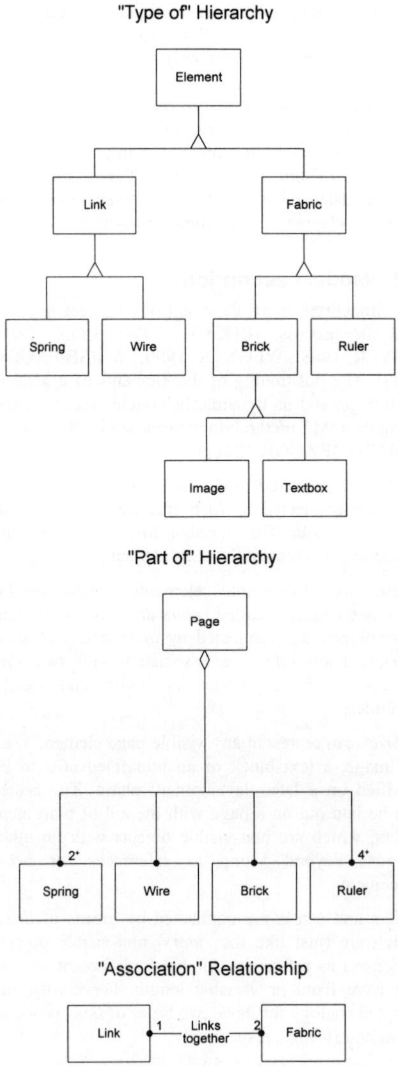

Figure 3: Sketch of the object model, following the OMT methodology

3 Support tools

3.1 A descriptive language

The proposed model can be implemented by use of an adequate language. The purpose of such a language is therefore that of the model, i.e., to accurately describe the behaviour of the elements on a Web page.

An automated interpreter for the language can be developed, for syntax and error checking. Such an interpreter can also perform other actions, such as automatic completion of the human specification. But even considering only the human specification, a page description using this language can be used as a companion document to a page's graphical design. The information forwarded to the developers in this way isn't as complete and error-free as it would be if processed by computer tools. Nonetheless, the human specification is a useful on-the-job implementation of this model, which fulfils the model's main objective: to convey clarification regarding the dynamic behaviour of a page's elements.

Each declaration produces an instantiation of one of the model's classes, with adequate properties.

The language is composed entirely by entity declarations; i.e., it has no command statements. This reflects the fact that the behaviour is attached to the objects, in an object-oriented paradigm.

The syntax of the proposed language, is partially described using Backus-Naur Form (BNF) rules:

```
Declaration ::= Entity | Comentary

Comentary ::= '//' {letter | digit |
    space}0+

Entity ::= Page | Link | Fabric

Page ::= 'PAGE' InstanceName LeftBorder
    TopBorder RightBorder BottomBorder
    Width Height Backcolor

Link ::= LinkIdentification InstanceName
    orientation ReferenceLength
    MinimumLength Source Target

LinkIdentification ::= 'WIRE' | 'SPRING'

Fabric ::= Ruler | Brick | Image | Textbox

Ruler ::= 'RULER' InstanceName Width Height
    orientation

Brick ::= 'BRICK' InstanceName Width Height
```

```
Image ::= 'IMAGE' InstanceName Width Height
    FilePath

Textbox ::= 'TEXTBOX' InstanceName Width
    Height text Textalignment

LeftBorder ::= InstanceName

TopBorder ::= InstanceName

RightBorder ::= InstanceName

BottomBorder ::= InstanceName

Width ::= InstanceName

Height ::= InstanceName

Backcolor ::= integer

orientation ::= 'HORIZONTAL' | 'VERTICAL'

Source ::= InstanceName

Target ::= InstanceName
```

Keywords	**Attributes**	
	Name	Data Type
PAGE	Id	String
	Top Border	Ruler Id
	Left Border	Ruler Id
	Right Border	Ruler Id
	Bottom Border	Ruler Id
	Left-to-Right Link	Link Id
	Top-to-Bottom	Link Id
BRICK	Id	String
	Width Link	Link Id
	Height Link	Link Id
IMAGE	Id	String
	Width Link	Link Id
	Height Link	Link Id
	Image To Display	Filename
TEXTBOX	Id	String
	Width Link	Link Id
	Height Link	Link Id
	Text To Display	String
	Text Alignment	One of: Left Right Centre Justified
WIRE	Id	String
	Orientation	One of: Horizontal Vertical
	Reference Length	Integer
	Minimum Length	Integer
	Source Anchor	Fabric Id
	Target Anchor	Fabric Id
SPRING	Id	String
	Orientation	One of: Horizontal Vertical
	Reference Length	Integer
	Minimum Length	Integer
	Source Anchor	Fabric Id
	Target Anchor	Fabric Id
RULER	Id	String
	Width Link	Link Id
	Height Link	Link Id
	Orientation	One of: Horizontal Vertical

Figure 4: Keyword list

At the time of writing, each *Attribute* has no identification keyword and is composed entirely by its value. All *Attributes* must be specified, i.e., there are no optional properties. If a given *Attribute* is an object, that object must be defined in another statement, and is referred to by its *InstanceName*. The language is case sensitive, and the keywords of the language are written in uppercase.

The language uses the keyword list shown in Figure 4. The list is extensive, assigning to each keyword (*ClassName*) the *Attributes* of its associated class and its superclass. The notation used follows the rule: "link id" means that either a *wire* id or a *spring* id can be used, and "fabric id" means that either a *brick* id or a *ruler* id can be used.

A piece of code illustrating the use of the language follows. The code has been commented for easier understanding. It contains apartial description of the dynamic behaviour of the Web page shown on Figure 2.

```
//Begin
//Page definition
PAGE Page1 TopBorder LeftBorder
  RightBorder BottomBorder PageWidth
  PageHeight None #FFFFFF
//Definition of the rulers that act
  as page borders
RULER TopBorder TBWidth TBHeight
  Horizontal
RULER BottomBorder BBWidth BBHeight
  Horizontal
RULER LeftBorder LBWidth LFHeight
  Vertical
RULER RightBorder RBWidth RBHeight
  Vertical
```

```
//Page border rulers' width and
  height links
SPRING TBWidth Horizontal 630 0
  TopBorder TopBorder
SPRING LBHeight Vertical 300 0
  LeftBorder LeftBorder
//Links between the page borders,
  setting the page's dimensions
SPRING PageWidth Horizontal 630 0
  LeftBorder RightBorder
SPRING PageHeight Vertical 300 0
  TopBorder BottomBorder
//One of the rulers present on figure
  2
RULER LeftMargin LMWidth LMHeight
  Vertical
//Link for placement of the
  "LeftMargin" ruler
WIRE LMPosLeft Horizontal 10 10
  LeftMargin LeftBorder
// One of the images present on
  figure 2
IMAGE Logo LogoW LogoH "Logo.jpg"
WIRE LogoW Horizontal 20 20 Logo Logo
WIRE LogoH Vertical 20 20 Logo Logo
//Links for placement of that image
//The "TopMargin" fabric is another
  ruler present on figure 3
WIRE LogoPosLeft Horizontal 0 0 Logo
  LeftMargin
WIRE LogoPosTop Vertical 0 0 Logo
  TopMargin
//Generic "Information Display Area",
  present on figure 2
BRICK InfoArea InfoAreaW InfoAreaH
SPRING InfoAreaW Horizontal 610 0
  InfoArea InfoArea
SPRING InfoAreaH Vertical 200 0
  InfoArea InfoArea
//Links for placement of that brick.
  The fabrics "Menu" and
  "RightMargin" are elements present
  on figure 2.
WIRE InfoAreaPosLeft Horizontal 0 0
  InfoArea LeftMargin
WIRE InfoAreaPosTop Vertical 10 10
  InfoArea Menu
WIRE InfoAreaPosRight Horizontal 0 0
  InfoArea RightMargin
WIRE InfoAreaPosBottom Vertical 10 10
  InfoArea BottomBorder
//End
```

3.2 A graphical implementation of the model

Another way of implementing the proposed model, and one that most designers are comfortable with, is to graphically define the behaviour of the page elements. A designer can draw symbolic lines

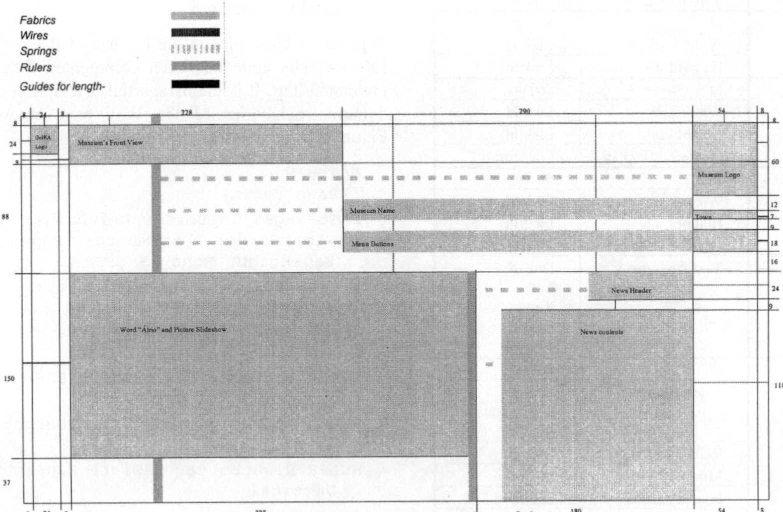

Figure 5: Graphic representation of the specification of a Web page.

between the elements of the page, or within the elements themselves to specify limits to movement, references or objects whose dimensions can vary. Colour coding can also be used to visually clarify the designer's intentions. An experimental graphic representation of the specification of a Web page is shown in Figure 5 (the original uses colour).

3.3 A layout tool

A prototype graphical layout tool is under development. It is based on the proposed model, and will allow designers to express page behaviour graphically, translating it into the description language, so that the page developers get a complete specification. The tool allows a designer to place elements on a page and specify *links* between them. The designer would then be able at any stage to experiment, changing the dimensions of the page, to see how the elements are positioned. This can reveal aspects of the design that were not anticipated, allowing for correction at the specification stage, with no page coding involved.

4 Conclusions

The paper describes a model for specifying the dynamic behaviour of a Web page. The proposed model is being well accepted by the development teams. It is an efficient form of clarifying the communication between designers and developers, when developing Web pages.

The amount of structural errors at Web page development is a major variable regarding the length of a Web page's development cycle. Diminishing the number of errors shortens this time and therefore the associated cost of Web page development also diminishes.

The proposed change in perspective of Web page design methodology, that includes dynamic behaviour, will also hopefully allow for development of new tools and methods. It is believed that the *fabric-and-link* model presented here is adequate for the proposed objectives. It can be implemented in most commercial Web tools, particularly in the layout-oriented ones, such as NetObject's Fusion [FUSION 1997].

Acknowledgements

This work has been supported by the EC Programm Interreg II (contract number 02/REGII/6/96), Feder and by Fundação para a Ciência e Tecnologia.

The authors would like to thank the cooperation and advice of Professor Alberto Proença, from the University of Minho. They are also in debt to the colleagues at CI-UTAD for their support, cooperation and helpful suggestions.

References

[BOOCH 1994] BOOCH, G. *Object Oriented Design with Applications*, The Benjamin/Cummings Publishing Company. California. USA, 1994.

[COX 1986] COX, B. J.. *Object-Oriented Programming: An Evolutionary Approach*. Addison-Wesley. Reading (Mass.). USA, 1986.

[FUSION 1997] *User Guide, Net Objects FUSION 2.0*, NetObjects Inc., Redwood City, California, USA, 1997.

[GORMAN 1997] GORMAN, T., *How CNET does it*. URL site: http://www.cnet.com/, and URL document: http://www.cnet.com/Content/Builder/Business/HowCnet/?dd. Cnet, Inc., USA, 1997.

[MEYER 1988] MEYER, B.. *Object-Oriented Software Construction*. Prentice-Hall International (UK) Ltd. Hertfordshire. UK, 1988.

[RUMBAUGH 1991] RUMBAUGH, J., BLAHA M., PREMERLANI, W., EDDY F., LORENSEN, W.. *Object Oriented-Modelling and Design*. Prentice-Hall International Editions. New York. USA, 1991.

[WEGNER 1990] WEGNER, P.. *Concepts and Paradigms of Object-oriented Programming*. Expansion of October 4 OOPSLA-89 Keynote Talk. OOPS Messenger. Vol 1, Number 1, August 1990. ACM Press, 1990.

[WIRSF-BROCK 1989] WIRSF-BROCK, R. and WILKERSON, B.. Object-Oriented Design: A Responsibility Driven Approach. OOPSLA-89 Proceedings, Special Issue of Sigplan Notices, vol. 24, number 10, Oct. 1989, Addison-Wesley, 1989.

Address translation in the PoP border - A mixed model of routing and IP masquerading for Internet access

Arsénio **Reis** (*), Álvaro **Lopes** (*), Filipe **Rebelo** (*),
Lino **Santos** (**), João **Luis** (**), João **Barroso**(*) and José **Bulas-Cruz** (*)

(*) Centro de Informática da Universidade de Trás-os-Montes e Alto Douro
Apt. 202, 5001 Vila Real Codex
Tel (059) 320356 Fax (059) 320480 Email: ars@utad.pt

(**) FCCN, Fundação de Computação Científica Nacional
Av. do Brasil, 101
1799 Lisboa Codex

Abstract

The Rede de Ciência Tecnologia e Sociedade (RCTS) is intended to provide Internet services to the Portuguese community. The "Internet na Escola" program is the first program to use this infrastructure, providing Internet services to the Portuguese secondary schools. To implement this infrastructure, covering the country territory, fourteen Internet Points of Presence (PoPs) have been created. This paper describes the proposed model for IP addressing and routing, for Internet access. The model has been implemented and is now fully operational in a number of PoPs. The RCTS management intends to implement the model in all PoPs, until the end of January 1998. In the model specification four issues where taken into consideration: security, IP v4 addressing limitations, future project developments and network performance. The solution is based on the concept of an IP Address Translator (the adopted solution uses the Linux IP Masquerading scheme [Au 1997]), supported by a proper routing configuration. This configuration has been implemented in a join effort, by the teams at the Centro de Informática da Universidade de Trás-os-Montes e Alto Douro (CI-UTAD) and at the Fundação de Computação Científica Nacional (FCCN).

1. Introduction

The Portuguese Government has decided the creation of the "Missão para a Sociedade da Informação em Portugal", a task force encharged of promoting the information society in Portugal. A number of directives has been issued, the "Livro Verde para a Sociedade da Informação" [COELHO 1997]. A national information infrastructure, Rede Ciência Tecnologia e Sociedade (RCTS), has been created by the Ministério da Ciência e Tecnologia (MCT).

The first phase of the RCTS implementation consisted of the creation of fourteen Internet PoPs, connected by the Rede da Comunidade Cientifica Nacional (RCCN) [RCCN 1997]. The "Internet na Escola" program is the first program to use this infrastructure, providing Internet services to around one thousand and six hundred secondary schools across the country. Other programs and initiatives are under way, in order to provide Internet services to museums, libraries and other entities.

Each PoP has an access router connected to the RCCN backbone, with ISDN Primary Interfaces (PRI) and a local Ethernet network connecting servers for basic services like DNS, email, etc. In the "Internet na Escola" program, schools are equipped with a personal computer connected to a ISDN Basic Rate Interface (BRI). Using this equipment, schools are able to establish ISDN connection to the PoP and use Point-to-Point Protocol (PPP) to access local servers or the Internet. IP protocol utilization implies proper IP addressing and routing policies, taking into consideration six aspects:

- Security;
- Accounting;
- Performance;
- Cost;
- Future project development aspects;
- Requirements concerning the hardware and software platforms already adopted.

These aspects where carefully examined and a solution has been designed based on a virtual addressing scheme. This scheme is suitable for dealing with security and IP v4 addressing limitations.

The paper is organized as follows. Next section describes the proposed solution. Section 3 is concerned with implementation aspects. Finally, section 4 presents the conclusions.

2. Proposed solution

The proposed solution, based on a virtual addressing scheme, is composed of two main modules:

- an IP Address Translator module, implemented with the Linux IP Masquerading scheme [AU 1997];
- a routing module, which implements a suitable routing configuration.

Regarding security between the schools and the Internet, a firewall is needed together with address screening mechanisms and advanced accounting capabilities, allowing accounting by address, protocol, port, and, if possible, others. Due to limitations in the address allocation space of the IP v4 Internet protocol, today's Internet is running out of addresses. This should not limit the implementation and future development of the project. So, a solution based on the school computers having one invalid IP address, not visible to the Internet beyond the PoP border, is adequate. This solution introduces a new element in the model, the IP Address Translator, which keeps track of the IP traffic between the schools and the Internet, translating the invalid schools IP addresses to one valid IP address and vice versa.

The IP Address Translator solves five of the six requirements stated earlier. It grants a good level of security [BRENT 1995]: as schools have invalid IP address, the connection establishment from the Internet to the school is impossible, and because all connections between the school and the Internet passes through the address translator, accounting actions can be performed. Also, the school's address space is not bounded to IP v4 addressing limitations [RFC1700 1994] and at any time it is possible to extend the project to other parties. As for the cost, it can be implemented is a cost-effective manner, with the hardware and software platforms already adopted.

Network performance [RFC0791] requirements, are satisfied by using a suitable routing configuration in the PoP Access Server (Figure 1). The adopted solution doesn't require any special configuration of the schools computers. It transparently routes IP packets destined to the PoP local servers directly to them and through the IP Address Translator the ones destined to the Internet. Local server's traffic to the Internet is directly routed through the Access Server.

A general overview is presented in Figure 1, showing the Access Server, the PoP Local Servers (Serverl, Server2) and a School Computer connected to the PoP.

The routing model is described by analyzing three possible paths: from the School Computer to Internet; from the School Computer to PoP Local Servers; and from PoP Local Servers to the Internet.

School Computers are configured in a Private Virtual Network (PVN) architecture [Tannenbaum 1996], which interfaces use reserved and private IP addresses. In order to provide global network access to schools, a maximum number of protocols and applications must be supported.

Other solutions, based on proxying, have been considered (e.g. SOCKS proxying). These solutions require special client configuration and only few protocols and client applications support these proxying models. This is a serious disadvantage to these solutions, for satisfying the requirements stated earlier for this project.

The proposed solution is implemented with IP masquerading [AU 1997]. IP masquerade allows clients using invalid IP addresses to connect to the Internet using the IP masquerade machine's valid IP address (this machine is referred to as Masquerade Server). The masquerading procedure is transparent to the client. There is no need of additional configuration on the client side. Suitable routing configuration in the access server and the IP Masquerade Server, accordingly to the proposed routing model, assures the overall system operation.

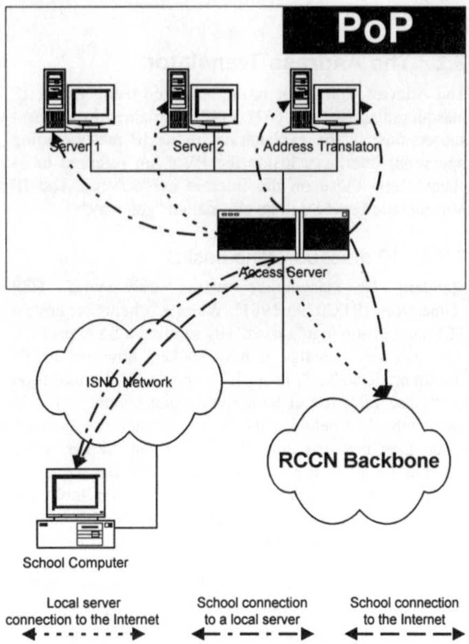

Figure 1 - Routing model

3. Implementation aspects

3.1. The hardware and software platforms

The hardware and software platforms are:

- Access Servers, ASCEND MAX ™ equipped with ISDN PRI ports, one Ethernet interface and one Serial interface;
- PoP Local Servers, Pentium™ based computers, running RedHat Linux;
- Masquerade Servers, Pentium™ 166MHz based computers, running RedHat Linux, with a 10Mbit Ethernet card;
- School Computers, Pentium™ 133MHz based computers, running Windows 95™, with an ISDN BRI card.

The PoP local network, connecting the Local Servers, the Masquerade Server and the Access Server, uses a 10Mbit Ethernet switch.

3.2. The Address Translator

The Address Translator is implemented using Linux IP masquerading features [AU 1997], explained in the next subsections. In the explanation of the IP masquerading operation, interfaces inside the PVN are refereed to as "client" and those on the Internet as “server”. The IP Masquerade Server will be also called "gateway".

3.2.1. IP masquerading basics

Standard IP masquerade works only with TCP connections [RFC0793 1981]. When a “client” requests a TCP connection to a “server” (by sending a SYN packet), the “gateway” creates a new socket, now on called "masquerade socket", using it to open a TCP connection to the “server”. It can be assumed that connection is in fact established between the “gateway” and the “server” rather than between the “client” and the “server”. The information about the "client" address and the requested connection parameters is recorded on a system table, the masquerading table. TCP packets and ICMP control packets received from the "client" are changed to reflect the "masquerade socket" properties (such as IP address, TCP port...), and then forwarded to the “server”. When TCP packets from the “server” are received, the demasquerade process is initiated by examining the destination port on the packet, in order to identify the “client” to whom the packet is destined. If the port does not match a "masquerading socket", then the packet is destined to the “gateway” and processed normally. If it does match one of the "masquerading sockets", then a lookup on the system masquerade table is performed and the original IP address and related TCP port are gathered from it. The packet is then changed accordingly, checksum is recalculated and it is finally forwarded to the "client".

3.2.2. UDP, ICMP and server-originated TCP connections

Some protocols require the “server” to originate TCP connections. The FTP protocol [STD0009 1985] operates this way, and it will be used as an example. In a common FTP session when a file transfer is initiated, the "client" opens a new socket, sends its IP address and port number to the “server”, and the latter opens the TCP connection back to the “client”. To handles this connection, the “gateway” packets received from the “client” are examined to determine if there it is necessary to create new sockets on the “gateway”, to allow the “server” to initiate connections between it and the "client". If a match is found (like FTP PORT command), then a new "masquerade socket" is created and the packet is modified to reflect this new socket instead of the one opened by the client. For example, the “gateway” identifies an FTP PORT command with this information: IP address 192.168.1.2 and port 8876. In this situation, when the “server” receives this information it will attempt to initiate a connection to that address and port. That connection would fail because the received address would be invalid. To avoid such failure, the “gateway” creates a new socket and binds it on, for example, port 1234. Then the packet that contains the PORT command is changed to reflect the new information IP=(router valid IP address) and PORT=1234. The original IP address and port are recorded on the system table and the packet is sent to the “server”. The newly created socket is now listening for connections and when the “server” connects to it, the “gateway” connects to the "client" (IP=192.168.1.2, PORT 8876) and subsequent packets are handled/masqueraded normally.

3.2.3. UDP packets

The principle for handling UDP [STD0006 19980] packets is the same as for standard TCP connections. However, since there is no connection information, the UDP packet stream is treated as a pseudo-connection. The pseudo-connection establishment occurs when the first packet is transmitted, and terminated after a timeout period of no traffic. As for TCP connections, a “server” cannot send UDP packets to a “client”. However, in many real time applications (e.g. video and sound streaming, games, etc.), multiple UDP streams are used, and “client” uses one stream to inform the “server” of address and port to which it must send UDP packets. This is the same case as the FTP, earlier used as an example. To handle these cases, it is possible to write specific masquerading modules.

3.2.4. ICMP masquerade

When encapsulated inside TCP packets ICMP packets [RFC0792 1981] are forwarded and the masquerade process passes all ICMP control messages to the client and vice versa. Special ICMP packets (echo and reply) are often very useful and several tools (like ping and Van

Jacobson traceroute) use it. All original rules are valid here though. The "client" can ping the "server", but the "server" cannot ping the "client".

3.3. Supported Protocols and Applications

Standard Internet protocols are supported by IP masquerade. These includes HTTP, POP/SMTP, Telnet, FTP (w/ specific module), Archie, NNTP, VRML, VJ traceroute, ICMP ping, IRC (w/ specific module), Gopher, WAIS, RealAudio, True Speech (1.1b), Internet Wave Player, Worlds Chat (0.9a), Alpha Worlds, Internet Phone (Originate calls only), Powwow (Originate calls only), CUSeeMe (w/ specific module) , VDOLive, NCSA Telnet (DOS), PC-Anywhere for Windows 2.0 (Only as a client, not as a server), NTP and Linux net-accounting package. Several network games are also supported with special modules installed.

Applications that are known not to work with IP masquerading are: Intel Internet Phone Beta 2, Intel Streaming Media Viewer Beta, Netscape Cooltalk, talk/ntalk, WebPhone and X-Windows.

3.4. The Routing Module

Routing implementation [HUNT 1997] is accomplished using only default routes on the PoP Local Servers and Access Server, and using default routes for the School Computers. These are implemented on the Access Server. In the Access Server there is a default route to the Internet (RCCN backbone Router which gives connection to Internet) and a "client" default gateway to the IP Masquerade Server. Therefore all traffic from the Schools Computers not destined to the IP subnetwork of PoP Local Servers is forwarded to the IP Masquerade Server, instead of being forwarded to the Internet. Each Local Server has a default route to the Access Server. Traffic between School Computers and PoP Local Servers is directly routed, by the Access Server, which forwards packets between the server's valid IP addresses and the school invalid ones.

This module has been implemented by suitable configuration of the ASCEND MAX TM, of the Local Servers, and of the IP Masquerade Server.

4. Conclusions

A methodology for network addressing and access in the RCTS has been presented and is now operational in the UTAD (Vila Real), UA (Aveiro) and LNEC (Lisbon) PoPs. The methodology is based on the concept of an IP Address Translator (the adopted solution uses the Linux IP Masquerading scheme [AU 1997]), supported by a proper routing configuration.

The proposed solution is, at the time of writing, the one that provides a better balance of the stated requirements and a wider range of services. Experience indicates that the solution is adequate for widespread use by the PoPs in RCTS.

5. Acknowledgments

The authors would like to thank the colleagues at FCCN, CI-UTAD and other PoPs for their support and helpful suggestions.

The authors are in debt to Pauline Middelink, Juan Jose Ciarlante, Richard Lynch, Nigel Metheringham, Keith Owens and Delian Delchev, who developed and implemented the IP masquerading software running on Linux. This high quality package is the base of the presented solution.

6. References

[UARTE 1998] *Projecto Internet na Escola* (1998). http://www.uarte.mct.pt.

[RCCN 1997] *Rede da Comunidade Científica Nacional* (1997). http://www.rccn.net.

[COELHO 1997] J. DIAS COELHO, e.t. (1997). *Livro Verde para a Sociedade da Informação em Portugal*. Missão para a Sociedade da Informação. Ministério da Ciência e Técnologia. HTTP://WWW.MISSAO-SI.MCT.PT

[TANNENBAUM 1996] ANDREW TANNENBAUM (1996). *Computer Networks*. Prentice-Hall International Editions. New York. USA.

[BRENT 1995] D. BRENT CHAPMAN & ELIZABETH D. ZWICKY (1995). *Building Internet Firewalls*. O'Reilly & Associates, Inc. Sebastopol. USA

[HUNT 1997] CRAIG HUNT (1997). *TCP/IP Network Administration*. O'Reilly & Associates, Inc. Sebastopol. USA

[AU 1997] AMBROSE AU AND KEN EVES, *The Linux IP-Masquerade mini-HOWTO*. http://www.sunsite.unc.edu/LDP (version 1.00, 01.Jan.1997).

[RFC0792 1981] *RFC0792 Internet Control Message Protocol*. J. Postel. Sep-01-1981. (Format: TXT=30404 bytes) (Obsoletes RFC0777) (Updated by RFC0950) (Status: STANDARD)

[RFC0793 1981] *RFC0793 Transmission Control Protocol*. J. Postel. Sep-01-1981. (Format: TXT=177957 bytes) (Status: STANDARD)

[RFC0791 1981] *RFC0791 Internet Protocol*. J. Postel. Sep-01-1981. (Format: TXT=97779 bytes) (Obsoletes RFC0760) (Status: STANDARD)

[RFC1700 1994] *RFC1700 ASSIGNED NUMBERS*. J. Reynolds,J. Postel. October 1994. (Format: TXT=458860 bytes) (Obsoletes RFC1340) (Also STD0002) (Status: STANDARD)

[STD0006 1980] *STD0006 User Datagram Protocol*. J. Postel. August 1980. (Format: TXT=5896 bytes) (Also RFC0768)

[STD0009 1985] *STD0009 File Transfer Protocol*. J. Postel, J. Reynolds. October 1985. (Format: TXT=148316 bytes) (Also RFC0959)

Anycast as an Application Layer Service

Miklós Berzsenyi[1] Hui Zhang[2] István Vajk[1]

[1] Technical University of Budapest, Department of Automation, H-1521 Budapest, Hungary
bermik@sun.aut.bme.hu, vajk@aut.bme.hu

[2] School of Computer Science, Carnegie Mellon University, Pittsburgh, USA 15213 hzhang@cs.cmu.edu

Abstract

In this paper, we present a new approach to application layer anycasting. The key to anycast is making it possible for clients to efficiently find the 'best' server for a given application in an unknown group of servers. We designed a selective anycast protocol, which is aimed at picking the right server based on application specific metrics, such as network delay and server load. This paper considers server-choosing metrics and efficient mechanisms to compute these metrics. We also present simulation results, which show our approach's merit, and proves that anycast can significantly improve the performance as compared to the traditional methods.

1 Introduction

On the Internet today, the World Wide Web is becoming an increasingly important application. Further, some of the most visited web sites consist of uncacheable data, either because the data is private, the data becomes stale quickly, or the data is customized for each user. We have also observed that network service has been degrading for the last few years, until currently, clients are able to retrieve only hundreds of bytes per second during the Internet's busiest periods.

The traditional method to overcome scarce network resources has been caching [3]. But caching becomes less and less effective as servers with uncacheable data become more common. Since only servers are able to deliver data to clients, we must consider server-initiated mechanisms for improving performance. Previously, server-initiated solutions have consisted mainly of infrastructure improvements such as using more powerful computers or buying faster network connections. While these solutions are certainly effective, they are not perfect. A congested link inside the network is the great equalizer among server hardware: regardless of how fast the server can push data into the network, the client will only receive it as fast as the congested link will allow.

In an attempt to avoid the congested link problem, server maintainers have begun to establish ``mirrors'' of a server at other locations in the network. If a client is dissatisfied with the performance of a server, it may switch to any of the mirrors. However, unless the client is clairvoyant, it will have difficulty picking the server that can supply it with the best performance. Still, as anyone who has ever beaten the odds and picked the right mirror will attest, this approach has merit. By scattering servers around the Internet, there is less of a chance that every path between a client and the servers will be congested. The missing piece of the puzzle is how to automatically choose the best server for a given client.

In 1993, Partridge et al [7] introduced the concept of anycast, a network service that would deliver a message to any one of a group of servers on the Internet. A selective anycast service is exactly what is needed to choose the best mirror server. By ``selective,'' we mean that the choice of server should be based on some application-specific metric. This paper will consider server-choosing metrics and efficient mechanisms to compute those metrics. The rest of the paper will be structured as follows: Section 2 will discuss previous work in this area. Section 3 will discuss the design space for anycast protocols. Section 4 will cover simulation experiments which explore the tradeoffs among our metrics. Finally, Section 5 will put our work in perspective.

2 Related Work

There have been several works dealing with network probing to choose a server from a group. Guyton et al [4] studied a number of mechanisms ranging from monitoring routing updates to using a series of statically-located hosts which probe the network. In Guyton's terminology, our work focuses on ''reactive'' mechanisms while his work focused on ``proactive'' mechanisms (though not to the exclusion of reactive mechanisms). In other words, Guyton's emphasis was on server-initiated network information collection, while our work emphasizes gathering information about a client from the client's query messages to the anycast group.

Anycast was first proposed by Partridge et al [7]. They envisioned a network-layer service which would route a client's datagrams to the server that is the fewest number of hops away. Levine et al [5] also developed a network-layer method of finding the closest host in a group. This version of anycast is not well-suited to the problem we have chose to solve because of its inflexible metric. We believe that server choice should be based on a variety of metrics including, but not limited to, hop count. Some servers may wish to use server load, or achievable throughput between the client and server. Also, we believe that the metric information, given that it is server-specific, is best left out of the network layer. Bhattacharjee et al [1] as well as Francis [3] have considered the infrastructure necessary to support application-layer anycast. Bhattacharjee's scheme involves altering clients' DNS resolvers to choose one server from a group when presented with an anycast address. Our work is meant to coexist with their work. Our mechanisms for finding anycast servers could be implemented inside the DNS framework.

Finally, we consider caching [2]. While caching has the same goal as our work, it takes the opposite approach. With caching, the first client to access a document forces the document to be cached so subsequent clients can take advantage of the nearby cached copy. Our work focuses on giving all clients quick access. In addition, as has already been mentioned, many services are uncacheable. In general, though, caching and anycast should complement each other.

3 Anycast proposal

The key to anycast is making it possible for clients to efficiently find the "best" server in an unknown group of servers. When designing an anycast protocol, there are a number of different metrics that might contribute to the determination of which server is "best". These include: (a) the network delay between the client and each server, (b) the available bandwidth between the client and each server, (c) whether or not the request can be served out of the cache at each server, and (d) the load at each server. For example, the importance of (a) varies depending on the amount of processing each request will require, the importance of (b) varies depending on the amount of data we expect to transmit, and the importance of (c) varies depending on the degree to which caching is beneficial and plausible for the application in question. Assuming that the amount of data transmitted is small (so that clients are indifferent to available bandwidth), and that caching behavior is either irrelevant or will be good regardless of the distribution of requests, we focus on (a) and (d); that is, we are primarily concerned with request latency, and we assume that latency mainly depends on network delay and server load, plus any overhead imposed by the anycast protocol.

3.1 Proposal overview

Since clients are initially unaware of the composition of the server group, they must be able to obtain the identity of one or more members by sending a request to some well-known authority. We call this request a FindServer request. The authority can be a single server contacted via ordinary unicast, but relying on a single server suffers from all of the well-known problems with centralized systems. A more scalable and fault-tolerant solution is for this authority to be a set of servers which can be contacted via multicast. Which of the anycast servers should subscribe to this multicast group? Clearly, having every anycast server receive every FindServer request would introduce unacceptable overhead. There are two ways to limit the number of anycast servers which receive a FindServer request: we can use TTL scoping to limit the range of a FindServer request, or the multicast group can include only a subset of the anycast servers.

Once the multicast servers receive a FindServer request, how do they ensure that the client is directed to the best server, i.e. the server which is least loaded and with whom it experiences the lowest network delay? If we are using TTL scoping, then each receiving server can simply respond with a local prediction of load (using some agreed upon metric), and the client will be able to determine relative loads and delays. If we are multicasting to a subset of the servers, then the members of the subset must obtain load information from the servers which are not in the subset. For simplicity and efficiency, this implies some hierarchical organization of the anycast servers into regular servers and representative servers, along with a grouping of the servers into clusters where each cluster has exactly one representative. Then, each regular server will report load information to its representative so that the representatives can respond to FindServer requests with the identity and load prediction of the predicted least-loaded server in their cluster. Notice that the delay that the client calculates will reflect its distance to the representative instead of its distance to the server identified in the response. To minimize this distortion, clustering needs to be based on delay between servers.

In the following two sections, we describe the basic TTL scoping scheme and the basic clustering scheme in greater detail. For each scheme, we present the protocols by which new servers are added to the server group (the Join protocol), the protocol with which clients obtain server identities and choose a server to receive their data request (the Anycast protocol), and the protocol by which the server group recovers from network and server failures (the Recovery protocol). In subsequent sections, we compare the two schemes, identify their weaknesses, and propose improvements.

3.2 Basic

TTL scoping scheme All servers subscribe to a multicast group, the AllServers group, and each server keeps track of its predicted future load based on its current load and the number of FindServer requests it has responded to in the last time period.

Join protocol. New servers simply subscribe to the AllServers group.
Anycast protocol. When using TTL scoping to limit the number of servers that receive a FindServer request, clients need to discover an appropriate TTL value; that is, clients must perform an expanding ring search (ERS). Servers which receive FindServer requests respond with their load prediction. When a client

receives a response, if the load prediction is below some threshhold, then it sends its data request to that server. Otherwise, it waits until it either receives a response which contains a sufficiently low load prediction, or the allowed waiting period has passed. If the allowed waiting period has passed and a minimum number of responses were received, then it sends its data request to one of the servers, selected based on response time and load prediction. Otherwise, it continues the ERS. The client caches its final TTL value. The server which receives the data request processes it and sends the appropriate response.

Recovery protocol. No recovery protocol is necessary.

3.3 Basic clustering scheme

All servers subscribe to a multicast group, the AllServers group, and representative servers also subscribe to another multicast group, the Representatives group. Each server keeps track of the identity of its representative and sends it a load information update once per time period. Each representative acknowledges its load information updates, combining them with information it maintains on the number of times it recommended each cluster member in the past period to predict each cluster member's load in the near future. Representatives also update their cluster membership information if necessary.

Join protocol. As mentioned in the overview, clusters have to be created carefully so that the delay calculated by a client, which is the delay between itself and each representative server, is a fairly accurate portrayal of the delay between the client and the server suggested in the representative's response. Therefore, new servers have to gather delay information before they can decide on which cluster to join. A new server multicasts to the AllServers group and uses the responses to build a list of the servers (this list need not be complete). It then measures the RTT between itself and every other server. If it discovers that the RTT between itself and at least one representative server is below some threshhold, then it sends an initial load information update to the closest of these in order to join an existing cluster. Otherwise, if it discovers that the RTT between itself and at least one regular server is below the threshhold, then it asks the other server to become a representative. The other server will promote itself by multicasting to the AllServers group, after which each regular member of its original cluster (and any other cluster) may choose to join the new cluster, and the new server will join the new cluster. Otherwise, the new server becomes its own representative (i.e. a one-member cluster).

Anycast protocol. A client multicasts a FindServer request to the Representatives group. Representative servers respond with the identity and load prediction of their predicted least-loaded cluster member. When the client receives a response, if the load prediction is below some threshold, then it sends its data request to that server. Otherwise, it waits until it either receives a response which contains a sufficiently low load prediction, or the allowed waiting period has passed. If the allowed waiting period has passed, then it sends its data request to one of the servers, selected based on response time and load prediction. The client caches at least the identity of the representative server whose recommendation it used. The server which receives the data request processes it and sends the appropriate response.

Recovery protocol. If a regular member does not receive an acknowledgment for one of its load information updates within a time period, it sends another. If this second update also times out, then it multicasts to the AllServers group that its representative is unresponsive. The regular servers who belonged to this cluster exchange messages to determine their RTTs to each other, and then each advertises the average of its RTTs. The server with the smallest average promotes itself by multicasting to the AllServers group, and the other servers either update their choice of representative or run the join protocol. If a representative doesn't receive a load information update from one of its cluster members within a time period, it explicitly requests this information from that member. If there is no response to this request, then it assumes that the member no longer exists and updates its cluster membership information.

3.4 TTL scoping versus clustering:

A comparison There are four drawbacks to the TTL scoping scheme. First, performing an ERS adds latency. Second, hop count may not correspond to network delay, so that the set of servers that receive the FindServer request may not include the set of closest servers. Third, the network topology and distribution of servers may be unfriendly to ERS; that is, the percentage of servers reached may always be either too small or too large. And, finally and most importantly, the servers will not be load balanced if the distribution of clients does not match the distribution of servers. This imbalance could get quite extreme. For example, if clients generally need to cross a backbone link to reach a server, but the servers are at vastly different numbers of hops from the backbone, then servers which are far from the backbone will never receive any requests. These drawbacks prevent the TTL scoping scheme from being a good, general solution.

In contrast, using clustering takes approximately the minimum additional latency for application-level anycast (i.e. one additional RTT for the FindServer request and response), is not dependent on hop count accurately reflecting network delay, is flexible with respect to network topology and server distribution, and allows some degree of load balancing across all of the servers. On the other hand, the server structure inherent in clustering imposes some additional complexity and overhead, requiring protocols to create and join clusters, to exchange load information between the regular members and the representative member in each cluster, and to maintain clustering in the face of network and server failures. In addition, there is no way to efficiently provide the accurate delay information obtained in the TTL scoping scheme, so clients must make their server choice based on less accurate information. Decreasing cluster sizes would increase the accuracy of the delay calculation, but it would also increase the percentage of servers which receive each FindServer request. This tradeoff between FindServer overhead and a client's ability to identify the best server is the greatest weakness of the basic clustering scheme.

3.5 The modified schemes

The main weakness of the TTL scoping scheme is its inability to automatically balance load among the servers if the distribution of servers and clients is not close to ideal. The problem is that, if a client increases its TTL in order to reach more servers (so that load can be more evenly distributed among the servers), then the FindServer request overhead will also increase. We can allow clients to reach more servers without adding to FindServer overhead by combining TTL scoping with clustering. This modified scheme, which we call clustered TTL scoping, is exactly like the basic clustering scheme described in section 3.3 except that clients use ERS to locate representative servers, and clients only need to cache a good TTL value. Although clustered TTL scoping no longer provides accurate delay information, and requires the additional complexity and overhead of clustering, it improves upon basic TTL scoping in two ways. First, as mentioned above, it has better load balancing properties because TTLs can be set much higher (reaching, through their representatives, a much larger number of servers) without increasing FindServer overhead. Second, it does not rely on having an ERS-friendly network topology and server distribution because reaching a large percentage of the representative servers simply causes this scheme to behave like the basic clustering scheme. If the topology and server distribution is ERS-friendly, then clustered TTL scoping also partially alleviates the problem with the basic clustering scheme; that is, clustered TTL scoping decreases the FindServer overhead for a given cluster size.

Another way to address the problem with the basic clustering scheme is to permit representative servers to quickly decide whether or not to ignore a FindServer request, where the cost of making this decision and the cost of discarding a request should be much less than the cost of servicing the request. Assuming that the representative servers are able to correctly identify and discard a significant percentage of FindServer requests, then this modified scheme, which we call clustering with discard, will decrease the FindServer overhead for a given cluster size. Note that permitting discards requires a mechanism for disallowing discards in order to ensure that all clients will eventually be able to obtain the identity of a server. This can be simply accomplished by adding a flag in the FindServer request, which should only set the flag if they are extremely concerned with latency or were unable to obtain service without the flag. In clustering with discard, there are three factors which could be used in the discard decision: the hop count from client to representative, past calculations of the relative load of the cluster, and the predicted load of the predicted least-loaded cluster member. The first two can be combined by using a hop count threshold which varies depending on the relative load experienced by a cluster. That is, a representative can keep track of what percentage of the data requests are being serviced by its cluster (calculated from information passed in the load information updates and by keeping track of the number of FindServer requests it received) and raise (or lower) its hop count threshold if the number of requests its cluster has serviced is below (or above) some low (or high) watermark of what constitutes its fair share of requests (based on what percentage of the servers are in its cluster). Upon receiving a FindServer request, the representative will discard it if the hop count is above its threshold and it predicts no idle cluster members. In other words, clustering with discard is like clustered TTL scoping except that the hop count is measured around the server instead of the client. The disadvantage of clustering with discard are that all representatives still receive all FindServer requests. The advantages are that it addresses the cluster size versus FindServer overhead issue even with ERS-unfriendly networks, it has no ERS overhead, and it has even better load balancing properties.

4 Evaluation

To evaluate and compare the performance of clustered TTL scoping and clustering with discard, we implemented both protocols as well as a base case in a packet-level simulator. The base case is to have a single well-known server, i.e. clients do not need to send FindServer requests.

4.1 Simulation environment

We use a discrete event packet-level simulator which supports unicast and multicast routing, and UDP and TCP communication. Routing minimizes the number of hops/packet. Links are characterized by minimum delay, d, and loss rate. UDP communication is simulated by forwarding undropped packets hop by hop with a delay uniformly distributed between d and 2d. TCP communication is simulated by calculating end-to-end delay as the sum of ave path delay and bytes transmitted/bandwidth, where ave path delay is calculated by summing the average link delays of the links on the route, and bandwidth is calculated by plugging ave path delay and the average loss rate of the links on the route into equation 3 from [8]. Thus, unlike the real world, loss and delay in the simulation are independent of the number of packets traversing a link (so, for example, the single server base case does not suffer from network congestion).

All of our experiments use a single, randomly generated network topology. The topology has two levels: a top level backbone network and a second level of regional networks. Each router in the backbone is connected to a regional router as well as being randomly connected to an average of four other backbone routers. Each regional network (of which there were 20) is connected to the top level backbone through a single router, and each regional router was randomly connected to an average of three other routers. Each backbone link was assigned a value for d of around 20ms to 40ms, while each regional link was assigned a value for d of around 1ms to 5ms. All links were assigned loss probabilities in the 0.1regional router is connected to one of the 400 hosts, and there are no multi-homed hosts. In our simulations, all hosts are either anycast clients or anycast servers. The servers are randomly distributed. Testing with less even distributions of clients and servers would have been informative, especially when comparing the two anycast protocols.

For the anycast simulations, we ran 10 server and 25 server tests. In the base case simulations, the single server was simulated as a 10 (or 25) processor machine; that is, each individual request took the same amount of time to process as in the anycast tests, but the single server could simultaneously process 10 (or 25) requests. In addition, the single server performs perfect load balancing amongst its processors. For simplicity, it was assumed that servers would process all non-data requests (e.g. FindServer requests) immediately and at no cost. This favors the anycast protocols. To partially account for the FindServer overhead in the anycast protocols, representative servers doubled their own load calculation when choosing a server to recommend in a FindServer response. Finally, servers were clustered with a RTT threshold of 100ms. For the 25 server case, this resulted in an average of 4 servers/cluster. In the 10 server, however, most of the clusters only contained a single member (there were 6 clusters).

4.2 Workload

The simulation was driven by a web server log. The log records 1,160,399 requests to the CMU CS web server from Nov. 23, 1997 to Nov. 30, 1997. For each request, the log contains a timestamp, a client identification, and the amount of data requested. Since the log records requests from 146,829 clients, each client in the simulation actually corresponds to many clients from the log. To avoid distorting client cache performance (i.e. a client's cache of an anycast server address), simulation clients maintain separate caches for each log client they represent. Server processing time for data requests is assumed to be linear with the amount of data requested.

4.3 Performance metrics

We primarily evaluate each technique based on perceived performance and server overhead. The perceived performance is measured as client response time, which is subdivided into FindServer response time and data request response time. Server overhead is measured as the ratio of FindServer requests processed to the number of data requests sent; that is, both of our anycast proposals may server. result in multiple servers processing each FindServer request, so we measure the degree of redundancy.

In order to gain a better understanding of the performance of our protocols, we also measure the service time of data requests at the servers. This allows us to determine how much of the client's perceived request latency was due to network latency. Also, by comparing the service times of the anycast protocols to that of the base case, we can determine how successfully each scheme loadbalanced the servers.

	10 servers			25 servers		
	ERS	CWD	Base	ERS	CWD	Base
Find	38.76	35.31	0	28.25	30.83	0
Fetch	679.69	672.56	659.71	747.93	745.67	741.67
Total	718.45	707.87	659.71	776.18	775.50	741.67

Table 1: Average Time (ms) for a client to receive data from the server

4.4 Results

In Table 1, we see a breakdown of average client waiting time for each of the protocols in each of the topologies. The columns are marked as follows: ``ERS" corresponds to clustered TTL scoping, ``CWD" corresponds to clustering with discard, and ``Base" corresponds to the single-server base case. The first row, marked ``Find," displays the average time to find a server to satisfy each request. The row marked ``Fetch," displays the average time to load the data. The row marked ``Total" is the sum of the two rows above. All times are in milliseconds. Note that the base case has no find overhead since each client only goes to one server each time.

There are several interesting details in Table 1. First, we see that the time required to find a suitable server is

	10 servers			25 servers		
	ERS	CWD	Base	ERS'	CWD	Base
Find	375.62	321.34	248.63	320.27	301.83	242.67
Total	3.97	2.73	n/a	3.93	2.93	n/a

Table 2: Average Time (ms) for a server to service a data request, and average number of servers that process each FindServer request

5% of the total time of each transfer for both ERS and CWD. The performance of the anycast protocols improve as the number of servers increases. This is also unsurprising as the average distance between a client and the closest server will decrease as the number of servers increases, and the same request stream should be more easily handled by a larger number of servers if the request stream is heavy enough to load the servers.

In Table 2, we see measurements of the service time as perceived by the server, and the degree of redundancy in processing FindServer requests. The columns are the same as in the previous table. The row marked ``Fetch," displays the average time (in milliseconds) to process a request at the server. The row marked ``Find Redundancy" is the average number of servers that process each FindServer request.

Comparing the server Fetch values to the client Fetch values, we can see that the majority of client-perceived latency for the base case was due to network latency. In contrast, the majority of the client-perceived latency of the anycast protocols is due to server processing time. Comparing the average times of the ERS and CWD protocols, we see that, as expected, CWD is the more successful at load balancing. We also see that, while adding more servers does decrease the average service time slightly, 2.5 times as many servers translates into a relatively small decrease in service time, even after factoring out the minimum time (as measured by the perfectly load-balanced base case). Finally, by comparing the network latencies experienced in each protocol, we see that, as expected, the anycast protocols were able to reduce network latency by directing client requests to nearby servers. We also see that ERS was slightly more successful at reducing network latency than CWD. This is due to ERS's strict adherence to hop count from the client. In CWD, a nearby cluster may choose to ignore a request because it is heavily loaded. Since the penalty of bad load balancing is significantly more severe than the penalty of being serviced by a slightly more distant cluster, this appears to be a good tradeoff. Finally, notice that the number of servers that process each FindServer request is fairly low, indicating that the server overhead in these protocols can probably be maintained at acceptable levels. We notice that the 25 server CWD case already has almost the same client request latency as the base case.

5 Conclusions

When a server's data in uncacheable, it makes sense to replicate that server around the network so that clients will have a better chance of avoiding congestion when communicating with it. Once the server is replicated, however, the challenge becomes choosing the correct mirror for a client to use. We have investigated mechanisms for picking a server based on a client's multicast query message. These mechanisms exist purely at the application layer and require no additional network probing. We used trace-based simulations to explore two anycast methods: clustered TTL with scoping, and clustering with discard. The former used a client-initiated expanding ring search to find the nearest cluster. The latter used the hop count from the client to the server to determine the appropriate cluster for a client. In both mechanisms, once a client found a cluster, its requests would be handed off to the least-loaded member of the cluster.

The simulations show that a reasonable method of application-layer anycast can be derived from our proposed mechanisms. The time to find a server imposes another 5% of overhead on data transfer time on a lightly congested network. With an amount of network congestion comparable to that in the Internet, we see that our anycast methods can outperform the base case.

References

1. S. Bhattacharjee, E. M. Ammar, E. Zegura, V. Shah, and Z. Fei. Application layer anycasting. In Proceedings of IEEE Infocom '97, 1997.
2. A distributed testbed for national information provisioning. http://ircache.nlanr.net/Cache/.
3. Paul Francis. A call for an internet-wide host proximity service (HOPS). http://www.ingrid.org/hops/wp.html.
4. James D. Guyton and Michael F. Schwartz. Locating nearby copies of replicated internet services. Technical Report CU-CS-762-95, University of Colorado at Boulder, 1995.
5. B. N. Levine and J. J. Garcia-Luna-Aceves. Improving internet multicast with routing labels. In Proceedings of ICNP '97, 1997.
6. M. Mathis, J. Semke, and J. Mahdavi. The macroscopic behavior of the tcp congestion avoidance algorithm. Computer Communication Review, 27(3), July 1997.
7. C. Partridge, T. Mendez, and W. Milliken. RFC 1546: Host anycasting service, October 1993.

Monotonicity Properties and Simple Bounds on the Mean Cycle Time in Acyclic Fork-Join Queueing Networks

Nikolai K. Krivulin*
Faculty of Mathematics and Mechanics, St.Petersburg State University
Bibliotechnaya Sq.2, Petrodvorets, St.Petersburg, 198904 Russia,
E-mail: nikolai@knk.usr.pu.ru
URL: http://www.math.spbu.ru/~krivulin

Abstract

The (max,+)-algebra approach is applied to establish some monotonicity properties and to get algebraic bounds on the service cycle completion times in acyclic fork-join queueing networks. The obtained results are extended to derive simple lower and upper bounds on the mean cycle time in stochastic networks.

1 Introduction

We consider acyclic fork-join queueing networks which consist of single-server nodes with infinite buffers [1, 4]. A network includes both source nodes representing external arrival streams of customers, and internal nodes. At the initial time, the buffers in the source nodes are assumed to have infinite number of customers, whereas the buffers in the internal nodes may have any fixed numbers of customers.

One of the problems of interest in the analysis of stochastic queueing networks is to evaluate the mean cycle time of a network. Both the mean cycle time and its inverse which can be regarded as a throughput, present performance measures commonly used to describe efficiency of the network operation.

It is frequently rather difficult to evaluate the mean cycle time exactly, even though the network under study is quite simple. To get information about the performance measure in this case, one can apply computer simulation to produce reasonable estimates. Another approach is to derive bounds on the mean cycle time (see [2, 4] for related examples).

The paper is concerned with the derivation of a lower and upper bounds on the mean cycle time for stochastic acyclic fork-join queueing networks. A useful way to represent dynamics of the networks is based on the $(\max,+)$-algebra approach [6, 4]. We apply the $(\max,+)$-algebra dynamic representation proposed in [10, 11] to establish some monotonicity properties with respect to the initial numbers of customers in the internal nodes and to get algebraic bounds on the cycle completion times. The obtained results are then extended to derive bounds on the mean cycle time in the stochastic case.

*This work was supported in part by the Russian Federation Ministry of Education Programme "The Universities of Russia" under Grant #4233

2 Algebraic Preliminaries

The $(\max,+)$-algebra is an idempotent commutative semiring (idempotent semifield) which is defined as $\mathbb{R}_{\max} = (\underline{\mathbb{R}}, \oplus, \otimes)$ with $\underline{\mathbb{R}} = \mathbb{R} \cup \{\varepsilon\}$, $\varepsilon = -\infty$, and binary operations $\oplus$ and $\otimes$ defined as

$$x \oplus y = \max(x, y), \quad x \otimes y = x + y \quad \forall x, y \in \underline{\mathbb{R}}.$$

As it is easy to see, the operations $\oplus$ and $\otimes$ retain most of the properties of the ordinary addition and multiplication, including associativity, commutativity, and distributivity of multiplication over addition. However, the operation $\oplus$ is idempotent; that is, for any $x \in \underline{\mathbb{R}}$, one has $x \oplus x = x$.

There are the null and identity elements, namely ε and 0, to satisfy the conditions $x \oplus \varepsilon = \varepsilon \oplus x = x$, and $x \otimes 0 = 0 \otimes x = x$, for any $x \in \underline{\mathbb{R}}$. The null element ε and the operation $\otimes$ are related by the usual absorption rule involving $x \otimes \varepsilon = \varepsilon \otimes x = \varepsilon$.

Non-negative power of any $x \in \mathbb{R}$ is defined as

$$x^0 = 0, \quad x^q = \underbrace{x \otimes \cdots \otimes x}_{q \text{ times}}, \quad q \geq 1.$$

Clearly, the new power x^q corresponds to qx in conventional algebra. In this paper, we will use the power notations only in the $(\max,+)$-algebra sense.

The $(\max,+)$-algebra of matrices is readily introduced in the regular way. Specifically, for any $(n \times n)$-matrices $X = (x_{ij})$ and $Y = (y_{ij})$, the entries of $U = X \oplus Y$ and $V = X \otimes Y$ are calculated respectively as

$$u_{ij} = x_{ij} \oplus y_{ij}, \quad \text{and} \quad v_{ij} = \sum_{k=1}^{n}{}_{\oplus}\, x_{ik} \otimes y_{kj},$$

where $\sum_{\oplus}$ stands for the iterated operation $\oplus$. As the null element, the matrix $\mathcal{E}$ with all entries equal to ε is taken in the algebra, whereas the diagonal matrix $E = \text{diag}(0, \ldots, 0)$ with the off-diagonal entries set to ε presents the identity.

For any square matrix $X \neq \mathcal{E}$, one can define

$$X^0 = E, \quad X^q = \underbrace{X \otimes \cdots \otimes X}_{q \text{ times}}, \quad q \geq 1.$$

However, idempotency in this algebra leads, in particular, to the matrix identity

$$(X \oplus Y)^q = X^q \oplus X^{q-1} \otimes Y \oplus \cdots \oplus Y^q.$$

As direct consequences of the above identity, one has

$$\begin{aligned}(X \oplus Y)^q &\geq X^p \otimes Y^{q-p}, \\ (E \oplus X)^q &\geq (E \oplus X)^p \geq X^p,\end{aligned}$$

for all $p = 0, 1, \ldots, q$.

For any matrix X, its norm is defined as

$$\|X\|_\oplus = \sum\nolimits_{\oplus}{}_{i,j} x_{ij} = \max_{i,j} x_{ij}.$$

The matrix norm possesses the usual properties. Specifically, for any matrix X, it holds $\|X\|_\oplus \geq \varepsilon$, and $\|X\|_\oplus = \varepsilon$ if and only if $X = \mathcal{E}$. Furthermore, $\|c \otimes X\|_\oplus = c \otimes \|X\|_\oplus$ for any $c \in \underline{\mathbb{R}}$, and

$$\begin{aligned}\|X \oplus Y\|_\oplus &= \|X\|_\oplus \oplus \|Y\|_\oplus, \\ \|X \otimes Y\|_\oplus &\leq \|X\|_\oplus \otimes \|Y\|_\oplus\end{aligned}$$

for any two conforming matrices X and Y. Note that for any $c > 0$, we also have $\|cX\|_\oplus = c\|X\|_\oplus$.

Consider an $(n \times n)$-matrix X with its entries $x_{ij} \in \underline{\mathbb{R}}$. It can be treated as an adjacency matrix of an oriented graph with n nodes, provided each entry $x_{ij} \neq \varepsilon$ implies the existence of the arc (i, j) in the graph, while $x_{ij} = \varepsilon$ does the lack of the arc.

It is easy to verify that for any integer $q \geq 1$, the matrix X^q has its the entry $x_{ij}^{(q)} \neq \varepsilon$ if and only if there exists a path from node i to node j in the graph, which consists of q arcs. Furthermore, if the graph associated with the matrix X is acyclic, we have $X^q = \mathcal{E}$ for all $q > p$, where p is the length of the longest path in the graph. Otherwise, provided that the graph is not acyclic, one can construct a path of any length, lying along circuits, and then it holds that $X^q \neq \mathcal{E}$ for all $q \geq 0$.

3 Further Algebraic Results

For any graph, its adjacency matrix G with the elements equal either to 0 or ε is said to be standard. It is easy to verify the next statement.

Proposition 1 *For any matrix X, it holds*

$$X \leq \|X\|_\oplus \otimes G,$$

where G is the standard adjacency matrix of the graph associated with X.

In particular, for a matrix $D = \operatorname{diag}(d_1, \ldots, d_n)$, we have $D \leq \|D\|_\oplus \otimes E$.

Proposition 2 *Let matrices $X_1, \ldots, X_k$ have a common associated acyclic graph, p be the length of the longest path in the graph, and*

$$X = X_1^{m_1} \otimes \cdots \otimes X_k^{m_k},$$

where $m_1, \ldots, m_k$ are nonnegative integers.

If it holds that $m_1 + \cdots + m_k > p$, then $X = \mathcal{E}$.

Proof: It follows from Proposition 1 that

$$\begin{aligned}X &= X_1^{m_1} \otimes \cdots \otimes X_k^{m_k} \\ &\leq \|X_1\|_\oplus^{m_1} \otimes \cdots \otimes \|X_k\|_\oplus^{m_k} \otimes G^m,\end{aligned}$$

where $m = m_1 + \cdots + m_k$.

Since the associated graph is acyclic, it holds that $G^q = \mathcal{E}$ for all $q > p$. Therefore, if $m > p$, then $G^m = \mathcal{E}$, and we arrive at the inequality $X \leq \mathcal{E}$ which leads us to the desired result. ∎

Lemma 1 *Let matrices $X_1, \ldots, X_k$ have a common associated acyclic graph, and p be the length of the longest path in the graph.*

If $\|X_i\|_\oplus \geq 0$ for all $i = 1, \ldots, k$, then for any nonnegative integers $m_1, \ldots, m_k$, it holds

$$\left\| \prod\nolimits_{\otimes}{}_{i=1}^{k} (E \oplus X_i)^{m_i} \right\|_\oplus \leq \left(\sum\nolimits_{\oplus}{}_{i=1}^{k} \|X_i\|_\oplus \right)^p,$$

where $\prod_\otimes$ denotes the iterated operation $\otimes$.

Proof: Consider the matrix

$$X = \prod\nolimits_{\otimes}{}_{i=1}^{k} (E \oplus X_i)^{m_i},$$

and represent it in the form

$$\begin{aligned}X &= (E \oplus X_1)^{m_1} \otimes \cdots \otimes (E \oplus X_k)^{m_k} \\ &= \sum\nolimits_{\oplus}{}_{i_1=0}^{m_1} X_1^{i_1} \otimes \cdots \otimes \sum\nolimits_{\oplus}{}_{i_k=0}^{m_k} X_k^{i_k} \\ &= \sum\nolimits_{\oplus}{}_{i_1=0}^{m_1} \cdots \sum\nolimits_{\oplus}{}_{i_k=0}^{m_k} X_1^{i_1} \otimes \cdots \otimes X_k^{i_k} \\ &\leq \sum\nolimits_{\oplus}{}_{0 \leq i_1 + \cdots + i_k \leq m} X_1^{i_1} \otimes \cdots \otimes X_k^{i_k},\end{aligned}$$

where $m = m_1 + \cdots + m_k$. From Proposition 2 we may replace the last term to get

$$X \leq \sum\nolimits_{\oplus}{}_{0 \leq i_1 + \cdots + i_k \leq p} X_1^{i_1} \otimes \cdots \otimes X_k^{i_k}.$$

Proceeding to the norm, with its additive and multiplicative properties, we arrive at the inequality

$$\|X\|_\oplus \leq \sum\nolimits_{\oplus}{}_{0 \leq i_1 + \cdots + i_k \leq p} \|X_1\|_\oplus^{i_1} \otimes \cdots \otimes \|X_k\|_\oplus^{i_k}.$$

Since $0 \leq \|X_i\|_\oplus \leq \|X_1\|_\oplus \oplus \cdots \oplus \|X_k\|_\oplus$ for all $i = 1, \ldots, k$, we finally have

$$\begin{aligned}\|X\|_\oplus &\leq \sum\nolimits_{\oplus}{}_{i=0}^{p} (\|X_1\|_\oplus \oplus \cdots \oplus \|X_k\|_\oplus)^p \\ &= (\|X_1\|_\oplus \oplus \cdots \oplus \|X_k\|_\oplus)^p.\end{aligned}$$

∎

4 Elements of Probability

In this section we present some probabilistic results associated with (max, +)-algebra concepts introduced above. We start with a lemma which states properties of the expectation with respect to the operations $\oplus$ and $\otimes$.

Lemma 2 *Let $\xi_1, \ldots, \xi_k$ be random variables taking their values in $\mathbb{R}$, and such that their expected values $\mathbb{E}[\xi_i]$, $i = 1, \ldots, k$, exist. Then it holds*

1. $\mathbb{E}[\xi_1 \oplus \cdots \oplus \xi_k] \geq \mathbb{E}[\xi_1] \oplus \cdots \oplus \mathbb{E}[\xi_k]$,
2. $\mathbb{E}[\xi_1 \otimes \cdots \otimes \xi_k] = \mathbb{E}[\xi_1] \otimes \cdots \otimes \mathbb{E}[\xi_k]$.

Proof: Clearly, it will suffice to prove the lemma only for $k = 2$, and then extend the proof by induction to the case of arbitrary k.

To verify the first inequality, first assume that one of the expectation on its right side, say $\mathbb{E}[\xi_2]$, is infinite; that is $\mathbb{E}[\xi_2] = \varepsilon$. Since it holds that $\xi_1 \oplus \xi_2 \geq \xi_1$, we have

$$\mathbb{E}[\xi_1 \oplus \xi_2] \geq \mathbb{E}[\xi_1] = \mathbb{E}[\xi_1] \oplus \xi_2 = \mathbb{E}[\xi_1] \oplus \mathbb{E}[\xi_2].$$

Suppose now that $\mathbb{E}[\xi_1], \mathbb{E}[\xi_2] > \varepsilon$, and consider the obvious identity

$$x \oplus y = \frac{1}{2}(x + y + |x - y|) \quad \forall x, y \in \mathbb{R}.$$

With ordinary properties of expectation, we get

$$\begin{aligned} \mathbb{E}[\xi_1 \oplus \xi_2] &\geq \frac{1}{2}(\mathbb{E}[\xi_1] + \mathbb{E}[\xi_2] + |\mathbb{E}[\xi_1] - \mathbb{E}[\xi_2]|) \\ &= \mathbb{E}[\xi_1] \oplus \mathbb{E}[\xi_2]. \end{aligned}$$

The second assertion of the lemma is trivial. ■

The next result [7, 8] provides an upper bound for the expected value of the maximum of independent and identically distributed (i.i.d.) random variables.

Lemma 3 *Let $\xi_1, \ldots, \xi_k$ be i.i.d. continuous random variables, and there exist $\mathbb{E}[\xi_1] < \infty$ and $\mathbb{D}[\xi_1] < \infty$. Then it holds*

$$\mathbb{E}\left[\sum_{i=1}^{k}{}_{\oplus}\, \xi_i\right] \leq \mathbb{E}[\xi_1] + \frac{k-1}{\sqrt{2k-1}}\sqrt{\mathbb{D}[\xi_1]}.$$

Consider a random matrix X with its entries x_{ij} taking values in $\mathbb{R}$. We denote by $\mathbb{E}[X]$ the matrix obtained from X by replacing each entry x_{ij} by its expected value $\mathbb{E}[x_{ij}]$. With Lemma 2, it is easy to verify the next statement.

Lemma 4 *For any random matrix X, it holds*

$$\mathbb{E}\|X\|_{\oplus} \geq \|\mathbb{E}[X]\|_{\oplus}.$$

Proof: It follows from Lemma 2 that

$$\begin{aligned} \mathbb{E}\|X\|_{\oplus} &= \mathbb{E}\left[\sum_{i,j}{}_{\oplus}\, x_{ij}\right] \\ &\geq \sum_{i,j}{}_{\oplus}\, \mathbb{E}[x_{ij}] = \|\mathbb{E}[X]\|_{\oplus}. \end{aligned}$$

■

5 Acyclic Fork-Join Networks

We consider a network with n single-server nodes and customers of a single class. The topology of the network is described by an oriented acyclic graph $\mathcal{G} = (\mathbf{N}, \mathbf{A})$, where $\mathbf{N} = \{1, \ldots, n\}$ represents the set of nodes, and $\mathbf{A} = \{(i, j)\} \subset \mathbf{N} \times \mathbf{N}$ is the set of arcs which determine the transition routes of customers. It is assumed that there are nodes in the graph which have no either incoming or outgoing arcs. Each node with no predecessors is assumed to represent an infinite external arrival stream of customers; provided that a node has no successors, it is considered as an output node intended to release customers from the network.

Each node of the network includes a server and infinite buffer which together present a single-server queue operating under the first-come, first-served queueing discipline. At the initial time, the server at each node is assumed to be free of customers, the buffers in nodes with no predecessors have infinite number of customers, whereas the buffers in the other nodes may have finite numbers of customers.

In addition to the usual service procedure, special join and fork operations [1] may be performed in a node respectively before and after service of a customer. The join operation is actually thought to cause each customer which comes into a node not to enter the buffer at the server but to wait until at least one customer from every preceding node arrives. As soon as these customers arrive, they, taken one from each preceding node, are united to be treated as being one customer which then enters the buffer to become a new member of the queue.

The fork operation at a node is initiated every time the service of a customer is completed; it consists in giving rise to several new customers one for each succeeding nodes. These customers simultaneously depart the node, each being passed to separate node related to the first one. We assume that the execution of fork-join operations when appropriate customers are available, as well as the transition of customers within and between nodes require no time.

For the queue at node i, we denote the kth departure epoch by $x_i(k)$, and the service time of the kth customer by τ_{ik}. We assume that $\tau_{ik} \geq 0$ are given parameters for all $i = 1, \ldots, n$, and $k = 1, 2, \ldots$, while $x_i(k)$ are considered as unknown state variables. With the condition that the network starts operating at time zero, it is convenient to set $x_i(0) = 0$ and $x_i(k) = \varepsilon$ for all $k < 0$, $i = 1, \ldots, n$. Finally, we denote the number of customers in the buffer at node i at the initial time by r_i with $0 \leq r_i \leq \infty$, and introduce $M = \max\{r_i | \, r_i < \infty;\ i = 1, \ldots, n\}$.

An example of an acyclic fork-join network with $n = 5$ is shown in Fig. 1.

It has been shown in [10, 11] that the dynamics of the network can be described by the state equation

$$\boldsymbol{x}(k) = \sum_{m=1}^{M}{}_{\oplus}\, A_m(k) \otimes \boldsymbol{x}(k-m), \qquad (1)$$

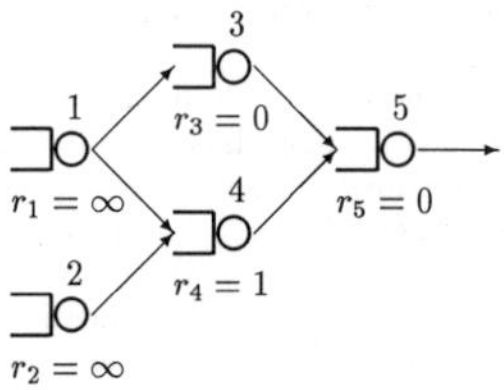

Figure 1: An acyclic fork-join network.

with the state transition matrices

$$\begin{aligned} A_1(k) &= (E \oplus \mathcal{T}_k \otimes G_0^T)^p \otimes \mathcal{T}_k \otimes (E \oplus G_1^T), \\ A_m(k) &= (E \oplus \mathcal{T}_k \otimes G_0^T)^p \otimes \mathcal{T}_k \otimes G_m^T, \\ & \quad m = 2, \ldots, M, \end{aligned}$$

where $\mathcal{T}_k = \mathrm{diag}(\tau_{1k}, \ldots, \tau_{nk})$ with ε as the off-diagonal entries, $G_m = (g_{ij}^m)$, $m = 0, 1, \ldots, M$, are matrices with their entries defined by the condition

$$g_{ij}^m = \begin{cases} 0, & \text{if } (i,j) \in \mathbf{A} \text{ and } m = r_j, \\ \varepsilon, & \text{otherwise,} \end{cases}$$

and p is the length of the longest path in the graph associated with the matrix G_0.

In fact, G_m presents the standard adjacency matrix of the partial graph $\mathcal{G}_m = (\mathbf{N}, \mathbf{A}_m)$ with $\mathbf{A}_m = \{(i,j) | \ (i,j) \in \mathbf{A}; \ r_j = m\}$. Since the graph of the entire network is acyclic, all its partial graphs $\mathcal{G}_m$, $m = 0, 1, \ldots, M$, possess the same property.

6 Monotonicity Properties

In this section, a useful property of monotonicity is established which relates the system state vector $\boldsymbol{x}(k)$ to the initial numbers of customers r_i. It is actually shown that the entries of $\boldsymbol{x}(k)$ for all $k = 1, 2, \ldots$, do not decrease when the numbers r_i with $0 < r_i < \infty$, $i = 1, \ldots, n$, are reduced to 0.

We prove this assertion in two steps: first we consider the effect of reducing the numbers $r_i > 1$ to 1, and then replace $r_i = 1$ with $r_i = 0$. Note that the change in the initial numbers of customers results only in modifications to partial graphs $\mathcal{G}_m$ and so to their adjacency matrices G_m. Specifically, reducing these numbers to 1 leads us to new matrices $\widetilde{G}_1 = G_1 \oplus \cdots \oplus G_M$, and $\widetilde{G}_m = \mathcal{E}$ for all $m = 2, \ldots, M$, whereas G_0 remains unchanged.

Lemma 5 *Let $\boldsymbol{x}(k)$ be determined by (1). Suppose that the vector $\widetilde{\boldsymbol{x}}(k)$ satisfies the dynamic equation*

$$\widetilde{\boldsymbol{x}}(k) = \widetilde{A}_1(k) \otimes \widetilde{\boldsymbol{x}}(k-1), \quad \widetilde{\boldsymbol{x}}(0) = \mathbf{0},$$

with $\widetilde{A}_1(k) = (E \oplus \mathcal{T}_k \otimes G_0^T)^p \otimes \mathcal{T}_k \otimes (E \oplus \widetilde{G}_1^T)$, where $\widetilde{G}_1 = G_1 \oplus \cdots \oplus G_M$.

Then for all $k = 1, 2, \ldots$, it holds

$$\boldsymbol{x}(k) \leq \widetilde{\boldsymbol{x}}(k).$$

Proof: Since $\boldsymbol{x}(k_1) \leq \boldsymbol{x}(k_2)$ for any $k_1 < k_2$, we have from (1)

$$\boldsymbol{x}(k) \leq \left(\sum_{i=1}^{M}{}_{\oplus} A_m(k) \right) \otimes \boldsymbol{x}(k-1).$$

Now we can define the matrix $\widetilde{A}_1(k)$ as

$$\begin{aligned} \widetilde{A}_1(k) &= \sum_{m=1}^{M}{}_{\oplus} A_m(k) \\ &= (E \oplus \mathcal{T}_k \otimes G_0^T)^p \otimes \mathcal{T}_k \otimes \left(E \oplus \sum_{m=1}^{M}{}_{\oplus} G_m^T \right). \end{aligned}$$

Starting with the condition $\boldsymbol{x}(0) = \widetilde{\boldsymbol{x}}(0) = \mathbf{0}$, we successively verify that the relations

$$\begin{aligned} \boldsymbol{x}(k) &\leq \widetilde{A}_1(k) \otimes \boldsymbol{x}(k-1) \\ &\leq \widetilde{A}_1(k) \otimes \widetilde{\boldsymbol{x}}(k-1) = \widetilde{\boldsymbol{x}}(k) \end{aligned}$$

are valid for each $k = 1, 2, \ldots$. ∎

The next lemma shows that in the system with finite initial numbers r_i equal either to 0 or 1, the entries of its transition matrix $A_1(k)$ do not decrease as all these numbers are set to 0. Clearly, this also involves nondecrease in the entries of the system state vector $\boldsymbol{x}(k)$.

Lemma 6 *For all $k = 1, 2, \ldots$, it holds*

$$A_1(k) \leq \widetilde{A}(k)$$

with $\widetilde{A}(k) = (E \oplus \mathcal{T}_k \otimes \widetilde{G}^T)^q \otimes \mathcal{T}_k$, where $\widetilde{G} = G_0 \oplus G_1$, and q is the length of the longest path in the graph associated with the matrix $\widetilde{G}$.

Proof: Consider the matrix

$$A_1(k) = (E \oplus \mathcal{T}_k \otimes G_0^T)^p \otimes \mathcal{T}_k \otimes (E \oplus G_1^T).$$

As one can see, to prove the lemma, it will suffice to verify both inequalities

$$\widetilde{A}(k) \geq (E \oplus \mathcal{T}_k \otimes G_0^T)^p \otimes \mathcal{T}_k, \tag{2}$$
$$\widetilde{A}(k) \geq (E \oplus \mathcal{T}_k \otimes G_0^T)^p \otimes \mathcal{T}_k \otimes G_1^T. \tag{3}$$

Let us write the obvious representation

$$(E \oplus \mathcal{T}_k \otimes \widetilde{G}^T)^q = \sum_{i=1}^{q}{}_{\oplus} (E \oplus \mathcal{T}_k \otimes G_0^T)^i \otimes (\mathcal{T}_k \otimes G_1^T)^{q-i}.$$

Since $q \geq p$, we get from the representation

$$\begin{aligned} (E \oplus \mathcal{T}_k \otimes \widetilde{G}^T)^q &\geq (E \oplus \mathcal{T}_k \otimes \widetilde{G}^T)^p \\ &\geq (E \oplus \mathcal{T}_k \otimes G_0^T)^p. \end{aligned}$$

It remains to multiply both sides of the above inequality by $\mathcal{T}_k$ on the right so as to arrive at (2).

To verify (3), let us first assume that $q > p$. In this case, we obtain

$$\begin{aligned} (E \oplus \mathcal{T}_k \otimes \widetilde{G}^T)^q &\geq (E \oplus \mathcal{T}_k \otimes \widetilde{G}^T)^{p+1} \\ &\geq (E \oplus \mathcal{T}_k \otimes G_0^T)^p \otimes \mathcal{T}_k \otimes G_1^T. \end{aligned}$$

Suppose now that $q = p$. Then it is necessary that $G_1 \otimes G_0^p = \mathcal{E}$. If this were not the case, there would be a path in the graph associated with the matrix $\widetilde{G} = G_0 \oplus G_1$, which has its length greater than p, and we therefore would have $q > p$.

Clearly, the condition $G_1 \otimes G_0^p = \mathcal{E}$ results in the equality $(\mathcal{T}_k \otimes G_0^T)^p \otimes \mathcal{T}_k \otimes G_1^T = \mathcal{E}$, and thus we get

$$\begin{aligned}(E \oplus \mathcal{T}_k \otimes \widetilde{G}^T)^p &\geq (E \oplus \mathcal{T}_k \otimes G_0^T)^{p-1} \otimes \mathcal{T}_k \otimes G_1^T \\ &= (E \oplus \mathcal{T}_k \otimes G_0^T)^p \otimes \mathcal{T}_k \otimes G_1^T.\end{aligned}$$

Since it holds $(E \oplus \mathcal{T}_k \otimes \widetilde{G}^T)^p \otimes \mathcal{T}_k \geq (E \oplus \mathcal{T}_k \otimes \widetilde{G}^T)^p$, one can conclude that inequality (3) is also valid. ∎

Lemmas 5 and 6 can be summarized as follows.

Theorem 1 *In the acyclic fork-join queueing network, reducing the initial numbers of customers from any fixed values to* 0 *does not decrease the entries of the system state vector* $\boldsymbol{x}(k)$ *for all* $k = 1, 2, \ldots$.

7 Service Cycle Time

We consider the evolution of the system (1) as a sequence of service cycles: the 1st cycle starts at the initial time, and it is terminated as soon as all the servers in the network complete their 1st service, the 2nd cycle is terminated as soon as the servers complete their 2nd service, and so on. Clearly, the completion time of the kth cycle can be represented as

$$\max_i x_i(k) = \|\boldsymbol{x}(k)\|_{\oplus}.$$

The next lemma provides simple lower and upper bounds on the kth cycle completion time.

Lemma 7 *For all* $k = 1, 2, \ldots$, *it holds*

$$\left\| \sum_{i=1}^{k} \mathcal{T}_i \right\|_{\oplus} \leq \|\boldsymbol{x}(k)\|_{\oplus} \leq \sum_{i=1}^{k} \|\mathcal{T}_i\|_{\oplus} + p \left(\sum_{i=1}^{k}{}_{\oplus} \|\mathcal{T}_i\|_{\oplus} \right).$$

Proof: To verify the left inequality, first note that

$$A_1(k) = (E \oplus \mathcal{T}_k \otimes G_0^T)^p \otimes \mathcal{T}_k \otimes (E \oplus G_1^T) \geq \mathcal{T}_k.$$

With this condition, we have from equation (1)

$$\begin{aligned}\boldsymbol{x}(k) &\geq \mathcal{T}_k \otimes \boldsymbol{x}(k-1) \\ &\geq \mathcal{T}_k \otimes \cdots \otimes \mathcal{T}_1 \otimes \boldsymbol{x}(0)\end{aligned}$$

with $\boldsymbol{x}(0) = \mathbf{0}$. Taking the norm, and considering that $\mathcal{T}_i$, $i = 1, \ldots, k$, are diagonal matrices, we get

$$\begin{aligned}\|\boldsymbol{x}(k)\|_{\oplus} &\geq \|\mathcal{T}_k \otimes \cdots \otimes \mathcal{T}_1\|_{\oplus} \\ &= \|\mathcal{T}_1 + \cdots + \mathcal{T}_k\|_{\oplus}.\end{aligned}$$

To obtain an upper bound, let us replace the general system (1) with that governed by the equation

$$\boldsymbol{x}(k) = A(k) \otimes \boldsymbol{x}(k-1), \quad \boldsymbol{x}(0) = \mathbf{0}, \qquad (4)$$

where $A(k) = (E \oplus \mathcal{T}_k \otimes G^T)^p \otimes \mathcal{T}_k$ with the matrix $G = G_0 \oplus G_1 \oplus \cdots \oplus G_M$, and p is the length of the longest path in the graph associated with G. As it follows from Theorem 1, such a replacement does not decrease the vector $\boldsymbol{x}(k)$ for all $k = 1, 2, \ldots$.

Let us denote $A_k = A(k) \otimes \cdots \otimes A(1)$. With the condition that $\boldsymbol{x}(0) = \mathbf{0}$, we can write from (4)

$$\|\boldsymbol{x}(k)\|_{\oplus} = \|A(k) \otimes \cdots \otimes A(1)\|_{\oplus} = \|A_k\|_{\oplus}.$$

From Proposition 1 we get for the matrix A_k

$$A_k \leq \prod_{i=1}^{k}{}_{\otimes} \|\mathcal{T}_i\|_{\oplus} \otimes \prod_{i=1}^{k}{}_{\otimes} (E \oplus \mathcal{T}_{k-i+1} \otimes G^T)^p.$$

By applying Lemma 1, we obtain the inequality

$$\begin{aligned}\|A_k\|_{\oplus} &\leq \prod_{i=1}^{k}{}_{\otimes} \|\mathcal{T}_i\|_{\oplus} \otimes \left(\sum_{i=1}^{k}{}_{\oplus} \|\mathcal{T}_i\|_{\oplus} \right)^p \\ &= \sum_{i=1}^{k} \|\mathcal{T}_i\|_{\oplus} + p \left(\sum_{i=1}^{k}{}_{\oplus} \|\mathcal{T}_i\|_{\oplus} \right),\end{aligned}$$

which provides us with the desired result. ∎

Let us define the average cycle time of the system:

$$y(k) = \frac{1}{k} \|\boldsymbol{x}(k)\|_{\oplus}.$$

In many applications, one is normally interested in investigating the steady-state mean cycle time; that is, the limit of $y(k)$ as k tends to ∞. We will consider this problem with relation to the stochastic network models in the next section.

8 Stochastic Networks

Suppose that for each node $i = 1, \ldots, n$, the service times $\tau_{i1}, \tau_{i2}, \ldots$, form a sequence of i.i.d. continuous non-negative random variables with $\mathbb{E}[\tau_{ik}] < \infty$ and $\mathbb{D}[\tau_{ik}] < \infty$ for all $k = 1, 2, \ldots$. With these conditions, $\mathcal{T}_k$ are i.i.d. random matrices, whereas $\|\mathcal{T}_k\|_{\oplus}$ present i.i.d. random variables with $\mathbb{E}\|\mathcal{T}_k\|_{\oplus} < \infty$ and $\mathbb{D}\|\mathcal{T}_k\|_{\oplus} < \infty$ for all $k = 1, 2, \ldots$.

In the analysis of the mean cycle time of the system, one first has to convince himself that the limit

$$\lim_{k \to \infty} \frac{1}{k} \|\boldsymbol{x}(k)\|_{\oplus} = \gamma \qquad (5)$$

exists. A standard technique to verify the existence of the above limit is based on the Subadditive Ergodic Theorem proposed in [9]. One can find examples of the implementation of the theorem in the $(\max, +)$-algebra framework in [5, 3, 4, 12].

With the above probabilistic conditions, it is not difficult to apply the theorem in the same way as in [5, 3, 4, 12] to prove existence of the limit in (5) for the system (1). In more exact terms, the theorem allows one to prove that this limit exists with the probability one, and, at the same time, it holds

$$\lim_{k \to \infty} \frac{1}{k} \mathbb{E}\|\boldsymbol{x}(k)\|_{\oplus} = \gamma. \qquad (6)$$

Now we present our main result which offers simple bounds on the mean cycle time γ.

Theorem 2 *In the stochastic dynamical system (1) the mean cycle time γ satisfies the double inequality*

$$\|\mathbb{E}[\mathcal{T}_1]\|_{\oplus} \le \gamma \le \mathbb{E}\|\mathcal{T}_1\|_{\oplus}. \qquad (7)$$

Proof: Note that according to the Subadditive Ergodic Theorem, we may represent the mean cycle time in the form (6).

Let us first prove the left inequality in (7). From Lemmas 7 and 4, we have

$$\begin{aligned} \frac{1}{k}\mathbb{E}\|x(k)\|_{\oplus} &\ge \frac{1}{k}\mathbb{E}\left\|\sum_{i=1}^{k}\mathcal{T}_i\right\|_{\oplus} \\ &\ge \left\|\frac{1}{k}\sum_{i=1}^{k}\mathbb{E}[\mathcal{T}_i]\right\|_{\oplus} = \|\mathbb{E}[\mathcal{T}_1]\|_{\oplus}, \end{aligned}$$

independently of k.

With the upper bound offered by Lemma 7, we get

$$\frac{1}{k}\mathbb{E}\|x(k)\|_{\oplus} \le \mathbb{E}\|\mathcal{T}_1\|_{\oplus} + \frac{p}{k}\mathbb{E}\left[\sum_{i=1}^{k}{}_{\oplus}\|\mathcal{T}_i\|_{\oplus}\right].$$

From Lemma 3, the second term on the right-hand side may be replaced by that of the form

$$\frac{p}{k}\left(\mathbb{E}\|\mathcal{T}_1\|_{\oplus} + \frac{k-1}{\sqrt{2k-1}}\sqrt{\mathbb{D}\|\mathcal{T}_1\|_{\oplus}}\right),$$

which tends to 0 as $k \to \infty$. ■

9 Concluding Remarks

In conclusion, we briefly discuss the behaviour of the bounds (7) under various assumptions concerning the service times in the network. First note that the derivation of the bounds does not require the kth service times τ_{ik} to be independent for all $i = 1, \ldots, n$. Moreover, if $\tau_{ik} = \tau_k$ for all i, we have $\|\mathbb{E}[\mathcal{T}_1]\|_{\oplus} = \mathbb{E}\|\mathcal{T}_1\|_{\oplus}$, and so the lower and upper bound coincide. Therefore, one can expect that the accuracy of the bounds increases with strengthening the dependency.

Furthermore, let us consider the effect of decreasing the variance $\mathbb{D}[\tau_{i1}]$ on the bounds on γ. Note that if τ_{i1} were degenerate random variables with zero variance, the lower and upper bounds in (7) would coincide. This leads us to the conclusion that with decreasing the variance of τ_{i1}, the bounds become more accurate.

Finally, let us choose a node of the network, say node $i = 1$. Suppose that, with the random variables τ_{i1}, $i \ne 1$, being fixed, the random service time τ_{11} is changed in such a way so that the probability

$$\mathbb{P}\Big\{\tau_{11} > \sum_{i \ne 1}{}_{\oplus}\tau_{i1}\Big\}$$

increases. It is easy to see that as the above probability tends to one, both the lower and upper bounds tend to the common value $\mathbb{E}[\tau_{11}]$.

Since, in particular, this probability increases as $\mathbb{E}[\tau_{11}]$ increases, we conclude that in this case, the greater difference between $\mathbb{E}[\tau_{11}]$ and $\mathbb{E}[\tau_{i1}]$ for all $i \ne 1$, the smaller difference between the lower and upper bounds in (7).

References

[1] F. Baccelli and A.M. Makowski, Queueing Models for Systems with Synchronization Constraints, *Proc. IEEE* 77 (1989), no.1, 138-160.

[2] F. Baccelli and P. Konstantopoulos, Estimates of Cycle Times in Stochastic Petri Nets, *Applied Stochastic Analysis*, Lecture Notes in Control and Information Sciences, 177, Springer-Verlag: New York, 1991, 1-20.

[3] F. Baccelli, Ergodic Theory of Stochastic Petri Networks, *Ann. Probab.* 20 (1992), no.1, 375-396.

[4] F. Baccelli, G. Cohen, G.J. Olsder, and J.-P. Quadrat, *Synchronization and Linearity*, Wiley: Chichester, 1992.

[5] J.E. Cohen, Subadditivity, Generalized Products of Random Matrices and Operations Research, *SIAM Review* 30 (1988), no.1, 69-86.

[6] R.A. Cuninghame-Green, *Minimax Algebra*, Lecture Notes in Economics and Mathematical Systems, 166, Springer-Verlag: Berlin, 1979.

[7] E.J. Gumbel, The Maxima of the Mean Largest Value and on the Range, *Ann. Math. Statist.* 25 (1954), 76-84.

[8] H.O. Hartly and H.A. David, Universal Bounds for Mean Range and Extreme Observations, *Ann. Math. Statist.* 25 (1954), 85-99.

[9] J.F.C. Kingman, Subadditive Ergodic Theory, *Ann. Probab.* 1 (1973), 883-909.

[10] N.K. Krivulin, An Algebraic Approach in Modelling and Simulation of Queueing Networks, in *Proc. Circuits, Systems and Computers '96, Hellenic Naval Academy, Piraeus, Greece, July 15-17, 1996* 2, 668-672.

[11] N.K. Krivulin, Max-Plus Algebra Models of Queueing Networks, in *Proc. International Workshop on Discrete Event Systems (WODES'96), 19-21 August 1996, University of Edinburgh, UK*, IEE: London, 1996, 76-81.

[12] J. Mairesse, Stochastic Linear Systems in the (max, +) Algebra, in *Proceedings of the 11th International Conference on Analysis and Optimization of Systems, Sophia-Antipolis, June 15-17, 1994 (G. Cohen and J.-P. Quadrat, Eds.)*, Springer-Verlag: London, 1994, 257-265.

Facilitating the Searching Methodologies in VLSI Circuit Design by Boundary Sampling

Kim T. Chan and A. Wu
EDA Centre, Department of Electronic Engineering,
City University of Hong Kong
Tat Chee Avenue, Kowloon, Hong Kong, P.R. China
Email: ktchan@ee.cityu.edu.hk; eeawueed@cityu.edu.hk

Abstract

Statistical VLSI circuits design requires the estimation for the Feasible region in the design parametric space because once this region is estimated, some searching methods such as the classical Yield Gradient Search [1][2] or the Design Centring Procedure [3] can be applied to it for obtaining the optimal circuit. However, the efficiencies of these searching methods depend very much upon the estimated region. More accurate the region is estimated; a better nominal circuit can be achieved ignoring whatever searching method is used. Hence, a new sampling approach known as the "Boundary Sample" will be introduced in this paper which enables the nominal circuit obtained produces the highest yield in a two-staged CMOS Operational Amplifier circuit by the two aforesaid searching methods than those Random or Stratified samples. Besides, this Boundary Sample requires a comparative lowest number of circuit simulations; and the original time-consuming Monte Carlo Analysis involved in the searching can be replaced by computing the circuit's performances representing equations.

Keywords – Boundary sample, Response modelling, *δ – Borel*

Introduction

One of the important keys to success in the modern micro-electronic industries is to introduce a new product to the market in time with a satisfactory manufacturing yield. However, due to the existence of the inherent disturbances in any IC fabrication process, it is hardly achievable to have hundred percent of production yield. In fact, these disturbances will significantly affect the yield when the complexity of the circuit increases like the VLSI circuits. Traditional method for yield enhancement using Monte Carlo though can attain a higher yield; however, it is rather inefficient because of its huge number of circuit simulations involved. Therefore, some sampling approaches for simplicial approximating the boundaries of the "Feasible Region" in the designed space is required. However, the accuracy of this approximation depends upon two things: the model used and the sample involved. Since many effort had already been put regarding the construction for the ideal model, sampling methodology will be concerned here in this paper. Some previously proposed samples like the Monte Carlo and Stratified samples required an unacceptable huge number of circuit simulations. Circuit simulation is a rather time consuming process and should be kept as small number as possible. Consequently, a new biased sample called the Boundary sample that contains mostly the points inside the δ – borels union of the boundary will be introduced in the following section.

Boundary Sampling Algorithm (BSA)

This Boundary Sampling is based upon the principal of closeness that states that if there is a higher proportion of closest points to the target function in the sample, the more accurate will be the approximation even with a minimum sample size.

DEFINITION: A δ-borel set for a point $x \in \Re^n$ with any arbitrary small $\delta > 0$ is

$$B_\delta(x) = \{y \in \Re^n : \|x - y\| < \delta\}$$

DEFINITION: Consider the infinity number of points on the function, each will form its own δ – borel set on the domain, then an infinity number of borel sets will be created which will union together to site a particular region called Neighbouring region N_f of the function f where

$$N_f = \left\{ x \middle| x \in \bigcup_{i=1}^{\infty} B_\delta(x_i) \right\}, \text{ where } x_i \text{ s are on } f$$

DEFINITION: A point, x, is known as the Boundary point of a function $f \Leftrightarrow x \in N_f$.

LEMMA: If a point x whose weight $w_x \in \left[w^T - \sigma, w^T + \sigma\right] \Leftrightarrow x \in N_f$, w^T is the specification weight for the function.

PROOF: If $w_x \in \left[w^T - \sigma, w^T + \sigma\right]$, this implies the point which bears the weight w_x should be included into the boundary sample. However, we have defined previously that any boundary sample is only a subset of N_f. $x \in N_f$.

Alternatively, if $x \in N_f \Rightarrow f(x) = w_x \approx w^T \Rightarrow \left|w_x - w^T\right| < \varepsilon, \varepsilon > 0$. Let $\varepsilon < \sigma$, then it implies that $\left|w_x - w^T\right| < \sigma \Rightarrow w_x \in \left[w^T - \sigma, w^T + \sigma\right]$.

Since it may be difficult to judge whether a point falls inside N_f, so we can use the above LEMMA to determine it indirectly by checking if its weight falls inside the weight interval of $w^T \pm \sigma$. The principle of the Boundary Sampling is simply to draw sample with the highest proportion of points in N_f as possible; thus, the following is the algorithm based on continuously revising the Boundary sample on hand until the finalised Boundary Sample is reached. The algorithm is:

Step 1: To start with an initial Boundary sample.

According to the response surface method which states that the boundary of the designed space is more important than the response function itself in order to accurately estimate the yield [4], Yu et al [5], this initial sample s_1 of size N for the function $f: \Re^n \to \Re$ contains points from the mid-points of all the surfaces as well as the centroid of the hyper-cube from the function's domain. But N depends on the nature of the model used. For instance, when the efficient quadratic model is employed, $N = 2n+1$ where n is the number of designed parameters.

The weight w_x for every point x in the sample will then be computed. Without loss of generality, these weights can be represented by the functional values, $f(x)$. Next, divide all the points in s_1 into 3 mutually exclusive sets denoted as L, H, E where $L = \{x \in \Re^n | w_x < w^T\}$; $H = \{x \in \Re^n | w_x > w^T\}$; $E = \{x \in \Re^n | w_x \in [w^T - \sigma, w^T + \sigma]\}$; and $\sum_{j=L,H,E} n(j) = N$, $n(j) \geq 0 \forall j = L,H,E$; and $L \cap H \cap E = \varnothing$.

We have to check the value for $n(E_1)$ in this step only in the beginning while the others $n(E_i), \forall i > 1$ will be checked in Step 2. It is because if $n(E_1)$ equals to N in the beginning, we do not need to continue, as this initial sample is already the finalised Boundary Sample. However, this is seldom the case. Indeed, most of the time we have $n(E_1) < N$. If so, point-pairs will be formed between the sets L_1 and H_1. Although the maximum number of point-pairs formed may differ in different models, they should not exceed $O(n^2)$.

DEFINITION:
$O(g(n)) = \{f(n): \exists c \& n_0 \ni 0 \leq f(n) \leq cg(n), \forall n \geq n_0\}$.

Step 2: To obtain a revised sample.

Consider a point-pair between the points $\bar{x}_1$ and $\bar{x}_2$ in the n-dimensional space with their corresponding weights $w_1 > w^T$ and $w_2 < w^T$ respectively. It is trivial that the line $\overline{\bar{x}_1\bar{x}_2}$ joining $\bar{x}_1$ and $\bar{x}_2$ will intersect the function somewhere on the line. Suppose, the interpolated point $\bar{x}$ is the intersection point where the line $\overline{\bar{x}_1\bar{x}_2}$ cuts the function. According to the general rule of point division, the co-ordinates of point $\bar{x}$ can be computed by the following formula

$$x_i = \frac{x_{1i} + (1+\pi_j)x_{2i}}{1+\pi_i}, \text{ where } i = 1,2,\ldots,n \text{ and}$$

$$\pi_i = \frac{|w_1 - w^T|}{|w_2 - w_1|}$$

This computation is valid only when the function is continuous and also under the assumption that the interpolated point will lie closer to the point that has a smaller absolute weight difference from w^T.

For $i > 1$, let I_i be the set of all the interpolated points got in this iteration. If $n(E_i) \geq \left(N - \sum_{j=1}^{i-1} n(E_j)\right)$ where $E_i = \{x \in I_i : w_x \in [w^T - \sigma, w^T + \sigma]\}$, then quit the process and the finalised Boundary Sample will be $\bigcup_{j=1}^{i} E_j$. However, in case of inequality, avoid choosing crowded Boundary points. However, If $n(E_i) < \left(N - \sum_{j=1}^{i-1} n(E_j)\right)$, draw another N points with the least $|w_x - w^T|$ from the set $(I_i \setminus E_i) \cup L_{i-1} \cup H_{i-1}$ to form the revised sample s_2. Replace s_1 by s_2 and repeat Step 1. Obviously, the sample s_i, starting with $i > 1$ contains no points in set E, we can omit the checking process for $n(E_i)$ again when repeating Step 1 after the first iteration.

Besides, if there happens that the revised sample s_i obtained after $(i-1)th$ iteration has all the points belong to either set L or H only, then stop the process and complete the finalised Boundary Sample by choosing the remaining points from the most updated set $(I_i \setminus E_i) \cup L_{i-1} \cup H_{i-1}$ which have the least $|w_x - w^T|$.

Step 3: Termination.

To make it clear, this algorithm will be terminated when either one of the following conditions occurs, they are:

a) when $n(E_1) = N$; or

b) $n(E_i) \geq \left(N - \sum_{j=1}^{i-1} n(E_j)\right), \forall i > 1$; or

c) No more new interpolated points can be generated when
   i. Only L_i or H_i exists in the revised sample after $(i-1)th$ iteration; or
   ii. The revised sample coincides exactly with any previous existence sample.

Two-staged CMOS Operational Amplifier

Operational amplifier, composed of many components, is one of the most versatile and important building blocks in analogue-circuit design. It usually has a sufficiently high forward gain. Figure 1 shows a block diagrammatic representation of a typical operational amplifier structure.

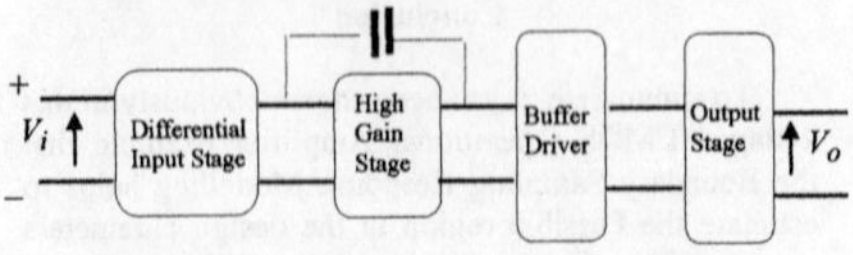

Figure 1 Typical structure for an operational amplifier

Suppose we are now considering the design for a 2-staged CMOS Operational Amplifier in Figure 2 with the following performances specifications:

Gain at DC $A_v \geq 16k$;
Power Dissipation $P \leq 6mW$;
Slew Rate $SR \geq 1.9V\,\mu s^{-1}$;
|Output voltage Swing| $|OVS| \geq 4.0$; and
Gain Bandwidth $GB \geq 0.75MHz$

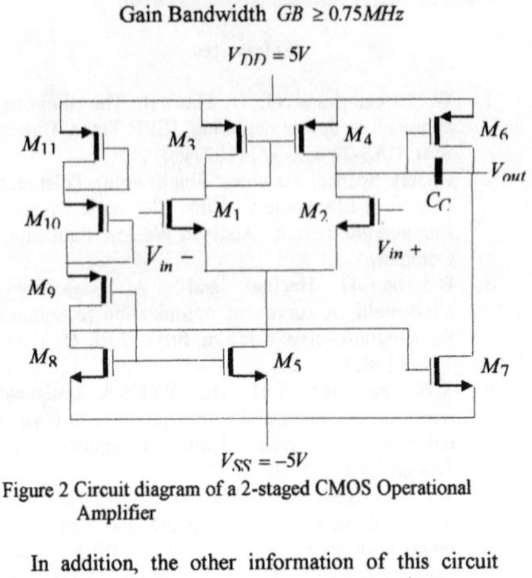

Figure 2 Circuit diagram of a 2-staged CMOS Operational Amplifier

In addition, the other information of this circuit design are $V_{DD} = 5V$; $V_{SS} = -5V$; $C_L = 20pF$ and $L = 10\mu m$. Thus, to begin with, we first let $p_i = \frac{W_i}{L} = \frac{W_i}{10\mu}$, for $i = 1,2,\ldots,11$ be the ratio of width and length of the *ith* transistor. If the first-cut design circuit obtained with $A_v = 16.01k$; $P_{diss} = 5.7mW$; $SR = 2.6\, V/_{\mu s}$; $|V_{out}(range)| = 4.877V$ as well as $GB = 0.842MHz$ is (5.4,5.4,2.4,2.4,5.1,30.9,94.9, 5.1,1,1.1,1). This circuit is obviously located inside the "Feasible Region", but it only has a 21% of manufacturing yield. Let the five circuit's response functions be $f_j(\bar{p}), \forall j = 1,2,\ldots,5$ where $\bar{p} = (p_1, p_3, p_6)^t$. Therefore, the approximations can be done separately with $\sigma = \pm 1\%$. Let W_2 varies as W_1 and W_4 as W_3. As the initial circuit point sounds optimal with respect to the performances of OVS, GB and SR within the designed parametric space of $[3.76, 7.04] \times [2.16, 2.64] \times [26.26, 35.54]$. Thus, without any loss of generosity, we only need to approximate the performances of the DC Voltage Gain as well as the Power Dissipation and the results with different sampling approaches will be shown in Table 1.

	Boundary sample		Random sample		Stratified sample	
	% error	Sim #	% error	Sim #	% error	Sim #
Gain	0.68	16	97.64	100	17.41	100
P	2.11	17	36.58	100	61.21	100

Sim # - the number of circuit's simulations
The percentage error is computed based upon 200 circuit simulations

Table 1 Comparison among the different sampling approximations for the 2-staged Op Amp

Searching Methodologies

After the Feasible region is well estimated, some searching methods like the traditional Yield Gradient Search [1][2] and the Design Centring Procedure (DCP) proposed by Director and Hachtel in 1977 [3] will be applied to it for obtaining the optimal design circuit.

I. Traditional Yield Gradient Search:-

This is the simplest gradient-based optimisation procedure depend on the steepest ascent of the yield prediction formula (YPF) [5]. This YPF enables the yield estimates to be extrapolated to new nominal circuit points in the design space by the same Monte Carlo analysis; however, this analysis can be replaced by those approximated analytical equations.

Let the YPF estimated by computing those analytical equations with N=500.

$$YPF \approx \hat{Y} = \sum_{i=1}^{N} g_i(x)$$

where $g(x)$ is the testing function and has a value 1 or 0 according to whether the point x satisfies all the equations. So we have

$$d\hat{Y} = \frac{\partial \hat{Y}}{\partial x_1} dx_1 + \frac{\partial \hat{Y}}{\partial x_3} dx_3 + \frac{\partial \hat{Y}}{\partial x_6} dx_6$$

The gradient vector will be defined as $\nabla \hat{Y} = \left\{ \frac{\partial \hat{Y}}{\partial x_1}, \frac{\partial \hat{Y}}{\partial x_3}, \frac{\partial \hat{Y}}{\partial x_6} \right\}$. If we represent $\hat{Y}$ in the designed space by the planes $\hat{Y} = \text{constant}$, then the grad $\hat{Y}$ is perpendicular to those contour planes. Since for the direction dx_t of the tangent to $\hat{Y} = \text{constant}$, we have

$$d\hat{Y} = \nabla \hat{Y} \bullet d\bar{x}_t = 0$$

However, we must first ascertain that in each direction we advance by the same amount

$$|d\bar{x}| = \sqrt{dx_1^2 + dx_3^2 + dx_6^2} = ds$$

Hence, the largest variation of $\hat{Y}$ can be maximised under the constraints of $ds^2 - \sum_{i=1,3,6}^{3} dx_i^2 = 0$ and the solution can be obtained by the usual mathematical approach with the aid of a Lagrange Multiplier from the necessary condition. It is quite self-evident to proceed from the initial circuit point $x^0 = (5.4, 2.4, 30.9)$ a certain distance Δs in the direction of $\nabla\hat{Y}$, the component for another new circuit point can be calculated by Δs. Thus,

$$x_i^{(p+1)} = x_i^{(p)} \pm \frac{\partial \hat{Y}}{\partial x_i}\Big|_{x_i^{(p)}} \bullet \Delta s \; ; \; p = 0,1,2,\ldots$$

II. Design Centring Procedure (DCP):-

The Design Centring Procedure (DCP) determined a set of $m \geq n+1$ boundary points of the estimated "Feasible Region". Based upon these points, a polyhedron can be formed which can inscribe the greatest hyper-sphere inside it. Then, another new boundary point will be selected which is located on the path passing through the mid-point of the greatest tangential face of the polyhedron and cuts the boundary. A new polyhedron with a larger inscribed hyper-sphere will then be formed. This procedure will be repeated until all the m boundary points are used. Monte Carlo Analysis will be run on the centroid of the finalised hyper-sphere.

However, this procedure can be facilitated by using those Boundary Sampling in two ways. Firstly, they can accurately locate the "Feasible Region" in the design parametric space for the procedure to work on. Similarly, the Monte Carlo Analysis can also be replaced by the approximated analytical equations.

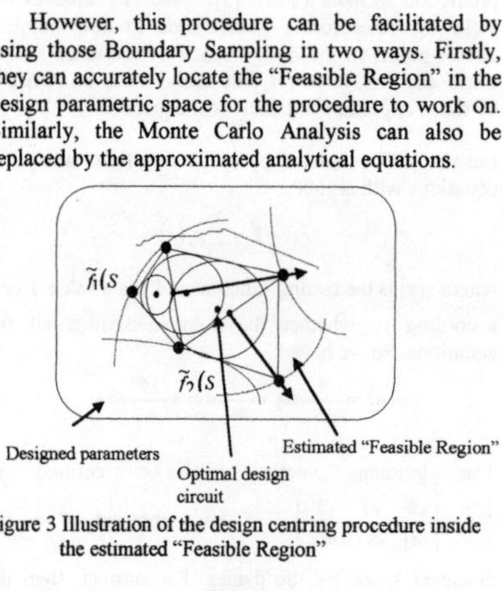

Figure 3 Illustration of the design centring procedure inside the estimated "Feasible Region"

Results

The optimal nominal circuit achieved when using different searching methods may be different which in turn will give different yields; however the following table shows that the yields for the above CMOS Operational Amplifier by these two common searching approaches.

	Yield %		
	Boundary (33 sims)	Random (200 sims)	Stratified (200 sims)
Yield Gradient	96%	53%	64%
DCP	85%	60%	64%

Table 2 Comparison the manufacturing yields between these searching methods in the 3 sampling approaches

Conclusion

To summarise, it has been shown obviously in this 2-staged CMOS Operational Amplifier example that the Boundary Sampling Response Modelling helps to estimate the Feasible region in the design parameters space accurately even with the smallest possible sample size than the random and stratified samples. Therefore, the yields by either the DCP or the Yield Gradient Search will be much greater than other sampling approximations. Although the yield appears to be lower in the DC procedure due to its convexity assumption for the Feasible region which is actually not the real situation, the Boundary Sampling Approximation (BSA) nevertheless can still be considered to facilitate the searching methods very much in finding the optimal design circuit.

References

1. W. Director and G. D. Hachtel, The simplical approach to design centering, IEEE Trans. Circuit Syst. CAS-24 363-372 (1977).
2. Robert Spence, Randeep Singh Soin, Tolerance Design of Electronic Circuits, Electronic Systems Engineering Series, Addison-Wesley Publishing Company.
3. Brayton, G. Hachtel, and A. Sagiovanni-Vincentelli, A survey of optimization techniques for integrated-circuit design, Proc. IEEE 69 1334-1346 (1981).
4. S.W. Pan and Y.H. Hu, PYFS-A statistical optimisation method for integrated circuit yield enhancement, IEEE Trans. Computer-Aided Design 12(2) 296-309 (1993).
5. T.K. Yu, S.M. Kang, I.N. Hajj and T.N. Trick, Statistical performance modeling and parametric yield estimation of MOS VLSI, IEEE Trans. Computer-Aided Design CAD-6 1013-1022 (1987).

Techniques for the Hardware Implementation of Modular Multiplication

by

Colin D. Walter

Computation Department, U.M.I.S.T.,
PO Box 88, Sackville Street, Manchester M60 1QD, U.K.

C.Walter@co.umist.ac.uk http://www.co.umist.ac.uk/

Index Terms: *Computer arithmetic, cryptography, RSA cryptosystem, Montgomery modular multiplication, redundant number systems, higher radix representation, optimal speed, area complexity.*

Abstract

Hardware for modular multiplication is required for strong cryptosystems so that large volumes of encrypted data can be safely stored in public areas and obtained over a public network (e.g. the WWW) but only understood by authorised users. This article reviews the main bottlenecks which may arise in the more obvious implementations of RSA and outlines a variety of solutions to them so that plain text can be recovered in real time.

1. Introduction

RSA [1] is an arbitrarily strong, two key cryptosystem which is generally only currently used for authentication protocols and for exchange of session keys to enable secure communication by arithmetically less intensive encryption methods. However, there is a growing need for secure encryption of large volumes of data. In particular, this is the case for data accessible over the internet which is commercially sensitive and should only be comprehensible to certain readers. It is also the case for much private data which is stored on public servers. The quantity of such data can make weak cryptosystems essentially useless in such situations. However, software implement-ations of a strong cryptosystem such as RSA are too slow for decrypting retrieved data in real time for viewing or editing purposes. Only dedicated hardware can achieve a speed equal to the disk access times, internal bus speeds, etc. which dictate the retrieval times for unencrypted data.

An RSA cryptosystem consists of a modulus M of around 1024 bits and two keys d and e with the property that $A^{de} \equiv A \bmod M$. Message blocks A satisfying $0 \le A < M$ are encrypted to $A' = A^e \bmod M$ and so uniquely decrypted by $A = A'^d \bmod M$ using the same algorithm for both processes. $M = PQ$ is chosen as a product of two large primes, e is often small with few non-zero bits so that encryption is relatively fast, and d chosen to satisfy $de \equiv 1 \bmod (P-1)(Q-1)$. Thus d has as many bits as M. The owner of the cryptosystem publishes M and e but keeps secret the factorization of M and the key d. Breaking the system requires discovering P and Q, which is computationally infeasible. Indeed, each addition of a small, almost constant number of bits (around 15) to the size of M doubles the effort required for this [2].

This paper discusses the major problems associated with space and time efficient hardware implementation of the cryptosystem and reviews their solution. Among the issues of concern are carry propagation, digit distribution, buffering, communication and use of available area.

2. Notation

The computation of $A^e \bmod M$ is split into two main processes: modular multiplication and exponentiation. The exponentiation is discussed last as it has to make repeated use of the modular multiplication hardware. Thus we look first at computing $(A{\times}B) \bmod M$.

Each number X has a representation of the form $X = \sum_{i=0}^{n-1} x_i r^i$ where r is the radix or base (usually a power of 2) and x_i is the ith digit (usually $0 \le x_i < r$). Let n be the number of digits for this representation of M. The representation is *redundant* if numbers can be represented in more than one way. Here this occurs by allowing digits in a range larger than $0..r-1$, and typically that given by an extra (carry) bit, that is, $0..2r-1$. For example, the output from a carry-save adder provides two bits for each digit and so, in effect, is a redundant representation where digits lie in the range 0..2 rather than the usual 0..1. We use k for the number of bits used to represent a digit, so that kn is approximately 2^{10} here, and $O(kn)$ is effectively constant.

The choice of k and n splits the formation of $A \times B$ into two multiplication levels: forming products of k-bit digits and forming products of n-digit numbers. More levels could be created. Different algorithms are used for each level. The lower level is of combinational logic, possibly pipelined to increase throughput. The hardware will be built around n k-bit digit multipliers, and this defines our choice of k. The upper level views a product as a sequence of additions of digits multiples a_iB of the multiplicand, and so will take a number of clock cycles.

3. Multiplication

Practical planar designs are well known for multipliers which are optimal with respect to some measure of time and area [3]-[8]. Under a model which assumes that wires take area but do not contribute to time, $Area \times Time^2$ complexity for a k-bit multiplication is bounded below by k^2 [3] and this bound can be achieved for any time in the range $log\ k$ to $\sqrt{k}$ [6]. Such designs tend to use the Discrete Fourier Transform and consequently involve large constants in their measures of time and area. There are more useful designs which are asymptotically poorer but perform better if k is not too large. Since the cross-over point is claimed to be around $k = 3 \times 10^3$ bits [5], i.e. greater than the size of the numbers here, classical methods are preferable. Indeed, it makes sense to pick a standard k-bit combinational multiplier off the shelf since it will contain years of optimisation, it will have a known latency and will be known to be correct. For a current standard chip of perhaps 10^7 transistors devoted entirely to RSA, $k = 32$ or 64 is the maximum practical [9] since there must be space for registers and for other operations such as modular reduction.

There is a direct trade-off between time and area. Doubling the number of digit multipliers allows the parallel processing of twice as many digits and so halves the time taken. If the k-bit multiplier works in one cycle with no pipelining and k is roughly the bandwidth of the internal bus, it is easy to calculate that sufficient throughput for real-time decryption requires n multipliers so that a complete multiplier digit times multiplicand a_iB (or equivalent) can be computed in one cycle. Then, in effect, each cycle processes all the multiplicand bits with k of the multiplier bits. A different regime would lead to more complex data paths and hence less efficient use of chip area, and so is not considered.

Suppose therefore that the n digit multipliers are used to add a_iB to a partial product in one clock cycle. If the carries are propagated then this takes extra time beyond the digit multiplic-ations. The digit multipliers ought not to lie idle while this happens. The equivalent of a carry save adder might be used to avoid carry propagation, so that the partial product has a redundant representation [10]. Alternatively, successive a_iB can be pipelined: either $a_{i+1}B$ can be formed as the previous carries are propagated or, if a_ib_j and its carry are calculated on one cycle, the next multiplier along should use this carry on the next cycle to compute a_ib_{j+1} and another carry [9].

4. Modular Reduction

The reduction of $A \times B$ to $(A \times B) \bmod M$ can be carried out in several ways, but each involves repeatedly choosing a suitable digit q and subtracting a shifted qM from the current remainder. The successive choices of digit q can be pieced together to form the integer quotient $Q = (A \times B) \text{ div } M$ or a closely related quantity if desired. Classically, shifted multiples of M are subtracted from the most significant end of $A \times B$:

```
{ Pre-condition: 0 ≤ A×B < M×r^n }
R := A×B ;
For i := n-1 downto 0 do
Begin
   q := R div (M×r^i) ;
   R := R - q×M×r^i   ;
   { Invariant: 0 ≤ R < M×r^i
               & R ≡ (A×B) mod M }
End ;
{ Post-Condition: R = (A×B) mod M }
```

This requires waiting for a full carry propagation with each subtraction if the largest possible multiple is to be removed. A better solution is just to use the top digit or two of M and the remaining product to determine a sufficiently good multiple of M to remove [10]. This reduces the result enough to guarantee an upper bound of rM, say, when the process terminates. This can be cleaned up properly at the end of the de-cryption. The critical path is now in the circuitry for computing q, but this can be reduced by scaling M [11,12]. M is replaced by a small multiple so that its top digits are known and simple, say, 10... Minor post-processing will again recover the correct residue.

If the product $A \times B$ is fully computed before the modular reduction starts, then a register of $2n$ digits is required. However, if the product is performed by repeated shifting and addition, the modular reductions can be interleaved with the additions to keep the partial sum down to only about n digits, thereby saving space. This has the added advantage that the multiplier hardware and modular reduction hardware can work simultaneously on the same modular product; otherwise full utilisation of these two parts of the hardware would require the complication of handling two modular products at once.

The modular reduction requires another n digit multipliers to compute qM, so that the main area taken up by the RSA circuitry is $2n$ $k \times k$-bit multipliers and an adder to combine their outputs. It has been suggested that a table be formed containing some or all digit multiples of M in order to avoid re-computing them so many times. This is unwise as it requires $O(2^k)$ entries, so the time and space requirements would exceed those of re-computation unless k were very small.

5. Montgomery's Algorithm

The above modular reduction method has several disadvantages. It requires a redundant representation (which takes up more space) to avoid carry propagation, makes a poor choice of multiple to subtract, takes time to compute the digit q, and requires the global broadcasting of q to each digit position. Peter Montgomery [13] has shown how to use the *least* significant digit of an accumulating product to determine the multiple of M to subtract. He reverses the usual multiplication order by choosing multiplier digits from *least* to *most* significant and shifting *down* on each iteration. If R is the current partial modular product, then q is chosen so that $R+qM$ is a multiple of r, and this is shifted down (i.e. divided by r) for use in the next iteration. Consequently, $(A \times B \times r^{-n}) \bmod M$ is computed:

```
{ Pre-condition: 0 ≤ A < r^n }
R := 0 ;
For i := 0 to n-1 do
Begin
    q := (-(r0+ai×b0)m0^-1) mod r;
    R := (R+ai×B+q×M) div r ;
    { Invariant: 0 ≤ R < M+B }
End ;
{ Post-Condition: R ≡ (A×B×r^-n) mod M }
```

The extra factor, a power of r, is easily cleared up in minor post-processing [14]. Any extra multiple of M is also easily removed.

With this algorithm, the digit q is computed from the lowest digits of R and M without waiting for any carry propagation. So pipelining of the digits can now take place with $a_i b_{j+1}$ computed on the cycle after $a_i b_j$ using its carry and the same values of q and a_i. Thus, a non-redundant representation can be used and q and a_i no longer need to be broadcast to all digit slices in the same clock cycle.

Once more the critical path length is in computing q. To reduce this path M is again scaled [15], this time ensuring that its lowest digits are known and simple, say ...01. This moves the critical path to within the multiplier of each digit slice, so that most of the hardware is operating at full capacity. Further optimisation must concentrate on the digit slice and improved communications.

6. Communications

Our goal is to have only local inter-communication because of the delays and wiring associated with global movement of data. The standard approach, namely parallel processing of digit operations for the same multiplier digit, requires broadcasting q and a_i to all digit slices on each cycle [10,12]. Avoiding this requires pipelining digits as described above and yields a systolic array [16,17,9].

If the term $a_i b_j$ were added to the partial result in digit slice j on cycle $i+j$, the first output digit would occur at time $n-1$. Full utilisation of the hardware could only occur if another modular multiplication were to start at time n when digit slice 0 becomes free again. Fortunately, the exponentiation involved in the cryptosystem means that the output from one modular multiplication is the input to the next modular multiplication, and so no time is lost and little wiring and buffering is required to achieve this. The precise timing details are actually slightly more complex because of the shift down in Montgomery's algorithm [16,17,9].

Since this system requires input digit serially, k bits at a time for each number and produces output similarly, its I/O matches internal bus speeds and bandwidth and so reduces the need for on chip buffering of data.

7. Exponentiation

The exponentiation required for encryption and decryption is generally achieved simply by incorporating several registers and making repeated use of the modular multiplier hardware. If the exponent d has the same size as M, namely about nk bits, then the usual square and multiply algorithm for exponentiation takes between nk and $2nk$ modular multiplications, and $1.5nk$ on average. There are ways to reduce this towards nk [18,19] but the possible improvements are very limited. Much more is achieved by good design for the modular multiplier.

8. Conclusion

We have reviewed the main bottlenecks which may arise in hardware for implementing the RSA cryptosystem and shown how to make the most efficient use of area. The key solutions are to use Montgomery's modular multiplication algorithm [13], scale the modulus, pipeline digit products and use an existing k-bit combinational multiplier. Finally, k is chosen as large as possible to make full use of the available chip area so that real time decryption is achieved.

References

[1] R. L. Rivest, A. Shamir & L. Adleman, "A Method for obtaining Digital Signatures and Public-Key Cryptosystems", *Comm. ACM*, vol. **21**, 1978, pp. 120-126.

[2] N. Koblitz, *A Course in Number Theory and Cryptography*, Graduate Texts in Mathematics, vol. **114**, Springer-Verlag, 1987.

[3] R. P. Brent & H. T. Kung, "The Area-Time Complexity of Binary Multiplication", *J. ACM*, vol. **28**, 1981, pp. 521-534.

[4] R. P. Brent & H. T. Kung, "A Regular Layout for Parallel Adders", *IEEE Trans. Comp.*, vol. **C-31**, no. 3, March 1982, pp. 260-264.

[5] W. K. Luk & J. E. Vuillemin, "Recursive Implementation of Optimal Time VLSI Integer Multipliers", *VLSI '83*, F. Anceau & E.J. Aas (eds.), Elsevier Science, 1983, pp. 155-168.

[6] K. Mehlhorn & F. P. Preparata, "Area-Time Optimal VLSI Integer Multiplier with Minimum Computation Time", *Information & Control*, vol. **58**, 1983, pp. 137-156.

[7] F. P. Preparata & J. Vuillemin, "Area-Time Optimal VLSI Networks for computing Integer Multiplication and Discrete Fourier Transform", *Proc. ICALP*, Haifa, Israel, 1981, pp. 29-40.

[8] C. S. Wallace, "A Suggestion for a Fast Multiplier", *IEEE Trans. Electronic Computers*, vol. **EC-13**, no. 2, Feb. 1964, pp. 14-17.

[9] C. D. Walter, "Redundant Arithmetic is not necessary for Fast Modular Exponentiation", submitted to *IEEE Trans on Comp*.

[10] E. F. Brickell, "A Fast Modular Multiplication Algorithm with Application to Two Key Cryptography", *Advances in Cryptology - CRYPTO '82*, Chaum *et al.* (eds.), New York, Plenum, 1983, pp. 51-60.

[11] C. D. Walter, "Faster Modular Multiplication by Operand Scaling", *Advances in Cryptology - CRYPTO '91*, J. Feigenbaum (ed.), Lecture Notes in Comp. Sci. vol. **576**, 1992, pp. 313-323, Springer-Verlag.

[12] C. D. Walter, "Space/Time Trade-offs for Higher Radix Modular Multiplication using Repeated Addition", *IEEE Trans. Comp.*, vol. **46**, 1997, pp. 139-141.

[13] P. L. Montgomery, "Modular Multiplication without Trial Division", *Math. Computation*, vol. **44**, 1985, pp. 519-521.

[14] S. E. Eldridge, "A Faster Modular Multiplication Algorithm", *Intern. J. Computer Math.*, vol. **40**, 1991, pp. 63-68.

[15] S. E. Eldridge & C. D. Walter, "Hardware Implementation of Montgomery's Modular Multiplication Algorithm", *IEEE Trans. Comp.*, vol. **42**, 1993, pp. 693-699.

[16] C. D. Walter, "Systolic Modular Multiplication", *IEEE Trans. Comp.*, vol. **42**, 1993, pp. 376-378.

[17] P. Kornerup, "A Systolic, Linear-Array Multiplier for a Class of Right-Shift Algorithms", *IEEE Trans. Comp.*, 1994, vol. **43**, no. 8, pp. 892-898.

[18] D. E. Knuth, *The Art of Computer Programming*, vol. **2**, "Seminumerical Algorithms", 2nd Edition, Addison-Wesley, 1981, pp. 441-466.

[19] C. D. Walter, "Exponentiation using Division Chains", *IEEE Trans. Comp.*, vol. **47**, 1998, no. 7, *to appear*.

26th May 1998

Integrated Partitioning and Scheduling for Hardware/Software Co-design

Huiqun Liu and D. F. Wong
Department of Computer Sciences, University of Texas, Austin, TX 78712, USA

Abstract—
Existing approaches to hardware/software co-design separate partitioning and scheduling in two steps. Since partitioning solutions affect scheduling results and vice versa, the existing sequential approach leads to sub-optimal results. In this paper, we explore an integrated hardware/software partitioning and scheduling strategy, where the partitioning process uses the information provided by the scheduling solution as a guide. We present an efficient algorithm for partitioning and scheduling the tasks for execution on the given software (2 CPUs) and hardware (k ASICs or FPGAs) resources with the objective of minimizing the total execution time and the hardware cost. Our algorithm have produced good results in all the task graphs we used in our experiments.

I. Introduction

In many real time and embedded applications, heterogeneous hardware/software architectures provide a more effective design solution for the target cost and performance. Hardware/software co-design systems are characterized by the presence of a set of software (m CPUs) and hardware (k AISCs or FPGAs) computing resources under both the performance and cost constraints. Hardware/software partitioning, which defines the boundary of the hardware/software implementation of a system specification, is one of the key aspects and the most challenging tasks of hardware/software co-design. Supporting the designer in choosing the right mixture of components and implementation technology is essential to the success of the final system.

A great deal of recent work has focused on hardware/software partitioning in one CPU system, including: greedy heuristics, iterative improvement, clustering, and mathematical programming approaches [2, 3, 4, 5, 6, 7, 10, 11, 12, 13, 14]. The algorithm in [2] achieves the hardware-software partitioning by moving operations from software to hardware to meet performance goals, while the algorithm in [3] moves operations from hardware to software on a processor to reduce system cost. [4] presents a binary-search algorithm which minimizes the hardware cost and satisfies other constraints. [5] presents a stepwise approach of partitioning with different granularity based on VHDL specification.

Existing approaches to hardware/software co-design separate partitioning and scheduling as two steps [12,13,14]. Usually a hardware/software partitioning is performed first, then scheduling and resource allocation is used as a feasibility checking and performance evaluation. If the scheduling result violates the performance requirement, then the partitioning solution is infeasible, and a new partition is generated and evaluated. This process is repeated until the system requirement is satisfied. Since partitioning solutions affect scheduling results and vice versa, the existing sequential approach may lead to sub-optimal results.

Hardware/software partitioning and scheduling are closely related. First, the execution time for a task depends on whether the task is placed in software or hardware. Secondly, the execution parallelism among hardware tasks, and between software and hardware tasks depends on the scheduling of all the tasks. This makes it difficult to evaluate the performance of a particular partition without considering scheduling at the same time. If partitioning is separated from the scheduling process, it can not guarantee a good scheduling result. For example, the partitioning process usually tries to minimize the total delay on the critical path. However, due to the precedence constraints among the tasks and the limited number of CPUs, even if the delay on the critical path is minimized, the scheduler may lead to sub-optimal result in the total execution time.

Instead of separating the scheduling and partitioning process as two steps, in this paper, we present an integrated hardware/software partitioning and scheduling strategy for a co-design system with 2 CPUs and k hardware resources. We start from a scheduling solution assuming all tasks are in software, then the partitioning process iteratively utilizes the information provided by the scheduler to select the best tasks to be implemented in hardware so as to minimize the total execution time as well as the hardware cost. In the meantime, re-scheduling is done efficiently and incrementally. The current scheduling provides the relative mobility information of the neighboring tasks and guides the partitioning process to select tasks to be moved to hardware to achieve the maximum parallelism among the software and hardware tasks. The parallelism not only reduces the total execution time, but also facilitates to lower the hardware cost. Experimental results show that the algorithm produced good results in term of total execution time in all the task graphs we used in our experiments.

II. Problem statement

A software/hardware co-design system is characterized by a set of software (CPUs or processors) and hardware (ASIC or FPGAs) computing resources. The system behavior is typically represented as a directed acyclic graph $G = (V, E)$. Each node $v \in V$ represents a task (or process), which can either run on one of the CPUs as a software process or can be implemented by hardware (*i.e* ASIC or FPGA). The edges in E defines the dependencies (precedence constraints) between the tasks. If there is an edge $u \rightarrow v$ from task u to task v, then u is a predecessor of v, and u must finish its execution before task v can start execution. A task v can only start its execution (either on hardware or software) after all its predecessors have finished execution. We consider the situation where both the software and hardware execution are non-preemptive, such that once a task starts execution, it must finish to the end.

Here we assume the CPUs are homogeneous and the tasks are designed to have uniform execution time in software, denoted by α. Each task i can have h_i different choices of hardware implementations, and each implementation has a different execution time β_{ij} and hardware cost c_{ij} (*e.g.* area, power consumption) for $1 \leq j \leq h_i$. A faster hardware implementation usually has a higher cost. A task in software has a lower cost but also a slower speed than its hardware implementation. Hence it is important to find a good trade off between cost and performance in the co-design process.

Let T_{exec} denote the total execution time of the system, which equals to the latest finishing time of any of the tasks. Minimizing T_{exec} or letting T_{exec} satisfy a pre-defined timing constraint is critical for many real time systems. Obviously, T_{exec} not only depends on the hardware/software partitioning solution, but also on the scheduling result.

Given a directed acyclic graph G and m homogeneous CPUs, our hardware/software partitioning problem is to select k tasks

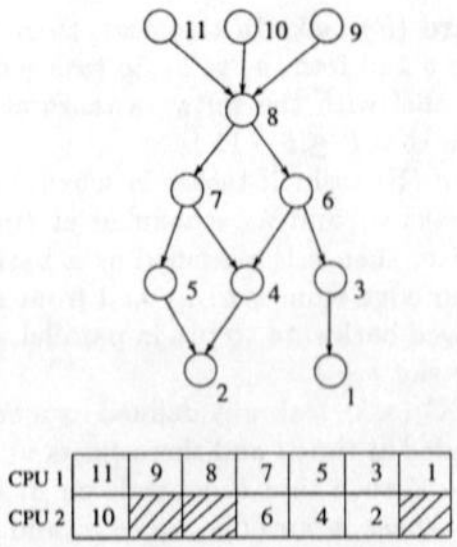

Fig. 1. *An example of an optimal 2-CPU scheduling*

to be implemented in hardware, with the objective of minimizing the total execution time T_{exec} as well as the total hardware cost. In this paper, we especially consider a co-design system with two CPUs (when $m = 2$) and k hardware resources. To meet both the performance and cost criteria, the hardware/software partitioning process that decides which tasks should be implemented in software or hardware is a non-trivial task, and has recently become a hot research topic.

III. Integrated hardware/software partitioning and scheduling

It is well known that if each task has uniform execution time α in software, an optimal two CPU scheduling solution can be found in polynomial time ([19]). The optimal scheduling solution is obtained by first assigning each task a label representing the priority of the task and then allocate the tasks to the two CPUs based on their priority and precedence constraints. Figure 1 shows an example of the labeling of the tasks and an optimal scheduling for a task graph which takes 7α total execution time. Let the time slot in a scheduling be marked as $0, ..., t, ...$ each with time duration α.

To facilitate the discussion in the rest of the paper, we introduce the following notations. Let $P_1(t)$, $P_2(t)$ denote the two tasks scheduled on CPU 1 and CPU 2 at time t. If $P_1(t) = i$ and $P_2(t) = \phi$ (*i.e.* CPU 2 is idle), we define i as a *singleton* task, and i is the only task running at time slot t on one CPU. Let T_1, T_2 denote the latest time any job finishes on CPU 1 and CPU 2. It is easy to show that $T_{exec} = max(T_1, T_2)$. For each task i, let $mc(i) = min(c_{ij})$ for $1 \leq j \leq h_i$. $mc(i)$ is the minimum cost among all the h_i hardware implementation choices for task i. When the CPU is idle, we define ϕ as a special task, whose cost is 0, *i.e.* $mc(\phi) = 0$.

It is easy to show that an optimal scheduling has the minimum number of singleton tasks and at most one CPU is idle at any time slot t. Though there may exist multiple optimal scheduling solutions, they all have the same number of singleton tasks. Figure 1 shows an example of an optimal scheduling. $T_{exec} = 7\alpha$, and tasks 9, 8 and 1 are singleton tasks.

A. A special case

Since the hardware execution time is usually much less than the software execution time, first we consider the case when the hardware execution time is small enough to be negligible from the software execution time (*i.e.* $\alpha \gg \beta_{ij}$ for task i). Though letting the hardware execution time be negligible is an unrealistic assumption for many real systems, it forms the basis of our discussion for the general case in the next section.

If the hardware execution time for each task can be ignored, we have the following two observations. First, when a singleton task scheduled at time t is moved from software to hardware, T_{exec} will be reduced by α. This is obvious because after the singleton task is moved, both CPUs will be idle at time slot t, we can do the re-scheduling by moving every task scheduled at time t' ($t' > t$) to time $t' - 1$. Since the singleton tasks may have different hardware cost, the one with a lower hardware cost will be a better choice. A simple strategy is to sort all the singleton tasks according to its cost $mc(i)$ and select the tasks with a lower cost first to move from software to hardware.

The second observation is that if there is no singleton tasks in the current schedule (*i.e.* both CPUs are busy in any time slot t), then $T_1 = T_2$ and at least two tasks have to be moved to hardware in order to reduce T_{exec}. The two tasks $P_1(t)$ and $P_2(t)$ can be moved together to hardware to reduce T_{exec} by α time, and the re-scheduling can be done by moving all the tasks at t' ($t' > t$) to $t' - 1$. Since $T_{exec} = max(T_1, T_2)$ and $T_1 = T_2$, it is easy to prove that two tasks have to be moved to hardware to reduce the total execution time. In order to minimize the hardware cost, we can sort the time slots in increasing order by $mc(i)+mc(j)$, such that $P_1(t) = i$ and $P_2(t) = j$. $mc(i)+mc(j)$ is the minimum total hardware cost for the two tasks scheduled at time t, and the two tasks with a smaller total cost should be moved to hardware first.

Based on the above observations, we have the following strategy to select k tasks to hardware while minimizing the execution time T_{exec} and the hardware cost.

Algorithm 1: Select k tasks to be implemented in hardware and minimize the total execution time.

1. Find an optimal two-CPU scheduling assuming each task runs in software.
2. Based on the optimal scheduling, find all the singleton tasks and sort them in increasing order by their cost $mc(i)$. If there are more than k singleton tasks, then select the first k to hardware. If there are less than k singleton tasks, select all of them to hardware.
3. If the number of tasks selected in step 2 is still less than k, then after step 2, both CPUs are busy (*i.e* $P_1(t) \neq \phi$ and $P_2(t) \neq \phi$ for any t). Sort all the time slots by their $mc(i)+mc(j)$ value. Move two tasks scheduled in the same time slot t to hardware, until k is reached.

Lemma 1: *If the hardware execution time of each task is negligible, then an optimal partitioning and scheduling in terms of minimum execution time can be found in polynomial time.*

Proof: An optimal two-CPU scheduling can be found in near linear time [19]. If k hardware tasks are selected in step 2, then the total execution time will be reduced by $k \cdot \alpha$, which is the maximum amount of delay that can be reduced from the initial optimal scheduling. Therefore, the execution time is minimized. If k is reached in step 3, then after the k tasks are moved to hardware, for the scheduling of the rest of the $n - k$ tasks run in software, both CPUs are kept busy until every task is finished. Since the hardware execution time is ignored, the execution time for task graph G is $\alpha \cdot \frac{(n-k)}{2}$, which is the minimum. □

B. The general case

However, if the hardware execution time is not negligible, then by selecting one or two tasks to hardware may not reduce the execution time by α. Figure 2 shows an example. If the two tasks $9, 8$ which are singleton tasks in the initial optimal scheduling, are moved to hardware, the total execution time is

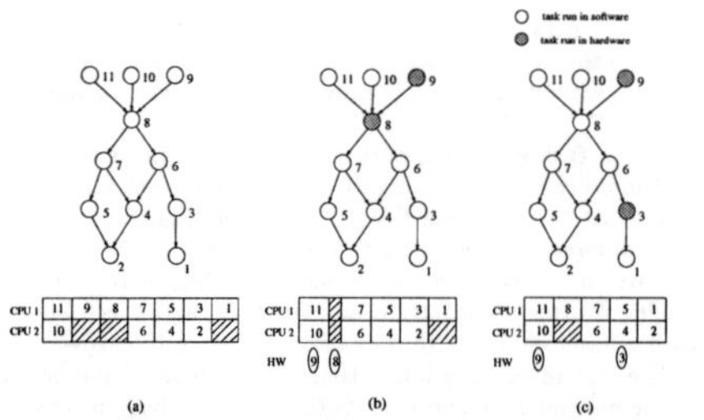

Fig. 2. *If the hardware execution time is not negligible, then moving a singleton task to hardware may not result in the optimal scheduling solution*

$5\alpha + \beta_8$ (Figure 2(b)). Task 8 can not run in parallel with any other task and it contributes β_8 in T_{exec}. Though task 3 is not a singleton task in the initial optimal scheduling (Figure 2(c)), it is a better choice to be moved to hardware than task 8. If task 3 is selected instead of task 8, the execution time is 5α which is optimal, since task 3 can run in parallel with the software tasks and contributes 0 time in T_{exec} (Figure 2(c)). This example illustrates that if the hardware execution is not 0, more careful strategy is needed to select the tasks to hardware in order to minimize the execution time T_{exec}.

To achieve the goal of better performance and lower cost, it is important to maximize the parallel execution among the software and hardware tasks, and among the hardware tasks. By fully exploring the parallelism among the hardware and software tasks, we can gain in two aspects. First, the total execution time can be maximally reduced. Secondly, the hardware cost can also be reduced by using the cheapest implementation. For example, if a hardware process i is running in parallel with a software process j, since usually software execution time of j is longer than the hardware execution time of i, the execution time of i will not affect the total execution time. Therefore we can select the cheapest hardware implementation for task i to reduce the cost.

In the following sections, we explain how to maximize parallelism among the hardware and software tasks and present an efficient integrated partitioning and scheduling algorithm. Section B.1 explains how to use the information from the scheduling result to mark the relative mobility of a task. Then, section B.2 discusses how the partitioning process can use a combination of the relative mobility information of the neighboring tasks to select a good task to move to hardware. Next, the integrated partitioning and scheduling algorithm is presented in section B.3.

B.1 Label the tasks with relative mobility

In this section, we show that the scheduling solution provides important information in how to explore the maximum parallelism while moving k tasks from software to hardware. And we will explain how to utilize the information provided by the scheduling process as much as possible to guide the partitioning process.

First, we study the relative mobility of the tasks in a scheduling solution and classify each task into one of the three categories: *forward, backward* and *stable* tasks.

(1) *forward* (F) task: if a task v is scheduled at time slot t and does not depend on u_1 and u_2 (one of them may be ϕ) which are scheduled at time slot $t-1$, then v is marked as a forward (F) task. In this case, there is no edge in G from u_1 to v and from u_2 to v. So task v can be moved to run in parallel with the software tasks at an earlier time slot t' such that $t' \leq t-1$.

(2) *backward* (B) task: if task v is scheduled at time t and the two tasks u_1 and u_2 scheduled at time $t+1$ do not depend on v, then v is classified as a backward (B) task. There is no edge from v to u_1 and from v to u_2. Task v can be moved backward to run in parallel with task u_1 and u_2 at time slot $t+1$.

(3) *stable* (X) task: task v is defined as a stable (X) task if it is scheduled at time t and there exists u_1 at time $t-1$, u_2 at time $t+1$, such that v depends on u_1 and u_2 depends on v (*i.e.* there is an edge $u_1 \rightarrow v$ and $v \rightarrow u_2$ in G). In this case, task v can not be moved either forward or backward in the current schedule unless its surrounding tasks are moved.

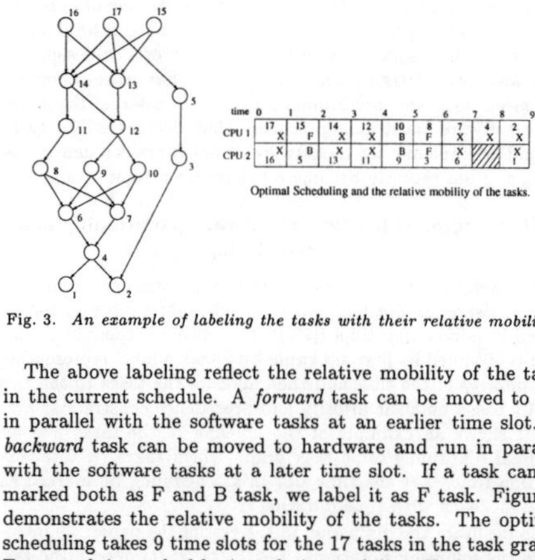

Fig. 3. *An example of labeling the tasks with their relative mobility*

The above labeling reflect the relative mobility of the tasks in the current schedule. A *forward* task can be moved to run in parallel with the software tasks at an earlier time slot. A *backward* task can be moved to hardware and run in parallel with the software tasks at a later time slot. If a task can be marked both as F and B task, we label it as F task. Figure 3 demonstrates the relative mobility of the tasks. The optimal scheduling takes 9 time slots for the 17 tasks in the task graph. Every task is marked by its relative mobility. Task 15 at time slot 1 is marked as F task because it does not have precedence constraints with the two tasks (task 17 and 16) at time 0. Task 5 is marked as B task because it is not a predecessor of task 13 and 14 scheduled at the next time slot, and can run in parallel with the two tasks 14 and 13.

After the labeling, a forward task i at time t can be moved to a set of earlier time slots. Let τ_1, τ_2 be the earliest and latest time slots that i can be moved to, that is, for any t', $\tau_1 \leq t' \leq \tau_2$, there is no dependency between i and $P_k(t')$, $k = 1, 2$. Task i can run in parallel with any tasks in time slots from τ_1 to τ_2. Let $S(i) = \{i\} \cup \{P_k(t')|k = 1, 2$ and $\tau_1 \leq t' \leq \tau_2\}$. An important observation is that not only i can be moved to hardware, any task in $S(i)$ can be moved to hardware as well. This gives us more flexibility in choosing a task from a subset of tasks to be moved to hardware in order to reduce the hardware cost. Let task j be the task such that $mc(j) = min\{mc(n)|n \in S(i)\}$. Then we can replace j by i and move j to hardware. Let $\gamma(i)$ denote the minimum cost while moving the task i, then $\gamma(i) = mc(j)$. Thus the task with the lowest hardware cost can be moved to hardware without influencing the total execution time. The same analysis applies to a backward task as well.

For example in Figure 3, task 3 is marked as F, $\tau_1 = 2$ and $\tau_2 = 7$. Task 9 is a B task with $\tau_1 = 5$ and $\tau_2 = 5$.

We define a function $move(i)$ to move a task i and find the best task to be implemented in hardware. We consider ϕ as a special task if $P_k(t) = \phi$, and we assign the cost of ϕ task as 0.

Function $move(i)$

1. find τ_1 and τ_2 for i;
2. $S(i) = \{i\} \cup \{P_k(t') | k = 1, 2 \text{ and } \tau_1 \leq t' \leq \tau_2\}$;
3. find task $j \in S(i)$ such that $mc(j) = min\{mc(n) | n \in S(i)\}$;
4. replace j by i; implement j in hardware with cost $mc(j)$;
5. set $\gamma(i) = mc(j)$;

B.2 Task selection

The relative mobility of a task depends on the current scheduling and will be dynamically changed with the moving of its neighboring tasks. It is important to note that we have to check a combination of the relative mobility of the neighboring tasks in order to decide which task is the best choice. Figure 4 illustrates an example that even if a task is a forward task (*e.g.* task 4) in the current schedule, it may not be a good choice to be moved to hardware since task 5, which runs in the same time slot is marked as X and the execution time can not be reduced when task 4 is moved.

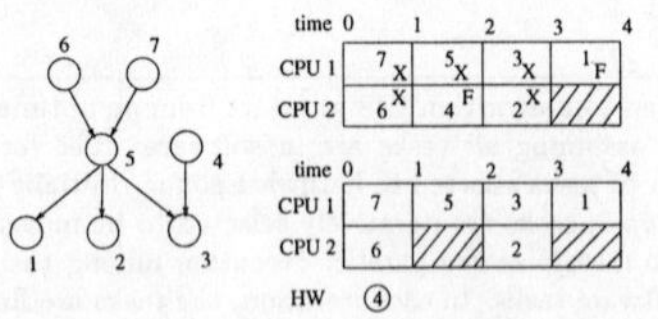

Fig. 4. *We need to consider a combination of the mobility of the surrounding tasks in order to decide which task should be moved to hardware. Though task 4 is marked as a forward task, it is not necessary to move it to hardware in this case*

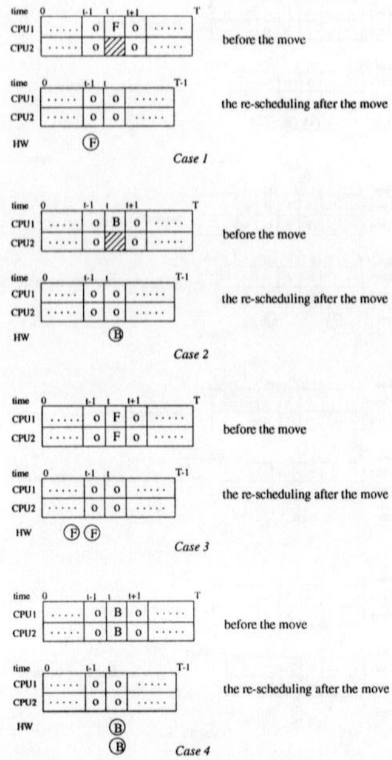

We have the following observations in how to utilize the patterns of the relative mobility of the neighboring tasks to move tasks from software to hardware, in order to minimize the execution time and the cost. In the following figures, 'o' represents any type of tasks, ϕ is a special task and we mark it as B task.

Case 1: If i is a singleton task at time slot t and i is a forward task, then i can be moved to an earlier time slot by the $move(i)$ function, and thus reduce α from T_{exec}. The re-scheduling is done by moving all task at t' ($t' > t$) to $t' - 1$.

Case 2: If i is a singleton task at time t and is a backward task, then i can be moved to a later time slot by the $move(i)$ function. T_{exec} will be reduced by α. The re-scheduling is done by moving all tasks at t' ($t' > t$) to $t' - 1$.

Case 3: If at time slot t, the two tasks allocated to the two CPUs are both forward tasks (both are marked as F), then both of them can be moved and run in an earlier time slot before t. After the move, we can re-schedule by moving every task scheduled at t' ($t' > t$) to $t' - 1$. Thus α time is reduced from T_{exec}.

Case 4: If at time slot t, the two tasks allocated to the two CPUs are both backward tasks (both are marked as B), then both of them can be moved and run in parallel with the tasks scheduled at time $t+1$. After the move, both CPUs are idle at time t, we can re-schedule by moving every task scheduled at t' ($t' > t$) to $t' - 1$. Thus α time is reduced from T_{exec}.

Case 5: If the two tasks scheduled at time t are marked as F and B, then both of them can be moved and reduce the execution time by α. The F task can be moved to an earlier time before t and the B task can be moved to time $t + 1$.

Case 6: If a forward (F) task is scheduled at time t and a backward (B) task is scheduled at time $t + 1$, and the task u at time $t + 1$ does not depend on v at time t, then the F and B task can be moved. The F task can be moved to an earlier time slot, while the B task can be moved to run in parallel with the tasks scheduled at time $t + 2$. We can do the re-schedule by moving task u to time slot t to run in parallel with v, and by moving all the tasks scheduled at t' ($t' \geq (t + 2)$) to $t' - 1$. By this re-scheduling, one time slot α is reduced from the execution time.

Case 7: If at time t, one CPU is idle and a stable task (X) if scheduled on the other CPU, then move this task to hardware will reduce the execution time by $\alpha - \beta$.

Case 8: If both tasks on the two CPUs are marked as X at any time slot t, then the length of the schedule equals to the length of the longest path. Two tasks have to be moved to hardware in order to reduce the total execution time and the execution time can only be reduced by $\alpha - \beta$.

In cases 1 to 6, by the $move(i)$ function, the task with the lowest cost in the subset $\{i\} \cup \{P_k(t') | k = 1, 2, \tau_1 \leq t' \leq \tau_2\}$ will be selected to hardware implementation. In each of the eight cases, the re-scheduling is done very efficiently, which only takes $O(1)$ time if we use a linked list to store the scheduled tasks on the two CPUs.

Lemma 2: *For Cases 1 to 6, the execution time is reduced by α after moving the tasks to hardware.*

Proof: In Cases 1 to 6, the tasks moved to hardware can run in parallel with some software tasks. After the rescheduling, the execution time is reduced by one time slot with a duration

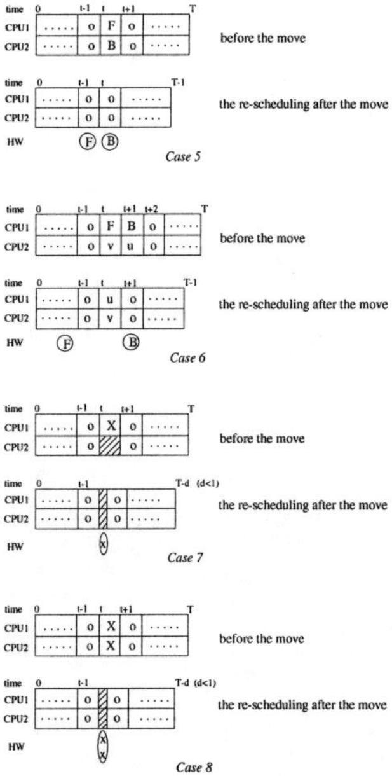

of α. □

Lemma 3: *In Case 8, if every task is marked as X, the delay on the longest path in G is equal to the length of the scheduling. We can not move any tasks to hardware to run in parallel with software to reduce α delay. Moving one or two tasks to hardware will at most reduce $\alpha - \beta$ time.*

Lemma 4: *In Cases 1 to 6, the tasks moved to hardware can use the implementation with the lowest cost.*

Proof: If a task i is moved to hardware in Case 1 to 6, it will run in parallel with a software task on CPU. Since $\beta_{ij} < \alpha$, task i can be implemented by any optional choices without influencing the total execution time. Therefore, the implementation with the minimum cost should be used. □

After some tasks are moved to hardware, they also form constraints on the relative mobility labeling and the scheduling of other tasks. We extend the definition of the relative mobility by considering the effect of these hardware tasks. A software task i at time t is marked as a *forward* task if it does not have precedence constraints between any of the tasks at time slot $t-1$, and if i is moved to hardware, the delay on the longest path of the hardware in time slot $t-1$ is less than α. A task i is marked as a *backward* task if i is not a predecessor of any of the software task at time slot $t+1$, and when i is moved to hardware, the delay on the longest path of the hardware in time slot $t+1$ is less than α.

B.3 Algorithm IPS: integrated partitioning and scheduling

In this section, we present the integrated partitioning and scheduling (IPS) algorithm. The analysis in the previous section presents a method to select which task to move to hardware based on the given scheduling result, and how to do the re-scheduling. We start from an optimal or near-optimal scheduling solution, and iteratively use the task selection method to move tasks from software to hardware. In each iteration, we select the task which can reduce the maximum amount of execution time and has the lowest hardware cost.

The following is the integrated hardware/software partitioning and scheduling (IPS) algorithm.

Algorithm IPS: Integrated partitioning and scheduling for two CPUs and k ASICs.

1. An optimal two-CPU scheduling is found by assuming each task is implemented in software. Let $total = 0$.
2. **While** $total < k$ **do**
   begin
   2.1 Mark the relative mobility of each task;
   2.2 **If** there are time slot satisfying Cases 1 to 6,
   find the tasks with the minimum cost $\gamma(i) + \gamma(j)$;
   else
   find the tasks with the minimum $\gamma(i) + \gamma(j)$ according to Cases 7, 8.
   2.3 Let (i, j) be the two tasks found in step 2.2;
   2.4 do $move(i)$ and $move(j)$;
   2.5 do the re-scheduling according to the move in step 2.4.
   2.6 Increment $total$;
   end

In step 1 of algorithm IPS, we start from an optimal scheduling by assuming all tasks are in software. Let $total$ be the number of tasks selected to hardware so far. Initially $total = 0$.

In step 2, tasks are iteratively selected to be moved to hardware to maximize the parallel execution among the hardware and software tasks. In each iteration, the tasks are first labeled with their relative mobility, then for each pair of tasks i, j satisfying Cases 1 to 8, $\gamma(i) + \gamma(j)$ is calculated, and the two tasks with the minimum cost is selected to be moved. Notice that one of i or j may be ϕ. Then the re-scheduling is done according to the move and $total$ is incremented. This process continues until the total number of hardware tasks is reached.

According to Cases 1 to 8, the re-scheduling takes O(1) time. In each iteration, the relative mobility labeling, selection of the best tasks will take $O(n)$. Since there are at most k iterations and the initial two-CPU optimal scheduling takes linear time, the time complexity for algorithm IPS is $O(kn)$.

In algorithm IPS, the scheduling and partitioning are integrated and interactively provide information to each other. Both the partitioning and re-scheduling process are incremental. The scheduling provides information to the partitioning process as which tasks are the best choice to be moved to hardware. The re-scheduling is efficiently performed according to the partitioning result, which in return provides information on how to do the partition in the next round.

Figure 5 illustrates an example of the IPS algorithm. If every task is in software, the optimal scheduling takes 9 time slots for the 17 tasks in the task graph. Every task is marked by its relative mobility. Task 15 at time slot 1 is marked as F task because it does not have precedence constraints between the two tasks (task 17 and 16) at time 0. Task 5 is marked as B task because it can run in parallel with the two tasks 14 and 13 scheduled at the next time slot. This matches Case 5, so task 15 and task 5 are moved to hardware and the total execution time is reduced by one time slot with duration α. In the next iteration, the relative mobility of the neighboring tasks are re-labeled and the two forward tasks 8 and 3 are selected to move

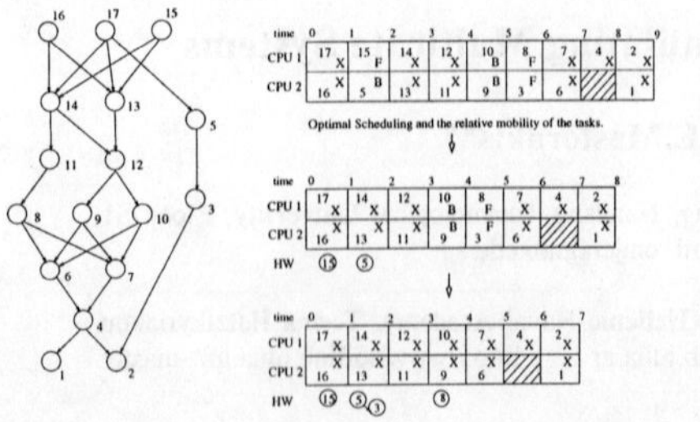

Fig. 5. *An example of the integrated partitioning and scheduling algorithm (IPS)*

to hardware since Case 3 is matched. The execution time is reduced by α with this move and the rest of the task are re-scheduled.

IV. Experimental results

The integrated partitioning and scheduling (IPS) algorithm is implemented in C++ and we experimented with some large directed acyclic task graphs (as shown in Table 1). The number of tasks in these task graphs ranges from 300 to 3000.

Table 1 shows the partitioning and scheduling results of the task graphs in a two-CPU and k-ASICs system. The execution time T_{exec} after the hardware/software partitioning and scheduling is compared with the best possible execution time T_{low}. We derive T_{low} by optimistically calculating the execution time on the software tasks assuming the two CPUs are always kept busy. If there are n tasks in a task graph and k tasks are implemented by hardware, then there will be $n - k$ software tasks and T_{low} would be $\frac{(n-k)}{2}$, which is a lower bound. We experimented when $\frac{k}{n}$ is set to be 20% and 50%.

TABLE I

Partitioning and scheduling result with two CPUs and k ASICs

		$\frac{k}{n} = 20\%$		$\frac{k}{n} = 50\%$	
Task graph	# Tasks	T_{exec}	T_{low}	T_{exec}	T_{low}
TG-432	217	87	87	54	54
TG-499	253	102	102	63	63
TG-880	390	156	156	98	98
TG-1355	650	260	260	163	163
TG-1908	390	156	156	94	94
TG-2670	924	370	370	202	202
TG-3540	1038	416	416	241	241
TG-5315	1778	712	712	445	445
TG-6288	2856	1143	1143	714	714
TG-7552	2247	899	899	562	562

The experiments show that for all the task graphs, the IPS algorithm yields good results in terms of execution time, as T_{exec} is equal to T_{low} in all our experiments. This proves that the IPS algorithm is effective in exploring the maximum execution parallelism among the software and hardware tasks, as well as among the hardware tasks. The IPS algorithm also results in low hardware cost, as in each iteration of the partitioning and re-scheduling process, the task with the lowest hardware cost is selected to be moved to hardware.

In our future research, we will further explore how to extend the IPS algorithm to deal with the more general case when each software process has different execution time. It is known that the scheduling is a NP-complete problem in this case. We will explore how to start from a near-optimal scheduling and fully use the information to guide the partitioning process to select tasks to be moved to hardware. We will also study how to extend the algorithm to m CPU systems ($m > 2$) and how to do hardware sharing to further reduce the hardware cost.

V. Conclusion

In this paper we propose an integrated hardware/software partitioning and scheduling algorithm. By first finding an optimal or near optimal scheduling and by analyzing the relative mobility of the tasks, the best tasks are selected to be implemented in hardware and run in parallel with the software in order to maximize the parallelism and therefore minimize the total delay. The parallel execution between the hardware and software tasks allows us to minimize the hardware cost by using the lowest cost hardware implementation among the different optional implementations for the hardware tasks.

Experimental results show that for two CPUs and k ASICs design, our integrated partitioning and scheduling algorithm have produced good results in all the task graphs we used in our experiments.

References

[1] Giovanni De Micheli and Mariagiovanna Sami, *Hardware/Software Co-Design*, Kluwar Academic Publishers, 1995.

[2] R. K. Gupta and G. D. Micheli, *hardware-software cosynthesis for digital systems*, IEEE Design & Test of Computers, Vol. 10, No. 3, pp29-41, September 1993.

[3] Rolf Ernst, Wei Ye, Thomas Benner and Jorg Henkel, *Fast timing analysis for hardware/software co-design*, In ICCD'93, 1993.

[4] R. Ernst, J. Henkel and D. D. Gajski, *Hardware/software co-synthesis for microcontrollers*. IEEE Design & Test of Computers, vol. 10, no. 4, December 1993.

[5] P. Eles, Z. Peng and A. Doboli, *VHDL system-level specification and partitioning in a hardware/software co-synthesis environment*, in Proceedings, International Workshop on Hardware-software Co-Design, pp 49-55, 1994.

[6] J. K. Adams and D. E. Thomas, *Multiple-process behavioral synthesis for mixed hardware-software systems*, IEEE International Symposium of System Synthesis, pp10-15, 1995.

[7] Rajesh K. Gupta and Giovanni De Micheli, *System synthesis via hardware/software co-design*, Technical Report CSL-TR-92-548, Computer System Laboratory, Stanford University, October 1992.

[8] Axel Jantsch, Peeter Ellervee, Johnny Oberg, Ahmed Hermani and Hannu Tenhunen, *Hardware/software partitioning and minimizing memory interface traffic*. In EURO-DAC'94, 1994.

[9] Asawaree Kalavade and Edward A. Lee. *A global criticality/local phase driven algorithm for the constrained hardware/software partitioning problem*. In Third International Workshop on Hardware/ software Codesign, pp42-48, September 1994.

[10] Frank Vahid, Jie Gong and Daniel D. Gajski, *A binary-constraint search algorithm for minimizing hardware during hardware/software partitioning*. In EURO-DAC'94, pp214-219, 1994.

[11] Jorg Henkel and Rolf Ernst, *A hardware/software Partitioner using a dynamically determined granularity*, DAC'97.

[12] Bharat P. Dave, Ganesh Lakshminarayana and Niraj K. Jha, *COSYN: hardware/software Co-synthesis of Embedded systems*, DAC'97.

[13] Samir Agrawal and Rajesh K. Gupta, *Data-flow Assisted behavioral partitioning for embedded systems*, DAC'97.

[14] Smita Bakshi and Danial D. Gajski, *Hardware/software partitioning and pipelining*, DAC'97.

[15] Jay K Adams and Donald E. Thomas, *The design of mixed hardware/ software systems*, DAC'96.

[16] Youngsoo Shin and Kiyoung Choi, *Enforcing schedulability of Multi-task systems by hardware-software Codesign*, International Workshop on Hardware/Software Codesign, 1997.

[17] Junwei Hou and Wayne Wolf, *Process partitioning for distributed embedded systems*, International Workshop on Hardware/software Codesign, pp70-76, 1996.

[18] Peter Voigt Knudsen and Jan Madsen, *PACE: a dynamic programming algorithm for hardware/software partitioning*, International Workshop on Hardware/software Codesign, pp85-92,

[19] E. G. Coffman and R. L. Graham, *Optimal scheduling for two-processor systems*, Acta Informatica 1, Vol 6, pp200-213, 1972.

MATLAB Programs for Simulating Multirate Systems

M.J.Er and N.E.Mastorakis**

(*) School of Electrical and Electronic Engineering, Nanyang Technological University, Block S1, Nanyang Avenue, 639798, SINGAPORE email: emjer@ntu.edu.sg

(**) Military Institutions of University Education, Hellenic Naval Academy, Terma Hatzikyriakou, 18539, Piraeus, GREECE. email: mastor@softlab.ntua.gr http://www.softlab.ntua.gr/~mastor

ABSTRACT

MATLAB programs to facilitate analysis and design of multirate systems are proposed in this paper. Algorithms for single-rate as well as multirate input sampling and multirate output sampling are developed. With the use of the MATLAB programs developed, the dynamic behaviour of the multirate system can be studied and analyzed. An example is presented to show the advantages of multirate-input controller and multirate output controller over the conventional single-rate digital controller. Simulation results show that both the multirate-input controller and the multirate output controller have higher flexibility and are more superior to the single-rate controller.

1. INTRODUCTION

In the last decade and particularly the last several years, multirate control has received considerable attention, motivated by the need to optimize the performance of sampled systems with varying dynamic modes and to make efficient use of available hardware resources. Multirate controllers used in conjunction with a linear time-variant plant can offer a new dimension of flexibility of the design process [1]-[38]. They have been used to achieve equivalent state feedback without observers, pole assignment, zero assignment, gain margin improvement, strong and simultaneous stabilization and the removal of decentralized fixed modes in decentralized control. Evidently, multirate controllers can offer substantially more design freedom than conventional LTI controllers; also a multirate controller can be implemented in practice without any significant difficulty since it does not violate the constraint of finite memory in a computer. Recent interests are reflected in the LQG/LTR designs by [4]-[8], the parameterization of all stabilizing controllers by [9]-[11] and the work by [12]-[17]. The controller parameterization in [9] and [11] provides a basis for designing optimal multirate systems.

There are several reasons for using a multirate sampling scheme in digital control systems:

- In complex, multivariable control systems, it is often unrealistic or sometimes impossible, to sample all physical signals uniformly at one single rate. In such situations, one is compelled to use multirate sampling. For example in a two time-scale control problem, multirate sampling allows slow sampling in the control loops associated with low-bandwidth control function and fast sampling in those associated with high-bandwidth control function.

- In general, one gets better performance if one can sample and hold faster. But, faster A/D and D/A conversions mean higher cost in implementation. For signals with different bandwidths, better trade-offs between performance and implementation cost can be obtained using A/D and D/A converters at different rates. A decrease in sampling rate will yield more time for control calculations. This means that a slower computer can be used for a given control function or more capability is available from a given computer. As for an increase in sampling rate, it will improve command signal tracking effectiveness, and decrease sensitivity to random plant disturbances, plant parameter variations and also measurement noise.

- Multirate controllers are in general time-varying. Thus, multirate control system can achieve what single-rate systems cannot. For example, gain margin improvement [18]-[19] and [33], simultaneous stabilization [19] and [20] and decentralized control [15], [21] and [22]..

- Multirate controllers are normally more complex than single-rate counterparts. But, they are often finite-dimensional and periodic in a certain sense and hence can be implemented on microprocessors via difference equations with finite number of coefficients. Therefore, like single-rate controllers, multirate controllers do not violate the finite memory constraint in microprocessors.

The existing multirate controllers in the literature often come in different forms and at times prove confusing to researchers who are new in this field. This confusion is often compounded by the use of different terminologies and notations in the literature. Furthermore, simulation study of multirate system cannot be directly carried out using Control System Toolbox owing to the different sampling rates in the underlying multirate system. In this paper, MATLAB programs for simulating multirate systems are developed so as to facilitate analysis and design of this class of systems. The developed programs will be used to design some multirate controllers whose performances will be compared with conventional single-rate controllers.

2. SINGLE-RATE SAMPLING ALGORITHM

When a system has a single output controlled by a single input, it is called single-rate control. For a conventional single-rate control, it performs a control calculation and sends the control signals at every frame of output measurement where T is the frame period. That means a single sample of feedback is obtained and after processing, a signal is output to drive the system. The single-rate PID control law can be represented by

$$\begin{aligned} u(kT) = Kp * e(kT) + Kd * [e(kT) - e((k-1)T)] \\ + Ki * \sum [e(kT) - e((k-1)T)] \end{aligned} \quad (1)$$

where e is the error signal, Kp, Kd, Ki are the controller's gain and u is the output signal of the controller. The figure below illustrates the single-rate sampling mechanism:-

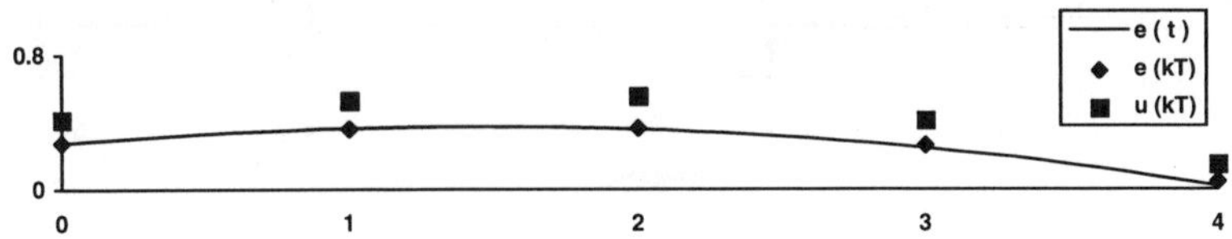

Figure 1 : Single rate sampling mechanism (T=1)

3. MULTIRATE SAMPLING ALGORITHMS

3.1 MULTIRATE INPUT SAMPLING ALGORITHM

For multirate input control, the output is measured at the frame period, T. With this sampler, N^I portions of different control signals are generated by multiplying the control signal u(kT) with different gain f1, f2, ..., fN^I respectively. That is, the input control signal, u(t) is updated at the multirate input-sampling rate T^I. These signals will be sent out consecutively to drive the plant before the next sample of error signal is obtained.

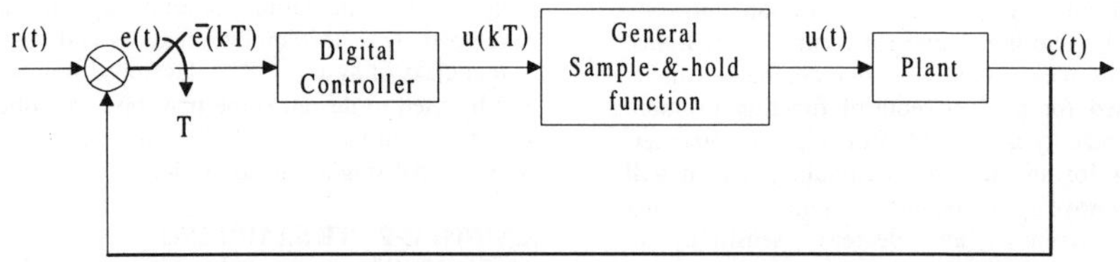

Figure 2 : Block diagram of multirate input sampling

The multirate input PID control law can be represented by the matrix equation given below :

$$u(kT) = Kp \times e(kT) + Kd \times [e(kT) - e((k-1)T)] + Ki \times 0.5 \times T \times \sum [e(kT) - e((k-1)T)] \qquad (2)$$

$$f(t) = \begin{cases} f1 & 0 \le t < T^I \\ f2 & T^I \le t < 2T^I \\ \vdots & \vdots \\ fN^I & (N^I - 1)T^I \le t < T \end{cases} \qquad (3)$$

$$u(t) = f(t) \times u(kT) \qquad (4)$$

where e is the sampled error signal, Kp, Kd, Ki are the controller's gains, u(kT) is the output signal of the controller, f is the set of gains of the general sample-hold function and u(t) is the input control signal to the plant.

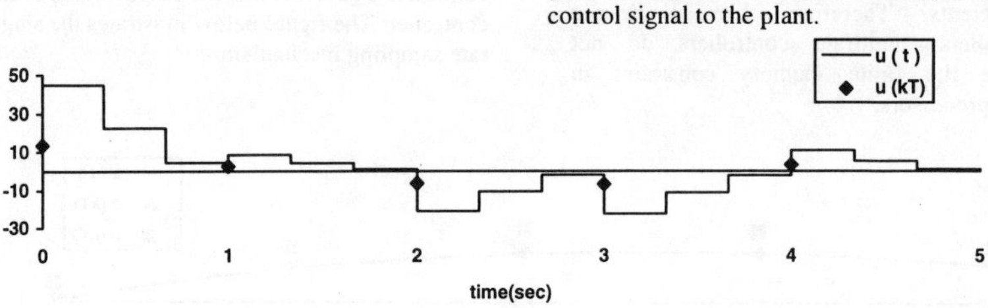

Figure 3 : Multirate input sampling mechanism for N^I=3, T=1

3.2 MULTIRATE OUTPUT SAMPLING ALGORITHM

For multirate output control, the output is measured at the base period T^O whereas the control signal is updated every frame period T by making used of the N^O number of sampled error signals over the interval kT to $kT+(N^O-1)T^O$.

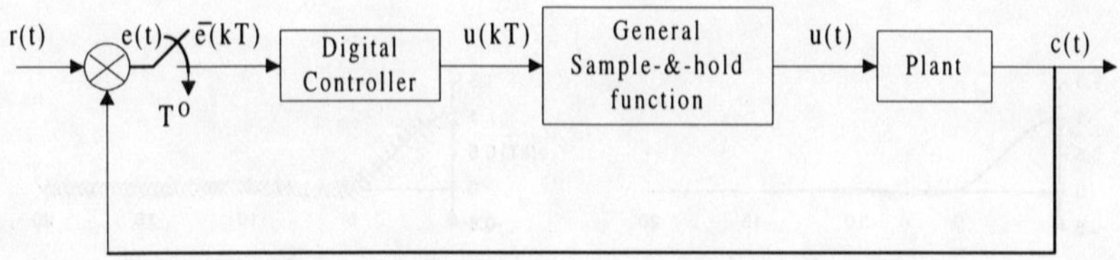

Figure 2 : Block diagram of multirate output sampling

The multirate output control law can be represented by

$$\bar{e}(kT) = \begin{bmatrix} e(kT) \\ \dot{e}(kT+T^O) \\ \vdots \\ e(kT+(N^O-1)T^O) \end{bmatrix} \qquad (5)$$

$$\begin{aligned} u(kT) = & \left[Kp1 \ldots KpN^O\right] \times \bar{e}(kT) \\ & + \frac{1}{T} \times \left[Kd1 \ldots KdN^O\right] \times \left(\bar{e}(kT) - \bar{e}((k-1)T\right) \\ & + \left[Ki1 \ldots KiN^O\right] \times 0.5 \times T \times \Sigma\left(\bar{e}(kT) - \bar{e}((k-1)T\right) \end{aligned} \qquad (6)$$

$$u(t) = f \times u(kT) \qquad \text{for } kT \le t < (k+1)T \qquad (7)$$

where e is the error signal, $\bar{e}$ is the sampled error signal, $Kp1 \ldots KpN^O$, $Kd1 \ldots KdN^O$, $Ki1 \ldots KiN^O$ are the controller's gains and u is the output of the controller.

The figure below illustrates the multirate output sampling mechanism:-

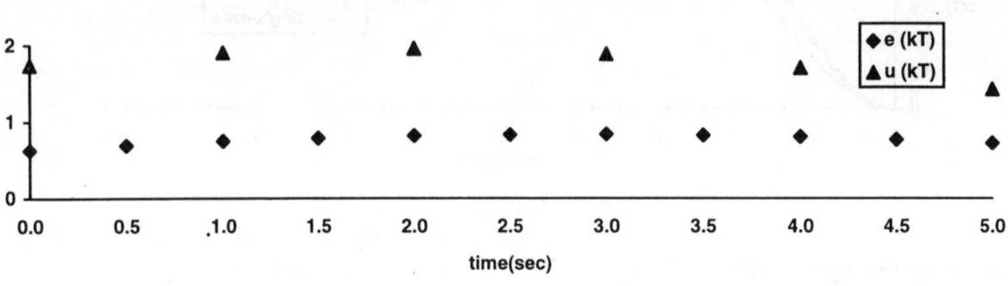

To verify the program algorithm, consider a robotic system of transfer function given by

4. EXAMPLES AND DISCUSSION

$$\frac{C(s)}{R(s)} = \frac{1.364579 \times 10^{14}}{s(s^4 + 8585.7704s^3 + 6.09245 \times 10^{11} s^2 + 5.19435 \times 10^{15} s + 3.75654 \times 10^{11})}$$

In order to satisfy the minimum requirements of 10% maximum overshoot, rise time of 3.5 sec, settling time of 8 sec with no steady-state error, a single-rate digital PD controller with Kp=9 and Kd=25 is used.

Now we consider multirate input controller with the same controller's gains, Kp=9 and Kd=25. The multirate input sampling-rate multiplicity, N^I, is chosen to be 3 with the set of gain [2.3, 0.5 0.1] used. Figures 4 to 8 show the signals at various stages of the multirate system:

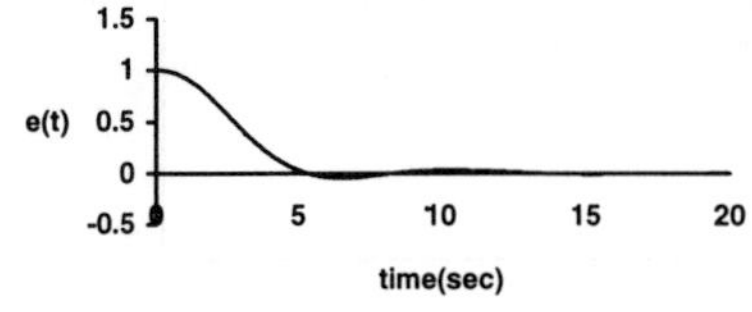

Figure 4 : Error signal

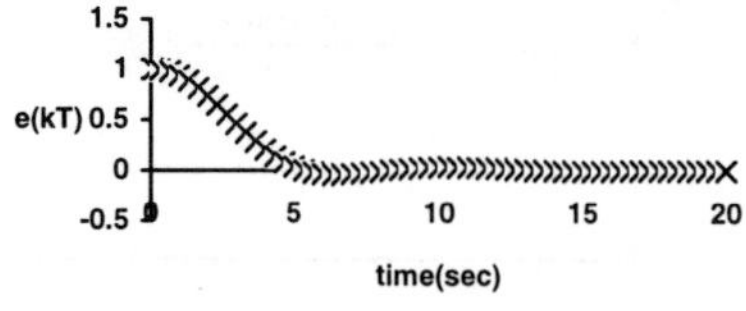

Figure 5 : Sampled error signal

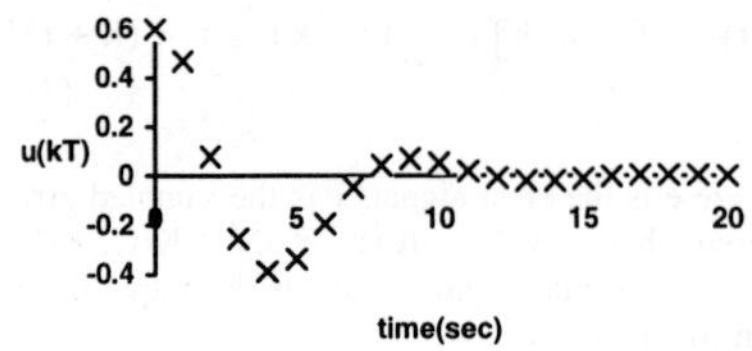

Figure 6 : Digital controller output signal

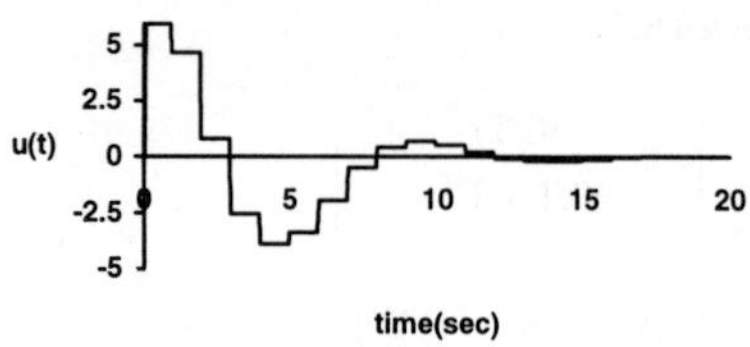

Figure 7 : Plant output control signal

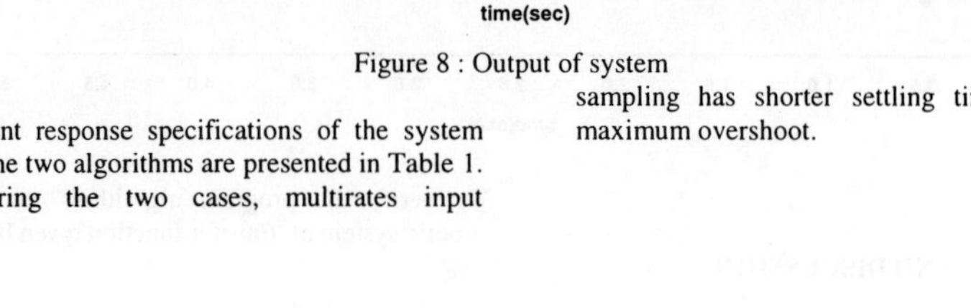

Figure 8 : Output of system

Transient response specifications of the system using the two algorithms are presented in Table 1. Comparing the two cases, multirates input sampling has shorter settling time and lower maximum overshoot.

Table 1. Transient response specifications of the system using single-rate & multirate input sampling algorithms

	Rise Time (sec)	Settling Time (sec)	Maximum Overshoot %
Single-rate sampling	2.631	8.6	5.2
Multirate input sampling	3.386	4.633	0.4

Now, consider the case where multirate output controller is used. The multirate output sampling-rate multiplicity is set to $N^O=3$ with the gain, f=10. The values of PD gains, Kp=[0.1 0.2 0.3] and Kd= [0.2 0.4 1.5] are used. Figures 9 to 13 show the signals at various stages.

Signals for the multirate output sampling system

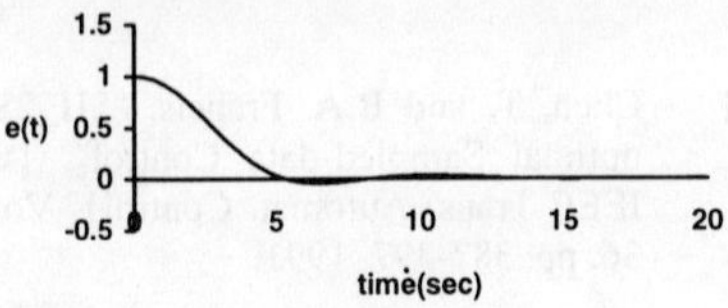

Figure 9 : Error signal

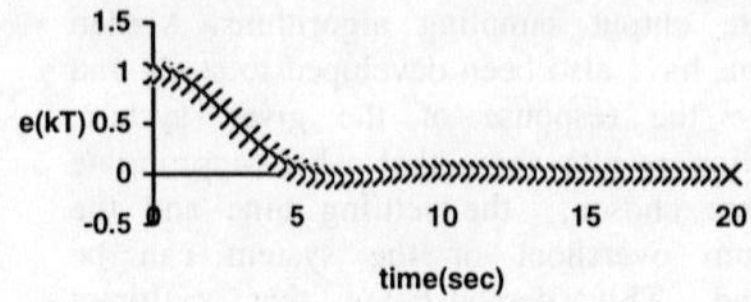

Figure 10 : Sampled error signal

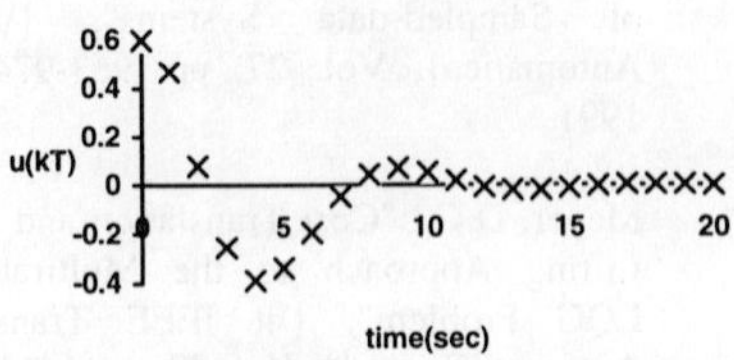

Figure 11 : Digital controller output signal

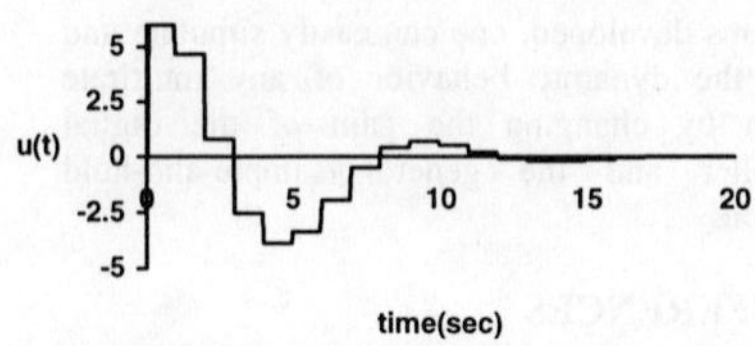

Figure 12 : Plant output control signal

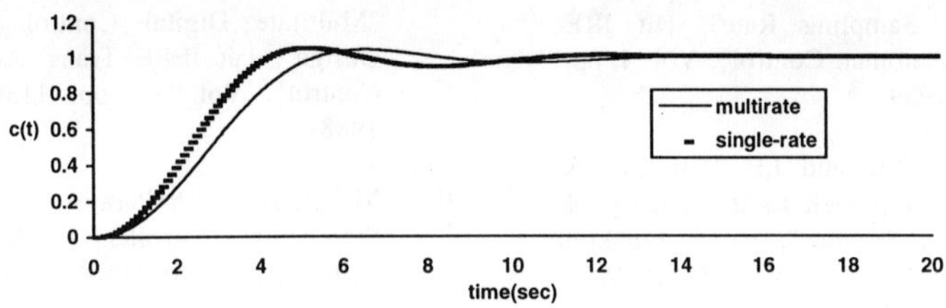

Figure 13 : Output of system

Transient response specifications of the system using the two algorithms are presented in Table 2.

Comparing the two cases, multirate output sampling, which has a lower gain, achieved a shorter settling time and lower maximum overshoot.

Table 2. Transient response specifications of the system using single-rate & multirate output sampling algorithms

	Rise Time (sec)	Settling Time (sec)	Maximum Overshoot %
Single-rate sampling	2.631	8.6	5.2
Multirate output sampling	3.319	4.833	4.4

5. CONCLUSIONS

This paper presents the algorithms of the single-rate as well as the two multirate sampling algorithms, namely multirate input sampling and multirate output sampling algorithms. Matlab programs have also been developed to study and simulate the response of the given system. Simulation results show that when appropriate gains are chosen, the settling time and the maximum overshoot of the system can be improved. This demonstrates that multirate controllers have more flexibility and are more superior to the conventional single-rate controllers. With the use of the MATLAB programs developed, one can easily simulate and study the dynamic behavior of any multirate system by changing the gain of the digital controller and the general sample-and-hold function.

6. REFERENCES

[1] Jury, E.I. and F.J. Mullin, "The Analysis of Sampled-data Control Systems with a. Periodically Time-varying Sampling Rate", {\it IRE Trans. Automat. Control}, Vol. 4, pp. 15-21, 1959.

[2] Kalman, R.E. and J.E. Bertram, "A Unified Approach to the Theory of Sampling Systems", {\it J. Franklin Inst.}, Vol. 267, pp. 405-436, 1959.

[3] Kranc, G.M. , "Input-output Analysis of Multirate Feedback Systems", {\it IRE Trans. Automat. Control}, Vol. 3, pp. 21-28, 1957.

[4] Al-Rahmani, H.M. and G.F. Franklin, "A New Optimal Multirate Control of Linear Periodic and Time-invariant Systems", {\it IEEE Trans. Automat. Control}, Vol. 35, pp. 406-415, 1990.

[5] Chen, T. and B.A. Francis, "H_2-optimal Sampled-data Control", {\it IEEE Trans. Automat. Control}, Vol. 36, pp. 387-397, 1991.

[6] Chen, T. and B.A. Francis, "Linear Time-varying H_2-optimal Control of Sampled-data Systems", {\it Automatica}, Vol. 27, pp. 963-974, 1991.

[7] Meyer, D.G., "Cost Translation and a Lifting Approach to the Multirate LQG Problem", {\it IEEE Trans. Automat. Control}, Vol. 37, pp. 1411-1415, 1992.

[8] Berg, M.C. , N. Amit and J. Powell, "Multirate Digital Control System Design", {\it IEEE Trans. Automat. Control}, Vol. 33, pp. 1139-1150, 1988.

[9] Meyer, D.G., "A Parameterization of Stabilizing Controllers for Multirate Sampled-data Systems", {\it IEEE Trans. Automat. Control}, Vol. 35, pp. 233-236, 1990.

[10] Meyer, D.G., "A New Class of Shift-Varying Operators, their Shift-

invariant Equivalents and Multirate Digital Systems", {\it IEEE Trans. Automat. Control}, Vol. 35, pp. 429-433, 1990.

[11] Ravi, R. , P.P. Khargonekar, K.D. Minto and C.N. Nett, "Controller Parameterization for Time-varying Multirate Plants", {\it IEEE Trans. Automat. Control}, Vol. 35, pp. 1259-1262, 1990.

[12] Araki, M. and K. Yamamoto, "Multivariable Multirate Sampled-data Systems: State-space Description, Transfer Characteristics and Nyquist Criterion", {\it IEEE Trans. Automat. Control}, Vol. 30, pp. 145-154, 1986.

[13] Colaneri, P., R. Scattolini and N. Schiavoni, "Stabilization of Multirate Sampled-data Linear Systems', {\it Automatica}, Vol. 26, pp. 377-380, 1990.

[14] Meyer, R.A. and C.S. Burrus, "A Unified Analysis of Multirate and Periodically Time-varying Digital Filters", {\it IEEE Trans. Circuits and Systems}, Vol. 22, pp. 162-168, 1975.

[15] Sezer, M.E. and D.D. Siljaik, "Decentralized Multirate Control",{\it IEEE Trans. Automat. Control}, Vol. 35, pp. 60-65, 1990.

[16] Araki, M. and T. Hagiwara, "Pole Assignment by Multirate Sampled-data Output Feedback", {\it Int. J. Contr.}, Vol. 44, pp. 1661-1673, 1986.

[17] Hagiwara, T. and M. Araki, "Design of a Stable Feedback Controller Based on the Multirate Sampling of the Plant Output", {\it IEEE Trans. Automat. Control}, Vol. 33, pp. 812-819, 1988.

[18] Francis, B.A. and T.T. Georgiou, "Stability Theory for Linear Time-invariant Plants with Periodic Digital Controllers", {\it IEEE Trans. Automat. Control}, Vol. 33, pp. 820-832, 1988.

[19] Khargonekar, P.P., K. Poolla and A. Tannenbaum, "Robust Control of Linear Time-invariant Plants Using Periodic Compensation", {\it IEEE Trans. Automat. Control}, Vol. 30, pp. 1088-1096, 1985.

[20] Olbrot, A.W. , "Robust Stabilization of Uncertain Systems by Periodic Feedback", {\it Int. J. Control}, Vol. 45, pp. 747-758, 1987.

[21] Anderson, B.D.O. and J.B. Moore, "Time-varying Feedback Laws for Decentralized Control", {\it IEEE Trans. Automat. Control}, Vol. 26, pp. 1133-1139, 1981.

[22] Wang, S.H. , "Stabilization of Decentralized Control Systems via Time-varying Controllers", {\it IEEE Trans. Automat. Control}, Vol. 27, pp. 741-744, 1982.

[23] Kando, H and Iwazumi, T "Multirate digital control design of as optimal regulator via singular perturbation theory" Int. J. Control, vol. 44, pp. 1555-1578, 1986

[24] Chammas, A.B. and C.T. Leondes, "On the Finite-Time Control of Linear Systems by Piecewise Constant Output Feedback", {\it Ibid}, Vol. 30, pp. pp. 227-234, 1979.

[25] Yan, W., B.D.O. Anderson and R.R. Bitmead, "On the Gain Margin Improvement Using Dynamic Compensation Based on Generalized Sampled-data Hold Functions", {\it IEEE Trans. on Automat. Contr.}, 39, pp. 2347-2354, 1994.

[26] Vidyasagar, M., "Robust Stabilization of Singularly Perturbed Systems", {\it Systems and Control Letters}, 5, pp. 413-418, 1985.

[27] Kabamba, K.T., "Control of Linear Systems Using Generalized Sampled-Data Hold Functions", {\it IEEE Trans. on Automat. Contr.}, 32, pp. 772-783, 1987.

[28] Er, M.J. and B.D.O. Anderson, "Practical Issues in Multirate Output Controllers", {\it Int. J. Contr.}, Vol. 53, No. 5, pp. 1005-1020, 1991.

[29] Er, M.J. and B.D.O. Anderson, "Performance Study of Multirate Output Controllers Under Noise Disturbances", {\it Int. J. Contr.}, Vol. 56, No. 3, pp. 531-545, 1992.

[30] Er, M.J. and B.D.O. Anderson, "Design of Reduced-order Multirate Input Compensators for Output Injection Feedback Laws", {\it Int. J. Contr.}, Vol. 58, No. 1, pp. 169-185, 1993.

[31] Er, M.J., "Avoidance of Large Controls in Multirate Input Controllers", {\it The EEE Journal}, Vol. 5, No. 1, July 1993.

[32] Er, M.J., "Multirate Approach Towards Observer-Based Deadbeat Controller Design", {\it J. Institution of Engineers, Singapore}, Vol. 33, No. 1, pp. 61-69, 1993.

[33] Er, M.J., B.D.O. Anderson and W.-Y. Yan, "Gain Margin Improvement Using Generalized Sampled-data Hold Function Based Compensator", {\it Automatica}, Vol. 30, No. 3, pp. 461-470, 1994.

[34] Er, M.J. and B.D.O. Anderson, "Discrete-time Loop Transfer Recovery via Generalised Sampled-data Hold Function Based Compensator",{\it Int. J. Robust and Nonlinear Control}, Vol. 4, pp. 741-756, 1994.

[35] Er, M.J., "Sensitivity Improvement via Generalized Sampled-data Hold Function Based Compensator", {\it J. Institution of Engineers, Singapore}, Vol. 34, No. 1, pp. 58-62, 1994.

[36] Er, M.J. and B.D.O. Anderson, "Design of Reduced-order Multirate Output Linear Functional Observer-based Compensators", {\it Automatica}, Vol. 31, No. 2, pp. 237-242, 1995.

[37] Er, M.J., "Periodic Controllers for Finite Dimensional Linear Time-invariant Systems", {\it Int. J. Systems Sci.}, Vol. 26, No. 10, pp. 1813-1822, 1995.

[38] Er, M. J. and S.Y. Chua, " Generalized Multirate linear Quadratic Gaussian Controllers for linear time invariant systems" Journal of IES, vol. 36, No. 1, pp. 47-53, 1996.

Integrated Reengineering: An Approach Towards Implementation of New Technologies

H.H. LIAKOS, NTUA
Zografou Campus, 15 780
Tel. (301) 772 3235, Fax. (301) 772 3228
e-mail: hliakos@chemeng.ntua.gr

D.I. TSELES, T.E.I. Piraeus
P. Ralli & Thivon 250, 122 44 Aegaleo, Greece
Tel. (301) 538 1249, Fax. (301) 545 0962

Abstract: **The paper presents the difficulties that companies from industrial and service sector business face in order to implement new technologies such as CAD/CAM/CAE, CNC and CIM, analyses the basic interrelated factors that are crucial for the successful application of such innovative techniques and finally develops an integrated reengineering approach.**

I. INTRODUCTION

For a variety of reasons a new technology may fail to provide all the predicted benefits or perform at specified levels and may have unforeseen adverse consequences beyond the directly affected areas of the production system. Hayes and Abernathy [1] research reveals the problems of USA manufacturing in managerial attitudes and organizational systems. They suggest that the existing top-down approach of the senior management of the implementation of new technologies leads to separation of strategic thinking and policy from technological decision making and short-term gains at the expense of long-term development. They argued that the lack of integrated management within manufacturing USA companies was a basic factor in order to understand and to initiate innovation steps.

Hackett [2] estimates that not only in manufacturing area, bur also in service sector companies the investments towards technological improvements yielded little in the way of positive benefits; particularly where comparisons are made with the manufacturing sector, despite the poor international performance of the latter. He explains this phenomenon that the fundamental problem is not systems design but that there is an inadequate coupling between operations and organizational systems-technology. He mentions that coupling technology with other operational drivers will be imperative for the service company for the future. Companies that persist in developing their operations strategy solely from a technology perspective can look forward to tougher competition as their rivals realize the incremental benefits of an integrated holistic approach. The above statements prove that our focus on implementation includes a wide range of activities and we view it as a broad change process and that the management of change is of particular importance.

II. BASIC FACTORS

Many firms in Western countries and also from Greece, when they implement new technologies they do not take into account the importance of the following interrelated factors that make technological change a dynamic, progressive, continuous improvement and broad long-term process.

Strategic: the strategic perspective that the company has and study the internal (within the company) and external environment (market and competitors) and how these factors affect the policy of the firm the next five or ten years.

Technological: The technology (the rate of innovation or change in products or in processes globally that concern the firm in comparison with its basic technological infrastructure, know-how and the status of its processes and other systems (information and communication systems). This comparison is usually the initial point to begin technological projects. In this area factors such as modifications in the existing layout, processes are included.

Organizational: These extend from the systems for control of work, for payment through to departmental divisions of concerns and methods of cost control. All these rules, procedures and guidelines are important in order to provide a framework which shapes people's motivation and commitment in relation to technological change and to develop mechanisms which either constrain or facilitate the initiation and completion of technological change. Training and education programs are also included.

Financial: These allocate the policy and forecast approaches (statistical methods such as payback or Annual Rate of Return ARR or the more complex Discounted Cash Flows methods DCF) that the firm follows in order to know if a suggested technological project will be valuable or not.

The above general categories of factors are interrelated, in conflict and many times express the policies of the different opinions and objectives of several profit-centres and departments within the firm. Most of the companies in Greece ignore the interdependence of the above broad four categories and mainly the organizational and strategic factors. Their focus on narrow financial short-term methods restrict the company to exploit the full benefits from a technological project. The crucial question is what is the best approach towards implementation of new technologies.

III. A FOUR-PHASE MODEL

The best way to apply implementation of new technologies is through a general four-phase model in which the phases are dynamic, continuous changing and provide feedbacks. The four phases are:

a) Initiation: the activities and concerns that are involved in the early simulation and elaboration of ideas about the possible shape of technological changes, through to commitment in firm decisions.

b) Planning: the associated activities necessary for organizing the technological change. Until here we mention the strategic and organizational factors that are important and allocate the possible innovation and that the costs are low.

c) Application: the activities, basic civil engineering work, the installation of new equipment and software, the training and educational program. The costs are high and the result of strategic plans (phases a and b) is shown here.

d) Consolidation: This phase includes the comparison and the effects of the technological change. It is mainly a post-project appraisal.

IV INTEGRATED REENGINEERING

Taking into account that we need a broad integrated approach to exploit the full benefits from a technological change we develop an integrated reengineering program through a theoretical example, basic case study that concerns Greek reality.

Alfa company was founded in 1977 by a group of venture capitalists. The organization manufactures heating and ventilation units for industrial, domestic usage and for automobiles. The company is progressive and aims to gain more market share. The industry is developed into a highly competitive environment with a number of companies fighting for the fast growing Greek market in this area of assembled heating units. The market in Greece for these heating systems can be divided into:

Domestic: This segment is highly developed and includes original equipment fitted to buildings (houses and offices) for heating and cooling internal rooms.

Industrial: The main use of these systems in industry is the heating and cooling of the huge buildings in industries. The company covers only the industrial area of south Greece.

Automobile: The objective in this segment is the air conditioning of means of transport. The operation manufactures heating systems only for buses of the public enterprise of transport (OAS) and for lorries and cars of the Greek army.

The total market is forecast to grow 10% a year for domestic heating systems, 8% for the automobiles and only 1% a year for the industrial heat-cool systems. The stability of Greek national economy (the value of national coin is steady against the European coins the last two years) and the effort of Greek government to catch the standards of European Community (Maastricht) creates the conditions of a strong without unexpected economic events market. Alfa's share in domestic segment in 1996 was 14%, behind Firogenis (33%), and Klimatair (16%) and equal to AVS. In industrial area Alfa's share was last year only 5% behind Toshiba 45%, Carrier 33% and AVS 6%. Toshiba and Carrier are multinational companies with increased rates of development in the industrial segment in Greece. In automobile, in the described sub area which was outlined above, predominate different conditions. Only companies from Greece can provide heat-cool systems for Greek army and OAS. In this sub-segment Alfa's share was in 1996 25%, behind Klimatair 50% and equal to AVS. The factory manufactures 10 types of domestic heating systems, 5 types of industrial systems and 12 types of air conditioning for cars. Each type has different size and performance. The operation follows a top-down approach to schedule its production. Production planning is based on an annual build plan (a part of a computerised MRP system which is applied since 1988) as estimated by marketing. The theoretical capacity of the company is rated at 30000 domestic machines, 2000 industrial and 4000 for automobiles yearly. Last year the company sold 16000 domestic heating systems, 1800 for automobiles and only 450 industrial heating systems. The machinery age is 20 years old, new relatively to the machinery of other competitors but with high annual maintenance cost. The factory operates two shifts and has about 280 employees.

The brief review of Alfa company shows the following discrepancies which affect the total performance of the operation:

- The perception inside the company is that if the finished items could not be sold it is a sales problem not a manufacturing problem. That means that there are not advanced contacts between the departments of the organization, or there is low level of integration.
- The central-computerised MRP leads to high level of inventory. These inventories not only tied up working capital, but also required extensive floor space. The operation has large overheaded expenses with this traditional production system. The numerous transactions in store room, shopfloor control, and the production and financial control mechanisms are key drivers of these expenses.
- Every effort for improvement is difficult with the existing production and control system, because work is scheduled in lots of one year worth of demand. Such scheduling caused that every problem (for example a quality problem or a bottleneck) is masked by inventories. There is slow feedback to the source of the problem, especially in quality problems and also there is low visibility of defects. The company seems to have no specific or focused policy. Alfa has 3 production lines. Each category of products belongs to a market with different philosophy. Domestic heating systems is a turbulent and competitive market mainly among the four Greek companies. Industrial heating systems is a more competitive market because large multinational operations allocate the rules of the competition. The third air-conditioning systems for the automobiles of the Greek army and OAS is a closed steady market (seem to be a monopoly among three Greek companies). Alfa needs a different management policy in every market if she wants to be progressive. The three production lines lead to high set up times and manufacturing lead times and make difficult the control of the raw materials and bought in components from suppliers.

The company needs a reengineering programme which is going to create the conditions for the development of the enterprise. The reengineering project is divided by stages.

The first motion is that everyone inside the operation must learn about the reengineering programme. The objective is that all employees know where the company is going in the long term and what its image in the market-place should be. This is the first part of the integration inside the operation that includes the company as a whole.

Stage 1

Alfa has to obtain focused manufacturing. Focused manufacturing means less product lines. The analysis of the turnover of each product line for 1996 is the following. Alfa has to withdraw from industrial heating system, because of the strong turbulent market. However that product does not add value to the profit of the company. The other two production lines are refereed to different markets as described above. The advantage is that Alfa does not need to improve its products dramatically for automobiles because of the character of the market and the long terms contracts with the Greek army and OAS. So the release of capital investments should help the development of the basic product line, the domestic heating systems.

Stage 2

Alfa has to differentiate its domestic products. The differentiation should be:

- In the performance of the domestic systems (intelligent systems with the use of high technology with computer based control for the less using up of electric energy). Mainly the manufacturing department and the financial have to work together here.
- In the design of the apparatus. All the departments have to cooperate and finally in the quality of the products. The same cooperation is needed as the above.

The above steps show the need for integration (mainly horizontal) and flexible manufacturing.

Stage 3

The above stages 1 and 2 allocate and demand the reorginization of the production, control system, human resources, the structure and the management of the company.

The production and the control must be allocated with a JIT system. It is severe to control the production through an MRP based system, because of the kind of products. The heating

systems especially in domestic segment have different characteristics (size, design, performance) and the standardisation is difficult to be achieved. The need for flexible manufacturing and for better quality shows the kind of the daily production system, the JIT. JIT shows the bottlenecks of production and the possible areas of quality problems through the reduction of inventories that do not add value to the product. This control system demands total quality management and a better flexible production flow (layout).
Firstly quality must be adjusted in all levels of the factory (manufacturing, service, suppliers) with the application of a Crosby's programme [3]. Everyone should try to improve the quality of products.

Secondly a new layout (U shape and the use of work cells) is a key driver for smoother flow of production. The relayout into work cells reduces set up times so that the production can be scheduled in small daily lot sizes.

The reengineering of the whole manufacturing system affects the human resources. JIT needs responsible and skilful personnel. Seminars, meetings, training programmes for employees are necessary for the successful implementation of the new systems. Every manager should transmit the new ideas to his/her subordinates and every employee should transmit every informal information about his/her work. This double approach (top-down and bottom-up) helps the development of the vertical integration inside the operation.

The existing structure of the company drives to a reactive style of management. The new quality programme through the whole manufacturing department (manufacturing, service and suppliers) introduces the changes in the structure of the company. The marketing department should advertise the new products and the new picture of the company to customers. The market should know about the change in Alfa's perception.

V. CONCLUSIONS

The above analysis shows that the successful implementation of new technologies depends on many factors. Using the general broad four phases approach we can firstly analyze the stimuli for possible technological change and then design it in detail. The integrated reengineering programme must take into account the importance of organizational and the human resource factors which are the most valuable resources within the firm.

VI REFERENCES

1. R.H. Hayes and W.J. Abernathy, Managing our way to Economic Decline, Harvard Business Review, 1980.
2. G.R. Hackett, Investment in Technology-the Service Sector Sinkhole?, Sloan Management Review, 1990
3. P.B. Crosby, Quality is free, pp 1149-222, Mc Graw Hill, 1977.
4. H. Scarbrough and R. Lannon, The Successful Exploitation of New Technology in Banking, Journal of General Management, vol. 13, 1988.
5. Quality, Postgraduate Course from the Open University, UK, 1997.
6. Implementation of new Technologies, Postgraduate Course from the Open University, UK, 1997.

Part 2

SIGNAL PROCESSING

Maximum likelihood estimation of the instantaneous optical carrier phase in coherent lightwave communications.

A. Arvizu, F.J. Mendieta
CICESE
km. 107, Ensenada, Baja California 22860, México
mailing address:
P.O. Box 430222, San Diego Ca 92143-0222, USA
tel:(52)61750502, fax: (52)61744729 email: jmendiet@cicese.mx

Abstract

We apply maximum likelihood techniques for the estimation the of instantaneous optical carrier phase in coherent lightwave communication systems. We synthesize an optimum estimator using a state variable representation of the optical fields and developing the corresponding Fokker Plánck equation. Finally we experimentally implemented a reduced simplicity coherent lightwave receiver with the estimator obtained and performed measurements.

INTRODUCTION

Two characteristics of the coherent optical communications systems are attractive in the synthesis of optimum receivers: a) a linear relationship existing between the received optical electric field and the post - detection photocurrent, and b) in the quantum limit case, a postdetection noise which is independent of the received optical signal.

These properties allow the use of several well developed synthesis methods from the statistical communication theory, where a structure for an optimum receiver can be obtained by the maximization of a suitable likelihood function. In this work we apply these principles in the synthesis of an optimum estimator of the instantaneous optical carrier phase for PSK coherent systems.

Previous works have derived synchronizing structures for heterodyne systems [1], and the contribution of our work is first the development of the analysis for the case of homodyne systems, which present additional complications related to the presence of higher order terms appearing in the likelihood function that cannot be neglected since they are in the system passband,

We next evaluate the performance of our structure with computer simulations.

Finally we present measurements on a demonstrative experimental work on a homodyne optical fiber communication system, with a synchronizer implemented accordingly with the theory.

1. THE STATE VARIABLE APPROACH

In the coherent optical receiver, with reference to figure 1, the phase modulated received optical field $E_S(t)$ of average optical power P_S is mixed with a local oscillator laser field $E_L(t)$ of power P_L, represented by:

$$E_S(t) = E_{SO} \sin[2\pi f_S t + \varphi_S(t) + m_k(t)],$$

$$E_L(t) = E_{LO} \sin[2\pi f_L t + \varphi_L(t)],$$

where E_{SO} and E_{LO} ; f_S and f_L ; are the signal and local oscillator amplitudes and central frequencies, respectively; φ_S $(t)$and φ_L (t) are independent processes modeling the phase instability in the signal and local fields, respectively,

$m_k(t)$ is the modulation waveform (PSK).

The coherently detected homodyne ($f_S = f_L$) photocurrent is:

$$i_{SL}(t) = i_{SL0} \sin[\varphi(t) + m_k(t)]$$

where $i_{SL0} = 2r\,(P_L P_S)^{1/2}$is the baseband photocurrent amplitude, and r is the photoreceiver responsivity.

$\varphi(t) = \varphi_S(t) - \varphi_L(t)$ is a random process representing the phase fluctuations in the photocurrent process.

As a result of the local oscillator shot noise, an additive white gaussian noise current $i_n(t)$ with two-sided spectral density $I_{n0}/2$, is superimposed onto the signal, resulting in the observable process:

$$i(t) = i_{SL}(t) + i_n(t)$$

In our analysis a state variable approach is used, as represented in figure 2, the output process is cast in the form of $i(t) = dy(t)/dt$ and the following equation [2] is used for the observation process:

$$dy(t) = i(t)dt = i_{SL}(t)dt + (I_{n0}/2)^{1/2} d\eta(t)$$

where the noise current has also been expressed in the form $i_n(t) = (I_{no}/2)^{1/2} d\eta/dt$, with $\eta(t)$ a standard

Wiener process.

The random phases in the signal and local oscillator fields can be modeled as independent Wiener processes [3], with parameters $(\Delta\nu_S)^{1/2}$ and $(\Delta\nu_L)^{1/2}$, respectively. This model corresponds well with experimental observations on the phase and frequency fluctuations of DFB semiconductor lasers:

$d\varphi_S/dt = (\Delta\nu_S)^{1/2} w_S(t)$

$d\varphi_L/dt = (\Delta\nu_L)^{1/2} w_L(t)$

where $w_S(t)$ and $w_L(t)$are normalized white noises representing the instantaneous optical frequency fluctuations around the means f_S and f_L, respectively.

Thus the random phase of the photocurrent process can be written as:

$d\varphi/dt = (\Delta\nu)^{1/2} w(t)$

where $w(t)$ is a normalized white noise generating the baseband phase process and $\Delta\nu = \Delta\nu_S + \Delta\nu_L$is the FWHM of the photocurrent spectrum,

2. THE FOKKER PLANCK ANALYSIS

We base our analysis on the Fokker Planck techniques developed by Snyder [2] to the problem of the continuous estimation in communications theory. We start from the estimator $\hat{\phi}(t) = E[\phi(t) \mid i(t), m_j]$ and variance $\Sigma(t) = E\{[\phi(t) - \hat{\phi}(t)]^2\}$ equations:

$$d\hat{\phi}(t) = \frac{2}{I_{no}} E\{[\phi(t)-\hat{\phi}(t)]i_{SL}(t)\}\{[dy(t)-E[i_{SL}(t)]dt\}$$

$$d\Sigma(t) = \Delta\nu dt + \frac{2}{I_{no}} E\{[\phi(t) - \hat{\phi}(t)]^2 [i_{SL}(t) - E[i_{SL}(t)]]\}\{dy(t) - E[i_{SL}(t)]dt\} - \frac{2}{I_{no}} E^2\{[\phi(t) - \hat{\phi}(t)]i_{SL}(t)\}dt$$

where E denotes conditional expectation with respect to the conditional density of the phase process $p(\phi(t) \mid i(t), m_j)$ given the observation $i(t)$ and assuming that m_j was sent.

The time evolution of the this conditional density (p for short notation) is described by:

$$\partial p/\partial t = \Delta\nu \partial^2 p/\partial x^2 + \frac{2}{I_{no}} p\{i_{SL}(t) - E[i_{SL}(t)]\}\{i(t) - E[i_{SL}(t)]\}$$

Using an a priori assumption of a gaussian conditional density for the phase error $\phi(t) - \hat{\phi}(t)$, we arrive at the following approximate solutions:

$$\phi^*(t) = \int \frac{2i_{SLO}}{I_{no}} \Sigma^* \exp(-\Sigma^*/2) \cos(\phi^*(t) + m_j) i(t) dt - \int \frac{i_{SLO}}{\sqrt{2} I_{no}} \Sigma^* \exp(-\Sigma^*) \sin\{2[\phi^*(t) + m_j]\} dt$$

$$\Sigma^* = \int \Delta\nu dt - \int \frac{2i_{SLO}}{I_{no}} \Sigma^{*2} \exp(-\Sigma^*/2) \sin(\phi^*(t) + m_j) i(t) dt - \int \frac{\sqrt{2} i_{SLO}}{I_{no}} \Sigma^{*2} \exp(-\Sigma^*) \cos\{2[\phi^*(t) + m_j]\} dt$$

Figure 3 shows a block diagram for the mechanization of this estimator

We evaluated the performance of our estimator using a communications system simulator. Several runs were made for different noise seeds and signal - to - noise ratios; eye diagrams, power spectra, histograms and time signals were obtained. Figure 4a shows the generates iener process for the optical phase; figure 4b is the phase estimate with no modulation; figure 4d is the phase error and figure 4d shows the pdf for the error process.

3.EXPERIMENTAL WORK

Our set up is a self - homodyne receiver consisting of a fiber optic interferometer as shown in figure 5. In one of the arms we place an electro-optical modulator in order to provide the digital phase modulation

We employ an external - cavity (ECC) laser at 1550 nm, with a spectral linewidth of approximately 100 kHz, , therefore virtually no phase noise is present in the detected photocurrent; now in order to introduce a controllable amount of phase noise we deliberately superimpose a noise waveform ($1/f^2$*spectrum*) onto the digital train using an adder circuit prior to the electro-optical modulation [4].

We developed a balanced detector configuration based on a 180^opolarization preserving directional coupler and a dual photodetector scheme, followed by baseband amplifying and filtering stages. We implemented the non linear electronic circuit based on a trigonometric function generator as shown in figure 6.

CONCLUSION

Using maximum - likelihood principles, we synthesized an optical phase estimator structure for homodyne communications systems, and evaluate its performance with computer simulations. We also developed a demonstrative experimental set up on a homodyne optical fiber communication system, with an estimator implemented accordingly with the theory.

REFERENCES

1. C. Georghiades, "A proposed receiver structure for optical communications systems that employ heterodyne detection and semiconductor laser as local oscillator", IEEE Trans. Com.Vol. 33, No. 4, pp. 382 - 384, (1995).

2. D. L. Snyder, "The State Variable Approach to Continuous Estimation", MIT Press, Cambridge, Mass. (1968).

3. O. Macchi, L.L. Scharf, "A dynamic programming algorithm for phase estimation and data encoding on random phase channels", IEEE Trans. Info. Theo., Vol 27, No. 5, pp. 581 - 595, (1981).

4. F.J. Mendieta, M.C. Leal, A. Arvizu, A coherent optical communications experiment with controlled laser field spectrum using electro - optical stochastic phase modulation " Proc. Ist. Int. Symp. Com. Syst. and Digital Signal Proc., Vol. 1, pp. 84 - 87, Sheffield, U.K., (1998).

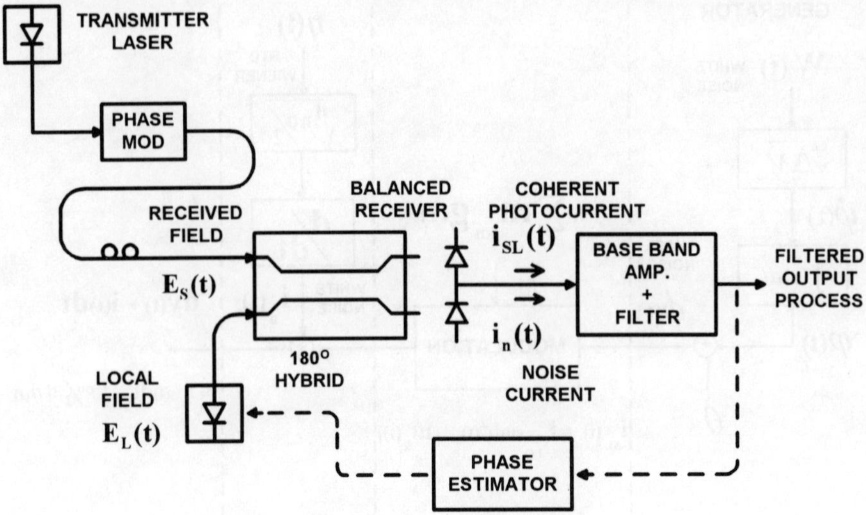

Figure 1. Homodyne Optical receiver.

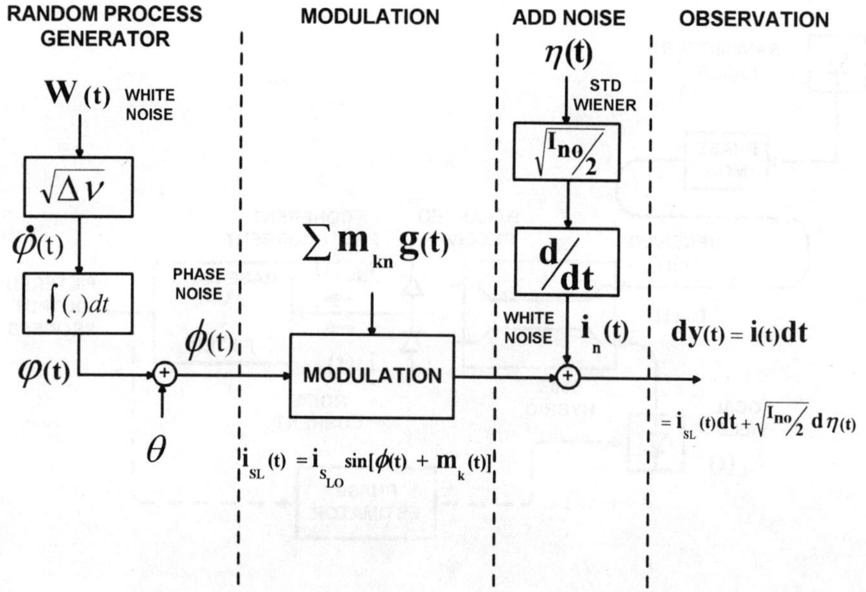

Figure 2. Coherent Comunications Channel model.

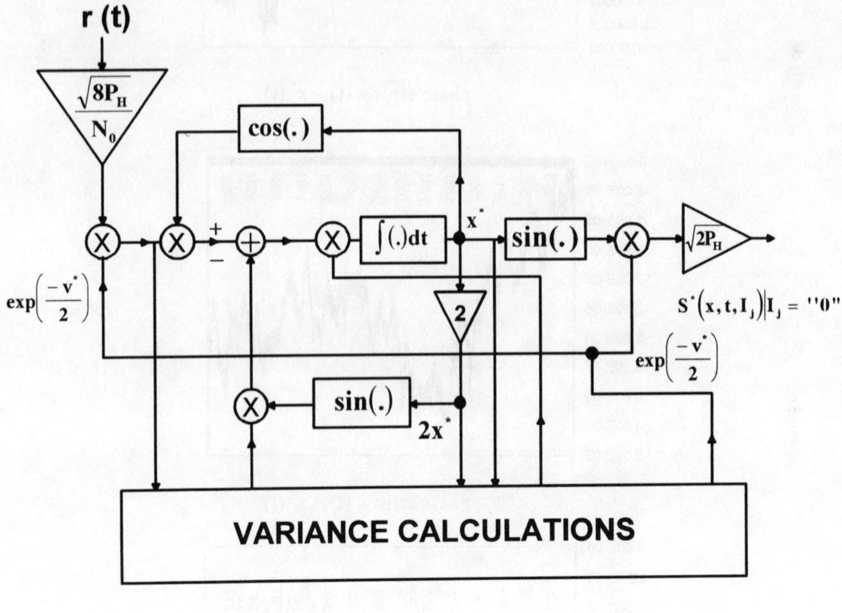

Figure 3. Phase estimator using a gaussian approximation for the homodyne case.

phase error x (t) – x^* (t)

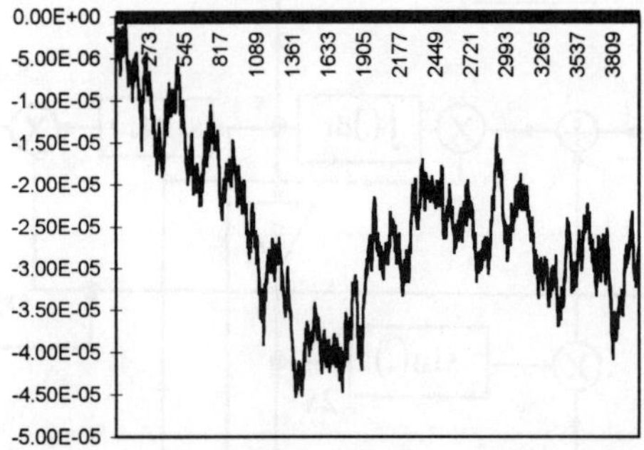

phase error x (t) – x^* (t)

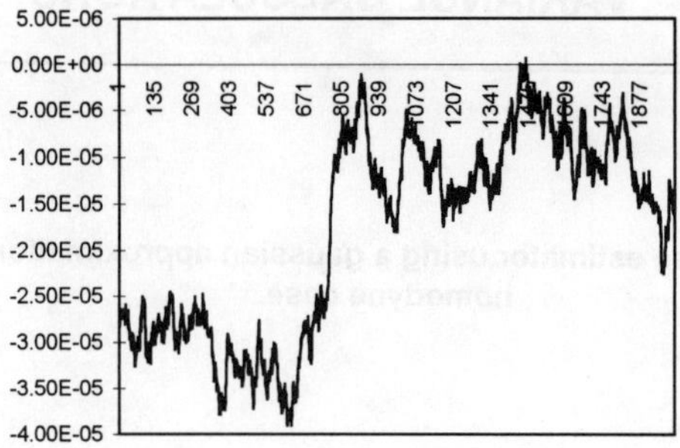

phase error x (t) – x^* (t)

Figure 4. Phase error waveforms.

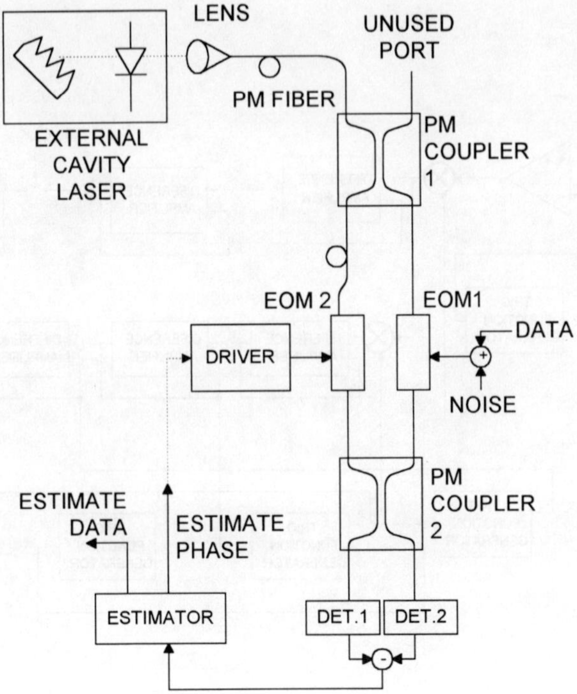

Figure 5. The homodyne receiver set up
EOM = Electro Optical Modulator
PM = Polarization Maintaining

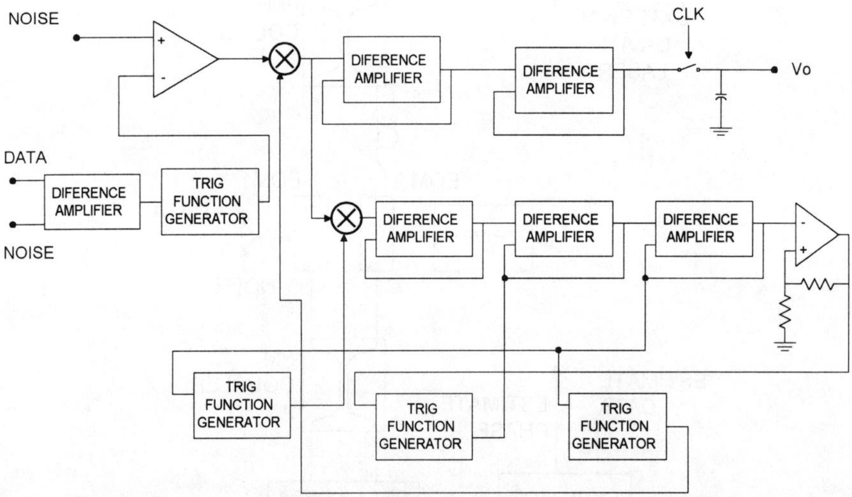

Figure 6. Non linear circuit for the phase estimator.

THE ANALYSIS OF DYNAMICS OF A COMPLICATED SYSTEM STATE ON PHASE PORTRAITS IN SPACE OF EIGENVECTORS*

ANATOLY A. BORISKEVICH, VALERY M. DEMKO, ALEXANDER M. KROT AND POLINA P. TKACHOVA

Institute of Engineering Cybernetics, National Academy of Sciences of Belarus, Surganov Str. 6, 220012, Minsk, Belarus, alxkrot@newman.basnet.minsk.by

Abstract. The approach to forming and analysis of phase portraits of dynamics of a behavior of complicated systems is offered. It is based on use of effective algorithm of an computation of eigenvalues and eigenvectors, and also choice of global and local structural indications possessing sufficient sensitivity to small distinctions of researched system states.

Key Words. Phase portrait, complicated system state, eigenvalues and eigenvectors, embedding dimensionality, real covariance matrix.

1. INTRODUCTION

The concept of a phase portrait of a dynamic system is the powerful tool of a local and global research of properties of systems, basis of the qualitative theory. The phase portraits comprise not only local characteristics of a system state, but also represent it globally, giving an obvious picture of behavior of a dynamic system in whole. A method of a construction of a phase eigenvector space [1] in which the system phase (or instant state) is displayed is important in the analysis of a complicated system state. However given method has not received a wide propagation till now in connection with a lack of effective methods of reconstruction of a phase eigenvector space and differential diagnostic indications of phase portraits for the visual and automatic analysis of a system state. For a solution of the given problem the approach based on using an effective algorithm of an computation of eigenvectors and eigenvalues and forming local and global indications, possessing sufficient sensitivity to small distinctions of researched system states is offered.

2. FAST KARHUNEN-LOEVE TRANSFORM FOR COVARIANCE MATRIX OF MARKOVIAN RANDOM PROCESSES

It is shown [2,3] that Karhunen-Loeve transform (KLT) is optimal one in connection to information compression. However, the procedure of KLT calculation has high computational complexity. Sequentially, it was necessary to found fast algorithm of KLT calculation. A method of KLT calculation applied for a class of random signal describing by Markov process is proposed.

Let us consider Markov first order process modeling a speech-like signal. Then it has to satisfy the following conditions:

$\{x_t\}$ is a stationary random sequence defined on the time interval T with

$$\begin{aligned} &M\{x_t\} = 0,\\ &M\{x_t^2\} = 1, \\ &M\{x_t x_s\} = r_{|t-s|},\ s,t = 1,2,\dots,N \end{aligned} \tag{1}$$

* This work was supported by International Science and Technology Center (ISTC) under project B-95

where M is mathematical expectation and $r_{|t-s|}$ is correlation coefficient.

The corresponding covariance matrix $\sum_x$ of size NxN will be defined as follows:

$$\sum_x = M\left(XX^T\right) \quad (2)$$

where X is a matrix of random sequences, T is a transform symbol.
As it is shown in [2,3] for such process with condition (1) the correlation coefficient is following:

$$r_{|t-s|} = \rho^{|t-s|}, \quad |\rho| \langle 1 \quad (3)$$

and covariance matrix $\sum_x$ is respectively:

$$\sum_x^{th} = \begin{bmatrix} 1 & \rho & \rho^2 & \cdots & \rho^{N-1} \\ \rho & 1 & \rho & \cdots & \cdot \\ \rho^2 & \rho & 1 & \cdots & \cdot \\ \vdots & \vdots & \vdots & \vdots & \vdots \\ \rho^{N-1} & \cdot & \cdot & \cdots & 1 \end{bmatrix}. \quad (4)$$

It is well known that discrete cosine transform (DCT) can be obtained as extreme case of KLT. In the case when $\rho \to \lambda_k$ KLT of first order Markov process can be expressed in closed form as follows

$$x_m = \sum_{k=0}^{N-1} \sqrt{2/(N+\lambda_k)} K_k \sin\{\omega_k[m-((N-1)/2)]+(k+1)\pi/2\} \quad (5)$$

where K_k are the KLT coefficients.

Let us introduce the following notions:

$$a(k) = \sqrt{2/(N+\lambda_k)}, \qquad 0 \le k \le N-1 \quad (6)$$

$$b(m,k) = \sin\{\omega_k[m-((N-1)/2)]+(k-1)\pi/2\}. \quad (7)$$

In this case (5) will be transformed to:

$$x_m = \sum_{k=0}^{N-1} a(k) K_k b(m,k). \quad (8)$$

To obtain $a(k)$ and $b(m,k)$ we use the methods suggested in [2,3]. To obtain $a(k)$ we use λ_k -eigenvalues of matrix $\sum_x^{th}$ defined by equation:

$$\lambda_k = \left(1-\rho^2\right)/(1-2\rho\cos\omega_k+\rho^2). \quad (9)$$

According to [2,3] ω_k are the positive roots of transcendental equation

$$tg(N\omega_k) = -\left(1-\rho^2\right)\sin\omega_k / \left(\cos\omega_k - 2\rho + \rho^2\cos\omega_k\right) \quad (10)$$

When the condition $\rho \to 1$ is imposed (10) will transform to $tg(N\omega_k)=0$ whose roots ω_k are:

$$\omega_k = k\pi/N \quad (11)$$

and (6) will be changed respectively to:

$$a(k) = \sqrt{2/N}, \quad 0 \le k \le N-1. \quad (12)$$

After the mentioned above transforms (5) will be as follows

$$x(m) = \frac{1}{\sqrt{N}} K_x(0) + \sqrt{\frac{2}{N}} \sum_{k=0}^{N} K_x(k) \cos\left[\frac{(2m+1)k\pi}{2N}\right]. \quad (13)$$

It means that on the imposing of the above conditions on signal together with $\rho \to 1$ KLT is approximated by DCT as follows:

$$K_x(0) = (N)^{-0.5} \sum_{m=0}^{N-1} x(m),$$

$$K_x(k) = \left(2/\sqrt{N}\right) \sum_{m=0}^{N-1} x(m) \cos\left[\frac{(2m+1)k\pi}{2N}\right]. \quad (14)$$

In connection with mentioned above covariance matrix of speech signal was calculated at first in [4]. Sets of data with length N were chosen from signal and located in a matrix NxN string-by-string. Then covariance matrix is calculated as follows:

$$\sum_x^{exp} = XX^T / \sigma_X^2.$$

According [4] further the optimal value of ρ was chosen. A recursive algorithm was used to do that:

Step1. The minimal matrix element is assumed to ρ_{min} and the maximal one –for ρ_{max} respectively. The medium point of segment $\rho_{min}\rho_{max}$ is chosen as an initial hypothesis for ρ

$$\rho_{min} = \min_{i,j} \sum_X (i,j), \quad \rho_{max} = \max_{i,j} \sum_X (i,j).$$

Step2. Two segments $\rho_{min}\rho_0$ and $\rho_0\rho_{max}$ are considered. Mean-root-square deviation $D(\rho)$ is calculated for medium points of them (ρ_A and ρ_B).

$$D(\rho_A) = N^{-2} \sum_{i,j=1}^{N} \left(\sum_X (i,j) - \rho_A^{|i-j|}\right)^2,$$

$$D(\rho_B) = N^{-2} \sum_{i,j=1}^{N} \left(\sum_X (i,j) - \rho_B^{|i-j|}\right)^2,$$

$$D(\rho_A) \rangle D(\rho_B): \rho_{min} = \rho_o, \; D(\rho_A) \rangle D(\rho_B): \rho_{max} = \rho_o.$$

Step2 is performed recursively while $(\rho_{max} - \rho_{min}) \rangle \varepsilon$ where ε is required precision. It was equal to 0.01 in our experiments with N=16 [4]. Value of ρ calculated for all phonemes of Belarusian speech was situated in range 0.78-0.89. The difference between ρ and 1 is not too much that allows us to continue.

According to formula (4) we can built matrix $\sum_x^{th}$ corresponded to matrix $\sum_x^{exp}$.

To calculate ω_k formula (12) has to be used. But that formula was obtained provided that $\rho \to 1$ whereas we used experimental value of ρ: 0.78-0.87 for calculation of λ. To analyze how large the possible deviation is we have calculated right part of formula (11) for ρ =0.8 and one period of $\omega = [0, \pi]$. It can be seen from [4] that there is one point where plot of function is differ from zero. These points correspond to points where denominator becomes zero: $\omega_k = arccos\left(2\rho/\left(1+\rho^2\right)\right)$. Therefore equation (11) will not be correct there. But these just a small part of all ω_k that are situated on this segment. It corresponds to N=1024 and for about 95% values of ω_k deviation is less than 0.064. To analyze behavior of eigenvalues λ_k we can use formula (9) to do that.

3. FAST EIGEN TRANSFORM ALGORITHM FOR COVARIANCE MATRIX

There is more general method for computing eigenvalues λ. The computation of eigenvectors $\vec{V}$ and eigenvalues λ of real covariance matrix $R_y = YY^T$ of dimensionality $N = 2^m$ (m-natural number, $m \geq 4$) is based on a solution of the following equation [5]:

$$S=\psi^{-1}R\psi=diag\left(\lambda_N,\dots,\lambda_N\right).$$

Here, ψ is a matrix of eigen transformation (ET) of dimensionality N; Y is a matrix of input data about a time signal on complex system output; S is a diagonal matrix of eigenvalues. The ET synthesis is carried out with use of a rotation operator (RO), representing a direct sum of Given's or Jacob's rotation matrixes. In a common case the procedure of ET synthesis consists of two stages: preliminary and basic. At the first stage the symmetric matrix R_Y is reduced with orthogonal transformation Q to persymmetric P (symmetric rather both principal and the secondary diagonal) in the correspondence with expression $P=Q^TR_YQ$, where Q is represented with a product of rotation operators. The second stage consists from n pitches ($n=log_2 N$). On each pitch the following operations sequentially are fulfilled. The persymmetric matrix P is transformed by a rotation operator H to block-diagonal form. $H^T PH = \left[\begin{array}{c|c} P_1 & 0 \\ \hline 0 & P_2 \end{array}\right]$ where $P1$ and $P2$ are matrix blocks of dimensionality $N/2$. Then the matrix blocks $P1$ and $P2$ are reduced to the persymmetric form. Thus, through n pitches we obtain eigenvalues located on a principal diagonal of a resulting matrix in decreasing order: $F^T PF = diag(\lambda_1,\dots,\lambda_N)$. Thus the matrix $\psi = QF$ of eigenvectors will represent a product of synthesized RO. For a persymmetric matrix $P = R_Y$ of dimensionality $N=8$ the matrix of eigenvectors ψ_8 has the following form

$$\psi_8 = \begin{bmatrix} \vec{V}_1 \\ \vec{V}_2 \\ -- \\ \vec{V}_8 \end{bmatrix}_{8\times8} = 2^{-3/2} H_8\left(H_4 \oplus H_4\right)\left(I_2 \oplus T_2 \oplus T_2 \oplus I_2\right)\left(H_2 \oplus H'_2 \oplus H_2 \oplus H_2\right)$$

where

$$H_8 = \begin{bmatrix} 1&0&0&0&0&0&0&1\\ 0&1&0&0&0&0&1&0\\ 0&0&1&0&0&1&0&0\\ 0&0&0&1&1&0&0&0\\ 0&0&0&1&-1&0&0&0\\ 0&0&1&0&0&-1&0&0\\ 0&1&0&0&0&0&-1&0\\ 1&0&0&0&0&0&0&-1 \end{bmatrix}; H_4 = \begin{bmatrix} 1&0&0&1\\ 0&1&1&0\\ 0&1&-1&0\\ 1&0&0&-1 \end{bmatrix}; H_2 = \begin{bmatrix} 1&1\\ 1&-1 \end{bmatrix}; H'_2 = \begin{bmatrix} -1&1\\ 1&1 \end{bmatrix};$$

$I_2 = \begin{bmatrix} 1&0\\ 0&1 \end{bmatrix}; T_2 = \begin{bmatrix} C_1 & S_1\\ S_1 & -C_1 \end{bmatrix}$ is a matrix of weight factors of a rotation operator; $c_1 = cos\ (\pi/8)$; $s_1 = sin\ (\pi/8)$; $\oplus$ is a sign of a direct sum.

The advantage of the offered algorithm on a comparison with known is that the values of weight factors ET ψ depend on a change of values of the elements of an initial covariance matrix R_Y only at the first stage and remain constant at the second stage of algorithm realization. Hence, the weight factors of transformation F are calculated beforehand and are stored in memory, and the factors of a matrix Q anew are calculated for each new covariance matrix. It allows to reduce time of a computation of eigenvectors and eigenvalues. Besides the algorithm using rotation operators is steady against round-off errors of intermediate computations, i.e. the round-off errors are minimized.

4. THE APPROACH TO THE ANALYSIS OF SYSTEM BEHAVIOR DYNAMICS BY PHASE PORTRAITS IN SPACE OF EIGENVECTERS

As one of global diagnostic indications of a researched system state in a phase space of eigenvectors it is expedient to use an embedding dimensionality M describing effective number of degree of freedoms connected to dynamics of a system behavior. For a reliable estimate of an embedding dimensionality M the relation mean square error ε_N of approximation of a point set of a phase space of dimensionality N by a set lying in a subspace of smaller dimensionality M from dimensionality N $\varepsilon_N = \left(\lambda_{N+1}\right)^{0,5}$ is used. The required an embedding dimensionality M is determined with first point of a characteristic plateau on a curve $\varepsilon_N = \varphi(N)$, as the further increase N does not raise an precision of approximation. Thus the average square of an approximation error is expressed with eigenvalues of a covariance matrix as follows $\varepsilon_M^2 = \sum_{i=M+1}^{N} \lambda_i$.

After a computation of an embedding dimensionality M informational capacity d_i of each eigenvector $\vec{V}_i$ is estimated with the formula $d_i = \lambda_i / \sum_{i=1}^{N} \lambda_i$ characterizing the relative contribution of i-th eigenvector $\vec{V}_i$ in a summarized variance. Besides the relative variance of a representation error of a system state in space of dimensionality M is estimated with relations $\delta_M^2 = 1 - r_M^2$ where magnitude $r_M^2 = \sum_{i=1}^{M} \lambda_i / \sum_{i=1}^{N} \lambda_i$ characterizes a convergence velocity of expansion of researched process on eigenvectors. At enough high velocity of convergence the given approach allows to include in the analysis those eigenvectors which contain in the structure statistically significant information. In this case each a researched complicated system state on a phase plane formed by i-th and j-th informative eigenvectors of a covariance matrix is characterized by a population of two-dimensional vectors $\vec{X}_{ijk} = (X_{ik}, X_{jk})$, where

$$X_{ik} = \vec{V}_i \vec{X}_k = \sum_{l=1}^{M} V_{il} X_{k+l}, \qquad X_{jk} = \vec{V}_j \vec{X}_k,$$

$k = \overline{(M+2, N_T)}$ and N_T is a number of values of observed signal $X(t)$, in discrete instants t_K and magnitudes of their norms $\|\vec{X}_{ijk}\| = (X_{ik}^2 + X_{jk}^2)^{0.5}$ coinciding with their lengths.

For a quantitative estimate of singularities of the constructed phase portraits or geometric structure of eigenvectors the following local geometric characters are offered:

$$\vec{X}_{ij} = N^{-1} \sum_{k=1}^{N} \vec{X}_{ijk}\ ; \quad r_{ij} = N^{-1} \sum_{k=1}^{N} \left\| \vec{X}_{ijk} - \vec{X}_{ji} \right\|;$$

$$R_{ijk} = \left\| \vec{X}'_{ijk} \right\|^3 \left[\left\| \vec{X}'_{ijk} \right\|^2 \left\| \vec{X}''_{ijk} \right\|^2 - \left(\vec{X}'_{ijk}, \vec{X}''_{ijk} \right)^2 \right]^{-0,5}$$

where $\vec{X}_{ij}$ is an average two-dimensional vector characterizing a center of points distribution of ij-th phase portrait on a plane formed by i-th and j-th eigenvectors of a covariance matrix; N is a number of two-dimensional vectors (points) ij-th phase portrait; r_{ij} is an average radius assigning a distance from a current vector $\vec{X}_{ijk}$ up to an average vector $\vec{X}_{ij}$ and defining circle with a center coinciding with coordinates $\vec{X}_{ij}$; R_{ijk} is current radius of a curvature serving by an deformation index of a trajectory of a phase portrait.

Being based on quantitative estimates of the offered indications, it is possible to make decisions about a belonging of a current phase portrait to one of the recognizing system state sample. The essential differences of phase portraits are generated by distinctions of initial signals on an investigated system output. However just in phase portraits these differences can be significant. Therefore the recognition of a system state even on one diagnostic parameter from all offered set is possible. At the same time the offered set of local and global characters for detection of a likeness or distinction between the various constructed phase portraits will allow to increase a number of recognizing classes and to extract an additional diagnostic and prognostic information about a researched system state.

For an estimate of a temporal statistical structure of chosen eigenvectors it is expedient to calculate their autocorrelated functions and spectra of their instantaneous frequencies.

5. CONCLUSION

The offered approach to forming and analysis of phase portraits of dynamics of a behavior of complicated systems is based on use of new algorithm of an effective estimate of eigenvalues and eigenvectors of real covariance matrix, and also effective choice of global and local structural characters possessing sufficient sensitivity to small distinctions of a researched system states. The given algorithm is steady against round-off errors of intermediate computations and allows to reduce time of an computation of eigenvectors and eigenvalues of real covariance matrix at the expense of use of rotation operators and precomputation of weight factors of orthogonal transformation F. The given approach is applicable in basic for a recognition of those functional states which easily is found out and is estimated on a phase portrait. The advantage of such approach lies in the possibility of characterizing the time series on the system by a single or several numbers. The quantitative estimate of a degree of a change of the offered diagnostic indications of phase portraits of current system state will allow to discover and to predict some physical regularities of a change of a researched system states.

6. REFERENCES

1. D.S.Broomhead and G.P.King, "Extracting qualitative dynamics from experimental data," Physica D, vol. 20, pp.217-236, 1986.

12. M.Flickner and N.Akhmed "A derivation for the discrete cosine transform" *Proceedings of IEEE*, vol.70, pp.1132-1134, Sept.1982.

3. M.Flickner and N.Akhmed "Some consederations of a discrete cosine transform" *Proceedings of IEEE*, vol.84, pp.295-299, March.1983.

4. A.M.Krot and N.N.Prokudina "Fast approximation of Karhunen-Loeve transform for problems of speech-like signal recognition" *Proc.13th Intern. conf. on Digital Signal Processing* (DSP'97), Santorini, Greece/ vol.2, pp.587-590, 3-5 July/ 1997

5. B.N.Parlett, The Symmetric Eigenvalue Problem. Berkeley, California, 1980.

AN ALGORITHM FOR FAST POLYNOMIAL REDUCTION IN DIGITAL SIGNAL PROCESSING PROBLEMS*

Alexander M. Krot, Helena B. Minervina

Institute of Engineering Cybernetics of the National Academy of Sciences of Belarus

Surganov Str., 6, 220012, Minsk, Belarus,

e-mail: alxkrot@newman.basnet.minsk.by

ABSTRACT

This paper estimate that the number of multiplications required for calculating the reduction of polynomial modulo an arbitrary polynomial q(z), whose coefficients do not belong to the field of constants. New fast algorithms are applied in digital signal filtering, restoration and interpolation problems.

1. INTRODUCTION

The theory of computational complexity [1]-[8] is important for solving problems in the areas of parallel computations, artificial intelligence and digital signal processing, especially multidimensional (some other relevant results can be found in [9]-[12]).

Many situations call for calculation of a product of polynomials modulo a third polynomial which is not cyclotomic and is not defined over the field of constant Ω, e.g. algorithm synthesis for optimal discrete control based on the polynomial equations method [1], [2].This paper examines the general case [2], [3].

2. DEFINITIONS OF THE GENERALIZED K_N -SHIFT, GENERALIZED K_N - CONVOLUTION AND VANDERMONDE TRANSFORM

The discrete Fourier transform (DFT) and linear and cyclic convolutions (LC and CC, respectively) are widely used in digital spectral analysis and digital filtering of signals [4], [5]. The CC matrix operator is a particular case of the matrix operator for generalized K_N -convolution which has the following form [2], [3]:

$$Z_N(\vec{h}) = \begin{bmatrix} \vec{h}^T K_N^0 \\ \vec{h}^T K_N^1 \\ \\ \vec{h}^T K_N^{N-1} \end{bmatrix} \qquad (1)$$

where $\vec{h}^T = (h_0, h_1, \cdots, h_{N-1})$, is the row vector of the impulse response, T indicates the transpose, K_N is the generalized K_N-shift represented by the Frobenius matrix:

$$K_N = \begin{bmatrix} 0 & 1 & & 0 \\ \vdots & & \ddots & \\ 0 & & & 1 \\ q_N & q_{N-1} & \cdots & q_1 \end{bmatrix} \qquad (2)$$

The generalized K_N-convolution of $\vec{x}^T = (x_0, x_1, \cdots, x_{N-1})$ and $\vec{h}^T = (h_0, h_1, \cdots, h_{N-1})$ can be written in the matrix notation as [2],[3]

$$\vec{y}^T = \vec{x}^T Z_N(\vec{h}) \qquad (3)$$

where $\vec{y}^T = (y_0, y_1, \cdots, y_{N-1})$ is the row vector of the generalized K_N-convolution. If the parameters of the generalized K_N-shift operator are defined as $q_N = 1$, $q_{N-1} = q_{N-2} = \dots q_1 = 0$, then $K_N = S_N(1)$ is the cyclic-shift matrix and $Z_N(\vec{h}) = C_N(\vec{h})$ is the matrix CC operator.

The eigentransform of the K_N-shift matrix (2) and the generalized K_N-convolution matrix (1) is the Vandermonde transform matrix:

$$\Lambda_N = \begin{bmatrix} 1 & 1 & \cdots & 1 \\ \lambda_0 & \lambda_1 & \cdots & \lambda_{N-1} \\ \lambda_0^2 & \lambda_1^2 & \cdots & \lambda_{N-1}^2 \\ \vdots & \vdots & \cdots & \vdots \\ \lambda_0^{N-1} & \lambda_1^{N-1} & \cdots & \lambda_{N-1}^{N-1} \end{bmatrix} \qquad (4)$$

where $\lambda_0, \lambda_1, \ldots, \lambda_{N-1}$ - are the eigenvalues of K_N, that is, the roots of the characteristic polynomial $q(z) = (-1)^N \left(z^N - q_1 z^{N-1} - \ldots - q_{N-1} z - q_N\right)$ over a certain field V. Assume that the eigenvalues λ_0, $\lambda_1, \ldots, \lambda_{N-1}$ and the coefficients $q_0, q_1, \ldots, q_{N-1}$ do not belong to $\Omega \in$ V, where Ω is the subfield of constants of the field V in the Winograd sense [4],[5]. This means that the multiplications $\lambda_n x_n$ and $q_n x_n$ ($\lambda_n, q_n, x_n \in$ V) cannot be regarded as trivial. The field V can for example be the field

* This work was supported by International Science and Technology Center (ISTC) under project B-95

of complex numbers. In the case where $K_N = S_N(1)$, the eigentransform matrix (4) is the DFT matrix F_N [2],[3].
The Vandermonde transform of the sequence $\{x_n\}$, $n = 0,1,...,N-1$, can be written:

$$\vec{X}^T = \vec{x}^T \Lambda_N \qquad (5)$$

where $\vec{X}^T = (X_0, X_1, \cdots, X_{N-1})$, and $X_k = \sum_{n=0}^{N-1} x_n \lambda_k^n$, $k=0,1,...,N-1$, that is, the Vandermonde transform is the first phase of Lagrangian interpolation. The Vandermonde transform of the generalized K_N-convolution (3) is:

$$\vec{Y}^T = \vec{X}^T \otimes \vec{H}^T \qquad (6)$$

where

$$\vec{Y}^T = \vec{y}^T \Lambda_N, \vec{X}^T = \vec{x}^T \Lambda_N, \vec{H}^T = \vec{h}^T \Lambda_N,$$

and $\otimes$ is the elementwise vector product. Using (6), it was shown in [2], [3] that the generalized K_N -convolution (3) of arbitrary sequences has the following polynomial form:

$$Y(z) \equiv H(z)X(z) \bmod q(z) \qquad (7)$$

where

$$Y(z) = \sum_{n=0}^{N-1} y_n z^n, H(z) = \sum_{n=0}^{N-1} h_n z^n, X(z) = \sum_{n=0}^{N-1} x_n z^n,$$

and mod means reduction modulo a polynomial. The polynomial interpretation of the generalized K_N^m -shift is also known from [2], [3]:

$$\vec{x}^T K_N^m \leftrightarrow z^m X(z) mod q(z) \qquad (8)$$

Generalized K_N -convolution is useful in several applications [2], [3]. For example, it may be used to synthesize a stable IIR filter providing a receipt of preassigned characteristic polynomial $Y(z)$ for a closed-loop system, i.e. for the system consisting of two filters with a feedback. Let the first filter have a preassigned transfer function $G(z) = H(z)/Q(z)$ where $H(z)$ and $Q(z)$ are known polynomials of z (z is a time delay operator for Δt). Second filter (adaptive corrector) has a transfer function $U(z) = X(z)/W(z)$ where $X(z)$ and $W(z)$ are unknown polynomials of z sought for. It is well-known that transfer function for a closed-loop system consisting of two filters $P(z) = F(z)/Y(z)$ ($Y(z)$ is desired polynomial chosen from a condition of stability of the system) is expressed by following relation:

$$P(z) = \frac{G(z)U(z)}{1 + G(z)U(z)}$$

By substituting in this equality the expressions for transfer functions $P(z)$, $G(z)$ and $U(z)$ we obtain that the synthesis of second filter (regulator) is reduced to solution of the following Diophantine equation in a polynomial ring:
$H(z)X(z) + Q(z)W(z) = Y(z)$.
This polynomial Diophantine equation is equivalent to the congruence over the polynomial residue-class ring V[z]/Q(z):

$$H(z)X(z) \equiv Y(z) \bmod Q(z)$$

which is the generalized K_N-convolution (7).

3. ALGORITHM AND MULTIPLICATIVE COMPLEXITY OF THE REDUCTION A MODULO ARBITRARY POLYNOMIAL

According to (7) and (8), we want to determine the multiplicative complexity the reduction modulo an arbitrary polynomial q(z), when the coefficients do not belong to the subfield of constants $\Omega \in V$ [3]. In this report the following statement is proved:

Lemma 1 (on the number of multiplications required for computing the reduction modulo an arbitrary polynomial).
The reduction of a polynomial A(z) over a field V of degree deg A(z)= L modulo a fixed polynomial q(z) over V of degree deg q(z)=N, where N= L/2 for even L and N=(L±1)/2 for odd L, can be executed in 2L multiplications.

The traditional computation of the residue R(z) over the field V requires N(L-N+1) arithmetic operations.
In Lemma 1, all coefficients of the polynomial $q(z) = z^N - q_1 z^{N-1} - q_2 z^{N-2} - \dots - q_{N-1} z - q_N$ are nontrivial in the sense that $q_i \in V$ and $q_i \notin \Omega$, where $\Omega \in V$. This implies that there exists no l such that $q_l \in \Omega$. Otherwise, the estimated number of multiplications necessary to reduce A(z) (of degree L) modulo the polynomial q(z) (of degree $N = L/2$ over V) might be smaller than 2L. For example, suppose that $L=5$, $N=(L+1)/2=3$ and $q(z)=z^3 - \lambda$ with $\lambda \notin \Omega$, but $\lambda \in \Omega$. Then, the remainder $R(z) \equiv \sum_{i=0}^{5} a_i z^i \bmod (z^3 - \lambda)$ can be calculated by replacing z^3 by λ so that the required number of multiplications is 3 < 2L for L = 5. The explanation is that in this degenerate case, the modulo polynomial $z^3 - \lambda$ is $q(z) = z^3 - q_1 z^2 - q_2 z - q_3$, where two of the coefficients, $q_1 = 0$ and $q_2 = 0$, belong to Ω and only one coefficient $q_3 = \lambda \notin \Omega$.
In practical applications of this algorithm to

compute polynomial residues, long LCs are computed using fast Fourier transforms (FFTs) [5], [6],[7], rather than the Cook-Toom algorithm. In this case, the number of multiplications to compute the polynomial reduction is $O(2L\log_2 L)$. For small L, the LC is computed by Winograd's algorithms [4], [5], which allows to $2L$.

Note that if N is not precisely equal to L/2 (or(L±1)/2 for odd L) accordingly Lemma 1, the multiplicative complexity of the reduction may exeed 2L. In this report the estimation of multiplications is derived.

Lemma 2. The reduction of a polynomial $A(z)$ over a field V of degree $\deg A(z)=L$ modulo a fixed polynomial q(z) over V of degree degq(z)=N where N<L and 2N≥L can be excecuted in 3L-2N multiplications..

4. DEVELOPMENT OF THE ALGORITHM FOR THE REDUCTION A MODULO AN ARBITRARY POLYNOMIAL

The algorithm leading to estimations of Lemma 1 [3] presents below. Let $R(z) \equiv A(z) \bmod q(z)$ be a polynomial residue modulo q(z) over V. According to the Euclid theorem,

$$A(z) = B(z)q(z) + R(z) \qquad (9)$$

where

$$A(z) = \sum_{i=0}^{L} a_i z^i,\ q(z) = z^N - \sum_{i=1}^{N} q_i z^{N-i},$$

$$B(z) = \sum_{i=0}^{L-N} b_i z^i,\ R(z) = \sum_{i=0}^{N-1} r_i z^i$$

with a_i, q_i, b_i, $r_i \in V$. The first term in (9), is the LC of the sequences $\{b_0, b_1, \ldots, b_{L-N}\}$, and $\{-q_N, -q_{N-1}, \ldots, -q_1, 1\}$[5]. For clarity, let us write (9) in the matrix form:

$$\begin{bmatrix} a_L \\ a_{L-1} \\ a_{L-2} \\ \vdots \\ a_N \\ a_{N-1} \\ \vdots \\ a_1 \\ a_0 \end{bmatrix} = \begin{bmatrix} 1 & & 0 \\ -q_1 & 1 & \\ -q_2 & -q_1 & \\ \vdots & \vdots & \\ -q_{L-N} & -q_{L-N-1} & 1 \\ -q_{L-N+1} & -q_{L-N} & -q_1 \\ & & \vdots \\ & \ddots & -q_{N-1} \\ 0 & & -q_N \end{bmatrix} \times \begin{bmatrix} b_{L-N} \\ b_{L-N-1} \\ b_{L-N-2} \\ \vdots \\ b_0 \end{bmatrix} + \begin{bmatrix} 0 \\ \vdots \\ 0 \\ 0 \\ r_{N-1} \\ \vdots \\ r_1 \\ r_0 \end{bmatrix} \qquad (10)$$

It follows from (9), that to determine the coefficients of the residue R(z) described by the vector $\vec{r} = (r_{N-1}, \ldots, r_1, r_0)^T$, first we have to find the coefficients of the incomplete quotient B(z), that is, $\vec{b} = (b_{L-N}, \ldots, b_{L-N-1}, b_0)^T$. If L=2N±1 or L=2N, this may be done by inverting the lower triangular matrix with unit diagonal:

$$\begin{bmatrix} b_{L-N} \\ b_{L-N-1} \\ b_{L-N-2} \\ \vdots \\ b_0 \end{bmatrix} = \begin{bmatrix} 1 & & & & 0 \\ -q_1 & 1 & & & \\ -q_2 & -q_1 & 1 & & \\ \vdots & \vdots & \vdots & \ddots & \\ -q_{L-N} & -q_{L-N-1} & -q_{L-N-2} & \cdots & 1 \end{bmatrix}^{-1} \times \begin{bmatrix} a_L \\ a_{L-1} \\ a_{L-2} \\ \vdots \\ a_N \end{bmatrix} \qquad (11)$$

Indeed, for L = 2N-1, the LC submatrix under consideration becomes NxN lower triangular matrix and, therefore invertible. As shown in [8], the matrix inverse of any lower triangular NxN matrix with a unit diagonal can be written as the product of N-1 elementary lower-column matrices.

Because 2N = L, i.e. L-N = N, and the elements q_i (i=1,...,N-1) are defined, the inverse matrix in (11) can be computed in advance according to [8]. It is a lower triangular matrix with a unit diagonal and the upper submatrix of the LC matrix of sequences $\{a_N, \ldots, a_{L-1}, a_L\}$ and $\{-q_N^{(-1)}, \ldots, -q_1^{(-1)}, 1\}$, where $-q_i^{(-1)}$, i = 1, 2,..., N, are elements of the inverse matrix.

Using the FFT algorithms [5], [6], [7] we can determine the minimal number of multiplications to compute the LC-product of two polynomials $\widetilde{B}(z) = \widetilde{A}(z)q^{(-1)}(z)$, where

$$\widetilde{B}(z) = z^N \sum_{i=0}^{L-N} b_i z^i + \sum_{i=0}^{N-1} \widetilde{b}_i z^i,\ \widetilde{A}(z) = \sum_{i=0}^{L-N} a_{i+N} z^i,$$

and $q^{(-1)}(z) = z^N - \sum_{i=1}^{N} q_i^{(-1)} z^{N-i}$.

Thus, the polynomial B(z) (which is a part of the polynomial $\widetilde{B}(z) = z^N B(z) + \sum_{i=0}^{N-1} \widetilde{b}_i z^i$) can be calculated using FFTs. According to (9), the determination of the residue R(z) can be reduced to computing the LC as well:

$R(z) = A(z) - B(z)q(z)$.

Note, however, that as long as the polynomials $q^{(-1)}(z)$ and q(z) are normalized. The products $z^N \widetilde{A}(z) \stackrel{\Delta}{=} \widetilde{B}_1(z)$ and $z^N B(z) \stackrel{\Delta}{=} W_1(z)$ can be computed by a shift without any multiplication, so the computation is reduced to the computation of the following polynomial products:

$$\widetilde{B}_2(z) = \widetilde{A}(z)\sum_{i=1}^{N} q_i^{(-1)} z^{N-i}, \qquad (12)$$

$$W_2(z) = B(z)\sum_{i=1}^{N} q_i z^{N-i},$$

(13)

where $\deg\widetilde{A}(z) = \deg B(z) = L - N$ and

$$deg\sum_{i=1}^{N} q_i^{(-1)} z^{N-i} = deg\sum_{i=1}^{N} q_i\, z^{N-i} = N-1.$$

In practical applications of this algorithm to compute polynomial residues, long LCs are computed using FFTs, [5], [6], [7].

Let us estimate the number of multiplications for the case when N is not precisely equal to L/2 (or(L±1)/2 for odd L). In Lemma 2 [3] the estimation of multiplications for this case was derived. In this report the algorithm based on Lemma 2 will be carried out by analogy with the one based on Lemma 1.

Let us obtain the arithmetic complexity for such algorithm. According to the algorithm based on Lemma 2 the reduction of the polynomial A(z) modulo q(z) over R, where deg A(z)=L= =2N-2 and degq(z)=N, amounts to the computation of LC of (N-2)-point sequences ($\widetilde{B}(z) = \widetilde{A}(z)q^{(-1)}(z)$) and LC of N-point sequences (*W(z) = B(z)q(z)*) and to N subtraction (*R(z)=A(z)-W(z)*). The algorithm for 2N-point CC may be used for the computation of each LC. Thus, the numbers of real multiplications and additions for the computation of R(z) ≡ A(z)modq(z) are

$$M(N,2N-2) = 2N(2\log_2 N - 1) + 6; \qquad (14)$$

$$A(N,2N-2) = N + 2N(6\log_2 N - 1) + 10 = N(12\log_2 N - 1) + 10 \qquad (15)$$

where M(N,2N-2) and A(N,2N-2) are functions depending both on N and L = 2N-2.

5. SUMMARY

The paper proves the following:

- polynomial reduction can be computed by efficient algorithms (see Lemmas 1 and 2, (14), (15));

- the proposed algorithms can be applied to digital filtering and restoration, Lagrangian interpolation of signals(images), optimal discrete control and also in some problems of parallel computations and artificial intelligence.

6. REFERENCES

[1] Polynomial methods in optimal control and filtering / Ed. by K.J.Hunt. Herts.: IEE Control Eng., Series no. 49, 1993.

[2] A.M.Krot, "On a class of discrete quasistationary linear dynamic systems", *Sov. Phys. Dokl.*, vol.35, no. 8, p.p. 711-713, 1990 (*a translation of Dokl. Akad. Nauk SSSR*, vol. 313, no. 6, pp. 1376-1380, Aug. 1990).

[3] A.M.Krot, "The multiplicative complexity of the reduction a modulo arbitrary polynomial, generalized K_N-convolution and fast Vandermonde transform", *Proc. 13th Intern. Conf. On Digital Signal Proc. (DSP'97)*, vol.2, Santorini, Greece, pp.893-897, 1997.

[4] S.Winograd, Arithmetic Complexity of Computations. *CBMSNSF Regional Conf. Series in Appl. Math.* Philadelphia, PA: SIAM, 1980.

[5] R.E.Blahut, Fast Algorithms for Digital Signal Processing. Reading, MA: Addison - Wesley, 1985

[6] H.V.Sorensen, D.L.Jones, M.T.Heideman and C.S.Burrus, "Real-valued fast Fourier transform algorithms", *IEEE Trans,* vol. ASSP-35, no. 6, pp. 849-863, 1987.

[7] A.M.Krot and H.B. Minervina, "Comment. Conjugate pair fast Fourier transform", *Electron. Letters*, vol. 28, no. 12, pp. 1143-1144, 1992.

[8] S.Pissanetzky. Space Matrix Technology. London: Academic Press, 1984.

[9] N.E.Mastorakis, N.J.Theodorou and S.G.Tzafestas, "Factorization of m-D Polynomials in Linear m-D Factors", International Journal of System Science, Vol.23, No.11, pp.1805-1824, 1992.

[10] N.E.Mastorakis, N.J.Theodorou and S.G.Tzafestas, "A General Factorization Method for Multivariable Polynomials" Multidimensional Systems and Signal Processing, Vol.5, pp.151-178, 1994.

[11] N.E.Mastorakis, S.G.Tzafestas and N.J.Theodorou, "Multidimensional Polynomial Factorization Through the Root Perturbation, Approach", Control Theory and Advanced Technology (C-TAT), Vol.10, No.4, Part 1, pp.901-911, 1994. ,

[12] N.E.Mastorakis,"Comments Concerning Multidimensional Polynomial Properties", IEEE Transactions on Automatic Control, Vol.41, No.2, p.260, Feb.1996.

MULTIVARIATE ARX MODEL IDENTIFICATION AND CONTROL WITH UNKNOWN PROCESS ORDER

E. N. DEMIRIS [1], S. D. LIKOTHANASSIS [1,2] and S .K. KATSIKAS [3]

[1] Department of Computer Engineering and Informatics, University of Patras, Patras 26500, GREECE
[2] Computer Technology Institute (C.T.I.), Patras 26100, GREECE
[3] Department of Mathematics, University of Aegean, Karlovassi 83200, GREECE
Tel: +30-61-997 755 ★ Fax: +30-61-997706
E-Mail: Demiris@cti.gr ★Likothan@cti.gr

ABSTRACT

A new adaptive method for simultaneously selecting the order, identifying the parameters of a multivariable ARX model and designing the control strategy is proposed. The method is based on the reformulation of the problem in the standard state space form and the subsequent implementation of a bank of minimum variance controllers, each fitting a different order model. The problem is thus reduced to selecting the true model, using the well known multi-model partitioning theory, for general (not necessarily Gaussian) data pdf's. Thus the cumulative control is the weighted average of the model conditional minimum variance controls, the weight being the respective a-posteriori probability that this particular model is the true model. Simulation experiments indicate that the proposed method is 100% successful in selecting the correct model order and that it accurately identifies the model parameters, in a small number of iterations.

1 INTRODUCTION

Many methods are known for the design of linear adaptive controllers. These methods are based on the availability of some process model as well as on the environment knowledge. Unfortunately, in many practical applications, the structure, i.e. the parameters and the order of the dynamical process model is usually unknown; therefore the controller design must be preceded by some identification or model construction technique [1],[2].

Consider the stochastic control system described by the following input-output equations:

$$y_k = \sum_{i=1}^{p} A_i y_{k-i} + \sum_{j=0}^{q} B_j u_{k-j} + e_k \qquad (1)$$

where process y is the output, u is the control input and e is a sequence of independent random variables with normal distributions $(0, R)$. The number of the unknown matrix coefficients A_i, $i = 1,\dots, p$ and B_j, $j = 1,\dots, q$, is obviously defined by the model order $n = (p, q)$. Since the parameters, as well as the order of the model are known, the control problem is stated as follows:

Given the output measurements $\lambda_K = y_k$, $k = 0,\dots, N-1$ as well as the previous control inputs u_K, $k = 0,\dots, N-1$, find the control strategy which minimizes the performance index:

$$J(N) = E\left\{\sum_{k=0}^{N-1} y_{k+1} \cdot C \cdot y_{k+1}\right\} \qquad (2)$$

where $C > 0$. In the case where the model order is known and the parameters are unknown but constant, one has to estimate the unknown coefficients and then a suitable control strategy, that minimizes the above performance index, calculates the control law as a function of y_k, y_{k-1}, ..., u_k, u_{k-1}, ... This is well known as the minimum variance strategy.

In the case where the order as well as the parameters of the model are unknown, the problem is twofold: one has both to select the model order and to estimate the model parameters. Perhaps the most crucial part of the problem is the former. Many methods exist for ARX model selection e.g.[3]-[7], the most well known and widely used among them being the ones proposed by Akaike [3]-[4]. Chen and Guo [8] have proposed that a consistent estimate of the order of feedback control systems with unknown parameters estimated by the least square method is derived by minimizing a modified version of the Bayesian information criterion, for uncorrelated driving noise. Recently, Wang and Libert [9], proposed a new method for identifying the ARX model order, combining pattern recognition techniques with Akaike's information criterion. All these methods are based on the assumption that the data are Gaussian and upon asymptotic results. Hence, strictly speaking, their applicability is limited only to the Gaussian case. Furthermore, they are two-pass methods, therefore they can not be used in an on line or adaptive fashion. Only Djuric and Kay [10] propose a method for simultaneous order selection and identification for ARX models, which, however, is applicable only to the Gaussian case and is computationally quite complicated.

In this paper, a new method for simultaneous multivariate ARX model order selection and identification is proposed, which is based on the adaptive multi-model partitioning theory [11]-[13]. The control law is derived using the minimum variance strategy to each one of the competitive models and the cumulative control is derived as the weighted average of the model conditional controls, each weighted by the respective a-posteriori probability that this particular model is the true model.

The method is not restricted to the Gaussian case, it is applicable to on-line/adaptive operation and is computationally efficient. Furthermore, it can be realized in a parallel processing fashion, a fact which makes it amenable to VLSI implementation. A similar method for simultaneous AR model order selection and parameter estimation was proposed in [14].

The paper is organized as follows: In section 2 the multivariate ARX model order selection and identification problem is reformulated, so that it can be fitted into the state space under uncertainty estimation problems framework. Section 3 presents the derivation of the multi-model adaptive minimum variance strategy. In the same section, the adaptive multi-model partitioning algorithm is presented and its application to the specific problem is discussed. In section 4 simulation experiments are presented, which demonstrate the performance of the new method. Finally, section 5 summarizes the conclusions.

2 REFORMULATION OF THE ARMAX MODEL ORDER SELECTION AND IDENTIFICATION

Consider the ARX model of (1) which can be represented as follows:

$$y_k = \sum_{i=1}^{p} A_i^k y_{k-i} + \sum_{j=1}^{q} B_j^k u_{k-j} + B_o u_k + e_k \tag{3}$$

where

$$A_i^k = \begin{bmatrix} a_{11}^i(k) a_{12}^i(k) \ldots a_{1m}^i(k) \\ a_{21}^i(k) a_{22}^i(k) \ldots a_{2m}^i(k) \\ \ldots \\ a_{m1}^i(k) a_{m2}^i(k) \ldots a_{mm}^i(k) \end{bmatrix}_{m \times m}$$

and

$$B_j^k = \begin{bmatrix} b_{11}^j(k) b_{12}^j(k) \ldots b_{1\ell}^j(k) \\ b_{21}^j(k) b_{22}^j(k) \ldots b_{2\ell}^j(k) \\ \ldots \\ b_{m1}^j(k) b_{m2}^j(k) \ldots b_{m\ell}^j(k) \end{bmatrix}_{m \times \ell} \tag{4}$$

The notations y_k , u_k denotes the $m \times 1$ output vector and the $\ell \times 1$ control vector respectively at time instant k .

Let us further define the vector:

$$\vartheta(k) = [a_{11}^1(k) a_{12}^1(k) .. a_{1m}^1(k) a_{21}^1(k) .. a_{mm}^p(k) \\ b_{11}^1(k) b_{12}^1(k) \ldots b_{1\ell}^1(k) b_{21}^1(k) \ldots b_{m\ell}^q(k)]^T \tag{5}$$

which contains all the elements of matrices A_i^k and B_j^k and is of dimension $(m^2 p + m\ell q) \times 1$.

Notice that A_i and B_j have been replaced by A_i^k and B_j^k respectively to reflect the possibility that the coefficients are subject to random perturbations. This fact can be modeled by assuming that:

$$\vartheta(k+1) = \vartheta(k) + w_k \tag{6}$$

where w_k is a zero-mean white noise process with variance Q (we assume that e_k and w_k are independent).

Assuming the case that the prediction coefficients are constant in time or slowly time varying ($Q = 0$), relation (6) is replaced by:

$$\vartheta(k+1) = \vartheta(k) \, , \; k = 0, \ldots, N-1 \tag{7}$$

Equation (3) can now be written as:

$$y_k = h^T(k) \vartheta(k) + B_o u_k + e_k \tag{8}$$

where the $m \times (m^2 p + m\ell q)$ matrix $h^T(k)$ is given by:

$$h^T(k) = [H_y^k H_u^k] \tag{9}$$

and

$$H_y^k = \begin{bmatrix} \left[y_{k-1}^T O_m y_{k-2}^T O_m \cdots y_{k-p}^T O_m \right]^0 \\ \left[y_{k-1}^T O_m y_{k-2}^T O_m \cdots y_{k-p}^T O_m \right]^m \\ \cdots \\ \left[y_{k-1}^T O_m y_{k-2}^T O_m \cdots y_{k-p}^T O_m \right]^{m^2-m} \end{bmatrix}$$

$$H_u^k = \begin{bmatrix} \left[u_{k-1}^T O_\ell \; u_{k-2}^T O_\ell \; \cdots \; u_{k-q}^T O_\ell \right]^0 \\ \left[u_{k-1}^T O_\ell \; u_{k-2}^T O_\ell \; \cdots \; u_{k-q}^T O_\ell \right]^\ell \\ \cdots \\ \left[u_{k-1}^T O_\ell \; u_{k-2}^T O_\ell \; \cdots \; u_{k-q}^T O_\ell \right]^{m\ell-\ell} \end{bmatrix} \tag{10}$$

where O_m, O_ℓ denotes the zero vectors of dimensions $1 \times (m^2 - m)$ and $1 \times (m\ell - \ell)$ respectively and the notation $[\ldots]^x$ is result of the xth right rotation of the vector $[\ldots]$.

Let us now assume that the order n , or the pair (p, q) is unknown and what we know is only that the true order satisfies the condition $n_0 \le n \le n_{\max}$. It is clear then that the true model is one of a family of models described by relations (7) and (8), the true model being specified by the true value of the pair of parameters (p, q) . The problem is then to select the correct model among various «candidate» models. In other words, we have to design an optimal solution to the derivation of the minimum variance control.

Remarks:

1. The formulation of equations (7) and (8) are in the standard state space form, so that state space estimation techniques can be readily used to estimate the values of the $\vartheta(k)$. This formulation is well known and widely used [8].
2. We assume that an a priori mean of the vector $\vartheta(0)$ can be set to zero in the case that no knowledge about

their values is available before any measurements are taken (we notice that is the most likely case). On the other the usual choice of the initial variance of the vector $\vartheta(0)$, denoted by $P(0/0)$ is $P(0/0)=cI$, where c is a large positive integer.

3. DERIVATION OF THE MINIMUM VARIANCE CONTROL STRATEGY

Consider the performance index of (2). We are seeking a feedback control, for every time instant $k=0,...,N-1$, which is a function of the measurements λ_k, such that, for every k, the sequence $\{u_j\}_{j=k}^{N-1}$ minimizes the performance index:

$$J_1(N)=\min_{u_k,...,u_{N-1}} E\left\{\left(\sum_{j=k}^{N-1} y_{j+1}\cdot C\cdot y_{j+1}\right)/\lambda_k\right\} \quad (11)$$

$J_1(N)$ is the optimal cost to proceed at time instant k, assuming that the observations λ_k are available. Using the smoothing property of the expectation operator, (11) takes the form:

$$J_1(N)=\min_{u_k,...,u_{N-1}} E\left\{E\left\{\left(\sum_{j=k}^{N-1} y_{j+1}\cdot C\cdot y_{j+1}\right)/\vartheta_i,\lambda_k\right\}/\lambda_k\right\} \quad (12)$$

where the index i denotes that the unknown system parameter vector ϑ_i belongs to a finite set. If a closed form solution could be found, then we would have an optimal solution for the problem. Given that such a solution is very difficult to obtain, we will perform the following approximation. Assume that the minimization and the first expectation operator can be interchanged [15]. Then, $J_1(N)$ becomes

$$J_2(N)=E\left\{\min_{u_k,...,u_{N-1}} E\left\{\left(\sum_{j=k}^{N-1} y_{j+1}\cdot C\cdot y_{j+1}\right)/\vartheta_i,\lambda_k\right\}/\lambda_k\right\} \quad (13)$$

Thus, if we minimize the above equations for every candidate model, with respect to the model (7), (8) the problem is reduced to the derivation of the minimum variance control [1], for every candidate model. Then, the cumulative control will be produced by the weighted average of the conditional minimum variance controls, with weight coefficients being the respective a-posteriori probabilities that is the true parameter vector.

Assuming that the maximum order of the conditional models is $n_{\max}$, then for $k=1,2,...,N-1$, the proposed adaptive minimum variance control is given by the relation:

$$u(k)=\sum_{i=n_o}^{n_{\max}} \hat{u}(k/k;\vartheta_i)p(\vartheta_i/\lambda_k) \quad (14)$$

where $\hat{u}(k/k;\vartheta_i)$ is the ϑ_i-conditional Minimum Variance Control (MVC). This is obtained [18] by the corresponding Kalman filter matched to the model with parameter vector $\vartheta(k)$, of dimension $(m^2p+m\ell q)\times 1$ and initialized with initial conditions $\hat{\vartheta}(0/0;\vartheta_i)$ and $P(0/0;\vartheta_i)$.

A presentation of the algorithm equations, adapted to the model partitioning theory, is given below:

1. The Kalman algorithm:

$$G(k/\vartheta_i)=\frac{F(k+1,k/\vartheta_i)P(k/k-1;\vartheta_i)h(k/\vartheta_i)}{h^T(k/\vartheta_i)P(k/k-1;\vartheta_i)h(k/\vartheta_i)+R}$$

$$\varepsilon(k/\vartheta_i)=y_k-h^T(k/\vartheta_i)\hat{\vartheta}(k/k-1;\vartheta_i)-B_o u_k$$

$$\tilde{z}(k/k-1;\vartheta_i)=y_k-h^T(k/\vartheta_i)F(k+1,k/\vartheta_i)*\hat{\vartheta}(k/k-1;\vartheta_i)-B_o u_k$$

$$\hat{\vartheta}(k+1/k;\vartheta_i)=F(k+1,k/\vartheta_i)\hat{\vartheta}(k/k-1;\vartheta_i)+G(k/\vartheta_i)\varepsilon(k/\vartheta_i)$$

$$\hat{\vartheta}(k/k;\vartheta_i)=F(k+1,k/\vartheta_i)^{-1}\hat{\vartheta}(k+1/k;\vartheta_i)$$

$$P(k/0;\vartheta_i)=P(k/k-1;\vartheta_i)-F(k+1,k/\vartheta_i)^{-1}*G(k/\vartheta_i)h^T(k/\vartheta_i)P(k/k-1;\vartheta_i)$$

$$P(k+1/k;\vartheta_i)=F(k+1,k/\vartheta_i)P(k/0;\vartheta_i)F^T(k+1,k/\vartheta_i)+QI$$

$$P_z(k/k-1;\vartheta_i)=h^T(k/\vartheta_i)P(k/0;\vartheta_i)h(k/\vartheta_i)+R$$

$$L(k/k;\vartheta_i)=\left|P_z(k/k-1;\vartheta_i)\right|^{-\frac{1}{2}}*\exp\left\{-\frac{1}{2}\left\|\tilde{z}(k/k-1;\vartheta_i)\right\|P_z^{-1}(k/k-1;\vartheta_i)\right\} \quad (15)$$

2. The model conditional MVC is given by:

$$\hat{u}(k/k;\vartheta_i)=-B_0^+h_i^T(k/\vartheta_i)\hat{\vartheta}_i(k/k) \quad (16)$$

where B_0^+ is

a) If $m=\ell$, $B_0^+=B_o^{-1}$

b) If $m>\ell$, $B_0^+=(B_o^TB_o)^{-1}B_o^T$

c) If $m<\ell$, $B_0^+=B_o^T(B_oB_o^T)^{-1}$

3. The model -conditional pdf $p(\vartheta_i/k)$ is given by:

$$p(\vartheta_i/k)=\frac{L(k/k;\vartheta_i)}{\sum_{i=n_o}^{n_{\max}}L(k/k;\vartheta_i)p(\vartheta_i/k-1)}p(\vartheta_i/k-1) \quad (17)$$

$$\hat{\vartheta}(k/k)=\sum_{i=n_o}^{n_{\max}}\hat{\vartheta}(k/k;\vartheta_i)p(\vartheta_i/k) \quad (18)$$

4. Initial Conditions

$$\hat{\vartheta}(0/0;\vartheta_i)=[O]_{(m^2p+m\ell q)\times 1}$$

$P(0/0;\vartheta_i)=cI$, c = large positive constant

$p(\vartheta_i/0)=\frac{1}{Kf}$, Kf = the size of Kalman's filter bank

An important feature of the adaptive multi-model partitioning algorithm is that all the filters needed to implement it can be independently realized. The solution adopted in this paper for the ARX identification problem is represented in Fig. 1. The parallelism in this block diagram emphasizes the ability to implement the algorithm in parallel, thus saving enormous computational time.

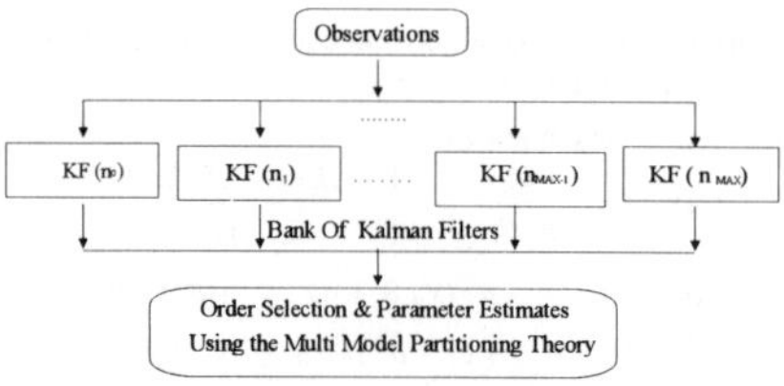

Figure 1: Solution Structure

Remarks:

1. It is well known that if the parameter estimates converge to the true values, then the control converges to the minimum variance control [1],[19]. If we assume that the system (1) is minimum phase, then the parameter estimates converge to the true values, while the respective a-posteriori probability almost surely tends to the unit [20]. Thus, as it is easily derived from relation (14), the adaptive control will converge to the minimum variance control which corresponds to the true model, because all the a-posteriori probabilities that weighs the model conditional controls become zero, except for the one which corresponds to the true model.
2. The use of matrix inversion in relation (16), restricts the application of the algorithm to the case where the matrix B_0 is inversible. Thus, this matrix must be nonsingular and the number of inputs equal to the number of outputs. Conditions for suitably selecting B_0 so as to produce unbiased estimates have been given in [19].
3. We can distinguish two criteria for the identification of the true model order. The true model can be taken as the one producing the maximum a-posteriori probability (MAP) or as that whose parameters are given by the weighted average of the model conditioned parameter's estimates, weighted by the respective a-posteriori probabilities. These criteria are referred to as "model competition scheme" and "model fusion scheme" respectively [19].
4. The method can be easily modified for the scalar case by simply replacing the matrices A, B by sets of scalar coefficients a and b.
5. The problem of the multivariable AR model order identification can be easily solved by the algorithm by simply setting $B = O$.

4. EXAMPLES

In order to assess the performance of the method, we conducted several simulation experiments. In this section two examples are discussed; first we present the case where the true order model belongs to the Kalman filters' bank and second the case where the correct order model satisfies the condition $n_0 \le n \le n_{\max}$ but it does not exists in the filters' bank.

To reduce realization dependency of the simulations we averaged over 100 Monte Carlo runs, the data record is of length 300, the added noise e_k is a zero mean white noise process with variance R equal unity, the initial value for $P(0/0;\vartheta_i)$ is $1000I$ and $Q = 0$.

Experiment 1: The model used was

$$y_k = \sum_{i=1}^{2} A_i\, y_{k-i} + \sum_{j=1}^{1} B_j u_{k-j} + B_o u_k + e_k$$

with

$$A_1 = \begin{bmatrix} 1.8 & -0.9 \\ 0.35 & 1.45 \end{bmatrix},\ A_2 = \begin{bmatrix} -1.6 & 0.65 \\ -1.72 & 1.4 \end{bmatrix}$$

and

$$B_1 = \begin{bmatrix} -0.98 & 0.78 \\ -1.2 & -0.54 \end{bmatrix},\ B_0 = \begin{bmatrix} -0.89 & 0.0046 \\ -0.02 & 1.88 \end{bmatrix}$$

We have realized a bank of Kalman filters which contains ten filters of order {[1,0], [1,1], [2,1]*, [1,2], [2,2], [3,1], [1,3], [3,2], [2,3], [3,3]} respectively.

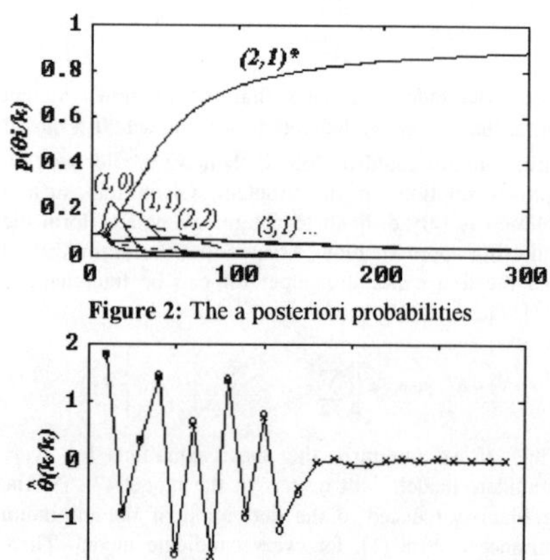

Figure 2: The a posteriori probabilities

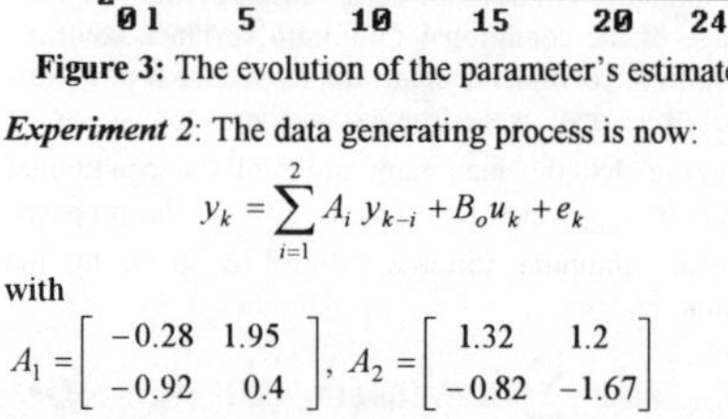

Figure 3: The evolution of the parameter's estimates

Experiment 2: The data generating process is now:

$$y_k = \sum_{i=1}^{2} A_i\, y_{k-i} + B_o u_k + e_k$$

with

$$A_1 = \begin{bmatrix} -0.28 & 1.95 \\ -0.92 & 0.4 \end{bmatrix},\ A_2 = \begin{bmatrix} 1.32 & 1.2 \\ -0.82 & -1.67 \end{bmatrix}$$

and

$$B_0 = \begin{bmatrix} -0.89 & 0.0046 \\ -0.02 & 1.88 \end{bmatrix}$$

We have realized a bank of Kalman filters which contains ten filters of order {[1,0], [1,1], [2,1], [2,2],

[3,2], [2,3], [3,3], [4,2], [2,4], [4,4]} respectively. Notice that the true order model (2,0) does not belong to the bank of Kalman filters.

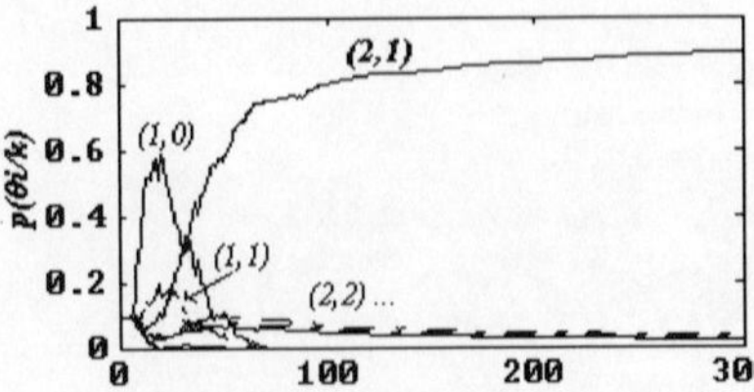

Figure 4: The a posteriori probabilities

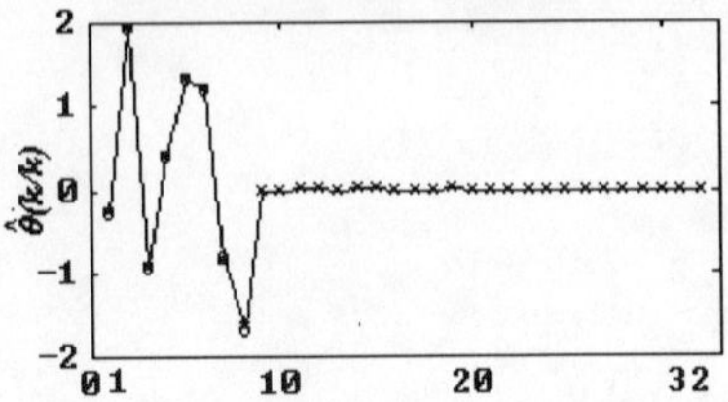

Figure 5: The evolution of the parameter's estimates

Experiment 3: The data generating process is the same with the experiment 2, but the non-squared (2×3) matrix B_o is given by:

$$B_o = \begin{bmatrix} 0.89 & -12.2 & 0.0046 \\ -0.02 & -0.42 & 8.84 \end{bmatrix}$$

We have realized a bank of Kalman filters which contains ten filters of order {[1,0], [1,1], [2,0]*, [1,2], [2,2], [3,1], [1,3], [3,2], [2,3], [3,3]} respectively.

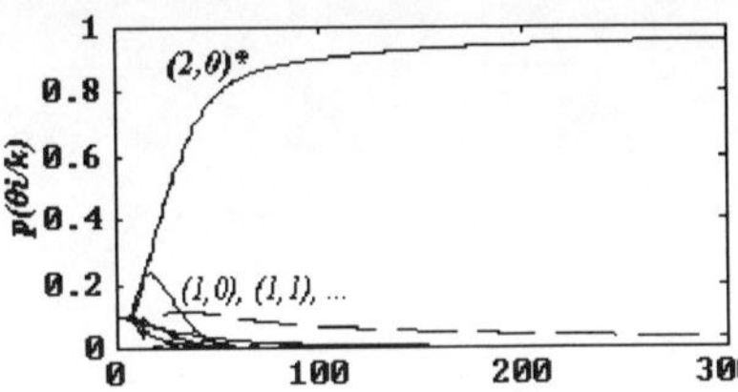

Figure 6: The a posteriori probabilities

Figure 2, 4 and 6, depict the a posteriori probabilities associated with each value of n, for the examples 1, 2 and 3 respectively.

Figure 3 for the example 1 and figure 5 for the example 2, shows how the true parameters' estimates (denoted by '+') tracks the true values of the parameters (denoted by '**o**') at time instant $k = 300$.

Figures 7 (a) and (b) shows how the parameters' estimates (solid lines) tracks the true parameter values (dashed lines), as a function of time. We denote the parameter's estimates by $A_1(1,1)$, $A_1(1,2)$, $A_1(2,1)$, $A_1(2,2)$ and $A_2(1,1)$, $A_2(1,2)$, $A_2(2,1)$, $A_2(2,2)$ for the matrixes A_1 and A_2 respectively.

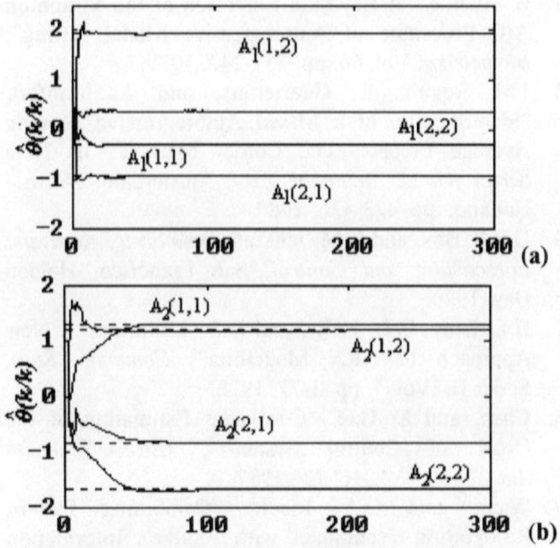

Figures 7 (a), (b): Parameter's estimates

4. CONCLUSIONS

A new method for simultaneously selecting the order, identifying the parameters of a multivariate ARX model and designing the control strategy has been developed, for the general case, where the number of inputs is different than the number of outputs. The method is based on the multi-model partitioning theory which is used for the selection of the true model and the minimum variance control strategy. Simulation experiments indicate that the proposed method is 100% successful in selecting the correct model order and that it accurately identifies the model parameters, in very few steps even in the case where the true model order is not included to the filters' bank. It has been proved, via simulations, that the method also performs well for correlated measurement noise. Since the MMSE criterion is used to produce the parameter estimates, the algorithm is applicable in cases with general (not necessarily Gaussian) data pdf's. The superiority of this method is that it operates in real time and it is adaptive, so that it has by nature the ability of tracking successfully changes in the model structure, in real time. The algorithm converges to the minimum variance control, if the system is minimum phase. Furthermore, the algorithm can be implemented in parallel and also a VLSI implementation is feasible.

REFERENCES

1. Astrom, "Theory and Applications of Adaptive Control - A Survey", *Automatica*, Vol. 19, pp. 471-486, 1983.
2. Lainiotis, J.G. Despande and T.N. Upadhyay, "Optimal Adaptive Control: A Nonlinear Separation Theorem", *Int. J. of Control*, Vol. 15, pp. 887-888, 1972.
3. Akaike, "A New Look at the Statistical Model Identification", *IEEE Trans. Automat. Contr.*, Vol. AC-19, pp. 716-723, 1974.

4. H. Akaike, "A Bayesian Extension of the Minimum AIC Procedure of Autoregressive Model Fitting", *Biometrika*, Vol. 66, pp. 237-242, 1979.
5. J.M. Beguin, C. Gourieroux, and A. Monfort, "Identification of a Mixed Autoregressive Moving Average Process: The Corner Method', in *Time Series (O. D. Anderson, Ed.),* Amsterdam: North - Holland, pp. 423-426, 1980.
6. G.E.P. Box, and G.M. Jenkins, *Time Series Analysis: Forecasting and Control*, San Francisco, Holden Day, 1970.
7. H.L. Gray, G.D. Kelly, and D.D. McIntire, 'A New Approach to ARX Modelling", *Commun. Stat.*, Series B, Vol. 7, pp. 1-77, 1978.
8. Chen, and L. Guo, "Consistent Estimation of the Order of Control Systems", *IEEE Trans.on Aut.Contr.*, Vol. ***AC-32***, 1987
9. Wang, and G.A. Libert, "Combining Pattern Recognition Techniques with Akaike's Information Criteria for Identifying ARX Models', *IEEE Trans.on Signal Process.*, Vol. SP-42, no. 6, pp. 1368-1396, 1994.
10. Djuric and S.M. Kay, "Predictive Probability as a Criterion for Model Selection', in *Proceedings, ICASSP 1990*, pp. 2415-2418, 1990.
11. D.G.Lainiotis, "Optimal Adaptive Estimation: Structure and Parameter Adaptation', *IEEE Trans. Automat.Contr.*, Vol. AC-16, pp. 160-170, 1971.
12. Lainiotis, "Partitioning: A Unifying Framework for Adaptive Systems I: Estimation', *Proceedings of the IEEE*, Vol. 64, pp. 1126-1143, 1976.
13. Lainiotis, "Partitioning: A Unifying Framework for Adaptive Systems II: Control', *Proceedings of the IEEE*, Vol. 64, pp. 1182-1198, 1976.
14. Katsikas, S.D. Likothanassis, and D.G. Lainiotis, "AR Model Identification with Unknown Process Order", *IEEE Trans. on Acoust. Speech and Sign. Proc.*, Vol. ASSP-38, no. 5, pp. 872-876, 1990.
15. Meier, R.E. Larson, and A.J. Tether, "Dynamic Programming for Stochastic Control of Discrete Systems", *IEEE Trans. on Aut. Contr.*, Vol. AC-16, pp. 767-775, 1971.
16. Shengbush and D.G. Lainiotis, "Simplified Parameter Quantization Procedure for Adaptive Estimation", *IEEE Trans. Autom. Contr.*, Vol. AC-14, pp. 424-425, 1969.
17. Lainiotis, S.K. Katsikas and S.D. Likothanassis, "Adaptive Deconvolution of Seismic Signals: Performance Evaluation, Computational Analysis and Parallelism", *IEEE Trans. on Acoust. Speech and Sign. Proc.*, Vol. ASSP-36, no. 4, pp. 1715-1734, 1988.
18. Likothanassis and S.K. Katsikas, "Multivariable AR Model Identification and Control", in *Proceedings IASTED Int. Symp. Modeling, Identification and Control*, pp. 248-252, Grindelwald, Switzerland, 1987.
19. Astrom and B. Wittenmark, "On Self-Tuning Regulators", Automatica, Vol. 9, pp. 185-199, 1973.
20. Hawkes and J.B. Moore, "Performance Bounds for Adaptive Estimation", *Proceedings of the IEEE*, Vol. 64, no 8, pp. 1143-1150, 1976.

LOW SNR TIME DELAY ESTIMATION BY ADAPTIVE POSTFILTERING OF CROSS-CORRELATOR OUTPUT SEQUENCE

Alexander N.DOLIA, Vladimir V. LUKIN, Alexander A. ZELENSKY

Dept. 507, Kharkov Aviation Institute, 17 Chkalova St., 310070, Kharkov, Ukraine.
Phone: +38 0572 442352, fax +38 0572 441186, e-mail lukin@xai.kharkov.ua

Abstract **- In case of low SNR and influence of other destructive factors the estimates of time delay between random wideband signals received by two displaced sensors are characterized by poor accuracy - abnormal errors occur with high probability. In this paper we briefly consider the properties of cross-correlator outputs (both elementary ones and their sequence) and then propose different algorithms of their postprocessing by means of 2-D linear and nonlinear filters. Their efficiency is quantitatively compared in respect to normal error variance and abnormal error probability. The methodology of filter type and parameter selection is presented and it is shown that it should be adaptive. The expedience of proposed algorithm application is demonstrated by numerical simulation data.**

Keywords: *time delay estimation, accuracy improvement, nonlinear filtering*

I. INTRODUCTION

The accuracy of time delay estimations (TDE) between random wideband signals irradiated by a source and received by two spatially displaced sensors (i.e. by interferometric antenna) is determined by several factors: irradiated signal and additive noise spectral densities $S(w)$ and $N(w)$, respectively, signal to noise ratio (SNR), elementary time of signal observation T [1]. For sonars the multipath and random medium propagation effects, signal source motion and spatial dimensions, different attenuation of signal spectral components dependent on frequency also influence the TDE accuracy [1, 2]. One more problem is the selection of T and the upper frequency of the processed wideband signal in conditions of lack of a priori information about signal and noise spectral characteristics, propagation medium properties, source dimension and motion parameter uncertainly. Usually T is constant because for hardware or software implementation of received signal cross-correlation processing it is difficult to vary it [3]. Then the TDE accuracy enhancement is provided due to postprocessing of TDE sequence or the sequence of cross-correlator outputs (CCO) [1,4].

The optimal techniques and algorithms of TDE for some particular situations are known [1]. For example, for high SNR, non-moving source and homogeneous unbounded medium it is a usual cross-correlation of received signals with "prewhitening" of Gaussian additive noise performed for the band of signal spectrum existence [2]. However, in any case the power spectrum $N(w)$ should be a priori known or preestimated. For low SNR the "prewhitening" and correction of received signal cross-spectrum is required, the other equivalent way is the elementary CCO postfiltering. In this case the ratio $S(w)/N(w)$ or coherence function have to be a priori known or preestimated. But for practical situations such kind of information is often absent, the corresponding estimates are not accurate enough, besides, this ratio can vary in time because of different effects. There also exist techniques of optimal simultaneous estimation of time delay and its first and second derivatives, but it is a great problem to implement them in real time operating processors [1]. It is even more difficult to design and, especially, to implement in practice the optimal signal processing algorithms for taking into account the other factors, in particular, the propagation and attenuation effects. Thus, the following approach seems reasonable: let us use the preliminary "prewhitening" of additive noise and, then, the standard correlation performing on basis of standard or modified FFT processor implementation [5]. Then it is proposed to apply the digital linear or nonlinear adaptive algorithms of signal/image postprocessing to cross-correlator output sequence represented as 2-D data array (image). The main goal is to improve the accuracy of TDE both in the sense of decreasing the abnormal error probability (the main criterion) and normal error variance reduction (the additional criterion).

The structure of the paper is the following. In Chapter II we discuss some peculiarities of elementary CCO for cases of low SNR and influence of other degrading factors. The used model is given as well. Then in Chapter III the assumptions concerning true time delay behavior in time are backgrounded and aspects of CCO sequence representation as 2-D image are considered. Some approaches to postprocessing algorithm parameter adaptation to signal and noise characteristics are put forward in Chapter IV. The accuracy characteristics of proposed novel algorithms are compared quantitatively in Chapter V. Finally, the Conclusions follow.

II. SIGNAL-NOISE MODEL AND PROPERTIES OF ELEMENTARY CROSS-CORRELATOR OUTPUT

Let us consider the simplest case of only two sensors. The most convenient way of received signal description is the presentation of current complex spectra as the following [6] :

$$\dot{S}_{U_1}(w) = \dot{S}_{ir}(w)e^{j\varphi_1(w)}e^{-\alpha(w)r} + \dot{N}_1(w) \quad (1)$$

$$\dot{S}_{U_2}(w) = \dot{S}_{ir}(w)e^{j\varphi_1(w)}e^{-jw\tau_0}e^{-\alpha(w)r} + \dot{N}_2(w) \quad (2)$$

where $\dot{S}_{U_1}(w)$ and $\dot{S}_{U_2}(w)$ define the spectra of received signal-noise mixtures U_1 and U_2, $\dot{S}_{ir}(w)$ is the irradiated signal current spectrum recalculated for the receiving sensors taking into account the distance to the source, $\alpha(w)$ denotes the factor showing acoustic wave attenuation, $\varphi_1(w)$ and $\varphi_2(w)$ are the random slowly changing functions with variance increasing approximately proportionally to w^2, $\dot{N}_1(w)$ and $\dot{N}_2(w)$ are the additive noise complex current spectra for the first and the second sensors, respectively. It is supposed for simplicity that the source is quasipoint; in general case τ_0 and both $\varphi_1(w)$ and $\varphi_2(w)$ depend on time t. The function $\alpha(w)$ values increase when $|w|$ becomes greater [4].Introducing the new notations

$$\dot{S}_{ir}(w)e^{-\alpha(w)r} = \dot{S}_1(w), \quad \Delta\varphi(w) = \varphi_1(w) - \varphi_2(w)$$

one gets the cross-spectrum as

$$\dot{S}_{12}(w) = \dot{S}_1(w)\dot{S}_1^*(w)e^{\Delta\varphi(w)}e^{jw\tau_0} + \{\dot{S}_1(w)e^{j\varphi_1(\omega)}N(w) + +\dot{S}_1(w)e^{-j\varphi_2(\omega)}e^{j\omega\tau_0}\dot{N}_1(w) + \dot{N}_1(w)\dot{N}_2(w)\} \quad (3)$$

and after "prewhitening" the CCO is described in the following way

$$Y(\tau) = \int_T \{\dot{S}(w)/N(w)\}e^{-jw\tau}d\omega = Y_0(\tau) + n(\tau) \quad (4)$$

where $Y_0(\tau)$ is the output signal component (the Fourier response of the first term in (4), $n(\tau)$ is the output noise component. The factor $e^{j\Delta\varphi(w)}$ as well as source motion also contribute to the output noise component.

Usually the CCO signal component has a mean main lobe width δ_S greater than an average width δ_A of other output side lobes. The latter parameter for low SNR is mainly determined by additive noise spectrum band (See (3)) and the other destructive factor characteristics. At the same time the multipath effects, signal absorption increasing with frequency growth, random medium inhomogenities and source motion influence in such a manner that they degrade the received signal spatial-temporal coherence mainly for the high frequency area of processed signal spectral band [1,3,7]. The consequence is the δ_S increasing in comparison to irradiated signal autocorrelation function main lobe width. The other practical consideration that evidences in favour of assumption that $\delta_S > \delta_A$ is the following. Usually the signal processing is performed for frequency band $w \in [-w_U, +w_U]$ for which $w_U > w_{US}$ where w_{US} is the upper frequency of received signal. It is often unknown or varies depending upon distance due to attenuation.

Let us illustrate this by numerical simulation data considering the model after prewhitening. Let us assume that the ratio of power spectra is of triangular shape

$$S(w)/N(w) = k_0(1 - |w|/w_U) \quad (5)$$

where $SNR = k_0/2$. Then analysing elementary CCO for cases of normal errors of TDE and abnormal errors the mean values of the ratios δ_S/δ_A have been found for different SNRs. The following data have been obtained: for SNR=0.3 it was 1.45, for 0.25 the ratio was 1.42 and for SNR=0.2 it was 1.38. This confirms the assumption introduced above. The other assumptions concerning the output getting are the following: a) the value T_l is more than 8..12 times greater than the maximal possible delay τ_{max} - this value is determined by the ratio of interferometer size L to acoustic wave propagation speed C; b) the received signal-noise mixture sampling rate $\Delta\tau$ or, at least, CCO discretization $\Delta\tau$ are not less than $8\pi/w_U$, i.e. data are oversampled. This requirement deals with necessity to provide enough high accuracy of δ_{Sl}, δ_{Al} and $\hat{\tau}_l$ estimation and to apply the output sequence processing algorithms described below.

III. CROSS-CORRELATOR OUTPUT SEQUENCE REPRESENTATION AND ITS PECULIARITIES

The assumptions and CCO peculiarities discussed above are put into the basis of the proposed algorithms of CCO sequence postprocessing that have the aim of TDE accuracy improvement. It was also supposed that $max\{\tau_{i+1} - \tau_i\} < 2\Delta\tau$, i.e. time delay varies slowly enough between time subintervals of signal observation and processing following each other.

There are different methodologies of CCO sequence representation as 2-D images. We used the following one. Let $\{Y[l,i]$ be an array of CCOs calculated for the l-th segment where true time delay is $\widetilde{D}_i^l = i_l\Delta\tau$, $i = \overline{-i_{max}, i_{max}}$ ($i_{max}\Delta\tau$ is the maximal physically possible delay). Let us map the real value array $\{Y[l,i]\}$ onto $\{Y^n[l,i]\} \in [0;255]$ in the following way

$$Y^n[l,i] = \begin{cases} 127 \cdot Y[l,i] / |Y_{max}[l]| + 128, \\ \quad if \ |Y_{max}[l]| > |Y_{min}[l]|, \\ 127 \cdot Y[l,i] / |Y_{min}[l]| + 128, \\ \quad \text{otherwise}, \end{cases} \quad (6)$$

where $|Y_{max}[l]|$ and $|Y_{min}[l]|$ are the absolute values of CCO maximum and minimum for the l -th segment (elementary subinterval), respectively. In this way one, first, gets the representation of the obtained image as 8-bit integer value array being traditional and suitable for image processing applications and, second, line data normalization makes negligible the influence of quantization errors.

For such representation the obtained image contains the information fragments visually observed as a continuous curve of mainly vertical orientation having several pixel width (for ratio (5) approximately equal to 7..8) for case of relatively high SNR and the region corresponding to noise. When the SNR is low and the probability of abnormal errors is high the curve is hardly observed even visually (See Fig.1,a) and the noise region is characterized by greater fluctuations. The signal time delay temporal variation function was $\tau_i = a_2 \sin(\pi b_2 i)$. It includes quasilinear changing and quasiconstant delay lots. Only the fragments of simulated data are presented in Fig.1.

It is possible and expedient to estimate both δ_S and δ_A analyzing the elementary CCO $Y^n[l,i]$ (if the TDE for it is normal) or the CCO sequence by zero-crossing (for considered representation zero level of initial representation approximately corresponds to 128) simultaneously with $\hat{\tau}$ estimations getting. Here and below we suppose that the cross-correlator operates sequentially, i.e. produces the outputs for equal time subintervals T_l following each other. In case of high probability of abnormal errors one can, at least, estimate δ_a. This information can be further used for initial selection of 2-D filter line (horizontal) size when the tracking of time delay is not yet performed.

In our papers [6] it was shown that 1-D filtering of elementary CCO or the sequence of TDEs obtained from elementary observations by means of even median filter provide some reduction of TDE abnormal error occurrence but it is not acceptable. 2-D filter application permitted to get essentially better results. That is why let us pay main attention here to analysis of 2-D filter properties and efficiency. One more advantage of 2-D filter application is that they are widely applied to image processing and, therefore, the results of their analysis are available. However, the filters should be selected or designed in such a way to preserve curves of predetermined width.

IV. PROPOSED PROCESSING ALGORITHMS

There are several approaches to time delay estimation accuracy improvement. The first one is the $1-D$ linear adaptive filtering of every cross-correlator output (image lines)

$$Y^f[l,i] = 1/K \sum_{j=-\frac{K-1}{2}}^{\frac{K-1}{2}} Y^n[l,i+j] \quad (7)$$

where $Y^f[l,i]$ here and below are the output sequence smoothed data array. It is shown in [6] that for this technique based on δ_S and δ_A estimation the adaptive selection of *K* is the following: $K \approx (\delta_S + \delta_A)/2\Delta\tau$ and *K* has to be odd. This recommendation is valid for both $1-D$ filters to be applied to elementary CCO and to $2-D$ ones concerning their horizontal size. Theoretically it should provide both P_a and σ_τ^2 reduction close to optimum. If the speed of time delay temporal variation is rather small an essential improvement can be got using cross-spectrum (or output sequence raw) recursive averaging $Y^f[l,i] = \frac{1}{M} \sum_{m=(M-1)/2}^{(M-1)/2} Y^n[l+m,i]$, but this method fails if time delay changes quickly and, moreover, the linear and nonlinear filters proposed by us in [6] perform better even for constant time delay. Thus, here we examined and compared to each other the following algorithms of cross-correlator output sequence postprocessing:

1) $2-D$ linear filtering in the scanning window with the size $M \times K$ (technique 2, several different *K* and *M* values are considered here, in [6] both *K* and *M* were equal to 5);

2) derivation of the median of 5 complex shape subaperture linear (mean) outputs; for this technique 3 the subaperture sizes should be approximately equal to $\frac{M+1}{2} \times \frac{K+1}{2}$, some subapertures can overlap but the total aperture size is *MxK* to provide correctness of data comparison, the sumaperture shapes for 7x7 apertures are presented in Fig.2;

3) a new proposed procedure of $2-D$ data processing that includes several stages. At the first one for every pixel the linear summation of values belonging to one-pixel width subapertures (See Fig.3) is done. In this way one gets 5 or 7 sums, i.e. the 5 or 7 elements vector. There are two algorithms of their further processing. Variant one assumes the derivation of the maximal value among vector elements and the assigning of it to the output image pixel. This technique can be interpreted as a suboptimal method of varying TDE supposing its linear changing. We called it technique

4. The other variant is to find the maximal value of vector components for current image line. Then one get intermediate binary data array for which units are assigned to the central and to all the other pixels of subaperture for which the sum is greatest in line. All the other elements of this intermediate array are zeroes. Then in the scanning (recursive) mode these intermediate arrays are summed up. So one obtains the image the values of which can vary from 0 to M, i.e. to the number of image lines included into subapertures. The final stage is to find the pixel index for every line having the greatest sum (characterized by the greatest value). Then it is decided that just it correspond to TDE. In case when $\delta_S > \delta_A$ the preliminary $1-D$ filtering of line data is expedient and it provides additional improvement of TDE accuracy

The increasing of filter aperture vertical size can be interpreted as making greater the observation time and while analysing the accuracy of different algorithms it should be taken into account.

V. COMPARISON OF THE TDE ACCURACY FOR DIFFERENT ALGORITHMS

In case of low SNR or when there exists the simultaneous influence of several destructive factors mentioned above the accuracy of TDE is characterized by two main parameters [2,6]: 1) the variance of normal errors σ_τ^2 (their absolute values are less than the output signal component mainlobe halfwidth $\delta_0/2$; 2) the probability of abnormal errors P_a., i.e. the cases when the time delay estimation greatly differs from its true value τ_0. The task to reduce P_a. is more important than to decrease σ_n^2. To show the necessity of filter parameter adaptation , for instance, its aperture size updating, we also analysed the other case of power spectra ratio:

$$S(w)/N(w) = const = k_0/2 . \quad (8)$$

The results of numerical simulations for initial data and algorithms 1-4 described above for time delay sinusoidal behavior are presented in Table 1 ($\delta_s = 8\Delta\tau$, $\delta_a = 4\Delta\tau$, $a_2 = 50\Delta\tau$, $b_2=0.02$) and for spectra ratio (5) and in Table 2 ($\delta_s = 4\Delta\tau$, $\delta_a = 4\Delta\tau$) for (8). For thorough analysis the results for different SNRs are given.

It is seen that the best results in respect to abnormal error removal are provided by technique 4 and, especially, if it is added by 1-D linear prefiltering for triangulat shape ratio. But for rectangular spectrum ratio 1-D prefiltering decreases the accuracy and this fact proves the expedience of CCO analysis and filter parameter adaptive selection. Technique 3 that combines linear and nonlinear data processing algorithms in a manner similar to that one described in [9,10] and technique 2 also give good results. At the same time due to output sequence postprocessing σ_τ^2 can be reduced not essentially in comparison to primary TDE normal errorvariance. It can even increase mainly because of dynamical errors for trajectory parts near its extrema.

The examples of different technique application to CCO sequence processing are presented in Fig.1,b,c,d. White dots indicate the locations of line global maxima. It is obvious that the trajectory can be well seen and the best results are obtained for proposed technique 4.

VI. CONCLUSIONS

New linear and nonlinear adaptive filtering techniques applicable to CCO sequence for TDE accuracy improvement are proposed. Some possibilities of their parameter updating (horizontal size of aperture or subapertures) are considered. Numerical simulation results permit to compare the algorithm efficiency and prove the expedience of proposed technique application.

References

[1] G.C.Carter, Time Delay Estimation for Passive Sonar Signal Processing, IEEE Trans. Acoust., Speech, Sign. Processing, Vol.ASSP-29 pp.463-470,June 1981.

[2] J.P.Ianiello, Lower Bounds on Worst Case Probability of Large Error for Two Channel Time Delay Estimation, IEEE Trans. Acoust., Speech, Sign. Processing, Vol. ASSP-33, pp.1102-1109, Oct.1985.

[3] V.V.Olshevskii, Statistical Methods in Hydroacoustics, Leningrad, Issued by Edit. Board "Sudostroyeniye", 1983, 280p.(in Russian).

[4] Olshevskii V.V. Statistical Methods in Sonar, C.B.Plenum Publishing Corporation, New York, 1978.

[5] A.N. Dolia, V.V.Lukin, A.A.Zelensky. A Fast Algorithm of Cross-Correlator Output Calculation for Interferometric System. Proceedings of the 1997 International Symposium on Signals Circuits and Systems, Iasi, Romania, Oct. 1997, V.1, pp. 223-226.

[6] A.N.Dolia, V.V.Lukin, V.P.Melnik, J.M.Yli-Hietanen, J.T.Astola. Techniques and algorithms of cross-correlator output sequence postprocessing for wideband signal time delay estimate accuracy improvement, Proceedings of the 1997 Finnish Signal Processing Symposium, May ,22,1997, pp.65-69.

[7] A.A. Zelensky, V.V. Lukin, Properties of Source Spatial Location Estimates in Random Inhomogeneous and Bounded Medii, in "Radioelectronic Systems of Flying Vehicles", Issued by Kharkov Aviation Institute, Kharkov, Ukraine, 1990,pp.3-13 (in Russian).

[8] Lukin V.V, Pogrebniak A.B., Application of nonlinear algorithms for wideband signal cross-correlation processing of signal-intensive additive noise mixture, Digest of All-Union Conference "Information Technologies of Radio System Efficiency Enhancement, Tashkent,1990,pp.96-98.(Russian).

[9] Risto Wichman, Design, Analysis and Application of Wieghted Median Sructures, Thesis for the Degree of Doctor of Technology, Tampere University of Technology, Tampere, Finland, 1995.

[10] P.Heinonen,Y. Neuvo, "FIR-Median Hybrid Filters", IEEE Trans. Acoust., Speech, Sign. Proc., Vol. ASSP-35, N6, pp.832-838, June 1987.

Table 1. Quantitative comparison of TDE technique accuracy for spectrum ratio (5)

Techniques		SNR=0.15		SNR=0.19		SNR=0.225	
		P_A	$(\sigma_\tau/\Delta\tau)^2$	P_A	$(\sigma_\tau/\Delta\tau)^2$	P_A	$(\sigma_\tau/\Delta\tau)^2$
For initial data		0.79	2.9	0.66	1.7	0.49	1.2
Cross-spectrum averaging	M=5	0.50	1.4	0.12	0.26	0.027	0.48
	M=7	0.40	1.4	0.086	0.3	0.01	0.48
2.Linear:	5x5	0.39	1.4	0.094	0.72	0.1	0.42
$M \times K =$	7x5	0.29	1.2	0.04	0.59	0.0017	0.37
	7x7	0.30	2.4	0.059	1.47	0.0051	1.04
3.Nonlinear:	5x5	0.48	1.7	0.15	1.0	0.26	0.64
$M \times K =$	5x7	0.47	2.	0.14	1.4	0.22	0.97
	7x7	0.34	1.8	0.06	1.1	0.0051	0.83
4.1 without prefiltering	5x5	0.49	1.6	0.16	0.88	0.025	0.48
with *1-D* prefiltering 1x5,	5x5	0.40	1.7	0.1	0.82	0.012	0.46
4.2 without prefiltering,	5x5	0.45	1.9	0.11	1.07	0.012	0.62
with *1-D* prefiltering 1x5,	5x5	0.35	1.8	0.066	0.91	0.00807	0.54
with *1-D* prefiltering 1x7,	5x5	0.37	2.9	0.09	1.9	0.011	1.4
without prefiltering,	5x7	0.31	1.7	0.045	0.71	0.0015	0.46
with *1-D* prefiltering 1x5,	7x7	0.24	1.6	0.022	1.71	0.00057	0.4
with *1-D* prefiltering 1x7,	7x7	0.27	2.6	0.033	0.88	0.0014	1.2

Table 2. Quantitative comparison of TDE technique accuracy for spectrum ratio (8)

Techniques		SNR=0.25		SNR=0.3		SNR=0.35	
		P_A	$(\sigma_\tau/\Delta\tau)^2$	P_A	$(\sigma_\tau/\Delta\tau)^2$	P_A	$(\sigma_\tau/\Delta\tau)^2$
For initial data		0.8	0.61	0.64	0.36	0.45	0.26
Cross-spectrum averaging	M=5	0.41	0.37	0.12	0.26	0.019	0.18
	M=7	0.34	0.40	0.086	0.3	0.014	0.21
2.Linear:	5x5	0.47	0.90	0.21	0.66	0.055	0.48
$M \times K =$	7x5	0.36	0.82	0.12	0.59	0.018	0.4
	7x7	0.46	2.39	0.22	2.41	0.067	2.3
3.Nonlinear:	5x5	0.50	0.72	0.22	0.59	0.054	0.5
$M \times K =$	5x7	0.53	1.13	0.26	0.97	0.075	0.84
	7x7	0.40	0.97	0.14	0.78	0.017	0.63
4.1 without prefiltering	5x5	0.43	0.45	0.12	0.25	0.014	0.15
with *1-D* prefiltering 1x5,	5x5	0.51	0.90	0.23	0.68	0.061	0.47
4.2 without prefiltering,	5x5	0.36	0.49	0.08	0.3	0.0045	0.18
with *1-D* prefiltering 1x5,	5x5	0.46	1.02	0.18	0.78	0.032	0.59
with *1-D* prefiltering 1x7,	5x5	0.55	2.38	0.32	2.56	0.134	2.6
without prefiltering,	5x7	0.20	0.41	0.016	0.23	not observed	0.15
with *1-D* prefiltering 1x5,	7x7	0.32	0.94	0.09	0.66	0.005	0.46
with *1-D* prefiltering 1x7,	7x7	0.45	2.41	0.2	2.56	0.062	2.7

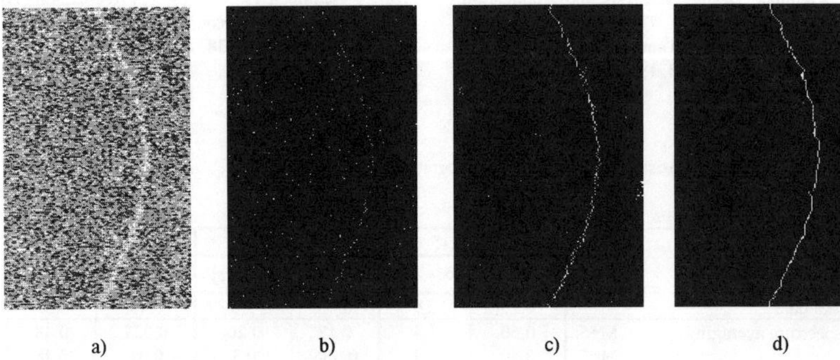

Fig. 1. a) 2-D representation of CCO sequence as 2-D image;
b) locations of line maxima for initial data;
c) locations of line maxima after processing by technique 3 (7x7);
d) location of line maxima after processing by technique 4
(variant 2, 1-D prefiltering K=5, M=7);

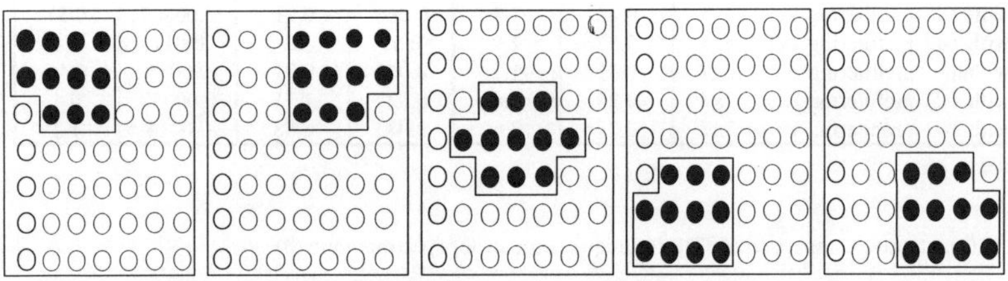

Fig.2 The substructures of $2-D$ nonlinear (hybrid) filter (7x7).

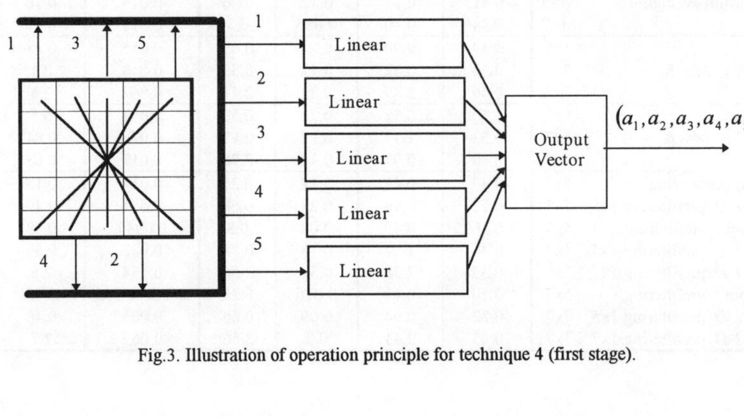

Fig.3. Illustration of operation principle for technique 4 (first stage).

Autoregressive Hidden Markov Models for Isolated Words Recognition

Evgeny I.Bovbel, Polina P.Tkacheva, Igor E.Kheidorov
Department of Radiophysics, Belarusian State University,
F.Scoriny av., 4, 220050, Minsk, BELARUS
tel. (0172) 770-890, fax (0172) 26 59 40
e-mail: ikheidorov@poboxes.com

Abstract. In this paper the autoregressive hidden Markov model was considered for the task of isolated belarusian words recognition. It was shown that for belarusian words close frames are not statistically independent in time. In this case standard hidden Markov model is not valid and has to be replaced by the autoregressive model.

Introduction

Statistical methods based on hidden Markov models find wide application to solve different practice tasks. Hidden Markov models are successfully used in automatic target recognition systems, for speaker identification and verification in secure access systems, in speech recognition systems [1,2,3]. Flexible and powerful mathematical apparatus lets to easily use them for effective temporal information modeling. But for the best results each task requires the development and designing of a hidden Markov model with special structure and parameters. Speech signal by its nature has two aspects. Firstly, speech of the person is defined by physical parameters, such as vocal tract length, glottal size and so on. Secondly, the speech producing is impossible without neural control of the articulators, which defines the personal learned abilities such as dialect or regional accents, pronunciation, speed and timing of the articulators. This two reasons find the reflection in speech signal non-linearity, and it is necessary to implement mmore or less nonlinear model. The purpose of this paper is to consider autoregressive hidden Markov models for isolated words recognition.

Autoregressive hidden Markov model

To design an autoregressive hidden Markov model (HMM) we assume:

- The given word model is presented by the sequence of elementary speech units (phones and phonemes). Discrete stationary HMM states are directly connected to the elementary speech units.
- Each word is presented by a single hidden Markov model, which described the statistical variations in word pronunciation speed.
- Acoustical signal belonged to the given word is a realization of part-stationary process (within 20-70ms intervals speech signal is assumed to be a stationary one).

Let we have M words constructed from L phonemes. Let $Q^* = \{1,2,\ldots,l,\ldots,L\}$ is a set of HMM states, which are used to build word models. The word can be modeled by the sequence of L_i discrete stationary states $q_n \in Q^*$, $L_i \le L$ with immediate transitions between states. For each word HMM defines:

a) stationary state sequence $Q = \{q_1, q_2, \ldots, q_n, \ldots, q_N\}$ which models the temporal speech structure.

b) acoustic vector sequence $O = \{O_1, O_2, \ldots, O_n, \ldots, O_N\}$ which models local-stationary properties of speech signal.

Formally the hidden Markov model for the word m, $m = 1,2,\ldots,M$, can be indexed as $\lambda_m = (\pi, A, B)$, where $A = (a_{ij}) = P(q_n = j \mid q_{n-1} = i)$ - state transition probabilities matrix with size $L_m x L_m$, $\Pi = (\pi_i) = P(q_1 = i)$ - initial probabilities matrix with size $L_m x1$. $B = \{b_j(O_n)\}$ - probability distribution of acoustic observation vector appearance at state j.

Training and decoding algorithms for usual hidden Markov models were developed in details with the following suggestions [3]:

- Hidden discrete HMM state sequence is described by the discrete 1-st order Markov chain

$$P(q_n = j \mid q_{n-1}.q_{n-2},...,q_1,O_{n-1},O_{n-2},...,O_1) =$$
$$P(q_n = j \mid q_{n-1} = i) = a_{ij}$$

- Acoustic observation vector O_n is supposed to be independent from previous vectors

$$P(O_n,q_n \mid q_{n-1},...,q_1,O_{n-1},...,O_1) = P(O_n,q_n \mid q_{n-1})$$

- Observation vector O_n is connected with state q_n only

$$P(O_n,q_n \mid q_{n-1},...,q_1,O_{n-1},...,O_1) =$$
$$P(O_n,q_n \mid q_{n-1}) = a_{ij}P(O_n \mid q_n)$$

For the considering model let suppose that the probability of acoustic vector $O_n = \{x_1, x_2,..., x_k\}$ appearance will depend on not only the state characteristics, but the relation between the speech signal characteristics x_m, $m = 1,...,k$ inside the state q_n. Let consider only linear dependence and according to [4] introduce autoregressive HMM. In this case for the acoustic vector components we can write down

$$x_n = -\sum_{k=1}^{P} a_k x_{n-k} + \sigma_n ,$$

where $a = (a_1, a_2,..., a_p)$-linear prediction coefficients, σ_i -noise dispersion.

Under these conditions we can write down

$$b_j(O_n) = \prod b_j(x_n \mid x_{n-1},...,x_{n-p}) =$$
$$\frac{1}{(2\pi\sigma_j^2)^{k/2}} exp\left\{-\frac{1}{2\sigma_j^2}\sum_{n=1}^{K}\left(x_n + \sum_{i=1}^{P} a_i^j x_{n-i}\right)^2\right\}$$

For such assumptions the training and decoding procedure of HMM are based on maximum likelihood function criteria. During training it is necessary to determine the parameters set α maximizing likelihood function for all training samples $O_j, j = 1,...,J$, connected with λ:

$$\underset{\alpha}{arg\,max} \prod_{j=1}^{J} P(O_j \mid \lambda_j, \alpha_j)$$

This is an ordinary maximum likelihood function criteria (ML-criteria). At the stage of word recognition it is necessary to find λ_m, $m = 1,2...,M$, for which $P(\lambda_m \mid \theta, \alpha)$ forms maximum for given fixed parameters set α and fixed observing set O:

$$m = \underset{\forall K}{arg\,max}\, P(O \mid \lambda_k, \alpha)$$

To solve these tasks it was developed effective algorithms, such as EM- algorithm in general case and "forward-backward" algorithm for HMM [5].

Data base and experiment

The speech data based was formed on the basis of belarusian language lexics, taking into consideration some features of belarusian pronunciation. All words are based on 17 mostly used belarusian phones (phonemes), among which 3 vowel and 14 consonant phonemes. Among vowels there are sonar (phones, which are produced by voice and noise, voice is louder then noise); звонкие (phones, which are produced by voice and noise, noise is louder then noise); глухие (phones, which are produced by noise only); свистящие.

Words are divided to blocks. First block includes verbs (152 words), which are selected to sub-blocks according to the base word. Second block contains nouns, adverbs and (48 words in total). Words are selected in manner to form sentences.

Each data base word was pronounced and recorded 10 times by 10 speakers. Recording was done with sampling frequency 11025Hz in 16-bit format and the achieved realizations were processed by digital second order filter. To form the sequence of acoustic vectors the methodic "frame-by-frame" was used with window length 30 ms and frame length 10 ms. Each signal sample was weights by Hamming function. Then linear prediction coefficients were used to estimate power spectrum according to

$$P(f) = \frac{T\rho}{\left|1 + \sum_{k=1}^{m} a[k] exp(-j2\pi fkT)\right|^2}$$

where T- sampling frequency. Coefficients ρ, a[1], a[2], ..., a[m] are determined using recursive Levinson algorithm [6] according to

$$\rho_0 = r_{xx}[0]$$
$$\Delta_m = \begin{cases} r_{xx}[1], m = 1 \\ \sum_{k=1}^{m-1} a_{m-1}[k] r_{xx}[m-k] + r_{xx}[m], m > 1 \end{cases}$$

$$a_m = \begin{cases} -\Delta_m / \rho_{m-1}, k = m \\ a_{m-1}[k] + a_m[m](a_{m-1}[m-k])^*, 1 \le k \le m-1, m > 1 \end{cases}$$

$$\rho_m = \rho_{m-1}\left(1 - |a_m[m]|^2\right)$$

Here r_{xx} - autocorrelation coefficients, ρ_m и Δ_m - help values.

The investigations of human ear perception shows that for speech recognition it is reasonable to use the transformation of linear spectrum to another scale, for example, to mel-scale according to:

$$f_{mel} = 2595 \, log_{10}\left(1 + f / 700\right).$$

As a rule, the accumulated spectrum values within the certain frequency range (channel) are used as speech parameters:

$$S_{avg} = \frac{1}{N} \sum_{n=0}^{N} \omega(f_{mel}, n) S(f_{mel}),$$

where N - number of spectral samples, $\omega(f_{mel}, n)$ - weight function.

Let S_i - spectral power of within the channel i.

Then $\{S_1, S_2, \dots, S_L\}$ - vector of speech parameters, where L- number of used channels. AFT spectrum can be estimated with any accuracy within the necessary range, that is why this method of spectrum estimation is very attractable to form mel-parameters. To increase the robustness of speech recognition we can perform the cos transformation of speech parameters. This transformation forms coefficients like the cepstral coefficients, but they are based on other principals. Thus, using the values of signal energy within the spectr range $E_i = log(S_i)^2$ we obtain the "mel-cepstr":

$$C_k = \sum_{i=1}^{L} E_i \, cos(k(i - 1/2)\pi / L), \; 1 \le k \le K,$$

where K- desired number of "mel-cepstr" values. To smooth parameters we can use the following transformation

$$W(k) = 1 + \frac{Q}{2} sin\left(\frac{\pi k}{Q}\right), \; 1 \le k \le K$$

$$\hat{C}_k = C_k W(k).$$

The obtained parameters are seemed to be robust to speech signal variations. It was found that the most optimal values are $8 \le K \le 20$. It is reasonable to use additional delta-parameters to include temporal information to speech parameter vector according to

$$\Delta\hat{C}_k(t) = \left[\sum_{m=-2}^{+2} m\hat{C}_k(t-m)G \right], \; 1 \le k \le K,$$

where t- time points, $0 \le t \le T$, usually G = *0,375*.

To form character vectors it was used K=20. During the experiment mel-cepstrums were built for all belarusian words from the data base. At fig.1 it is shown the mel-cepstrum for the belarusian word "byada". Let define k mel-cepstrum coefficient at time n as $c_k(n)$. For each $c_k(n)$, $1 \le k \le 20$ autocorrelation functions were built. At fig.2 we can see such function for k=2 in belarusian word "byada". At fig. 3 there are scatterplots for $c_2(n)$ at various lags l, $l = 0,1,4,7$. Each subplot presents $c_2(n)$ against $c_2(n+l)$. It is obvious that close frames separated up to 70 ms are not statistically independent in time. The statistical independence assumption of standard hidden Markov models is not valid and must be removed. For large models such word possibly the hybrid HMM/ neural approaches are more suitable.

References

1. H. A. Bourlard and N. Morgan Connectionist Speech recognition: A Hybrid Approach. Kluwer Academic Publishers, Boston M.A., 1994

2. L. R. Rabiner and B.H.Juang. Fundamentals of Speech Recognition. PTR Prentice Hall inc., NJ, 1993

3. L.R.Rabiner A tutorial on hidden Markov models and selected applications in speech recognition, Proc. of the IEEE, 77(2):257-286, Feb 1989.

4.B.H.Juang, L.R.Rabiner, Mixture autoregressive hidden markov models for speech signals. IEEE Trans. on Acoustic Speech and Signal Processing, ASSP-33(6):1404-1412, Dec. 1985

5. A.P.Dempster, N.M.Laird, and D.B.Rubin Maximum likelihood from incomplete data via the EM algorithm, J.Rojal Stat. Society, 39(1):1-38, 1977

6. 1. J.Picone,"Signal Modeling Techniques in Speech Recognition", Proc. of the IEEE, vol.81, No.9, Sept. 1993.

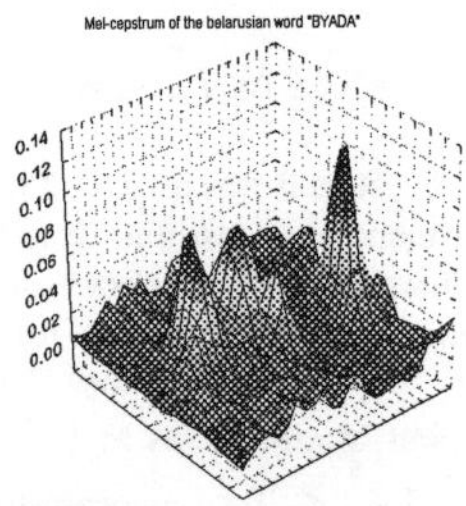

Fig.1 Mel-cepstrum of the belarusian word "BYADA"

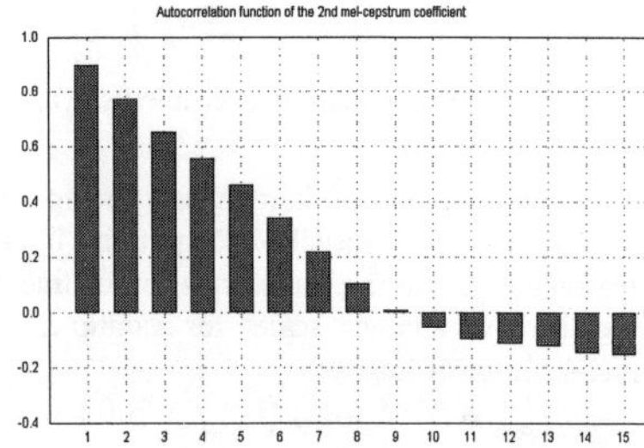

Fig.2. Autocorrelation function of the 2nd mel-cepstrum coefficient-

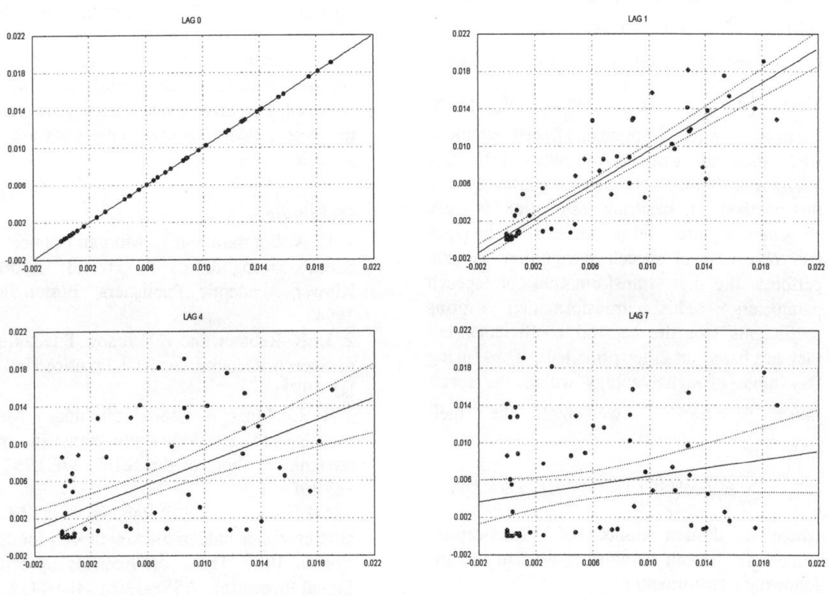

Fig.3. Scatterplot of the 2nd mel-cepstrum coefficient for lags 0,1,4 and 7.

Multiprocessor DSP system for real-time digital signal processing applications

N.-A.I.Livanos* and E.Zigouris**

Electronics Laboratory,
Division of Electronics and Computers,
Department of Physics, University of Patras

*email: nlivanos@physics.upatras.gr
**email: ez@physics.upatras.gr
fax: 3061 997456, phone:+3061 997465

Abstract

In this paper a multiprocessor system for digital signal processing applications is described. The whole system consists of two DSP modules and a microprocessor one. The DSP modules are parallel interfaced in order to achieve high data transfer rates. The microprocessor module provides an easy way to control the signal processing procedures, in applications independent from the personal computer (PC). The architecture of the system, the interconnection schemes, as well as the developed OS will be briefly presented. As a demonstration of the system a high quality audio mixer that supports equalization, echo control and mixing of two audio signals was implemented.

1. Introduction

In the last few years the development of modern Digital Signal Processing applications and algorithms is increasing rapidly. Concurrently, the processing power and the communication facilities of the modern Digital Signal Processors permit the implementation of rather complex algorithms by the interconnection of multiple processors in various network and parallel configurations. The recent DSP multi-processor systems provide the essential demands for applications in communication systems, audio processing, image processing, etc. Some of these systems are described in [2],[4],[6],[10],[11].

Most of the implementations require large host-computers (such as personal computers or workstations) in order to provide a method for reprogramming and reconfiguring the multiprocessor, as well as to provide a methodology for the control of the applications. Our effort is focused in the separation of the reprogramming and the control of the developed applications. The latter is achieved by the realization of a general-purpose compact microcontroller unit, enhanced with a user interaction methodology (LCD and keyboard), in order to support stand-alone operation.

The second development procedure was to interface DSP modules, so as to provide the desired computational power for the implementation of digital signal processing applications. For the time being two such DSP modules are interfaced. The inter-communication between these modules is based in a master-slave scheme, through a parallel data bus, so as to achieve high data transmission rates. This structure of the DSP modules is interfaced with the control system via an interconnection scheme. This interconnection is based on a FIFO buffer, which is controlled by optimized low-level software from the master DSP module. In order to improve the ability for developing digital signal processing applications a naiv (low-level) micro-kernel was implemented.

2. System Overview

The architecture of the system is depicted in Fig.1, [5]. The system can be subdivided in three parts:

- Generic microprocessor
- DSP modules
- User communication

The Development Board for Parallel System Control (DBPSC) characterizes the generic microprocessor part and the user interface. The CPU is a simple microcontroller (AT89c52), which is well suited for the control of the display (LCD) and the keyboard. The latter external devices are interfaced via special interfacing devices. The basic operations of the generic microprocessor module are the following:

- Reception and translation of data commands from the keyboard
- Transmission and reception of data to/from LCD
- Graphic display computations
- Transmission of data commands to the master DSP module

- Control of the serial communication port of the system

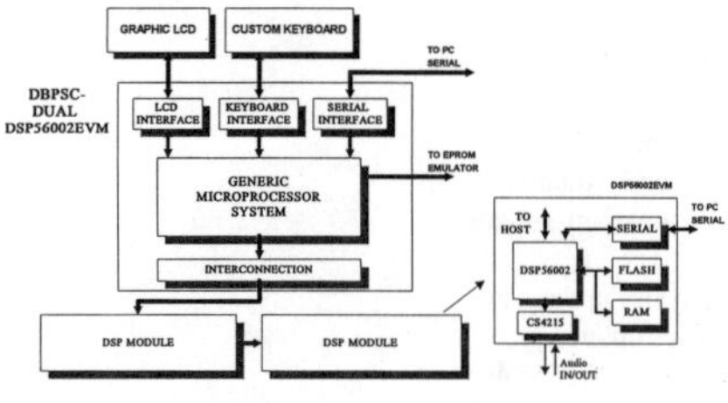

Figure 1 - Block Diagram of the DBPSC-DUAL DSP56002EVM

Up to this point the DSP56002EVM was selected as DSP module. This evaluation module is based on the Motorola 24-bit DSP56002 processor, [3]. It provides the basic demands for the development of a variety of DSP applications, especially in audio signal processing. The architecture of this platform is shown in Fig. 2.

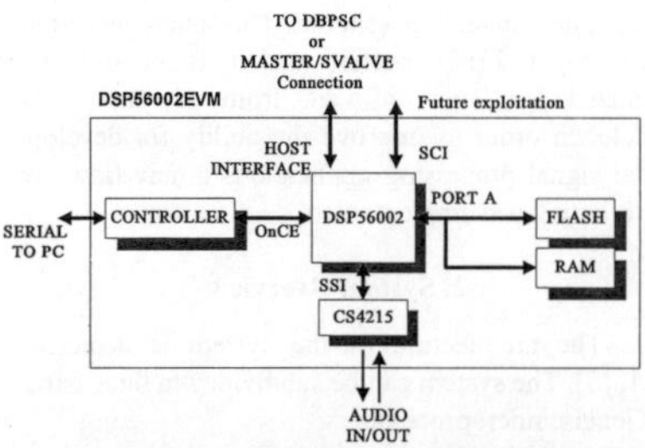

Figure 2 - DSP56002EVM architecture

The DSP56002 provides special on-chip interfacing circuits for easy connection with external modules. More specifically, the port A is utilized to interface additional external memory (RAM and ROM), port C to interface serial synchronous (codec and AD/DA Converters) and asynchronous devices and port B for the interconnection with other DSP and microprocessors. Furthermore, there is a dedicated circuit (OnCE) for real-time emulation of the processor. Except the port B, the above on-chip circuits are efficiently used in the EVM board. Port B is utilized either for the interconnection with the control system, or for the communication between the two DSPs. The interfacing and communication schemes between the devices are handled with optimized low-level software, as the DSP56002 on-chip peripherals minimize the necessity of additional external logic. The communication modes within the system are the following:

- **Command Data Transfer** - Microcontroller to master DSP data transfer
- **DSP Data Transfer** - DSP to DSP parallel data transfer
- **User Interface** - LCD and Keyboard interface, used for controlling the system
- **SSI (Synchronous Serial Interface)** - Codec and DSP synchronous serial data transfer
- **Serial link for PC** - Used for PC to board communication
- **Serial Message Passing** - Future serial exploitation for DSP communication (full-dublex)

3. Interconnection Schemes

The interconnection between the processors of the system is divided in two different schemes, [5]. The first one (Command Data Transfer) is dedicated for the data (command) passing from the control system to the master DSP module, Fig.3. The microcontroller simply sends the data command in a FIFO memory. The master DSP reads the contents of the FIFO memory in appropriate moments. It is obvious that this communication mode is unidirectional, from the microcontroller to the master DSP.

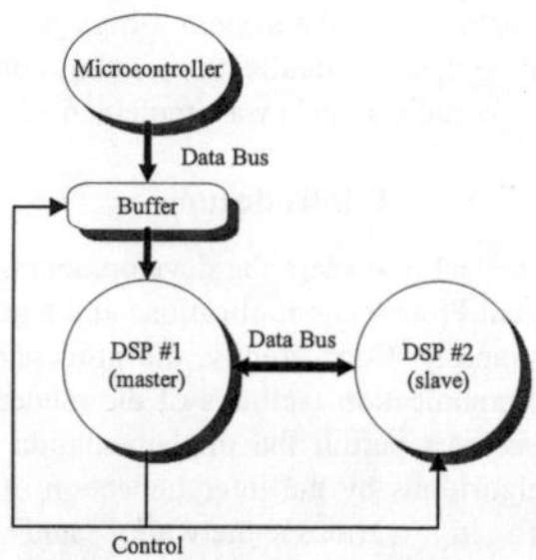

Figure 3 - DBPSI-DUAL DSP56002EVM interconnection

The two DSP units are simply interfaced in a master-slave configuration (DSP Data Transfer), Fig.3. In this scheme there is no need of external logic, as the master DSP provides the necessary control and timing signals for the communication. It is noted that the master DSP utilizes the port B as general-purpose pins. In contrast, the slave DSP utilizes the port B as Host Interface, [3], in order to simplify the communication software.

4. Operating System

The main operation of the microcontroller system is the handling of application controls, such as menus/submenus, sliders, messages, buttons, pop-up menus, etc. Every control consists of three main operations: Display, Handling and Communication. The display refers to the appearance of the controls on the liquid crystal display (LCD), the handling refers to the management of the control properties and finally the communication refers to the interface with the corresponding digital signal processing application, enabled to a specific DSP module. The operating system of the microcontroller is based on an object-oriented structure, in a way to allow efficient management of the user's controls, as well as easy development of applications, [8],[12]. The structure is depicted in Fig. 4.

The kernel of the operating system consists of two parts: low-level and application interface. The low-level part includes the basic procedures for the management of the system's resources. It is sub-divided in a multi layer structure in order to achieve modularity, and extendibility. The first layer, called "Handler", consists of the keyboard handling routines, as well as the total memory management of the system. The second layer, called "Display", includes a plethora of low-level routines for the interface and the communication with the liquid crystal display (LCD). Furthermore, some additional higher-level routines are useful for the realization of general-purpose graphical patterns and shapes, such as lines, frames, text, etc. The third layer, called "Communication", consists of low-level routines that control the interconnection logic and the interfacing with the DSP modules.

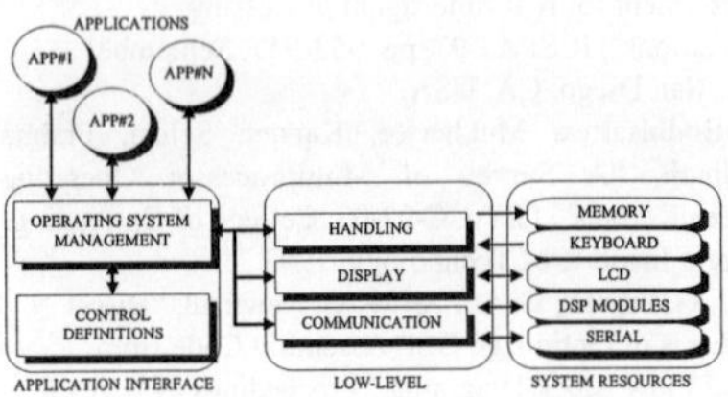

Figure 4 – Structure of the operating system for the microcontroller

The second part of the operating system is dedicated to higher-level procedures. This part essentially provides an efficient interface between the developed applications and the system's resources. It is sub-divided in two sections: the Control Definitions and the Operating System Management. The Control Definition section provides a reference basis for all the types of the developed objects. The Operating System Management is the most important section of the kernel as it performs the scheduling policy of the application's processes. Furthermore, it utilizes the Control Definition section as a reference for the run-time control objects, in means of having knowledge of the structure, the properties and the execution function of the objects.

The DSP modules compose a distributed multi-processor system. In such cases a micro-kernel operating system represents the suitable approach, [8]. It provides a transparent methodology for installing applications, as well as supports the system with the primitive operations. The micro-kernel is placed in every processing module and performs the management and communication operations through the system. More specifically, the basic operations of a micro-kernel are the process management, the synchronization, the event-handling concept and the network-wide communications.

In order to provide all the above operations in the DSP modules of the proposed system, a similar DSP real-time operating system has been developed. The structure of the operating system of the DSP modules consists of two sections, fig.5:

- Interface Section
- Management Section

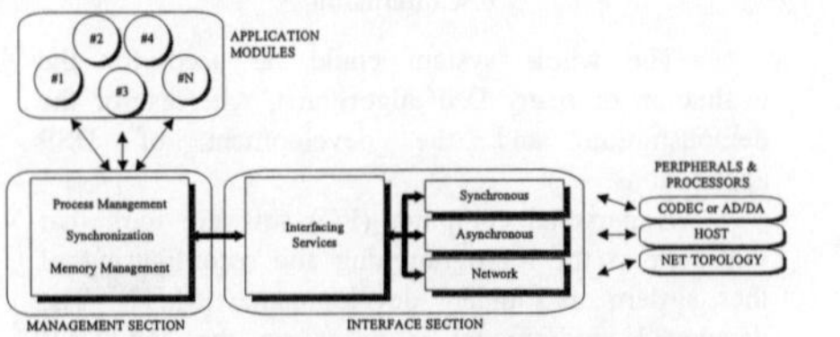

Figure 5 - Operating system structure for the DSP modules

The first section refers to the interfacing services for the external and internal peripherals, as well as the processors. This section is sub-divided in two parts: the Interfacing Services and the low-level interfacing routines. This structure aims to general-purpose utilization, as the first part is developed in high-level language. The low-level interfacing routines are developed in low-level language, in respect with the selected processor and the hardware interface. The Interfacing services currently support simple communications schemes, such as pipes and packets.

The second section refers to the management operations. These are the process management, the synchronization and the memory management. The above operations are currently under research. It is desired to support various static-scheduling policies, as well as priority based, preemptive, and time sliced scheduling. For the memory management it is investigated a method to swap large memory block, between on-chip and off-chip memory, in order to reduce the memory access overhead.

5. Demonstration Application

As a demonstration application a stereo audio signal mixer was implemented, [5]. It is a high quality audio processing application that supports 10-band stereo equalization for both audio signal, as well as echo control for every one of the ten bands. In Fig.6 the flow chart of the procedures for every DSP module is depicted. The codec of every EVM board receives the audio signal. The main processing parts are the equalization and the echo part. Then the master DSP module sends the processed audio data to the slave DSP for the appropriate signal mixing. Finally the audio data is transmitted to the codec of the slave DSP, in order to form the desired output audio signal.

A graphical environment has been developed at the DBPSC system for the control of the application. The user can easily select to control either the equalization, or the echo in every of the two input audio signals. The control commands are transmitted to the master DSP. After receiving the commands there is a dedicated application part in the master DSP that decodes and executes the commands.

6. Conclusion

The whole system could be used for the evaluation of many DSP algorithms, whereas for the demonstration and the development of DSP applications.

A personal computer (PC) software tool, that will support the reprogramming and reconfiguring of the system is under development, [9],[1]. The developed environment is based on the MATLAB software platform, as the latter provides many DSP design capabilities, [7].

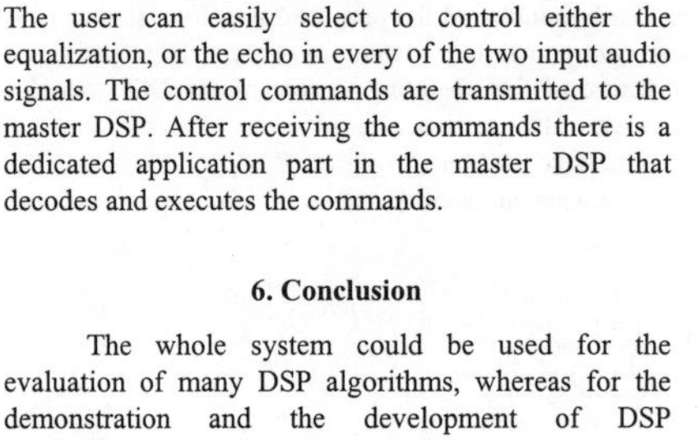

Figure 6 - Flowchart for the audio mixer operations in the DSP modules

References

[1] Shuvra S. Bhattacharyya, Sundararajan Sriram, and Edward A. Lee, "Optimizing Synchronization in Multiprocessor DSP Systems", IEEE Transactions on Signal Processing, vol.45, no.6, June 1997

[2] V.Michael Bove, Jr. And John A.Watlington, "Cheops: A Reconfigurable Data-Flow System for Video Processing", IEEE Transactions on Circuits and Systems for Video Technology, 5, April 1995, pp.140-149.

[3] DSP56002 User's manual, Motorola, 1993

[4] Anton Gunzinger, Urs A. Muller, Walter Scott, Bernhard Baumle, Peter Kohler, Hansruedi Vonder Muhll, Florian Muller-Plathe, Wilfried F. Van Gunsteren, and Walter Guggenbuhl, "Achieving super computer performance with a DSP array processor", In Robert Werner, editor, Supervomputing 92, pages 543-550, Loas Alamitos, California, November 16-20, 1992, Minneapolis, Minesote 1992. IEEE/ACM, IEEE Computer Society Press

[5] N.-A.I.Livanos, "Multiprocessor system for DSP applications", Electronics Lab, Division of Electronics and Computers, University of Patras, MSc Thesis (in Greek), Jan.1998, Patras, Greece.

[6] N.-A.I.Livanos, E.Zigouris, "A multi - DSP system for pipeline real-time applications", Accepted to be presented in ICSPAT98, Torondo, Canada

[7] Nikolaos-Antonios I. Livanos,Panagiotis D. Papadimitriou, Evangelos Zigouris, "An open software environment for real-time signal processing applications", ICSPAT'97, pp. 953-957, September 1997, San Diego, CA, USA.

[8] Bodhisattwa Mukherjee, Karsten Schan, Prabha Gopinath, "A Survey of Multiprocessor Operating System Kernels", GIT-CC-92/05, College of Computing, Georgia Institute of Technology, 1993

[9] D. G. Powell, E. A. Lee, W. C. Newman, "Direct Synthesis of Optimized DSP Assembly Code from Signal Flow Block Diagrams," Proceedings of ICASSP, San Francisco, March, 1992.

[10] M. Rosenthal, M. Klebl, A. Gunzinger, G. Tr ster. A Freely Configurable Audio-Mixing Engine with Automatic Loadbalancing. In 98th AES Convention, Paris. AES Convention Preprint I5, 1995

[11] Peter Schulz, "A multi-DSP interconnection structure for real-time applications", Proc. ICSPAT 95, pp. 1319-1323, Boston, USA, October 1995

[12] Steven Vercauteren, Bill Lin, Hugo De Man, "A Strategy for Real-Time Kernel Support in Application-Specific HW/SW Embedded Architectures", ACM/IEEE Design Automation Conference, June 1996

STRUCTURE SELECTION OF SEMI-LINEAR SYSTEMS WITH SIGNAL-DEPENDENT PARAMETERS

J.-Y. DIEULOT, H. BAUSSART
APAB, IAAL, bat C6, Cité Scientifique, 59650 Villeneuve d'Ascq, France,
dieulot@univ-lille1.fr

Abstract

The identification of "linear" systems with signal-dependent parameters is performed using Euler approximation; the variance of the continuous time equation parameters can be derived from the variances of the discretized equation parameters. A criterion is found that can be used for model selection. This criterion is compared with the criterion AIC_4.

Introduction

The paper deals with the identification of a "linear" system with signal-dependent parameters; this class of models has been developed in (Haber and Keviczky, 1985). It consists in a linear input-output differential equation, where each parameter (gain, time constant,...) depends on a computable or measurable variable $x(t)$ (e.g. a first-order equation where the time constant is a function of $x(t)$).
This representation allows to describe non-linear systems in a handy fashion for users familiar with the linear systems theory. It makes possible to use linear identification and control methods (Haber and Unbehauen, 1990), and avoids to use complex methods such as Volterra series. Parameters depend on a signal $x(t)$, which can be time-varying, or be characterised by a change or a change in direction of another signal. The model is thus a tool which may represent the "changes" of the parameters of a linear system with respect to the change of set-points, or with respect to the action of an internal variable. Further, it can be of a help to understand a change in regime of a process where parameters evolve according to physical conditions, as pointed out in (Haber et al, 1987).

A polynomial static dependence of the signal $x(t)$ is assumed for the expression of the parameters of the differential equation.
Previous identification procedures have shown that using Euler or bilinear approximation for the discretisation of the differential equation yields a difference equation linear in the parameters (Haber and Keviczky, 1985). This is an advantage over other sampling methods: a non linear regression can be performed to obtain an estimation of the discrete parameters. The parameters of the difference equation are signal dependent, and can be easily derived from the parameters of the continuous differential equation. The reverse relation is given for example in (Roostgaard et al., 1993). This relation allows the computation of the continuous parameters, the identification of the discrete parameters being performed with a LS algorithm. Another method proposed for the determination the parameters (Haber and Keviczky, 1985) is the use of steps of small amplitude, identification of the dynamic parameters with graphoanalytical methods and static regression to determine the polynomials; this method requires a long identification procedure and needs to quantize the input.
If the signal $x(k\text{-}1)$ (the sampling time will be kT, where T is defined as the sampling period) is a combination of previous inputs or outputs, the model can be seen as a polynomial NARMAX model (Leontaritis and Billings, 1985). This model is shown to be able to approximate a wide class of non linear systems; the estimated degrees of the polynomials depend on the required approximation accuracy (Chen and Billings, 1989).

In the first section of the paper, the relation between continuous and discrete parameters for a polynomial signal-dependent parameters model is recalled.
The second section deals with the determination of the model structure and the validation of the model.
A subclass of previous systems, where parameters of the differential equation are signal dependent within an interval of the values of the variable $x(t)$, and are constant outside this interval, is considered. The polynomial variation realises a continuous transition between the lower bound and the upper bound parameters values. Within the interval where the parameters are signal-dependent, the associated difference equation components will be products of the powers of the signal $x(t)$ and of the input and output signals.
Among all possible components that can be entered in the model, only the most significant should be selected, which may be performed using several statistical tests (Freeman, 1985), or spectral analysis (Roostgaard et al, 1994, Aguirre et al., 1997). AIC_4 (Modified Aikake's Information Criterion) seems to be a good experimental criterion (Leontaritis and Billings, 1987), which will be used to determine the order of the piecewise linear parts. Experimental comparison studies (Kortmann and Unbehauen, 1988, Kortmann et al., 1988 ; Freeman, 1985) show nevertheless that the use of only one criterion among the most popular, is not sufficient to validate a model. An additional criterion to AIC_4 can be provided by comparing the variances of the continuous parameters at the boundaries of the interval, for several structures with the same differential equation order but with different polynomial degrees. This will allow to determine the

best degrees for the polynomials. These variances will be calculated, given the discrete parameter covariance matrix, using the results of section 1.

Relation between continuous and discrete systems via Euler approximation

A "linear" dynamic system with signal-dependent parameters consists in a differential linear equation where the parameters are considered as a static function of a measurable or computable signal (Haber and Keviczky, 1985). We will consider for the sake of simplicity a all-pole equation.

A polynomial static function is assumed for the parameters so that the equation of the model can be written as:

$$\sum_{i=0}^{i=n} P_i(x(t))y^{(i)}(t) = P_u(u(t)), \qquad (1)$$

where $x(t)$ is a signal , n is the order of the "linear" equation, $y^{(i)}(t)$ is the nth derivative of the output $y(t)$, $u(t)$ is the input, and the P_i are polynomials defined by :

$P_i(x) = \sum_{j=0}^{d_i} p_{i,j}x^j$. Let us define $d = \max(d_i)$, where d_i is the degree of polynomial P_i, so that we can write

$$P_i(x) = \sum_{i=0}^{d} a_{i,j}x^j. \qquad (2)$$

If the parameters are signal-dependent as in (2), it is shown in (Haber and Unbehauen, 1985) that, using methods such as Euler or bilinear approximation for the discretisation of the differential equation, a difference equation non linear in the variables, but linear in the parameters, is obtained. The regressors are chosen to be products of $u(k\text{-}1)$, $y(k)$, $y(k\text{-}1)$, $y(k\text{-}2)$,..., and of the successive powers of $x(k\text{-}1)$. If $P_0(x) \neq a_{0,0}$, the model will not be predictive. The equation being linear in the parameters, an unbiased estimation of the parameters can be provided with a LS algorithm -white noise is assumed to affect the output- (Ljung, 1987). The Z-transform does not lead to a difference equation linear in the parameters. With Euler or bilinear approximations, the parameters of the difference equation are each a linear combination of the continuous time parameters (Haber and Keviczky, 1985). This can be written :

$$\sum_{i=0}^{n}\left(\sum_{j=0}^{d} \alpha_{i,j}x^j(k-1)y(k-i)\right) = P_u(u(k-1)), \qquad (3)$$

where $\alpha_{i,j}$ are the discrete equation parameters.

Several methods can be applied to estimate the parameters of the difference equation, among them :

- use "gate functions" which interpolate non-linear functions (Haber and Keviczky, 1985); the input signal is approximated by stepwise constant values; the choice of the gate functions can be complex and the system has to be linearised and identified at different operating points;

- use step-response identification and graphoanalytical methods, which is interesting for industrial processes (Haber et al., 1987), to estimate the parameters for different values of $x(t)$; polynomial interpolation or a regression can be used to determine the parameters of polynomials P_i, using relation (2). This method is quite straightforward but requires many identification experiments.

- see equation (3) as a non-linear difference equation, which is linear in the parameters; the regressors are non-linear functions of the input and output variables, and of $x(k\text{-}1)$; parameters estimation can be solved by an appropriate linear regression method such as Least Squares (Haber and Unbehauen, 1990).

We will use the Euler backward approximation to discretise equation (1), for a purpose of simplicity, i.e.

$$s = \frac{d}{dt}(.) = \frac{1-q^{-1}}{T}, \qquad (4)$$

where T is the sampling time and q is the forward operator, s is the Laplace operator..

This approximation is shown to be exact for $s = 0$ and good for $s = j\omega$, where $\omega << \frac{1}{T}$ (Goodwin and Middleton, 1990).

Equation (1) can be put under the form given by equation (3), the correspondence between the discrete parameters $\alpha_{i,j}$ and the continuous parameters $a_{i,j}$ is given by (Roostgaard et al, 1994):

$$\alpha_{i,j} = \sum_{l=i}^{n} \frac{a_{l,j}}{T^l} C_l^i (-l)^i, \quad \text{for} \quad i \geq 2,$$

$$\alpha_{1,j} = -\sum_{l=1}^{n} \frac{a_{l,j}}{T^l} C_l^1 + a_{0,j}, \quad \alpha_{0,j} = \sum_{l=0}^{n} \frac{a_{l,j}}{T^l} - a_{0,j}. \qquad (5)$$

We have from the Euler equation :

$$\frac{dy}{dt} = \frac{y(k) - y(k-1)}{T} \qquad (6)$$

and

$$y^{(i)}(t) = \sum_{l=0}^{i} \frac{C_i^l y(k-l)(-l)^l}{T^i}. \qquad (7)$$

Remarking that the equivalence of $y(t)$ is $y(k\text{-}1)$, equation (1) can be discretised and written as:

$$\sum_{i=1}^{n}\left(\sum_{j=0}^{d} a_{i,j}x^{j}(k-1)\right)\sum_{l=0}^{i}\frac{C_i^l y(k-l)(-1)^l}{T^i}= \quad (8)$$
$$P_u(u(k-1))-P_0(y(k-1)).$$

Polynomials in (4) and (8) are identical, it is trivial that the term in $\alpha_{i,j}$ will be as given in (5).

The $a_{i,j}$ are given as the following equation :

$$\frac{a_{i,j}}{T^i}(-1)^i=\sum_{m=i}^{n}\alpha_{m,j}C_m^i\ , \text{ for } i\neq 1, \quad (9)$$

$$-\frac{a_{1,j}}{T}=\sum_{m=1}^{n}\alpha_{m,j}C_m^1-a_{0,j}\,. \quad (10)$$

We can write : $1-Ts=q^{-1}$

Replacing in (3), we have :

$$\sum_{i=1}^{n}\left(\sum_{j=0}^{d}\alpha_{i,j}x^j(1-Ts)^i(y)\right)=P_u(u)-P_0(y),$$

$$\sum_{i=1}^{n}\left(\sum_{j=0}^{d}\alpha_{i,j}x^j\left(\sum_{l=0}^{i}C_i^l(Ts)^l(-1)^l\right)(y)\right)=$$
$$P_u(u)-P_0(y)$$

the term in $x^j s^i(y)$ is given by :

$$\sum_{l=i}^{n}\alpha_{l,j}C_l^i(T)^i(-1)^i\,.$$

We have to correct this for i = 1, for which we obtain, as $y(t)$ is discretised in $y(k\text{-}1)$:

$$a_{1,j}=\sum_{l=1}^{n}-\alpha_{l,j}C_l^1(T)+a_{0,j}\,.$$

For i = 0, the terms in $\pm a_0$ compensates in the expressions of α_1 and α_0 such that the general formula can be used.

This formula allows to get directly the continuous parameters from the discrete parameters which can be identified with a non-linear regression.

Model validation

Since the continuous equation parameters can be computed from the difference equation parameters, classical validation techniques for discrete time non linear equations can be used. Yet, it does not take possible available information on the continuous system parameters into account.

We want to study the special case where equation (1) represents a transition between two phases; the process can be described by a differential equation, with constant parameters θ_1 if $x(t)$ is above a threshold s_1, with parameters θ_2 if $x(t)$ is below a threshold s_2 , and a by "linear" equation with polynomial signal-dependent parameters in the interval $]s_1,s_2[$:

$$\begin{cases}\sum_{i=0}^{i=n}\theta_i^1 y^{(i)}(t)=k_1u(t) \text{ if } x(t)\geq s_1, & (11a)\\ \sum_{i=0}^{i=n}P_i(x(t))y^{(i)}(t)=P_u(u(t)) \text{ if } s_2<x(t)<s_1, & (11b)\\ \sum_{i=0}^{i=n}\theta_i^2 y^{(i)}(t)=k_2u(t) \text{ if } x(t)\leq s_2. & (11c)\end{cases}$$

We suppose that the parameters variation is continuous so that :

$$\forall i,\ \ P_i(s_1)=\theta_i^1,\ \ P_i(s_2)=\theta_i^2\,. \quad (12)$$

Model validation of linear in parameters systems (linear or not in the variables) has been intensively considered in the literature (Ljung, 1987). Using the Euler approximation, the equivalent difference equation will be a linear combination of the powers of several variables as in equation (3) (where regressors are combinations of $u(k)$, $y(k\text{-}1)...y(k\text{-}n)$, and of the powers of $x(k\text{-}1)$). Only the significant components among all possible have to be selected. The discrete model should be accurate enough without suffering from overparametrisation.

A first class of validation tests is based on residuals; the use of the criterion AIC_4 seems to be a good experimental choice for the validation of a model as recommended in Leontaritis and Billings (1987). It should avoid overparametrisation. We recall that :

$$AIC_4=N\,log(\hat{\sigma}^2)+4p, \quad (13)$$

where N is the number of data points, $\hat{\sigma}^2$ is the estimated residuals variance and p the number of parameters.

A first step in the identification procedure is to use this criterion for the selection of the order of equations (11a) and (11c). It can be remarked that the transition part differential equation order (equation 11b) has been chosen to be the same than that of (11a) and (11c), so that a comparison can be made between these equations.

The problem will now be to find the appropriate degrees d_i of the polynomials P_i defined in equations (1) or (11b).

A second step is to perform regressions for a range of models with different values of d (which is the maximum of degrees d_i.). The components in the equivalent difference equation are products of previous values of u and y and of $x(k\text{-}1)^j$, j ranging from 0 to d. A preliminary test is to check the model components with a partial F-test and to discard some of them.

From a comparison study in (Kortmann and Unbehauen, 1988, Kortmann et al., 1988), it is recalled that the overall F-test may lead to overparametrisation; many other criteria based on the residuals are investigated. The conclusion, drawn from simulations, is that several tests have to be applied to validate the possible structure of a model. The choice of the model should not be entirely based on the variance of residuals, but also on the parameter covariance matrix that brings information on the parsimony of the model (Ljung, 1987). It is pointed out in (Freeman, 1985) that one should be careful with criteria derived from the use of this matrix.
Another validation method is based on term clusters : similar terms (supposed to yield the same dynamical properties) are grouped together and a selection is performed on clusters with the help of correlation methods [Aguirre, 1997].
The idea is to give an additional acceptance criterion on the value of the continuous parameters for the validation of system (11b). A gaussian distribution of noise is assumed. The outputs in (11a), (11b), (11c) should have the same variance, and parameters values of (11a) and (11b), and (11b) and (11c) should be the same at the boundaries s_1 and s_2. The quality of the estimation of parameters in (11b) should be comparable to that obtained in (11a) and (11c).
The variance of the linear models parameters and the non-linear ones will thus be compared. The calculus of the variances of parameters $a_{i,j}$ will use the discrete parameters covariance matrix. The criterion will be shown to be :

$$\forall k = 1..2,\quad \forall i, j,\quad (s_k)^{2j}\,\mathrm{var}\big(a_{i,j}\big) \le \frac{2\lambda\,\mathrm{var}(\theta_i^k)}{\big((d_i+1)(d_i+2)\big)} \tag{14}$$

This will lead to compare the values

$$D_{ijk} = \frac{(s_k)^{2j}\,var\big(a_{i,j}\big)\big((d_i+1)(d_i+2)\big)}{2}.$$

Systems (11a) and (11c) are linear systems and an estimate of the parameters of the equivalent linear difference equation is given by the LS algorithm. Moreover, an estimate of the discrete parameters covariance matrix is given by (Ljung, 1987) :

$$\mathrm{cov}(\Theta_N) = \lambda_0\left(\Phi_N\Phi_N^T\right)^{-1}, \tag{15a}$$

where N is the number of measures, Φ_N the matrix of regressors , λ_0 the variance of the residuals, Θ_N the estimated discrete parameters.

An unbiased estimator of λ_0 is given (assuming white noise) by :

$$\lambda_N = \frac{1}{N-\dim(\Theta)}\sum_{j=1}^{N}\left(Y_i - \Theta_N^T\varphi_i\right)^2, \tag{15b}$$

where Y is the output, φ_i is the regressor at time i.
In order to accept the model, we want that the parameter estimation in (11b) be comparable to that in (11a) or (11c), that is to say that the variance of the estimated value $P_i(s_k)$ is comparable to that of the θ_i^k. The variance of parameters of the equivalent difference equation are found by equation (15a) and (15b). The variance of both the continuous parameters θ_i^k and the $P_i(s_k)$ can be calculated with formula (10). This gives a condition on the variance of the continuous parameters $a_{i,j}$.

Using (12), the criterion can be put under the form :

$$\forall k = 1..2,\quad \forall i > 0,\quad var\big(P_i(s_k)\big) \le \lambda\, var(\theta_i^k),$$

where λ is a chosen value, which is equivalent to :

$$\forall k = 1..2,\quad \forall i > 0,$$
$$\mathrm{var}\left(\sum_{j=0}^{d_i} a_{i,j}(s_k)^j\right) \le \lambda\,\mathrm{var}(\theta_i^k) \tag{17}$$

The variance of the $a_{i,j}$ can be expressed with equation (10) as :

$$var\left(\frac{a_{i,j}}{T^i}(-1)^i\right) = var\left(\sum_{m=i}^{n}\alpha_{m,j}C_m^i\right). \tag{18}$$

The $\alpha_{m,j}$ can be considered as random variables, though not independent.
We thus have:

$$\frac{1}{T^{2i}}\mathrm{var}\big(a_{i,j}\big) = \sum_{m=i}^{n}\mathrm{var}\big(\alpha_{m,j}C_m^i\big) + 2\sum_{m=i}^{n}\sum_{l>m}\mathrm{cov}\big(\alpha_{m,j}C_m^i, \alpha_{l,j}C_l^i\big), \tag{19}$$

which leads to :

$$\mathrm{var}\big(a_{i,j}\big) = T^{2i}\left(\begin{array}{l}\sum_{m=i}^{n}\left(C_m^i\right)^2\mathrm{var}\big(\alpha_{m,j}\big) + \\ 2\sum_{m=i}^{n}C_m^i\sum_{l>m}C_l^i\,\mathrm{cov}\big(\alpha_{m,j},\alpha_{l,j}\big)\end{array}\right).$$

(20)

The variance of the $a_{i,j}$ can be obtained given the covariance matrix of the $\alpha_{m,j}$ (calculated with formulas (15a) and (15b)).
Assuming that the s_k are perfectly known so that $\mathrm{var}(s_k) = 0$, equation (17) can be transformed into :

$$\forall k = 1...2, \quad \forall i > 0,$$
$$\sum_{j=0}^{d_i} (s_k)^{2j} \mathrm{var}\left(a_{i,j}\right) + \sum_{j=0}^{d_i} (s_k)^j \sum_{l>j} (s_k)^l \mathrm{cov}\left(a_{i,j}, a_{i,l}\right)$$
$$\leq \lambda \, \mathrm{var}(\theta_i^k) \tag{21}$$

which gives the sufficient condition :

$$\forall k = 1...2, \quad \forall i > 0,$$
$$\sum_{j=0}^{d_i} \sum_{l>j} (s_k)^j (s_k)^l \sqrt{\mathrm{var}\left(a_{i,j}\right)} \sqrt{\mathrm{var}\left(a_{i,l}\right)} + . \tag{22}$$
$$\sum_{j=0}^{d_i} (s_k)^{2j} \mathrm{var}\left(a_{i,j}\right) \leq \lambda \, \mathrm{var}(\theta_i^k)$$

A strong sufficient condition on the value of the a_{ij}s' that fulfils equation (22) is:

$$\forall k = 1...2, \quad \forall i > 0, \forall j,$$
$$\left((d_i + 1) + \frac{(d_i + 1)d_i}{2}\right)(s_k)^{2j} \mathrm{var}\left(a_{i,j}\right) \leq \lambda \, \mathrm{var}(\theta_i^k) \tag{23}$$

yielding :

$$\forall k = 1...2, \quad \forall i > 0, \forall j,$$
$$(s_k)^{2j} \mathrm{var}\left(a_{i,j}\right) \leq \frac{2\lambda \, \mathrm{var}(\theta_i^k)}{\left((d_i + 1)(d_i + 2)\right)} \tag{24}$$

The condition in (24) is quite strong; it is nevertheless possible to compare the amplitudes of the variances of the $a_{i,j}$ that is to say to compare the values of the $D_{i,j,k}$ defined by:

$$\forall k = 1...2, \quad \forall i, j,$$
$$D_{i,j,k} = \frac{(s_k)^{2j} \mathrm{var}\left(a_{i,j}\right)\left((d_i + 1)(d_i + 2)\right)}{2}. \tag{25}$$

The following procedure is undertaken for the determination of the model: the linear model order is determined thanks to criterion AIC_4. The transition phase differential equation order is chosen to be the same than the linear model order. Regression is then performed for different values of the d_i. The variance of the of the $a_{i,j}$ are computed with formula (20). The D_{ijk} are computed with formula (25) and then compared to each other. The model selected should have the lower D_{ijk}s. A comparison is then given with criterion AIC_4.

Example

The real system is the following :

$$\begin{cases} 210y^{(2)}(t) + 24\dot{y}(t) + y(t) = u(t) \\ \qquad \text{if} \quad u(t) \geq 1 \quad \text{or} \quad u(t) \leq -1, \\ \left(75u(t)^2 + 135\right)y^{(2)}(t) + 24\dot{y}(t) + y(t) = u(t). \\ \qquad \text{if} \quad -1 < u(t) < 1, \end{cases} \tag{26}$$

We choose $T = 1$, so that the equation be transformed into :

$$\begin{cases} 159y(k) - 293y(k-1) + 135y(k-2) = u(k-1) \;, \\ \qquad \text{if} \quad u(t) \geq 1 \;\; or \;\; u(t) \leq -1, \\ \left(75u^2(k-1) + 159\right)y(k) - \left(150u^2(k-1) + 293\right)y(k-1) \\ + \left(75u^2(k-1) + 135\right)y(k-2) = u(k-1) \\ \qquad \text{if} \quad -1 < u(t) < 1. \end{cases} \tag{27}$$

Small noise is added on $y(t)$. Models with a differential equation of order 2 are proposed. The values tried for d_i range from 1 to 4. For models with $d_i > 1$, the use of the partial F-test shows that the terms in $u(k-1)y(k)$ and $u^3(k-1)y(k)$ are non significant. 3 models are thus compared, M_1, M_2 and M_3, with $d_i = 1$, $d_i = 2$ and $d_i = 4$, defined as:

$$\begin{cases} \left(\alpha_{0,1}u(k-1) + \alpha_{0,0}\right)y(k) + \left(\alpha_{1,1}u(k-1) + \alpha_{1,0}\right)y(k-1) \\ + \left(\alpha_{2,1}u(k-1) + \alpha_{2,0}\right)y(k-2) = K_1 u(k-1) \qquad : M_1 \\ \left(\beta_{1,2}u(k-1) + \beta_{1,0}\right)y(k-1) + \left(\beta_{0,2}u(k-1)^2 + \beta_{0,0}\right)y(k) \\ + \left(\beta_{2,2}u(k-1) + \beta_{2,0}\right)y(k-2) = K_2 u(k-1) \qquad : M_2 \\ \left(\gamma_{0,4}u(k-1) + \gamma_{0,2}u(k-1) + \gamma_{0,0}\right)y(k) + \\ \left(\gamma_{1,4}u(k-1) + \gamma_{1,2}u(k-1) + \gamma_{1,0}\right)y(k-1) \qquad : M_3 \\ + \left(\gamma_{2,4}u(k-1) + \gamma_{2,2}u(k-1) + \gamma_{2,0}\right)y(k-2) = K_3 u(k-1). \end{cases}$$

Since the values of the parameters are the same for $s_1 = 1$ and $s_2 = -1$, we have $D_{ij1} = D_{ij2} = D_{ij}$. The values of the D_{ij} are given in Table 1 :

	M_1	M_2	M_3
D_{01}	2.10^{-8}	X	X
D_{02}	X	$3.7.\ 10^{-7}$	$1.7.10^{-8}$
D_{04}	X	$3.7.\ 10^{-7}$	X
D_{10}	3.10^{-6}	$4.9.\ 10^{-6}$	$1.8.\ 10^{-6}$

D_{11}	$5.6.10^{-6}$	X	X
D_{12}	X	$1.5.\ 10^{-4}$	6.10^{-6}
D_{14}	X	$1.3.\ 10^{-4}$	X
D_{20}	3.10^{-6}	$5.1\ 10^{-6}$	$1.8.10^{-6}$
D_{21}	1.10^{-4}	X	X
D_{22}	X	4.10^{-3}	$1.7\ 10^{-4}$
D_{24}	X	3.110^{-3}	X
AIC_4	$-3.2.\ 10^{4}$	-35154	-35185

Table 1 Values of the D_{ijk} for models M_1, M_2 and M_3

It can be seen from Table 1 that the D_{ij} in M_1 and M_2 are comparable. M_3 is discarded. It can be seen from results in (Kortmann et al., 1988) that the difference in the value of the AIC_4 criterion for the true model (M_2), and a little more complex model (M_3) is not very important. In our case, M_1 should be discarded by the value of the criterion AIC_4. The two approaches are thus complementary as the parameter variance approach discards more complex models, and AIC_4 discards too complex and too simple models.

Conclusion

A "linear" with polynomial signal dependent parameters has been discretised using Euler approximation. The procedure for the validation of a model where parameters are signal dependent within a range of values of the signal and constant outside has been performed in three steps. A first step is a classical determination of the constant parameter model order. The order of the signal-dependent differential equation is chosen to be the same as the constant parameter part. A second step is the selection of components to enter in the model which is performed with the use of a partial F-test. As pointed out, this approach may not be sufficient and an additional criterion is provided which compares the values of the parameters variances. This provides a tool which is used, along with an AIC_4 criterion, to determine the degrees of the polynomials. The continuous parameters variances are deducted from the discrete parameters covariance matrix.

References

Aguirre L.A., "On the Structure of Nonlinear Polynomial Models : Higher Order Correlation Functions, Spectra, and Term Clusters », IEEE Trans. Circ. And Systems, I, **44**, 450-453, (1997).

Chen S., and S.A. Billings, "Representations of Non-Linear Systems: the NARMAX Model", Int. J. Control, **49**, 1013-1032, (1989).

Freeman T.G., "Selecting the Best Linear Transfer Function Model", Automatica, **22**, 543-554, (1986).

Haber R., and L. Keviczky, "Identification Of "Linear" Systems Having Signal Dependent Parameters", Int. J. Syst Sci., **16**, 869-884, (1985).

Haber R., and H. Unbehauen, "Structure Identification Of Nonlinear Dynamic Systems-A Survey On Input-Output Approaches", Automatica, **26**, 651-677, (1990).

Haber R., L. Keviczky, M. Hilger, "Modelling And Identification Of A Cement Mill By A "Linear" System Model With Signal Dependent Parameters", in Applied Modelling and Identification of Technology Systems, P. Borne and S.G. Tzafestas Editors, Elsevier Science, 17-23, (1987).

Kortmann M., and H. Unbehauen, "Structure Detection in the Identification of Non Linear Systems", APII **22**, 5-25, (1988).

Kortmann M., K. Janiszowski, and H. Unbehauen, "Application and Comparison of Different Identification Schemes Under Industrial Conditions", Int. J. of Control, (1988).

Leontaritis I.J., and S.A. Billings, "Input-Output Parametric Models for Non Linear Systems, Part I: Deteministic Non Linear Systems; Part II: Stochastic Non Linear Systems", Int. J. Control, **41**, 303-344, (1985).

Leontaritis I.J., and S.A. Billings, "Model Selection and Validation for Non Linear Systems ", Int. J. Control, **45**, 311-341, (1987).

Ljung L. "System Identification: Theory For the User", Prentice Hall, (1987).

Middleton R.H. and G.C. Goodwin, "Digital Control and Estimation", Prentice Hall, (1990).

Roostgaard M., N.K. Poulster, O. Ravn, "A Rapproachment Between Discrete-Time Operators", Proc. ECC Conference, Grenoble, France, vol 2, 426-431, (1993).

Roostgaard M., N.K. Poulster, O. Ravn, "Spectral Factorisation Using Delta Operator", Systems Control Letters, **22**, 293-301, (1994).

Adaptive Event Recognition with the use of Limited Training Data

Georgios Paliouras[+] [•] and David S. Brée
Computer Science Department
University of Manchester
Oxford Road
Manchester, M13 9PL
UK

Abstract: This paper presents a novel event recognition system, which is capable of adapting itself to improve its performance on a small set of training data. The event recognition system is represented by a network of events, related to each other by temporal constraints. This symbolic representation is particularly suitable to the treatment of overlapping events, which have been overlooked in most of the work on event recognition. Additionally, a method for refining the temporal parameters of the recognition system is presented here. The method uses a small set of preclassified training examples to improve the performance of the system. The principle of minimal model change is used to overcome the sparseness of the training data. Particular emphasis is given to the issue of multiple positive examples, which is prevalent when allowing overlapping events. The new system has been applied to the thematic analysis of humpback whale songs with encouraging results.

Keywords: learning, adaptive systems, event recognition, network models

1. Introduction

The fascinating properties of the sounds emitted by humpback whales have attracted the attention of marine biologists during the past few decades. The usual method of analysis of the song is by examination of the spectrogram of a recording. A spectrogram is a plot of the acoustic signal in the frequency domain. It depicts the frequency components of the uttered sounds, as acquired by a Fourier transformation, against time. Figure 1 shows a piece of such a spectrogram. The basic sounds identifiable in the spectrogram and separated by silence are called *units*. In order to aid the analysis of the song, experts in the field have developed a hierarchical model which groups units into *subphrases*, *phrases* and *themes* [Payn71,Payn83]. Phrases and themes are identified in Figure 1.

The hierarchical model of the humpback whale song allows the identification and comparison of song components in different recordings. This is an instance of the class of *event recognition* tasks, which are the subject of this paper. The song components, i.e., units, subphrases, phrases and themes, are the events and recognition is achieved by applying the song model to the recording. Similar tasks occur in a variety of domains, ranging from speech recognition [Rabi89,Waib90,Lipp90] and signal understanding [Nii88,Less95] to process monitoring [Kock94] and fault diagnosis [Hewi89,Dous96].

In this paper, event recognition is viewed as the process of analysing a stream of symbolic, time-indexed data, in order to recognise interesting events that have occurred. In the case of the humpback whale song the input data consist of time-stamped occurrences of the basic song units. The aim of the system is to recognise the occurrence of other events in the sequence, i.e.,

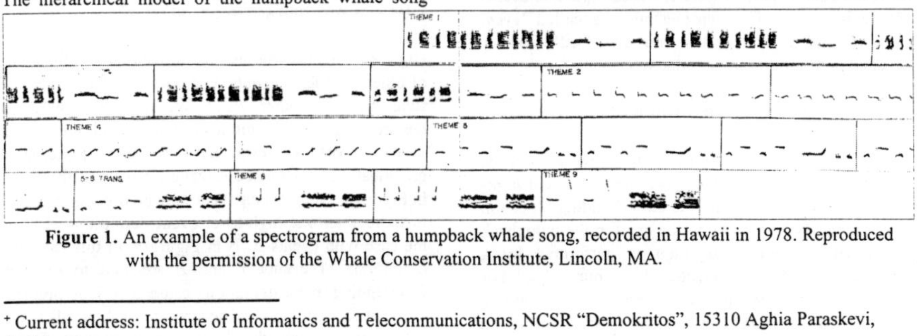

Figure 1. An example of a spectrogram from a humpback whale song, recorded in Hawaii in 1978. Reproduced with the permission of the Whale Conservation Institute, Lincoln, MA.

[+] Current address: Institute of Informatics and Telecommunications, NCSR "Demokritos", 15310 Aghia Paraskevi, Attikis, Greece.

[•] This work was funded by Thomson Marconi Sonar UK Ltd. and the Engineering and Physical Sciences Research Council, UK.

subphrases, phrases and themes. Event recognition is based on an *event model,* which can be thought of as a temporal expert system. This model consists of a set of dependencies between events and temporal parameters, constraining the recognition of events. Section 2 describes in some detail the representation of the recognition system.

The manual assignment of the temporal parameters in the event recognition system is a tedious and error prone process. For this reason, we present here a method that partially automates the assignment of the temporal parameters. The initial values of the parameters are assumed to be incorrect, but near misses of the true values. Under this assumption, the parameters are refined using a small set of training examples. The relational nature of the event recognition task introduces a number of challenging issues, in addition to the small size of the training set. Such issues are the extent of supervision provided by the preclassified data and the construction of training examples from the continuous input stream. Section 3 examines these issues and provides solutions.

The method of refining the temporal parameters of the system was evaluated on the problem of analysing humpback whale songs to identify song components. The results obtained in these experiments, presented in section 4, are very encouraging, showing that the new method is useful for refining event recognition systems, especially under the constraint of a small training set. Section 5 briefly examines related work in event recognition and section 6 discusses the advantages and shortcomings of the methods presented in the paper.

2. Event network

In order to facilitate parameter refinement, especially under the constraint of sparse data, the event recognition system needs to be represented in a simple and well-structured way. For this purpose, a network representation is proposed here, which organises events into a hierarchy. This representation is called '*event network*' and its main features are described below. A detailed description can be found in [Pali97].[1]

2.1 Hierarchical decomposition of events

The basic entities of the event network are events, which are divided into two types: *low-level* and *high-level.* Low-level events are the basic building blocks in the system, corresponding to the units in the humpback whale song. Their recognition is performed by a separate system, not considered in our work. For instance, assume the signal in Figure 2, which could be a simplified and cleaned up version of a small piece of a spectrogram.[2] The low-level event recognition system identifies four events in this spectrogram: A, B, C, D. The output of the low-level system is the sequence of recognised events, with their time stamps:

A(0,200), B(200,400), C(300,500), D(500,600),

where the numbers in brackets correspond to the start and the end of each *event occurrence.* The start time for the recording sets the zero point for time stamps. Time may be measured in any unit, e.g. msec. So A starts at time 0, the start of the recording, and ends after 200 msec. The recognition of an event is notified by the low-level recognition system, as soon as the event ends, so that the event can be associated with its time stamp. The above sequence of low-level event occurrences is the input to the high-level recognition system, which is the subject of this article.

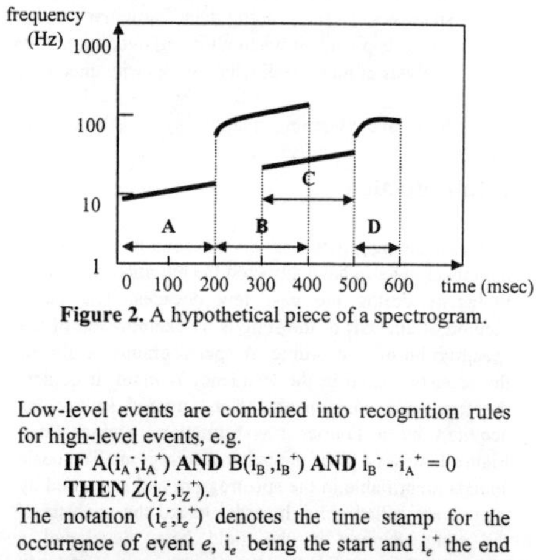

Figure 2. A hypothetical piece of a spectrogram.

Low-level events are combined into recognition rules for high-level events, e.g.

IF $A(i_A^-, i_A^+)$ **AND** $B(i_B^-, i_B^+)$ **AND** $i_B^- - i_A^+ = 0$
THEN $Z(i_Z^-, i_Z^+)$.

The notation (i_e^-, i_e^+) denotes the time stamp for the occurrence of event *e*, i_e^- being the start and i_e^+ the end time. The above rule is called the *definition* of event Z and the low-level events A, B are called its *subevents.* The time stamp of the event being defined is assumed to exactly cover the subevent occurrences. Thus, the high-level event Z(0,400) will be recognised, combining subevents A(0,200) and B(200,400).

High-level events can also be defined as combinations of other high-level events. For instance, Z could be the subevent of another event W. In this manner, a hierarchy of event definitions is constructed, forming an event network. The event network can be represented graphically as a Directed Acyclic Graph, e.g. the graph in Figure 3. Note that an event may be used as subevent in more than one high-level event definitions. This is the case with events A, B in Figure 3. In this case, the definitions of events Y and Z are said to *overlap.* Overlapping event definitions cause a serious problem in event recognition. The occurrence of A and B is not sufficient to say whether Y or Z is happening. Events

[1] The term *temporal classification network*, instead of *event network*, was used in [Pali97].

[2] The term "cleaned up" refers to the removal of harmonics.

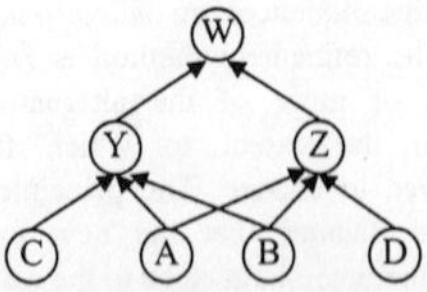

Figure 3. A simple event network.

C and D are necessary for distinguishing between Y and Z. Under certain conditions, e.g. noisy signal, both C and D might be recognised making it impossible to decide whether Y or Z should be recognised. This could be the case if the following sequence of events is recognised:

A(0,200), B(200,400), C(300,500), D(500,600)

and both the definitions of Y and Z are satisfied. In such situations, the system notifies the occurrence of both events, i.e., Y(0,500) and Z(0,600), using the same occurrences of subevents A and B.

The implicit assumption so far is that the recognition of a high-level event requires the occurrence of *all* of its subevents. In other words, event definitions correspond to rules with a conjunctive condition. Such rules are not sufficient for the representation of a realistic event recognition system. For this reason, two more types of event are used in the event network: *disjunctive* and *repeating*. Disjunctive events require simply that one of the subevents in the definition occurs. Repeating event definitions contain a single subevent, which is required to occur repeatedly. The number of repetitions of the subevent is constrained within a range, e.g. 20 to 30 times.

2.2 Temporal relations and parameters

As mentioned above, the event network represents a temporal expert system. Thus, event definitions are augmented with temporal parameters constraining the recognition of events. The example definition for event Z above contains such a constraint, i.e., $i_B^- - i_A^+ = 0$, which requires that subevent B starts when A ends. In general, the subevents in an event definition are not required to meet in time; there may be a gap between them or they may overlap. This is an important advantage of the explicit representation of temporal constraints in a symbolic system.

Three types of temporal constraint are used in an event network:

- A *precedence* qualitative constraint, *precedes*(x,y), which requires that subevent x *ends before* y *ends*. Note that x and y may still overlap.
- A quantitative constraint on the *duration* of subevents, *duration*(x,[d_1,d_2]), where [d_1,d_2] is an integer range of valid values for the duration of x.
- A quantitative constraint on the temporal *distance* between subevents, *distance*(x,y,[s_1,s_2]), [s_1,s_2] being the range of valid distances between x and y.

The use of ranges, instead of exact values, is needed to deal with noise and variation in real-world data. Disjunctive event definitions do not contain relations between subevents, since a single subevent is used for the recognition of the high-level event. Only the duration of the subevent is constrained. In repeating event definitions, there is just a single subevent which precedes itself. Thus, only one duration and one distance constraint are defined, which apply to all repetitions of the subevent.

The use of the *precedes* relation in conjunctive events is further constrained for efficient event recognition:

- No cycles in the precedence of subevents, e.g. *precedes*(A,B) and *precedes*(B,A), are allowed.
- Each subevent can only be used in two *precedes* relations: in one of them it should *precede* another, say *precedes*(B,C) and in the other it must be *preceded*, e.g. *precedes*(A,B).

In this manner a *precedence sequence* of subevents is constructed in each conjunctive definition. One of the subevents in this sequence does not precede any other and is called *terminal* subevent, since its end coincides with the end of the high-level event. Thus if Z is defined as the sequence of subevents A, B, C, where *precedes*(A,B) and *precedes*(B,C), C is the terminal subevent in the definition.

2.3 Recognition algorithm

In the design of the representation that was presented in this section, particular attention was paid to the performance of the recognition system. In particular two properties of the representation are used to achieve efficient recognition:

- The partial ordering of events in the event network.
- The precedence sequence in conjunctive events.

In brief, the recognition algorithm stores the occurrences of events in a dynamic database and for each incoming event occurrence it checks whether it could act as the terminal subevent in a definition. If not, no action is needed, otherwise the appropriate event definition is used to recognise potential occurrences of the corresponding event. These occurrences are appended to the database and recognition is propagated to the higher levels of the network. This algorithm is described in more detail in [Pali97].

3. Adaptation of the event network

The event network for a realistic event recognition problem may involve a large number of event definitions with an equally large number of temporal constraints. Incorrect assignment of values to these constraints may cause unacceptably high levels of misrecognition. However, manual setting of these constraint values can be very difficult and time-consuming. Therefore, any automation of this process would be welcome by the experts who design the recognition system. This section presents a method which starts with a set of initial constraint values and improves them to achieve correct recognition on a small set of preclassified training data. The initial constraint values may be only rough estimates of the correct values. These values will then be refined according to the performance of the system on the training data. Two versions of the *parameter refinement* method are presented in the following two subsections of this section. The two versions differ in the level of supervision which is provided by the training data.

3.1 Refinement under full supervision

The first version of the refinement method makes the assumption that the training data provide information about *all the high-level events which should be recognised*, given a sequence of low-level event occurrences. For instance, assuming the network in Figure 3 - where events A, B, C, D may correspond to the units of a whale song, Y and Z to phrases and W to a complete theme - the following sequence of unit occurrences may be part of the training data:

A(0,200), B(200,300), A(250,350), B(400,500), C(410,500), D(500,600)

and supervision is provided in the form of phrases and themes that should be recognised, e.g.

Y(0,500), Z(250,600), W(0,600).

All relevant themes and phrases which should be recognised in the above sequence of unit occurrences are assumed to be provided in the training data. This mode of supervision is called here '*full supervision*.'

Note that the representation of the training data deviates significantly from the feature vector of typical classification problems, which is assumed in most of the machine learning and knowledge refinement literature, e.g. [Quin93] and [Craw90]. Here the data are presented in two separate streams of event occurrences:

- The *input stream,* consisting of unit occurrences in our examples.
- The *feedback stream,* consisting of themes and phrases that should be recognised.

No information is provided about which occurrences of low-level events should be combined to recognise a particular high-level event. To a certain extent this information can be deduced by the event network and the time stamps in the feedback data. For instance, it is clear that the unit occurrence C(410,500) can only be used in the recognition of Y(0,500), since event C participates only in the definition of Y. Similarly, A(0,200) is used in the recognition of Y(0,500), because there is no other event starting at time 0. However, the use of overlapping event definitions in an event network complicates matters, e.g. either of the two occurrences of B, B(200,300) and B(400,500), may be used to recognise Y(0,500). Thus, there may be more than one sequence of low-level events which could cause the recognition of one high-level event, e.g. for Y(0,500):

A(0,200), B(200,300), C(410,500),
A(0,200), B(400,500), C(410,500).

These alternative sequences are called '*multiple positive instances.*'[3] The refinement method is responsible for covering one or more of the alternative positives, depending on the extent to which the temporal parameters need to change. The principle of *minimal model change* dictates that the new values of the temporal parameters remain close to the original values.

In order to make the problem solvable by a machine learning method, the data pass through two pre-processing stages, which provide the required representation shift to the space of the temporal parameters. The first stage of pre-processing enumerates the sequences of subevent occurrences that could lead to the recognition of an event.[4] In the example of the event Y(0,500) above, the two alternative sequences of A, B, C will be generated. This process is initiated when the terminal subevent - C in this case - is recognised. The alternative subevent sequences are organised into a tree structure, called *'event support tree'* (EST). The EST for the above positive example for event Y(0,500) is presented in Figure 4.

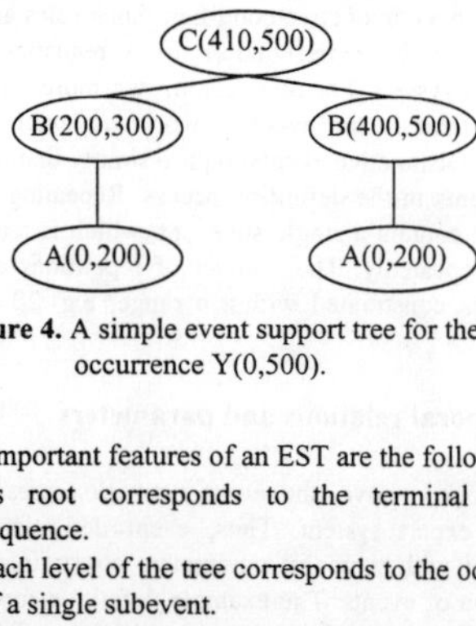

Figure 4. A simple event support tree for the event occurrence Y(0,500).

The important features of an EST are the following:

- Its root corresponds to the terminal subevent sequence.
- Each level of the tree corresponds to the occurrences of a single subevent.
- Each path from the root to a leaf is a sequence of subevents, which could lead to the recognition of the high-level event.

Each EST that is generated is considered a single example to be used for the refinement of the temporal parameters. The EST in Figure 4 is a positive example for event Y. In addition to positive ESTs, negative ones are constructed for those subevent sequences which lead to the recognition of events not in the feedback data. For instance, the sequence of unit occurrences

A(250,350), B(400,500), C(410,500)

could cause the recognition of Y(250,500), which is not in the feedback data and thus its recognition is undesirable.

---

[3] This term was coined in [Diet97].

[4] A user-defined window parameter is used to avoid combinatorial explosion.

In the second stage of pre-processing, a set of ESTs is collected to form a training set for the refinement of the temporal parameters in an event definition. Thus, all the ESTs for event Y - both positive and negative - are collected into a training set. This training set is also organised in a tree structure, which is called the '*relative event support tree*' (REST). The REST maintains the structural features of an EST, but instead of absolute time, the relative parameter values are used to label the nodes. Furthermore, lists of positive and negative examples are associated with each node to assist in the refinement decision. Figure 5 shows the REST for the running example of event Y(0,500).

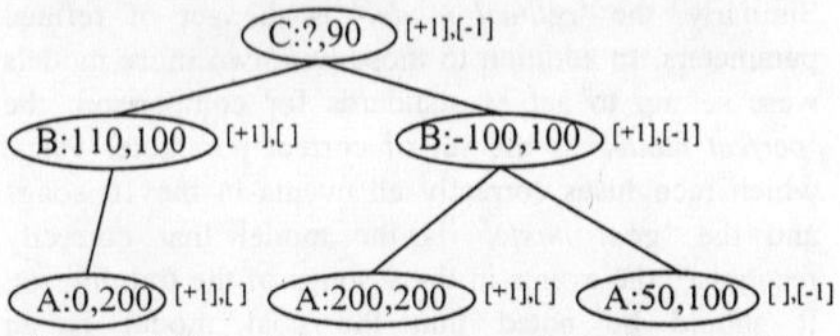

Figure 5. The relative event support tree for event Y.

Each node in the REST contains two parameter values: the first is the distance of the subevent occurrence from the occurrence that it precedes and the second is the duration of the subevent occurrence. For instance, the root of the tree does not precede any other subevent and its distance value is undefined (=?). Its duration is 90 msec, which is the difference between the end and the start of the event occurrence C(410,500). Similarly, the distance between B(400,500) and C(400,500) is 400-500=-100 msec and the duration of B(400,500) is 100 msec, resulting in the node B:-100,100 of the REST in figure 5. The lists next to the nodes of the tree contain labels for positive and negative examples. These labels are given by global example counters. In the example of figure 5 there is one positive (+1) and one negative example (-1). The positive example corresponds to two alternative paths through the tree, as explained above. The cumulative construction of the REST, allows the use of a batch learning method which is independent of the order in which examples are presented in the data.

Given the data in the form of RESTs, a number of alternative search algorithms can be applied to look for the optimal set of new parameter values. The algorithm that we developed performs a simple best-first search, traversing the tree from the root to the leaves. The optimality criterion combines two subcriteria:

- *purity*, which gives an indication of how many positive and negative examples are covered by each solution;
- *proximity*, measuring the closeness of a solution to the original values.

The user is allowed to determine the relative weight of these parameters, depending on the amount of noise in the data and his/her confidence in the original parameter values. The details of the algorithm can be found in [Pali97].

3.2 Refinement under partial supervision

In subsection 3.1 we have assumed that the feedback stream contains information about all of the events in an event network. This assumption cannot easily be satisfied when a realistically large event network is used. It is, therefore, desirable to reduce the amount of supervision required for refinement. This section presents briefly an extension to the original method, which makes the assumption that supervision is provided for only part of the training data. In particular only the top-level nodes in the network - the themes in the case of the whale song - are identified in the feedback data. In our running example, this would shrink the feedback data to a single event occurrence: W(0,600).

The problem that appears under this weaker supervision scenario is the labelling - as positive or negative - for the occurrences of all intermediate events in the network. In our example, we need to decide, which of the following occurrences of Y and Z should really be recognised:

Y(0,500), Y(250,500), Z(0,600), Z(250,600).

Almost any combination of the above two pairs of Y and Z occurrences could be used to recognise W(0,600), the only exception being the combination of Y(250,500) and Z(250,600), which does not give the right start time for W.

The solution that we adopted was to maintain a set of weights, one for each event occurrence in the network. These weights are called *recognition beliefs* and provide an estimate of whether an occurrence should be recognised or not. Recognition beliefs are initially set according to how easy it would be to recognise an event occurrence, i.e., how much the original model parameters should be modified, if at all, in order for the occurrence to be recognised. This initial model-based estimate is updated according to the feedback data. The recognition belief for the top-level event occurrences that are explicitly identified in the data is set to the maximum (1.0), while those events that should not be recognised are given minimum belief (0.0). This information is propagated backwards to their subevents to obtain the final belief for each event occurrence in the network.

After this two-stage calculation of the recognition beliefs, each training example is associated with a weight. At this stage, a heuristic could be applied to decide on a single set of event occurrences that would lead to the recognition of the required high-level events. For instance, a winner-takes-all strategy could be adopted. The problem with such heuristics is that they are local in nature and can thus cause brittleness, throwing away useful information, i.e., the actual weights. For this reason, we have opted for a simple modification to the optimality criteria used under full supervision, which allows the use of weights, resulting in finer distinctions between alternative solutions. The details of the extended refinement method can be found in [Pali97].

4. Experimental evaluation

The event recognition system that was briefly introduced in this paper was tested on a real-world problem: the recognition of song components in humpback whale songs. The structure of the song has been studied in detail in the biological literature, e.g. [Payn71,Payn83], and a number of interesting observations were made. The following are of particular interest here:

- In each recording season (roughly December to April) and for a particular population of humpback whales, the same song is sung by all individuals, with only small aberrations.
- The song is structured hierarchically into themes, phrases, subphrases and units, i.e., themes are broken down into phrases, which consist of subphrases and can be further decomposed into units.
- The temporal features of the song components, e.g. duration and distance, are highly variable, even for the same individual.

Each whale song consists of a sequence of themes, which differ structurally from each other. The task that was set for the event recognition system was to identify the themes and their structural components, i.e., phrases, subphrases and units. This task is named here '*theme analysis*' of the whale song. The data that we used for the test were provided by the Whale Conservation Institute in the form of spectrogram print-outs. These spectrograms corresponded to several hours of recording in one season in Hawaii. The same data were used in the detailed study presented in [Payn83].

The event network representation suited nicely the hierarchical structure of the whale song. Each theme was represented by an event network, using information from the study in [Payn83]. We also manually extracted sequences of unit occurrences from 10 of the spectrograms. Manual extraction was necessary due to the lack of a low-level event recognition system. The goal of our system was to learn the correct parameter settings, so that the subphrases, phrases and themes that are identified by the event networks are the correct ones. For this purpose, we performed a 10-fold cross-validation experiment, using the 10 songs that were coded from the spectrograms. In each of the ten runs, one of the songs was held out as test data and the rest were used for training.

The literature in marine biology does not provide detailed information on the temporal aspects of song components. For this reason, a parameter initialisation algorithm was developed, which uses a set of data to approximate the values of the temporal parameters in the event networks. The use of problem-specific information allows this algorithm to achieve close approximations of the real parameter values. Applying this algorithm on a subset of the 9 songs in the training data, the parameters were assigned initial values, which were further refined with the use of the remaining training data. For instance, 4 songs could be used to initialise the parameters and 5 to refine them. The performance of the algorithm for different sizes of the initialisation set is reported in the results below.

The initial set of parameters, generated by the above-mentioned algorithm is called an '*expert model.*' Similarly, the '*refined model*' is the set of refined parameters. In addition to those two, two more models were set up to act as standards for comparison: the '*perfect model*' is the set of correct parameter vales, which recognises correctly all events in the 10 songs and the '*goal model*' is the model that correctly recognises the events in the 9 songs of the training set. It should be noted that the goal model is an approximation of the parameters that we expect the refinement method to generate, but does not provide a uniquely correct solution.

Figure 6 presents the results of the experiment, using an evaluation metric called '*model displacement.*' This metric is simply the sum of absolute differences between the parameter values of a model and the perfect model. Results both under full and partial supervision are presented. The number of songs that are used in the initialisation of the parameters is varied on the x-axis of the diagram. When the initialisation set is small, e.g. 1 song, the expert model is far from the desired perfect model. As expected, for larger initialisation sets the expert model approaches the perfect model. When 8 of the 9 songs are used for initialisation the difference between the expert and the goal model is minimal. The goal model, which is generated on the 9 songs of the training set remains largely unaffected by the size of the initialisation set.

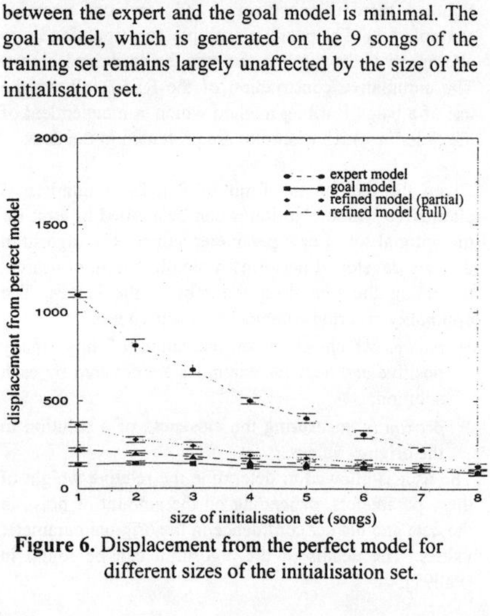

Figure 6. Displacement from the perfect model for different sizes of the initialisation set.

The goal and the expert model form an envelope, within which the refined model is expected to lie. The performance of the refinement method is judged by the distance of the refined model from the expert and the goal model. The closer the refined model is to the goal the better the method. On this basis, the results presented in Figure 6 are very encouraging. Both under full and partial supervision, the refined model is very close to the goal. The expected fall in performance under partial supervision is also small, when compared to the improvement that is achieved over the expert model. Under partial supervision, the amount of feedback provided for training is minimal: only the theme occurrences are given. Thus, the results of figure 6 suggest that our refinement method has handled the test problem very well.

These good results are reinforced by *the recognition accuracy* of the system on the unseen data, i.e., the tenth song that was not used for training. Recognition accuracy corresponds to the standard evaluation measure in machine learning literature, i.e., the proportion of objects being correctly classified. Figure 7 presents the results along this dimension. The picture is similar to that in Figure 6: the refined models achieve the desired performance. Under full supervision, the refined model outperforms even the goal model, which suffers small approximation errors.

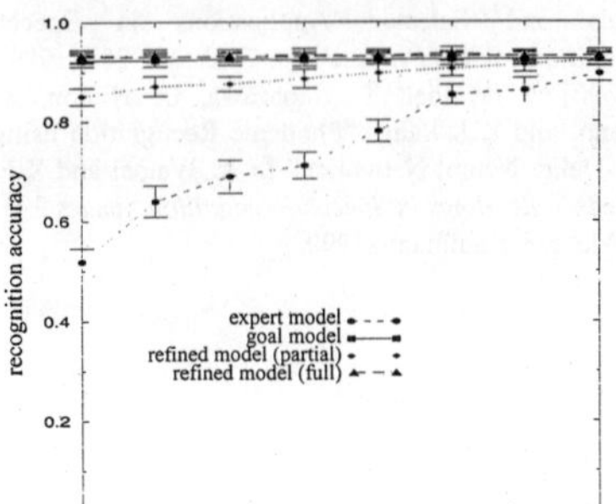

Figure 7. Recognition accuracy of the various models on the held-out song data.

5. Related work

Most of the work on event recognition, e.g. [Rabi89, Waib90, Lipp90] adopts numeric approaches such as Artificial Neural Networks and Hidden Markov Models. These methods can provide accurate and effective models, when there is enough data to estimate the necessary parameters. This was not the case in our work. Furthermore, these approaches cannot deal with overlapping events and do not provide an easy way to use domain knowledge, provided by a human expert.

Early symbolic signal understanding systems which also perform event recognition [Erma80, Lowe90] have meanwhile been abandoned, due their inefficiency. The main problem with these approaches was the use of a blackboard architecture, which is a flexible and powerful, but also inefficient, problem solving method. This architecture has been used in a more recent system which is presented in [Samm90]. In this system, the authors tried to improve recognition efficiency by structuring the use of the blackboard inference strategy into four distinct levels of event definitions. All the above-mentioned systems do not deal with overlapping events and are not adaptive, i.e., no learning takes place.

The event recognition system, as described in section 2, belongs in a small class of systems, grouped under the label '*temporal event recognition systems.*' Examples of this work can be found in [Kock94] and [Dous96]. These systems use a temporal logic to represent the event model and *Temporal Constraint Satisfaction* algorithms for event recognition. The first important difference of these approaches to the system presented here is that they are not adaptive. Additionally, there are practical differences in the recognition system, such as the kind of event that is used and the recognition algorithm. These differences are discussed in detail in [Pali97].

6. Conclusions

In this paper we presented an event recognition system, which is able to adopt itself in order to improve its performance on a small set of training data. In addition to the restriction of the small training set, the system was required to handle overlapping events, which are commonly ignored and are difficult to handle. The solution that we proposed was based on a simple, but well-structured hierarchical representation of events. This representation allows the use of explicit temporal constraints, making the handling of overlapping events easier.

Due to the small size of the training set, we restricted the scope of the learning method on the refinement of the temporal parameters. The parameters are initially assigned approximate values, which can be refined in the light of the training information. Particular attention was paid to the extent of supervision that the expert designer needs to provide, as this can be decisive for the usability of the system. We extended our method to handle a situation where a minimal amount of supervision is provided.

The evaluation of the method was performed on real data that was drawn from the "realm" of marine mammals. 10 songs of the humpback whale were coded and used to test our method. The results of the experiment are very encouraging. The refinement method consistently managed to improve the initially inaccurate model and reach close to the expected maximum on two different measures.

While these results are encouraging, they are just indicative, as only a single problem was used for evaluation. Further evaluation on more data and different problems is needed to verify the effectiveness of our system. This effort should be combined with the use of an automatic system for the recognition of low-level events, i.e., units in the case of the whale song.

Another direction for further work is to expand the scope of refinement to include the restructuring of the event network. Although the confidence of the human expert on the structure of the recognition system is higher than on the exact values of the temporal constraints, errors can also be made at that level. A prerequisite for a method that would perform such restructuring is the use of more training data, in order to make reliable decisions.

Acknowledgements

We are both indebted to the people doing work on the sounds of the humpback whale for their invaluable help, in particular to Roger Payne for providing the data and the much-needed insight on the acoustics of the whale sounds.

References

[Craw90] S. Craw and D. Sleeman. "Automating the Refinement of Knowledge-Based Systems." *Proceedings of the European Conference on Artificial Intelligence*, 167-172, 1990.

[Diet97] T.G. Dietterich, R.H. Lathrop and T. Lozano-Pérez. "Solving the Multiple Instance Problem with Axis-parallel Rectangles." *Artificial Intelligence*, 89:31-71, 1997.

[Dous96] C. Dousson. "Alarm Driven Supervision for Telecommunication Network II - on-line chronicle recognition." *Annales des Télécommunication*, 51(9-10):501-508, 1996.

[Erma80] L.D. Erman, F.Hayes-Roth, V.R. Lesser, and D.R. Reddy. "The Hearsay-II Speech-Understanding System: integrating Knowledge to resolve uncertainty." *ACM Computing Surveys*, 12(2):214-253, 1980.

[Hewi89] P.D. Hewitt, P.J.C. Skitt, and R.C. Witcomb. "A Self-organising Feedforward Network Applied to Acoustic Data." In J.G. Taylor and C.L.T. Mannion (eds.), *New Developments in Neural Computing*, pages 71-78, Adam Hilger, 1989.

[Kock94] S. Kockskämper, B. Neuman, and M. Schick. "Extending Process Monitoring by Event Recognition." In Proceedings of the 2nd International Conference on Intelligent Systems Engineering, pages 455-460, 1994.

[Less95] V.R. Lesser, S.H. Nawab, and F.I. Klassner. "IPUS: an architecture for the integrated processing and understanding of signals." *Artificial Intelligence*, 77:129-171, 1995.

[Lipp90] R.P. Lippmann. "Review of Neural Networks for Speech Recognition." In A. Waibel and K.F. Lee (eds.), *Readings in Speech Recognition*, pages 374391, Morgan-Kaufmann, 1990.

[Lowe90] B. Lowerre and R. Reddy. "The HARPY Speech Understanding System." In A. Waibel and K.F. Lee (eds.), *Readings in Speech Recognition*, pages 576-586, Morgan-Kaufmann, 1990.

[Nii88] H.P. Nii, E.A. Feigenbaum, J.J. Anton, and A.J. Rockmore. "Signal-to-Symbol Transformation: HASP/SIAP case study." In R. Engelmore and T. Morgan, (eds.), *Blackboard Systems*, pages 135157, Addison-Wesley, 1988.

[Pali97] G. Paliouras. *Refinement of Temporal Constraints in an Event Recognition System using Small Datasets*. Ph.D. Thesis, Computer Science Department, University of Manchester, 1997.

[Payn71] R.S. Payne and S. McVay. "Songs of Humpback Whales." *Science*, 173(3997):585-597, 1971.

[Payn83] K. Payne, P. Tyack, and R. Payne. "Progressive Changes in the Songs of Humpback Whales (Megaptera Novaeangliae): a detailed analysis of two seasons in Hawaii." In R. Payne, (ed.) *Communication and Behaviour of Whales*, pages 9-57, Westview Press, 1983.

[Quin93] J.R. Quinlan. *C4.5: Programs for Machine Learning*. Morgan Kaufmann, San Mateo, CA, 1993.

[Samm90] T.M. Sammon Jr. "The Transient Expert Processor." *Conference Record - Asilomar Conference on Signals, Systems and Computers*, 612-617, 1990.

[Rabi89] L.R. Rabiner. "A Tutorial on Hidden Markov Models and Selected Applications in Speech Recognition." *IEEE Proceedings*, 77(2):257-285, 1989.

[Waib90] A. Waibel, T. Hanazawa, G. Hinton, K. Shikano, and K.J. Lang. "Phoneme Recognition using Time-Delay Neural Networks." In A. Waibel and K.F. Lee (eds.), *Readings in Speech Recognition*, pages 393-404, Morgan-Kaufmann, 1990.

A Novel Weighted Hough Transform for Robust Detection of Linear Formations

S. J. Perantonis, N. Vassilas, K. Seretis and Th. Tsenoglou

Institute of Informatics and Telecommunications, National Center for Scientific Research "DEMOKRITOS", 153 10 Agia Paraskevi, Athens, Greece.

Abstract

A method based on a modified implementation of the Hough transform is presented and applied to the location of prevalent linear formations in digital images. A given image is segmented into its connected components and appropriate shape descriptors (elongation, area, orientation of the principal axis) are calculated for each component. The contribution of each component to the accumulator array is determined by a suitably defined function that depends on the shape descriptors. The method is applied with success to various image processing and computer vision applications where the original Hough transform fails to produce satisfactory results.

1 Introduction

The Hough transform [1] has emerged in recent years as a very powerful method for detecting parametrically described shapes in images. Its main advantages are its robustness to noise and its relative insensitivity to missing parts of the required shapes. Even in its simplest application, which is the detection of straight lines or line segments, it has been successfully applied to numerous image processing and computer vision problems [2].

Despite its robustness, the Hough trasform is still susceptible to the presence of outliers, especially in complicated and noisy images. In many cases, a large number of pixels that do not originate from the existence of a straight line in the image may accidentally be aligned, resulting to the occurence of spurious maxima in the Hough transform accumulator array. The problem is especially acute in cases where the required lines are axes located in the interior of objects, so that edge detection followed by application of the Hough transform is not appropriate for locating them [3]. It is thus highly desirable to have methods of hindering these non-interesting pixels from contributing to the accumulator array. To this end, weighting factors must be introduced that suppress the contribution of unwanted pixels. In the original formulation of the Hough transform, this is not possible, because each foreground pixel contributes the same amount (equal to 1) to all accumulator array points that correspond to lines passing through this pixel.

The concept of a "voting kernel" that enables the contribution of a pixel to the accumulator array to be weighted has been introduced in order to allow a pixel to contribute to neighbouring bins of the accumulator array, thus minimizing aliasing effects or achieving increased (even subpixel) accuracy in the evaluation of the direction of straight lines [4] [5].

In this paper, we present a novel modified Hough transform method that weights the contribution of each foreground pixel in order to reduce interference effects from outliers even in highly noisy images. After segmenting the image into connected components of foregroung pixels, we compute the weighting factor for each pixel by taking into account appropriate shape descriptors of the connected component to which the pixel belongs. The method is highly successful in detemining prevalent linear directions in demanding image processing and computer vision applications.

2 Methodology

Given a binary image, we are interested in the detection of straight lines parametrized by

$$r = x\cos\theta + y\sin\theta \qquad (1)$$

as shown in fig. 1. To this end, we firstly form a decomposition of the image into connected regions. For each region, we consider its geometrical center ($\overline{x}$, $\overline{y}$) and increment for various values of θ the corresponding cells in the Hough accumulator array. To evaluate the contribution of each region to various cells in the accumulator array we take into account appropriately chosen shape descriptors related to the region. To express the dependence formally, we introduce a "voting kernel", which is a continuous function of the shape descriptors. Each step of our method is described in detail in the following subsections.

2.1 Decomposition into Connected Regions

To specify the connected regions of the binary image, we follow the label assignment procedure outlined in [6], whereby a linked-list is constructed for storing simultaneously the following:

- labels belonging to different regions using vertical pointers

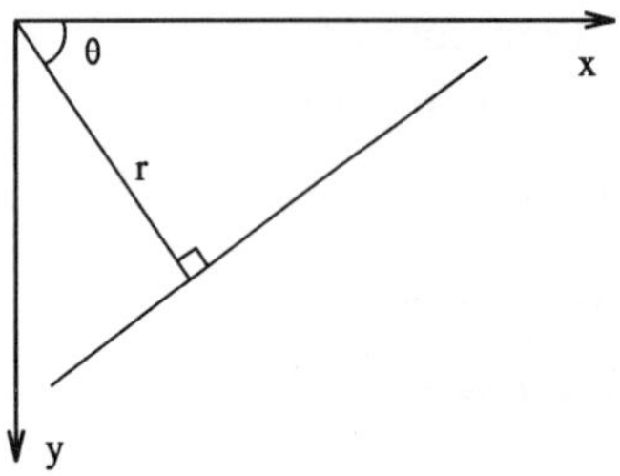

Figure 1: Parametrization of a straight line for application of Hough transform.

- equivalence classes, i.e. labels assigned to pixels of the same region using horizontal pointers.

The image is scanned top to bottom and left to right, skipping background pixels, until a new foreground pixel is found. If all the top and left connected neighbors (e.g. assuming 4- or 8- connectedness) belong to the background, a new label is added to the bottom of the linked-list and the pixel points to this label (the pointers from pixels to labels are stored in a 2-D array with the same dimensions as the original image). Otherwise, the pixel is made to point to the first label found among the foreground top and left neighbors. Inconsistencies due to two different neighboring pixels having different labels are easily resolved as follows: the second found label is first removed from the vertical label list, then placed to the equivalence class (horizontal list) of the first found label and finally changed to the first found label (also specifying the equivalence class). Such a technique has the advantage of speed, since it does not require a second image scanning in order to assure uniformity in region labelling, i.e., changing all equivalent labels to one.

2.2 Shape Descriptors

For each region, we calculate three descriptors, all of which can be evaluated in terms of the central moments m_{ij} of the region:

- The area $A = m_{00}$.
- The angle ϕ of the principal axis relative to the x-axis, given by the equation:

$$\phi = \frac{1}{2}\tan^{-1}\frac{2m_{11}}{m_{20} - m_{02}} \qquad (2)$$

- The elongation of the region. This is evaluated by finding the ellipse that best fits to the region (in the sense that it has the same moments of inertia). The elongation ϵ is then equal to the major to minor axis length ratio (so that $\epsilon > 1$) and can be found as:

$$\epsilon = \left(\left|\frac{I_{max}}{I_{min}}\right|\right)^{1/2} \qquad (3)$$

where

$$I_{min} = m_{20}\sin^2\phi + m_{02}\cos^2\phi - m_{11}\sin 2\phi \quad (4)$$

and

$$I_{max} = m_{20}\cos^2\phi + m_{02}\sin^2\phi + m_{11}\sin 2\phi \quad (5)$$

Details of the derivation of these formulae are found in [7].

2.3 The Voting Kernel

The presence of an elongated region in the image is taken as strong evidence for the existence of a line whose direction is parallel or approximately parallel to the principal axis of the region. Thus, the contribution to the accumulator array

- should increase with the elongation ϵ of the region
- should be maximum for $\phi = \theta$ and drop with increasing $|\phi - \theta|$ for a given value of ϵ.

The rate of change with increasing $|\phi - \theta|$ should clearly depend on the elongation itself: For very large ϵ, only the direction $\theta = \phi$ should be incremented. At the other extreme, regions with $\epsilon \approx 1$, which are nearly circular, should be allowed to vote equally for all directions.

Finally, a dependence of the kernel on the area should be also introduced in order to minimize the effects of interference from unwanted regions and avoid spurious maxima in the accumulator array. Regions of relatively small elongation and large area are a major source on interference and their contribution to the accumulator array should be suppressed. At the other extreme, regions of very small area should also be discarded as noise. Inbetween these extreme cases, regions of small elongation whose area is comparable to a characteristic intermediate area scale A_0 can be part of a chain of aligned regions contributing to a disrupted linear structure and should be therefore taken into account for forming the accumulator array. In short, for small elongations, the voting kernel should have the structure of a band-pass filter which suppresses voting from regions of very small and very large areas, but allows regions of intermediate areas to contribute to the accumulator array.

To summarize, given a region whose center is located at x, y and a value of the angle θ, its contribution to the accumulator array cell (r, θ) is of the form $f(A, \epsilon, \phi - \theta)$ where f must fulfill the following conditions:

1. f should be asymptotically proportional to ϵ as $\epsilon \to \infty$.
2. f should not depend on θ as $\epsilon \to 1$ and should tend to $\delta(\phi - \theta)$ as $\epsilon \to \infty$.
3. $f \to 0$ as $A \to 0$ or $A \to \infty$ for $\epsilon \approx 1$.

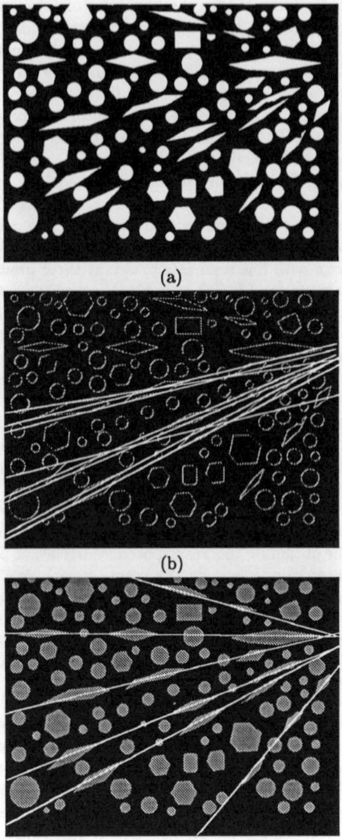

Figure 2: Determination of linear formations in a synthetic image. (a) Original image. (b) Result of Hough transform applied to image after edge detection. (c) Result of method proposed in this paper.

The following function is modelled to conform with the above conditions:

$$f = \epsilon \exp[-(\epsilon - 1)(\phi - \theta)^2] A \exp[-\frac{(A - A_0)}{A_0 \epsilon^2}] \quad (6)$$

In this relation, the factor ϵ explicitly weights elongated regions in accordance with condition 1; the factor $\exp[-(\epsilon - 1)(\phi - \theta)^2]$ is inserted to conform with condition 2; and the factor $A \exp[-\frac{(A-A_0)}{A_0 \epsilon^2}]$, which has a maximum at $A = A_0$ for given ϵ, plays the role of a band-pass filter for values of ϵ close to 1 (so that condition 3 is fulfilled), but further enhances the contribution of elongated regions proportionally to their area for large values of ϵ.

The characteristic area A_0 can be chosen statistically as the average area of connected image regions whose elongation exceeds a certain threshold. However, our simulations have shown that the method is robust, so that no fine tuning of A_0 is required. In all applications described in the experimental section, good performance was observed for a relatively wide range of values for A_0.

3 Experimental results

In order to demonstrate the efficiency of our approach, we consider various computer vision and image processing applications.

Fig. 2a is a synthetic black and white image displaying a number of linear directions that originate from a common focus of expansion. Other shapes of various dimensions play the role of interfering noise. In fig. 2b, the result of Hough transform application on the edge image is shown. The result is poor, because the method places too much empasis on the local orientations of the edges. We note that an equally poor result was obtained using the Hough transform on the original image (without edge detection) because of extensive interference from irrelevant pixels originating mainly from other shapes of large area. In fig. 2c, lines detected by our method are shown, which adequately match the prevalent linear formations in the original image.

Fig. 3a is part of an image displaying sparkles originating from a common center of expansion that lies outside the image. The objective is to determine prevalent lines in the image that correspond to the orbits of the sparkles. Fig. 3b shows a thresholded version of the original image, to which edge detection has been applied. Superimposed are the lines corresponding to the seven most prominent maxima of the Hough transform accumulator array, which are clearly unacceptable. By contrast, applying our method to the thresholded image we obtain the very good result shown in fig. 3c.

Recently, the Hough transform has been applied to the problem of finding an orientation which might be prevalent in an entire image, rather than locating individual straight lines. This is especially useful for finding the skew of printed documents [8] [9] [10]. In these

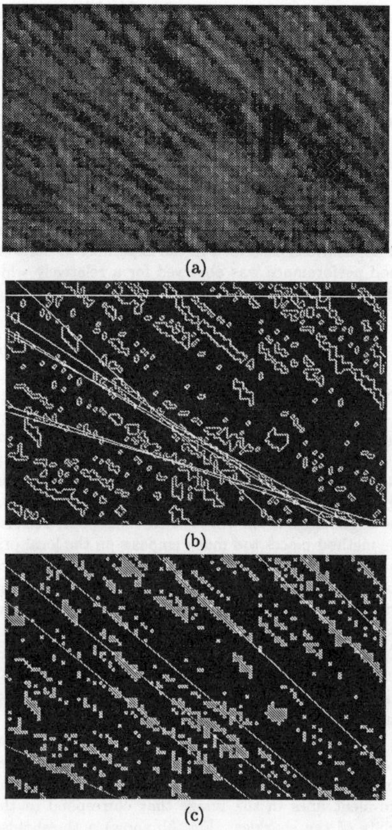

Figure 3: (a) The sparkle image. (b) Edge extraction from thresholded image and result of Hough transform. (c) Thresholded image and result of proposed method.

applications, where the distinction between foreground and background is clear and there is only one prevalent orientation in the image (parallel to the lines of the document), the Hough transform is very successful in finding the prevalent orientation with considerable accuracy.

To find prevalent orientations using the Hough transform, we compute the accumulator array, apply a lower threshold T_0 to eliminate cells with small contributions and add the contributions of all remaining cells that correspond to a certain value of θ [10]. The result is a one-dimensional array (integrated accumulator array) of values, with each value corresponding to a certain θ. The prevalent orientations can be located by finding the maxima in this array.

Distinguishing many prevalent orientations in the presence of superimposed noise is a task that can cause difficulties to the human visual system [11], as pointed out by Marr. Following Marr's work, we show in fig. 4a an image with line segments drawn at three prevalent orientations (at 9^0, 75^0 and 135^0), to which a number of line segments with random orientations are superimposed. Interference from irrelevant pixels causes difficulties to the Hough transform, whose integrated accumulator array exhibits peaks at many irrelevant orientations (4b) Moreover, this result is very sensitive to the value of the threshold T_0 selected for forming the integrated accumulator array. By contrast, the integrated accumulator array of our method, shown in fig. 4c, displays three clear maxima at 12^0, 74^0 and 136^0, which are very good approximations to the true prevalent orientations. No thresholding was necessary for obtaining this result, because irrelevant pixels have been suppressed by the voting kernel. We note the smoothness of the integrated accumulator for our method, which facilitates the determination of maxima and originates from the fact that the voting kernel was modeled as a smooth function of the shape descriptors.

4 Conclusion

In this paper, a novel method was presented for finding linear formations and prevalent orientations in digital images. A plausible voting kernel for Hough transform implementation was constructed by taking into account the shape and orientation of connected regions. As a result, the contribution of outlier pixels to the accumulator array was suppressed and the method was successfully applied to problems where the original Hough transform failed to determine the required lines or orientations. More generally, our method introduces useful *a priori* local information about the shape and properties of the neighborhood of a certain pixel into the accumulator array. In this way, we can obtain more robust detection of shapes at the global scale.

Acknowledgment

The authors wish to thank Erwan Lecren for writing the code of the program that decomposes images into connected components.

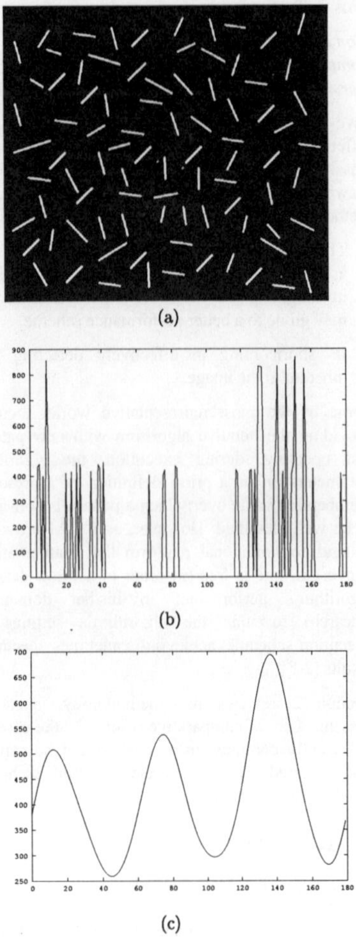

Figure 4: (a) Textured image with three prevalent orientations. (b) Typical integrated Hough transform accumulator array (number of pixels versus θ). (c) Integrated accumulator array of proposed method, displaying clear maxima corresponding to the prevalent orientations.

References

[1] R. D. Duda and P. E. Hart, "Use of the Hough transform to detect lines and curves in pictures,", *Commun. ACM*, vol. 15, pp. 11-15, 1972.

[2] V. F. Leavers, "Which Hough Transform?," *CVGIP: Image Understanding*, vol. 58, pp. 250-264, 1993.

[3] B. Gatos, S. J. Perantonis, and N. Papamarkos, " Accelerated Hough transform using rectangular image decomposition," *Electronics Letters*, vol. 32, pp. 730-732, 1996.

[4] P. L. Palmer, J. Kittler, and M. Petrou, "An optimizing line finder using a Hough transform algorithm," *Computer Vision and Image Understanding*, vol. 67, pp. 1-23, 1997.

[5] P. L. Palmer, J. Kittler, and M. Petrou, "A Hough transform algorithm with a 2D hypothesis testing kernel," *CVGIP: Image Understanding*, vol. 58, pp. 221-234, 1993.

[6] M. Sonka, V. Hlavac, and R. Boyle, *Image Processing, Analysis and Machine Vision*. London: Chapman and Hall, 1993.

[7] A. K. Jain, *Fundamentals of Digital Image Processing*. Englewood Cliffs, NJ: Prentice Hall, 1989.

[8] D. S. Le, G. R. Thoma, and H. Wechsler, "Automated page orientation and skew angle detection for binary document images," *Pattern Recognition*, vol. 27, pp. 1325-1344, 1994.

[9] S. C. Hinds, J. L. Fisher, and D. P. d'Amato, "A document skew detection method using run-length encoding and the Hough transform," *Proc. 10th Int. Conf. on Pattern Recognition*, pp. 464-468, 1990.

[10] B. Yu and A. K. Jain, "A robust and fast skew detection algorithm for generic documents", *Pattern Recognition*, vol. 29, pp. 1599-1629, 1996.

[11] D. Marr, "Representing visual information - a computational approach," *Lectures on Mathematics and Life Sciences*, vol. 10, pp. 61-80, 1978.

Comparison of Two Fuzzy Pixel-Clustering Algorithms: The Optimal Number of Clusters Approximation Issue

Sotiris N. Raptis and Spyros G. Tzafestas

Intelligent Robotics and Automation Laboratory (I.R.A.L.)
Department of Electrical & Computers Engineering
National Technical University of Athens

Abstract

In this paper two major methods for pixel clustering, namely the classical Fuzzy C-Means (F.C.M.) and the Iterative Fuzzy C-Means (I.F.C.M.) methods, are considered and compared. In both algorithms the patterns to classify are pixels.. The study of the results obtained for complex images leads to the conclusion that an essential improvement to the F.C.M. class of algorithms can be achieved by using iterative schemes that allow to preview algorithm's execution under changing operational conditions.

1. Introduction

Very often in image processing research and practice one deals with pixels for getting better results, instead of dealing with image blocks. The fact that the patterns to classify are pixels makes demanding a clustering policy which is more powerful, efficient and quick than a block clustering method. The basic concepts of both block and pixel clustering methods are founded on the fuzzy set theory and reasoning, allowing a pixel or a block to belong to more than one clusters, i.e. to simultaneously "resemble" to more than one pixels or blocks which are considered as clusters. Since an ordinary image contains a great deal of data, and this number becomes huge for detailed and complicated images where more pixel information is required, the need for efficient, fast and reliable algorithms becomes more demanding [1].

I.F.C.M. algorithms are based on the idea that more accurately, quickly and reliably will be classified those pattern-pixels whose association with a cluster through a membership value is over a certain level of confidence, while those with lower membership values will be reorganized and transferred to the next iteration as not yet well classified patterns. It is shown that this concept is not only more reliable and quick than the classical single-step F.C.M. class of methodologies, but also can guide us to figure out an optimized computational scheme in terms of the algorithm's initial settings, like the optimum number of clusters.

The idea of iterative implementing the F.C.M. method can be realized in more than one ways. Researchers have developed iterative schemes in order to study different aspects of fuzzy logic application into classification issues or to eliminate classical F.C.M drawbacks. The major drawbacks of the F.C.M. method are :

1. The requirement to classify the input patterns into a predefined number of clusters without investigating the nature of input patterns which may guide to a better performance scheme.
2. Its shortcoming in effectively detecting noise inherent to the image.

Some of the most representative works focus on providing the iterative algorithm with new patterns, and updating, during execution, the algorithm's parameters or the a priori definition of a prescribed membership value over which a pattern is considered to be well classified. However, as F.C.M provides a general computational platform that mathematically converges, one is free (in order to achieve desirable algorithm's performance in his/her domain of research) to tune the algorithm's settings and execution schedule, achieving sometimes spectacular results [2-8].

Section 2 reviews the methodology, Section 3 presents a set of comparative results for the case of a sufficiently complex image that cannot be captured and detected by a block-classification technique. Finally, Section 4 provides the conclusions.

2. Methodology

In image F.C.M. methodology, clusters are represented by pixels as the clusters' centers do. The membership matrix contains information that relates any pixel to any prototype-cluster pixel. The prototype pixels are updated during the iterations of the algorithm and the same is true for the membership matrix. However it is observed that the number of iterations needed for the algorithm to converge becomes unacceptable, although the final quality is much better compared to that obtained using the block classification.

A solution to this problem is to use and implement F.C.M. iteratively using a new algorithm (called Iterative Fuzzy C-Means (I.F.C.M.) algorithm) which is a generalization of the classical F.C.M. one. The

I.F.C.M. algorithm is briefly discussed here. The pixels, initially (during the first few iterations) used and considered as clusters, are taken from a fraction of the pixels to classify. The clusters are not determined from the beginning of the algorithm's execution. The pixels that are to be used as clusters and the classified patterns are obtained iteratively until the end of the algorithm. This means that during each iteration, new pixels are estimated that fulfill the clusters' properties and the clusters' criteria which are set up prior to the algorithm execution. These new pixels-patterns are then classified into the current set of clusters and are added to the matrix of classified input patterns. Hence, the classified pixels (number is gradually raised until it reaches the predefined number of input patterns, while the non classified pixels' set gradually reduces. This iterative selection depends on whether the pixels examined pertain to a cluster through a membership value contained within the partition matrix. To do this selection a pixel has to be associated with a specific cluster via a membership value greater than a prespecified level of confidence. This simply means that at each iteration of the algorithm as classified pixels will be considered only those ones which belong to a certain cluster with a minimum degree of membership. All the other pixels will not be classified at this iteration and will be passed to the next iteration as new patterns to classify. The set of pixels-clusters will be at the same time updated and reevaluated as the output of a new implementation of the algorithm. The new updated clusters' vector derived at a given iteration has the property that it contains pixels which are related to the current vector of input patterns with a membership value greater than a prespecified level. This level is the one of the algorithm's input arguments. This set of newly classified patterns is subtracted from the current input patterns'set. At the end of the algorithm an overall set of clusters is made up iteratively while the input pattern set is empty.

In the following, the I.F.C.M. algorithmic steps are briefly described :

step 1

step 1.1 Define the vector of input patterns x=[x1,…,xN], where (N) is the number of image pixels to classify

step 1.2 Define the number of clusters (c)

step 1.3 Define the level of confidence (ε_L)

step 1.4 Initialize the iterations(counter (b=0)

step 1.5 Initialize the vector of clustered pixels $\underline{x}_c^{(b)}$=[], and the vector of unclustered pixels $\underline{x}_u^{(b)}=\underline{x}$

step 1.6 Define randomly the initial set of clusters $\underline{c}^{(b)} = \{x_i, i = 1,\ldots,c | x_i \in \underline{x}\}$

step 2

step 2.1 Increase by 1 the iterations' counter b=b+1;

step 2.2 Set $\underline{x}^{(b)}=\underline{x}_u^{(b-1)}$, the vector of unclustered patterns at the b-th iteration and $\underline{x}_c^{(b)}=\underline{x}$-{ x_i: x_i ($\underline{x}^{(b-1)}$ and $\underline{\mu}_{c(b-1)}(\underline{x}_i)$ (ε_L}, where $\underline{\mu}_{c(b-1)}(\underline{x}_i)$ represents the vector of membership values that relate the i-th pattern to the current set of pixels clusters ($\underline{c}^{(b-1)}$) derived from the previous iteration (b-1). In an analogous way the set of currently unclustered patterns $\underline{x}_u^{(b)}$ is computed using the 'smaller than (<) instead of the 'greater than or equal(($\geq$) inequality sign within the membership function condition expression;

step 2.3 Compute the number of clustered and unclustered pixels ($n_c^{(b)}$ =|$\underline{x}_c^{(b)}$|) and ($n_u^{(b)}$ =|$\underline{x}_u^{(b)}$|).

step 3

step 3.1 *if* n_c=N *then* stop *else* go to step 2.

A general theoretical framework of the iterative fuzzy classification and coding schemes is discussed in [5], where the concept of fuzzy to crisp mode transition is introduced using hyperspheres of clusters' that surround the patterns to classify. These, hyperspheres are shrinking iteratively around the patterns until the transition from the fuzzy to crisp pattern state is complete. However, the general framework of the proposed scheme in this paper supports constant clusters, with only the number of related patterns changing iteratively. Membership threshold notion is also used for the shrinking of the hyperspheres.

The general mathematical methodology discussed in this paper is also partially formulated in [7] where the iterative implementation is applied in order to achieve a better noise canceling. Noise reduction within images and original image restoration are among the most known and useful applications of fuzzy logic into the image processing field. Working and carrying out experiments on some iterative implementation techniques of fuzzy methodologies, we have verified that the overall procedure not only becomes faster but can provide insight about optimal image treatment which consists a subject only sparsely addressed in the literature. In [8] an iterative methodology is also reported based on iterative relaxation techniques of some pixel assignment probability function which depends on the assignment of pairs of pixels into corresponding clusters.

3. Results

In the following some results are provided which concern the application of both algorithms on a given image which exhibits some complexity and cannot be captured and detected by a block-based classification scheme.

The original image is shown in Fig. 1. Figure 2 contains in its first column the reconstructed images obtained through the application of the classical F.C.M. algorithm, and in its second column the images obtained through the application of the I.F.C.M. algorithm. In Fig. 3 the convergence curves for the algorithms are given. The first column contains the convergence curve for F.C.M. and the second the convergence curve for the I.F.C.M. algorithm. The two algorithms have been compared using a variable number of clusters so as to examine their classification performance in different conditions. This number of clusters varies from 10 to 100.

The measures of comparison used are:

1. The number of iterations needed for the algorithm to converge.
2. The final mean classification error per pixel defined by the formula:

$$E = \frac{1}{N}\sum_{i=1}^{N}|x_i - c_i|,$$

where N is the number of input patterns, x_i is the i-th input pattern, and c_i is the cluster to which the i-th pattern is most likely attributed with the greatest membership value.

Table 1, presents and explains the abbreviations used in the reconstructed images shown in Figures 2 and 3. Table 2, gives the summarized results obtained from the performance comparison of the two algorithms when the mean classification error per pixel is considered. Finally Table 3, contains the corresponding results when the number of iterations needed for the twos algorithms to converge is considered.

4. Conclusions - Discussion

Some conclusions that can be directly drawn from the tables 2 and 3 are the following :

- Convergence is faster in the I.F.C.M. case.
- The mean error per pixel is also smaller in I.F.C.M. than in F.C.M., which means that one can achieve better image representation using I.F.C.M. .
- The number of iterations is constant in I.F.C.M. and variable in F.C.M.
- The mean classification error per pixel in the I.F.C.M. case possesses the same behavior remaining practically constant with the number of initial clusters.
- The same tendency is also observed in the F.C.M. case where the term "practically constant" implies that the classification error per pixel is constant when the number of clusters increases.
- Looking also at the segmented images one can observe a constant behavior.

Putting the above conclusions into a more general framework one could inference that:

- Performance characteristics tend to remain stable over the algorithm's initial settings.
- The same performance can be reached even for small number of clusters.
- There must be a "nearly optimum" set of parameters that can be chosen to initialize the algorithm in order to make it work more efficiently with better performance, if optimality is yet an elusion for the same quality of output results.

It is the authors' intention to assist and improve classification techniques considering, besides absolute gray level values, other types of information (such as neighbors' information) to construct more generic clustering schemes.

Table 1 : Abbreviations used to represent the performance parameters of the algorithms

'no. cl.(	stands for the number of clusters
'er.'	stands for the mean classification error per pixel
'no. iter.'	stands for the number of iterations needed for algorithm's convergence

Figure 1 : Original tree image

Figure 2 : Reconstructed images using both F.C.M. and I.F.C.M. algorithms for fuzzy pixel classification

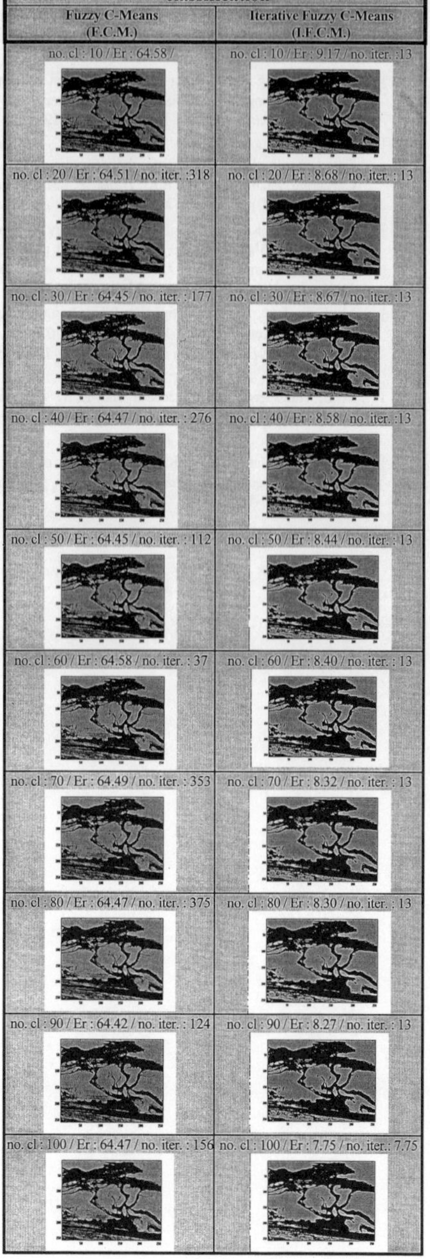

Figure 2 : Convergence curves of both F.C.M. and I.F.C.M. algorithms for fuzzy pixel classification

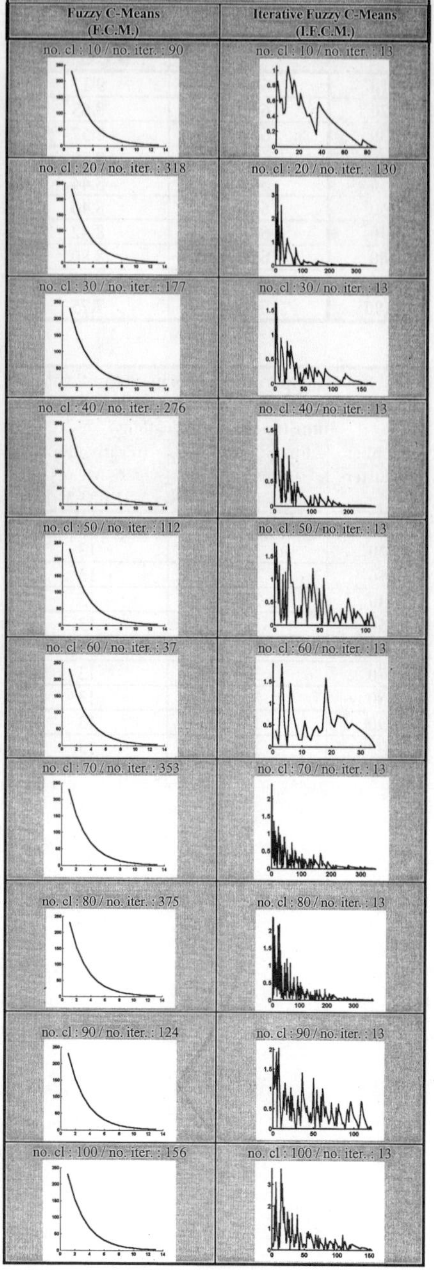

Table 2 : Comparative performance of F.C.M. and I.F.C.M. algorithms in terms of mean classification error		
Number of clusters	Fuzzy C-Means (F.C.M.)	Iterative Fuzzy C-Means (I.F.C.M.)
10	64.88	9.17
20	64.51	8.68
30	64.45	8.57
40	64.47	8.58
50	64.45	8.44
60	64.58	8.40
70	64.49	8.42
80	64.47	8.80
90	64.42	8.47
100	64.47	7.75

Table 3 : Comparative performance of F.C.M. and I.F.C.M. algorithms in terms of convergence time (number of iterations)		
Number of clusters	Fuzzy C-Means (F.C.M.)	Iterative Fuzzy C-Means (I.F.C.M.)
10	90	13
20	378	13
30	177	13
40	276	13
50	112	13
60	37	13
70	353	13
80	375	13
90	124	13
100	156	13

5. References

[1] Fu & J. K. Mui, 'As survey of image segmentation', *Pattern Recognition*, Vol. 13, pp. 3-16, 1981

[2] M.A. Ismail, 'Fuzzy C-means : Optimality of solutions and effective termination of the algorithm', *Pattern Recognition*, Vol. 19, No. 6, pp. 481-485, 1986.

[3] Zheru Chi, Jing Wu & Hong Yan, 'Handwritten numeral recognition using self organizing maps and fuzzy rules', *Pattern Recognition*, Vol. 28, No. 1, pp. 59-66, 1995.

[4] Robert L. Cannon, Jitendra V. Dave & James C. Bezdek, 'Efficient Implementation of the Fuzzy c-means Clustering Algorithms', *I.E.E.E. Trans. P.A.M.I.*, Vol. PAMI-8, No. 2, pp. 248-255, March 1986.

[5] Nicolaos B. Karayiannis, Pin-I Pai, 'Fuzzy Vector Quantization Algorithms and their Application in Image Processing Compression', *I.E.E.E. Trans. on Image Processing,* Vol. 4, No. 9, Sep. 1995, pp. 1193-1201.

[6] Mu-King Tsay, Jen-Fa Huang, Wei-Ping Chang-Chung, 'Image Compression Using V.Q. and Fuzzy Classified Algorithm', *I.E.E.E. Proc. on image processing*, 1996, pp. 466-471.

[7] T. L. Huntsberger, C. L. Jacobs and R. L. Cannon, 'Iterative fuzzy image segmentation', Pattern Recognition

[8] Nikhil R. Pal and Sankar K. Pal, 'A review of image segmentation techniques', *Pattern Recognition*, Vol. 26, No. 9, pp. 1277-1294, 1993.

A FUZZY MODEL FOR THE PITCH PERCEPTION OF COMPLEX TONES

D. K. Fragoulis, C. N. Papaodysseus and J. N. Avaritsiotis

National Technical University of Athens
Department of Electrical and Computer Engineering
9 Heroon Polytechniou St., 157 73 Zographou, Athens, Greece
E-mail: frag@mlab.ece.ntua.gr

ABSTRACT

In this work, we consider the problem of pitch perception and we propose a fuzzy model that can account, in a qualitative way, for all the possible cases of complex tones. The model includes two distinct stages. The first stage is a frequency analyzer that determines the frequencies of some of the individual sinusoidal components of the complex tone. This information proceeds to the second stage of the model, which is a fuzzy processor. The processor receives the frequencies of the components and performs all the necessary computations in order to derive the pitch. The use of a fuzzy processor that represents and manipulates information, which is not precise, makes the model capable to predict the ambiguities of pitch that have been observed.

1. INTRODUCTION

Pitch may be defined as that attribute of auditory sensation in terms of which sounds may be ordered in a musical scale. Like loudness and timbre, it is a subjective attribute that cannot be expressed in physical units. Essentially, pitch is related to the repetition rate of the waveform of a sound. In the case of a pure tone, it is primarily correlated with tone's frequency, despite the fact that intensity, duration and temporal envelope of the tone may have an influence on pitch. Assigning a pitch value to a complex tone is generally understood to mean determination of the frequency of a pure tone having the same subjective pitch as the complex tone. It is noticed that even sounds not formed of well-defined discrete sinusoids may evoke a pitch sensation.

In music, pitch is related with the features of melody and harmony. Since a simple tone evokes a pitch, then a sequence of tones with appropriate frequencies should evoke the percept of melody. However, it seems that a sequence of tones evokes a sense of melody only when tones lie below 4-5 kHz [1]. Also, experimental results on pitch identification have shown that the pitch of a complex tone can be ambiguous, especially if low order components are weak or missing, or if only a few components are present.

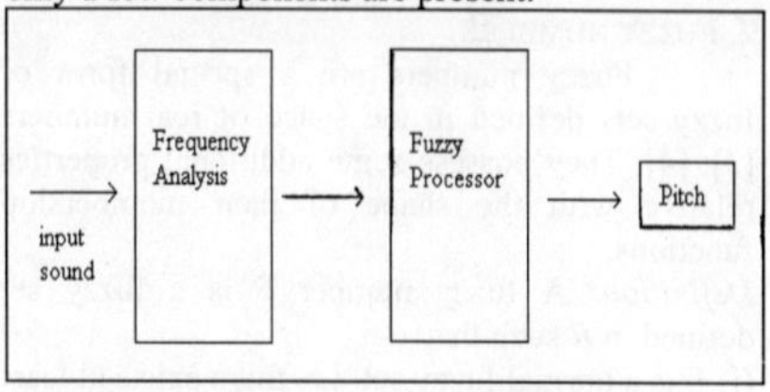

Figure 1. A schematic model for a pitch perception system

The pitch of a complex tone could be derived from pitches of the individual components using a pattern recognition model [2]. Generally, such a model involves two stages, as illustrated in figure 1. The first stage is a frequency analyzer, which simulates the procedure of spectral analysis performed in the inner ear, so that different frequencies are separated. The second stage is a pattern recognizer, which determines the pitch of the complex tone from the frequencies of the resolved components. This is obtained by searching for a fundamental frequency whose "harmonics" match the frequencies of the resolved components of the stimulus as closely as possible.

The pattern recognizer should be able to work properly in all possible types of complex tones. Consider as an example a sound consisting of the frequencies 200Hz, 400Hz, 600Hz, 800Hz,etc. This sound has a low pitch, which is the same to the pitch of a 200Hz pure tone. However, it is possible to filter the sound in order to remove the 200Hz component and we will find that the pitch does not alter. The same result will be observed if we eliminate all except a small group of mid frequency harmonics, say 1800Hz, 2000Hz, 2200Hz. This phenomenon is well known as the "missing fundamental". As an other example we could consider a sound that consists of three sinusoidal components at 1840Hz, 2040Hz and 2240Hz. The perceived pitch of this sound is about that of a 204Hz pure tone. Actually, there is an ambiguity of the exact pitch value since it seems to lie around 180Hz, 204Hz and 227Hz.

In order to have an effective pitch identification system the pattern recognizer should be able to manage with pitch ambiguities. To achieve this, a fuzzy processor is used which performs all the manipulations using fuzzy numbers. This feature of the processor provides the ability to adjust the calculation precision. Thus, if we represent the frequency values as fuzzy numbers, the system is able to derive vague values of pitch.

2. FUZZY NUMBERS

Fuzzy numbers are a special form of fuzzy sets defined in the space of real numbers [3], [4]. They possess some additional properties relative with the shape of their membership functions.

Definition: A fuzzy number F is a fuzzy set defined in ***R*** such that:

(i) F is a normal fuzzy set, i.e. there exists at least one element x of ***R*** which F(x)=1.

(ii) F is convex.

(iii) F is upper semicontinuous ⇔ All α-cuts of F are convex.

(iv) F has a bounded support ⇔ All α-cuts are closed intervals of ***R***.

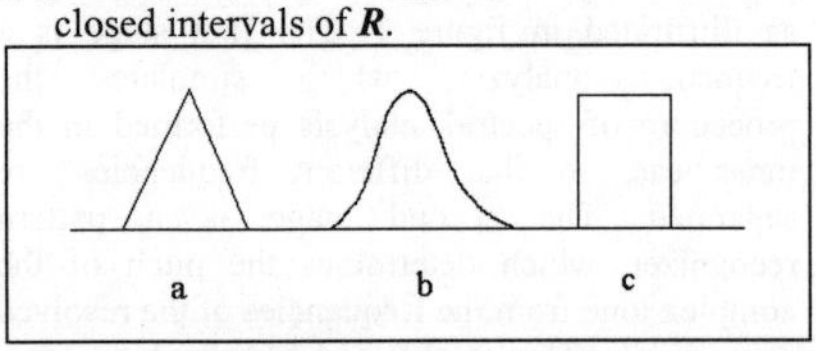

Figure 2. Examples of fuzzy numbers

A fuzzy number may be considered as a suitable model of approximate notions, as for example, near zero, about 5, etc. Some shapes of fuzzy numbers are illustrated in figure 2. The membership function of the fuzzy number visualizes a grade membership of a given element of a concept (near, about, etc.). Unimodality of F assures us that exactly one region exists, in which the relevant elements have the highest grades of membership. Of course, the shape of a membership function reflects different situations in which a variety of shapes can be observed. In figure 2a, a triangle-like fuzzy number is presented, where three characteristic points are interpreted as upper and lower values of the range, and the element of x corresponding to the highest grade of membership is called a modal value of the fuzzy number. In figure 2b, a so-called bell shaped fuzzy number is given, while in figure 2c an interval that is a particular case of fuzzy number, is presented.

We observe that the shapes of the membership functions are similar in that one modal and two extreme limits are evident. This enables us to use a parametric representation of the fuzzy numbers. For this purpose, L(left side) and R(right side) fuzzy numbers are introduced. By an L fuzzy number we mean a fuzzy number of this membership function:

(i) L(-x)=L(x)

(ii) L(0)=1

(iii) L is increasing in [0,+∞)

The same definition holds for the R fuzzy number. An L-R fuzzy number possesses the following membership function:

$$F(x) = \begin{cases} L\left(\dfrac{m-x}{a}\right), & if\ x \le m \\ R\left(\dfrac{x-m}{b}\right), & if\ x \ge m \end{cases}$$

where a, b>0 are parameters controlling fuzziness of the fuzzy number. For the case a=b=0 we get a genuine real number. Including the above parameters (m,a,b) the fuzzy number is denoted by A(m,a,b).

3. THE FUZZY PROCESSOR

The fuzzy processor is composed of two blocks, as illustrated in figure 3. The first block takes as input the frequencies of the individual components of the sound. We notice that the phases and amplitudes of the components are ignored. Next, every component is resolved in order all the potential subcomponents to be derived. Essentially, computing all the submultiples of the frequency of all the components performs the resolution procedure. Subsequently, the fuzzyfication of all the subcomponents is performed, by assigning a fuzzy number at each subcomponent. The shape of the membership function of the fuzzy numbers is given below:

$$F(x) = e^{\left(-b\left(x-x_0\right)^2\right)}$$

The value of b determines how narrow the membership function will be. We notice that the width of the membership function is related to the description explicitness of the subcomponent frequency. The frequency discrimination ability

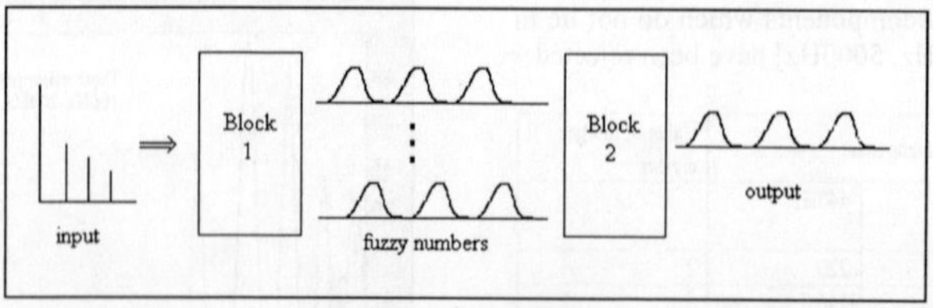

Figure 3. The fuzzy processor

of the human ear appears a logarithmic dependence on frequency. Thus we should select an appropriate value for b, according to the harmonic interval where each fuzzy number belongs.

After assigning a membership function at each subcomponent, the union operation is applied on the groups of subcomponents that have been generated by the same component of the sound. Therefore, some non-unimodal fuzzy numbers derived, which correspond to the components of the input sound. Finally, the intersection operation is applied on the aforementioned fuzzy numbers. The result of this operation is a fuzzy number whose membership function appear some local peaks, and the greatest of them determines the pitch. If there exist more than one peaks having an almost common value, then all of them contribute to the formation of the pitch.

The union and the intersection operations are defined as follows:

$$A_1 \cap A_2 = \min\{A_1, A_2\}$$

$$A_1 \cup A_2 = \max\{A_1, A_2\}$$

4. Simulation Results

The developed fuzzy model has been used to derive the pitch in three special cases of complex tones, as discussed in following. As a first example, we considered a harmonic sound consisted of three components at 200Hz, 300Hz and 400Hz. Figure 4 shows the resolved subcomponents, while in figure 5 the membership

Frequency of component			Value of integer divisor
200Hz	300Hz	400Hz	
100	150	200	2
rejected	100	133.3	3
rejected	rejected	100	4
rejected	rejected	rejected	5

Figure 4. The derived subcomponents for the first example

functions of the corresponding fuzzy numbers are presented. The output of the model is shown in figure 6.

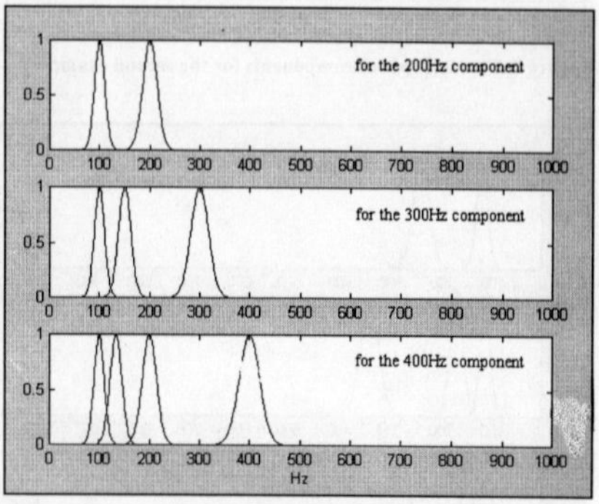

Figure 5. The derived fuzzy numbers for the first example

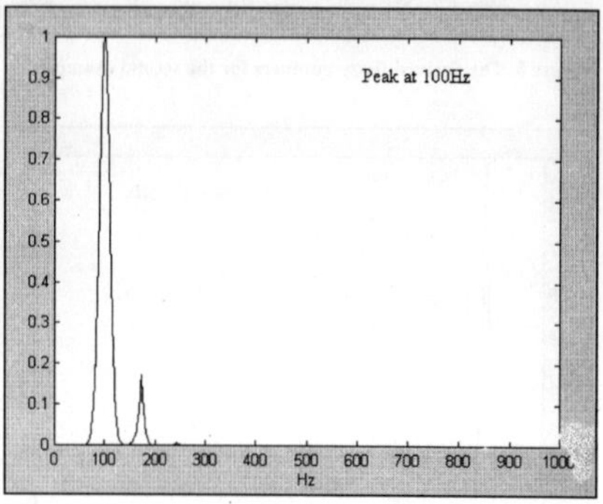

Figure 6. Output of the model for the first example

In a second example, a non-harmonic sound with three components at 240Hz, 340Hz and 440Hz has been used. The results are presented in figures 7, 8 and 9. It is apparent that the proposed model derives a pitch despite the fact that the subcomponents do not coincide (see fig. 7). As a third example a non-harmonic sound with components at 1840Hz, 2040Hz and 2240Hz has been treated. The values of sound components chosen, have been used by researchers [5] to show experimentally that pitch cannot be determined univocally in some cases. The output of the model is illustrated in figure 10. It is apparent that the output appears in the form of three dominant peaks. We notice that, in all the examples, the subcomponents which do not lie in the interval [100Hz, 5000Hz] have been rejected.

Frequency of component			Value of integer divisor
240Hz	340Hz	440Hz	
120	170	220	2
rejected	113.3	146.6	3
rejected	rejected	110	4
rejected	rejected	rejected	5

Figure 7. The derived subcomponents for the second example

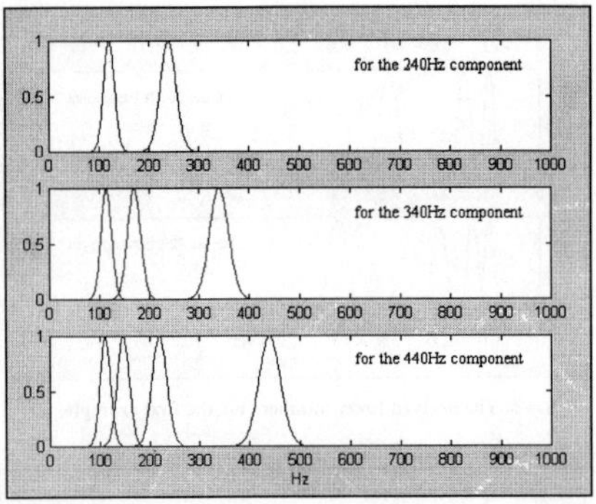

Figure 8. The derived fuzzy numbers for the second example

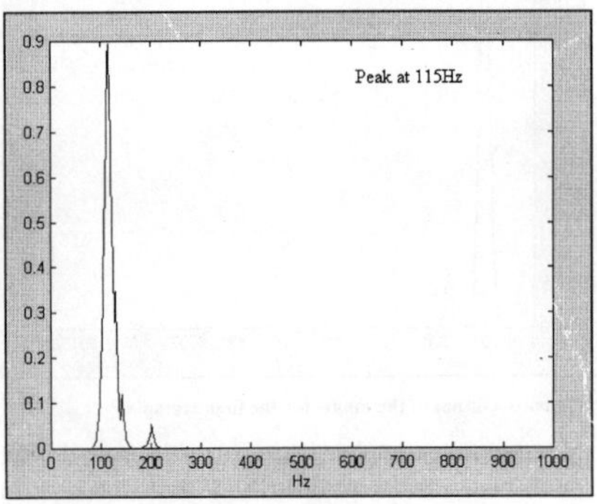

Figure 9. Output of the model for the second example

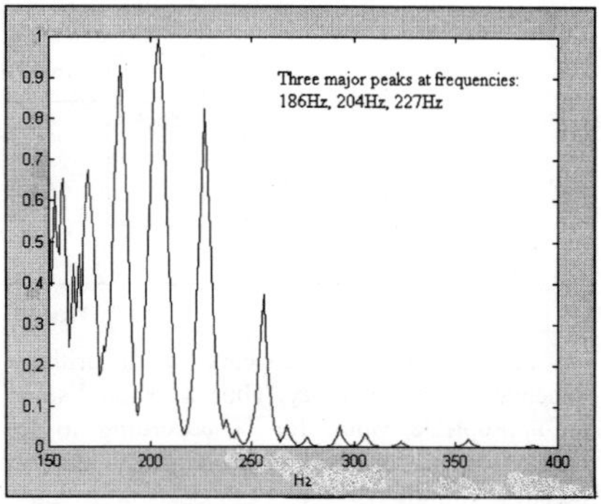

Figure 10. Output of the model for the third example

5. CONCLUSION

A fuzzy model for pitch identification has been developed, that is able to derive the pitch of a complex tone using the information of individual components. The basic feature of the model is that it performs all the manipulations using fuzzy numbers. Considering frequency components as fuzzy numbers with adjustable membership function width, provides the ability to impose to the manipulation a precision which is relative to the logarithm of components frequency. Thus, the necessary distance between the central frequencies of two subcomponents in order the intersection of them to cause a local peak to the output of the system is much smaller when components correspond at low frequencies than when correspond at high. Generally, the greatest peak of the derived output corresponds to the pitch of the complex tone. In the case of more than one peak with close values, the pitch can't be determined univocally.

REFERENCES

[1] W. D. Ward, *Subjective musical pitch*, J. Acoust. Soc. Am. 26, 369-380, (1954).

[2] E. Terhardt, *Pitch, consonance and harmony*, J. Acoust. Soc. Am. 55, 1061-1069, (1974).

[3] Witold Pedrycz, "Fuzzy Control and fuzzy Systems", Research Studies Press LTD, (1993).

[4] Earl Cox, "The fuzzy systems handbook", Academic Press Professional, (1994).

[5] J. F. Schouten, R. J. Ritsma and B. L. Cardozo, *Pitch of the residue*, J. Acoust. Soc. Am. 34, 1418-1424, (1962).

A Voice Scripting Language Interface of N-Arity for an OO Formant Synthesizer

Dionysios V. Politis, Ioannis A. Tsoukalas, Panagiotis Linardis

Department of Computer Science, Aristotle University of Thessaloniki
Thessaloniki 540 06, Greece
dpolitis@csd.auth.gr, http://www.csd.auth.gr

Abstract

In this paper a scripting language of N-class arity is presented. This language is used as an interface for a real-time formant synthesizer encompassing object-oriented (OO) software engineering technology. The synthesizer uses physical modeling techniques and acts as a generic interface for MIDI and vocal reproduction of music. The vocal part of the synthesizer-'singer' is event driven in terms of formant arithmetic according to the SKINI (Synthesis toolKit Network Interface) format. A new script-language interface is devised in order to program the 'singer' in terms of music ambient factors. The interface is adaptable up to arity N vectors, where N is the factor of the voice quality complexity adequately reproduced by the formant description at the synthesizer.

1 Introduction: the semantics

The exact performance of synthetic 'singers' for non-tempered, chromatic vocal reproduction of songs, especially in the East, has to cope with two major issues: the one has to do with the scales (where one finds the successors of the ancient Dorian, Lydian, Phrygian, Mixolydian Modes [1]) and the other with the notation, or the *microtones* of the perceived octaves.

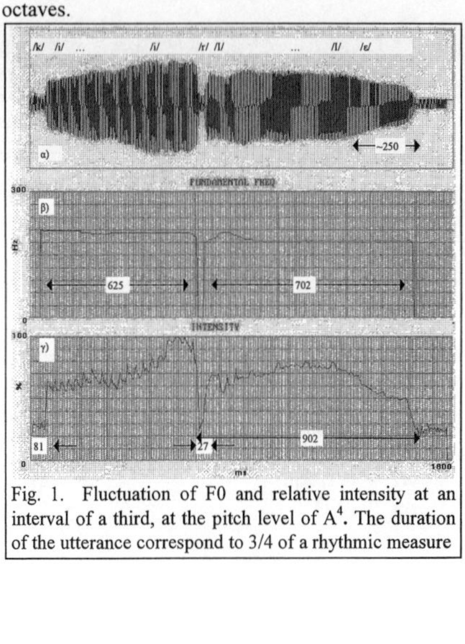

Fig. 1. Fluctuation of F0 and relative intensity at an interval of a third, at the pitch level of A^4. The duration of the utterance correspond to 3/4 of a rhythmic measure

As it can be readily seen by the spectrogram of fig. 1, the real singer reproduces phonemes by accelerating and fluctuating his voiced utterance bilaterally to the pronounced note. These frequency curves correspond to a 'quality' bending of voice, which is difficult to describe in arithmetic terms and other musical notation symbols when driving a formant synthesizer. This situation which is not sufficiently described in terms of 'flat' note description is resolved by using "quality curves" in order to describe periods of spectral disorder and variation, like attack transients or musical morphemes like *petasti* [2].

On the other hand, apart from the usual music notation which implies specific diatonic and chromatic scales, there are various other regional systems [3] [4] which have an entirely different microtonal distribution. In order to use these one has either to use the coarse approximation of the usual music system and notation or to use a generic Δ system of arity N, like the one proposed by the authors of this paper.

2. The OO synthesizer

The synthesizer used was originally devised by P. Cook [5]. Using object-oriented technology and software design it is able to encapsulate a hierarchy of classes, amongst which resonance and anti-resonance FIR filters in order to shape the formants of the utterance. This formation has the characteristics of a *spectral envelope enforcement* function having the form of:

$$sef : AS \times \begin{bmatrix} EN \\ \ldots \\ EN \end{bmatrix} \rightarrow AS$$

where AS is the audio signal array.

The *sef* function enforces the formant envelopes on the excitation signal of the class RawWvIn of the synthesizer (see fig. 4).

$$sef\left(es \begin{bmatrix} en_1 \\ \ldots \\ en_4 \end{bmatrix} \right) = \sum_{i=1}^{4} gain(fb^{(i)}(es)en_i - env^{(i)}(es))$$

Thus, the special envelopes of quantitative speaker characteristics are enforced on the excitation source *es*. On the software design part of the 'singer', the basic and the derived classes are shown in fig. 4.

3 The N-arity scripting client/server network

On the prototype we have used, the server is an SGI Indigo-2 real time implementation of the 'singer' and the client is a Tcl/Tk GUI shell acting as the visual client. The client part can be on the same computer or, on any other networked computer using the GUI shell. In the latter case, a TCP/IP *socket* can be used to transmit data. On our implementation we have used, apart from the SGI client, a Winsock 1.1 client [6], which is an implementation of the BSD Unix sockets on the TCP and IP layers of the Windows OS.

The visual client is virtually implementing a Δ arity system as follows:

1. A scale is chosen. The number of commas per octave is denoted (for instance, 100 for *hindu* music [3], or 80 for *traditional* Greek; however, the default is 55).
2. A signed interval is denoted. The maximum alteration is that of a twelfth.
3. The time duration is noted. Taken into account that the default duration is that of a *noire* the alterations are additive or multiplying. Again, a user defined basic rhythmic foot can be declared in *ms*.
4. The envelope quality operator is declared; for instance, a common instrumental and vocal as well quality characteristic of traditional Greek Music is *petasti* [2] [8].
5. *Dieses, bemols* and alterations of scale are denoted.
6. Intonation *(accents)* are also marked.

Taking all these into account, one could describe the utterance of fig. 1 as follows:

S(d,2), Δ(+1, 1,pi) [k I], Δ(0,1) [r I], Δ(0,1) [epsilon]

where
S(d,2) : defines the diatonic scale, and the second note of the middle octave,
Δ(+3,1,pi) : is an alteration of a fourth, a time duration of a *noire* and a quality effect of *petasti*,
Δ(0,1) [epsilon] : is the same note with the previous one, a time duration of a *noire*, and the utterance of the phoneme /ε/, according to the notation of the International Phonetic Alphabet.

Sampling four times this utterance by five different male subjects we have taken the mean value of /e/ as seen at fig. 2.

Phoneme	ASCII description	formants (Hz)	Freq. Width	Relative amplitudes (dB)
/ε/	ehh	515	0.977	0
		1805	0.810	-10
		2526	0.875	-10
		3103	0.400	-13

Fig. 2. Estimated mean values for a phoneme out of 4 samples of the same utterance at different pitch levels out of 5 speakers. The frequency width of the formants is not denoted in Hz but as it is inserted into the synthesizer, i.e. exp(2W/Fp)

The arity of the script can be deduced as follows:

N = max (dim v_1, dim v_2, …, dim v_n)
where

v1 = (+1, 1,pi)
v2 = (0,1)
… …

We have found that usually an arity of 5 is adequate to describe the most complex voicing phenomena.
Some of the operators used and their approximate action can be seen in fig. 3 [7].

Operator	Scripting description	Alteration of F0
κ (kappa)	Fluctuation for 1.5 of time duration with an increase of a semitone	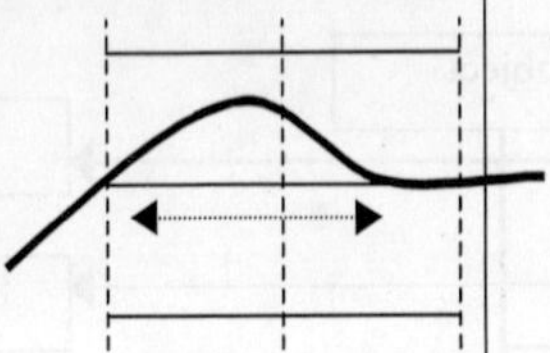
ψ (psi)	Accent 20% increase of pitch level	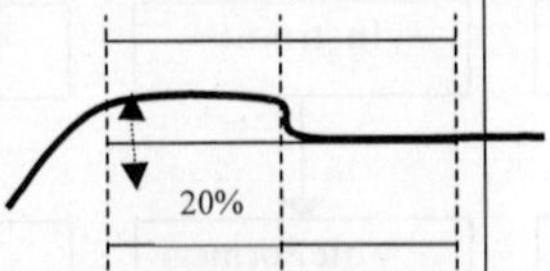

Fig. 3. Description of the alterations caused on F0 by the action of operands. The ψ operator alters the gain of the utterance as well (not shown in this diagram)

4 Conclusions

Usually formant synthesizers lack the appropriate interface to describe voice intonation and quality of speech. As a result, they can not be driven properly and furthermore they lack the scripting semantics for a client/server coupling.
This paper proposes an encoding methodology acting as an interpreted script language interfacing the user semantics with the synthesizer formant arithmetic description.

5 Acknowledgments

The authors would like to acknowledge that the model sounds have been estimated from the voices of N. Lefkopoulos, D. Papageorgiou, N. Kougias, D. Voultsios and S. Triantafyllidis. We are grateful for their assistance.

References

[1] Balaban, M. and Irish, S., "Automatic Jazz Accompaniment Computation : An Open Advice-Based Approach" ", *International Computer Music Conference ICMC96*, Hong-Kong, Proceedings, pp. 145-148, August 19-24, 1996.

[2] Pikrakis, A., Kamarotos, D., "Recognition of Isolated Musical Patterns in the Context Greek Tradional Music", Special Session: Voice/Audio Processing Systems, *Third IEEE International Conference on Electronics, Circuits and Systems ICECS '96*, Rhodes, Vol. II, pp. 1223-1226, October 13-16, 1996.

[3] Mastorakis, N., "Interpretation of Byzantine Music Notatuion as Adaptive Δ-Modulation", Special Session: Voice/Audio Processing Systems, *Third IEEE International Conference on Electronics, Circuits and Systems ICECS '96*, Rhodes, Vol. II, pp. 1219-1222, October 13-16, 1996

[4] Spyridis, H.C., Politis, D.V., "Information Theory Applied to the Structural Study of Byzantine Ecclesiastical Hymns", *ACUSTICA*, Vol. 71, No. 1, May 1990, pp. 41-49.

[5] Cook, P.R., "SIGGRAPH: Synthesis ToolKit in C++, Version 1.0", Department of Computer Science, Princeton University, May 1996.

[6] Oliphant, Z., "Windows-to-Unix Sockets", *PC Magazine*, Vol. 16, No. 41, pp.173-177, February 18, 1997.

[7] Rader, G.M, "Creating Printed Music Automatically", *IEEE Computer Magazine,* June, 1996.

[8] Politis, D., Tsoukalas, A., Linardis, P., "VIDI-A Voice Instrument Digital Interface for Byzantine Music", *International Computer Music Conference ICMC97*, Thessaloniki, Proceedings, pp. 403-407, September 25-30, 1997.

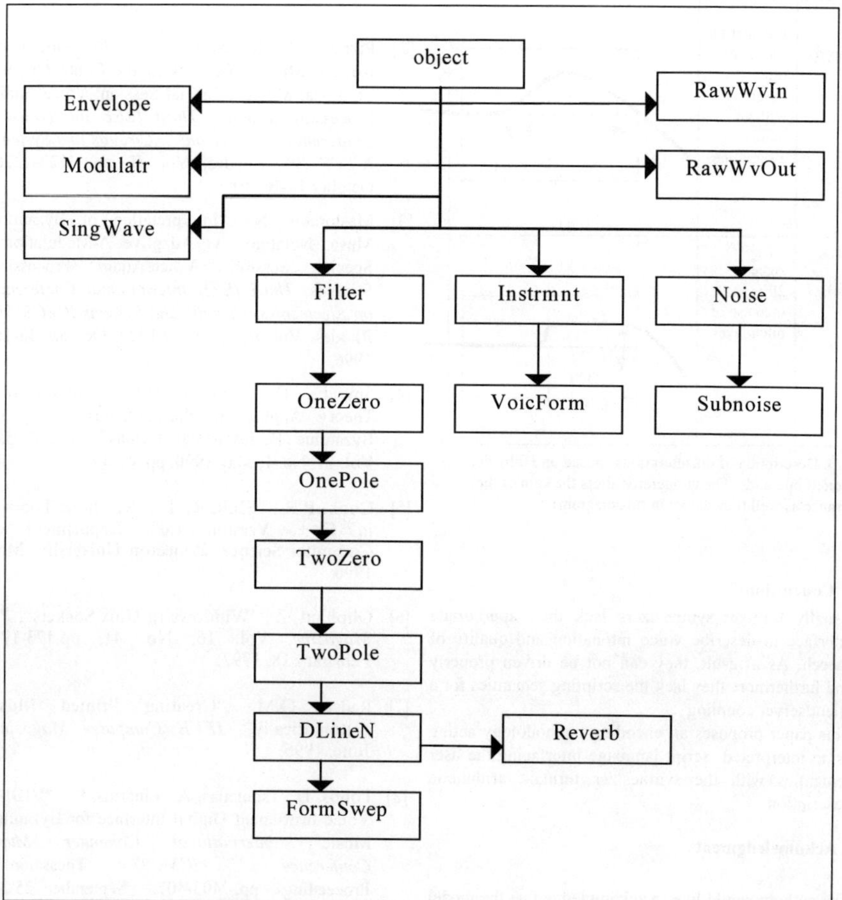

Fig. 4. Class Hierarchy for the formant synthesizer acting as a synthetic singer.

IDENTIFICATION OF DISCRETE INPUT NONLINEAR SYSTEMS FOR DIGITAL CHAOTIC SIGNAL PROCESSING

Alexander M. Krot[a], *Mikhail A. Shcherbakov*[b]

[a]Institute of Engineering Cybernetics of the National Academy of Sciences of Belarus
Surganov Str., 6, 220012, Minsk, Belarus
e-mail: alxkrot@newman.basnet.minsk.by
Tel.: (375) 172 685086, Fax.: (375) 172 318403
[b]State Technical University of Penza
Krasnaya Str., 40, 440017, Penza, Russia
e-mail: mike@dimond.stup.ac.ru
Tel.: (841-2) 663744; Fax.: (841-2) 550212

1. INTRODUCTION

The problem of finding the functional relationship that determines the output of a system in response to any relevant input is known as the problem of system identification or system characterization.

Wiener [1] considered the class of causal systems that produce an output with finite mean-square value when their input is Gaussian white noise. The output, $y(t)$, of an unknown nonlinear "black-box" system can be approximated by a series of functionals, $G_m[h_m, x(t)]$, of the input, $x(t)$ as

$$y(t)=\sum_{m=0}^{M}G_m[h_m,x(t)]. \qquad (1)$$

The first three G-functionals are given by

$$G_0[h_0,x(t)]=h_0,$$

$$G_1[h_1,x(t)]=\int_{-\infty}^{\infty}h_1(\tau)x(t-\tau)d\tau,$$

$$G_2[h_2,x(t)]=\int_{-\infty}^{\infty}\int_{-\infty}^{\infty}h_2(\tau_1,\tau_2)x(t-\tau_1)x(t-\tau_2)d\tau_1d\tau_2-$$

$$-P\int_{-\infty}^{\infty}h_2(\tau,\tau)d\tau.$$

where the power density spectrum of the zero mean white Gaussian process $x(t)$ is P.

Several methods have been presented to find the Wiener kernels of nonlinear systems from given input and output pairs. Lee and Shetzen [2] showed that the kernels can be estimated by input-output crosscorrelation. French and Butz [3] used the fast Fourier transform (FFT) and Walsh transform algorithms for the Wiener kernels calculation. However, there are some difficulties in these methods:

a) A white Gaussian process is unrealizable;
b) Formula for kernels, $m \geq 2$, contains Dirac delta functions, when two or more kernel's arguments are equal;
c) The necessary computations increase very rapidly depending on the order of Wiener kernels that are being calculated.

This paper will resolve these problems by investigating discrete systems with discrete inputs generated using FFT algorithm. We will construct the G-functionals for such inputs, and the formula for Wiener kernels and efficient identification algorithm will be presented in frequency domain [4]. For more efficient computation of Fourier coefficients the split-radix FFT algorithms will be used [5], [6], [7].

2. FORCING FUNCTIONS FOR NONLINEAR SYSTEMS TESTING

It is necessary that the stimulant system must, on the one hand, be like a random noise to get maximum information about unknown system and, on the other hand, to simplify the G-functionals and procedure of identification on the whole.

Taking into consideration these circumstances, select as test input periodic noise approximation

$$x(n)=\sum_{k=0}^{N_x-1}X(k)exp(j2\pi kn/N_x). \qquad (2)$$

Here $X(k)=A(k)exp(j\varphi(k))$ are complex Fourier coefficients where the amplitudes $A(k)$ determinate the power spectrum of input and phases $\varphi(k)$ are independent random values with uniform distribution.

For real zero mean signal, the complex valued Fourier coefficients have the following relationship $X(0)=0$, $X(N_x-k)=X^*(k)$. According to Central Limit Theorem, the signal in the form of (2), being a sum of independent random quantities, has a nearly Gaussian distribution for large N_x. For every set $\varphi_l(k)$ random phases, formula (2) determinates the sequence $x_l(n)$ having N samples which may be formed by inverse FFT of coefficients $X_l(k)=A(k)exp(j\varphi_l(k))$. This inverse FFT (IFFT) is calculated by split-radix FFT for Hermitian symmetric sequences [6], [7].

In order to joint the separate sequences into long random process the following way can be proposed. Every time the set $\varphi_l(k)$ random phases is formed by random permutation of the totality $2\pi i/N_x$, $i=0,..,N_x-1$. In this case for any sequence $x(0)=0$ and joint of the sequences may be reduce to change sign of the blocks of data so that the condition $x(1)>x(0)$ is satisfied.

3. G-FUNCTIONALS AND WIENER KERNELS IN FREQUENCY DOMAIN

According to method of generation of the test signal the l-th sequence $x_l(n)$ of the random process $x(n)$ is determinated by the set of input Fourier coefficients $X_l(k)$, $k=0,...,N_x-1$, and the corresponding response $y_l(n)$ can be characterized by the set of output Fourier coefficients $Y_l(k)$, $k=0,...,N_y-1$. Therefore, it is possible to rewrite input-output relationship for nonlinear systems in frequency domain as

$$Y_M(k)=\sum_{m=0}^{M} G_m[H_m, X(k)], \qquad (3)$$

where $H_m(k_1,..., k_m)$ is multidimensional discrete Fourier transformation (DFT) of the Wiener kernel $h_m(n_1,..., n_m)$.

Using a Gram-Schmidt orthogonalization procedure, the G-functionals can be shown as

$$G_m[H_m, X(k)]=\sum_{\Omega_m} H_m(k_1,...k_m)\delta^k_{k_1+...+k_m}\prod_{i=1}^{m} X(k_i), \qquad (4)$$

where the summation must extend over the m-D region Ω_m consisting various combination $(k_1,..., k_m)$ from integers $\{0, 1,..., N_x-1\}$, such that $k_1 \geq k_2 \geq ... \geq k_m$, $k_i \neq k_j$, and δ_i^j is a Kronecker delta.

The Wiener kernels in frequency domain for model (3) can be determined by minimization the mean square error between the DFT of the system output $Y(k)$ and $Y_M(k)$ - DFT of model response:

$F = E\{\Delta^T\Delta^*\} \rightarrow min,$

where $\Delta = [\delta_1, ..., \delta_N]$ is the vector of the complex errors having elements $\delta_k = (Y(k) - Y_M(k))$, and $E\{\cdot\}$ denotes the average operation.

Minimizing this function, the optimal Wiener kernels become

$$H(k_1,...,k_m)=E\{Y(k_1,...,k_m)\times \times\prod_{i=1}^{m} X^*(k_i)\Big/\prod_{i=1}^{m} A^2(k_i)\}. \qquad (5)$$

In order to construct the estimation of kernel $H_m(k_1,...,k_m)$ which will be suitable in practice let us introduce the periodogram

$$I^l_{y_{x..x}}(k_1,...,k_m)=Y_l(k_1,...,k_m)exp[-j\sum_{i=1}^{m}\varphi_l(k_i)] \qquad (6)$$

Then as the estimation of kernel $H_m(k_1,...,k_m)$ may be use

$$\overline{H}_m(k_1,...,k_m)=\sum_{l=1}^{L} I^l_{y_{x..x}}(k_1,...,k_m)\Big/ L\prod_{i=1}^{m} A(k_i) \qquad (7)$$

The statistical properties of the estimation have been investigated in [4]. In particular it has been proved that estimation (7) is unbiased and its variance goes to zero if $L \rightarrow \infty$.

4. ALGORITHM OF IDENTIFICATION

Taking into account that the random phases is formed by random permutation of the values $2\pi i/N_x$, $i=0,...,N_x-1$, the equation (6) for periodogram can be rewritten as

$$I^l_{y_{x..x}}(k_1,...,k_m)=Y_l(k_1,...,k_m)\times$$
$$\times exp[-j(2\pi/N_x)\{s^l_{k_1}+...+s^l_{k_m}\}mod N_x]$$

where s_k^l is l-th set of random integers obtained by permutation of the totality $\{0,...,N_x-1\}$.

The calculation of Wiener kernels may be performed more effectively if it is noted that periodogram (8) may take limited number of values $Y_l(k)exp[-j(2\pi i/N_x)]$, $k=0,...,N_y-1$, $i=0,...,N_x-1$. This allows us in advance to form the array of possible products for every DFT $Y_l(k)$. Thus the algorithm of identification consists of the following steps:

1) Generation of random integers $s^l_1,...,s^l_{N_x}$ by means of permutation of set $\{0,...,N_x-1\}$ and forming the complex Fourier coefficients

$$X(k)=\begin{cases} A(k)exp(j2\pi s^l_k/N_x), k=0,...,N-1; \\ 0, \quad k=N,...,N_x-N-1; \\ A(N_x-k)exp(-j2\pi s^l_k/N_x), k=1,...,N. \end{cases}$$

2) Calculation of the l-th block of input by means of the inverse FFT based on the Hermitian-valued split-radix FFT algorithm [6], [7]:

$x_l(n)=IFFT\{X_l(k)\}$, $n=0,..., N_x-1$.

3) Stimulation of the system by the input $x_l(n)$ and registration of the response $y_l(n)$.

4) Calculation of the complex Fourier coefficients by means of the real-valued split-radix FFT algorithm:

$Y_l(k) = FFT\{y_l(n)\}$, $k=0,...,N_y-1$.

5) Definition of the array $Z(k,i)$ of all possible values of the periodograms

$Z_l(k,i)=Y_l(k)exp(-j2\pi i/N_x)$,
$k=0,...,N_y-1$, $i=0,...,N_x-1$.

6) Forming from the array $Z_l(k,i)$ periodograms

$$\Gamma^{l}_{y_{x..x}}(k_1,\ldots,k_m)=Z(k_1+\ldots+k_m,\{s^{l}_{k_1}+\ldots+s^{l}_{k_m}\}mod N_x),$$

$m = 1,...,M$.

7) Calculation of the estimation of kernels using eqn. (7).

Since the number C_m of combination $k_1,...,k_m$ containing in the kernel definition region Ω_m increases rapidly with a growth of kernel order m and the number of multiplications, demanding for calculation of array $Z_l(k,i)$ of all possible values of periodograms, do not depend on m, proposed algorithm as compared with methods [2], [3] allows to decrease the number of multiplications to a marked degree.

Actually, the most effective method [3] demands approximately $L(C_1+2C_2+...+mC_m)$ complex multiplications just as proposed method requires only $LNxNy/2$ multiplications.

5. CONCLUSIONS

An algorithm for identification of discrete nonlinear systems in terms of the orthogonal series was presented. The process generated by inverse FFT algorithm was used as a test signal. For this input the *G*-functionals and Wiener kernels was defined in frequency domain. The proposed algorithm offers a significant reduction in computational complexity compared with the known methods as a number of multiplications do not depend on kernel order. The additional reduction on a number of arithmetic operations is achieved by the use of the Hermitian and real-valued split-radix FFT algorithms. These results are used for construction of algorithms and software of digital chaotic signal processing for diagnostic and prediction of the complex nonlinear systems of different physic nature.

REFERENCES

[1] N. Wiener, Nonlinear problems in random theory. MIT press, 1958.

[2] Y.W. Lee, M. Schetzen, Measurement of the Wiener kernels of nonlinear system by cross-correlation. Int. J. Control 2, 237-254 (1965).

[3] A.S. French, E.G. Butz, Measuring the Wiener kernels of nonlinear system using the fast Fourier algorithm. Int. J.Control 17, 529-539 (1973).

[4] Shcherbakov M.A. The digital polynomial filtering: theory and applications. – Penza: State Technical University of Penza Publ. 1997. – 246 p. (in Russian).

[5] A.M Krot, Discrete models of dynamic systems based on polynomial algebra. Minsk: Nauka i tekhnika, 1990 (in Russian).

[6] A.M Krot, E.B. Minervina, Synthesis of FFT split-radix algorithms for real-valued and Hermite-symmetrical series Radioelectronics & Communication Systems 12, 10-15 (1989) (a translation from Izv.VUZ, Radioelektronika, Vol.32, No.12, pp.12-17, 1989).

[7] A.M Krot, E.B. Minervina, Identification and modelling of complex system based on series from the orthogonal Wiener-Volterra functionals. IVth Annual Seminar "Nonlinear Phenomena .in complex systems". Minsk, Febr., 1995, p. 153-158.

Part 3

MULTIDIMENSIONAL SYSTEMS THEORY AND APPLICATIONS

On the dynamic motion of a towed array in the ocean

Nikitas V. Nikitakos [1], Assimakis K. Leros [2] and Sokratis K. Katsikas [3]

[1] Cdr, Hellenic Navy, PO Box 80318, Piraeus 18510,Greece
[2] Dept. of Informatics, T.E.I. of Athens, Egaleo 12210, Greece
[3] Dept. of Mathematics, University of the Aegean, Karlovassi 83200, Greece

Abstract

The problem of towed array shape estimation is re-formulated and shown to be mathematically equivalent to the problem of state estimation with abruptly changing bias of the plant noise process. An algorithm belonging to the family of adaptive multi-model partitioning algorithms is subsequently applied to this problem and its performance is comparatively evaluated with that of non-adaptive algorithms previously proposed through simulation experiments.

1. INTRODUCTION

The problem of towed array shape estimation has received considerable attention in the past few years due to its importance in sonar and seismic applications [1]. It is widely recognized that the shape of the towed array plays a critical role in the sophisticated processing of hydrophone data. In the past many methods have been proposed for estimating the shape of a towed array; one such method is the use of Kalman filters [2]. With this method one starts from the Paidoussis equation (which describes the dynamical behavior of a thin towed array through the water) and discretizes it in space and time, so that a Kalman filter representation is derived that describes the physics of the propagation of motion down the array. The Kalman filter, at each instant in time, gives the least mean square estimate of the state of the system, when all the previous sampled time history of the measurement sensors is taken into account.

The approaches based on the Kalman filter do not usually perform adequately when facing a gross maneuver (such as a turn) or a perturbation of the equilibrium array shape under steady tow conditions. In such cases adaptive algorithms outperform the conventional Kalman filter-based ones. In this paper, the use of such an algorithm, based on the generic partitioning filtering theory of Lainiotis is proposed.

2. TOWED ARRAY SHAPE ESTIMATION VIA KALMAN FILTERS

Paidoussis [3], [4] formulated the problem describing the dynamics of a neutrally buoyant array of circular cross-section towed at a constant speed through the water. Dowling [5] presented an extensive analysis of the Paidoussis equation for the dynamics of towed flexible arrays, according to which the Paidoussis equation can be written as

$$M\frac{\vartheta^2 y}{\vartheta t^2}+M(\frac{\vartheta}{\vartheta t}+U\frac{\vartheta}{\vartheta x})^2 y-\frac{\vartheta}{\vartheta x}\left\{\left[2C_T\left[\frac{L-x}{d}\right]+\frac{1}{2}C_T^{'}\right]MU^2\frac{\vartheta y}{\vartheta x}\right\}+2C_N\frac{MU}{d}\left[\frac{\vartheta y}{\vartheta t}+U\frac{\vartheta y}{\vartheta x}\right]=0 \qquad (1)$$

where y=y(t,x) is the transverse displacement, M is the mass per unit of the neutrally buoyant cylinder, d is the diameter of the array, U is the tow speed along the x-axis, L is the array length, C_T, C_N are the tangential and normal drag coefficients of the cylinder.

The Paidoussis equation is discretized in both space and time using first-order differences in order to obtain a simple and useful finite dimensional state-space representation of the system. Subsequently, a Kalman filter is derived for estimating the array shape at "water pulley" conditions (i.e. the effects propagate undamped down the array at close to the tow speed of the array). A detailed description of this discretization procedure can be found in [2]. For wavelengths comparable to or greater than the length of the array, the final approximation for a state equation, which describes the time evolution of the system state, has the form

$$\underline{x}(k+1)=\Phi\underline{x}(k)+\underline{b}(k)+\underline{w}(k) \qquad (2)$$

where $\underline{x}(k)$ are the transverse displacements of each of the *n* segments of a piecewise linear approximation of the array shape at time kh_r where *k*=1,2......*n*, *h* is the length of each segment and $r=t\frac{U}{L}$ (a dimensionless variable). The vector $\underline{b}(k)$ can be interpreted as the driving term and the vector $\underline{w}(k)$ represents additive noise, which is assumed to be Gaussian, white, zero-mean and of variance *Q*. Finally, Φ is the transition matrix which relates the displacement of any segment at time kh_r to the displacement of the two immediately upstream segments of the array at time $(k-1)h_r$. An extremely simple expression for the transition matrix in water pulley motion of a towed array is of the form:
$\Phi=\alpha L_l$
where a is the damping coefficient and L_l is a lower triangular matrix whose only nonzero elements are equal to one in the first diagonal below the main diagonal. The measurement equation relating the output of the jth sensor at time *k*, denoted as $z_j(k)$, to the states of the system is (in vector form):

$$\underline{z}(k)=H\,\underline{x}(k)+\underline{v}(k) \qquad (3)$$

where *H* is the measurement matrix and $\underline{v}(k)$ represents additive noise that is associated with the measuring device and is assumed to be white, Gaussian, zero-mean and of variance equal to *R*.

Finally, given the above state space representation, a Kalman filter can be designed, which recursively predicts the state of the system one time interval ahead, denoted as $\hat{\underline{x}}(k+1/k)$. This one-time-ahead prediction allows the correct beamforming delays to be precalculated.

Two approaches can be used for treating $\underline{b}(k)$: one can either consider it an unknown, stochastic quantity and incorporate it in $\underline{w}(k)$ or one can consider it an unknown but deterministic quantity and subsequently attempt to somehow estimate its value. The former approach leads to the design of a simple linear Kalman filter whereas the latter approach transforms the problem to the problem of estimating the state of a system whose bias term in the plant noise is unknown. It should be noted that since the driving term is hardly constant in time, we are actually faced with a problem of time-varying bias estimation. In fact, $\underline{b}(k)$ is expected to be equal to zero most of the time and becomes non-zero only at certain times, corresponding to abrupt motions of the towed array induced by -for example- maneuvers of the towing vessel.

3. BIAS ESTIMATION USING MULTIMODEL PARTITIONING

Several bias estimation algorithms have been proposed in the literature [7]-[15]. Some of them [7]-[11] have been designed for systems with unknown but constant or slowly time-varying bias terms while others [12]-[15] for systems with slowly time varying bias terms. All bias estimation algorithms of the former type consist of three basic building blocks :

- a nominal state estimation filter (e.g. a linear Kalman filter), conditioned on the absence of a bias term;
- a bias estimator (which can be a filter [9] or a smoother [10]);
- a correction block, for updating the nominal state estimate, based on the bias estimate.

In this paper we use an alternative algorithm for estimating a time-varying bias term, which was originally developed and used for underwater passive target tracking [16]. Our model of the bias is the same as in [13] i.e. it is assumed that $b(k+1) = b(k)$ as long as no turns are made; however, when a maneuver is executed at time k, the bias term becomes $b(k+1) = b(k) + u$, where u is an unknown control input. Both the amplitude of the input u and the time instant of its occurrence are unknown to the observer and have to be estimated in order for a correct state estimate to be obtained.

The algorithm operates on the model of eqs. (2) and (3), and has been developed using the multimodel partitioning approach [17]. The algorithm comprises the same building blocks as a typical constant bias estimation algorithm does, but the bias estimator is implemented as

- a nominal bias estimator, conditioned on the hypothesis that no change occurred in the bias term in the time period $[k-N, k-1$, where N is some time horizon;
- a bank of N bias estimators, the i-th one conditioned on the hypothesis that a change in the bias term occurred at time T_i, with $k-N < T_i < k-1$;
- a bias estimate correction block, for updating the nominal bias estimate, based on the results of the bias change (conditional) estimators.

The algorithm is described by equations (4)-(25). Details on the algorithm development process can be found in [16].

$$\hat{x}(k/k-1) = \hat{x}_n(k/k-1) + U(k)\hat{b}(k-1/k-1) \tag{4}$$

$$\hat{x}(k/k) = \hat{x}_n(k/k) + V(k)\hat{b}(k/k) \tag{5}$$

$$(k) = \Phi V(k-1) \tag{6}$$

$$V(k) = \left[I - K_n(k)H\right]U(k) \tag{7}$$

$$\hat{b}(k/k) = \sum_{i=1}^{N} \hat{b}(k/k;T_i)p(T_i/k) = \hat{b}(k/k;0) + \sum_{i=1}^{N} M(T_i,k)\hat{u}_i p(T_i/k) \tag{8}$$

$$M(T_i,k) = \prod_{\ell=i}^{k} \left[I - K_b(\ell)HU(\ell)\right) \tag{9}$$

$$\hat{u}_i = \sum_{\ell=i+1}^{k} \left[A(\ell,T_i)\right]^{-1} \sum_{\ell=i+1}^{k} B(\ell,T_i)\tilde{z}_b(\ell/\ell-1;0) \tag{10}$$

$$A(\ell,T_i) = \left\|HU(\ell)M(T_i+1,\ell-1)\right\|^2 P_{\tilde{z}_b}^{-1}(\ell/\ell-1;0) \tag{11}$$

$$B(\ell,T_i) = \left[HU(\ell)M(T_i+1,\ell-1)\right]^T P_{\tilde{z}_b}^{-1}(\ell/\ell-1;0) \tag{12}$$

$$p(T_i,k) = N(T_i,k)/D(T_i,k) \tag{13}$$

$$N(T_i,k) = \exp\left\{-\tfrac{1}{2}\sum_{\ell=0}^{k}\left\|\tilde{z}_b(l/l-1;0)\right\|^2 P_{\tilde{z}_b}^{-1}(\ell/\ell-1) + \tfrac{1}{2}\sum_{\ell=i+1}^{k}\left\|B(\ell,T_i)\tilde{z}_b(\ell/\ell-1;0)\right\|^2 \times \sum_{\ell=i+1}^{k} A(\ell,T_i^{-1})\right\}$$

$$D(T_i,k) = \sum_{i=1}^{N}\exp\left\{-\tfrac{1}{2}\left\|\tilde{z}_b(k/k-1;0)\right\|^2 P_{\tilde{z}_b}^{-1}(k/k-1) + \tfrac{1}{2}\sum_{\ell=i+1}^{k}\left\|B(\ell,T_i)\tilde{z}_b(\ell/\ell-1;0)\right\|^2 \times \sum_{\ell=i+1}^{k} A(\ell,T_i^{-1})\right\}$$

$$\hat{x}_n(k/k-1) = \Phi\hat{x}_n(k-1/k-1) \tag{14}$$

$$P_n(k/k-1) = \Phi P(k-1/k-1)\Phi^T + Q \tag{15}$$

$$P_{\tilde{z}_n}(k/k-1) = HP_n(k/k-1)H^T + R \tag{16}$$

$$K_n(k) = P_n(k/k-1)H^T P_{\tilde{z}_n}^{-1}(k/k-1) \tag{17}$$

$$\tilde{z}_n(k/k-1) = z(k) - H\hat{x}_n(k/k-1) - m(k) \tag{18}$$

$$\hat{x}_n(k/k) = \hat{x}_n(k/k-1) + K_n(k)\tilde{z}_n(k/k-1) \tag{19}$$

$$P_n(k/k) = \left[I - K_n(k)H\right]P_n(k/k-1) \tag{20}$$

$$P_{\tilde{z}_b}(k/k-1;0) = HU(k)P_b(k-1/k-1;0)U^T(k)H^T P_{\tilde{z}_b}^{-1}(k/k-1;0) \tag{21}$$

$$K_b(k) = P_b(k-1/k-1;0)U^T(k)H^T P_{\tilde{z}_b}^{-1}(k/k-1;0) \tag{22}$$

$$P_b(k/k;0) = \left[I - K_b(k)HU(k)\right]P_b(k-1/k-1;0) \tag{23}$$

$$\tilde{z}_b(k/k-1;0) = \tilde{z}_n(k/k-1) - HU(k)\hat{b}(k-1/k-1;0) \tag{24}$$

$$\hat{b}(k/k;0) = \hat{b}(k-1/k-1;0) + K_b(k)\tilde{z}_b(k/k-1;0) \tag{25}$$

where $\hat{x}_n(k/k-1), \hat{x}_n(k/k), P_n(k/k-1), P_n(k/k)$ are the predicted and filtered state estimates and the associated error covariances, respectively, conditioned on the absence of any bias term (i.e. matched to the model of (2) with $b(k)=0$ for all k) and initialized with $\hat{x}(0/0) = \hat{x}_0$ and $P(0/0) = P_0$. $\hat{b}(k/k)$ and $P_b(k/k)$ are the bias estimate and the associated error covariance, respectively, initialized by $\hat{b}(0/0)$ and $P_b(0/0) = P_{b0}$.

4. SIMULATION RESULTS

In order to assess the proposed algorithm's performance, a number of scenarios were simulated. The simulated towed array system consisted of a 100m array with 10 hydrophones towed through the water at a speed of 8 knots. The array remains at a nominal depth by a leveling device (array stability module) mounted at the head of the array. A vibration isolation module assembly provides mechanical isolation from vibrations generated and transmitted by the tow cable. We assume that the head of the array is actively controlled by a leveling device and that the state space water pulley model and the incorporating damping coefficient hold as discussed in the previous section. Motion in the horizontal plane due to yaw is not considered here. The array is equipped with a number of calibrated depth sensors that enable the vertical displacements of the array section to be measured. It can be shown [2] that, under these conditions, the transverse displacement propagates down the array through the water and is only lightly damped.

For our simulation studies we assume that for some reason (violent maneuver, man overboard maneuver, etc.) a relative motion of the second hydrophone occurs, which then propagates down the array. The vertical displacement of this motion has a nominal value of 1m. We examine the performance of three different filters, namely the Kalman Filter, a pseudolinear partitioning filter [11] and the proposed adaptive filter. 100 Monte Carlo runs are being made in all our simulation studies. We report the relative position error of a hydrophone with respect to the tow point (first hydrophone) versus time. In all runs we use a process noise standard deviation equal to 0.1 m , and an observation interval of 1 sec. We now proceed with the discussion of several simulation experiments.

<u>Experiment 1:</u> Assuming that the standard deviation of the measurement noise is 0.1m, at time instant 50 the second hydrophone moves 1m down. The relative position error of the fifth hydrophone is depicted in figure 1.

<u>Experiment 2:</u> Assuming that the standard deviation of the measurement noise is 0.5 m, at time instant 50 the second hydrophone moves 1m down. The relative position error of the fifth hydrophone is depicted in figure 2.

<u>Experiment 3:</u> Assuming that the standard deviation of the measurement noise is 0.1m, at time instant 50 the second hydrophone moves 1m down and at time instant 130 it moves 1m up. The relative position error of the fifth hydrophone is depicted in figure 3.

<u>Experiment 4:</u> Assuming that the standard deviation of the measurement noise is 0.5m, at time instant 50 the second hydrophone moves 1m down and at time instant 130 it moves 1m up. The relative position error of the fifth hydrophone is depicted in figure 4.

It should be noted that the assumed noise level is extremely low, and that these experiments served to demonstrate the failure of the conventional (i.e. non-adaptive) algorithms even in favorable conditions (high SNR). Indeed, the results show that the conventional algorithms perform very well as long as the tow ship does not maneuver, but fail to respond to a maneuver that results in a bias change.

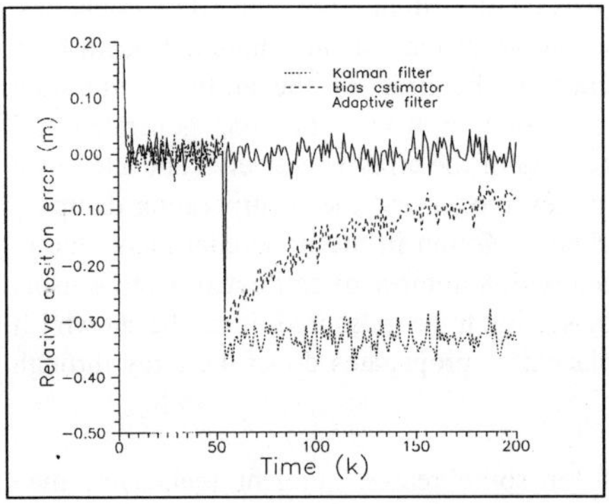

Figure 1

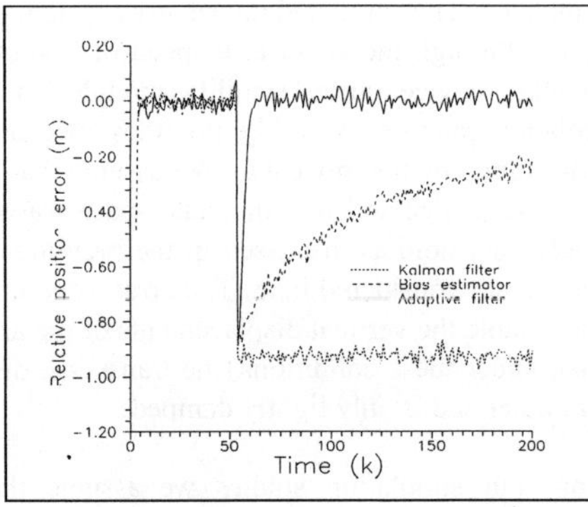

Figure 2

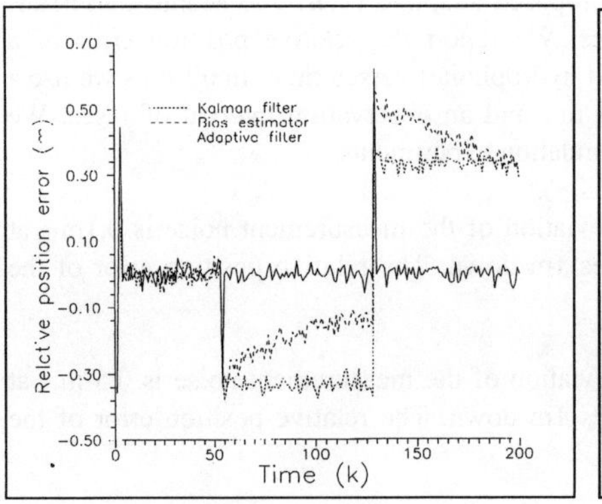

Figure 3

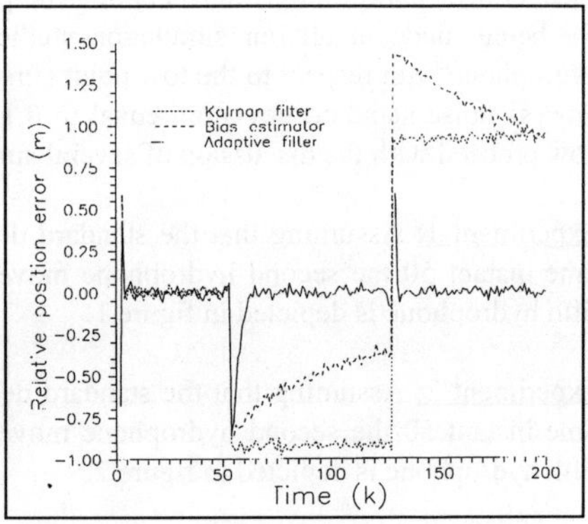

Figure 4

5. CONCLUSIONS

In this paper a multi-model partitioning adaptive algorithm has been applied to the problem of towed array shape estimation. The problem examined herein has been shown to be equivalent to the problem of state estimation with an unknown time-varying bias term being present in the plant noise process. Abrupt changes of this bias term model large-scale pilot-initiated towed array maneuvers. The proposed algorithm operates on a bank of elemental filters, each of which is conditioned on a change in bias taking place at a central point of time. Several simulation runs have been carried out in order to test the algorithm under various operating conditions. In all cases the proposed algorithm performs very well and it is able to detect fast enough and cope with abrupt large - scale towed array shape changes.

REFERENCES

[1] S.M.Kay and H.C. Woodsum, "Sonar Technology", in *Trends and Perspectives in Signal Processing,* 1993, pp. 1-7.

[2] D.Gray, B.Anderson, R.R.Bitmead, "Towed Array shape estimation using Kalman Filters- Theoretical Model", *IEEE J. Oceanic Eng.* ,Vol. OE-18, 1993, pp. 543-556.

[3] M.P.Paidoussis, "Dynamics of flexible slender cylinders in axial flow", *Journal of Fluid Mechanics,* Vol. 26, 1966, pp. 717-736.

[4] M.P.Paidoussis, "Dynamics of cylindrical structures subjected to axial flow", *Journal of Sound and Vibration,* Vol. 29, 1973, pp. 365-385.

[5] A.P. Dowling, "The dynamics of towed flexible cylinders Part 1. Neutrally buoyant elements", *J. of Fluid Mechanics*, Vol. 187, 1988, pp. 507-532.

[6] R.M. Kennedy and E.S. Strahan, *A linear theory of transverse cable dynamics at low frequencies*, NUSC Tech. Rep. 6463, Naval Underwater Systems Center, New London, CT, 1981

[7] B. Friedland, "Treatment of Bias in Recursive Filtering", *IEEE Trans. on Autom. Control*, Vol. AC-14, 1969, pp. 359-367.

[8] B. Friedland, "Notes on Separate-Bias Estimation", *IEEE Trans. on Autom. Control,* Vol. AC-23, 1978, pp. 735-738.

[9] M.B. Ignagni,, "An Alternate Derivation and Extension of Friedland's Two-stage Kalman Estimator", *IEEE Trans. on Autom. Control*, Vol. **AC-26,** 1981.

[10] K. Watanabe, "Two-stage Correction Estimators Based on Generalized Partitioning Estimation Method", *Int. J. Control*, Vol. 38, 1983, pp. 621-637.

[11] K. Watanabe, "Partitioned Estimators Based on the Perturbed Kalman Filter Equations", *Int. J. of Syst. Sci.,* Vol. 14, 1983, pp. 1115-1128.

[12] M.B. Ignagni, "Separate-bias Kalman Estimator With Bias State Noise", *IEEE Trans. on Autom. Control*, Vol. AC-35, 1990, pp. 338-341.

[13] B. Friedland, "Maximum-Likelihood Estimation of a Process with Random Transitions (Failures)", *IEEE Trans. on Autom. Control*, Vol. AC-24, 1979, pp. 932-944.

[14] B. Friedland, "Multidimensional Maximum Likelihood Failure Detection and Estimation", *IEEE Trans. on Autom. Control*, Vol. AC-26, 1981, pp. 567-570.

[15] B. Friedland and S.M. Grabousky, "Estimating Sudden Changes of Biases in Linear Dynamic Systems", *IEEE Trans. on Autom. Control*, Vol. AC-27, 1982, pp. 237-240.

[16] S.K. Katsikas, A.K. Leros and D.G. Lainiotis, "Underwater tracking of maneuvering targets using time delay measurements", *Signal Processing*, Vol. 41, 1995, pp. 17-29.

[17] D.G.Lainiotis, "Partitioning: A unifying framework for adaptive systems I; Estimation", *Proceeding of the IEEE*, Vol. 64, 1976, pp. 1126-1143.

Equivalent standard systems for singular discrete-time systems with delays

Tadeusz Kaczorek
Warsaw Technical University, Faculty of Electrical Engineering
Institute of Control and Industrial Electronics
00-662 Warszawa, Koszykowa 75, Poland
Tel. (+48 2) 6256278, 6280665, fax (+48 2) 6256633
e mail: kaczorek @ nov.isep.pw.edu.pl

Abstract. A standard system which has the same solution for admissible initial conditions as a given singular discrete-time linear system with delays in state and input is derived. Some basic properties of the fundamental matrices of the singular discrete-time linear systems with delays are characterised. A method of determination of the standard system based on the shuffle algorithm is proposed.

1. Introduction.

Analysis and synthesis of linear systems with delays has been considered in many papers and books [1,8,10]. A survey of linear singular systems is given in [5]. Recently in [3,4] a standard system which is equivalent (has the same solution) to the singular (regular) linear system has been derived.

The main purpose this paper is to extend this approach for discrete-time linear systems with delays in state and input. Some basic properties of the fundamental matrices of the singular discrete-time linear systems with delays will be characterised. A standard system which has the same solution for admissible initial conditions as a given singular discrete-time linear system will be derived. A method of determination of the standard system based on the shuffle algorithm [7,2] will be proposed.

2. Preliminaries and fundamental matrices.

Let Z_+ be the set of nonnegative integers. The set of $m\times n$ real matrices will be denoted by $R^{m\times n}$ and $R^m := R^{m\times 1}$.

Consider the linear discrete-time system with delays

(1) $$Ex_{i+1} = A_1x_i + A_2x_{i-d_1} + B_1u_i + B_2u_{i-d_2} \quad i,d_1,d_2 \in Z_+$$

where $x_i \in R^n$ is the state vector, $u_i \in R^m$ is the input vector, $E, A_1, A_2 \in R^{n\times n}$, $B_1, B_2 \in R^{n\times m}$ with E possibly singular and d_1 and d_2 is the delay in state and input, respectively.

To compute x_i for $i \in Z_+$ we have to know u_i for $i \geq -d_2$ and the initial conditions

(2) $$x_{-d_1}, x_{-d_1+1}, \ldots, x_0$$

The system (1) is called standard if $E = I_n$ (the identity matrix) and it is called singular if $\det E = 0$.

It is assumed that

(3) $$\det\left[Ez - A_1 - A_2z^{-d_1}\right] \neq 0 \quad \text{for some } z \in \mathbf{C} \text{ (the field of complex numbers)}$$

The system (1) is called regular if (3) holds.

If (3) is satisfied then

(4) $$\left[Ez - A_1 - A_2 z^{-d_1}\right]^{-1} = \sum_{i=-\mu}^{\infty} \Phi_i z^{-(i+1)}$$

where μ is the index of nilpotence and Φ_i is the fundamental matrix.

Substitution of (4) into the equality $\left[Ez - A_1 - A_2 z^{-d_1}\right]^{-1}\left[Ez - A_1 - A_2 z^{-d_1}\right] = I_n$ yields

(5) $$\left(\sum_{i=-\mu}^{\infty} \Phi_i z^{-(i+1)}\right)\left[Ez - A_1 - A_2 z^{-d_1}\right]^{-1} = \left[Ez - A_1 - A_2 z^{-d_1}\right]^{-1}\left(\sum_{i=-\mu}^{\infty} \Phi_i z^{-(i+1)}\right) = I_n$$

Comparison the coefficients at the like power of z of (5) yields

$$E\Phi_i - A_1\Phi_{i-1} - A_2\Phi_{i-d_1-1} = \Phi_i E - \Phi_{i-1}A_1 - \Phi_{i-d_1-1}A_2 = I_n\delta_i := \begin{cases} I_n & for\ i = 0 \\ 0 & for\ i = -\mu+1, -\mu+2, \ldots, -1, 1, 2, \ldots \end{cases}$$

(6)

and $E\Phi_{-\mu} = \Phi_{-\mu}E = 0$.

where δ_i is the Kronecker delta.

Lemma. The fundamental matrices Φ_i and E, A_2 satisfy the equalities

(7) $$\Phi_j E\Phi_i + \Phi_{i-d_1-1}A_2\Phi_j + \Phi_{i-d_1-2}A_2\Phi_{j+1} + \cdots + \Phi_{j-d_1-1}A_2\Phi_{i-2} + \Phi_{j-d_1}A_2\Phi_{i-1} =$$

$$= \Phi_i E\Phi_j + \Phi_{i-1}A_2\Phi_{j-d_1} + \Phi_{i-2}A_2\Phi_{j-d_1-1} + \cdots + \Phi_{j+1}A_2\Phi_{i-d_1-2} + \Phi_j A_2\Phi_{i-d_1-1} \quad \text{for } i, j \in Z_+$$

(8) $$\Phi_1 E\Phi_i + \Phi_{1-d_1}A_2\Phi_{i-1} + \Phi_{2-d_1}A_2\Phi_{i-2} + \cdots + \Phi_0 A_2\Phi_{i-d_1} = \Phi_{i+1} \quad \text{for } i \in Z_+$$

Proof. From (6) we have

(9a) $$E\Phi_i = A_1\Phi_{i-1} + A_2\Phi_{i-d_1-1} \quad \text{for } i > 0$$

and

(9b) $$\Phi_{i-1}A_1 = \Phi_i E - \Phi_{i-d_1-1}A_2 \quad \text{for } i > 0$$

Using successively (9a) and (9b) we obtain for $i \in Z_+$

$$\Phi_1 E\Phi_i = \Phi_1 A_1\Phi_{i-1} + \Phi_1 A_2\Phi_{i-d_1-1} = \Phi_2 E\Phi_{i-1} - \Phi_{1-d_1}A_2\Phi_{i-1} + \Phi_1 A_2\Phi_{i-d_1-1} =$$

$$= \Phi_2 A_1\Phi_{i-2} + \Phi_2 A_2\Phi_{i-d_1-2} - \Phi_{1-d_1}A_2\Phi_{i-1} + \Phi_1 A_2\Phi_{i-d_1-1} =$$

$$= \Phi_3 E\Phi_{i-2} - \Phi_{i-d_1-2}A_2\Phi_{i-2} + \Phi_2 A_2\Phi_{i-d_1-2} - \Phi_{1-d_1}A_2\Phi_{i-1} + \Phi_1 A_2\Phi_{i-d_1-1} = \cdots$$

$$= \Phi_i E\Phi_1 - \Phi_{i-d_1-1}A_2\Phi_1 + \Phi_{i-1}A_2\Phi_{i-d_1} - \Phi_{1-d_2-2}A_2\Phi_2 + \Phi_{i-2}A_2\Phi_{2-d_1} - \cdots +$$

$$\Phi_1 A_2\Phi_{i-d_1-1} - \Phi_{1-d_1}A_2\Phi_{i-1}$$

Similarly

$$\Phi_2 E\Phi_i = \Phi_2 A_1\Phi_{i-1} + \Phi_2 A_2\Phi_{i-d_1-1} = \Phi_3 E\Phi_{i-1} - \Phi_{2-d_1}A_2\Phi_{i-1} + \Phi_2 A_2\Phi_{i-d_1-1} =$$

$$= \Phi_3 A_1\Phi_{i-2} + \Phi_3 A_2\Phi_{i-d_1-2} - \Phi_{2-d_1}A_2\Phi_{i-1} + \Phi_2 A_2\Phi_{i-d_1-1} =$$

$$= \Phi_4 E\Phi_{i-2} - \Phi_{3-d_1}A_2\Phi_{i-2} + \Phi_3 A_2\Phi_{i-d_1-2} - \Phi_{2-d_1}A_2\Phi_{i-1} + \Phi_2 A_2\Phi_{i-d_1-1} = \cdots$$

$$= \Phi_i E \Phi_2 - \Phi_{i-d_1-1} A_2 \Phi_2 + \Phi_{i-1} A_2 \Phi_{2-d_1} - \Phi_{1-d_1-2} A_2 \Phi_3 + \Phi_{i-2} A_2 \Phi_{3-d_1} - \cdots +$$

$$\Phi_2 A_2 \Phi_{i-d_1-1} - \Phi_{2-d_1} A_2 \Phi_{i-1}$$

and for any $j \in Z_+$

$$\Phi_j E \Phi_i = \Phi_j A_1 \Phi_{i-1} + \Phi_j A_2 \Phi_{i-d_1-1} = \Phi_{j+1} E \Phi_{i-1} - \Phi_{j-d_1} A_2 \Phi_{i-1} + \Phi_j A_2 \Phi_{i-d_1-1} =$$

$$= \Phi_{j+1} A_1 \Phi_{i-2} + \Phi_{j+1} A_2 \Phi_{i-d_1-2} - \Phi_{j-d_1} A_2 \Phi_{i-1} + \Phi_j A_2 \Phi_{i-d_1-1} =$$

$$= \Phi_{j+2} E \Phi_{i-2} - \Phi_{j-d_1+1} A_2 \Phi_{i-2} + \Phi_{j+1} A_2 \Phi_{i-d_1-2} - \Phi_{j-d_1} A_2 \Phi_{i-1} + \Phi_j A_2 \Phi_{i-d_1-1} =$$

$$\cdots = \Phi_i E \Phi_j - \Phi_{i-d_1-1} A_2 \Phi_j + \Phi_{i-1} A_2 \Phi_{j-d_1} - \Phi_{i-d_1-2} A_2 \Phi_{j+1} +$$

$$\Phi_{i-2} A_2 \Phi_{j-d_1+1} - \cdots - \Phi_{j-d_1} A_2 \Phi_{i-1} + \Phi_j A_2 \Phi_{i-d_1-1}$$

The equality (8) may be proved in a similar way using (6),(7) and (9). □

Remark 1. For $A_2 = 0$ from (7) we obtain the equality $\Phi_j E \Phi_i = \Phi_i E \Phi_j$ which was shown in [6].

3. Solution of the system.

Let $P \in R^{n \times n}$ be a nonsingular matrix of elementary row operations such that

(10) $$PE = \begin{bmatrix} E_1 \\ 0 \end{bmatrix}$$

where $E_1 \in R^{r \times n}$ has full row rank.

Premultiplying (1) by P and using (10) we obtain

(11a) $$E_1 x_{i+1} = A_{11} x_i + A_{21} x_{i-d_1} + B_{11} u_i + B_{21} u_{i-d_2} \qquad i \in Z_+$$

and

(11b) $$0 = A_{12} x_i + A_{22} x_{i-d_1} + B_{12} u_i + B_{22} u_{i-d_2} \qquad i \in Z_+$$

where

$$PA_1 = \begin{bmatrix} A_{11} \\ A_{12} \end{bmatrix}, PA_2 = \begin{bmatrix} A_{21} \\ A_{22} \end{bmatrix}, PB_1 = \begin{bmatrix} B_{11} \\ B_{12} \end{bmatrix}, PB_2 = \begin{bmatrix} B_{21} \\ B_{22} \end{bmatrix}$$

$$A_{11} \in R^{r \times n},\ A_{21} \in R^{r \times n},\ B_{11} \in R^{r \times m},\ B_{21} \in R^{r \times m}$$

Definition 1. A set X_a of initial conditions (2) satisfying (11b) for $i = 0,1,\dots,d_1$ for a given input sequence u_i for $i > -d_2$ is called the set of admissible initial conditions of the system (1).

Definition 2. A set U_a of input sequences u_i for $i > -d_2$ satisfying (11b) for $i = 0,1,\dots,d_2$ for given input conditions (2) is called the set of acceptable input sequences of the system (1).

Note that the system (1) has a solution $x_i, i \in Z_+$ for a given input sequence u_i for $i > -d_2$ only if initial conditions (2) belong to set X_a. Similarly the system (1) has a solution $x_i, i \in Z_+$

for given initial conditions (2) only if the input sequence $u_i, i \in Z_+$ belongs to the set U_a.
In what follows it is assumed that the input sequences are given and the initial conditions (2) belong to X_a.
Application of the Z-transform to (1) yields

$$X(z) = \left[Ez - A_1 - A_2 z^{-d_1}\right]^{-1} \left\{Ex_0 + A_2 z^{-d_1}\left(x_{-1}z + x_{-2}z^2 + \cdots + x_{-d_1}z^{d_1}\right) + \right. \tag{12}$$

$$\left. +\left(B_1 + B_2 z^{-d_2}\right)U(s) + B_2 z^{-d_2}\left(u_{-1}z + u_{-2}z^2 + \cdots + u_{-d_2}z^{d_2}\right)\right\}$$

where $X(z)$ and $U(z)$ are the Z-transform of x_i and u_i, respectively.
Substituting (4) into (12) we obtain

$$X(z) = \sum_{i=-\mu}^{\infty} \Phi_i z^{-(i+1)}\left[zEx_0 + A_2\left(x_{-d_1} + x_{-d_1+1}z^{-1} + \cdots + x_{-1}z^{1-d_1}\right) + \left(B_1 + B_2 z^{-d_2}\right)U(s) + \right. \tag{13}$$

$$\left. +B_2\left(u_{-d_2} + u_{-d_2+1}z^{-1} + \cdots + u_{-1_2}z^{1-d_2}\right)\right]$$

Using the convolution theorem to (13) we obtain

$$x_i = \Phi_i Ex_0 + \Phi_{i-1}A_2 x_{-d_1} + \Phi_{i-2}A_2 x_{1-d_1} + \cdots + \Phi_{i-d_1}A_2 x_{-1} + \sum_{k=0}^{i+\mu-1}\Phi_{i-k-1}B_1 u_k + \tag{14}$$

$$\sum_{k=0}^{i+\mu-d_2-1}\Phi_{i-k-d_2-1}B_2 u_k + \Phi_{i-1}B_2 u_{-d_2} + \Phi_{i-2}B_2 u_{1-d_2} + \cdots + \Phi_{i-d_2}B_2 u_{-1} \quad \text{for } i > 0$$

Therefore, we have proved the following

Theorem 1. Let (2) hold. Then the solution x_i to the equation (1) with admissible initial conditions (2) is given by (14).

4. Equivalent standard system.

Knowing the fundamental matrices Φ_i for $i = -\mu, 1-\mu, \ldots, 0, 1, \ldots$ of (1) we may compute the matrices T_j for $j \in Z_+$ which are defined by the expension

$$\left[I_n z - \Phi_1 E - \Phi_{1-d_1}A_2 z^{-1} - \Phi_{2-d_1}A_2 z^{-2} - \cdots - \Phi_0 A_2 z^{-d_1}\right]\left[\sum_{k=0}^{\infty} T_k z^{-(k+1)}\right] = \tag{15}$$

$$\left[\sum_{k=0}^{\infty} T_k z^{-(k+1)}\right]\left[I_n z - \Phi_1 E - \Phi_{1-d_1}A_2 z^{-1} - \Phi_{2-d_1}A_2 z^{-2} - \cdots - \Phi_0 A_2 z^{-d_1}\right] = I_n$$

it follows that

$$T_0 = I_n, T_1 = \Phi_1 E, T_2 = \Phi_1 ET_1 + \Phi_{1-d_1}A_2, T_3 = \Phi_1 ET_2 + \Phi_{1-d_1}A_2 T_1 + \Phi_{2-d_1}A_2, \ldots$$

$$T_{d_1} = \Phi_1 ET_{d_1-1} + \Phi_{1-d_1}A_2 T_{d_1-2} + \cdots + \Phi_{-1}A_2, T_{d_1+1} = \Phi_1 ET_{d_1} + \Phi_{1-d_1}A_2 T_{d_1-1} + \cdots + \Phi_0 A_2, \ldots, \tag{16}$$

$$T_{d_1+k} = \Phi_1 ET_{d_1+k-1} + \Phi_{1-d_1}A_2 T_{d_1+k-2} + \cdots + \Phi_0 A_2 T_{k-1} \qquad \text{for } k \geq 2$$

Consider the standard discrete-time system described by the equation

$$x_{i+1} = F_0 x_i + F_1 x_{i-1} + F_2 x_{i-2} + \cdots + F_{d_1}x_{i-d_1} + H_{-d_2}u_{i-d_2} + H_{1-d_2}u_{i-d_2+1} + \cdots + \tag{17}$$

$$H_{\mu-d_2}u_{i-d_2+\mu} + H_0 u_i + H_1 u_{i+1} + \cdots + H_\mu u_{i+\mu}$$

where

$$F_0 := \Phi_1 E, \quad F_1 := \Phi_{1-d_1} A_2, \quad F_2 := \Phi_{2-d_1} A_2, \ldots, F_{d_1} := \Phi_0 A_2$$

(18) $$H_\mu := \Phi_{-\mu} B_1, \quad H_{\mu-1} := \Phi_{1-\mu} B_1 - T_1 H_\mu,$$

$$H_{\mu-2} := \Phi_{2-\mu} B_1 - T_1 H_{\mu-1} - T_2 H_\mu, \ldots,$$

$$H_{\mu-d_2} := \Phi_{-\mu} B_2 + \Phi_{d_2-\mu} B_1 - T_{d_2-\mu} H_0 - \cdots - T_{d_2} H_\mu$$

$$H_{\mu-d_2-1} := \Phi_{-\mu+1} B_2 + \Phi_{\mu-d_2+1} B_1 - T_{\mu-d_2+1} H_0 - \cdots - T_{d_2+1} H_\mu - T_1 H_{\mu-d_2}$$

....

$$H_{1-d_2} := \Phi_{-1} B_2 + \Phi_{d_2-1} B_1 - T_{d_2-1} H_0 - \cdots - T_{\mu+d_2-1} H_\mu - T_1 H_{2-d_2} - \cdots - T_{\mu-1} H_{\mu-d_2}$$

$$H_{-d_2} := \Phi_0 B_2 + \Phi_{d_2} B_1 - T_{d_2} H_0 - \cdots - T_{\mu+d_2} H_\mu - T_1 H_{1-d_2} - \cdots - T_\mu H_{\mu-d_2}$$

Theorem 2. The equations (1) and (17) with admissible initial conditions (2) have the same solution (14).

Proof. We shall show that (14) is also the solution of (17) with admissible initial conditions (2). Using (17), (14), (7) and (8) we obtain

$$F_0 x_i + F_1 x_{i-1} + F_2 x_{i-2} + \cdots + F_{d_1} x_{i-d_1} + H_{-d_2} u_{i-d_2} + H_{1-d_2} u_{i-d_2+1} + \cdots + H_{\mu-d_2} u_{i-d_2+\mu} + H_0 u_i +$$

$$+ H_1 u_{i+1} + \cdots + H_\mu u_{i+\mu} = F_0 \Big[\Phi_i E x_0 + \Phi_{i-1} A_2 x_{-d_1} + \Phi_{i-2} A_2 x_{1-d_1} + \cdots + \Phi_{i-d_1} A_2 x_{-1} +$$

$$+ \sum_{k=0}^{i+\mu-1} \Phi_{i-k-1} B_1 u_k + \sum_{k=0}^{i+\mu-d_2-1} \Phi_{i-k-d_2-1} B_2 u_k + \Phi_{i-1} B_2 u_{-d_2} + \Phi_{i-2} B_2 u_{1-d_2} + \cdots + \Phi_{i-d_2} B_2 u_{-1} \Big] +$$

$$+ F_1 \Big[\Phi_{i-1} E x_0 + \Phi_{i-2} A_2 x_{-d_1} + \Phi_{i-3} A_2 x_{1-d_1} + \cdots + \Phi_{i-d_1-1} A_2 x_{-1} + \sum_{k=0}^{i+\mu-2} \Phi_{i-k-2} B_1 u_k +$$

$$\sum_{k=0}^{i+\mu-d_2-2} \Phi_{i-k-d_2-2} B_2 u_k + \Phi_{i-2} B_2 u_{-d_2} + \Phi_{i-3} B_2 u_{1-d_2} + \cdots + \Phi_{i-d_2-1} B_2 u_{-1} \Big] + \cdots +$$

$$F_{d_1} \Big[\Phi_{i-d_1} E x_0 + \Phi_{i-d_1-1} A_2 x_{-d_1} + \Phi_{i-d_1-2} A_2 x_{1-d_1} + \cdots + \Phi_{i-2d_1} A_2 x_{-1} + \sum_{k=0}^{i+\mu-d_1-1} \Phi_{i-d_1-k-1} B_1 u_k +$$

$$+ \sum_{k=0}^{i+\mu-d_1-d_2-1} \Phi_{i-k-d_1-d_2-1} B_2 u_k + \Phi_{i-d_1-1} B_2 u_{-d_2} + \Phi_{i-d_1-2} B_2 u_{1-d_1-d_2} + \cdots + \Phi_{i-d_1-d_2} B_2 u_{-1} \Big] +$$

$$+ H_{-d_2} u_{i-d_2} + H_{1-d_2} u_{i-d_2+1} + \cdots + H_{\mu-d_2} u_{i-d_2+\mu} + H_0 u_i + H_1 u_{i+1} + \cdots + H_\mu u_{i+\mu} =$$

$$= \Phi_{i+1} E x_0 + \Phi_i A_2 x_{-d_1} + \Phi_{i-1} A_2 x_{1-d_1} + \cdots + \Phi_{i-d_1+1} A_2 x_{-1} + \sum_{k=0}^{i+\mu} \Phi_{i-k} B_1 u_k +$$

$$+\sum_{k=0}^{i+\mu-d_2}\Phi_{i-k-d_2}B_2u_k+\Phi_iB_2u_{-d_2}+\Phi_{i-1}B_2u_{1-d_2+1}+\cdots+\Phi_{i-d_2+1}B_2u_{-1}=x_{i+1}$$

Therefore (14) is also the solution of (17). □

Remark 2. For $A_2=0$ and $B_2=0$ the equation (17) has the form [4]

$$x_{i+1}=F_0x_i+H_0u_i+H_1u_{i+1}+\cdots+H_\mu u_{i+\mu}= \tag{19}$$

$$=\Phi_0A_1x_i+\Phi_0B_1u_1+\Phi_{-1}B_1u_{i+1}+\cdots+\Phi_{-\mu}B_1u_{i+\mu}$$

where the fundamental matrices $\Phi_0,\Phi_{-1},\ldots,\Phi_{-\mu}$ are defined by [6,9,4]

$$[Ez-A_1]^{-1}=\sum_{i=-\mu}^{\infty}\Phi_iz^{-(i+1)} \tag{20}$$

Example 1.
Consider the system (1) with

$$E=\begin{bmatrix}1&0\\0&0\end{bmatrix},A_1=\begin{bmatrix}1&0\\0&1\end{bmatrix},A_2=\begin{bmatrix}0&1\\1&0\end{bmatrix},B_1=\begin{bmatrix}1\\2\end{bmatrix},B_2=\begin{bmatrix}1\\1\end{bmatrix},d_1=2,d_2=3 \tag{21}$$

The system is regular since

$$\det\left[Ez-A_1-A_2z^{-d_1}\right]=\begin{vmatrix}z-1, & z^{-2}\\ -z^{-2}, & -1\end{vmatrix}=1-z-z^{-4} \tag{22}$$

and

$$\left[Ez-A_1-A_2z^{-d_1}\right]^{-1}=\begin{bmatrix}z-1, & -z^{-2}\\ -z^{-2}, & -1\end{bmatrix}^{-1}=\frac{1}{1-z-z^{-4}}\begin{bmatrix}-1\ , & -z^{-2}\\ -z^{-2}\ , & z-1\end{bmatrix}= \tag{23}$$

$$=\Phi_{-1}+\Phi_0z^{-1}+\Phi_1z^{-2}+\Phi_2z^{-3}+\Phi_3z^{-4}+\cdots$$

where

$$\Phi_{-1}=\begin{bmatrix}0&0\\0&-1\end{bmatrix},\Phi_0=\begin{bmatrix}1&0\\0&0\end{bmatrix},\Phi_1=\begin{bmatrix}1&0\\0&0\end{bmatrix},\Phi_2=\begin{bmatrix}1&-1\\-1&0\end{bmatrix},\Phi_3=\begin{bmatrix}1&-1\\-1&0\end{bmatrix},\Phi_4=\begin{bmatrix}1&-1\\-1&1\end{bmatrix},\ldots \tag{24}$$

In this case the equality (8) has the form

$$\Phi_1E\Phi_i+\Phi_{-1}A_2\Phi_{i-1}+\Phi_0A_2\Phi_{i-2}=\Phi_{i+1}\quad \text{for}\quad i\in Z_+ \tag{25a}$$

or

$$\begin{bmatrix}1&0\\0&0\end{bmatrix}\Phi_i+\begin{bmatrix}0&0\\-1&0\end{bmatrix}\Phi_{i-1}+\begin{bmatrix}0&1\\0&0\end{bmatrix}\Phi_{i-2}=\Phi_{i+1} \tag{25b}$$

It is easy to check that the matrices (24) satisfy the equality (25b) for $i\in Z_+$
Using (18), (16) and (21) we obtain

$$F_0=\Phi_1E=\begin{bmatrix}1&0\\0&0\end{bmatrix},F_1=\Phi_{1-d_1}A_2=\Phi_{-1}A_2=\begin{bmatrix}0&0\\-1&0\end{bmatrix},F_2=\Phi_{2-d_1}A_2=\Phi_0A_2=\begin{bmatrix}0&1\\0&0\end{bmatrix}$$

$$T_0=I_n=\begin{bmatrix}1&0\\0&1\end{bmatrix},T_1=\Phi_1E=F_0=\begin{bmatrix}1&0\\0&0\end{bmatrix},T_2=\Phi_1ET_1+\Phi_{1-d_1}A_2=F_0T_1+F_1=\begin{bmatrix}1&0\\-1&0\end{bmatrix}$$

$$T_3=\Phi_1ET_2+\Phi_{1-d_1}A_2T_1+\Phi_{2-d_1}A_2=F_0T_2+F_1T_1+F_2=\begin{bmatrix}1&1\\-1&0\end{bmatrix}$$

$$T_4 = F_0T_3 + F_1T_2 + F_2T_1 = \begin{bmatrix} 1 & 1 \\ -1 & 0 \end{bmatrix}$$

$$H_1 = \Phi_{-1}B_1 = \begin{bmatrix} 0 \\ -2 \end{bmatrix}, H_0 = \Phi_0 B_1 - T_1 H_1 = \begin{bmatrix} 1 \\ 0 \end{bmatrix}, H_{-2} = \Phi_{-1}B_2 + \Phi_2 B_1 - T_2 H_0 - T_3 H_1 = \begin{bmatrix} 0 \\ -1 \end{bmatrix},$$

$$H_{-3} = \Phi_0 B_2 + \Phi_3 B_1 - T_3 H_0 - T_4 H_1 - T_1 H_{-2} = \begin{bmatrix} 1 \\ 0 \end{bmatrix}$$

Hence in this case the equation (17) has the form

$$x_{i+1} = \begin{bmatrix} 1 & 0 \\ 0 & 0 \end{bmatrix} x_i + \begin{bmatrix} 0 & 0 \\ -1 & 0 \end{bmatrix} x_{i-1} + \begin{bmatrix} 0 & 1 \\ 0 & 0 \end{bmatrix} x_{i-2} + \begin{bmatrix} 1 \\ 0 \end{bmatrix} u_i + \begin{bmatrix} 0 \\ -2 \end{bmatrix} u_{i+1} + \begin{bmatrix} 0 \\ -1 \end{bmatrix} u_{i-2} + \begin{bmatrix} 1 \\ 0 \end{bmatrix} u_{i-3} \tag{26}$$

and the set of admissible initial conditions (2) for given $u_i, i \geq d_2$ is defined by the equality

$$[0 \;\; 1] x_i + [1 \;\; 0] x_{i-2} + 2u_i + u_{i-3} = 0 \quad \text{for} \quad i = 0,1,2 \tag{27}$$

5. Application of the shuffle algorithm to determination of the standard system.

The shuffle algorithm was proposed by Luenberger [5] for time invariant linear systems. In this section the shuffle algorithm will be applied to determination of the equaivalent standard system (17) for singular discrete-time system (1).

Knowing the matrices E, A_1, A_2, B_1, B_2 of (1) we construct the array

$$E, A_1, A_2, B_1, B_2 \tag{28}$$

Performing elemenatry row operations on the array (28) we reduce it to the form

$$\begin{matrix} E_1, A_{11}, A_{21}, B_{11}, B_{21} \\ 0,\; A_{12}, A_{22}, B_{12}, B_{22} \end{matrix} \tag{29}$$

where $E_1 \in R^{n_1 \times n}$ is of full row rank and $A_{11}, A_{21} \in R^{n_1 \times n}, B_{11}, B_{21} \in R^{n_1 \times m}$.

Shuffle the array (29) to the form

$$\begin{matrix} E_1, & A_{11}, A_{21}, & 0, & B_{11}, & 0, & B_{21}, & 0 \\ A_{12}, & 0, & 0, -A_{22}, & 0, & -B_{12}, & 0, & -B_{22} \end{matrix} \tag{30}$$

If the matrix

$$\begin{bmatrix} E_1 \\ A_{12} \end{bmatrix} \tag{31}$$

is nonsingular then

(32)

$$x_{i+1} = \begin{bmatrix} E_1 \\ A_{12} \end{bmatrix}^{-1} \left\{ \begin{bmatrix} A_{11} \\ 0 \end{bmatrix} x_i + \begin{bmatrix} A_{21} \\ 0 \end{bmatrix} x_{i-d_1} + \begin{bmatrix} 0 \\ -A_{22} \end{bmatrix} x_{i-d_1+1} + \begin{bmatrix} B_{11} \\ 0 \end{bmatrix} u_i + \begin{bmatrix} 0 \\ -B_{12} \end{bmatrix} u_{i+1} + \begin{bmatrix} B_{21} \\ 0 \end{bmatrix} u_{i-d_2} + \begin{bmatrix} 0 \\ -B_{22} \end{bmatrix} u_{i-d_2+1} \right\}$$

If the matrix (31) is singular, performing elementary row operations on (30) we obtain

$$\begin{matrix} E_2, A_{11}^1, A_{21}^1, A_{31}, B_{11}^1, B_{21}^1, B_{31}, B_{41} \\ 0,\; A_{12}^1, A_{22}^1, A_{32}, B_{12}^1, B_{22}^1, B_{32}, B_{42} \end{matrix} \tag{33}$$

where E_2 is of full row rank and $rankE_2 \geq rankE_1$.

Shuffle the array (33) to the form

(34) $$\begin{matrix} E_2, A_{11}^1, A_{21}^1, A_{31}, & 0, & B_{11}^1, & B_{21}^1, & 0, & B_{31}, B_{41}, 0 \\ A_{12}^1, 0, & 0, -A_{22}^1, -A_{32}, & 0, & -B_{12}^1, -B_{22}^1, & 0, -B_{32}, -B_{42} \end{matrix}$$

If the matrix is nonsingular then

(35) $$\begin{bmatrix} E_2 \\ A_{12}^1 \end{bmatrix}$$

$$x_{i+1} = \begin{bmatrix} E_1 \\ A_{12}^1 \end{bmatrix}^{-1} \left\{ \begin{bmatrix} A_{11} \\ 0 \end{bmatrix} x_i + \begin{bmatrix} A_{21}^1 \\ 0 \end{bmatrix} x_{i-d_1} + \begin{bmatrix} A_{13} \\ -A_{22}^1 \end{bmatrix} x_{i-d_1+1} + \begin{bmatrix} 0 \\ -A_{32} \end{bmatrix} x_{i-d_1+2} + \begin{bmatrix} B_{11}^1 \\ 0 \end{bmatrix} u_i + \begin{bmatrix} B_{21}^1 \\ -B_{12}^1 \end{bmatrix} u_{i+1} + \right.$$

(36) $$\left. + \begin{bmatrix} B_{31} \\ 0 \end{bmatrix} u_{i-d_2} + \begin{bmatrix} B_{41} \\ -B_{32} \end{bmatrix} u_{i-d_2+1} + \begin{bmatrix} 0 \\ -B_{42} \end{bmatrix} u_{i-d_2+2} \right\}$$

If the matrix (35) is singular we repeat the procedure for (34). If the system (1) is regular and (3) holds then after k steps we obtain a nonsingular matrix $\begin{bmatrix} E_k \\ A_{12}^{k-1} \end{bmatrix}$ [2]. The shuffle algorithm can be justified as follows. Elementary row operations do not change the rank of $\left[Ez - A_1 - A_2 z^{-d_1} \right]$ and the shuffle of the array is equivalent to multiplication of the lower rows by $-z$. [7,2]

Example 2. (continuation of Example 1)

The find the equivalent standard system (26) for the singular system (1) with (21) we apply the shuffle algorithm.
In this case the array (28) has already the form (29)

(37) $$E, A_1, A_2, B_1, B_2 = \left[\begin{array}{cc:cc:cc:c:c} 1 & 0 & 1 & 0 & 0 & 1 & 1 & 1 \\ 0 & 0 & 0 & 1 & 1 & 0 & 2 & 1 \end{array}\right]$$

with $E_1 = [1\ 0], A_{11} = [1\ 0], A_{12} = [0\ 1], A_{21} = [0\ 1], A_{22}[1\ 0], B_{11} = [1], B_{12} = [2], B_{21} = [1], B_{22} = [1]$
The shuffle of (37) yields

$$\begin{matrix} E_1, A_{12}, A_{21}, 0, & B_{11}, & 0, & B_{21}, 0 \\ A_{21}, 0, & 0, -A_{22}, & 0, -B_{12}, 0, -B_{22} \end{matrix} = \left[\begin{array}{cc:cc:cc:cc:c:c:c:c} 1 & 0 & 1 & 0 & 0 & 1 & 0 & 0 & 1 & 0 & 1 & 0 \\ 0 & 1 & 0 & 0 & 0 & 0 & -1 & 0 & 0 & -2 & 0 & -1 \end{array}\right]$$

The matrix $\begin{bmatrix} E_1 \\ A_{21} \end{bmatrix} = \begin{bmatrix} 1 & 0 \\ 0 & 1 \end{bmatrix}$ is nonsingular and the equivalent standard system (32) has the form

$$x_{i+1} = \begin{bmatrix} 1 & 0 \\ 0 & 0 \end{bmatrix} x_i + \begin{bmatrix} 0 & 1 \\ 0 & 0 \end{bmatrix} x_{i-2} + \begin{bmatrix} 0 & 0 \\ -1 & 0 \end{bmatrix} x_{i-1} + \begin{bmatrix} 1 \\ 0 \end{bmatrix} u_i + \begin{bmatrix} 0 \\ -2 \end{bmatrix} u_{i+1} + \begin{bmatrix} 1 \\ 0 \end{bmatrix} u_{i-3} + \begin{bmatrix} 0 \\ -1 \end{bmatrix} u_{i-2}$$

6. Concluding remarks.

A standard system (17) which has the same solution (14) for admissible initial conditions (2) as the singular system (1) has been derived. Some basic properties of the fundamental matrices defined by (4) of the system (1) have been characterised. A method based on the shuffle algorithm for determination of the matrices of the standard system (17) has been proposed. Using the equivalent standard system (17) all results based on the solution concerning for example reachability, controllability, observability, minimum energy control obtained for the standard discrete-time linear systems (17) can be immediately extended for singular system (1). An open problem is to extend this approach for singular 2D linear systems described by the singular 2D Roesser type model and the singular 2D Fornasini-Marchesini type models [2].

References

[1] H. Górecki, S. Fuksa, P. Grabowski, A. Korytkowski, *Analysis and Systhesis of Time Delay Systems*, PWN J. Wiley, Warszawa - New Yoork 1989.

[2] T. Kaczorek, *Linear Control Systems*, vol. I and II, Reserach Studies Press, J. Wiley, New York 1992.

[3] T. Kaczorek, *Weakly positive continuous-time linear systems*, Bull. Pol. Acad. Techn. Sci., vol. 46, No. 2, 1998, pp. 231-243.

[4] T. Kaczorek, *Positive descriptor discrete-time linear systems*, Problems of Nonlinear Analysis in Engineering Systems 1998 (in press).

[5] F.L. Lewis, *A survey of linear singular systems*, Circuits Syst. Signal Process, vol. 5, No 1, 1986, pp. 1-36.

[6] F.L. Lewis and B.G. Metrzios, *On the analysis of discrete linear time-invariant singular systems*, IEEE Transactions on Automatic Control, vol. 35, No. 4, 1990, pp. 506-511.

[7] D.G. Luenberger, *Time-invariant descriptor systems*, Automatica, vol. 14, 1978, pp. 473-480.

[8] A. Medvedev, *Disturbance attenuation in finite-spectrum-assignment controllers*, Automatica, vol. 33, No 6, 1997, pp. 1163-1168.

[9] B.G. Mertzios and F.L. Lewis, *Fundamental matrix of discrete singular systems*, Circuits Systems Signal Process, vol. 8, No 3, 1989, pp. 341-355.

[10] A. Olbrot, *Stabilizability, decectability and spectrum assignment for linear systems with general time delays*, IEEE Trans. Autom. Contr. AC_23, 1978, pp. 887-890.

COMPUTATION OF THE VECTOR POWERS OF MATRICES WHICH ARE USED IN 2-DIMENSIONAL SYSTEMS

Nikos E.Mastorakis
Military Institutions of University Education (MIUE), Hellenic Naval Academy,
Chair of Computer Science, Terma Hatzikyriakou, 18539, Piraeus, GREECE,
Tel-Fax: +301 777 5660 and Fax: +301 4181768
email: mastor@softlab.ntua.gr URL: http://softlab.ntua.gr/~mastor

Abstract: A new method for the computation of the vector powers of two-dimensional (2-D) state-space models is presented. The method can be applied to all 2-D models that are commonly used and consists in presenting the vector power of a matrix as a definite integral, which can then be computed numerically. This approach is illustrated by means of two examples.

I.Introduction

The vector powers of matrices in 2-D and m-D (m>2) systems is of fundamental importance since they always appear in the general response formula, in controllability and observability tests and in problems related to the stability of all these models. Givone and Roesser's model, [1]÷[3], and Fornasini-Marchesini's model, [4], were the first 2-D dynamical models and they are the most widely used models though there exist many other models such as Theodorou's model, [5], Eising's model, [6] and Galkowski's model [7]. A great number of recent papers and books has been already published on the mathematical theory, mainly, of the first two models, [8]÷[13]. The computation of the various two-dimensional vector powers that appear in these 2-D models is one of the primary processes in the field of 2-D systems [1]÷[7], [16].

The following definition can be considered as a unified definition of the vector power (of a square matrix A) for all the above models:

i) $A^{i_1,i_2} = \boldsymbol{0}$ if $i_1 < 0$ or $i_2 < 0$ $\; i_1, i_2 \in \boldsymbol{Z}, \boldsymbol{Z}$ is the set of the integer numbers.

ii) $A^{0,0} = I$ (identity matrix).

iii) $A^{i_1,i_2} = A^{1,0}A^{i_1-1,i_2} + A^{0,1}A^{i_1,i_2-1}$ for $(i_1,i_2) > (0,0)$ with

- $A^{1,0} = \begin{bmatrix} A_1 & A_2 \\ 0 & 0 \end{bmatrix}$ and $A^{0,1} = \begin{bmatrix} 0 & 0 \\ A_3 & A_4 \end{bmatrix}$ for Roesser's model (where $A = \begin{bmatrix} A_1 & A_2 \\ A_3 & A_4 \end{bmatrix}$ is the block companion matrix with A_1, A_4 square sub-matrices) [1]÷[3].

- $A^{1,0} = A_1$ and $A^{0,1} = A_2$ for Fornasini-Marchesini's model with A_1, A_2 the two companion (square) matrices of this model [4].

- $A^{1,0} = \begin{bmatrix} A_1 & 0 \\ A_3 & 0 \end{bmatrix}$ and $A^{0,1} = \begin{bmatrix} 0 & A_2 \\ 0 & A_4 \end{bmatrix}$ for Theodorou's model (where

$A = \begin{bmatrix} A_1 & A_2 \\ A_3 & A_4 \end{bmatrix}$ is the block companion matrix with A_1, A_4 square sub-matrices) [5].

In the other models analogous definitions can be stated. As we mentioned above, the computation of the power A^{i_1,i_2} is of fundamental importance in the 2-D systems theory. Surely, the definition offers a method. However, it appears high computational complexity and rather useless for big i_1 and i_2. For this reason, some efforts have already been made in order to simplify the computation of A^{i_1,i_2}. In [3], except the definition, another method is also proposed. However, in [11], the method of [3] is proved insufficient and incorrect in most cases and for this reason a different method is recommended. Nevertheless, the method in [11] appears to be complicated and difficult for big i_1 and i_2 (but simpler and better than the one in [3]).

In the present paper, a new method for the computation of the power A^{i_1,i_2} is proposed. First some theoretical results are given and then the method is presented. The method has the advantage of the direct computation of A^{i_1,i_2} even if we would have big i_1, i_2 in the superscript. On the contrary, the other methods [3], [11] require the previous evaluation of all or almost all the powers of A^{j_1,j_2} with $j_1 < i_1$ and $j_2 < i_2$.

II. Main Results

Consider the double power series:

$$\Phi(x,y) = \sum_{i_1=0}^{\infty}\sum_{i_2=0}^{\infty} \frac{A^{i_1,i_2}}{i_1!i_2!} x^{i_1} y^{i_2} \tag{1}$$

It will be proved that the convergence radii of this double power series are ∞ and ∞. More precisely, the following theorem holds. The proof can be found in the Appendix.

Theorem 1 : The power series (1) converges uniformly and absolutely $\forall\ (x,y) \in D_1 \times D_2$ where D_1 and D_2 are closed and bounded subsets of $\Re$ (the set of the real numbers). ∎

Now, one can find the double Laplace transform of $\Phi(x,y)$

Theorem 2 : Suppose that the double Laplace transform: $\Phi(s_1,s_2)=\mathrm{L}_x\mathrm{L}_y\Phi(x,y)$ exists (for proper domains of s_1, s_2). Then

$$\Phi(s_1,s_2) = \left[s_1 s_2 I - s_2 A^{1,0} - s_1 A^{0,1}\right]^{-1} \tag{2}$$

Proof: From (1), we obtain

$$L_x L_y \Phi(x,y) = \sum_{i_1=0}^{\infty}\sum_{i_2=0}^{\infty} A^{i_1,i_2} \frac{1}{s_1^{i_1+1}} \frac{1}{s_2^{i_2+1}}$$

Suppose that for appropriate values of s_1, s_2 this double power series converges. Then, it is easy to verify, by equating of like powers, that:

$$\left(\sum_{i_1=0}^{\infty}\sum_{i_2=0}^{\infty} A^{i_1,i_2} \frac{1}{s_1^{i_1+1}} \frac{1}{s_2^{i_2+1}}\right)\left(s_1 s_2 I - s_2 A^{1,0} - s_1 A^{0,1}\right) = I \tag{3.1}$$

as well as

$$\left(s_1 s_2 I - s_2 A^{1,0} - s_1 A^{0,1}\right)\left(\sum_{i_1=0}^{\infty}\sum_{i_2=0}^{\infty} A^{i_1,i_2} \frac{1}{s_1^{i_1+1}} \frac{1}{s_2^{i_2+1}}\right) = I \tag{3.2}$$

One should notice that eqn. (3.1) and (3.2) hold if the double infinite sum $\left(\sum_{i_1=0}^{\infty}\sum_{i_2=0}^{\infty} A^{i_1,i_2} \frac{1}{s_1^{i_1+1}} \frac{1}{s_2^{i_2+1}}\right)$ exists, i.e. this double power series converges. The following theorem provides a necessary condition for this convergence.

Theorem 3 : A necessary condition for the absolute convergence of the double power-series

$$\Phi(s_1, s_2) = \sum_{i_1=0}^{\infty}\sum_{i_2=0}^{\infty} A^{i_1,i_2} \frac{1}{s_1^{i_1+1}} \frac{1}{s_2^{i_2+1}} \tag{4}$$

(and consequently for the validity of (2)) is

$$M_1\left|\frac{1}{s_1}\right| + M_2\left|\frac{1}{s_2}\right| < 1 \tag{5}$$

where $M_1 = \|A^{1,0}\|$, $M_2 = \|A^{0,1}\|$, and $\| \ \|$ is a matrix norm - for example the Frobenius norm.

Proof: The power series $\Phi(s_1, s_2) = \sum_{i_1=0}^{\infty}\sum_{i_2=0}^{\infty} A^{i_1,i_2} \frac{1}{s_1^{i_1+1}} \frac{1}{s_2^{i_2+1}} = \frac{1}{s_1}\frac{1}{s_2}\sum_{i_1=0}^{\infty}\sum_{i_2=0}^{\infty} A^{i_1,i_2} \frac{1}{s_1^{i_1}} \frac{1}{s_2^{i_2}}$ converges absolutely if and only if the power series $\sum_{i_1=0}^{\infty}\sum_{i_2=0}^{\infty} A^{i_1,i_2} w_1^{i_1} w_2^{i_2}$ ($w_i = \frac{1}{s_i}$, $i = 1,2$) converges absolutely too. Now, one can obtain that

$$\left\|\sum_{i_1=0}^{\infty}\sum_{i_2=0}^{\infty} A^{i_1,i_2} w_1^{i_1} w_2^{i_2}\right\| \le \sum_{i_1=0}^{\infty}\sum_{i_2=0}^{\infty} \left\|A^{i_1,i_2}\right\| |w_1|^{i_1} |w_2|^{i_2}.$$

On the other hand, it is easily seen (Proof of Theorem 1 in Appendix) that $\left\|A^{i_1,i_2}\right\| \le \frac{(i_1+i_2)!}{i_1!i_2!} M_1^{i_1} M_2^{i_2}$. Therefore:

$$\left\|\sum_{i_1=0}^{\infty}\sum_{i_2=0}^{\infty} A^{i_1,i_2} w_1^{i_1} w_2^{i_2}\right\| \le \sum_{i_1=0}^{\infty}\sum_{i_2=0}^{\infty}\left\|A^{i_1,i_2}\right\| |w_1|^{i_1} |w_2|^{i_2} \le \sum_{i_1=0}^{\infty}\sum_{i_2=0}^{\infty}\frac{(i_1+i_2)!}{i_1!i_2!} M_1^{i_1} M_2^{i_2} |w_1|^{i_1} |w_2|^{i_2} \quad (6)$$

From the Rearrangement Theorem for double series, [14, Paragraph 8.22], one can conclude that $\sum_{i_1=0}^{\infty}\sum_{i_2=0}^{\infty}\frac{(i_1+i_2)!}{i_1!i_2!} M_1^{i_1} M_2^{i_2} |w_1|^{i_1} |w_2|^{i_2}$ converges if and only if the series $\sum_{k=0}^{\infty}\sum_{i_1=0}^{k}\frac{(k)!}{i_1!(k-i_1)!} M_1^{i_1} M_2^{k-i_1} |w_1|^{i_1} |w_2|^{k-i_1}$ converges too. The last series can be written as $\sum_{k=0}^{\infty}\left(M_1|w_1|+M_2|w_2|\right)^k$ which converges if $M_1|w_1|+M_2|w_2|<1$ or equivalently if (5) holds. ∎

We recall that a *complete Reinhardt domain* [17], is an open set $D \subseteq \boldsymbol{C}^2$ (where $\boldsymbol{C}$ denotes the set of the complex numbers) having the property that for every $(s_1,s_2) \in D$ and every pair of complex numbers σ_i such that $|\sigma_i| \le 1$ (i=1,2), $(\sigma_1 s_1, \sigma_2 s_2) \in D$. An open set is an *inverse complete Reinhardt domain* if the condition $|\sigma_i| \le 1$ is replaced by $|\sigma_i| \ge 1$. Therefore, a simple corollary of the Theorem 3 is that the domain given in (5) is an *inverse complete Reinhardt domain.* So, we can always find appropriate positive numbers R_1, R_2 such that the convergence for $|s_1| \ge R_1$, $|s_2| \ge R_2$ is guaranteed.

Suppose now that $adj\left[s_1 s_2 I - s_2 A^{1,0} - s_1 A^{0,1}\right] = \sum_{j_1=1}^{N_1}\sum_{j_2=1}^{N_2} F_{j_1,j_2} s_1^{N_1-j_1} s_2^{N_2-j_2}$, then

$$\left[s_1 s_2 I - s_2 A^{1,0} - s_1 A^{0,1}\right]\sum_{j_1=1}^{N_1}\sum_{j_2=1}^{N_2} F_{j_1,j_2} s_1^{N_1-j_1} s_2^{N_2-j_2} = p(s_1,s_2)\cdot I \quad (7)$$

where $p(s_1,s_2) = det\left[s_1 s_2 I - s_2 A^{1,0} - s_1 A^{0,1}\right] = \sum_{i=0}^{N_1}\sum_{j=0}^{N_2} a(i,j) s_1^i s_2^j$. Then, from (7), one has equivalently

$$\sum_{j_1=1}^{N_1}\sum_{j_2=1}^{N_2}\left(s_1^{N_1-j_1+1} s_2^{N_2-j_2+1} - A^{1,0} s_1^{N_1-j_1} s_2^{N_2-j_2+1} - A^{0,1} s_1^{N_1-j_1+1} s_2^{N_2-j_2}\right) F_{j_1,j_2} = \sum_{i=0}^{N_1}\sum_{j=0}^{N_2} a(i,j) s_1^i s_2^j \cdot I$$

Then, by equating of like powers in the last relation, the following Theorem can be proved.

Theorem 4 : The inverse matrix $\left[s_1s_2I - s_2A^{1,0} - s_1A^{0,1}\right]^{-1}$ is computed from the relation

$$\left[s_1s_2I - s_2A^{1,0} - s_1A^{0,1}\right]^{-1} = \frac{\sum_{j_1=1}^{N_1}\sum_{j_2=1}^{N_2} F_{j_1,j_2} s_1^{N_1-j_1} s_2^{N_2-j_2}}{det\left[s_1s_2I - s_2A^{1,0} - s_1A^{0,1}\right]} \tag{8}$$

where

$$F_{j_1,j_2} = A^{1,0}F_{j_1-1,j_2} + A^{0,1}F_{j_1,j_2-1} + a(N_1 - j_1 + 1, N_2 - j_2 + 1)I \tag{9}$$

with $F_{1,1} = I$, $F_{j_1,j_2} = \boldsymbol{0}$ for $j_1 < 1$ or $j_2 < 1$, and $a(i,j)$ are the i,j coefficients in the N_1, N_2 degree polynomial $p(s_1,s_2) = det\left[s_1s_2I - s_2A^{1,0} - s_1A^{0,1}\right] = \sum_{i=0}^{N_1}\sum_{j=0}^{N_2} a(i,j)s_1^is_2^j$ and $a(N_1,N_2) = 1$. ■

Theorem 4 actually provides a fast algorithm for computing the matrix inverse $\left[s_1s_2I - s_2A^{1,0} - s_1A^{0,1}\right]^{-1}$.Now, we are ready to state a new method for the computation of the matrix A^{i_1,i_2}.

III. The proposed method

Theorem 5: The matrix A^{i_1,i_2} is computed by the double integral

$$A^{i_1,i_2} = \frac{1}{(2\pi \cdot i)^2} \oint_{|s_1|=R_1} \oint_{|s_2|=R_2} \left[s_1s_2I - s_2A^{1,0} - s_1A^{0,1}\right]^{-1} s_1^{i_1}s_2^{i_2} ds_1 ds_2 \tag{10}$$

$$\left(i = \sqrt{-1}\right)$$

where R_1, R_2 satisfy the relation $\frac{M_1}{R_1} + \frac{M_2}{R_2} < 1$.

Proof: The proof of the last inequality is based on Theorem 3. The Laplace transformation of: $\Phi(x,y) = \sum_{i_1=0}^{\infty}\sum_{i_2=0}^{\infty} \frac{A^{i_1,i_2}}{i_1!i_2!} x^{i_1}y^{i_2}$ is given by (4) from which following the classic complex analysis we obtain:

$$A^{i_1,i_2} = \frac{1}{(2\pi \cdot i)^2} \oint_{|s_1|=R_1} \oint_{|s_2|=R_2} \Phi(s_1,s_2) s_1^{i_1}s_2^{i_2} ds_1 ds_2 \tag{11}$$

where R_1, R_2 ought to satisfy the relation $\frac{M_1}{R_1}+\frac{M_2}{R_2}<1$. Substituting (2) into (11), we obtain (10). ∎

Remark 1: The integral in (10) can be evaluated using any suitable numerical technique for real integrals since one can substitute

$s_1 = R_1 \cdot (\cos(t_1)+i\cdot\sin(t_1)),\quad s_2 = R_2\cdot(\cos(t_2)+i\cdot\sin(t_2)),$

$ds_1 = R_1(-\sin(t_1)+i\cdot\cos(t_1))dt_1,\quad ds_2 = R_2(-\sin(t_2)+i\cdot\cos(t_2))dt_2$ with $t_1, t_2 \in [0, 2\pi]$.

Remark 2: Numerical "experiments" using a software package (for example *Mathematica* 2.2) confirm that the presented method is better than those of [3] and [11] especially for big i_1, i_2. So, we present the example of [11] with $i_1 = 2,\ i_2 = 1$. Then another example is provided in which one can verify the applicability and the power of the present method.

Example 1, [11]: For the Roesser model (see Introduction), we consider $A_1 = [-0.1]$, $A_2 = [-0.09]$, $A_3 = [1]$, $A_4 = [-0.1]$. Using the algorithm of Theorem 4, we find

$$\Phi(s_1,s_2)=\frac{\begin{bmatrix} s_1s_2+0.1s_1 & -0.09s_2 \\ s_1 & s_1s_2+0.1s_2\end{bmatrix}}{s_1^2s_2^2+0.1s_1s_2^2+0.1s_1^2s_2+0.1s_1s_2}.$$ Then, one has

$$A^{i_1,i_2}=\frac{1}{(2\pi\cdot i)^2}\oint_{|s_1|=1}\oint_{|s_2|=2}\frac{\begin{bmatrix} s_1s_2+0.1s_1 & -0.09s_2 \\ s_1 & s_1s_2+0.1s_2\end{bmatrix}}{s_1^2s_2^2+0.1s_1s_2^2+0.1s_1^2s_2+0.1s_1s_2}s_1^{i_1}s_2^{i_2}ds_1ds_2$$

Setting for example $i_1 = 2,\ i_2 = 1$ and after the numerical calculation one finds the same result as in [11]: $A^{2,1}=\begin{bmatrix} 0.018 & 0.0072 \\ 0.01 & 0.009\end{bmatrix}$.

Example 2: For the Roesser model, we consider now $A_1 = [1]$, $A_2 = [-0.2]$, $A_3 = [0.3]$, $A_4 = [0.5]$. Similarly, we find

$$\Phi(s_1,s_2)=\frac{\begin{bmatrix} s_1s_2-0.5s_1 & -0.2s_2 \\ 0.3s_1 & s_1s_2-s_2\end{bmatrix}}{s_1^2s_2^2-s_1s_2^2-0.5s_1^2s_2+0.56s_1s_2}.$$ Therefore

$$A^{i_1,i_2}=\frac{1}{(2\pi\cdot i)^2}\oint_{|s_1|=2}\oint_{|s_2|=1}\frac{\begin{bmatrix} s_1s_2-0.5s_1 & -0.2s_2 \\ 0.3s_1 & s_1s_2-s_2\end{bmatrix}}{s_1^2s_2^2-s_1s_2^2-0.5s_1^2s_2+0.56s_1s_2}s_1^{i_1}s_2^{i_2}ds_1ds_2$$

Setting for example $i_1 = 5,\ i_2 = 8$ one finds: $A^{5,8} = \begin{bmatrix} 3.194 & 6.294 \\ -17.732 & 5.111 \end{bmatrix} \cdot 10^{-4}$.

IV. Conclusion

A new fast and efficient method for the computation of the 2-dimensional vector powers of matrices is presented. Some indispensable theoretical results are also investigated. These results are the background for the proposed method and they are extended to the m-D (m>2) vector powers in a straightforward manner.

References:

[1].D.D.Givone and R.P.Roesser, "Multidimensional Linear Iterative Circuits - General Properties", *IEEE Transactions on Computers,* Vol.C-21, No.10, pp. 1067-1073, Oct.1972.

[2].D.D.Givone and R.P.Roesser, "Minimization of Multidimensional Linear Iterative Circuits", *IEEE Trans. Computers,* Vol.C-22, No.7, pp. 673-678, July1973.

[3].R.P.Roesser, "A discrete state-space model for image processing," *IEEE Transactions on Automatic Control,* vol. AC-20, pp. 1-10, Feb. 1975.

[4].E.Fornasini and G.Marchesini, "Doubly-indexed dynamical systems: State-space models and structural properties", *Mathem. System Theory,* vol.12, pp.59-72, 1978.

[5].N.J.Theodorou, "State-Space Representation and Error Analysis od Two-Dimensional Systems", Ph.D.Thesis, Imperial College, Univ. London, 1978.

[6].R.Eising, "Realization and Stabilization of 2-D systems", *IEEE Trans. Automat. Contr.,* vol. AC-24, pp. 793-799, Oct. 1978.

[7].K.Galkowski, "The State-Space Realization of an n-Dimensional Transfer Function", *Circuit Theory and Applications,* Vol.9, pp.189-197, 1981.

[8].T.Kaczorek, *Two-Dimensional Linear Systems,* Springer-Verlag, Lecture Notes in Control and Information Sciences, Berlin-Heidelberg, 1985.

[9].N K.Bose (Editor), *Multidimensional Systems Theory, Progress, Directions and Open Problems in Multidimensional Systems,* D. Reidel Publishing Company, Dordrecht, Holland 1985.

[10].S.G.Tzafestas (Editor), *Multidimensional Systems, Techniques and Applications,*Marcel Dekker, N. York, 1986.

[11].N.J.Theodorou and R.A.King, "State-Space Discrete Systems: Computation of the Transition Matrix", *IEEE Trans. on Autom. Control,* Vol. AC-25, No 2, pp.296-297, 1980.

[12].N.E.Mastorakis, N.J.Theodorou and S.G.Tzafestas: "Multidimensional polynomial Factorization in linear m-D factors", *International Journal of System Science,* Vol.23, pp.1805-1824, 1992.

[13].N.E.Mastorakis, N.J.Theodorou and S.G.Tzafestas : "A general Factorization method for multivariable polynomials", *Multidimensional Systems and Signal Processing,* Vol.5, pp.151-178, 1994.
[14].Tom M. Apostol, *Mathematical Analysis,* Addison-Wesley Publishing Company, 1974, (Fifth Printing 1981).
[15].Louis Brand, *Advanced Calculus,* John Wiley and Sons, 1955.
[16].N.E.Mastorakis and N.J.Theodorou, "Stochastic Analysis of systems described by the Roesser model", *Journal of the Franklin Institute,* Vol.330, No.4, pp.767-773, 1993.
[17].R.C.Gunning, *Introduction to Holomorphic Functions of Several Variables,* Wadsworth & Brooks/Cole Publishing Company, California, USA, 1990.

APPENDIX

Proof of Theorem 1: From the recursive relation $A^{i_1,i_2} = A^{1,0}A^{i_1-1,i_2} + A^{0,1}A^{i_1,i_2-1}$ one can conclude that A^{i_1,i_2} is the sum of $\frac{(i_1+i_2)!}{i_1!i_2!}$ terms. Every term is a product of i_1 factors of the form $A^{1,0}$ and i_2 factors of the form $A^{0,1}$. Taking all the possible combinations of $A^{1,0}$ and $A^{0,1}$, the sum is proved to have $\frac{(i_1+i_2)!}{i_1!i_2!}$ terms.

Denoting $M_1 = \|A^{1,0}\|$, $M_2 = \|A^{0,1}\|$, where $\| \ \|$ is a matrix norm - for example the Frobenius norm - and based on the triangular inequality, we obtain:

$$\|A^{i_1,i_2}\| \le \frac{(i_1+i_2)!}{i_1!i_2!} M_1^{i_1} M_2^{i_2} \tag{A.1}$$

thus

$$\left\|\frac{A^{i_1,i_2}}{i_1!i_2!}\right\| \le \frac{(i_1+i_2)!}{(i_1!i_2!)^2} M_1^{i_1} M_2^{i_2} \tag{A.2}$$

Furthermore, from the double power series

$$S_1(x,y) = \sum_{i_1=0}^{\infty}\sum_{i_2=0}^{\infty} \frac{(i_1+i_2)!}{(i_1!i_2!)^2} M_1^{i_1} M_2^{i_2}\, x^{i_1} y^{i_2} \tag{A.3}$$

one can find the single power series (the bracketed sum is a finite sum)

$$S_2(x,y) = \sum_{k=0}^{\infty}\left(\sum_{i_1=0}^{k} \frac{k!}{(i_1!(k-i_1)!)^2} M_1^{i_1} M_2^{k-i_1} x^{i_1} y^{k-i_1}\right) \tag{A.4}$$

$S_1(x,y)$ converges absolutely if and only if $S_2(x,y)$ converges absolutely too (Rearrangement Theorem for Double Series, Paragraph 8.22 in [14]). It is easy to verify (ratio test) that $S_2(x,y)$ converges absolutely $\forall\ (x,y) \in \Re^2 = \Re \times \Re$, $\Re$ is the set of the real numbers. Therefore $S_1(x,y)$ converges absolutely as well as $\Phi(x,y)$ converges absolutely $\forall\ (x,y) \in \Re^2$ too. Using Weierstrass test [15], one finds that $S_1(x,y)$ converges uniformly $\forall\ (x,y) \in D_1 \times D_2$ where D_1 and D_2 are closed and bounded subsets of $\Re$. Therefore $S_1(x,y)$ converges uniformly and $\Phi(x,y)$ converges uniformly too $\forall\ (x,y) \in D_1 \times D_2$. ■

Two–Dimensional Positive Systems: Minimal State Space Realization and Transfer Functions [1]

George Antoniou, Apostolos Papis and Angie Chilmaza

Computer Science Department
Montclair State University
Montclair, New Jersey, 07043
antoniou@pegasus.montclair.edu

Abstract

New minimal state space realizations are presented 2-D positive systems. The corresponding 2–D transfer functions have special structures state space realizations various problems in system theory man be studied.

Key Words

Realization, Positive Systems, System theory, Multidimensional systems

1 Introduction

Two–Dimensional(2–D) positive systems are dynamic systems having all coefficients, of the state space representation, non–negative [1]. These systems can be represented, in state space, using the multidimensional models of Roesser, Fornasini–Marchesini and Attasi.

Applications, for the case of one–dimensional (1–D) systems, have been reported in the areas of Image Processing, Biomathematics, For 2–D systems, Kaczorek studied the realization, reachability, controllability and minimum energy control related to their asymptotic and dynamic behavior. Klamka studied the constrained controllability of 2–D positive systems of the Fornasini-Marchesini type.

In this paper minimal state realizations, of Roesser type, are presented for special 2–D (x, /, \ structured) positive systems [2]–[5]

It is worth mentioning that the general problem of minimal state space realization has not been solved even for two–dimensional systems. Minimal 2–D realizations exist only for special cases, i.e. all–pole, all–zero, separable, factorable, systems expandable to continued fractions [6]–[10].

2 Problem formulation

Let us consider the following 2–D state space model of Roesser type [11]:

$$\begin{aligned} \dot{\mathbf{x}}(i_1, i_2) &= \mathbf{A}\mathbf{x}(i_1, i_2) + \mathbf{b}u(i_1, i_2) \\ y(i_1, i_2) &= \mathbf{c}'\mathbf{x}(i_1, i_2) + du(i_1, i_2) \end{aligned} \tag{1}$$

where,

[1]Part of this work was supported by the MSU Faculty–Student grant FY97.

$$\dot{\mathbf{x}}(i_1,i_2) = \begin{bmatrix} \mathbf{x}^{d_1}(i_1+1,i_2) \\ \mathbf{x}^{d_2}(i_1,i_2+1) \end{bmatrix}$$

$$\mathbf{x}(i_1,i_2,i_3) = \begin{bmatrix} x^{d_1}(i_1,i_2) \\ x^{d_2}(i_1,i_2) \end{bmatrix}$$

and where, $x^{d_1}(i_1,i_2)$ is the horizontal state vector, $x^{d_2}(i_1,i_2)$ is the vertical state vector, $u(i_1,i_2)$ is the input and $y(i_1,i_2)$ is the output.

$$\mathbf{A} = \begin{bmatrix} \mathbf{A}_{11} & \mathbf{A}_{12} \\ \mathbf{A}_{21} & \mathbf{A}_{22} \end{bmatrix}$$

$$\mathbf{b} = \begin{bmatrix} \mathbf{b}_1 \\ \mathbf{b}_2 \end{bmatrix}, \quad \mathbf{c}' = \begin{bmatrix} \mathbf{c}_1 & \mathbf{c}_2 \end{bmatrix}$$

The above 2–D state space model of Roesser type is considered to be positive if for the following boundary conditions [1].

$$x^{d1}(0,i_2) \in R_+, i_2 \in Z_+, x^{d2}(i_1,0) \in R_+, i_2 \in Z_+$$

and for all $u(i_1,i_2) \in R_+, \forall i_1, i_2 \in Z_+$ and $y(i_1,i_2) \in R_+, \forall i_1, i_2 \in Z_+$, the following holds

$$\mathbf{A} \in R_+, \mathbf{b} \in R_+, \mathbf{c} \in R_+, d \in R_+$$

3 Realizations and transfer functions

In the following subsections minimal state space realizations and their corresponding transfer functions are presented.

3.1 X-structure

Consider the 2–D transfer function

$$TF(n) = \frac{z_1 + z_2 - a_{0,n} + a_{1,n} + a_{2,n} - a_{3,n}}{(z_1 - a_{0,n})(z_2 - a_{3,n}) - a_{1,n}a_{2,n}} + TF(n-1) \tag{2}$$

where

$$TF(0) = \frac{z_1 + z_2 - a_{0,0} + a_{1,0} + a_{2,0} - a_{3,0}}{(z_1 - a_{0,0})(z_2 - a_{3,0}) - a_{1,0}a_{2,0}} \tag{3}$$

The generalized 2–D state space model of Roesser type (1) has the following x-structure, where

$$\mathbf{A}_{11} = \begin{bmatrix} a_{0,n} & 0 & \cdots & 0 \\ 0 & \ddots & \ddots & \vdots \\ \vdots & \ddots & \ddots & 0 \\ 0 & \cdots & 0 & a_{0,0} \end{bmatrix}, \quad \mathbf{A}_{12} = \begin{bmatrix} 0 & \cdots & 0 & a_{1,n} \\ \vdots & \ddots & \ddots & 0 \\ 0 & \ddots & \ddots & \vdots \\ a_{1,0} & 0 & \cdots & 0 \end{bmatrix} \tag{4}$$

$$\mathbf{A}_{21} = \begin{bmatrix} 0 & \cdots & 0 & a_{2,0} \\ \vdots & \ddots & \ddots & 0 \\ 0 & \ddots & \ddots & \vdots \\ a_{2,n} & 0 & \cdots & 0 \end{bmatrix}, \quad \mathbf{A}_{22} = \begin{bmatrix} a_{3,0} & 0 & \cdots & 0 \\ 0 & \ddots & \ddots & \vdots \\ \vdots & \ddots & \ddots & 0 \\ 0 & \cdots & 0 & a_{3,n} \end{bmatrix}$$

$$\mathbf{b} = \begin{bmatrix} 1 \\ \vdots \\ 1 \end{bmatrix}, \quad \mathbf{c}' = \begin{bmatrix} 1 & \cdots & 1 \end{bmatrix}$$

3.2 \ -structure

Consider the 2–D transfer function

$$TF(n) = \frac{z_1 + z_2 - a_{0,n} - a_{3,n}}{(z_1 - a_{0,n})(z_2 - a_{3,n})} + TF(n-1) \tag{5}$$

where

$$TF(0) = \frac{z_1 + z_2 - a_{0,0} - a_{3,0}}{(z_1 - a_{0,0})(z_2 - a_{3,0})} \tag{6}$$

The generalized 2–D state space model of Roesser type (1) has the following \ -structure, where

$$\mathbf{A}_{11} = \begin{bmatrix} a_{0,n} & 0 & \cdots & 0 \\ 0 & \ddots & \ddots & \vdots \\ \vdots & \ddots & \ddots & 0 \\ 0 & \cdots & 0 & a_{0,0} \end{bmatrix} \quad \mathbf{A}_{12} = \begin{bmatrix} 0 & \cdots & 0 & 0 \\ \vdots & \ddots & \ddots & 0 \\ 0 & \ddots & \ddots & \vdots \\ 0 & 0 & \cdots & 0 \end{bmatrix}$$

$$\mathbf{A}_{21} = \begin{bmatrix} 0 & \cdots & 0 & 0 \\ \vdots & \ddots & \ddots & 0 \\ 0 & \ddots & \ddots & \vdots \\ 0 & 0 & \cdots & 0 \end{bmatrix} \quad \mathbf{A}_{22} = \begin{bmatrix} a_{3,0} & 0 & \cdots & 0 \\ 0 & \ddots & \ddots & \vdots \\ \vdots & \ddots & \ddots & 0 \\ 0 & \cdots & 0 & a_{3,n} \end{bmatrix}$$

$$\mathbf{b} = \begin{bmatrix} 1 \\ \vdots \\ 1 \end{bmatrix}, \quad \mathbf{c}' = \begin{bmatrix} 1 & \cdots & 1 \end{bmatrix}$$

3.3 /-structure

Consider the 2–D transfer function

$$TF(n) = \frac{z_1 + z_2 + a_{1,n} + a_{2,n}}{z_1 z_2 - a_{1,n} a_{2,n}} + TF(n-1) \tag{7}$$

where

$$TF(0) = \frac{z_1 + z_2 + a_{1,0} + a_{2,0}}{z_1 z_2 - a_{1,0} a_{2,0}} \tag{8}$$

where

$$\mathbf{A}_{11} = \begin{bmatrix} 0 & 0 & \cdots & 0 \\ 0 & \ddots & \ddots & \vdots \\ \vdots & \ddots & \ddots & 0 \\ 0 & \cdots & 0 & 0 \end{bmatrix} \quad \mathbf{A}_{12} = \begin{bmatrix} 0 & \cdots & 0 & a_{1,n} \\ \vdots & \ddots & \ddots & 0 \\ 0 & \ddots & \ddots & \vdots \\ a_{1,0} & 0 & \cdots & 0 \end{bmatrix}$$

$$\mathbf{A}_{21} = \begin{bmatrix} 0 & \cdots & 0 & a_{2,0} \\ \vdots & \ddots & \ddots & 0 \\ 0 & \ddots & \ddots & \vdots \\ a_{2,n} & 0 & \cdots & 0 \end{bmatrix} \quad \mathbf{A}_{22} = \begin{bmatrix} 0 & 0 & \cdots & 0 \\ 0 & \ddots & \ddots & \vdots \\ \vdots & \ddots & \ddots & 0 \\ 0 & \cdots & 0 & 0 \end{bmatrix}$$

$$\mathbf{b} = \begin{bmatrix} 1 \\ \vdots \\ 1 \end{bmatrix}, \ \mathbf{c}' = \begin{bmatrix} 1 & \cdots & 1 \end{bmatrix}$$

Note that the following equation relates a 2-D state space representation, of Roesser type, with its corresponding 2–D trasfer function.

$$H(z_1, z_2, \ldots, z_3) = \mathbf{c}'[\mathbf{I}\mathcal{Z} - \mathbf{A}]^{-1}\mathbf{b}' \tag{9}$$

where, $\mathcal{Z} = w\mathbf{I}_n \oplus z\mathbf{I}_n$, with $\oplus$ denoting the direct sum.

4 Conclusions

In this paper new 2–D state space realizations for positive systems were proposed. Their state space vectors and the state space matrices $\mathbf{A}, \mathbf{b}, \mathbf{c}'$, and the scalar d of the Givone–Roesser model are of minimal dimension.

REFERENCES

[1] Kaczorek, T "Realization problem, reachability and minimum energy control of positive 2–D Roesser type model", 6th Annual International Conference on Advances in Communication and Control, pp. 765–776, Corfu, Greece, 1997.

[2] Kaczorek, T, "Reachability and Controllability of nonnegative 2–D Roesser type models", Bulletin Polish Academy of Sciences, 1996.

[3] Klamka, J "Constrained controllability of positive 2–D Systems", 6th Annual International Conference on Advances in Communication and Control, pp. 777–784, Corfu, Greece, 1997.

[4] Fornasini, E., and M.E. Valcher, "Dynamic behavior of 2–D positive systems" 2nd Portugese Conference on automatic control. Vol. 2, pp. 31-37, Porto, Portugal, 1996.

[5] Valcher, M.E., and E. Fornasini, "State Space Models and asymptotic behavior of 2–D positive systems" IMA Journal of Mathematical Control and Information, No. 12, pp. 17-36, 1995.

[6] Antoniou, G.E., Varoufakis, S.J., and Paraskevopoulos, P.N., 1986, I.E.E.E. Trans. Circuits and Systems, 33, 926.

[7] Antoniou, G.E., Paraskevopoulos, P.N., and Varoufakis, S.J., 1988, Proc. Inst. Elect. Electron. Engrs, 135, 65.

[8] Antoniou, G.E., Varoufakis, S.J. and Paraskevopoulos, P.N., 1988, I.E.E.E Trans. Circuits and Systems, 35, 1055.

[9] Varoufakis, S.J., Paraskevopoulos, P.N., and Antoniou, G.E., 1987, I.E.E.E. Trans. Circuits and Systems, 34, 289.

[10] Antoniou, G.E., 1991, Control Theory and Advanced Technology, 7, 129.

[11] Roesser, P.R., 1975, I.E.E.E. Trans. Autom. Control, 20, 1.

Primitivity of 2D positive systems

Ettore Fornasini
Dip. di Elettronica ed Informatica - Univ. di Padova
via Gradenigo 6a, 35131 Padova, ITALY
phone: +39-49-827-7605, fax: +39-49-827-7699
e-mail:fornasini@dei.unipd.it

Abstract

Necessary and sufficient conditions are provided, guaranteeing that the free state evolution of a positive 2D system becomes asymptotically strictly positive
Periodic initial conditions are first assumed, and strict positivity is reduced to the primitivity of a suitable circulant matrix. General conditions are next assumed, and a general description of primitive matrix pairs is finally derived, that includes both spectral and combinatorial constraints on the pair.

Keywords : primitive matrices, circulant matrices, directed graphs, integer matrices, multidimensional systems

1 Introduction

Positive systems make their appearance when modelling processes in which variables represent nonnegative quantities, such as pressures, concentrations, densities, population levels, etc....They have been the object of a long stream of research, aiming to explore basic issues of system theory, like controllability, reachability and realizability, under positivity constraints.

In this context, the notion of primitivity arises quite naturally when analyzing the asymptotic behavior of an homogeneous linear discrete time positive system

$$\mathbf{x}(t+1) = F\mathbf{x}(t), \qquad t = 0, 1, \dots, \tag{1}$$

the primitivity of the positive matrix F meaning that every positive initial condition $\mathbf{x}(0)$ induces a state evolution that becomes strictly positive within a finite number of steps.

When considering a positive matrix pair (A, B), with A and B in $\mathbb{R}_+^{n\times n}$, it is easy to figure out a reasonable extension of the dynamical behavior we have just described. To this end, we associate with the pair (A, B) the discrete homogeneous two-dimensional (2D) system [4]

$$\mathbf{x}(h+1, k+1) = A\mathbf{x}(h, k+1) + B\mathbf{x}(h+1, k), \qquad h, k \in \mathbb{Z}, \tag{2}$$

where the doubly indexed *local states* $\mathbf{x}(h, k)$ are elements of the orthant $\mathbb{R}_+^n$ and *initial conditions* are a sequence $\mathcal{X}_0 := \{\mathbf{x}(\ell, -\ell) : \ell \in \mathbb{Z}\}$ of nonnegative local states on the *separation set* $\mathcal{C}_0 := \{(\ell, -\ell) : \ell \in \mathbb{Z}\}$. A system of this kind is called a 2D *positive system.*

By assuming the aforementioned dynamical viewpoint, we express the primitivity of the pair (A, B) as a strict positivity constraint on the behavior of (2) as $h + k$ goes to $+\infty$. It is easy to see, however, that the structure of the initial sequence $\mathcal{X}_0$ has to be somehow restricted. In fact, if $\mathcal{X}_0$ includes $N + 1$ consecutive zero local states

$$\mathbf{x}(h, -h) = \mathbf{x}(h+1, -h-1) = \dots = \mathbf{x}(h+N, -h-N) = \mathbf{0},$$

then zero local states occur also on the separation sets

$$\mathcal{C}_t := \{(t + \ell, -\ell) : \ell \in \mathbb{Z}\}, \qquad t = 1, 2, \dots, N,$$

irrespective of the remaining initial conditions on $\mathcal{C}_0$. So, in order to guarantee that for some finite t all local states on $\mathcal{C}_t$ can be strictly positive, we must confine our attention to *admissible* sequences of initial conditions, namely to nonnegative sequences $\mathcal{X}_0$ which satisfy the following assumption: *there is an integer* $N > 0$ *such that* $\sum_{\ell=h}^{h+N} \mathbf{x}(\ell, -\ell) > 0$ *for all* $h \in \mathbb{Z}$. We are now in a position to introduce the following definition of primitivity for a nonnegative matrix pair.

Definition A pair of nonnegative matrices (A, B) is *primitive* if, for every admissible sequence $\mathcal{X}_0$ of initial conditions, all local states $\mathbf{x}(h, k)$ become strictly positive when $h + k$ is sufficiently large.

When a 2D system is described by a primitive matrix pair, eventually all its variables appear "permanently excited", independently of the particular set of admissible initial conditions that originated its evolution. This seems to be quite relevant when the system describes, for instance, a diffusion process, and the two independent variables represent a spatial and a temporal coordinate. In that case, primitivity guarantees that, after a certain time instant, at every point all system variables represent strictly positive quantities.

The paper is organized as follows. Section 2 investigates the spectral and combinatorial features of (A, B)

by means of the complex matrices $e^{i\theta}A+e^{i\omega}B$, $\theta,\omega\in\mathbb{R}$, and of suitably associated directed graphs. It has a preliminary character w.r.t. the remaining sections, as it provides the mathematical tools for the subsequent discussion. Basing on the circulant matrices $C_T(A,B)$, $T=1,2,\ldots$ associated with (A,B), section 3 analyses the primitivity condition when (2) undergoes a periodic state evolution. Finally, in section 4, the primitivity of (A,B) is considered in a general setting. It is shown to be equivalent to a variety of conditions, involving the cyclic structure of the directed graphs, the spectra of $e^{i\theta}A+e^{i\omega}B$, $\theta,\omega\in\mathbb{R}$, and the positivity of at least one Hurwitz product.

If $F=[f_{ij}]$ is a matrix (in particular, a vector), we write $F\gg 0$ (F *strictly positive*), if $f_{ij}>0$ for all i,j; $F>0$ (F *positive*), if $f_{ij}\geq 0$ for all i,j, and $f_{hk}>0$ for some pair (h,k); $F\geq 0$ (F *nonnegative*), if $f_{ij}\geq 0$ for all i,j. To every pair of $n\times n$ nonnegative matrices (A,B) we associate a digraph of order n, $\mathcal{D}^*(A,B)$, with arcs of two different kinds, namely A-arcs and B-arcs. There is an A-arc from vertex i to vertex j iff $a_{ij}>0$, and a B-arc iff $b_{ij}>0$.

Example 1 Consider the pair of positive matrices

$$A=\begin{bmatrix}0&0&2\\1&4&0\\0&0&0\end{bmatrix}\qquad B=\begin{bmatrix}0&0&6\\0&0&0\\0&4&0\end{bmatrix}.$$

The associated digraph $\mathcal{D}^*(A,B)$ is given in Fig. 1.1, where A-arcs and B-arcs have been represented (as in the sequel) by thicklines and thinlines, respectively.

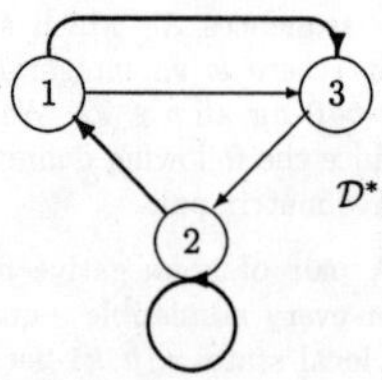

Fig. 1.1

When assigning a path p in $\mathcal{D}^*(A,B)$, we have to specify, for each pair of consecutive vertices, which kind of arc they are connected by, so that p will have a representation like $(i_0,i_1)_A,(i_1,i_2)_B,\ldots,(i_{k-1},i_k)_B$. Thus, it is natural to associate p with a couple of nonnegative integers, $\alpha(p)$ and $\beta(p)$, representing the number of A-arcs and B-arcs occurring in it, respectively. A path whose extreme vertices coincide, i.e. $i_0=i_k$, is called a *cycle*. In particular, if each vertex in a cycle appears exactly once as the first vertex of an arc, the cycle is called a *circuit*.

Given a pair of square matrices (A,B), the *Hurwitz products* of A and B are inductively defined [6] as

$$A^i \sqcup\!\sqcup^0 B = A^i,\quad i\geq 0,$$

$$A^0 \sqcup\!\sqcup^j B = B^j,\quad j\geq 0,$$
$$A^i \sqcup\!\sqcup^j B = A(A^{i-1}\sqcup\!\sqcup^j B)+B(A^i\sqcup\!\sqcup^{j-1}B)\quad i,j>0$$

For notational convenience sometimes we allow either i or j to be negative integers, and in these cases we assume $A^i\sqcup\!\sqcup^j B=0$. Using Hurwitz products, we can express any local state $\mathbf{x}(h,k)$ of system (2) in terms of the sequence of initial conditions. Actually, if $\mathcal{X}_0=\{\mathbf{x}(\ell,-\ell):\ell\in\mathbb{Z}\}$ is an arbitrary sequence of initial conditions on $\mathcal{C}_0$, for all $h,k\in\mathbb{Z}$, $h+k\geq 0$, $\mathbf{x}(h,k)$ can be represented as

$$\mathbf{x}(h,k)=\sum_{\ell}(A^{h-\ell}\sqcup\!\sqcup^{k+\ell}B)\,\mathbf{x}(\ell,-\ell). \tag{3}$$

In particular, if the initial conditions on the separation set $\mathcal{C}_0$ are all zero, except at $(0,0)$, we have

$$\mathbf{x}(h,k)=(A^h\sqcup\!\sqcup^k B)\,\mathbf{x}(0,0),\qquad\forall\ h,k\geq 0.$$

The *characteristic polynomial* of (A,B) is defined as

$$\Delta_{A,B}(z_1,z_2):=\det(I_n-Az_1-Bz_2).$$

2 Spectrum of $e^{i\theta}A+e^{i\omega}B$

Perron-Frobenius theory estabilishes, for an $n\times n$ irreducible matrix F, tight connections among its characteristic polynomial, the invariance under rotation of its spectrum and the lengths of all cycles in the standard digraph $\mathcal{D}(F)$ associated with F. These connections can be specialized to primitive matrices, thus leading to a set of characterizations of primitivity which represent suitable strengthenings of those available for irreducibility.

Trying to determine conditions for the primitivity of a positive matrix pair (A,B), it is natural to ask to what extent these results admit a generalization, once the spectrum of F is replaced by the variety of $\Delta_{A,B}(z_1,z_2)$ and the digraph of F by $\mathcal{D}^*(A,B)$.

To this purpose, in this section and throughout the paper, we will steadily assume that the matrix pair (A,B) has the following properties: a) A and B are both positive; b) $A+B$ is irreducible; c) $A+B$ has a unitary maximal eigenvalue. The set of $n\times n$ pairs endowed with these properties will be denoted by $\mathcal{I}_n$. Assumptions a) and b) easily prove to be necessary conditions for 2D primitivity, which is our final goal. Assumption c) entails no loss of generality. Actually, we can divide both A and B by $\rho(A+B)$ without affecting the properties we aim to investigate, which are independent of the spectral radius of $A+B$. The case when $A+B$ is nilpotent would constitute the unique exception to this rescaling procedure, but then $A+B$ would not be irreducible.

The answer to the previous question is given by the following Proposition, which enlightens, under different points of view, which rotations in the z_1- and z_2-planes leave the variety of $\Delta_{A,B}(z_1,z_2)$ invariant. The proof, based on Wielandt's theorem [8], is rather technical and will not included here for sake of brevity. The interested reader is referred to [9].

Proposition 2.1 *Let $(A,B) \in \mathcal{I}_n$. For any θ and $\omega \in \mathbb{R}$ the following facts are equivalent:*

i) *1 is an eigenvalue of $e^{i\theta}A + e^{i\omega}B$;*

ii) *there exists a diagonal matrix*

$$D = \operatorname{diag}\{e^{i\omega_1}, e^{i\omega_2}, \ldots, e^{i\omega_n},\},\ \omega_1, \omega_2, \ldots, \omega_n \in \mathbb{R},$$

such that

$$A = e^{i\theta} DAD^{-1} \quad \text{and} \quad B = e^{i\omega} DBD^{-1};$$

iii) *for every cycle γ in $\mathcal{D}^*(A,B)$, including $\alpha(\gamma)$ A-arcs and $\beta(\gamma)$ B-arcs,*

$$\alpha(\gamma)\theta + \beta(\gamma)\omega \equiv 0 \mod 2\pi; \tag{4}$$

iv) *the characteristic polynomial of (A,B) satisfies*

$$\Delta_{A,B}(z_1, z_2) = \Delta_{A,B}(z_1 e^{i\theta}, z_2 e^{i\omega}). \tag{5}$$

Remark In order to check condition iii) , it is not necessary to consider all cycles but only the circuits $\gamma_1, \gamma_2, \gamma_t$ in $\mathcal{D}^*(A,B)$. So, point iii) reduces to a finite number, say t, of congruence relations which can be expressed in matrix form as

$$L_{A,B}\begin{bmatrix}\theta\\ \omega\end{bmatrix} = \begin{bmatrix}\alpha(\gamma_1) & \beta(\gamma_1)\\ \alpha(\gamma_2) & \beta(\gamma_2)\\ \vdots & \vdots\\ \alpha(\gamma_t) & \beta(\gamma_t)\end{bmatrix}\begin{bmatrix}\theta\\ \omega\end{bmatrix} \equiv \mathbf{0} \mod 2\pi. \tag{6}$$

Next Corollary deals with the situation when $A+B$ is primitive and only trivial rotations leave invariant the variety of $\Delta_{A,B}(z_1, z_2)$. This corresponds to the right primeness $L_{A,B}$ and will provide later a necessary and sufficient primitivity condition for the matrix pair.

Corollary 2.2 *Let $(A,B) \in \mathcal{I}_n$ and assume that $A+B$ is primitive. The following facts are equivalent:*

i) *$1 \in \Lambda(e^{i\theta}A + e^{i\omega}B)$ implies $\theta \equiv \omega \equiv 0$ mod 2π;*

ii) *the integer matrix $L_{A,B}$ is right prime;*

iii) *$\Delta_{A,B}(z_1, z_2) = \Delta_{A,B}(e^{i\theta}z_1, e^{i\omega}z_2)$ implies $\theta \equiv \omega \equiv 0$ mod 2π.*

PROOF i) $\Rightarrow$ ii) We show, first, that $L_{A,B}$ has full column rank. Consider the integer matrix

$$\bar{L}_{A,B} := \begin{bmatrix}\alpha(\gamma_1) & \alpha(\gamma_1)+\beta(\gamma_1)\\ \alpha(\gamma_2) & \alpha(\gamma_2)+\beta(\gamma_2)\\ \vdots & \vdots\\ \alpha(\gamma_t) & \alpha(\gamma_t)+\beta(\gamma_t)\end{bmatrix} = L_{A,B} \cdot \begin{bmatrix}1 & 1\\ 0 & 1\end{bmatrix},$$

whose second column consists of the lengths of all circuits in $\mathcal{D}^*(A,B)$. The primitivity assumption on $A+B$ implies that the g.c.d. of these lengths is 1, and hence integer coefficients x_h can be found such that $\sum_h x_h\,[\alpha(\gamma_h) + \beta(\gamma_h)] = 1$. If $\bar{L}_{A,B}$ were not full column rank, its first column, which is nonzero as (A,B) is in $\mathcal{I}_n$, would be a scalar multiple of the second one, namely

$$\bar{L}_{A,B}\begin{bmatrix}1\\ -q\end{bmatrix} = \mathbf{0},$$

for some rational number q, $0 < q < 1$. Consequently, we would have $0 < \sum_h x_h \alpha(\gamma_h) < 1$, which is impossible, as all addenda $x_h\alpha(\gamma_h)$ are integer numbers. So, $\bar{L}_{A,B}$, and hence $L_{A,B}$, have rank 2.
We prove, now, that $L_{A,B}$ is right prime. If not, it would factor over the ring $\mathbb{Z}$ as $L_{A,B} = L\Delta$, where L is a $t \times 2$ right prime matrix and Δ a square matrix with $\det\Delta \neq \pm 1$ [?]. As Δ^{-1} is not an integer matrix, the pair

$$\begin{bmatrix}\theta\\ \omega\end{bmatrix} := \Delta^{-1}\begin{bmatrix}2\pi\\ 2\pi\end{bmatrix} \not\equiv \mathbf{0} \mod 2\pi$$

satisfies $L_{A,B}\begin{bmatrix}\theta\\ \omega\end{bmatrix} \equiv \mathbf{0}$ mod 2π. By Proposition 2.1, this implies $1 \in \Lambda(e^{i\theta}A + e^{i\omega}B)$.
ii) $\Rightarrow$ i) If $L_{A,B}$ is right prime, it admits a $2 \times t$ integer left inverse S, so that $SL_{A,B} = I_2$. Consequently, $L_{A,B}\begin{bmatrix}\theta\\ \omega\end{bmatrix} \equiv \mathbf{0}$ mod 2π implies $\begin{bmatrix}\theta\\ \omega\end{bmatrix} \equiv \mathbf{0}$ mod 2π. By Proposition 2.1, this proves the result.
i) $\Leftrightarrow$ iii) Obvious from Proposition 2.1. ■

The situation when in Proposition 2.1 θ is zero is particularly interesting for the subsequent analysis of circulant matrices. Clearly, the problem of determining for which ω's the matrix $A + e^{i\omega}B$ has eigenvalue 1 can be solved by resorting to the above propositions and, in particular, by analysing the cyclic structure of $\mathcal{D}^*(A,B)$. It seems more convenient, however, to associate with the pair (A,B) a simpler (strongly connected) digraph, $\mathcal{D}_A(B)$, obtained as follows: for all vertices $h \in \{1, 2, \ldots, n\}$ shrink into a single vertex $[h]$ all vertices of the communicating class of h in $\mathcal{D}(A + A^T)$, and then connect $[h]$ and $[k]$ with the arc $([h],[k])$ if there is an arc (ℓ, m) in $\mathcal{D}(B)$ for some $\ell \in [h]$ and $m \in [k]$.
The structure of the shrinked digraph $\mathcal{D}_A(B)$ of a pair (A,B) is better clarified by means of an example.

Example 2 The positive matrices

$$A = \begin{bmatrix}0&1&0&0&0\\0&0&1&0&0\\0&0&0&0&0\\0&0&0&0&0\\0&0&0&0&0\end{bmatrix} \qquad B = \begin{bmatrix}0&6&0&0&0\\0&0&0&0&0\\0&0&0&2&0\\0&0&0&0&3\\4&0&0&0&0\end{bmatrix}$$

are associated with the following digraphs

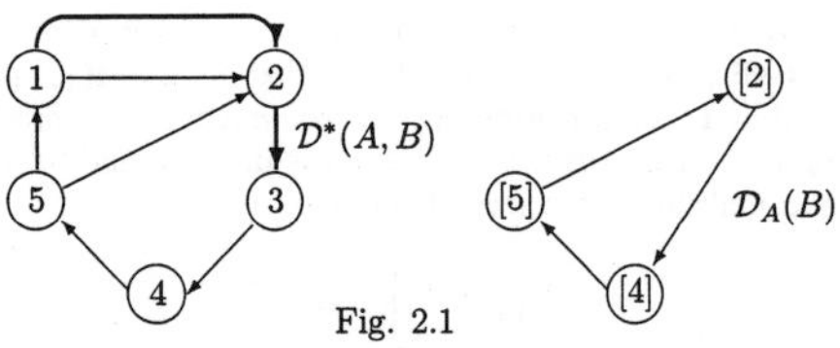

Fig. 2.1

The following Proposition enlightens some connections between the combinatorial properties of $\mathcal{D}_A(B)$ and $\mathcal{D}^*(A,B)$ and the spectral properties of $A + e^{i\omega}B$

Proposition 2.3 [9] *Let $(A,B) \in \mathcal{I}_n$. $1 \in \Lambda(A+e^{i\omega}B)$ for some real number ω if and only if the imprimitivity index $h_A(B)$ of $\mathcal{D}_A(B)$ satisfies*

$$h_A(B)\ \omega \equiv 0 \qquad \text{mod } 2\pi. \tag{7}$$

Moreover, the following are equivalent:

i) $1 \in \Lambda(A+e^{i\omega}B)$ *implies* $\omega \equiv 0$ *mod* 2π;

ii) g.c.d.$\{\beta(\gamma) : \gamma$ a cycle in $\mathcal{D}^*(A,B)\} = 1$;

iii) $h_A(B) = 1$.

Remarks 1. Analogous results can be obtained for the family of matrices $e^{i\theta}A + B$, $\theta \in \mathbb{R}$, by simply referring to the shrinked digraph $\mathcal{D}_B(A)$ and to the occurrencies of the A-arcs in the cycles of $\mathcal{D}^*(A,B)$. It is worthwhile to notice, however, that the digraphs $\mathcal{D}_A(B)$ and $\mathcal{D}_B(A)$ can be endowed with different structural properties and, in particular, their imprimitivity indices $h_A(B)$ and $h_B(A)$ need not coincide.

2. When $L_{A,B}$ *is right prime*, we have only the trivial solution $\theta \equiv \omega \equiv 0$ mod 2π.

3 Periodic initial conditions

In this section we turn our attention to some conditions on the pair (A,B) which ensure a strictly positive asymptotic dynamics for the associated 2D system (2), under the assumption that the initial conditions $\mathcal{X}_0$ have a periodic pattern. Although this situation is admittedly restrictive, it deserves a thorough discussion for at least two reasons. First, it develops intuitive insights into the combinatorial and spectral properties of a positive matrix pair, meanwhile enlightening some interesting features of block-circulant positive matrices. Second, this analysis leads the way to the solution of the general problem, we shall afford in the subsequent section.

If $\mathcal{X}_0$ is nonzero and periodic with period T, i.e.

$$\mathbf{x}(\ell,-\ell) = \mathbf{x}(\ell+T,-\ell-T) \geq 0, \qquad \forall\, \ell \in \mathbb{Z}. \tag{8}$$

it is clear that the local states $\mathbf{x}(t+\ell,-\ell)$ on each subsequent separation set $\mathcal{C}_t$ still constitute a periodic sequence of period T. It is a matter of simple computation to check that the nT-dimensional vector

$$\mathbf{p}_T(t) := \begin{bmatrix} \mathbf{x}(t,0) \\ \mathbf{x}(t+1,-1) \\ \vdots \\ \mathbf{x}(t+T-1,-T+1) \end{bmatrix}, \tag{9}$$

obtained by stacking T consecutive local states on $\mathcal{C}_t$, updates according to the following equation

$$\mathbf{p}_T(t+1) = C_T(A,B)\ \mathbf{p}_T(t), \tag{10}$$

where $C_T(A,B)$ denotes the $nT \times nT$ block circulant matrix

$$C_T(A,B) = \begin{bmatrix} A & B & & & \\ & A & B & & \\ & & \ddots & \ddots & \\ & & & & B \\ B & & & & A \end{bmatrix}, \tag{11}$$

if $T > 1$, and the $n \times n$ matrix $A + B$ if $T = 1$, i.e. if all initial local states on $\mathcal{C}_0$ coincide.

It is worth noticing that $\mathbf{p}_T(t)$ is completely determined by the initial condition, $\mathbf{p}_T(0) > 0$, and by the structure of $C_T(A,B)$. In particular

• if $C_T(A,B)$ is irreducibile, no component of $\mathbf{p}_T(t)$ remains permanently unexcited. Vice versa, if $C_T(A,B)$ is reducibile, a positive vector $\mathbf{p}_T(0)$ can be found such that for some $j \in \{1,2,\ldots,nT\}$, the j-th entry of $\mathbf{p}_T(t)$ is zero for all $t \in \mathbb{N}$.

• The matrix $C_T(A,B)$ is primitive if and only if for every $\mathbf{p}_T(0) > 0$ the vector $\mathbf{p}_T(t)$ eventually becomes strictly positive.

So, under the assumption of periodic initial conditions with period T, the asymptotic strict positivity of every state evolution of (2) is equivalent to the primitivity of $C_T(A,B)$, which describes the system dynamics according to (10). Consequently, our primary goal in this section is to investigate how the properties of a positive pair (A,B) affect those of $C_T(A,B)$, and, in particular, under what conditions $C_T(A,B)$ is irreducible or primitive.

The solution of this problem relies on the spectral properties of circulant matrices [3] and on the following result, whose proof is given in [9]

Proposition 3.1 *Let $(A,B) \in \mathcal{I}_n$ and $T \in \mathbb{N}$. The circulant matrix $C_T(A,B)$ is*

i) irreducible if and only if 1 is not an eigenvalue of anyone of the following matrices

$$A+e^{i\omega}B, A+e^{2i\omega}B, \ldots, A+e^{(T-1)i\omega}B, \quad \omega = 2\pi/T. \tag{12}$$

ii) primitive if and only if $A+B$ is primitive and none of the above matrices has an eigenvalue of unitary modulus.

It is easy to obtain dual statements for the block circulant matrices $C_T(B,A)$, $T = 1,2,\ldots$, thus relating the irreducibility and primitivity of these matrices to the spectra $\Lambda(e^{i\theta\ell}A + B)$, $\theta = 2\pi/T$, $\ell = 1,2,\ldots,T-1$. In general, the irreducibility of $C_T(B,A)$ needs not imply that of $C_T(A,B)$.
Differently from the case of irreducibility, A and B play a symmetric role in determining the primitivity of $C_T(A,B)$. Actually, if $C_T(A,B)$ is primitive, none of the matrices $A + e^{i\omega\ell}B$, $\omega = 2\pi/T$ and $\ell = 1,2,\ldots,T-1$, has an eigenvalue of unitary modulus, and this happens if and only if the same holds true for the family $B + e^{i\omega\ell}A$, $\ell = 1,2,\ldots,T-1$. Thus, $C_T(B,A)$ is primitive, too.

Corollary 3.2 *Let $(A,B) \in \mathcal{I}_n$. The following facts are equivalent:*

i) all matrices $C_T(A,B)$, $T = 1,2,\ldots$, are irreducible;

ii) $1 \in \Lambda(A + e^{i\omega}B)$ for some real number ω implies $\omega \equiv 0 \bmod 2\pi$.

PROOF i) $\Rightarrow$ ii) Assume, by contradiction, that 1 is an eigenvalue of $A + e^{i\omega}B$, for some $\omega \not\equiv 0 \bmod 2\pi$. By Proposition 2.3, ω must be a rational multiple of 2π, i.e. $\omega = 2\pi(\nu/\bar{T})$, for some nonzero integers ν and $\bar{T}$, $\nu \not\equiv 0 \bmod \bar{T}$. But in this case, by Proposition 3.1, $C_{\bar{T}}(A,B)$ is a reducible matrix, which contradicts assumption i).
ii) $\Rightarrow$ i) follows from Proposition 3.1, too. ∎

Corollary 3.3 *Let $(A,B) \in \mathcal{I}_n$, with $A + B$ primitive. The following facts are equivalent:*

i) all circulant matrices $C_T(A,B)$, $T = 1,2,\ldots$, are primitive;

ii) $1 \in \Lambda(e^{i\theta}A + e^{i\omega}B)$ implies $\theta \equiv \omega \equiv 0 \bmod 2\pi$.

PROOF i) $\Rightarrow$ ii) As remarked at the end of the previous section, $L_{A,B}$ has rank 2. So, all solutions of

$$L_{A,B}\begin{bmatrix}\theta\\ \omega\end{bmatrix} \equiv \mathbf{0} \mod 2\pi,$$

and, consequently, all the pairs (θ,ω) for which 1 belongs to $\Lambda(e^{i\theta}A + e^{i\omega}B)$, must be rational multiples of 2π, namely $(\theta,\omega) = 2\pi(q_1,q_2)$, $q_1,q_2 \in \mathbb{Q}$. However, if 1 would be in $\Lambda(e^{i\theta}A + e^{i\omega}B)$, for certain θ and ω rational multiples of 2π, we would have $e^{-i\theta} \in \Lambda(A + e^{i(\omega-\theta)}B)$, thus contradicting Proposition 3.1.
ii) $\Rightarrow$ i) Immediate from Proposition 3.1. ∎

Tying together Corollary 2.2 and Proposition 2.3 with the above results, several alternative characterizations of the irreducibility and the primitivity of all circulant matrices $C_T(A,B)$, $T \in \mathbb{N}$, can be obtained, based on the digraphs $\mathcal{D}_A(B)$ and $\mathcal{D}^*(A,B)$, respectively. In particular, graph-theoretic criteria are available for checking the above properties and hence the strict positivity of the asymptotic dynamics of (2), starting from periodic initial conditions.

4 Arbitrary initial conditions

In this section we drop the periodicity assumption, and turn our attention to general (admissible) initial conditions. As every periodic $\mathcal{X}_0$ is admissible, it is clear that the primitivity of all $C_T(A,B)$, $T \in \mathbb{N}$, is necessary for 2D primitivity. We aim to prove that it is also sufficient.
In fact, we will show that when all $C_T(A,B)$, $T \in \mathbb{N}$, are primitive, and hence $L_{A,B}$ is right prime, there exists a solid convex cone $\mathcal{K}$ in $\mathbb{R}^2_+$ such that for all (h,k) in $\mathcal{K} \cap \mathbb{Z}^2$ the Hurwitz products $A^h \sqcup^k B$ are strictly positive. Consequently, every nonzero local state $\mathbf{x}(\ell,-\ell) > 0$ produces a strictly positive state evolution inside the cone $(\ell,-\ell) + \mathcal{K}$, as we have $\mathbf{x}(h+\ell,k-\ell) \geq (A^h \sqcup^k B)\mathbf{x}(\ell,-\ell) \gg 0$ for all $(h+\ell,k-\ell) \in (\ell,-\ell) + \mathcal{K}$. The admissibility assumption on $\mathcal{X}_0$ guarantees that the union of all cones $(\ell,-\ell)+\mathcal{K}$, which correspond to positive initial states $\mathbf{x}(\ell,-\ell)$, includes all separation sets $\mathcal{C}_t$, for t greater than a suitable $t_{\min}$. Consequently, for $t > t_{\min}$ all local states on the separation set $\mathcal{C}_t$ are strictly positive.

The subsequent discussion is based on the following number theoretic result, which extends a well-know lemma attributed to Schur [2].

Lemma 4.1 [9] *Let $\mathcal{S}$ be a nonempty subset of $\mathbb{N}^2$, closed under addition, such that the $\mathbb{Z}$-module generated by $\mathcal{S}$ is $\mathbb{Z}^2$. Then there exists a solid convex cone $\mathcal{K}^*$ in $\mathbb{R}^2_+$ such that all elements in $\mathcal{K}^* \cap \mathbb{Z}^2$ are in $\mathcal{S}$.*

Proposition 4.2 *Let (A,B) be in $\mathcal{I}_n$. The following facts are equivalent*

i) the integer matrix $L_{A,B}$ is right prime;

ii) there is a solid convex cone $\mathcal{K}$ in $\mathbb{R}^2_+$ such that for every pair of integers (h,k) in $\mathcal{K}$ and every couple of vertices i and j, there is a path p in $\mathcal{D}^*(A,B)$, from i to j, including h A-arcs and k B-arcs;

iii) there is a solid convex cone $\mathcal{K}_H$ in $\mathbb{R}^2_+$ such that for every pair of integers (h,k) in $\mathcal{K}_H$ the Hurwitz product $A^h \sqcup^k B$ is strictly positive;

iv) the pair (A,B) is primitive.

PROOF i) $\Rightarrow$ ii) Let $\mathcal{S}_\ell$ be the set of integer vectors $[\alpha(\gamma)\ \beta(\gamma)]$ corresponding to all cycles γ in $\mathcal{D}^*(A,B)$ passing through vertex ℓ. Clearly, $\mathcal{S}_\ell$ is nonempty and closed under addition. Moreover, the $\mathbb{Z}$-module generated by $\mathcal{S}_\ell$ coincides with the $\mathbb{Z}$-module generated by the rows of $L_{A,B}$, namely with $\mathbb{Z}^2$. Actually, consider a positive vector $[\alpha(\gamma)\ \beta(\gamma)]$, γ a circuit in $\mathcal{D}^*(A,B)$, which is not included in $\mathcal{S}_\ell$, and let j be any vertex γ passes through. As $\mathcal{D}^*(A,B)$ is strongly connected, it includes a cycle γ' passing through ℓ and j, and another cycle, γ'', obtained by connecting γ and γ'. So, both $[\alpha(\gamma')\ \beta(\gamma')]$

and $[\alpha(\gamma") \ \beta(\gamma")]$ are in $\mathcal{S}_\ell$, and

$$[\alpha(\gamma) \ \beta(\gamma)] = [\alpha(\gamma") \ \beta(\gamma")] - [\alpha(\gamma') \ \beta(\gamma')]$$

is in the $\mathbb{Z}$-module generated by $\mathcal{S}_\ell$. By the above lemma, then, there exists a solid convex cone $\mathcal{K}_\ell^*$ in $\mathbb{R}_+^2$ such that all integer vectors in $\mathcal{K}_\ell^*$ are in $\mathcal{S}_\ell$.

If i and j are arbitrary vertices in $\mathcal{D}^*(A,B)$ and $p_{i\ell}$ and $p_{\ell j}$ are two fixed paths connecting i to ℓ and ℓ to j, respectively, all integer vectors in the cone

$$\mathcal{K}_{ij}^* := [\alpha(p_{i\ell}) + \alpha(p_{\ell j}) \quad \beta(p_{i\ell}) + \beta(p_{\ell j})] + \mathcal{K}_\ell^*$$

correspond to paths connecting i to j. Clearly, $\mathcal{K} := \cap_{ij}\mathcal{K}_{ij}^*$ is a solid convex cone which satisfies ii).

ii) $\Rightarrow$ iii) Obvious, once assuming $\mathcal{K}_H = \mathcal{K}$.

iii) $\Rightarrow$ iv) Under assumption iii), it is easy to see that every admissible $\mathcal{X}_0$ eventually produces a strictly positive state evolution, and hence the pair (A,B) is primitive, by definition.

iv) $\Rightarrow$ i) When (A,B) is primitive, all nonzero periodic initial conditions eventually produce strictly positive dynamics. This implies that all $C_T(A,B)$, $T \in \mathbb{N}$, are primitive matrices and hence, by Propositions 2.2 and 3.3, $L_{A,B}$ is right prime. ■

To conclude, observe that the above proposition reduces the primitivity of the pair (A,B) to the existence of a solid cone $\mathcal{K}_H$ in $\mathbb{R}_+^2$, whose integer coordinates points correspond to strictly positive Hurwitz products. Indeed, this condition can be considerably simplified, as the existence of a primitive, and hence of a strictly positive, Hurwitz product ensures that of a whole cone $\mathcal{K}_H$ of strictly positive Hurwitz products. This property nicely extends to matrix pairs the well-known fact that a positive matrix F is primitive if and only if it has a strictly positive power.

Proposition 4.3 *Let (A,B) be in $\mathcal{I}_n$. The following facts are equivalent:*

i) there is a solid convex cone $\mathcal{K}_H$ in $\mathbb{R}_+^2$ such that for every pair of integers (h,k) in $\mathcal{K}_H$ the Hurwitz product $A^h \sqcup\!\sqcup^k B$ is strictly positive ;

ii) there exists a positive pair $(\ell,m) \in \mathbb{N}\times\mathbb{N}$ such that $A^\ell \sqcup\!\sqcup^m B$ is primitive.

PROOF i) $\Rightarrow$ ii) Obvious.

ii) $\Rightarrow$ i) Assume that $A^\ell \sqcup\!\sqcup^m B$ is primitive. Then there exists a positive integer r such that $A^{r\ell} \sqcup\!\sqcup^{rm} B \geq (A^\ell \sqcup\!\sqcup^m B)^r \gg 0$. So, it is not restrictive to assume that $A^\ell \sqcup\!\sqcup^m B$ is strictly positive.

As A and B are both positive and $\mathcal{D}^*(A,B)$ is strongly connected, there exists a vertex j with an outgoing A-arc, (j,u), and an ingoing B-arc (e,j). By the assumption on $A^\ell \sqcup\!\sqcup^m B$, in $\mathcal{D}^*(A,B)$ one can find a cycle γ passing through j, a path p_{uj} from u to j and a path p_{je} from j to e, each of them including ℓ A-arcs and m B-arcs. So, the path p_{ju} can be completed into a cycle with $\ell+1$ A-arcs and m B-arcs, and similarly p_{ej} can be completed into a cycle including ℓ A-arcs and $m+1$ B-arcs. Clearly, the $\mathbb{Z}$-module $\mathcal{M}$ generated by the pairs (ℓ,m), $(\ell+1,m)$ and $(\ell,m+1)$ is $\mathbb{Z}^2$, as the integer matrix

$$\begin{bmatrix} \ell & m \\ \ell+1 & m \\ \ell & m+1 \end{bmatrix}$$

is right prime. Moreover, as the $\mathbb{Z}$-module generated by the rows of $L_{A,B}$ includes $\mathcal{M}$, $L_{A,B}$ is a right prime matrix, too, and the conclusion follows from the above proposition. ■

References

[1] A. BERMAN AND R.J. PLEMMONS, *Nonnegative matrices in the mathematical sciences*, Academic Press, New York (NY), 1979.

[2] R.A. BRUALDI AND H.J. RYSER, *Combinatorial matrix theory,* Cambridge Univ. Press, Cambridge (GB), 1991.

[3] P.J. DAVIS, *Circulant matrices*, J.Wiley & Sons, New York (NY), 1979.

[4] E. FORNASINI AND G. MARCHESINI, *Doubly indexed dynamical systems*, Math. Sys. Theory, 12 (1978), pp. 59-72.

[5] E. FORNASINI, *A 2D systems approach to river pollution modelling*, Multid. Sys. Sign. Process., 2 (1991), pp. 233 -65.

[6] E. FORNASINI AND M.E. VALCHER, *Matrix pairs in 2D systems: an approach based on trace series and Hankel matrices*, SIAM J. on Contr. and Optim., 33 (1995), pp.1127-1150.

[7] E. FORNASINI AND M.E. VALCHER, *On the spectral and combinatorial structure of 2D positive systems*, Lin. Alg. and Appl., 245 (1996), pp. 223-258.

[8] H. MINC, *Nonnegative matrices*, J.Wiley & Sons, New York (NY), 1988.

[9] E. FORNASINI AND M.E. VALCHER, *Primitivity of positive matrix pairs: algebraic characterizaton, graph theoretic description, and system theoretic interpretation*, Siam J. Matrix Anal. Appl., 19 (1998), pp. 71-88.

Reduced Order Two-Dimensional Adaptive State-Space Filters

Takao HINAMOTO, Hiroshi MANABE, Akimitsu DOI and Mitsuji MUNEYASU

Faculty of Engineering, Hiroshima University, Higashi-Hiroshima 739-8527, Japan
hinamoto@ecl.sys. hiroshima-u.ac.jp

Abstract— **To reduce computational complexity and to attain fast convergence, a 2-D adaptive state-space filtering structure is developed by regarding an ideal output signal as an input signal. This is possible by choosing the coordinate transformation appropriately. As a result, a 2-D state-space filter of (m,n) order is transformed to be of either $(m,n-1)$ order or $(m-1,n)$ order. A least mean square (LMS) algorithm is then applied to the reduced order 2-D state-space filter in which new systems are used to generate the gradient signals. Finally, an illustrative example is given to illustrate the utility of the proposed reduced order 2-D adaptive state-space filter.**

I. Introduction

In recent years, there has been considerable interest in two-dimensional (2-D) adaptive filtering. 2-D adaptive filters have found applications such as image noise reduction, interference cancellation, image restoration, 2-D filter design, etc. 2-D adaptive filters possess the ability of tracking the inherent nonstationary statistical properties of images. Several different structures and algorithms have been presented for 2-D adaptive filters [1]–[15]. Among them, 2-D adaptive state-space filters enable us to enjoy freedom to explore the performance advantages of different structures, due to the capability of adapting arbitrary state-space filters [12]. A drawback of 2-D adaptive state-space filters is to require more computational complexity than an alternative described by a differnce equation.

This paper develops a 2-D adaptive state-space filtering structure to reduce computational complexity and to attain faster convergence. This is done by regarding an ideal filter output signal as a filter input signal. As a result, a 2-D adaptive state-space filter of (m,n) order is transformed to that of either $(m,n-1)$ or $(m-1,n)$ order. Finally, a numerical example is solved to demonstrate the validity of the proposed reduced order 2-D adaptive state-space filter.

II. Reduced Order State-Space Description

Consider the following LSS model for 2-D recursive digital filters:

$$\begin{bmatrix} \boldsymbol{x}_o^h(i+1,j) \\ \boldsymbol{x}_o^v(i,j+1) \end{bmatrix} = \begin{bmatrix} \boldsymbol{A}_{o1} & \boldsymbol{A}_{o2} \\ \boldsymbol{A}_{o3} & \boldsymbol{A}_{o4} \end{bmatrix} \begin{bmatrix} \boldsymbol{x}_o^h(i,j) \\ \boldsymbol{x}_o^v(i,j) \end{bmatrix} + \begin{bmatrix} \boldsymbol{b}_{o1} \\ \boldsymbol{b}_{o2} \end{bmatrix} u(i,j) \tag{1}$$

$$y(i,j) = \begin{bmatrix} \boldsymbol{c}_{o1}^T & \boldsymbol{c}_{o2}^T \end{bmatrix} \begin{bmatrix} \boldsymbol{x}_o^h(i,j) \\ \boldsymbol{x}_o^v(i,j) \end{bmatrix} + d_o u(i,j)$$

where $\boldsymbol{x}_o^h(i,j)$ is an $m \times 1$ horizontal state vector, $\boldsymbol{x}_o^v(i,j)$ is an $n \times 1$ vertical state vector, $u(i,j)$ is a scalar input, $y(i,j)$ is a scalar output, and $\boldsymbol{A}_{o1}$, $\boldsymbol{A}_{o2}$, $\boldsymbol{A}_{o3}$, $\boldsymbol{A}_{o4}$, $\boldsymbol{b}_{o1}$, $\boldsymbol{b}_{o2}$, $\boldsymbol{c}_{o1}$, $\boldsymbol{c}_{o2}$ and d_o are real matrices of appropriate dimensions. Without loss of generality, it can be assumed that

$$\boldsymbol{c}_{o2}^T = [\ 0 \cdots 0\ 1\ ]\ . \tag{2}$$

This enables us to decompose $\boldsymbol{x}_o^v(i,j)$ into two parts:

$$\boldsymbol{x}_o^v(i,j) = \left[\frac{\boldsymbol{x}^v(i,j)}{x_n^v(i,j)}\right] \tag{3}$$

where

$$x_n^v(i,j) = y(i,j) - \boldsymbol{c}_{o1}^T \boldsymbol{x}^h(i,j) - d_o u(i,j)\ .$$

According to the partition, the state-space matrices can now be represented as

$$\boldsymbol{A}_{o2} = [\,\boldsymbol{A}_2 \,|\, \boldsymbol{h}_1\,], \qquad \boldsymbol{A}_{o3} = \left[\frac{\tilde{\boldsymbol{A}}_3}{\tilde{\boldsymbol{c}}_1^T}\right]$$
$$\boldsymbol{A}_{o4} = \left[\begin{array}{c|c} \boldsymbol{A}_4 & \boldsymbol{h}_2 \\ \hline \boldsymbol{g}_2^T & d_1 \end{array}\right], \qquad \boldsymbol{b}_{o2} = \left[\frac{\tilde{\boldsymbol{b}}_2}{\tilde{b}}\right]. \tag{4}$$

Substisuting (3) and (4) into (1) and eliminating $x_n^v(i,j)$ from (1) leads to

$$\begin{bmatrix} \boldsymbol{x}^h(i+1,j) \\ \boldsymbol{x}^v(i,j+1) \end{bmatrix} = \begin{bmatrix} \boldsymbol{A}_1 & \boldsymbol{A}_2 \\ \boldsymbol{A}_3 & \boldsymbol{A}_4 \end{bmatrix} \begin{bmatrix} \boldsymbol{x}^h(i,j) \\ \boldsymbol{x}^v(i,j) \end{bmatrix} + \begin{bmatrix} \boldsymbol{h}_1 \\ \boldsymbol{h}_2 \end{bmatrix} y(i,j) + \begin{bmatrix} \boldsymbol{b}_1 \\ \boldsymbol{b}_2 \end{bmatrix} u(i,j)$$
$$y(i,j) = \boldsymbol{c}_1^T \boldsymbol{x}^h(i,j) + [\ \boldsymbol{g}_1^T\ \boldsymbol{g}_2^T\ ] \begin{bmatrix} \boldsymbol{x}^h(i,j-1) \\ \boldsymbol{x}^v(i,j-1) \end{bmatrix} + d_1 y(i,j-1) + d_2 u(i,j-1) + d_o u(i,j) \tag{5}$$

where

$$\boldsymbol{A}_1 = \boldsymbol{A}_{o1} - \boldsymbol{h}_1 \boldsymbol{c}_1^T, \quad \boldsymbol{A}_3 = \tilde{\boldsymbol{A}}_3 - \boldsymbol{h}_2 \boldsymbol{c}_1^T$$
$$\boldsymbol{b}_1 = \boldsymbol{b}_{o1} - d_o \boldsymbol{h}_1, \quad \boldsymbol{b}_2 = \tilde{\boldsymbol{b}}_2 - d_o \boldsymbol{h}_2$$
$$\boldsymbol{x}_o^h(i,j) = \boldsymbol{x}^h(i,j), \quad \boldsymbol{c}_1 = \boldsymbol{c}_{o1}$$
$$d_2 = \tilde{b} - d_o d_1 \quad \boldsymbol{g}_1 = \tilde{\boldsymbol{c}}_1 - d_1 \boldsymbol{c}_1.$$

If the actual output, $y(i,j)$, is replaced by the ideal output, $y_d(i,j)$, on the right-hand side of (5), the LSS model described by (5) can be viewed as a new system with two kinds of inputs where $\boldsymbol{x}^v(i,j)$ is an $(n-1) \times 1$ vertical state vector. For simplicity, (5) can be expressed as

$$\begin{aligned} \boldsymbol{x}_{11}(i,j) &= \boldsymbol{A}\boldsymbol{x}(i,j) + \boldsymbol{B}\boldsymbol{u}(i,j) \\ y(i,j) &= \boldsymbol{c}_1^T \boldsymbol{x}^h(i,j) + \boldsymbol{g}^T \boldsymbol{x}(i,j-1) \\ &\quad + \boldsymbol{d}^T \boldsymbol{u}(i,j-1) + d_o u(i,j) \end{aligned} \tag{6}$$

where

$$\boldsymbol{x}_{11}(i,j) = \begin{bmatrix} \boldsymbol{x}^h(i+1,j) \\ \boldsymbol{x}^v(i,j+1) \end{bmatrix}, \quad \boldsymbol{x}(i,j) = \begin{bmatrix} \boldsymbol{x}^h(i,j) \\ \boldsymbol{x}^v(i,j) \end{bmatrix}$$

$$u(i,j) = \begin{bmatrix} y_d(i,j) \\ u(i,j) \end{bmatrix}, \quad A = \begin{bmatrix} A_1 & A_2 \\ A_3 & A_4 \end{bmatrix}, \quad g = \begin{bmatrix} g_1 \\ g_2 \end{bmatrix}$$

$$B = \begin{bmatrix} B_1 \\ B_2 \end{bmatrix} = \begin{bmatrix} b_1 & h_1 \\ b_2 & h_2 \end{bmatrix}, \quad d = \begin{bmatrix} d_1 \\ d_2 \end{bmatrix}.$$

Applying z-transforms to (6) yields

$$\begin{aligned} X(z_1,z_2) &= (S-A)^{-1}BU(z_1,z_2) \\ Y(z_1,z_2) &= \Big[\left([\, c_1^T \;\; 0\,] + z_2^{-1}g^T \right)(S-A)^{-1}B \qquad (7) \\ &\quad + z_2^{-1}d^T \Big] U(z_1,z_2) + d_o U(z_1,z_2) \end{aligned}$$

where $X(z_1,z_2)$, $U(z_1,z_2)$ and $U(z_1,z_2)$ denote the z-transform of $x(i,j)$, $u(i,j)$ and $u(i,j)$, respectively, and

$$S = \begin{bmatrix} z_1 I_m & 0 \\ 0 & z_2 I_{n-1} \end{bmatrix}.$$

Definition 1: Let Q be an $m \times n$ real matrix and let $f(Q)$ be a scalar complex function of Q, differentiable w.r.t. all the entries of Q. The sensitivity function of f w.r.t. Q is then defined as

$$S_Q = \frac{\partial f}{\partial Q} \quad \text{with} \quad (S_Q)_{kl} = \frac{\partial f}{\partial q_{kl}}$$

where q_{kl} denotes the (k,l)th entry of the matrix Q.

To obtain gradient signals, the derivatives of the output signal w.r.t. each of the filter coefficient matrices are derived from (7) as follows:

$$\begin{aligned} &\frac{\partial Y(z_1,z_2)}{\partial A} \\ &= \left[\left([\, c_1^T \;\; 0\,] + z_2^{-1}g^T \right)(S-A)^{-1} \right]^T X^T(z_1,z_2) \\ &\frac{\partial Y(z_1,z_2)}{\partial B} \\ &= \left[\left([\, c_1^T \;\; 0\,] + z_2^{-1}g^T \right)(S-A)^{-1} \right]^T U^T(z_1,z_2) \\ &\frac{\partial Y(z_1,z_2)}{\partial c_1} = X^h(z_1,z_2) \\ &\frac{\partial Y(z_1,z_2)}{\partial g} = z_2^{-1} X(z_1,z_2) \qquad (8) \\ &\frac{\partial Y(z_1,z_2)}{\partial d} = z_2^{-1} U(z_1,z_2) \\ &\frac{\partial Y(z_1,z_2)}{\partial d_o} = U(z_1,z_2). \end{aligned}$$

From (8) it is clear that the gradient signals required to adapt the c_1 and g vectors are available as the output states $x^h(i,j)$ and $x(i,j-1)$, respectively, whereas the gradient signals for the d_o scalar and the d vector are the signals $u(i,j-1)$ and $u(i,j)$, respectively. However, the gradient signals required to adapt the A and B matrices must be created by two types of new systems.

III. Adaptive Mechanism

Define an error signal, $e(i,j)$, by the difference between the ideal output, $y_d(i,j)$, and the actual output, $y(i,j)$, in the form

$$e(i,j) = y_d(i,j) - y(i,j). \qquad (9)$$

During adaption, the coefficients of an adaptive filter are updated to minimize the mean-squared error signal, $E[e^2(i,j)]$. In order to find a minimum of the mean-squared error performance surface, the steepest descent method can be used with the gradient signals. Let the data size be $M \times N$, that is, $\{(i,j) \mid 0 \le i \le M{-}1,\ 0 \le j \le N{-}1\}$ and let $k = Mj+i$. The same data are repeatedly used during adaption. Applying the steepest descent method, any coefficient, p, of the adaptive filter is updated according to

$$p(k+1) = p(k) - \mu \frac{\partial E[e^2(i,j)]}{\partial p(k)} \qquad (10)$$

where μ is a step-size parameter which controls the convergence of the algorithm. As usual, in approximating the expected value in the LMS algorithm by the instantaneous value of the squared error signals, (10) is changed to

$$p(k+1) = p(k) + 2\mu e(i,j) \frac{\partial y(i,j)}{\partial p(k)}. \qquad (11)$$

Referring to (8) and (11), adaption equations for the adaptive filter coefficients are written as

$$\begin{aligned} A_\xi(k+1) &= A_\xi(k) + 2\mu e(i,j)\alpha_\xi(i,j) \\ B_\zeta(k+1) &= B_\zeta(k) + 2\mu e(i,j)\beta_\zeta(i,j) \\ c_1(k+1) &= c_1(k) + 2\mu e(i,j)x^h(i,j) \\ g(k+1) &= g(k) + 2\mu e(i,j)x(i,j-1) \qquad (12) \\ d(k+1) &= d(k) + 2\mu e(i,j)u(i,j-1) \\ d_o(k+1) &= d_o(k) + 2\mu e(i,j)u(i,j) \\ &\xi = 1,2,3,4; \quad \zeta = 1,2 \end{aligned}$$

where the gradient signals $\alpha_\xi(i,j)$ and $\beta_\zeta(i,j)$ are created by using

$$\begin{aligned} \begin{bmatrix} \alpha_1(i+1,j) & \alpha_2(i+1,j) \\ \alpha_3(i,j+1) & \alpha_4(i,j+1) \end{bmatrix} &= A^T(k) \begin{bmatrix} \alpha_1(i,j) & \alpha_2(i,j) \\ \alpha_3(i,j) & \alpha_4(i,j) \end{bmatrix} \\ &+ \begin{bmatrix} c_1(k) \\ 0 \end{bmatrix} x^T(i,j) + g(k)x^T(i,j-1) \\ \begin{bmatrix} \beta_1(i+1,j) \\ \beta_2(i,j+1) \end{bmatrix} &= A^T(k) \begin{bmatrix} \beta_1(i,j) \\ \beta_2(i,j) \end{bmatrix} \\ &+ \begin{bmatrix} c_1(k) \\ 0 \end{bmatrix} u^T(i,j) + g(k)u^T(i,j-1). \end{aligned}$$

From the above arguments, a reduced order 2-D adaptive state-space filter can be implemented.

IV. Numerical Example

In this section, an example is solved to demonstrate the validity of the proposed reduced order 2-D adaptive state-space filter.

Let an ideal output signal be given by the following 2-D Gaussian filter:

$$y_d(i,j) = 0.256322\exp[-0.103203\{(i-4)^2 + (j-4)^2\}] \quad (i,j) \in S_h$$

where $S_h = \{(i,j) \mid 0 \le i \le 10,\ 0 \le j \le 10\}$. The original 2-D adaptive state-space filter is assumed to be of order $(m,n) = (3,3)$ and let the input signal be specified by

$$u(i,j) = \begin{cases} 1, & i=j=0 \\ 0, & \text{otherwise.} \end{cases}$$

As is well known [16], a part of the ideal output signals, $\{y_d(i,j) \mid 0 \le i \le 3,\ 0 \le j \le 3\}$, can be realized in terms of a canonical form LSS model whose transfer function is separable in the denominator as follows:

$$\boldsymbol{A}_{o1} = \begin{bmatrix} 0.0 & 1.0 & 0.0 \\ 0.0 & 0.0 & 1.0 \\ 0.0 & 0.0 & 0.0 \end{bmatrix}, \quad \boldsymbol{A}_{o4} = \begin{bmatrix} 0.0 & 0.0 & 0.0 \\ 1.0 & 0.0 & 0.0 \\ 0.0 & 1.0 & 0.0 \end{bmatrix}$$

$$\boldsymbol{A}_{o2} = \boldsymbol{0},\ \boldsymbol{A}_{o3} = \begin{bmatrix} 0.208519 & 0.152997 & 0.091323 \\ 0.152997 & 0.112259 & 0.067007 \\ 0.091323 & 0.067007 & 0.039996 \end{bmatrix}$$

$$\boldsymbol{b}_{o1} = [\,0.0 \quad 0.0 \quad 1.0\,]^T$$

$$\boldsymbol{b}_{o2} = [\,0.044344 \quad 0.032537 \quad 0.019421\,]^T$$

$$\boldsymbol{c}_{o1}^T = [\,0.044344 \quad 0.032537 \quad 0.019421\,]$$

$$\boldsymbol{c}_{o2}^T = [\,0.0 \quad 0.0 \quad 1.0\,]$$

$$d_o = 0.009430.$$

It should be noted that $y(i,j) = y_d(i,j)$ holds for $i,j = 0,1,2,3$. The above canonical form realization can be represented by using (6) in the form

$$\boldsymbol{A}_1 = \begin{bmatrix} 0.0 & 1.0 & 0.0 \\ 0.0 & 0.0 & 1.0 \\ 0.0 & 0.0 & 0.0 \end{bmatrix}, \quad \boldsymbol{A}_4 = \begin{bmatrix} 0.0 & 0.0 \\ 1.0 & 0.0 \end{bmatrix}$$

$$\boldsymbol{A}_2 = \boldsymbol{0}, \quad \boldsymbol{A}_3 = \begin{bmatrix} 0.208519 & 0.152997 & 0.091323 \\ 0.152997 & 0.112259 & 0.067007 \end{bmatrix}$$

$$\boldsymbol{B}_1 = \begin{bmatrix} 0.0 & 0.0 \\ 0.0 & 0.0 \\ 0.0 & 1.0 \end{bmatrix}, \quad \boldsymbol{B}_2 = \begin{bmatrix} 0.0 & 0.044244 \\ 0.0 & 0.032537 \end{bmatrix}$$

$$\boldsymbol{c}_1^T = [\,0.044344 \quad 0.032537 \quad 0.019421\,]$$

$$\boldsymbol{g}_1^T = [\,0.091323 \quad 0.067007 \quad 0.039996\,]$$

$$\boldsymbol{g}_2^T = [\,0.0 \quad 1.0\,]$$

$$\boldsymbol{d}^T = [\,0.0 \quad 0.019421\,], \quad d_o = 0.009430.$$

This will serve an initial estimate of the reduced order 2-D adaptive state-space filter.

The same data are repeatedly used in the adaptive process. The step-size parameter is chosen to be $\mu = 1 \times 10^{-1}$. The reduced order 2-D adaptive state-space filter obtained after iterations $k = 24.1879 \times 10^6$ was as

$$\boldsymbol{A}_1 = \begin{bmatrix} 0.743009 & 0.625012 & 0.011607 \\ -0.093857 & 0.614114 & 0.731062 \\ 0.029888 & -0.229384 & 0.672232 \end{bmatrix}$$

$$\boldsymbol{A}_2 = \begin{bmatrix} 0.102855 & 0.039893 \\ 0.072330 & -0.042516 \\ -0.043758 & -0.001533 \end{bmatrix}$$

$$\boldsymbol{A}_3 = \begin{bmatrix} 0.084730 & 0.064965 & 0.038635 \\ 0.141471 & 0.105900 & 0.063067 \end{bmatrix}$$

$$\boldsymbol{A}_4 = \begin{bmatrix} 0.848660 & -0.290589 \\ 0.855834 & 0.673360 \end{bmatrix}$$

$$\boldsymbol{B}_1 = \begin{bmatrix} -0.016435 & 0.074152 \\ 0.023029 & 0.077067 \\ -0.000502 & 0.708920 \end{bmatrix}$$

$$\boldsymbol{B}_2 = \begin{bmatrix} 0.100366 & 0.019009 \\ 0.009106 & 0.030790 \end{bmatrix}$$

$$\boldsymbol{c}_1^T = [\,0.044344 \quad 0.032537 \quad 0.019421\,]$$

$$\boldsymbol{g}_1^T = [\,0.066705 \quad 0.049776 \quad 0.029663\,]$$

$$\boldsymbol{g}_2^T = [\,-0.042295 \quad 0.742777\,]$$

$$\boldsymbol{d}^T = [\,0.526442 \quad 0.014457\,], \quad d_o = 0.009430.$$

The resulting filter can be evaluated by using the following deviation:

$$\varepsilon_2 = \frac{\left[\sum_{i=0}^{M-1}\sum_{j=0}^{N-1}(y_d(i,j) - y(i,j))^2\right]^{1/2}}{\left[\sum_{i=0}^{M-1}\sum_{j=0}^{N-1} y_d^2(i,j)\right]^{1/2}} \times 100$$

where $M = N = 11$. Through the adaptive process, $\varepsilon_2 = 92.8707$ in the initial estimate was reduced to $\varepsilon_2 = 1.2683$ after iterations $k = 24.1879 \times 10^6$. This result is better than $\varepsilon_2 = 1.2732$ reported in [12].

In the computation of (5), it is obviously possible to use the actual output, $y(i,j)$, instead of $y_d(i,j)$ on the right-hand side of (5). In such a case, $\varepsilon_2 = 92.8707$ in the initial estimate was reduced to $\varepsilon_2 = 1.4285$ after iterations $k = 24.1879 \times 10^6$ and the resulting filter was as

$$\boldsymbol{A}_1 = \begin{bmatrix} 0.721090 & 0.439582 & -0.156401 \\ -0.301697 & 0.543708 & 0.617026 \\ 0.061250 & -0.159058 & 0.790024 \end{bmatrix}$$

$$\boldsymbol{A}_2 = \begin{bmatrix} 0.053435 & -0.001516 \\ -0.022105 & 0.000012 \\ -0.007558 & 0.000528 \end{bmatrix}$$

$$\boldsymbol{A}_3 = \begin{bmatrix} 0.125436 & 0.091912 & 0.054800 \\ 0.287326 & 0.210717 & 0.125734 \end{bmatrix}$$

$$\boldsymbol{A}_4 = \begin{bmatrix} 0.750252 & -0.296842 \\ 0.612452 & 0.631658 \end{bmatrix}$$

$$\boldsymbol{B}_1 = \begin{bmatrix} 0.003851 & -0.139596 \\ -0.001247 & 0.161666 \\ -0.000093 & 1.053181 \end{bmatrix}$$

$$\boldsymbol{B}_2 = \begin{bmatrix} 0.110363 & 0.026654 \\ -0.078118 & 0.061222 \end{bmatrix}$$

$$\boldsymbol{c}_1^T = [\,0.044344 \quad 0.032537 \quad 0.019421\,]$$

$$\boldsymbol{g}_1^T = [\,0.058795 \quad 0.043159 \quad 0.025726\,]$$

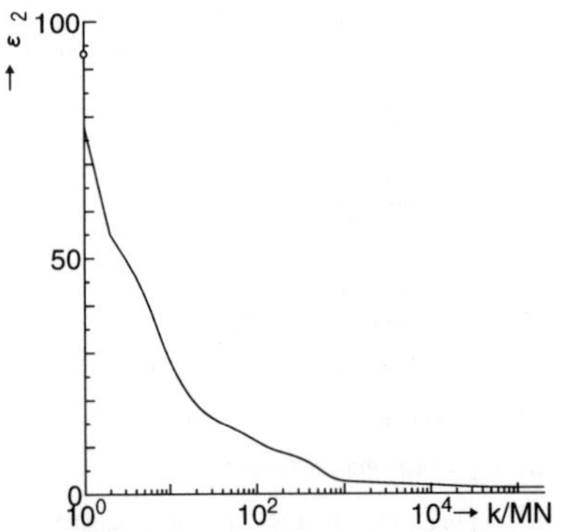

Fig.1 Convergence of parameters in regarding $y_d(i,j)$ as an input where o indicates the inital value of ε_2 at $k=0$.

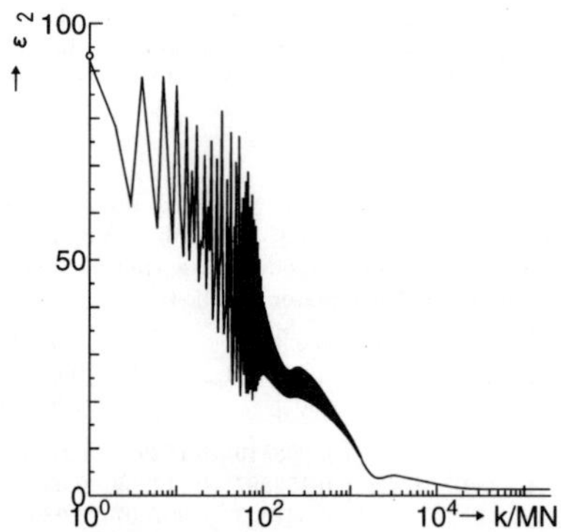

Fig.2 Convergence of parameters in using $y(i,j)$ as an input where o indicates the initial value of ε_2 at $k=0$.

$$\boldsymbol{g}_2^T = [\ -0.245488 \quad 0.414011\ ]$$

$$\boldsymbol{d}^T = [\ 0.730761 \quad 0.012533\ ]\ , \quad d_o = 0.009430\ .$$

The convergence of parameters in the adaptive process for each case is depicted in Figs.1 and 2.

V. Conclusion

The reduced order 2-D adaptive state-space filter has been developed in this paper. This makes it possible to reduce computational complexity and attains faster convergence. A numerical example has demonstrated the validity of the proposed reduced order 2-D adaptive state-space filter. The same arguments can be applied to the Fornasini-Marchesini second local state-space model and the results will appear elsewhere.

References

[1] M. M. Hadhoud and D. W. Thomas, "The two-dimensional adaptive LMS (TDLMS) algorithm", *IEEE Trans. Circuits Syst.*, vol.CAS-35, pp.485-494, May 1988.

[2] W. K. Jenkins and R. P. Faust, "A constrained two-dimensional adaptive digital filters with reduced computational complexity", in *Proc. of IEEE Int. Symp. Circuits and Systems*, pp.2655-2658, June 1988.

[3] M. Ohki and S. Hashiguchi, "Two-dimensional LMS adaptive filters", *IEEE Trans. Consumer Electronics*, vol.37, pp.66-73, Feb. 1991.

[4] W. B. Mikhael and S. M. Ghosh, "Two-dimensional variable step-size sequential adaptive gradient algorithms with applications", *IEEE Trans. Circuits Syst.*, vol.CAS-38, pp.1577-1580, Dec. 1991.

[5] W. B. Mikhael and S. M. Ghosh, "Two-dimensional block adaptive filtering algorithms", in *Proc. of IEEE Int. Symp. Circuits and Systems*, pp.1219-1222, May 1992.

[6] S.-C. Pei, C.-Y. Lin and C.-C. Tseng, "Two-dimensional LMS adaptive linear phase filters", in *Proc. of IEEE Int. Symp. Circuits and Systems*, pp.311-314, May 1993.

[7] W. B. Mikhael and S. M. Ghosh, "Two-dimensional optimum block adaptive filtering algorithms for image restoration and enhancement", in *Proc. of IEEE Int. Symp. Circuits and Systems*, pp.419-422, May 1993.

[8] J. C. Strait and W. K. Jenkins, "A fast two-dimensional quasi-newton adaptive filter", in *Proc. of IEEE Int. Symp. Circuits and Systems*, vol.2, pp.149-152, May-June 1994.

[9] S.-G. Chen and Y.-A. Kao, "A new efficient 2-D LMS adaptive filtering algorithm", in *Proc. of IEEE Int. Symp. Circuits and Systems*, vol.2, pp.233-236, May-June 1994.

[10] M. Kawamata, E. Kawakami and T. Higuchi, "Realization of lattice-form separable-denominator 2-D adaptive filters", in *Proc. of IEEE Int. Symp. Circuits and Systems*, pp.295-298, May 1993.

[11] A. C. Tan and S.-T. Chen, "Two-dimensional adaptive LMS IIR filter", in *Proc. of IEEE Int. Symp. Circuits and Systems*, pp.299-302, May 1993.

[12] M. Muneyasu and T. Hinamoto, "2-D adaptive state-space digital filters using LMS algorithm", in *Proc. of IEEE Int. Symp. Circuits and Systems*, vol.2, pp.65-68, May-June 1994.

[13] M. R. Azimi-Sadjadi and H. Pan, " Two-dimensional block diagonal LMS adaptive filtering", *IEEE Trans. Signal Proceeding*, vol.42, pp.2420-2429, Sept. 1994.

[14] M. Muneyasu and T. Hinamoto, "Parallel-form realization of 2-D adaptive separable-denominator state-space filters", in *Proc. of IEEE Int. Symp. Circuits and Systems*, pp.29-32, May 1996.

[15] T. Nakachi, K. Yamashita and N. Hamada, "A two-dimensional adaptive joint-process estimator using new lattice form", in *Proc. of IEEE Int. Symp. Circuits and Systems*, vol.2, pp.33-36, May 1996.

[16] T. Hinamoto and F. W. Fairman, "Separable-denominatorstate-space realization of two-dimensional filters using a canonic form", *IEEE Trans. on Acoustics, Speech, and Signal Process.*, vol.ASSP-29, pp.846-853, Aug. 1981.

MULTIDIMENSIONAL FILTERS AND ALGORITHMS FOR AUTOMATIC REALTIME DETECTION AND CLASSIFICATION OF RAILROAD SLEEPERS IN VIDEO IMAGES

J.Velten, A.Kummert*, D.Maiwald***

*
Laboratory for Communication Theory
Department of Electrical Engineering
University of Wuppertal
D-42097 Wuppertal
Germany
phone: +49-202-439-2961
fax: +49-202-439-2959
email: kummert@uni-wuppertal.de
velten@uni-wuppertal.de

**
STN ATLAS Elektronik GmbH
Simulation Division

D-28305 Bremen
Germany
phone: +49-421-4573001
fax: +49-421-4573903
email: maiwald@stn-atlas.de

Abstract

The automatic inspection of railroad tracks is a new and challenging field of application of multidimensional systems. Making a machine able to understand which parts of an image belong to a sleeper without giving any special information about its form, needs implementation of sophisticated algorithms. In this paper this task is realized by using a model of the railroad and the application of multi-dimensional filters and algorithms. This implemented artificial intelligence is of course not perfect, but leads to good results with an appropriate expenditure. In order to decompose the railroad image, a modified Marr-Hildreth operator is proposed, where the sensitivity with respect to brightness is adaptable.

1. Introduction

To guarantee a proper and secure operation, railroad tracks have to be checked and, if required, repaired from time to time. Until now this control has to be done by a track-inspector, a person who walks along the whole track and controls the fastenings, the rails, and the sleepers. In this paper a multidimensional system is introduced that can handle the detection and classification of railroad sleepers automatically by the evaluation of images. Such a video based detection algorithm is limited to handle faults like splits or complete breaks which look like wider splits. The rotting of timber sleepers can only be detected by knocking on them. The demand for realtime processing and the detection of even unknown sleeper types have been severe constraints. Image data is collected by a high speed line camera which is mounted on an inspection vehicle (cf. fig. 1). The acquisition speed of the camera is adjusted to the speed of the vehicle so that the ratio of distance in the image to that in the real scene is constant.

2. Improvement in image quality

The acquired images are of poor quality (cf. fig. 2), so that an improvement is required before any further processing. At first an illumination homogenization process is applied, that means the result should look

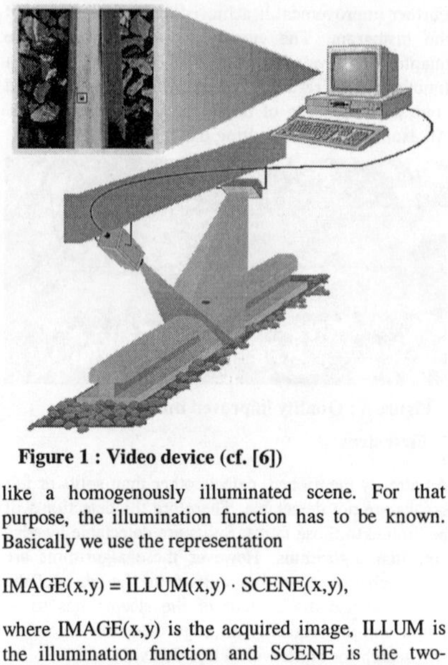

Figure 1 : Video device (cf. [6])

like a homogenously illuminated scene. For that purpose, the illumination function has to be known. Basically we use the representation

IMAGE(x,y) = ILLUM(x,y) · SCENE(x,y),

where IMAGE(x,y) is the acquired image, ILLUM is the illumination function and SCENE is the two-dimensional representation of the image. Since the

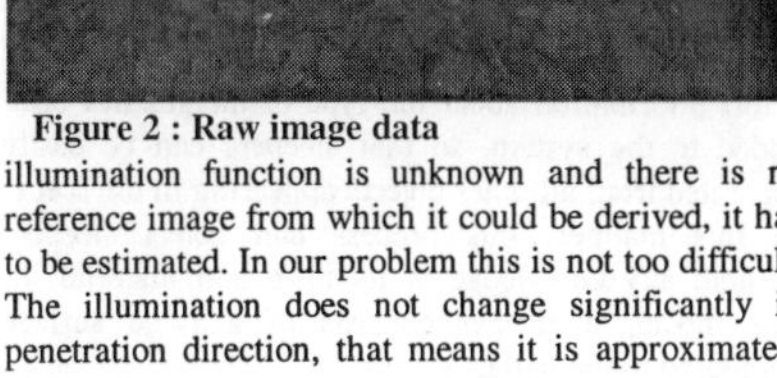

Figure 2 : Raw image data

illumination function is unknown and there is no reference image from which it could be derived, it has to be estimated. In our problem this is not too difficult. The illumination does not change significantly in penetration direction, that means it is approximately constant

ILLUM(x,y) = ILLUM(x),

with y as penetration direction. The mean value of brightness of the scene is approximately independent of x, so that fluctuations have to be caused by the illumination function. So we obtain the illumination by

$$E(IMAGE(x,y)) = E(ILLUM(x) \cdot SCENE(y)) = ILLUM(x) \cdot E(SCENE(y)),$$

where E denotes the expectation operator. Homogenous illumination can now be achieved by multiplying the image by the inverse illumination function. Since the illumination changes slowly, dependent on changing illumination angles in curves, this estimation has to be repeated from time to time.
Further improvement is achieved by an equalization of the histogram. The cumulative distribution of the quantization levels is used to deduce a transformation function. The resulting image will show increased contrast in regions of dominant quantization levels. An example for the resulting image is shown in fig. 3.

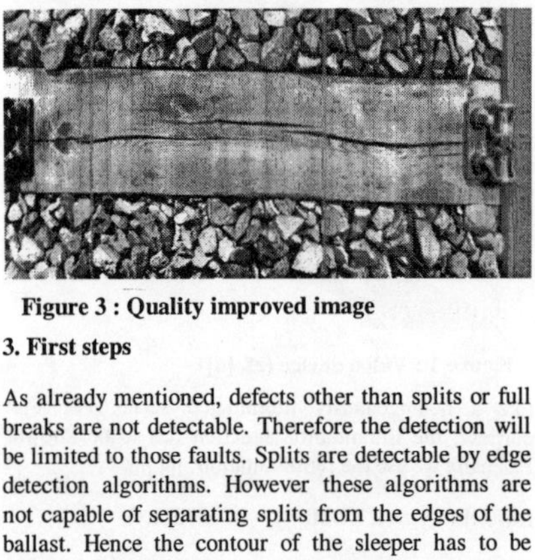

Figure 3 : Quality improved image

3. First steps

As already mentioned, defects other than splits or full breaks are not detectable. Therefore the detection will be limited to those faults. Splits are detectable by edge detection algorithms. However these algorithms are not capable of separating splits from the edges of the ballast. Hence the contour of the sleeper has to be found and subsequently an edge detection algorithm will search for faults within this domain.
The contour detection algorithm should be applicable to different types of sleepers, so a non-template based algorithm had to be designed. For this task an intelligent system would be required. It is nearly impossible to design such a device with realtime capabilities in a cost effective manner. To solve this problem, a simpler model was developed which allows to replace this intelligence by multidimensional filters and algorithms which are fitted to our images. In other words, the a-priori information about the type of images has been added to the system, so that sleepers can be easily separated from all other objects appearing in the scene. In this manner, this process can detect sleepers without any knowledge of its form and material. In this model, a sleeper consists of a large surface compared to the ballast stones.
The rails which have a large surface too can be detected and eliminated by known procedures (cf. [1]). A system based on this model is of course not as perfect as the human visual system and brain. If there are objects with large surfaces other than the sleepers, the process fails. Fortunately such situations (e.g. level crossings) are very seldom, so that this model is a good description of reality.

4. Segmentation

An often used method for segmentation is to start with pixels as segments, calculate suitable measures, and to classify them with respect to the two classes "sleeper" and "not sleeper". This type of processing is not possible here, because the contours have to be detected exactly. The surfaces of ballast stones and those of sleepers seem to be very similar in some cases. Even the human visual system needs a larger neighborhood of the pixel to decide whether a pixel belongs to a sleeper or to the ballast, and a larger neighborhood causes growing complexity for processing. On the other hand, the classificator for large domains changes little, if it is moved from one pixel to the next. Hence, a good and robust classification becomes improbable.
The system introduced in this work searches for edge segments as probable boundaries and decides whether they belong to the class "sleeper" or to the class "ballast". For this purpose, closed segments are of advantage. A good edge-detector would be one which generates many edges in the ballast region and none or little in the sleeper region. Especially, timber sleepers are problematic here. The wood grain of timber is a texture which generates much edges. Figure 4 shows the different results obtained by different edge detectors (cf. [2]): a) Sobel operator, b) Laplace operator, and c) Marr-Hildreth operator. It is obvious that none of the standard operators can be used directly. But we will take a closer look at the Marr-Hidreth operator.

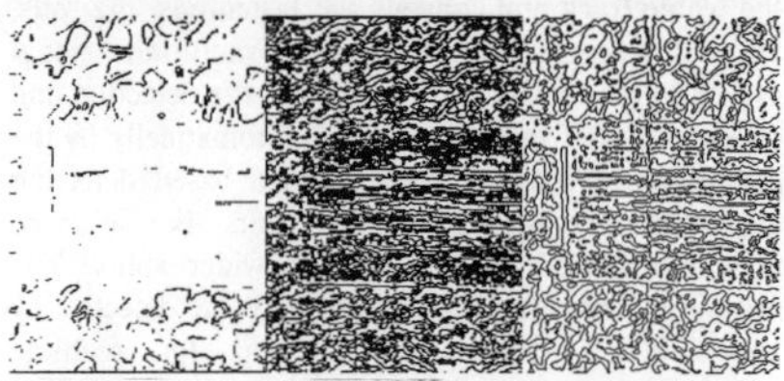

Figure 4 : Part of the sleeper image, processed with a) Sobel, b) Laplace and c) Marr-Hildreth operator

5. Marr-Hildreth operator

The Marr-Hildreth operator (cf. [3],[4]) uses the isotropic Laplace operator, to calculate some kind of second derivative to search for zero-crossings of the result. Because of the Laplace operator being very sensitive to noise, the image is filtered with a low-pass filter first. This filter has to have a narrow pass band in the time and frequency domain simultaneously, in order to achieve exact boundary contours with a small size operator. This requirements are met best by a Gaussian low pass filter which is the essential part of the Marr-Hildreth operator. The Laplace operator and the low pass filter can be unified which is called Laplacian of Gaussian or shorter LoG.

$$L(\,G(x,y) ** B(x,y)\,) = L(\,G(x,y)\,) ** B(x,y)$$

where B(x,y) is the image, G(x,y) the impulse response of the low pass, and ** denotes the two-dimensional convolution. Impulse response and frequency response of a discrete LoG filter are shown in figure 5. The continuous filter is a real band pass, i.e. the DC

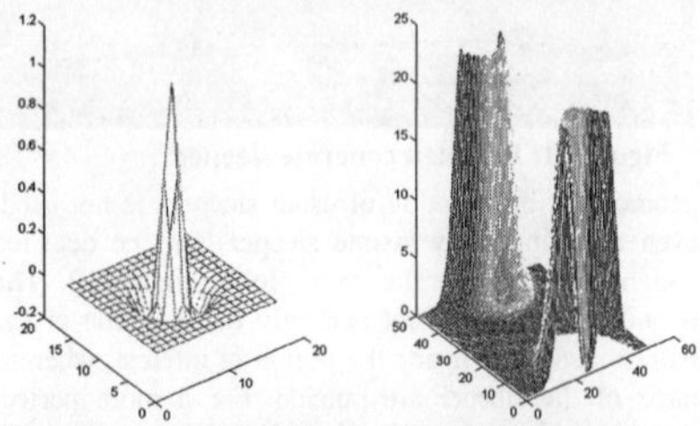

Figure 5 : Impulse response and frequency response of a 2-D 17x17 LoG filter (frequency-response is shifted for better visualisation)

component lies in the stop band of the filter. By filtering the image and searching for zero-crossings the edges are detected.

The attempt to use a discrete relaization of the Marr-Hildreth operator exhibits the following problems.

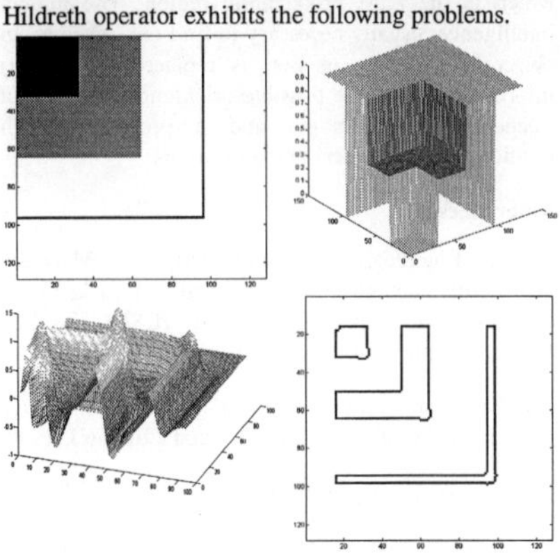

Figure 6 : The test image, its 3-D representation, the LoG filtered image and the resulting edges (convolution was calculated only for valid pixels)

While searching for steep transitions (edges) in the image, saddle points have to be excluded. Hence, the simple search for zero-crossings displays more edges then there are present in the image. On the other hand, the operator generates closed segments which are easier to classify. The problem of wrong edges is illustrated in figure 6. On the upper left, the test image is depicted, on the upper right its three dimensional representation. On the lower left side, one finds the three dimensional representation of the LoG-filtered image and on the right the resulting edges.

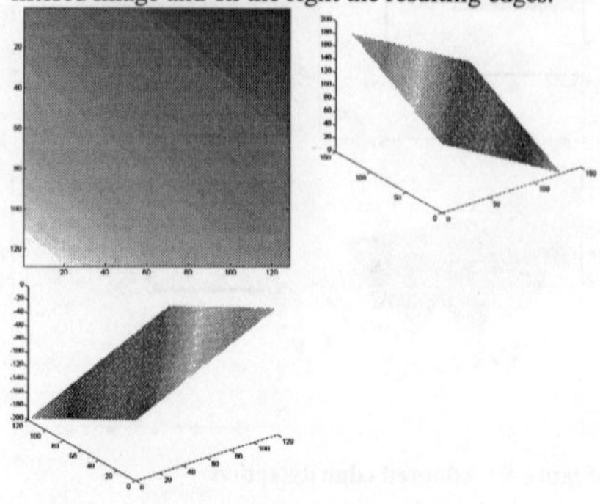

Figure 7 : The problem with an increasing gray level

Obviously some of the edges detected by the applied operator are incorrect. In realizations of the Marr-Hildreth operator, thresholds are used often, to suppress such wrong edges. However, this is not a suitable tool to distinguish between correct and incorrect edges. Another problem of the operator results in the imperfect discrete realization of the LoG. The LoG-function has to be cut in order to use it. As a consequence, the DC component is no longer suppressed which is illustrated in figure 7.

The gray level in the test image depicted in figure 7 is linearly varied in the diagonal direction. The three dimensional representation in the top right position shows the corresponding plane. The result of the LoG-filter has to be a constant and not the plane shown in the bottom of the left.

6. Solution of the segmentation problem

Segmentation is problematic since there are too many edges near the boundaries of the sleepers, so that usual edge detectors are not applicable. These contours, for example wood grain, can not be suppressed by the Gaussian of the Marr-Hildreth operator. These edges are simply too dominant to be suppressed. Often the sleepers are brighter than the ballast so that an edge-detector which is more sensitive in darker regions would be suitable. However, exactly that is realized if the LoG filter mentioned above is applied. After LoG-filtering, bright regions are torn away from the 0-plane by superimposed low frequency components of the original. So zero-crossings only occur if an edge is very strong. Furthermore, the range of suppressed edges can be controlled by the width of the filter or, by the coefficient of the Gaussian of the LoG-filter. In this work, the second possibility has been chosen due to its practicability. The complete effect is explained in figure 8. The processing of the test image from figure 6 is shown.

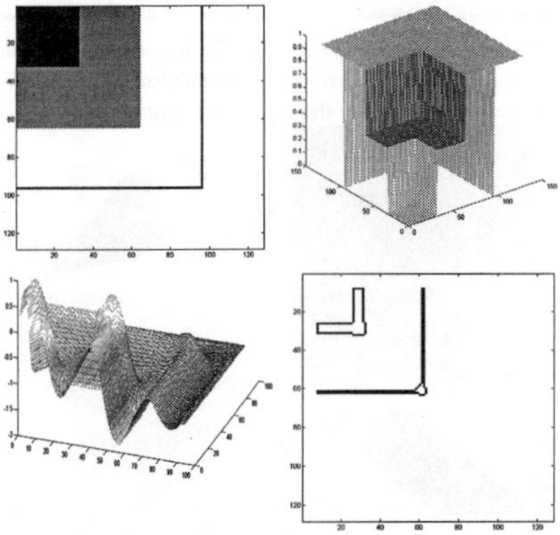

Figure 8 : Adapted edge detection

7. Morphological operators

The resulting images are still not completely segmented, i.e. there are intervals between the edge-segments. Hence, these edge segments have to be connected. This can be done by the application of the morphological operation dilation (cf. [5]) followed by the operation erosion in which the split of a region into two regions is prevented.

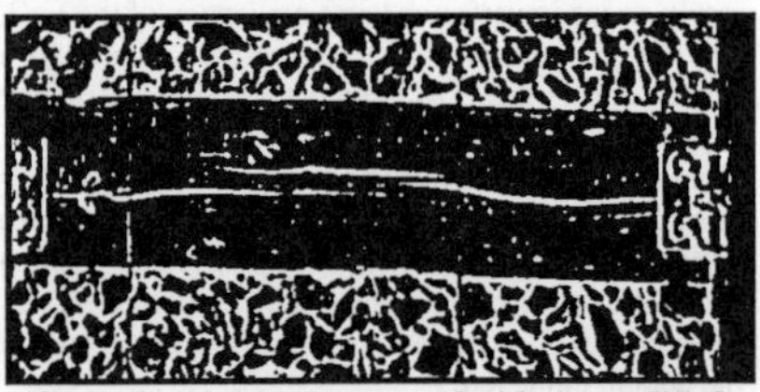

Figure 9 : An image processed with the modified Marr-Hildreth operator

8. Classification

The resulting segments can be classified with respect to its location and size, which are suitable features separating the two classes "sleeper" and "not sleeper".

Figure 10: Detected boundary contour

To proceed in this manner with sleepers of different quality and material, different coefficients of the Gaussian filter have to be chosen. Hence, for the detection of different qualities, some parallel working processes with different coefficients or one process with an adaptive coefficient is necessary. The implementation of parallel processes is more reliable, whereas one adapted process is cheaper in implementation.

The latter will require post processing, because the expense for prediction of the coefficients is very high. It is much easier to estimate it from older results, i.e. the last image, showing which segmentation was not satisfying. The next image shows an example of an image processed in the proposed way. Since the

Figure 11: Detected concrete sleeper

geometrical information of usual sleepers is not used, even not completely visible sleepers can be detected which is shown by the example in figure 10. The boundary contour is not perfectly found, some of the ballast stones are inside the region of interest, whereas parts of the sleeper are outside. For a more perfect detection iterative processing is necessary. On the other hand, the found boundary contour is appropriate to search for dangerous splits, since those would generate larger edges.

9. Conclusion

The proposed system, is capable of separating sleepers from its neighborhood, especially from the ballast which is the most problematic region. The human intelligence, usually necessary to find out, whether an object is a sleeper or not, is replaced by a-priori information about the possible orientation and size of sleepers in our images and a processing with multidimensional filters and algorithms.

References

[1] I. Khandogin, A. Kummert, D. Maiwald, "Automatic damage detection for railroad tracks by the analysis of video images," *in Proc. ICSPAT'97*, San Diego, CA, pp. 1130-1134, 1997.

[2] J.S. Lim, *Two-dimensional signal and image processing*. Prentice-Hall, Englewood Cliffs, NJ, 1990.

[3] D. Marr, *Vision*, Freeman, San Francisco, 1982.

[4] D. Marr, E. Hildreth, "Theory of edge detection," *Proc. R. Soc. Lond.*, B204, pp. 301-328, 1982.

[5] X.Zhuang, R.M. Haralick, S.R.Sternberg, "Image analysis using mathematical morphology," *IEEE Trans., PAMI-9(4)*: pp. 532-550, 1987.

[6] STN ATLAS Elektronik GMBH, Bremen, *RAIL CHECK, Automated Inspection of Rail Networks*, Company Prospect, May 1996.

Stable Factorization of 2-D Filters Using a Constrained Optimization Algorithm

S. J. Perantonis, N. Ampazis and S. J. Varoufakis

Institute of Informatics and Telecommunications,
National Center for Scientific Research "DEMOKRITOS",
153 10 Agia Paraskevi, Athens, Greece.

Abstract-In this paper we present a constrained optimization algorithm in order to obtain factorized vesrions of the transfer functions of 2-D filters. For 2-D IIR filters in particular, the algorithm achieves simultaneous factorization of the numerator and denomenator polynomials of the transfer functions, while special care is taken so that the resulting factorized filter is stable and, hence, it can be reliably implemented in cascade form.

I. Introduction

Factorability is a very important issue in the design of digital filters since a factorized filter transfer function can be efficiently implemented in cascade form. However, the cascade form is not a general structure that can be used in the implementation of 2-D FIR or IIR filters because their transfer functions consist of bivariate polynomials that cannot, in general, be factored as a product of lower-order polynomials. Hence, an efficient method for the factorization of a 2-D filter's tranfer function would be most beneficial. Many methods have been proposed for dealing with the two-dimensional polynomial factorization problem (see [2]-[4] and references cited therein), including recent work on the important subject of approximate factorization [5]-[8]. Recently, we also proposed a neural network based Constrained Learning Algorithm (CLA) for factorizing 2-D polynomials [9]. In this paper, we extend this neural network approach to a more general constrained optimization method in order to deal not only with the problem of bivariate polynomial factorization but directly with the problem of finding appropriate 2-D filter cascade structures that match the specifications of an original unfactored filter. This is achieved by minimizing a cost function based on the difference between the frequency responses of the original and of the factorized filter, while simultaneously satisfying appropriate constraints, so that factorization is facilitated. The proposed technique gives the exact factor polynomials of the transfer functions in the case of 2-D factorable filters, while for unfactorable transfer functions, it produces good approximate solutions as far as the polynomial factorization is concerned, and excellent match between the characteristics of the original and the factorized filter. In addition, for the case of 2-D IIR filters, by incorporating additional stability constraints into the formalism, the stability (in the sense of Huang [10]) of the transfer function with the resulting factorized polynomial in the denominator (of up to second order) is also ensured.

II. Algorithm Derivation Outline

Consider the 2-D IIR filter transfer function

$$H(z_1, z_2) = \frac{B(z_1, z_2)}{A(z_1, z_2)} \tag{1}$$

where

$$B(z_1, z_2) = \sum_{i=0}^{N_B} \sum_{j=0}^{N_B} b_{ij}\, z_1^i\, z_2^j \tag{2}$$

and

$$A(z_1, z_2) = \sum_{i=0}^{N_A} \sum_{j=0}^{N_A} a_{ij}\, z_1^i\, z_2^j \tag{3}$$

with N_A, N_B even and $b_{00} = a_{00} = 1$. For the above polynomials, we seek to achieve an exact or approximate factorization of the form:

$$B(z_1, z_2) \approx \prod_{i=1,2} B^{(i)}(z_1, z_2) \tag{4}$$

where

$$B^{(i)}(z_1, z_2) = \sum_{j=0}^{M_B} \sum_{k=0}^{M_B} u_{jk}^{(i)}\, z_1^j\, z_2^k \tag{5}$$

and

$$A(z_1, z_2) \approx \prod_{i=1,2} A^{(i)}(z_1, z_2) \tag{6}$$

where

$$A^{(i)}(z_1, z_2) = \sum_{j=0}^{M_A} \sum_{k=0}^{M_A} v_{jk}^{(i)}\, z_1^j\, z_2^k \tag{7}$$

with $M_A = N_A/2$, and $M_B = N_B/2$ so that the transfer function of eqn (1) can be approximated by

$$\hat{H}(z_1, z_2) = \frac{\prod_{i=1,2} B^{(i)}(z_1, z_2)}{\prod_{i=1,2} A^{(i)}(z_1, z_2)} \tag{8}$$

In this case, we should ask in what sense are $H(z_1, z_2)$ and $\hat{H}(z_1, z_2)$ similar? The answer is that we would expect at least the amplitude spectra of $H(z_1, z_2)$ and $\hat{H}(z_1, z_2)$ to be roughly equal so that the specifications of the original and of the factorized filter match as close as possible. Hence, the main purpose of the factorization algorithm is to minimize the Mean Square Error (MSE) cost function based on the magnitude of the frequency responses of the original and the resulting filter:

$$E = \frac{1}{2} \sum_{\theta_1=-\pi}^{\pi} \sum_{\theta_2=-\pi}^{\pi} (T - O)^2 \tag{9}$$

with $T = \ln(|H(e^{j\theta_1}, e^{j\theta_2})|)$ and $O = \ln(|\hat{H}(e^{j\theta_1}, e^{j\theta_2})|)$. The double summation is carried over a regular grid of points. The logarithmic functions are used to supress deep valleys of the cost function landscape and thus facilitate convergence. Since E is a highly non-linear function of the polynomial coefficients, gradient based techniques can run into problems in the presence of valleys or ridges in the MSE's landscape. However, for such cases it has proved beneficial to incorporate into the adaptation rule additional *a priori* problem-specific information. This often facilitates the convergence of the algorithm and leads to better solutions. For the problem at hand, additional information is available in the form of constraints between the coefficients of the given numerator and denominator polynomials and the coefficients of the corresponding desired factor polynomials. More explicitly, if we assume that $B(z_1, z_2)$ and $A(z_1, z_2)$ are factorable, then these constraints can be expressed as follows:

$$\Phi^u_{j+(N_B+1)i} = b_{ij} - \sum_{l=1}^{i} \sum_{m=1}^{j} u^{(1)}_{lm} u^{(2)}_{i-l,j-m} = 0 \tag{10}$$

with $0 \le i \le N_B, 0 \le j \le N_B$, and

$$\Phi^v_{j+(N_A+1)i} = a_{ij} - \sum_{l=1}^{i} \sum_{m=1}^{j} v^{(1)}_{lm} v^{(2)}_{i-l,j-m} = 0 \tag{11}$$

with $0 \le i \le N_A, 0 \le j \le N_A$. Thus, for the general case in which $B(z_1, z_2)$ and $A(z_1, z_2)$ are non-factorable, the objective of the adaptation process is to reach a minimum of the cost function of eqn (9) with respect to the variables $u^{(i)}_{jk}$ and $v^{(i)}_{jk}$, which satisfies as best as possible the constraints $\boldsymbol{\Phi} = \mathbf{0}$, where $\boldsymbol{\Phi}^T = (\boldsymbol{\Phi}^u, \boldsymbol{\Phi}^v)$ with $\boldsymbol{\Phi}^u = (\Phi^u_{j+(N_B+1)i}, 0 \le i \le N_B, 0 \le j \le N_B)$, and $\boldsymbol{\Phi}^v = (\Phi^v_{j+(N_A+1)i}, 0 \le i \le N_A, 0 \le j \le N_A)$. For the rest of this section, it is convenient, for reasons of compactness in terminology, to construct the vector of all polynomial coefficients $\boldsymbol{w} = (\boldsymbol{u}, \boldsymbol{v})^T$. To achieve rapid convergence of $\boldsymbol{\Phi}$ towards its target (zero), we propose an iterative algorithm for adapting $\boldsymbol{w}$, whose objectives are outlined as follows:

1. At each epoch of the learning process, the vector $\boldsymbol{w}$ will be incremented by $d\boldsymbol{w}$, so that the search for an optimum new point in the space of $\boldsymbol{w}$ is restricted to a hypersphere of known radius δP centered at the point defined by the current $\boldsymbol{w}$. If δP is small enough, the changes to the cost function E and to each component Φ_i of $\boldsymbol{\Phi}$ induced by changes in the weights can be approximated by the first differentials dE and $d\Phi_i$.
2. At each epoch it is desirable to change each Φ_i at a rate proportional to Φ_i, so that the Φ_i tend to zero at an exponential rate. Therefore, we should have $d\Phi_i = -\kappa\Phi_i$ with $k > 0$. In this expression, the maximum possible value of κ should be used.
3. Maximization of κ must be attempted subject to the constraint that the change dE in E is equal to a predetermined vector quantity δQ.

Based on these considerations, the following optimization problem can be formulated for each epoch of the algorithm, whose solution will determine the adaptation rule for $\boldsymbol{w}$:

Maximize $\kappa > 0$ with respect to $d\boldsymbol{w}$, subject to the following constraints:

$$d\boldsymbol{w}^T d\boldsymbol{w} = (\delta P)^2 \tag{12}$$

$$\kappa = -d\Phi_i/\Phi_i \tag{13}$$

$$dE = \delta Q \tag{14}$$

This constrained optimization problem can be solved analytically by introducing and evaluating suitable Lagrange multipliers. Solving this problem by following the general optimization framework introduced by Bryson and Denham [11], leads to the update rule for $\boldsymbol{w}$. To formulate the update rule, we introduce the primary quantities:

- A vector $\boldsymbol{G}$ with elements $G_i = \partial E/\partial w_i$
- A matrix $\boldsymbol{F}$ whose elements are defined by $F_{mi} = (1/\Phi_m)(\partial\Phi_m/\partial w_i)$.

and the quantities resulting from combinations of the primary quantities:

$$I_{GG} = \boldsymbol{G}^T\boldsymbol{G} \tag{15}$$

$$I_{GF} = \boldsymbol{F}\boldsymbol{G} \tag{16}$$

$$I_{FF} = FF^T \tag{17}$$

$$R = \frac{1}{I_{GG}}(I_{GG}I_{FF} - I_{GF} \times I_{GF}) \tag{18}$$

$$Z = 1 + \frac{(R^{-1})_a(I_{GF}{}^T R^{-1} I_{GF}) - (1^T R^{-1} I_{GF})^2}{(R^{-1})_a I_{GG}} \tag{19}$$

$$L_2 = -\frac{1}{2}\left[\frac{I_{GG}}{(R^{-1})_a[I_{GG}(\delta P)^2 - Z(\delta Q)^2]}\right]^{1/2} \tag{20}$$

$$\Lambda = -\frac{R^{-1}1}{(R^{-1})_a} - \frac{2L_2\delta Q}{I_{GG}}\left[\frac{1^T R^{-1} I_{GF}}{(R^{-1})_a}R^{-1}1 - R^{-1}I_{GF}\right] \tag{21}$$

$$L_1 = -\frac{2L_2\delta Q + \Lambda^T I_{GF}}{I_{GG}} \tag{22}$$

where $(.)_a$ denotes the sum of all elements of a matrix and 1 is a column vector whose elements are all equal to 1. In terms of these quantities, the update rule is given by:

$$dw = -\frac{L_1}{2L_2}G - \frac{1}{2L_2}F^T\Lambda \tag{23}$$

A full derivation of the above update rule is given in the Appendix, where it is also shown that δQ must be chosen adaptively according to the relation $\delta Q = -\xi\delta P\sqrt{I_{GG}}$. Here ξ is a real parameter with $0 < \xi < 1$. Consequently, the proposed algorithm has two free parameters, namely δP and ξ.

III. Stability Constraints

For the filter $H(z_1, z_2)$ defined in eqn (1), it is reasonable to assume that for most practical purposes the numerator polynomial $B(z_1, z_2)$ does not affect the system stability [1]. In the important special case of a second order denominator polynomial $A(z_1, z_2)$ ($N_B = 2$), the stability conditions according to Huang [10] for the factor polynomials can be written as $X_k < 1, k = 1, \ldots, 6$, as shown in Table 1. These conditions can be incorporated in the formalism as follows: At a certain iteration of the algorithm, let a number M of the stability constraints be violated, so that $X_{k_r} \geq 1, r = 1, \ldots, M$. We can augment the vector Φ^v of the previous section by adding extra components $\Phi^v_{[j+(N_A+1)i]+r} = X_{k_r}, r = 1, \ldots M$. By following the formalism of section II using the augmented vector Φ^v, the quantities X_{k_r} are driven towards the stability region. Note that the dimensionality of the vector Φ^v is adaptive, as only the violated constraints are included in each iteration. Iterative application of this scheme can lead to a final stable solution.

IV. Simulation Results

We seek an approximate factorization of the second order 2-D IIR filter whose (non-factorable) numerator and denominator polynomial coefficients are shown in Tables 2 and 3 respectively. Fig. 1a shows the amplitude spectrum of the original low-pass IIR filter. Using the constraints Φ^u_1, Φ^u_3, Φ^u_4, Φ^v_1, Φ^v_3 and Φ^v_4 and all stability constraints of section III, we have applied the proposed method using a regular grid of 32^2 training points. Fig. 1b shows the amplitude spectrum of the filter obtained (with $\delta P = 0.005$ and $\xi = 0.5$). Clearly, there is very good agreement between the amplitude spectra of Fig. 1a and 1b, and therefore the proximity to the original amplitude spectrum, enables us to design the cascade filter that meets as closely as possible the specifications of the original non-factorable filter. The factorization results are summarized in Tables 2 and 3. Note that due to the maximum similarity achieved between the frequency responses there is an small expense in terms of coefficient similarity, which is however distributed both along the numerator and denominator coefficients.

V. Conclusion

In this paper, an efficient algorithm was proposed for factorizing simultaneously the numerator and denominator polynomials of the transfer functions of 2-D IIR filters. The method is useful for designing IIR filters in cascade form for more efficient hardware implementation. By introducing a cost function based on the difference of frequency responses between the original and cascade filter and using a flexible framework for incorporating additional information in the form of constraints, we obtained optimal stable solutions for non-factorable filters.

APPENDIX: Derivation of Constrained Optimization Algorithm

The constrained optimization problem defined in section II.can be solved analytically by introducing two Lagrange multipliers L_1 and L_2 to take account of eqns (14) and (12) respectively and a vector of multipliers Λ to take account of eqn (13). We thus introduce the quantity

$$\begin{aligned}\kappa' &= \kappa + L_1(dE - \delta Q) + L_2[dw^T dw - (\delta P)^2] \\ &+ \sum_c \Lambda_c(\frac{1}{\Phi_c}d\Phi_c + \kappa)\end{aligned} \tag{24}$$

where the index c runs over all constraints.

On evaluating the differentials involved in the right hand side, we readily obtain:

$$\begin{aligned}\kappa' &= \kappa + L_1(G^T dw - \delta Q) \\ &+ L_2[dw^T dw - (\delta P)^2] + \Lambda^T(F dw + \kappa 1)\end{aligned} \tag{25}$$

To maximize κ under the required constraints, we demand that:

$$\begin{aligned}d\kappa' &= d\kappa(1 + \Lambda^T 1) \\ &+ (L_1 G^T + \Lambda^T F + 2L_2 dw^T)d^2 w = 0\end{aligned} \tag{26}$$

$$d^2\kappa' = 2L_2 d^2 w^T d^2 w < 0 \tag{27}$$

Hence, the factors multiplying $d^2 w$ and $d\kappa$ in eqn (26) should vanish, and therefore we obtain:

$$dw = -\frac{L_1}{2L_2}G - \frac{1}{2L_2}F^T\Lambda \tag{28}$$

$$\Lambda^T 1 = -1 \tag{29}$$

Note that eqn (28) is identical to the weight update rule of eqn (23). It therefore remains to evaluate L_1, L_2 and Λ in terms of known quantities.

By multiplying both sides of eqn (28) by G^T and by taking into account eqn (14) we obtain:

$$\delta Q = -\frac{L_1}{2L_2}I_{GG} - \frac{1}{2L_2}\Lambda^T I_{GF} \tag{30}$$

Solving for L_1 readily yields eqn (22), which evaluates L_1 in terms of L_2 and Λ.

By left multiplication of both sides of eqn (28) by F and taking into account eqns (13) and (22), we obtain

$$\kappa 1 + \frac{\delta Q I_{GF}}{I_{GG}} = \frac{R\Lambda}{2L_2} \tag{31}$$

where the matrix R is defined by eqn (18). Solving eqn (31) for Λ yields

$$\Lambda = 2L_2\kappa R^{-1}1 + \frac{2L_2\delta Q}{I_{GG}}R^{-1}I_{GF} \tag{32}$$

By substituting this equation into eqn (29) we arrive at:

$$\kappa = -\frac{1 + \frac{2L_2\delta Q}{I_{GG}}1^T R^{-1} I_{GF}}{2L_2(R^{-1})_a} \tag{33}$$

We can now substitute this equation into eqn (32) to obtain eqn (21) which evaluates Λ in terms of L_2.

To evaluate L_2, we must substitute our expression for dw into eqn (12). To make the algebra easier, we note that on account of eqn (22), eqn (28) can be written as:

$$dw = \frac{\delta Q}{I_{GG}}G + \frac{1}{2L_2}A \tag{34}$$

where

$$A = \frac{\Lambda^T I_{GF}}{I_{GG}}G - F^T\Lambda \tag{35}$$

From the definition of A we can readily derive the following properties:

$$||A||^2 = \Lambda^T R\Lambda, \quad A^T G = 0 \tag{36}$$

Substituting eqn (34) into eqn (12) and taking into account eqn (36), we can obtain a relation involving only L_2 and Λ:

$$L_2 = -\frac{1}{2}\left[\frac{I_{GG}(\Lambda^T R\Lambda)}{I_{GG}(\delta P)^2 - (\delta Q)^2}\right]^{1/2} \tag{37}$$

where the negative square root sign has been selected on account of inequality (27).

By substituting eqn (21) into eqn (37) and solving for L_2, eqn (20) is obtained, with Z given by eqn (19). Evaluation of all Lagrange multipliers in terms of known quantities is now complete.

As a final note, let us discuss our choice for δQ. This choice is dictated by the demand that the quantity under the square root in eqn (37) be positive. It can readily be seen by the first of eqn (36) that $\Lambda^T R\Lambda \geq 0$. Since $I_{GG} = G^T G \geq 0$, it follows from eqn (37) that care must be taken to ensure that $I_{GG}(\delta P)^2 > (\delta Q)^2$. The simplest way to achieve this is to set $\delta Q = -\xi\delta P\sqrt{I_{GG}}$ with $0 < \xi < 1$.

References

[1] J. S. Lim, *Two-Dimensional Signal and Image Processing*, Prentice-Hall International, 1990.

[2] Z. Mou-Yan and R. Unbehauen, "On the approximate factorization of 2-D polynomials," *IEEE Trans. Acoust., Speech, and Signal Processing*, vol. ASSP-35, pp. 577–579, 1987.

[3] N. E. Mastorakis, N. J. Theodorou, and S .G. Tzafestas, "A general factorization method for multivariable polynomials," *Multidimensional Systems and Signal Processing*, vol. 5, pp. 151–178, 1994.

[4] P. Misra and R. V. Patel, "Simple factorizability of 2-D polynomials," in *Proc. Int. Symp. Circ. Syst.*, New Orleans, 1990, pp. 1207–1210.

[5] N. E. Mastorakis and N. J. Theodorou, "Exact and approximate multidimensional polynomial factorization. Application on measurement processing," *Foundations of computing and decision science*, vol. 19, no. 4, pp. 309–317, 1994.

[6] N. E. Mastorakis, "Approximate multidimensional polynomial factorization into general m-D polynomial factors," *Control and Cybernetics*, vol. 25, no. 4, pp. 809–821, 1996.

[7] N. E. Mastorakis, "Approximate and stable separable polynomial factorization," *Foundations of Computing and Desicion Science*, vol. 21, no. 1, pp. 55–64, 1996.

[8] N. E. Mastorakis, "A method of approximate multidimensional factorization via the singular value decomposition," *Found. of Comput. Desic. Sci.*, vol. 21, no. 3, pp.137–144, 1996.

[9] S. J. Perantonis, N. Ampazis, S. Varoufakis, and G. Antoniou, "Constrained learning in neural networks: Application to stable factorization of 2-D polynomials," *Neural Proc. Lett.*, vol. 7, pp. 5–14, 1998.

[10] T. S. Huang, "Stability of two-dimensional recursive filters," *IEEE Trans. Audio Electoacoust.* , vol. AU-20, pp. 158-163, 1972.

[11] A. E. Bryson and W. F. Denham, "A steepest ascent method for solving optimum programming problems," *Journal App. Mech.*, vol. 29, pp. 247-257, 1962.

$$
\begin{aligned}
X_1 &= (v_{10}^{(1)})^2 \\
X_2 &= (v_{10}^{(2)})^2 \\
X_3 &= (v_{01}^{(1)})^2 + (v_{11}^{(1)})^2 + 2v_{01}^{(1)}v_{11}^{(1)} - (v_{10}^{(1)})^2 - 2v_{10}^{(1)} \\
X_4 &= (v_{01}^{(1)})^2 + (v_{11}^{(1)})^2 - 2v_{01}^{(1)}v_{11}^{(1)} - (v_{10}^{(1)})^2 + 2v_{10}^{(1)} \\
X_5 &= (v_{01}^{(2)})^2 + (v_{11}^{(2)})^2 + 2v_{01}^{(2)}v_{11}^{(2)} - (v_{10}^{(2)})^2 - 2v_{10}^{(2)} \\
X_6 &= (v_{01}^{(2)})^2 + (v_{11}^{(2)})^2 - 2v_{01}^{(2)}v_{11}^{(2)} - (v_{10}^{(2)})^2 + 2v_{10}^{(2)}
\end{aligned}
$$

Table 1: Stability constraints for the denominator polynomial.

	Original non-factorable	Proposed method
Numerator Polynomial Coefficient Matrix $\boldsymbol{B}$	$\begin{bmatrix} 1 & 0.4000 & 0.0300 \\ 0.2500 & 0.3350 & 0.0700 \\ 0.0100 & 0.0450 & 0.0200 \end{bmatrix}$	$\begin{bmatrix} 1 & 0.3998 & -0.2742 \\ 0.2499 & 0.3387 & 0.0837 \\ -0.2556 & 0.0247 & 0.1840 \end{bmatrix}$
1st Factor Polynomial Coefficient Matrix	--	$\begin{bmatrix} 1 & 0.7605 \\ 0.6461 & 0.5175 \end{bmatrix}$
2nd Factor Polynomial Coefficient Matrix	--	$\begin{bmatrix} 1 & -0.3607 \\ -0.3962 & 0.3556 \end{bmatrix}$

Table 2: Factorization results for the numerator polynomial.

	Original non-factorable	Proposed method
Denominator Polynomial Coefficient Matrix $\boldsymbol{A}$	$\begin{bmatrix} 1 & -1.1636 & 0.3385 \\ -1.1636 & 1.2888 & -0.3327 \\ 0.3385 & -0.3327 & 0.0817 \end{bmatrix}$	$\begin{bmatrix} 1 & -1.1633 & 0.3338 \\ -1.1633 & 1.2939 & -0.3550 \\ 0.3298 & -0.3474 & 0.0909 \end{bmatrix}$
1st Factor Polynomial Coefficient Matrix	--	$\begin{bmatrix} 1 & -0.5146 \\ -0.6739 & 0.3263 \end{bmatrix}$
2nd Factor Polynomial Coefficient Matrix	--	$\begin{bmatrix} 1 & -0.6487 \\ -0.4895 & 0.2786 \end{bmatrix}$

Table 3: Factorization results for the denominator polynomial.

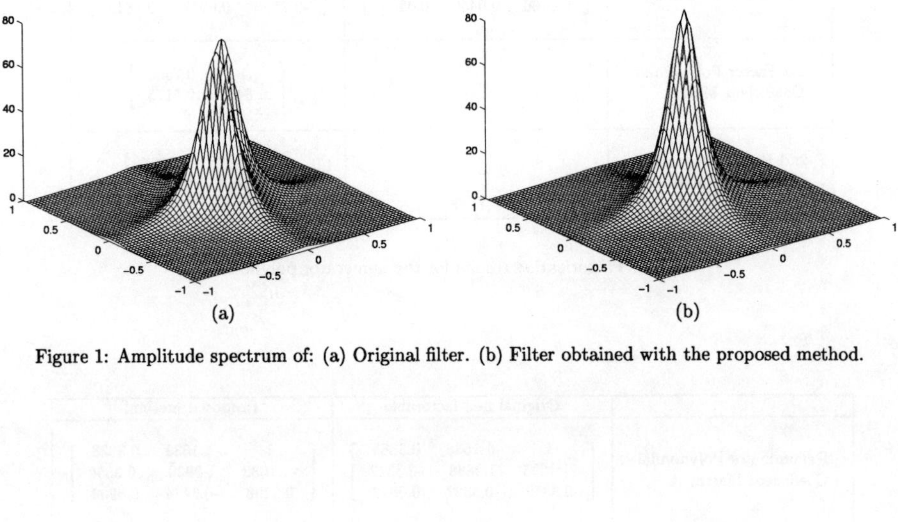

Figure 1: Amplitude spectrum of: (a) Original filter. (b) Filter obtained with the proposed method.

A Method for Computing the 2-D Stability Margin Based on a New Stability test for 2-D Systems

Nikos E. Mastorakis,
Military Institutions of University Education (MIUE),
Hellenic Naval Academy, Chair of Computer Science,
Terma Hatzikyriakou, 18539, Piraeus, GREECE.
Tel-Fax: +301 7775660, Fax: +301 4181768
email: mastor@softlab.ntua.gr
http://www.softlab.ntua.gr/~mastor

ABSTRACT

A new method to compute the stability margin of 2-D discrete systems is considered. The method is based on a recently proposed 2-D stability test by the author. The method is supported by illustrative examples.

1. INTRODUCTION

Nowadays, 2-D and *m*-D (*m*>2) system theory possess a "high" position in the systems theory and in general in applied mathematics and modern computer science. In particular, Discrete Linear and Shift Invariant (LSI) 2-D systems are attracting the attention of many engineers and scientists due to their extended applications in Digital Image Processing, Applied Mathematics, Biomedicine, Underwater Acoustics, Modelling, and Modern Computer Architecture.

In order to ensure that any bounded input will produce a bounded output, the considered 2-D (LSI) system should be (Hurwitz) stable. Consider a Discrete LSI single-input single-output 2-D system described by the transfer function:

$$G(z_1,z_2)=\frac{A(z_1,z_2)}{B(z_1,z_2)} \quad (1)$$

$A(z_1,z_2)$ and $B(z_1,z_2)$ are coprime polynomials in the independent complex variables z_1 and z_2. It is assumed that there are no nonessential singularities of the second kind on the closed unit bidisk, i.e. there are no points (z_1,z_2) with $|z_1|\le 1$ and $|z_2|\le 1$ such that $A(z_1,z_2)=B(z_1,z_2)=0$.

It is also well known that the system (1) is (Hurwitz) stable if and only if

$$B(0,z_2)\neq 0, \quad \text{for} \quad |z_2|\le 1 \quad (2.1)$$

$$B(z_1,z_2)\neq 0, \quad \text{for} \quad |z_1|\le 1, \quad |z_2|=1 \quad (2.2)$$

Henceforth, the following notation will be used

$$B(z_1,z_2)=\sum_{i_1=0}^{N_1}\sum_{i_2=0}^{N_2} b_{i_1,i_2} z_1^{i_1} z_2^{i_2}=\sum_{i=0}^{N_1} b_i(z_2) z_1^i \quad (3)$$

where $b_i(z_2)=\sum_{i_2=0}^{N_2} b_{i,i_2} z_2^{i_2}$. Equation (2.1) is relatively easy to check using any 1-D stability test. Equation (2.2) is more difficult since it includes two variables. Additionally, the polynomial $B(z_1,z_2)$ is said to be *(Hurwitz) Stable* if and only if (2.1) and (2.2) are fulfilled.

There exist several algebraic methods for testing the stability of 2-D discrete systems or, equivalently, checking the Hurwitz character of 2-D polynomials [1].

In the study of 2-D systems, we are interested not only in whether the system is stable but also whether the system will remain stable in the presence of system parameter deviations.

For this reason, for a stable 2-D (discrete) system, the following definitions have been introduced [3]:

Definition 1: Given a 2-D discrete system LSI described by the transfer function (1), we call stability margin σ_1 the supremum (i.e. the lower upper bound) of the positive real numbers for which $B((1+\sigma_1)\cdot z_1, z_2)$ is a *(Hurwitz) Stable Polynomial.*

Definition 2: Given a 2-D discrete system described by the transfer function (1), we call stability margin σ_2 the supremum of the positive real numbers for which $B(z_1,(1+\sigma_2)\cdot z_2)$ is a *(Hurwitz) Stable Polynomial.*

Definition 3: Given a 2-D discrete LSI system described by the transfer function (1), we call stability margin σ the supremum of the positive real numbers for which $B((1+\sigma)\cdot z_1,(1+\sigma)\cdot z_2)$ is a *(Hurwitz) Stable Polynomial.*

One should notice that the special case where the stable system has nonessential singularities of the second kind on the closed unit bidisk is excluded, since all three stability margins will be zero.

For the evaluation of the stability margin several methods already exist [3÷8]. In this paper, a new method is proposed. It is based on a recently proposed method for checking the stability of a 2-D system [9].

2 COMPUTATION OF THE STABILITY MARGINS FOR A 2-D (DISCRETE, LSI etc) SYSTEM

In [9], a new test for checking Condition (2.2) is proposed. This test is formulated by way of a theorem:

Theorem:: $B(z_1,z_2)\neq 0$, for $|z_1|\leq 1$, $|z_2|=1$, if and only if the matrix

$$C(z_2)= = a_0^*(z_2)A^{N_1}+a_1^*(z_2)A^{N_1-1}+\ldots+a_{N_1-1}^*(z_2)A+I_{N_1}$$

(the asterisk indicates complex conjugate)

(i) is positive definite for a z_2 with $|z_2|=1$, and

(ii) det{$C(z_2)$}>0 for all z_2 with $|z_2|=1$, where

$$A=\begin{bmatrix} 0 & 1 & 0 & \cdot\ \cdot & 0 \\ 0 & 0 & 1 & \cdot\ \cdot & 0 \\ & & \vdots & & \\ 0 & 0 & 0 & \cdot\ \cdot & 1 \\ -a_0(z_2) & -a_1(z_2) & -a_2(z_2) & \cdot\ \cdot & -a_{N_1-1}(z_2) \end{bmatrix} \tag{4}$$

where

$$a_i(z_2)=\frac{b_{N_1-i}(z_2)}{b_0(z_2)} \tag{5}$$

$$i=0,\ldots,N_1-1$$ ♦

In [13], the evaluation of C is achieved properly (Please, see [13]). Here C=$C(z_2)$.

In this paragraph, a new method of computing the stability margins of 2-D systems is presented. First, we introduce the notation

$$k_1=1+\sigma_1 \tag{6}$$

For a stable 2-D discrete system, we recall that the polynomial $B(z_1,z_2)$ is a *(Hurwitz) Stable Polynomial* if and only if: (2.1) holds and (i) and (ii) of the above Theorem are fulfilled. Therefore $B(k_1z_1,z_2)$ remains *(Hurwitz) Stable Polynomial* if and only if (2.1) holds and (i) and (ii) of the above Theorem are fulfilled. However, because of the assumed stability of the considered system, (2.1) holds independent of k_1. (Note that (2.1) does not contain z_1, consequently it does not contain k_1). Thus, $B(k_1z_1,z_2)$ remains *(Hurwitz) Stable Polynomial* if and only and (i) and (ii) of the above Theorem are fulfilled. It is easy to verify (for a detailed justification see Appendix), that for the supremum of k_1 for which $B(k_1z_1,z_2)$ is *(Hurwitz) Stable* the matrix $C(k_1,z_2)$ will be singular i.e.

$detC(k_1,z_2)$=0 (for some z_2, $z_2 = e^{j\phi_2}$ and $\phi_2 \in [0,2\pi]$). Therefore, the supremum of k_1 for which $B(k_1 z_1, z_2)$ is *(Hurwitz) Stable* is simultaneously the *minimum* of all k_1 with $detC(k_1,z_2)$=0 (for some z_2, $z_2 = e^{j\phi_2}$ and $\phi_2 \in [0,2\pi]$). This implies that the computation of k_1 can be achieved by solving the following minimization problem

$$min\ k_1 \tag{7.1}$$

under the constraint

$$detC(k_1,z_2)=0 \tag{7.2}$$

where $C(k_1,z_2)$ is evaluated in the same way as $C(z_2)$. See [13]. Then, we easily obtain σ_1 from Equation (6).

By interchanging the roles of the variables z_1 and z_2, a completely analogous method for the computation of σ_2 is obtained.

Analogously, for the computation of σ we denote

$$k=1+\sigma \tag{8}$$

Here, instead of (2.1) and (2.2), we use the equivalent condition $B(z_1,z_2) \neq 0$, for $|z_1| \leq 1$, $|z_2| \leq 1$, [1]. So, k is the supremum of the real numbers (≥ 1) for which $B(kz_1, kz_2) \neq 0$, for $|z_1| \leq 1$, $|z_2| \leq 1$. Varying only z_2, one can obtain that this condition is equivalent to

$B(kz_1, kz_2) \neq 0$, for $|z_1| \leq 1$, $|z_2| = 1$.

This latter equation is analogous to Equation (2.2). Therefore, following exactly the same steps as in the case of the stability margin σ_1, we state the following method for the stability margin σ.

$$min\ k \tag{9.1}$$

under the constraint

$$detC(k,z_2)=0 \tag{9.2}$$

where $C(k,z_2)$ is evaluated in the same way as $C(z_2)$. See [13]. The following example illustrates the implementation of this method.

Example 1 [3÷8]: Let us consider the general first order characteristic polynomial of a stable system

$$B(z_1,z_2) = 1 + az_1 + bz_2 + cz_1z_2 \tag{10}$$

where *a, b, c* are real numbers. We always assume that the corresponding 2-D system has no nonessential singularities of the second kind. For the computation of the stability margin σ_1, one forms the matrix $C(k_1,z_2)$. This is

$$C(k_1,z_2) = -k_1\left(\frac{a+cz_2}{1+bz_2}\right)^* k_1 \frac{a+cz_2}{1+bz_2} + 1 \tag{11}$$

where $z_2 = e^{j\phi_2}$ and $\phi_2 \in [0,2\pi]$ and the asterisk denotes complex conjugate. Then

$$detC(k_1,z_2) = \frac{-(a^2+c^2+2acx)k_1^2 + (1+b^2+2bx)}{1+b^2+2bx}$$

where $x = cos\,\phi_2$ ($x \in [-1,1]$). So, the problem of (7.1) and (7.2) is reduced to

$$min\ k_1 \tag{12.1}$$

under the constraint

$$-(a^2+c^2+2acx)k_1^2 + (1+b^2+2bx)=0 \tag{12.2}$$

One obtains that

$$-(a^2+c^2+2acx)k_1^2 + (1+b^2+2bx)$$

is linear in *x*. So, for a certain k_1 the minimum value of $-(a^2+c^2+2acx)k_1^2 + (1+b^2+2bx)$

is obtained for $x=+1$ (if $ack_1^2-b\geq 0$) or for $x=-1$ (if $ack_1^2-b<0$). Thus, for the *minimum* k_1 with $-\left(a^2+c^2+2acx\right)k_1^2+\left(1+b^2+2bx\right)=0$, $detC\left(k_1,z_2\right)$ will be zero for $x=\pm 1$. Therefore, for the minimum k_1, we obtain:

$$\left(a^2+c^2+2ac\right)k_1^2-\left(1+b^2+2b\right)=0 \qquad (13.1)$$

or

$$\left(a^2+c^2-2ac\right)k_1^2-\left(1+b^2-2b\right)=0 \qquad (13.2)$$

Solving (13.1) and (13.2), we find

$k_1=min\left[\frac{|1+b|}{|a+c|},\frac{|1-b|}{|a-c|}\right]$. From which

$$\sigma_1=min\left[\frac{|1+b|}{|a+c|},\frac{|1-b|}{|a-c|}\right]-1 \qquad (14)$$

Consequently, interchanging the variables z_1 and z_2, one evaluates

$$\sigma_2=min\left[\frac{|1+a|}{|b+c|},\frac{|1-a|}{|b-c|}\right]-1 \qquad (15)$$

The results agree with those of [3]÷[8]. Note that here they derived in a very simple manner.

Let us also compute σ. We form the matrix $C\left(k,z_2\right)$. This is

$$C\left(k,z_2\right)=-k\left(\frac{a+ckz_2}{1+bkz_2}\right)^{*}k\frac{a+ckz_2}{1+bkz_2}+1 \qquad (16)$$

Then

$$detC\left(k,z_2\right)=$$

$$\frac{-k^2\left(a^2+c^2k^2+2ackx\right)+\left(1+b^2k^2+2bkx\right)}{1+b^2k^2+2bkx}$$

where $x=cos\,\phi_2$ ($x\in[-1,1]$). So, the problem of (9.1) and (9.2) is reduced to

$$min\ k \qquad (17.1)$$

under the constraint

$$k^2\left(a^2+c^2k^2+2ackx\right)-\left(1+b^2k^2+2bkx\right)=0 \qquad (17.2)$$

where $x=cos\,\phi_1$. One also obtains that $k^2\left(a^2+c^2k^2+2ackx\right)-\left(1+b^2k^2+2bkx\right)$ is also linear in *x*. So, for a certain *k* the minimum value of

$$k^2\left(a^2+c^2k^2+2ackx\right)-\left(1+b^2k^2+2bkx\right)$$

is obtained for $x=\pm 1$. Thus, for the minimum *k* with

$$k^2\left(a^2+c^2k^2+2ackx\right)-\left(1+b^2k^2+2bkx\right)=0,$$

$k^2\left(a^2+c^2k^2+2ackx\right)-\left(1+b^2k^2+2bkx\right)$ will be zero for $x=\pm 1$. Therefore, we obtain for the minimum *k*:

$$k^2\left(a^2+c^2k^2+2ack\right)-\left(1+b^2k^2+2bk\right)=0 \qquad (18.1)$$

or

$$k^2\left(a^2+c^2k^2-2ack\right)-\left(1+b^2k^2-2bk\right)=0 \qquad (18.2)$$

Solving (18.1), (18.2) we find $k=$ *minimum* of the real positive values of the set

$$\left\{\frac{a+b\pm\sqrt{(a+b)^2-4c}}{2c}, \frac{-a+b\pm\sqrt{(-a+b)^2+4c}}{2c},\right.$$

$$\left.\frac{a-b\pm\sqrt{(a-b)^2+4c}}{2c}, \frac{-a-b\pm\sqrt{(-a-b)^2-4c}}{2c}\right\}$$

From which $\sigma = k-1$. All the results agree with those derived in [3]÷[8], but here they derived in an easier manner.

Example 2 [6]: Consider $B(z_1,z_2)=3-z_1-z_2$. Following the above procedure we obtain $\sigma_1=1,\sigma_2=1$ as well as $\sigma=0.5$. The latter can be obtained from (15.1) and (15.2) if we put $a=b=-1/3$ and $c=0$.

Remark: An interesting genaralization of the Definitions of σ_1,σ_2,σ could be the following:

Definition of the stability margin σ with weights λ_1,λ_2 ($\lambda_1+\lambda_2=1, \lambda_1\geq 0$ & $\lambda_2\geq 0$) Given a 2-D discrete system described by the transfer function (1), we call stability margin σ the supremum of the positive real numbers for which $B((1+\lambda_1\sigma)\cdot z_1,(1+\lambda_2\sigma)\cdot z_2)$ is a *(Hurwitz) Stable Polynomial.*

Taking into account this definition, we can consider Definitions 1÷3 as special cases of the previous definition (Definition 3 needs a slight modification). Moreover, modifying the above method, one can easily derive a general algorithm for evaluating the stability margin σ with weights λ_1,λ_2.

3 CONCLUSIONS

A new method for computing the stability margins have been proposed. The method is based on a constrained optimization problem of a real positive parameter. Since the present formulation of the determinant is better, with respect to the computational complexity, than the formulation of the Schour-Cohn matrix [1], [9], the method, is better than the method of [3]. The significance of the proposed computational method and the improvement with respect to previous work in [3]÷[8] is that we have to solve a constrained minimization problem without computing various partial derivatives and solving a problem of non-linear equations as in [4]÷[8]. Other recent results can also be found in [2].

4. APPENDIX

Consider the mapping $\delta\colon k_1\to\delta(k_1)$ where $\delta(k_1)=C(k_1,z_2)$. This is a *continuous* mapping since the matrix $C(k_1,z_2)$ consists of rational functions in k_1,z_2. Also, consider the mapping *det* : $\delta(k_1)\to det\,\delta(k_1)$. This is also a continuous mapping.

Therefore, their synthesis $det\,\delta\colon k_1\to det\,\delta(k_1)$ is also a continuous mapping. We denote S, the set S = $\{\delta(k_1)\text{ with }\delta(k_1)>0\}$, where > denotes positive definiteness for all z_2 with $z_2=e^{j\phi_2}$ and $\phi_2\in[0,2\pi]$, [9]. We also denote *det*{S} the subset of the real numbers which consists of all the determinants of $\delta(k_1)$ that belong to S. Evidently, *det*{S} is the set of all the (strictly) positive real numbers. Thus, the only limit point of *det*{S} is the 0.

S is an *open* set and because of the continuity of the mapping δ, the corresponding set of k_1 will also be *open* (see any standard textbook of *Real Analysis* or *Topology*, [12]). Thus, the supremum of k_1 is a limit point of this set and because of the continuity of the mapping δ, for this k_1, $\delta(k_1)$ is also a limit point of S. Furthermore by the continuity of the mapping $det\colon\delta(k_1)\to det\,\delta(k_1)$, $det\delta(k_1)$ is limit point in the set *det*{S}, for this k_1. Since the only limit point of *det*{S} is the 0, we conclude that for this k_1, we have $det\delta(k_1)=0$.

As a result, we obtain that for the supremum of k_1 for which $B(k_1 z_1, z_2)$ is *(Hurwitz) Stable*, the matrix $C(k_1, z_2)$ will be singular (for some z_2, $z_2 = e^{j\phi_2}$ and $\phi_2 \in [0, 2\pi]$).

5. REFERENCES

[1] E.I.Jury, "Stability of Multidimensional Systems and Related Problems", *in Multidimensional Systems (Techniques and Applications)*, Marcel Dekker, Inc, New York 1986, edited by Spyros G. Tzafestas.

[2] N.E.Mastorakis, "Recursive Algorithms for Two-Dimensional Filters' Spectral Transformations" *IEEE Trans.Signal Processing* , Vol. SP-44, No.10, p.2647-2651, Oct.1996.

[3] P.Agathoklis, E.I.Jury and M.Mansour, "The margin of stability of 2-D linear discrete systems", *IEEE Trans. Acoust. Speech Signal Process.*, Vol. ASSP-30, No.6, Dec.1982, pp.869-873.

[4] E.Walach and E.Zeheb, "*N*-Dimensional stability margins computation and a variable transformation", *IEEE Trans. Acoust. Speech Signal Process.*, Vol. ASSP-30, No.6, Dec.1982, pp.887-893.

[5] W.-S. Lu, A.Antoniou and P.Agathoklis, "Stability of 2-D digital filters under parameter variations", *IEEE Trans. Circuits and Systems*, Vol. CAS-33, No.5, May 1986, pp.476-482.

[6] L.M.Roytman, M.N.S.Swamy and G.Eichmann, "An efficient numerical scheme to compute 2-D stability thresholds", *IEEE Trans. Circ. Syst.*, vol.CAS-34, No.3, March 1987, pp.322-324.

[7] M.Wang, E.B.Lee and D.Booley, "A simple method to determine the stability and the margin of stability of 2-D recursive filters". *IEEE Trans. Circ. Syst.-I: Fundamental Theory and Applications*, vol.39, No.3, March 1992, pp.237-239.

[8] D.Hertz and E.Zeheb, "Simplifications in Multidimensional stability margin computations, *IEEE Trans. Acoust. Speech Signal Process.*, Vol. ASSP-35, No.4, April 1987, pp.566-568.

[9] N.E.Mastorakis, "New Stability Test for 2-D Systems", *Foundations of Computing and Decision Sciences*, Vol.21, No.2, 1996, pp.115-122.

[10] R.P.Roesser, "A discrete state-space model for image processing," *IEEE Trans. Automat. Contr.*, vol. AC-20, Feb. 1975, pp. 1-10.

[11] E.I.Jury, "Modified Stability Table for 2-D Digital Filters", *IEEE Trans. Circuits and Systems*, Jan.1988, pp.116-119.

[12] W.Sutherland. *Introduction to Metric and Topological Spaces*. Clarendon Press, Oxford, 1975.

[13] S.Barnett, "Number of zeros of a complex polynomial inside the unit circle", Electronics Letters, Vol. 6, No. 6, 1970, pp.164-165.

UNSUPERVISED CLASSIFICATION AND FUSION OF MULTIDIMENSIONAL SIDESCAN SONAR DATA

U. Hoelscher-Hoebing and D. Kraus

STN ATLAS Elektronik GmbH
Sebaldsbrücker Heerstraße 235
D-28305 Bremen
Tel. : 0421/457-2583
Fax.: 0421/457-2020,
e-mail: hoelscher.u@stn-atlas.de

ABSTRACT

In the development of future sonar systems computer aided classification (CAC) becomes increasingly important. One element in a Multi-Beam/Multi-Aspect sidescan sonar CAC system is the classification and image fusion of the multidimensional data. In this context, recent developments have been made to prevent the effects of aspect dependent backscattering strength (target strength) of objects lying on the sea floor. Because the target strength of an object varies with aspect angle, the sonar echo and consequently its representation in the sidescan image is rather random. To make sure that a maximum echo strength is obtained, overlapping bottom areas are insonified by temporal successive pings giving the echoes of the target under different aspect angles. The resulting images of successive pings are fusioned to one sidescan image. The existing image fusion algorithms [6] now require an operator to set threshold values distinguishing target and shadow zones from bottom reverberation zones. Here we propose an unsupervised method for classification and optimal fusion of multidimensional sidescan sonar images for Multi-Beam/Multi-Aspect sidescan sonars.

1 INTRODUCTION

The new procedure has been developed for unsupervised classification and image fusion of successive ping images. Its basic steps are

- image segmentation by means of the EM algorithm.
- clustering of image segments applying the Markov random field approach.
- fusion of successive pings images following a minimum/mean/maximum strategy according to the results of image segmentation and clustering.

The image segmentation and image clustering steps together are considered as a classification step.

Sidescan sonar performs imaging of the sea floor and the objects lying there. It shows bottom reverberation, target and the corresponding shadow zones. The data from the different sources represent three different image pixel classes:

- class 1: shadow - low intensity pixel
- class 2: bottom reverberation - medium intensity pixel
- class 3: target - high intensity pixel

Due to the signal processing performed on the raw data the image pixels are independent and their distribution is the Rayleigh probability density function (PDF)

$$f(y)=\begin{cases}\frac{y}{\sigma^2}e^{\frac{-y^2}{2\sigma^2}}, & \text{for } y\geq 0\\ 0, & \text{otherwise}\end{cases}, \quad (1)$$

cf. [1]. The analyzed Multi-Beam/Multi-Aspect sidescan sonar images have been taken from sea trials.

The organization of this paper is as follows. In section 2 the image segmentation algorithm and its result for sidescan sonar images is shown. Section 3 presents the image clustering procedure and its application. Finally in section 4, the fusion strategy based upon the previously performed processing is demonstrated. The advantages of the unsupervised method are then addressed in section 5.

2 IMAGE SEGMENTATION

Image segmentation is considered as the process of separating the image into a set of disjunct regions associated with a number of classes that are modelled as distinct random fields. The observed image is regarded as a mixture of several data classes with the class status of each pixel unknown; that is the correct segmentation is not known. The problem of estimating the model parameters of the data classes directly from the image leads to the incomplete data problem.

Let $\mathbf{z}=(\mathbf{x},\mathbf{y})$ be a set of random data, where $\mathbf{y}=(y_1,y_2,\dots y_N)$, N = number of image pixels, is the observed data and $\mathbf{x}=(x_1,x_2,\dots x_N)$ is the part of $\mathbf{z}$ that is not observable. Here $\mathbf{y}$ is the set of image pixel intensities with $\mathbf{y}\in R$ whereas $\mathbf{x}$ is the class status of the pixels which is not observable taking its values in $\Omega=(\omega_1,\omega_2,\dots,\omega_l)$. Usually $\mathbf{y}$ is called the incomplete data and $\mathbf{z}$ is called the complete data.

Let $f(\mathbf{z}|\Theta)$ be the PDF of the complete data, where Θ is a set of parameters that characterize the density function. The incomplete data problem is to estimate Θ based only on the observations represented by the incomplete data $\mathbf{y}$. A maximum likelihood approach is used to find an estimate $\hat{\Theta}$. The most effective algorithm for solving the problem is the iterative Expectation Maximization (EM) algorithm which consists of the following steps

- Initialization
  Initial guess of the parameter set Θ
- Expectation-Step (E-step)
  At each iteration step k calculate
  $$Q(\Theta,\hat{\Theta}^k) = E\left[\log f(z|\Theta)|y,\hat{\Theta}^k\right] \quad (2)$$
- Maximization-Step (M-step)
  At each iteration step k solve
  $$\hat{\Theta}^{k+1} = \arg\max_{\Theta} Q(\Theta,\hat{\Theta}^k) \quad (3)$$

Solutions for this approach exist only for a limited number of PDFs, e. g. normal-, beta- or gamma-distribution ([2], [3], [4]). In case of sidescan sonar images the following assumptions are made:

The PDF (1) of the image pixels $\mathbf{y}$ can be approximated by a gamma distribution with q=4 degrees of freedom (DOF):

$$f(y) = \begin{cases} \dfrac{q^q}{\mu^q \Gamma(q)} y^{q-1} e^{-\frac{yq}{\mu}}, & \text{for } y \geq 0 \\ 0, & \text{otherwise} \end{cases} \quad (4)$$

where $\Gamma(q)$ = gamma-function, and $\mu > 0$.

Due to the three different classes in the sidescan sonar image x is taking its values in $\Omega = (\omega_1,\omega_2,\omega_3)$. $\mathbf{x}$ and $\mathbf{y}$ are independent and the set of parameters Θ characterizing the PDF is

$$\Theta = (\pi_1,\pi_2,\pi_3,\mu_1,\mu_2,\mu_3), \quad (5)$$

where

$$\pi_p = f(x = \omega_p|y), \; p=1,2,3 \quad (6)$$

$$\pi_1 + \pi_2 + \pi_3 = 1, \quad (7)$$

and μ_p denotes the parameter of the pth PDF.

The steps of the EM-Algorithm are then in detail:

Initialization

Let

$\hat{\Theta}^0 = (\pi_1^0,\pi_2^0,\pi_3^0,\mu_1^0,\mu_2^0,\mu_3^0)$

be the initial estimate of

$\Theta = (\pi_1,\pi_2,\pi_3,\mu_1,\mu_2,\mu_3)$.

Maximum Likelihood Estimation

Calculate

$\hat{\Theta}^{k+1} = (\pi_1^{k+1},\pi_2^{k+1},\pi_3^{k+1},\mu_1^{k+1},\mu_2^{k+1},\mu_3^{k+1})$

from the estimation in the previous iteration step k

$\hat{\Theta}^k = (\pi_1^k,\pi_2^k,\pi_3^k,\mu_1^k,\mu_2^k,\mu_3^k)$

and $\mathbf{y}$ by:

a) E-Step
In each iteration step k estimate the PDF of $\mathbf{x}$ conditioned on $\mathbf{y}$ for each y_i, $1 \leq i \leq N$. (N = Number of pixels). Let f_1^k, f_2^k, f_3^k be the PDFs f_1, f_2, f_3 of the three classes at iteration step k with the parameter set

$$\hat{\Theta}^k = (\pi_1^k,\pi_2^k,\pi_3^k,\mu_1^k,\mu_2^k,\mu_3^k)$$

$$f_p^k(y_i) = f(y_i|\omega_p,\hat{\Theta}^k) \quad (8)$$

and

$$\pi_{p,i}^k = E\left[x_i|y_i,\hat{\Theta}^k\right] = f(x_i = \omega_p|y_i) = \frac{\pi_p^k f_p^k(y_i)}{\sum_{m=1}^{3} \pi_m^k f_m(y_i)}. \quad (9)$$

b) M-Step
In each iteration step calculate

$$\pi_p^{k+1} = \frac{1}{N}\sum_{i=1}^{N} \pi_{p,i}^k \quad (10)$$

$$\mu_p^{k+1} = \frac{1}{N\pi_p^{k+1}} \sum_{i=1}^{N} \frac{y_i \pi_p^{k+1} f_p^k(y_i,\mu_p^k)}{g^k(y_i)} \quad (11)$$

where:

$$g^k(y_i) = \sum_{m=1}^{3} \pi_{m,i}^k f_m^k(y_i,\mu_m^k). \quad (12)$$

Iteration is stopped when

$\hat{\Theta} = (\pi_1,\pi_2,\pi_3,\mu_1,\mu_2,\mu_3)$

stabilizes. The result is a soft estimate of the class status of each pixel.

An example of a detail single ping sidescan sonar image showing sea floor, target and corresponding shadow is given in Fig. 1. Figs. 2 and 3 show the result of the segmentation of Fig. 1 which has to be chosen with a significant number of pixels in each class. Fig. 2 shows the segmentation result after 50 iterations, when the estimate $\hat{\Theta}$ has converged. The resulting image segments (red = target, blue = shadow, green = bottom) represent the size of visually expected target, shadow, and bottom zones corresponding to the sea trial conditions. The segmentation is noisy due to the widely overlapping PDFs of the shadow and bottom reverberation class as shown in Fig. 3 giving the overall-PDF and the PDFs of the three classes in the images are target class = red, shadow class = blue and bottom class = green. To adapt the segmentation results to image fusion application clustering of the noisy image segments is required.

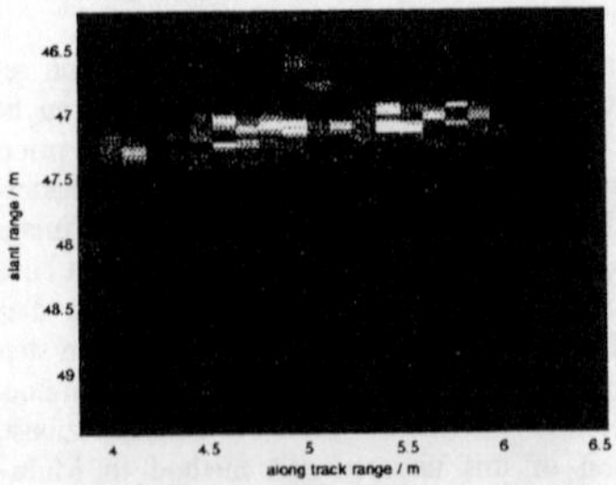

Fig. 1: Detail from a sidescan sonar image

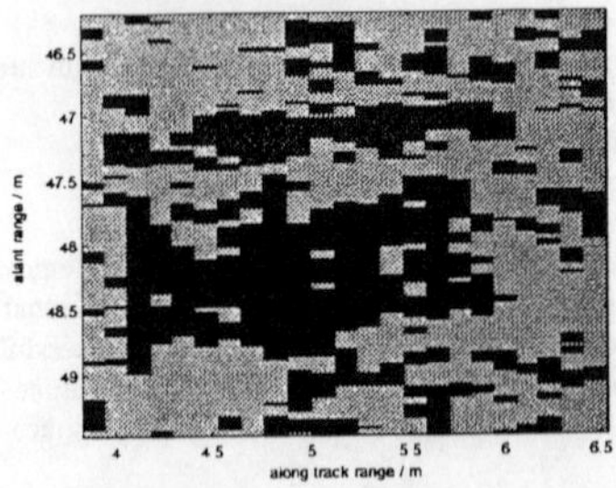

Fig. 2: Segmentation result of the EM algorithm

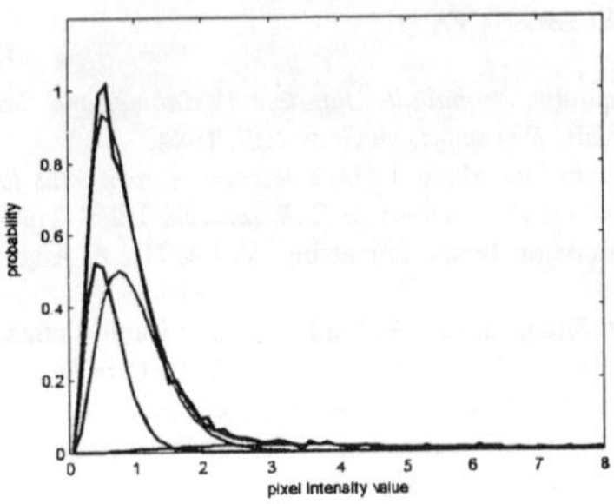

Fig. 3: PDFs of the three data classes

3 CLUSTERING OF IMAGE SEGMENTS BY MARKOV-RANDOM-FIELD (MRF) MODELING

In the segmentation step it has been assumed that the variables y and x are independent. In sidescan sonar images the target, bottom or shadow zones are extended and connected structures and not isolated pixels. If several neighbours of a pixel have the same class status the probability that the pixel has the same class status is high. Independence of the variables is not given. The neighbourhood dependence of the variables can be described by a MRF image model ([3], [4], [5])

$$f(x|\Theta_x) = \frac{1}{x} e^{-U(x|\Theta_x)}. \quad (13)$$

Here this function is approximated by the local characteristic

$$f(x_{i,j} = \omega_p | x_{\eta_{i,j}}, \Theta_x) = \frac{e^{\beta\delta_{i,j}(p)}}{\sum_{p=1}^{P} e^{\beta\delta_{i,j}(p)}}. \quad (14)$$

where:

- $x_{i,j}$ - unknown state vector at pixel position i,j.
- $x_{\eta_{i,j}}$ - state in the specified neighbourhood $\eta_{i,j}$.
- $\delta_{i,j}(p)$ - sum of elements of $\eta_{i,j}$ in state p.
- $\beta>0$ - parameter controlling the degree of spatial clustering.
- Θ_x - parameter vector of the conditional PDF of $x_{i,j}$ (in this case $\Theta_x = \beta$).

Furthermore it is assumed that β is either known or observable.

Application of the local PDF to the segmentation results, choosing an estimate for β and the neigbourhood according to the resolution of the sidescan sonar gives a result shown in Fig. 5. The isolated pixels of each class have been clustered to larger regions, which correspond with the expectations from sea trial conditions. The size of the target was approximately 2m length and 0.5m diameter casting a shadow of approximately 2m x 1.3m. They have not been distorted by segmentation and clustering.

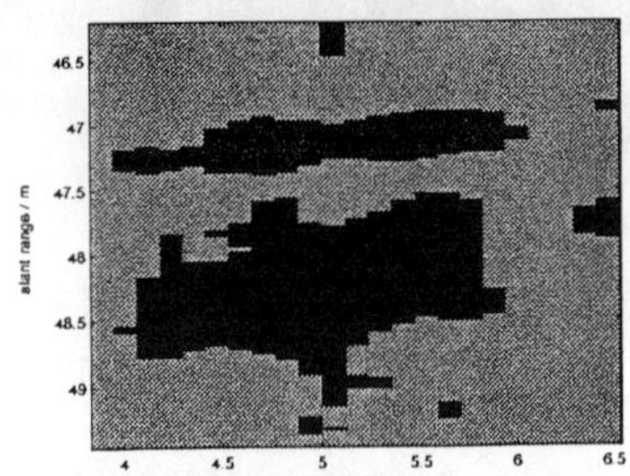

Fig. 4: Clustering and segmentation result

4 IMAGE FUSION

In case of Multi-Beam/Multi Aspect sidescan sonar images of temporal successive pings the spatial overlapping is considerable. In the overlapping region they can be fusioned to a single image. To achieve optimum detectability of target and shadow zones the following image fusion algorithm based on the result of image segmentation and clustering is applied.

In the target zone a maximum strategy is adequate to minimize the effect of aspect dependence of the target echoes

$$y_{i,j}^{\max} = \max(y_{i,j}^{l_1} \ldots\ldots y_{i,j}^{l_N}) . \quad (15)$$

where $y_{i,j}^{l_k}$ is the intensity of the pixel at position i, j at ping l_k and N = number of images for fusion. In the bottom reverberation zone a mean strategy

$$y_{i,j}^{mean} = \frac{1}{N} \sum_{n=1}^{N} y_{i,j}^{l_n} \quad (16)$$

is preferred to reduce the reverberation in the fused image. In the shadow zone a minimum strategy

$$y_{i,j}^{\min} = \min(y_{i,j}^{l_1} \ldots\ldots y_{i,j}^{l_N}) \quad (17)$$

is chosen to attain a better perception of the shadow.

The decision which fusion strategy is to be chosen is based on the segmentation and clustering result. Decision for target (= maximum strategy) is made, if the class status of $y_{i,j}^{l_k}$ is the target class in at least one l_k. The mean strategy for shadow zone is chosen if the class status of $y_{i,j}^{l_k}$ is the shadow class in more than one ping. The mean strategy for bottom reverberation is selected if none of the other conditions is satisfied.

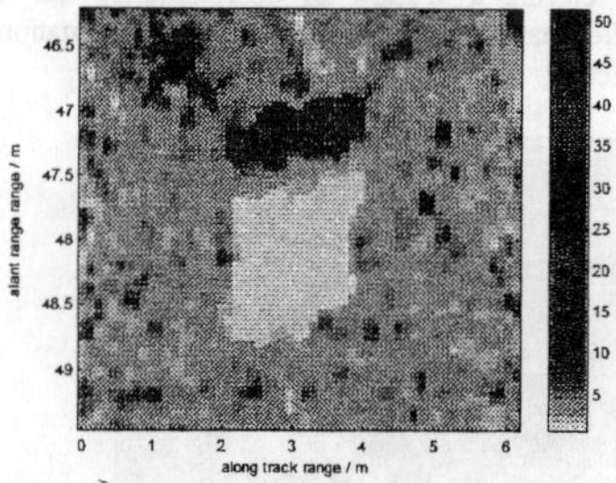

Fig. 5: Fused sidescan sonar image

Fig. 5 shows the result of the fusion of 18 successive sidescan sonar images. Compared to the single images it shows significantly improved detectability of the shadow region and non aspect dependent target. The size of target and shadow zones are not distorted.

5 CONCLUSIONS

An unsupervised algorithm for classification and fusion of multidimensional sidescan sonar images has been presented consisting of the steps

- classification by image segmentation and clustering of image segments and
- image fusion based upon classification results.

Classification requires apart from the information regarding the sidescan sonar resolution, which can be fixed for a specific sidescan sonar, additional a priori information regarding the size of the target and shadow zone to determine the appropriate sector of the image containing a significant number of pixels of each class and initial estimates of the parameters of the data classes. These data can be prepared in a detection step. Regarding the choice of initial estimates of the parameters of the PDF, this method seems to be quite robust. Application of this unsupervised method to Multi-Beam/Multi-Aspect sidescan sonar images provides comparable or even better results than those achieved with the supervised method. It was shown that

- effects of aspect dependence of target strength are avoided,
- bottom reverberation can be reduced,
- the perception of shadow zones is improved.

The proposed method can be considered as one element in a future Multi-Beam/Multi-Aspect sidescan sonar CAC-system. We expect this method to be successful also in forward looking sonars, data fusion for autonomous underwater vehicles (AUVs) and further applications.

6 REFERENCES

[1] Papoulis, *Probability, Random Variables, and Stochastic Processes*, McGraw-Hill, 1984,

[2] Ramin Samadani, *A Finite Mixture Algorithmus for Finding Proportions in SAR Images*, IEEE Transactions on Image Processing, Vol 4, No. 8, August 1995

[3] Jun Zhang, James W. Modestion and David Langan, *Maximum Likelihood Parameter Estimation for Unsupervised Stochastic Model-Based Image Segmentation*, IEEE Transaction on Image Processing, Vol. 3, No. 4, July 1994

[4] Yves Delignon, Abdelwaheb Marzouki and Wojciech Pieczynski, *Estimation of Generelized Mixtures and Its Application in Image Segmentation*, IEEE Transaction on Image Progessing, Vol. 6, No. 10, October 1997

[5] Stuart Geman and Donald Geman, *Stochastic Relaxation, Gibbs Distribitions, and the Bayesian Restoration of Images*, IEEE Transactions on Pattern Recognition and Machine Inteligence, Vol. PAMI-6, No. 6, November 1984

[6] Kraus D. *Auswertung von Multi-Beam/Multi-Aspekt Seitensichtsonar-Daten*, BL 4788 T 219, STN ATLAS Elektronik, Bremen, Juli 1997

Transfer Function Models for Non Self-Adjoint Multidimensional Systems

R. Rabenstein
Lehrstuhl für Nachrichtentechnik, Universität Erlangen-Nürnberg
D-91058 Erlangen, Cauerstr. 7, Germany
rabe@nt.e-technik.uni-erlangen.de

ABSTRACT

Transfer function models for the description of multidimensional physical systems have recently been introduced. They provide an alternative to the conventional representation by partial differential equations. Multidimensional transfer functions are input-output models for physical phenomena with more than one independent variable (e.g. time and space). They allow to treat the effects of initial conditions, boundary conditions, and excitation functions on the resulting output signal separately. Transfer function models are an excellent starting point for the development of discrete-variable representations of physical systems. They offer the following advantages: suitability for computer implementation by iteration free algorithms, stability in the sense of systems theory, and high numerical accuracy without prohibitively small step sizes. Multidimensional transfer function models have already been derived for physical systems with self-adjoint differential operators. This paper provides an extension to non self-adjoint problems.

1 Introduction

The conventional tools for the description of time and space dependent physical phenomena are partial differential equations (PDEs). The solution of a PDE represents a physical quantity depending on excitation functions, initial and boundary conditions. However, this formulation is not optimally suited for the derivation of computer models for simulation or control. These applications call for descriptions of the physical process itself, not just one of its output quantities.

There is a variety of suitable input-output models for one-dimensional physical systems, described by ordinary differential equations. Examples are signal flow graphs, network models, state space models, and transfer functions. These models are well established and in widespread use.

Corresponding models for multidimensional (MD) physical systems have emerged only recently. One example is the description of physical processes by MD Kirchhoff circuits, leading to the concept of MD wave digital filters [1].

Another approach are transfer function models for MD systems [4]. They allow to study the response to initial values, boundary values and excitations separately. This makes them well suited for physical processes described as initial-boundary-value problems. The derivation of discrete simulation models from these transfer functions is shown in [3].

So far, transfer function models have been presented for physical systems with self-adjoint spatial differential operators. This special case comprises a number of technically important problems like diffusion, heat flow, and wave propagation. On the other hand, there are also physical effects with non self-adjoint operators (e.g. convection-diffusion problems). Transfer function models for this more general class of problems are presented here.

The remainder of the paper is organized as follows: Section 2 describes a working problem. Section 3 briefly reviews the self-adjoint case. The extension to non self-adjoint problems is shown in Section 4. A short example is given in Section 5.

2 Problem Description

The basic idea for turning a differential equation into a transfer function is simple: Remove the differential operators by applying suitable functional transformations for each independent variable. The resulting algebraic equation can be solved for the transform of the output quantity. The desired transfer function follows immediately. The choice of the functional transformation depends on the nature of the additional conditions for the corresponding independent variable. Although this approach is rather general, this paper focuses on initial-boundary value problems with time and space as independent variables.

The Laplace transformation with respect to time is well suited for initial value problems. It is the standard method in electrical network theory and in control theory. The reason is, that the differentiation theorem of the Laplace transformation has two useful properties: Firstly, it replaces time derivatives with multiplications by the complex frequency. Secondly, it includes the initial conditions as an additive term into the resulting equation. The key step is to find a transformation for the spatial variable, which acts on the boundary conditions in a similar way. Then we can obtain transfer functions for initial-boundary value problems by applying both functional transformations.

This procedure is illustrated by considering a multidimensional system, which is described by the following PDE

$$\dot{y}(\mathbf{x},t) + L\{y(\mathbf{x},t)\} = 0, \quad \mathbf{x} \in V \tag{1}$$

$$y(\mathbf{x},0) = y_i(\mathbf{x}), \quad \mathbf{x} \in V \tag{2}$$

$$f_b\{y(\mathbf{x},t)\} = \phi(\mathbf{x},t), \quad \mathbf{x} \in S \tag{3}$$

$y(\mathbf{x},t)$ is a physical quantity depending on the vector of spatial coordinates $\mathbf{x}$ and time t. $\dot{y}$ denotes first order time derivation. $L\{y\}$ is a linear operator of spatial derivatives. The initial conditions at $t = 0$ are specified by the initial value $y_i(\mathbf{x})$. $y(\mathbf{x},t)$ and $y_i(\mathbf{x})$ are defined on a spatial domain V. On its surface S, boundary conditions are specified by a boundary operator f_b and the boundary value function $\phi(\mathbf{x},t)$. A detailed account of a more general problem is given in [4].

Laplace transformation $Y(\mathbf{x},s) = \mathcal{L}\{y(\mathbf{x},t)\}$ with the derivation theorem

$$\mathcal{L}\{\dot{y}(\mathbf{x},t)\} = sY(\mathbf{x},s) - y(\mathbf{x},0) \tag{4}$$

turns the initial-boundary-value problem (1-3) into a pure boundary value problem

$$sY(\mathbf{x},s) + L\{Y(\mathbf{x},s)\} = y_i(\mathbf{x}), \quad \mathbf{x} \in V \tag{5}$$

$$f_b\{Y(\mathbf{x},s)\} = \Phi(\mathbf{x},s), \quad \mathbf{x} \in S \tag{6}$$

Note that $\dot{y}$ is replaced by sY and that the initial value y_i shows up as an additive term on the right hand side.

The next step is to construct a spatial transformation $\mathcal{T}$, which removes the spatial derivatives L in (5) and which correctly considers the boundary value in (6).

This spatial transformation may be expressed as a scalar product $\langle Y, K\rangle$ between $Y(\mathbf{x},s)$ and the transformation kernel $K(\mathbf{x},\beta)$ (s omitted)

$$\begin{aligned} \bar{Y}(\beta_\mu) &= \mathcal{T}\{Y(\mathbf{x})\} = \int_V Y(\mathbf{x})K(\mathbf{x},\beta_\mu)\, dV \\ &= \langle Y(\mathbf{x}), K(\mathbf{x},\beta_\mu)\rangle . \end{aligned} \tag{7}$$

The discrete spatial frequencies β_μ with index μ and the transformation kernel $K(\mathbf{x},\beta_\mu)$ have to be determined such that a suitable differentiation theorem for $\mathcal{T}$ exists. More precisely, the term $\mathcal{T}\{L\{Y\}\}$ which results from application of (7) to (5) has to be expressed by $\bar{Y}(\beta_\mu)$ and an additive boundary value term.

The solution to this problem depends on the properties of the differentiation operator $L\{Y\}$. For certain problems of practical importance, $L\{Y\}$ is a self-adjoint operator. This situation has been discussed in [4] and will be mentioned only briefly in Section 3. If $L\{Y\}$ is not self-adjoint, then it has an adjoint operator $\tilde{L}\{Y\}$. This case is covered in section 4.

3 Self-Adjoint Systems

A spatial differential operator $L\{Y\}$ is self-adjoint, if it satisfies a Green's formula of the form (independent variables are omitted)

$$\begin{aligned} &\langle L\{Y\}, K\rangle - \langle Y, L\{K\}\rangle = \\ &= \int_S g_b\{Y\}\, f_b\{K\}\, dS - \int_S g_b\{K\}\, f_b\{Y\}\, dS . \end{aligned} \tag{8}$$

g_b is a boundary operator associated with f_b. The yet to be determined transformation kernel K is now chosen to satisfy the Sturm-Liouville problem

$$L\{K(\mathbf{x},\beta)\} = \beta^m K(\mathbf{x},\beta), \quad \mathbf{x} \in V \tag{9}$$

$$f_b\{K(\mathbf{x},\beta)\} = 0, \quad \mathbf{x} \in S . \tag{10}$$

The integer m is the order of the differentiation operator L.

From (7,8,9), and (10) follows the required differentiation theorem for the spatial operator

$$\mathcal{T}\{L\{Y(\mathbf{x},s)\}\} = \beta_\mu^m \bar{Y}(\beta_\mu,s) - \bar{\Phi}_b(\beta_\mu,s) \tag{11}$$

with the boundary value term

$$\bar{\Phi}_b(\beta_\mu,s) = \int_S g_b\{K(\mathbf{x},\beta_\mu)\}\, \Phi(\mathbf{x},s)\, dS . \tag{12}$$

Note the formal similarity between (4) and (11).

Now we can summarize the procedure for setting up the transfer function description of a MD system described by (1)-(3) as follows:

1. Apply the Laplace transformation with respect to time. This turns the initial-boundary-value problem (1)-(3) into the boundary value problem (5,6).

2. Establish the Green's formula (8) for the operator L to
   - verify that L is self-adjoint,
   - obtain the boundary operator g_b.

3. Set up the Sturm-Liouville problem (9,10) associated with (5,6) and solve it for the eigenvalues β_μ and the eigenfunctions $K(\mathbf{x}, \beta_\mu)$ of the operator L.

4. Calculate the boundary term $\bar{\Phi}_b(\beta_\mu, s)$ from (12) by surface integration.

5. Use the differentiation theorem (11) to turn the boundary value problem (5,6) into an algebraic equation.

6. Solve this algebraic equation and obtain the transfer function description

$$\bar{Y}(\beta_\mu, s) = \bar{G}(\beta_\mu, s)\left[\bar{y}_i(\beta_\mu) + \bar{\Phi}_b(\beta_\mu, s)\right] \quad (13)$$

$$\bar{G}(\beta_\mu, s) = \frac{1}{s+\beta_\mu^m}\,. \quad (14)$$

7. Since the eigenfunctions of the Sturm-Liouville problem are orthogonal, the inverse spatial transform is given by the orthogonal expansion

$$Y(\mathbf{x}) = \mathcal{T}^{-1}\{\bar{Y}(\beta_\mu)\} = \sum_\mu \frac{1}{N_\mu}\bar{Y}(\beta_\mu)K(\mathbf{x}, \beta_\mu) \quad (15)$$

   with the normalization factor N_μ.

4 Non Self-Adjoint Systems

The procedure outlined above is also suitable for MD systems where the operator L in (1) is not self-adjoint. However, some modifications and extensions are required. They are presented in this section. The key point is to consider not only the operator L of the PDE (1), but also a second operator, the so called adjoint operator $\tilde{L}$. Self-adjoint operators are a special case with $\tilde{L} = L$.

The operator L and its adjoint $\tilde{L}$ satisfy an extended Green's formula [2]

$$\langle L\{Y\}, K\rangle - \langle Y, \tilde{L}\{K\}\rangle = \quad (16)$$
$$= \int_S g_b\{Y\}\,\tilde{f}_b\{K\}\,dS - \int_S \tilde{g}_b\{K\}\,f_b\{Y\}\,dS$$

with the boundary operators f_b from (3) and $\tilde{f}_b$, g_b, $\tilde{g}_b$.

In order to derive a differentiation theorem for $\mathcal{T}\{L\{Y\}\}$, we chose the transformation kernel K again as solution of a Sturm-Liouville problem. In contrast to (9,10), it is here determined by the adjoint differential operator $\tilde{L}$ and the adjoint boundary operator $\tilde{f}_b$.

$$\tilde{L}\{K(\mathbf{x},\beta)\} = \beta^m K(\mathbf{x},\beta), \quad \mathbf{x} \in V \quad (17)$$
$$\tilde{f}_b\{K(\mathbf{x},\beta)\} = 0, \quad \mathbf{x} \in S\,. \quad (18)$$

Inserting $\tilde{L}\{K\}$ and $\tilde{f}_b\{K\}$ into the extended Green's formula (16) leads to the same differentiation theorem as in (11). However, $\bar{\Phi}_b(\beta_\mu, s)$ is now given by

$$\bar{\Phi}_b(\beta_\mu, s) = \int_S \tilde{g}_b\{K(\mathbf{x},\beta_\mu)\}\,\Phi(\mathbf{x}, s)\,dS\,. \quad (19)$$

The procedure for obtaining the transfer function model of a non self-adjoint MD system is as follows:

1. As above.

2. Establish the Green's formula (16) for the operator L to obtain the adjoint operator $\tilde{L}$ and the boundary operators $\tilde{f}_b$, g_b, $\tilde{g}_b$.

3. Set up the Sturm-Liouville problem (17,18) and solve it for the eigenvalues β_μ and the eigenfunctions $K(\mathbf{x}, \beta_\mu)$ of the operator $\tilde{L}$.

4. Calculate $\bar{\Phi}_b(\beta_\mu, s)$ from (19).

5., 6. as above

The derivation of the transfer function is very similar to the self-adjoint case. The only difference so far is that the transformation kernel $K(\mathbf{x}, \beta_\mu)$ consists of the eigenfunctions of the adjoint operator $\tilde{L}$.

The remaining problem is the inverse transformation $\mathcal{T}^{-1}$. It is no longer an orthogonal expansion, since the eigenfunctions $K(\mathbf{x}, \beta_\mu)$ are not orthogonal for $\tilde{L} \neq L$. To establish the proper form of $\mathcal{T}^{-1}$, we need also the eigenfunctions of L. They are now denoted by $J(\mathbf{x},\beta_\mu)$ and follow from the Sturm-Liouville problem (9,10)

$$L\{J(\mathbf{x},\beta)\} = \beta^m J(\mathbf{x},\beta), \quad \mathbf{x}\in V \quad (20)$$
$$f_b\{J(\mathbf{x},\beta)\} = 0, \quad \mathbf{x}\in S\,. \quad (21)$$

The Sturm-Liouville problem (17,18) is also called the adjoint boundary value problem to (20,21) and vice versa.

In general, neither $K(\mathbf{x},\beta_\mu)$ nor $J(\mathbf{x},\beta_\mu)$ are orthogonal functions. Instead, they form a pair of biorthogonal functions. This is easily shown by forming the following scalar products for different eigenvalues β_μ and β_ν and using (17) and (20)

$$\langle L\{J(\beta_\mu)\}, K(\beta_\nu)\rangle = \beta_\mu^m\langle J(\beta_\mu), K(\beta_\nu)\rangle, \quad (22)$$
$$\langle J(\beta_\mu), \tilde{L}\{K(\beta_\nu)\}\rangle = \beta_\nu^m\langle J(\beta_\mu), K(\beta_\nu)\rangle. \quad (23)$$

Subtraction of (23) from (22) gives

$$\langle L\{J(\beta_\mu)\}, K(\beta_\nu)\rangle - \langle J(\beta_\mu), \tilde{L}\{K(\beta_\nu)\}\rangle \quad (24)$$
$$= (\beta_\mu^m - \beta_\nu^m)\langle J(\beta_\mu), K(\beta_\nu)\rangle\,.$$

From the Green's formula (16), it follows with (18) and (21) that the left hand side of (24) is zero. Thus $J(\beta_\mu)$ and $K(\beta_\nu)$ are biorthogonal

$$\langle J(\beta_\mu), K(\beta_\nu)\rangle = 0 \quad \text{for} \quad \mu\neq\nu\,. \quad (25)$$

The inverse transformation is now given as an expansion in $J(\mathbf{x},\beta_\mu)$

$$Y(\mathbf{x}) = \mathcal{T}^{-1}\{\bar{Y}(\beta_\mu)\} = \sum_\mu \frac{1}{N_\mu}\bar{Y}(\beta_\mu)J(\mathbf{x},\beta_\mu) \quad (26)$$

with $N_\mu = \langle J(\beta_\mu), K(\beta_\mu)\rangle$.

5 Example

As an example we consider a convection-diffusion problem in one spatial dimension ($V = \{x|0 < x < 1\}$) with first order boundary conditions. It is given by (5,6) with (prime denotes spatial derivation)

$$L\{Y\} = -aY'' + 2bY', \quad f_b\{Y\} = Y\,. \quad (27)$$

The Green's formula (16) is established using integration by parts. It yields the adjoint operator and the boundary operators

$$\tilde{L}\{Y\} = -aY'' - 2bY', \quad \tilde{f}_b\{Y\} = Y \quad (28)$$

$$g_b\{Y\} = -aY' + bY, \quad \tilde{g}_b\{Y\} = -aY' - bY \quad (29)$$

The solutions of the Sturm-Liouville problems (17,18) and (20,21) are

$$J(x,\beta_\mu) = \exp(+bx/a)\sin(\mu\pi x), \quad (30)$$
$$K(x,\beta_\mu) = \exp(-bx/a)\sin(\mu\pi x). \quad (31)$$

Since L is a second order differential operator, the transfer function $G(\beta_\mu, s)$ is given by (14) with $m = 2$.

6 Conclusion

The multidimensional transfer function models previously presented for self-adjoint systems have been extended to general linear spatial differential operators. The approach shown in this paper can be applied similarly to PDEs with higher order time derivatives and space and time dependent excitation functions.

The basic structure of the underlying PDE determines the resulting transfer functions. They contain the complex frequency variable of the Laplace transformation and the eigenvalues of the spatial transformation. These eigenvalues and the eigenfunctions follow from the spatial differential operator and the type of boundary conditions. Note, that the initial and boundary values are not part of the transfer functions. Rather, they act as input signals. This shows that the presented transfer functions are indeed a multidimensional equivalent to their one-dimensional counterparts from network and control theory.

References

[1] A. Fettweis. Multidimensional wave-digital principles: From filtering to numerical integration. In *Proc. Int. Conf. Acoustics, Speech, and Signal Processing (ICASSP 94)*, pages VI–173 – VI–181. IEEE, April 1994.

[2] C. Lanzcos. *Linear Differential Operators.* D. Van Nostrand Company, London, 1961.

[3] R. Rabenstein. Discrete simulation models for multidimensional systems based on functional transformations. In J. G. McWhirter, editor, *Mathematics in Signal Processing IV.* Oxford University Press, 1998. In print.

[4] R. Rabenstein. Transfer function models for multidimensional systems with bounded spatial domains. *Mathematical Modelling of Systems*, 1998. In print.

Efficient Implementation of Digital 3-D IIR Filters for Separation of Velocity Components in Data-Streams

G. Runze

University of Erlangen-Nuremberg, Telecommunications Institute I
Cauerstrasse 7, D-91058 Erlangen, Germany
Email: {runze}@nt.e-technik.uni-erlangen.de

Abstract

In this paper an implementation structure for three-dimensional recursive filters is proposed. This structure turns out as a result of a filter design method, which has been published in [1]. For the application of velocity separation (velocity-filters), its execution speed, e.g. measured as frame rate, will be compared to those of another filter implementation structure that uses the Fast Fourier Transform in the spatial domain.

1 Introduction

For a long time one-dimensional and especially multi-dimensional signal-processing real-time algorithms could be applied only on digital signal processors (DSPs), but along with the increasing availability of memory and computational power of general-purpose processors, many multi-dimensional algorithms seem to be also feasible on non-DSPs.
One class of application is the multi-dimensional linear filtering by recursive systems, which will be investigated further in this paper. While the implementations of those systems have been optimized due to the number of numerical operations (multiplication and addition), other time-consuming parts have not been taken into account. When a filter algorithm is applied on a general-purpose processor, it can be easily shown that much time is spent on accessing memory – sometimes even more than for the numerical operations.

In the following we are going to point out the most important basic operations that have to be considered, when an execution-time efficient implementation is to be developed. After this general view, a standard filter design method and an alternative filter design method [1] for three-dimensional velocity-filters will be compared due to their approximation quality. Further their implementations will be compared due to their processing speed on a non-DSP system.

2 General Implementation-Aspects

As it was pointed out in the introduction, more than the pure number of numerical operations has to be considered, when time consuming operations are to be determined. Following basic operations should be taken into account:

- Numerical operations
- Memory access
- Index conversion to the linear address space

While the processors increased their speed of computation, memory access became the main bottleneck for almost every application. For this reason the memory-cache, a fast accessible block of memory, became a standard expansion of many processors, and is most efficiently used, when the memory is addressed in subsequent order. This is even more interesting in multi-dimensional signal processing, when index conversion can be avoided by a subsequent memory access.

3 Standard Implementation of 3-D Recursive Filters

When a three-dimensional data-stream with two spatial dimensions, and one temporal dimension is processed, we assume the signal to be limited in space but not necessarily in time. To achieve a fast processing of those signals, we avoid a lot of indexing operations in setting the recurrence direction along the time axis. This yields a transfer-function of the recursive system with a multi-variate numerator-polynomial B and a uni-variate denominator-polynomial C

$$H(z_x, z_y, z_t) = \frac{B(z_x, z_y, z_t)}{C(z_t) z_x^{l_x} z_y^{l_y}}. \quad (1)$$

Without loss of generality l_x and l_y can be set to zero. As a consequence of the uni-variate denominator-polynomial the stability of those systems – in opposite to multi-variate denominator-polynomials – can be guaranteed by the filter design procedure.

An easy, but slow implementation yields the direct evaluation of the difference equation, which follows from (1), with the input signal v and the output y

$$\sum_{\mu} c_\mu y(k_x, k_y, k_t + \mu) = \sum_{\kappa}\sum_{\lambda}\sum_{\mu} b_{\kappa,\lambda,\mu} v(k_x + \kappa, k_y + \lambda, k_t + \mu). \quad (2)$$

A very fast implementation [4] is achieved by applying a fast convolution algorithm, by a Fast Fourier Transform (FFT), within the spatial coordinates. For a given spatial size of the input signal ($N_x \times N_y$), and

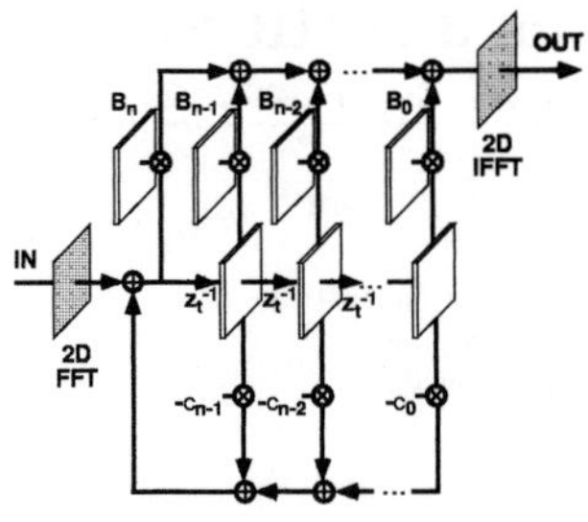

Figure 1: Implementation structure of the reference filter

a given filter order of n_x and n_y in the spatial dimensions, equation (2) can be written as

$$\sum_{\mu} c_\mu Y_{k_t-\mu}(m_x,m_y)e^{-j2\pi/(M_xM_y)} = \sum_{\mu} B_\mu(m_x,m_y)V_{k_t-\mu}(m_x,m_y), \quad (3)$$

while $B_\mu(m_x,m_y)$ denotes the two-dimensional FFT of the zero-padded numerator coefficients $b_{\kappa,\lambda,\mu}$ up to $M_x \times M_y$ values in the spatial directions κ and λ, where

$$M_x \geq n_x + N_x - 1, \quad \text{and}$$
$$M_y \geq n_y + N_y - 1.$$

$V_{k_t}(m_x,m_y)$ and $Y_{k_t}(m_x,m_y)$ denote the two-dimensional FFTs, also zero-padded to $M_x \times M_y$ samples in spatial dimensions, of the input and output signal at time step k_t.

To find a good approximation of a desired frequency-response $D(\Omega_x,\Omega_y,\Omega_t)$, with spatial frequencies Ω_x and Ω_y, and time-frequency Ω_t, we have applied a multi-dimensional version of a filter-design method [3], which minimizes a complex mean squared error on a dense frequency-grid.

The implementation of a three-dimensional IIR-Filter of equation (1), which is given by figure 1, will be the reference for further comparisons.

While it seems that this implementation is most efficient as it uses the 2-D FFT, it is also well known that for a small number of coefficients the advantage of the fast convolution degrades. This fact is of great interest when signals of large spatial extension have to be processed.

4 Alternative Filter Design and Implementation

As it was mentioned in the previous section, the advantage of the FFT-Solution degrades on large input signals and a small number of coefficients. Instead of going back to the direct convolution, which has another disadvantage, the multi-dimensional indexing, we propose the implementation of another type of filter design [1, 2] which leads to the same type of transfer functions as in equation (1):

Given an arbitrary desired frequency response $D(\Omega_x,\Omega_y,\Omega_t)$, with spatial frequencies Ω_x and Ω_y, and time-frequency Ω_t, we can express this function by an infinite series using the two-dimensional inverse discrete time Fourier transform,

$$D(\Omega_x,\Omega_y,\Omega_t) = \sum_{k_x=-\infty}^{\infty}\sum_{k_y=-\infty}^{\infty} D_{k_x,k_y}(\Omega_t)e^{-jk_x\Omega_x}e^{-jk_y\Omega_y}. \quad (4)$$

Here $D_{k_x,k_y}(\Omega_t)$ denotes the inverse discrete time Fourier transform of $D(\Omega_x,\Omega_y,\Omega_t)$, and is given by:

$$D_{k_x,k_y}(\Omega_t) = \frac{1}{4\pi^2}\int_{-\pi}^{\pi}\int_{-\pi}^{\pi} D(\Omega_x,\Omega_y,\Omega_t)e^{j(k_x\Omega_x+k_y\Omega_y)}d\Omega_x d\Omega_y \quad (5)$$

In many cases of interest (5) can be evaluated in closed form. As a first step of approximation the infinite two-dimensional series in equation (4) is truncated to a limited number of terms, restricting the spatial indices to $k_x \in [-L_x, L_x]$ and $k_y \in [-L_y, L_y]$. As a second step, these filters are approximated by rational transfer functions,

$$D_{k_x,k_y}(\Omega_t) \approx \frac{B_{k_x,k_y}(e^{j\Omega_t})}{C_{k_x,k_y}(e^{j\Omega_t})}. \quad (6)$$

For this, we have chosen the one-dimensional IIR-filter approximation [3], which minimizes a complex mean squared error criterion.
Substituting these $(2L_x+1)(2L_y+1)$ one-dimensional transfer-functions into (4), one ends up with the three-dimensional transfer function which can be written as,

$$H(z_x,z_y,z_t) = \sum_{k_x=-L_x}^{L_x}\sum_{k_y=-L_y}^{L_y} \frac{B_{k_x,k_y}(z_t)}{C_{k_x,k_y}(z_t)} z_x^{-k_x} z_y^{-k_y}, \quad \text{with } z_{x,y} = e^{j\Omega_{x,y}}. \quad (7)$$

This sum of rational functions could be composed to one, and would yield an expression of equation (1). But the definition of the re-composed transfer function in equation (7) leads directly to the proposed implementation structure, which can be simply described by a parallel connection of separable systems, composed of a delay in both spatial dimensions, and the previously designed one-dimensional IIR filters.
The advantage of this Parallel Shift-and-Filter (PSF) implementation structure lies in the simple shift-stages, which can be realized by linear indexing functions (figure 2).

For symmetric frequency responses, some of the tailoring IIR filters are identical and the preceding spatial delays can be combined to a shift-and-add stage. This simplification can be applied, when velocity filters are designed. Figure 3 shows the reduction of parallel one-dimensional recursive systems with increasing symmetry properties. The number of systems can be reduced further by a restriction of the Fourier-series coefficients of eqn. (4) within a circular k_x, k_y-range instead of square one (Fig. 3c).

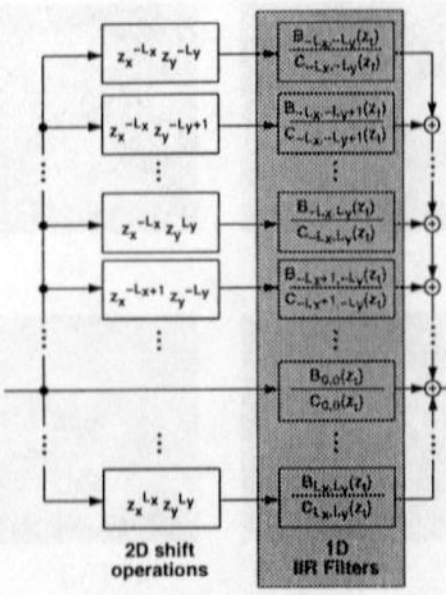

Figure 2: *Implementation structure of the proposed alternative filter: a parallel connection of simple spatial shifts with tailoring one-dimensional recursive systems*

5 Design of Velocity Filters

For three-dimensional signals, with two spatial coordinates and one temporal variable, the term "velocity" can be addressed in two different ways:

1. the velocity of a two-dimensional spatial texture, moving with linear trajectory, or
2. the velocity of a planar wave with a certain direction.

Any three-dimensional signal can be described by a superposition of elementary signals, either of the first or the second kind of moving objects or propagating waves. In this paper we assume the signals to be composed of planar waves, propagating with constant speed. Each of those wave-components has a Dirac-line as a spectrum with an orientation that corresponds directly to the velocity-vector of the spatial-time-domain signal (figure 4).

A *velocity filter* in our terminology has to attenuate those wave-components that propagate with a velocity slower (or faster) than a fixed value, and pass wave-components that are faster (or slower) than this velocity.

While all spectral frequencies, that correspond to waves, propagating faster that certain velocity reside inside a double-cone in the spectral domain, the ideal frequency-response is a double-cone shape with a certain cut-off velocity, that corresponds to its slope. In the ideal case the frequency-response is 1 inside the cone, and 0 outside. Figure 5 (left) shows the passband region of the ideal frequency-response.

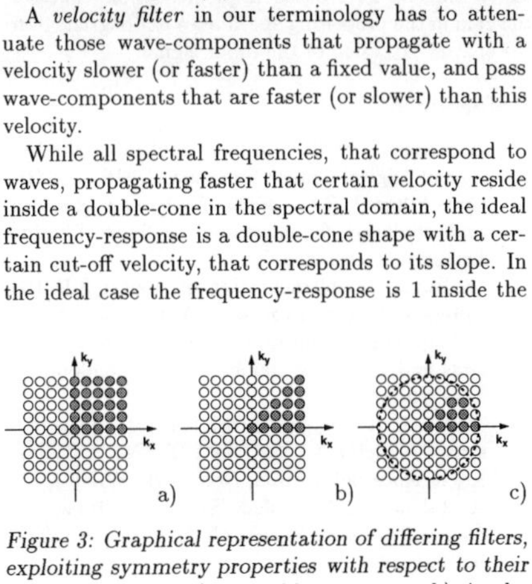

Figure 3: *Graphical representation of differing filters, exploiting symmetry properties with respect to their indices k_x and k_y: a) k_x- and k_y-symmetry, b) circular symmetry, and c) circular symmetry with a further reduced number of filters within a circular region.*

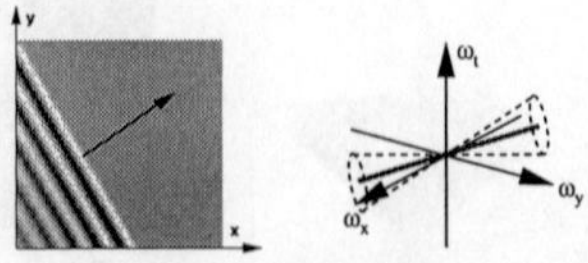

Figure 4: *Time-domain signal and frequency support for a planar wave, propagating with a velocity vector. The dashed region in the frequency-domain may be the passband of a velocity-filter*

6 Approximation Error of Design Methods

To ensure that the both filter design methods, which will be compared, will yield nearly the same L_2 approximation error, this error has been evaluated for both designs, while the number of free coefficients is kept nearly the same (as far as it was possible). Table 1 shows the approximation results for the standard FFT and the alternative PSF design method, where N_{FFT} denotes the number of free parameters in the standard design, and N_{PSF} in the alternative design method.

Figure 5 visualizes the magnitude frequency-responses of both filter-designs using a volume rendering method. The magnitude of the transfer-function was encoded as the opacity of each volume element.

7 Implementation Comparison

For comparison both implementations were realized in C++ on an SGI Workstation.

Two questions should be answered by the experiments

- How does the frame rate degrade with increasing input image sizes ?
- Up to which filter-size (free parameters) is the alternative implementation (without FFT) faster than the standard FFT-implementation?

For each implementation five different filter complexities have been compared, from 11 to 143 free parameters for the FFT-Implementation, and from 10 to

Table 1: *Comparison of the two investigated filter-design methods due to their mean squared error*

Standard Design		PSF Design	
N_{FFT}	MSE	N_{PSF}	MSE
11	0.302	10	0.259
15	0.228	15	0.237
34	0.213	36	0.203
76	0.174	78	0.171
143	0.149	153	0.146

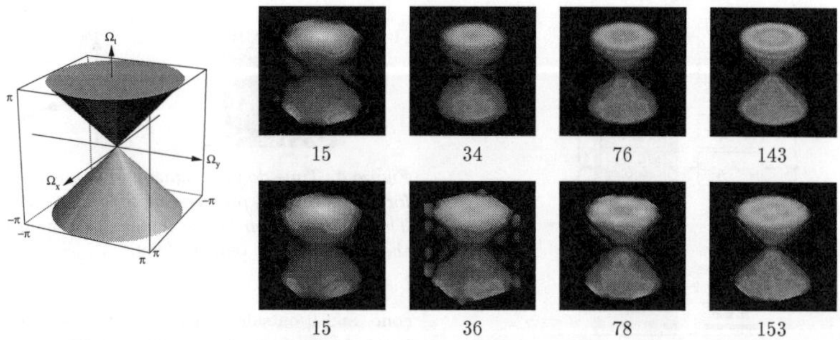

Figure 5: Left: Ideal shape of a velocity-filter with a cut-off velocity of 1 pixel per frame, and no direction sensitivity. Right: The upper row visualizes magnitude frequency-responses of the standard filter design with the number of free coefficients below. The lower row visualizes magnitude frequency-responses of the proposed PSF filter design.

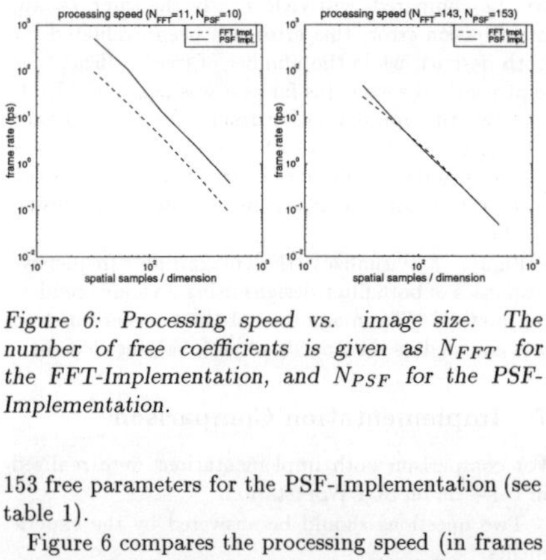

Figure 6: Processing speed vs. image size. The number of free coefficients is given as N_{FFT} for the FFT-Implementation, and N_{PSF} for the PSF-Implementation.

153 free parameters for the PSF-Implementation (see table 1).

Figure 6 compares the processing speed (in frames per second) of both implementations for different spatial sizes of the input sequence (32, 64, 128, 256 and 512 samples in each spatial dimension), while the number of free parameters N_{FFT} and N_{PSF} was kept nearly the same.

The results show that the frame rate degrades nearly the same for both structures, and the gain in the processing speed for the PSF-Implementation seems not to break down even for spatially large input signals, but it decreases with the number of free parameters (figure 7). Even though the processing speed of the PSF-Implementation decreases faster than the FFT-Implementation, it has a better performance up to large number of free parameters (approx. 150), which is more than it could be reached by the direct evaluation of equation 2.

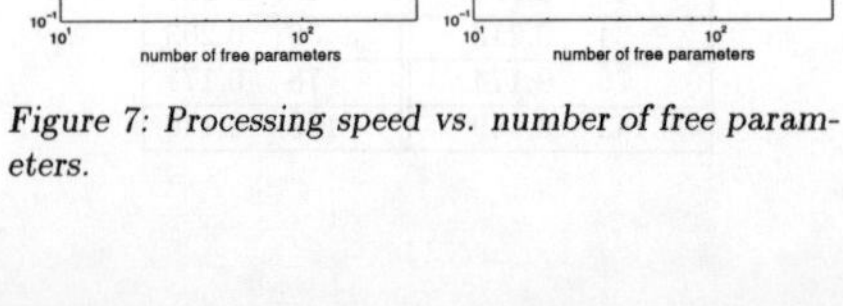

Figure 7: Processing speed vs. number of free parameters.

8 Conclusions

In this paper an implementation structure for three-dimensional recursive filters was proposed, which accelerates the processing speed of those filters significantly. Experimental results have shown that up to about 150 free coefficients, the implementation is faster than an FFT-based implementation. Further the gain in the processing speed does not degrade over the spatial extension of the input signal.

References

[1] G. Runze, P. Steffen "A Contribution to the Design of Digital Three-Dimensional FIR and IIR Cone Filters," *Proceedings of 3D Image Analysis und -synthesis '96*, November 1996, pp. 179–182 Erlangen (Germany)

[2] G. Runze "Implementation of digital 3-D IIR Filters for Stream-Processing Applications," IEE Colloquium on Multidimensional Systems: Problems and Solutions, January 1998, London, pp. 4/1–4/5

[3] T. W. Parks, C. S. Burrus "Digital filter design," Chapter 3.7.4.2, pp 221–224, A Wiley-Interscience publication, New York, Wiley 1987.

[4] R. Rabenstein, P. Steffen "Stability of Image Sequence Processing Systems," *AEÜ*, Bd. 37 (1983) pp. 261–266

Part 4

COMMUNICATION SYSTEMS

Capacity Related Reliability (CRR) as Topology Performance Measure Tool for ATM Transport Networks

Kyamakya Kyandoghere
University of Hagen, Electrical Engineering, FTK,
Feithstrasse 142 / TGZ, 58084 Hagen, Germany.
e-mail: kyamakya.kyandoghere@fernuni-hagen.de

Reader Aids-
Purpose: Widen state of the art.
Results useful to: telecommunication engineers, network operators, and reliability analysts.

Abstract- Since high availability requirements are expected to increase in the B-ISDN era, adequate methods are needed, which allow network designers and operators to outline the relation between available network resources and actual traffic demands on one hand and the reachable availability for either the whole network or individual source-destination VP[1] connections on the other hand. Performance index for a transport network is defined as a composite index integrating the important aspects of reliability, heterogeneous link capacities, non-uniform traffic demands, instantaneous paths layout, resource sharing, and re-routing capability. This paper suggests a simple and thus fast method for deriving the symbolic expression of the performance index in a compact form, from which a "capacity related reliability polynom" may easily be derived. Since the capacity of several subnetworks must be computed taking re-routing capability into account, an efficient procedure for capacity determination is also suggested. This performance index, the CRR, is then used as performance measure tool of topology evolution scenarios. An example illustrates the whole procedure and particularly points out the tradeoff between CRR improvement by connectivity increase on one hand and CRR improvement by capacity extension of existent links on the other hand.

I. Introduction

While evaluating reliability, successful communication is interpreted as the existence of at least one path being available between nodes s and t. The flow capability of network links and the traffic demand of the system is generally ignored. This implies that the required amount of information can always be transmitted from s to t whenever a path is available, which implies that every link is capable of the required flow- an implication which is neither valid nor economically justifiable in the design of telecommunications networks. Similarly, while finding the maximum capacity[2], the failure probability of links is implicitly neglected --which again is an assumption that is neither valid nor feasible. Although these two measures are independently used, neither is a true measure of the performance of a transport network.

Lee [1], Aggarwal [2], Rai and Soh [3], and Schanzer [4] may be credited for their pioneering works in modifying the definition of reliability as the probability of successfully transmitting the required amount of information from s to t. The available path(s) in any success state must be able to carry the intended information content. But the main drawbacks of all these methods are that: (a) they consider only two-terminal reliability, (b) they don't take capacity sharing (resource sharing among different SD[3]-pairs) into account since they assume that a SD pair has the whole network capacity at its disposal, while the situation in real networks (particularly transport networks) is such that many SD pairs share the available network resources, and (c) they don't take re-routing (or restoration) capability into account, which uses redundant available capacity in order to restore traffic in failure case.

In this paper we extend the methods previously cited for capacity related reliability evaluation for the context of an ATM transport network and we integrate other features such as resource sharing, restoration capability [5-8], heterogeneous traffic demands, and paths layout in the non-failure state. Then we use the obtained method for evaluation of two possible CRR enhancement schemes: (a) connectivity increase by providing additional links to the network; (b) redundant capacity increase on the already existent network links (branches).

II. Assumptions

1. The telecommunication network[4] is modeled by a graph wherein each link is characterized by its reliability and its capacity.
2. Links and paths are bi-directional.
3. Each link can have only two states, up or down, and no information can be transmitted through a down link.
4. The network nodes are perfect or supposed to be such. Consider for example the fact that a modern telecommunication switch is designed with an unavailability goal of 2 hours within 40 years of operation.
5. There is no limit on the capacity of any node of the system.
6. The minimal paths (in the 2-terminal reliability case) and the minimal spanning trees (in the case of all-terminal reliability) considering connectivity only, are known.
7. Cost of interconnection of a link to an already existing node is negligible.
8. Cost of installing every possible link is specified. It generally includes fiber cost, equipement cost, and

[1] VP: Virtual Path.
[2] Refer to Mincut-Maxflow Algorithms.
[3] SD: source-destination.
[4] We consider an ATM VP transport network; its inherent features (inherent rate adaptation and non-hierarchical multiplexing) allow among others flexible network reconfiguration and dynamic bandwidth control, all of which can be combined in order to optimize both restoration and resource sharing.

placement cost. According to references [16,17] it has the general form[5]:

COST=CONST1 + (CONST2 + CAP)*LENGTH (1)

whereby CONST1 may be neglected according to assumption 7; CAP is the total link capacity (including active and redundant capacity); LENGTH is the geographical link length; and CONST2 represent all other factors. So we obtain the simplified expression:

COST= (CONST + CAP)*LENGTH (2)

9. The locations of the various nodes and the possible locations of the connecting links are known.

III. Notations

C_j	capacity (or traffic demand) of path S_j (See Table I)
p_i, q_i	reliability, unreliability of branch i
C(●)	capacity (or contribution to the throughput) of the subnetwork formed by (●)
b	number of branches
m	number of minpaths (spanning trees or paths)
n_j	number of qualifying subsets of minpath P_j
QSS	Qualifying Subset
QSP_{jk}	QSS k from path P_j
SPC_{jk}	set of paths containing QSP_{jk}
ΔC_{jk}	increment in throughput (or capacity) due to QSP_{jk}
$WC\Delta C_{jk}$	worst-case value of ΔC_{jk}
PI	performance index
ΔPI_{jk}	increment in PI due to QSP_{jk}
$\Pr_{jk}$	probability of set QSP_{jk}
CRR	Capacity Related Reliability
GR	Graph Reliability (the traditional definition)

IV. Nomenclature

Branch: An element X of a reliability (logic) diagram which connects two nodes (branches represent links).

Path: A group of branches connecting a source node to a terminal node.

Connecting tree: a group of branches connecting all nodes of the network.

Subset: a group of branches included in the set of branches constituting a tree or a path.

Qualifying Subset: a subset of a minpath (path of spanning tree) which is either contained in one or more of the paths P_j (j<i) or disjoint with each of them (see Fig.1).

Performance Index PI: is the ratio between the traffic demand admitted in the non-failure state and the mean capacity available to transmit it (of course taking both link reliabilities and capacities into account).

V. Method for CRR Evaluation

The quintessence of the method is based on Boolean algebra, consideration of minpaths (in the case of all-terminal reliability minpaths are spanning trees; in the 2-terminal reliability case minpaths are simple paths), optimal restoration, and "survivability"(as defined in references [6,8]):

- Each minpath is expanded (split) so that each of its terms is either disjoint with or absorbed in previously considered minpaths; one obtains QSS's.
- We consider all possible non-zero states (QSS).
- For each QSS (state) optimal restoration is performed, after which ΔPI_{jk} is calculated.

1. Algorithm

<u>*Step 1*</u>

1. Find all minpaths of the network $P_1, P_2, \ldots, P_m$.
2. Define a b-dimensional vector E_i (i=1,2, ..., m) corresponding to P_i such that element at position corresponding to branch K of this vector is 1 if the set $K \subset P_i$ and 0 otherwise.
3. Define $TE_j = \sum_{i \le j} E_i, j = 1,2,\ldots,m$.
4. For QSS P_1 perform optimal restoration (see section V.2) and compute respectively ΔC_1 (see section V.3) and $\Delta PI_1 = \Delta C_1 . \Pr_1$.

<u>*Step 2*</u>

$j \leftarrow 1$ (initialize).

5. Let $j \leftarrow j+1$. If there are any non-zero entries in TE_j corresponding to zero entries in E_j, record their positions as $k_1, k_2, \ldots$
6. Expand P_j successively according to $k_1, k_2, \ldots$ until QSS's are obtained, in a way such as $P_j = P_j K_1 \cup P_j \overline{K_1}$ [6], etc.
7. Ultimately, let $P_j = QSP_{j1} \cup QSP_{j2} \cup \ldots \cup QSP_{jn_j}$.
8. Also record SPC_{jk} for every QSP_{jk}.

<u>*Step 3*</u>

$k \leftarrow 0$ (initialise)

[5] slovenly formulated and compressed.

[6] k_i is the position in E_i corresponding to branch K_i

9. Let $k \leftarrow k+1$. For QSP_{jk}, perform optimal restoration (see section V.2), and calculate ΔC_{jk} (see section V.3).

10. Then calculate $\Delta PI_{jk} = \Delta C_{jk} \Pr_{jk}$.
Let $PI \leftarrow PI + \Delta PI_{jk}$.

11. If $k < n_j$, go to #9.

12. If $j < m$, go to #5.

13. Performance Index = PI.

2. Optimal Restoration (or optimal path layout for restoration)

The goal of an optimal restoration is to restore as much traffic as possible taking a fair resource sharing among all failed paths into account. Nevertheless it is clear that the restoration process in the practice is not always going to be optimal [5,8] so that the results we obtain should be rather considered as theoretical upper bounds of the capacity related reliability.
The paths layout is optimal (or near optimal) if we apply the following steps[7]:

Procedure 1

1. The failed paths are ordered applying following rules:
   - If the some paths have different lengths[8], then the shortest first.
   - If some paths have the same length, then consider first the paths with the highest traffic demand.
2. Re-route (place) the now already ordered paths successively. Each path is placed on a min-cost route such that the total residual capacity (considering all until now already placed paths) is maximal.
3. Repeat #2 (but with a little change in the formulation: a path is first deallocated[9] and then newly placed) until one obtains the same solution after two consecutive allocation cycles[10].

3. Capacity/Throughput Determination

It is evident that a 100%-restoration is not always possible. But we follow a strategy such that available resources are fairly shared among all restorable[11] paths. The throughput of a path is determined as follows:

Procedure 2

1. The throughput is 1 for all non-failed paths; it is 0 for all non-restorable paths.
2. For the restorable paths, do:
   a. determine the "<u>load demand</u>" of each link, which is the sum of the traffic demands of the paths going through this link according to Procedure 1.
   b. for each link, calculate the "<u>load factor</u>", which is the ratio between its capacity and its "load demand".
   c. if all load factors are higher or equal 1, then all restorable paths have a throughput equals 1. Go to #d.
   else:
   - consider the link with the lowest "load factor";
   - all paths going through this link (after Procedure 1) are accorded a throughput equals to this "load factor". The respective traffic demands are updated[12] accordingly. Go to #a[13].

   d. ΔC_{jk} is the sum of the so obtained throughputs over all paths (non-failed and restorable).

   <u>Note</u>:
   - In the two-terminal case ΔC_{jk} is the throughput of the sole path between the terminals in consideration.
   - If a QSP_{jk} is included in SPC_{jk}, then ΔC_{jk} is determined by the formula[14]

$$\Delta C_{jk} = C(SPC_{jk} \cup QSP_{jk}) - C(SPC_{j}$$

4. Theorem

The throughput provided by Procedures 1 and 2 is (near) optimal.

<u>Proof</u>: The results follows directly from both intuition[15] and references [9,10] ■

---

7 we suppose that only the failed paths are rearranged, and we consider the network formed by both redundant capacities and the capacities earlier occupied by failed paths.

8 In the topology provided by the QSS in consideration, the length of a path is the distance between its end nodes (expressed in "number of hops"; a consideration of the geographical length in miles is also conceivable).

9 Since all paths have bin till now allocated (or placed).

10 Procedure 1 is a simplification and thus an acceleration of the so-called simulated allocation (see reference [10]). In subsequent work it was established that about 2-5 cyles are in general sufficient for obtainig the optimal solution, depending on network size & connectivity and heterogeneity of the traffic demands.

11 A path is restorable if its end nodes are still connectable regarding the connectivity of the topology provided by the QSS in consideration.

12 The new "virtual traffic demand" of a path is the product of the "load factor" and the initial traffic demand.

13 Each path S_i is considered only once, the residual link capacities are accordingly updated.

14 It relies on the probability (formula) that one of two non-disjoint events occurs.

15 The arrangement of Procedure 1 is really the one obtained by the so called "simulated allocation"(see reference[10]); the intuition relies on the potential for a path (with a certain traffic demand) to be routed in a way that consumes minimal resources. Moreover reference [10] demonstrates the superiority of "simulated allocation" compared with Linear

VI. CRR Enhancement Strategies

It is clear that there are two ways to improve the CRR of a network:

- **Way A:** topology connectivity optimization is the traditional way and consists in placement of additional links, subject to some cost and performance constraints;
- **Way B:** an other conceivable way is, while maintaining the same topology, to place additional spare capacity on the existent links of the network.

A very important question is then, "which of these two ways is the best, particularly in regards of both generally high placement costs of an additional link and the resulting increase of management complexity consecutive to a higher connected topology?" A global answer is not possible since most of the parameters can not be easily compressed and included in a general theoretical model: costs structure, type and level of traffic demands, location of the different nodes, kind of network (military or civil), etc. Thus the analysis must be performed on a network-by-network basis. Such an analysis is called *trend analysis,* and helps formulate economical factors into a single measurement that represents the total network cost. The numerical example of section VII analyzes (for the sample scenarios considered) some of the factors that may be crucial to determining the economical merit of either Way A or Way B.

1. CRR enhancement by topology optimization

A heuristic method is used for extending a transport network to maximize the overall reliability. We use an optimal link allocation strategy subject to the locations of the network nodes, the installation costs of links in all possible locations along with their reliability. For all the presently available branch positions, a ratio of increase in the overall reliability to increase in the cost is worked out if any particular link is to be added to the network. That link for which this ratio is maximum is added (eventually subject to the permissible cost constraint). The augmented network thus obtained becomes the starting point and the the whole procedure is repeated for the remaining possible links. This is carried out either as long as permitted by the cost constraint or until the reliability level wished is reached. See reference [14] for a similar way of thinking.

2. CRR enhancement by redundancy extension

An alternative to topology extension is the increase of the redundant capacity[16] for CRR enhancement. Two placement strategies are conceivable:

- **Way A1**: the present redundant capacity is uniformly extended (increased) on all links (whereby the requirement that channels must be integer is respected) until either the required CRR is reached or as long as permitted by the (total) cost constraint. This scheme is indeed simple but not necessarily guarantees the optimal CRR to COST ratio.
- **Way A2**: for all presently available branch capacities (active and redundant ones) a ratio of increase in the overall reliability to increase in the cost is worked out if an additional spare channel is placed on a particular branch. That branch (link) for which this ratio is maximum is selected for placement (subject to the permissible cost constraint). The augmented network thus obtained becomes the starting point and the whole procedure is repeated. This is carried out either as long as permitted by the (total) cost constraint or until the CRR wished is reached.

3. Spare Capacity Dimensioning

The problem is to find the appropriate level and distribution of spare capacity in order to have a robust network which is able to cope with a given set of possible failure scenarios. Assignment of spare capacity is driven by several basic factors such as:

- the failure scenarios for which a "100% or less"-restorability is to be guaranteed,
- cost of adding redundant capacity to the various physical links,
- integrality of spare channels, and
- modularity of transmission systems carrying both working and spare capacity (PDH or SONET/SDH systems).

An usual dimensioning basis for redundant capacity is that "100%-restoration is guaranteed" for all one-link failure scenarios [5,8,15]. According to this requirement, optimal redundancy calculation is an easy task using Procedures 1 & 2.

VII. Example

Consider the networks shown in Fig.2, where we assume for simplicity that all links have the same length & reliability, and the same installation cost. For each topology link capacities[17] are caculated as explained in section VI.3. Table I presents the different paths, and their traffic demands. **Net2Ext (see Fig.5 & 6)** is the network topology Net2 for which redundant capacity[18] has been uniformly extended to 130% (the links have in Net2Ext the capacity (equal for all) of 4.6 BU).

As resource sharing & VP bandwidth control scheme we assume that only failed paths are optimally rearranged and they share fairly both the redundant capacity and the capacity earlier occupied from failed paths on non-failed links.

We examine following CRR scenarios:

Programming, Mixed-Integer Programming, and even "simulated annealing [11]".

[16] One should also take the fact in consideration, that an ATM network oft uses bandwith supplied by synchronous systems such as SONET/SDH. For this case restoration flows can still be non integer, however, spare channel assigned to each link in the ATM network are required to be integer. See also reference [15] for a more detailled discussion.

[17] should be expressed in Bandwidth Units (BU); 1 BU can be for example a DS3 or STM-n/OC-n, etc.

[18] initially (for Net2) calculated as explained in section VI.3.

- Two-terminal reliability. For illustration let us consider path S5. Note that nodes 2 and 4 are 3-connected[19]. The results for **Net2** are condensed in Table II[20] (similar tables can be established for the other networks and for the other CRR scenarios (two- & all-terminal).
- All-terminal reliability: the results are condensed in Figures3-6.

Table I: Paths: traffic demands and end nodes

Path Index	Path ID	Path Terminals	Traffic Demand in BU
1	S1	1-2	2
2	S2	1-3	1
3	S3	1-4	1
4	S4	2-3	2
5	S5	2-4	2
6	S6	3-4	1

VIII. Results comment and conclusion

The method presented is very effective since:

- its complexity is polynomial, depending on the number of minpaths, which makes it suitable specially for large networks;
- it allows the derivation of a symbolic expression for the performance index (CRR or availability), what is very advantageous from several point of view such as reduced computer time for numerical evaluation and ease of obtaining derivatives in sensitivity studies (see Table II as illustration).

The main teachings from Figures 3-6 (which are self-explaied) is that depending on link reliability, costs structure & traffic demands --among others-- ***"a higer network connectivity is not necessarily the best & economical way to increase network CRR".*** *Further it has been emphasized that the trend analysis should be performed network-by-network, taking specific network data (which can considerably be different from a network to another) into accout.*

References

[1] S. H. Lee, "Reliability Evaluation of a Flow network", IEEE Trans. Reliability, vol 29, 1980 Apr, pp.24-26.

[2] K. .K. Aggarwal, "A fast Algorithm for the Performance Index of a Telecommunication Network", IEEE Trans. Reliability, vol.37, No.1, 1988 Apr. pp. 65-69.

[3] S. Rai and S. Soh, "Survivability Analysis of Complex Computer Networks with Heterogenous Link-Capacities", IEEE Trans. Reliability, vol 40, 1991 Oct, pp 441-451.

[4] R. Schanzer, "Comment on: Reliability Modeling and Performance of Variable Link-Capacity Networks", IEEE Trans. Reliability, vol.44, No.4, 1995 December, pp.620-621.

[5] J. Anderson et al., "Fast Restoration of ATM Networks", IEEE Journal of Selected Areas in Communication, vol.12, January 1994.

[6] A. Zolfghari and F.J. Kaudel, "Framework for Network Survivability Performance", IEEE Journal of Selected Areas in Communication, vol.12, no.1, January 1994.

[7] B. Sanso and F. Soumis, "Communication & Transportation Network Reliability Using Routing Models", IEEE Trans. Reliability, vol.40. no.1, April 1991.

[8] K. Kyandoghere, "Survivability Functions as Performance Measure Tool for Rerouting Strategies in an ATM/VP Mesh Transport Network",Proceedings of The joint IEEE ICCS'96 / ISPACS'96, 25-29 November 1996, Singapore, pp. 25.4.1-25.4.7.

[9] A. Gersht and A. Shulman, "Optimal Routing in Circuit Switched Communication Networks", IEEE Transactions on Communications, vol.37, Nov.1989, pp.1203-1211.

[10]M. Pioro, P. Gajowniczek, "Stochastic allocation of virtual paths to ATM links", in Performance Modelling and Evaluation of ATM Networks, Chapman & Hall, 1995.

[11]D.S. Johnson, C.R. Aragon, L.A. McGeoch, and C. Schevon, "Optimization by Simulated Annealing: an Experimental Evaluation", in Operations Research, Vol.39, No.1, 1991.

[12]K. Kyandoghere, "VP Control for ATM Networks with Call-Level QOS Guarantees", in the IEICE Transactions on Communications, Vol..E1-B, No.1, January 1998, pp.32-44.

[13]K. Kyandoghere, "A customized Service Availability Concept based on Traffic Segregation, Path Diversity and Hierarchical Restoration in Public Telecommunication Transport Networks", in Proceedings of The Third IEEE International Conference on Electronics, Circuits, and Systems ICECS'96, October 13-16, 1996, Rodos, Greece., pp. 1190-1193.

[14] K.K. Aggarwal, "Topological layout of links for optimizing the overall reliability in a computer communication system", Microlectron. Rel.22, No.3, pp.347-351,1982.

[15] M.H. Herzberg, S.J. Bye, and A. Utano, "The Hop-Limit Approach for Spare-Capacity Assignment in Survivable Networks", IEEE/ACM Transactions on Networking, Vol.3, No.6, December 1995.

[16] E.I. Tsai, B.A. Coan, M.Kerner, and M.P. Vecchi, "A comparison of Strategies for Survivable Network Design: Reconfigurable and Conventioanal Approaches", Proc. of the IEEE GLOBECOM'90, San Diego, CA, December 1990, pp.301.1.1-301.1.7.

[17] Tsong-Ho Wu, Fiber Network Service Survivability, Artech House, MA, 1992.

[19] We consider link-connectivity since nodes are assumed to be perfect or near of that.

[20] For Net2 we obtain that all link have the same capacity L=4 BU, including redundant capacity of 100% (2 BU on each link).

Path	Subset	QSP_{jk}	(**)	SPC_{jk}	ΔC_{jk}	$\Pr_{jk}$
P_1:E			d	---	1	p_E
P_2:AC	AC	ACE	a	P_1	0	---
		$AC\bar{E}$	d	---	$(L-2)/2$	$p_A p_C q_E$
P_3:BD	BD	$BDACE$	a	P_1, P_2	0	---
		$BDAC\bar{E}$	a	P_2	0	---
		$BDA\bar{C}E$	a	P_1	0	---
		$BDA\bar{C}\bar{E}$	d	---	$(L-2)/4$	$p_A p_B q_C p_D q_E$
		$BD\bar{A}CE$	a	P_1	0	---
		$BD\bar{A}C\bar{E}$	d	---	$(L-2)/4$	$q_A p_B p_C p_D q_E$
		$BD\bar{A}\bar{C}E$	a	P_1	0	---
		$BD\bar{A}\bar{C}\bar{E}$	d	---	$(L-2)/2$	$q_A p_B q_C p_D q_E$

(**)a: absorbed; d: disjoint; e: expand.

Table II: Net2: Solution for the two-terminal CRR(S5) case, path S5(2-4). Minpaths are paths between 2 and 4. L=4 BU.

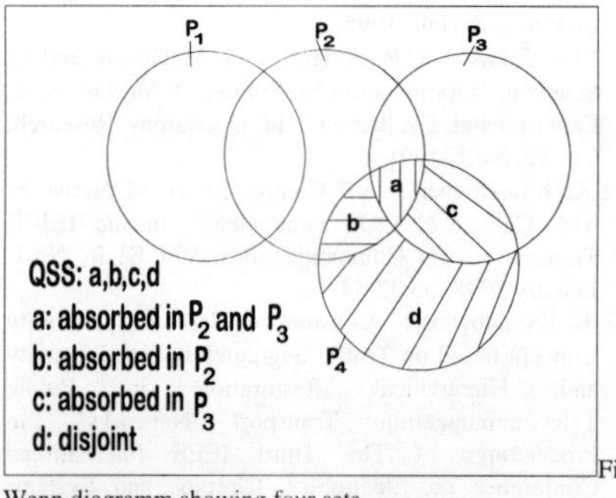

Fig.1: Wenn diagramm showing four sets.

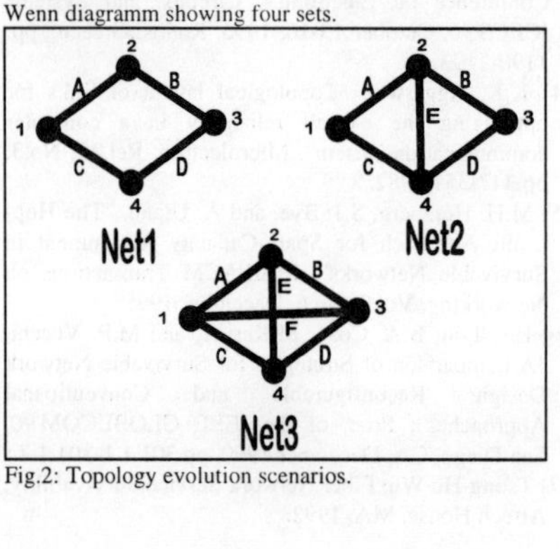

Fig.2: Topology evolution scenarios.

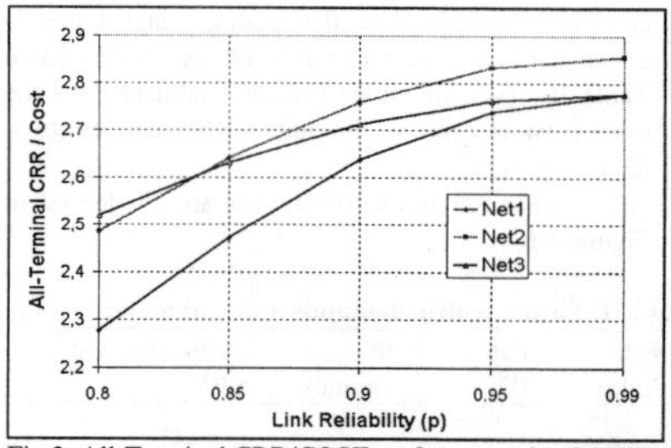

Fig.3: All-Terminal CRR/COST performance for CONST=3.

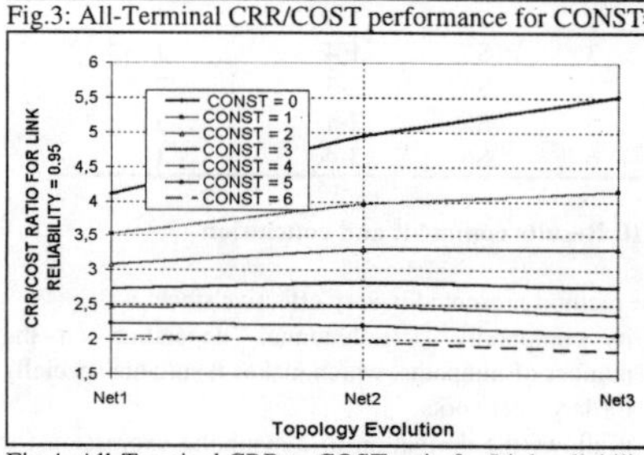

Fig.4: All-Terminal CRR to COST ratio for Link reliability p=0.95.

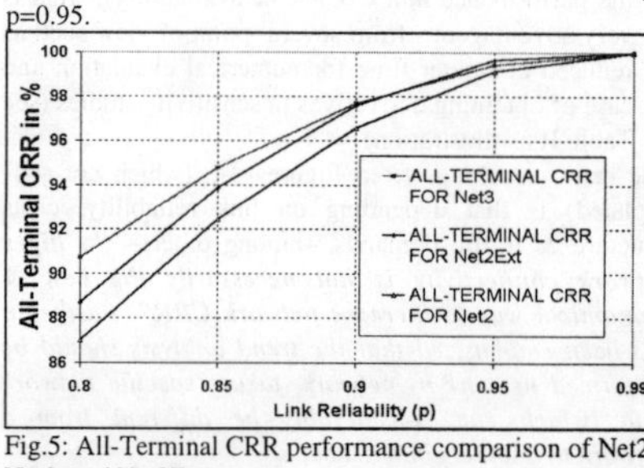

Fig.5: All-Terminal CRR performance comparison of Net2, Net3, and Net2Ext.

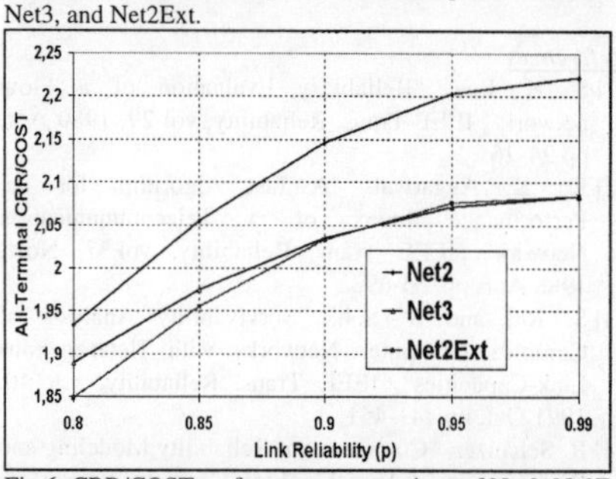

Fig.6: CRR/COST performance comparison of Net2, Ne2Ext and Net3 for CONST=5.

THE DESIGN OF PASSIVE OPTICAL NETWORKS ACCORDING TO FSAN

G.A. Pikrammenos , J. D. Angelopoulos

National Technical University of Athens
Electrical and Computer Science Dptm.
157 73 Polytechniopolis Zographou

Abstract

The need for specialized low cost solutions to the residential last mile which will enable the photonization of the local loop led to the Full Services Access Network (FSAN) initiative among the major world Public Network Operators and manufacturers. The result of a two year effort by this forum is a low level specification of a Passive Optical Network (PON) architecture which can be the basis for the design of components for an open broadband ATM based PON system expediting the development and deployments of such access solutions. The functions, formats, and expediencies for the design of an FSAN compliant PON are presented in this work.

Introduction

The photonization of the local loop has stayed far behind that of the transmission plant for reasons of cost and low traffic intensities. The high cost of introducing dedicated fibers into residential access networks inhibits a widespread deployment of broadband services, which in turn could finance the fiber upgrade of the local loop. To fuel the initial boost out of this vicious circle, requires special technological solutions which take into account the peculiarities and cost sensitivity of residential customers. Business customers can afford the dedicated access links because they have already concentrated traffic from an economically viable number of terminals by means of cheaper shared media Customer Premises Networks (CPNs), typically Local Area Networks (LANs). Traffic concentration, infrastructure sharing and re-use of the drop lines are cost saving measures which must also be offered to domestic sites by the access architecture. Although interim solutions like Asymmetric Digital Subscriber Loop (ADSL) can extend the useful life of the copper plant and play an important role in stimulating demand for broadband services, they inevitably exhaust their capabilities at some point sooner or later in the steadily rising bandwidth demand curve. In contrast, PONs constitute a medium and long term solution which can offer an affordable, flexible and robust access system to the domestic customer with virtually unlimited expandability [8]. Initial low cost architectures feature a TDMA approach, but the prospects of Wavelength Division Multiplexing (WDM) expansion on the same fiber infrastructure make PONs a future-proof system, a feature not found in competitive solutions. In such an upgrade the full system capacity is made available to smaller clusters of customers by means of separate wavelengths carried on the same initial fiber plant.

PON systems with narrow-band interfaces are already in commercial exploitation but also ATM-based broadband PONs (APONs) have been repeatedly demonstrated in several field trials e.g. [2], [3].

These first generation APONs built a few years ago were designed for a distance of a few kilometers and a splitting ratio of 16 to 32, serving around 100 customers by Fiber To The Curb (FTTC). Their evaluation gave promising even if not spectacular results in terms of robustness, flexibility and cost reduction. Compared to the dedicated fiber solution, the cost per customer can be halved [3].

Recognizing the special needs of the residential market attention to access solutions is growing as reflected in the activities of the RBB (Residential BroadBand) working group of ATM Forum [4] and the FSAN (Full Services Access Network) initiative [1]. This initiative was taken by the largest PTTs and Telecom system manufacturers with an aim to expedite the deployment of residential access systems by focusing on the most promising system choices and assisting the mass production of components by narrowing down the array of options. In relation to PONs, the effort has resulted

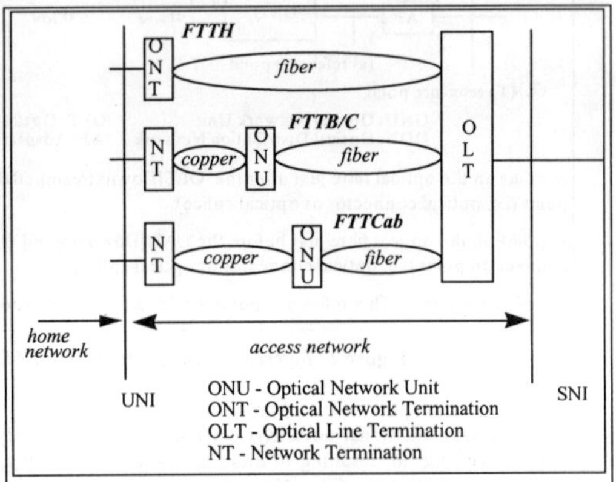

Figure 1 *Network Architecture (form page 10 of [1])*

in a system specification which is now offered for resolution by the ITU Study Group 15 as recommendation G.983 [N]. This specification defines a PON system which can be the basis of a cost-effective and open design approach. The main features of this specification are the focus of this paper.

The Architecture

The optical section of a Local Access Network system could be either a point-to-point, active, or passive point-to-multipoint architecture. Figure 1 shows the architectures considered.

FTTB/C (Fiber to the Building /Curb) and FTTCab (Fiber to the Cabinet) network options are the same from a technical point of view. Within the FTTCab/C/B scenario the following service categories have been considered: (i) Asymmetric broadband services; (ii) Symmetric broadband services; (iii) PSTN and ISDN.

FTTH (Fiber to the Home) despite higher initial costs, offers the following additional advantages: (i) Indoor ONU's can be considered, resulting in more favorable environmental conditions; (ii) No change of intermediate ONU is required to upgrade access network capabilities to accommodate future evolution of broadband and multimedia services; (iii) Maintenance is easier, because of lack of metallic part; (iv) FTTH is a driver for the development of advanced optoelectronics technologies.

The OAN (Optical Access Network) is common to all architectures shown in Figure 1, and this commonality in this system has the potential to generate large world-wide volumes.

Figure 2 shows the reference configuration of the PON according to the ITU G.982. The ODN offers one or more optical paths between one OLT and one or more ONUs. The OLT is connected over the Service Node Interface (SNI) to service nodes and to the PON. The OLT is responsible for managing all the PON specific aspects of the ATM transport system. The ONU interfaces over the IF_{PON} to the OLT and to the User Network Interface (UNI). Together with the OLT, the ONU is responsible for providing a transparent ATM transport service between the UNI and the SNI over the PON. The ODN provides the optical transmission means from the OLT towards the users and vice versa. It utilizes passive optical components. Each optical path is defined between reference points S and R in a specific wavelength window. The two directions for optical transmission in the ODN are identified as follows: downstream direction for signals traveling from the OLT to the ONU(s), and upstream direction for signals traveling from the ONU(s) to the OLT.

ONU's share the capacity of one fiber which is passively split between them. Because of the passive splitting, special actions are required with respect to privacy and security. Moreover, in the upstream direction a TDMA MAC protocol is required [5], [6]. The interface at the reference points S/R and R/S is defined as IF_{PON}. This is a PON-specific interface that supports all the protocol elements necessary to allow the transmission between OLT and ONUs. The ONU may have an adaptation function (AF), for digital subscriber line (DSL) transmission over copper to the customer. The OAN is the system between the 'V' and 'T' reference points and is managed as one element, through a Q3 management interface.

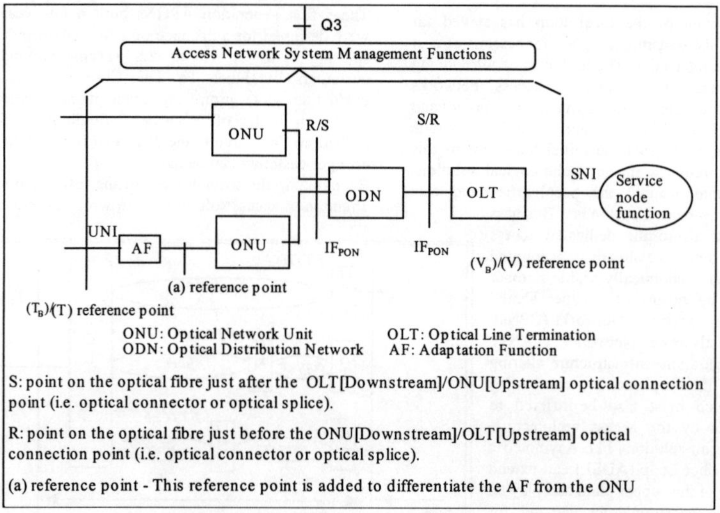

Figure 2 *Reference Configuration for an ATM based PON*

Layered structure of optical network

The protocol reference model is divided into Physical Medium (G.902), TC (Transmission Convergence) layer (I.326), and Path Layer (G.982). In the ATM-PON network, Path Layer corresponds to the VP (Virtual Path) of the ATM layer.

For the Physical Medium dependent layer the transmission line rate should be a multiple of 8 kHz. The target standardized system will have the following nominal line rates: (i) Symmetric 155.52 Mbit/s for FTTCab /C/B/H and (ii) Asymmetric 155.52 Mbit/s upstream / 622.08 Mbit/s downstream for FTTCab/C/B.

addressing tables in the ONU and enables efficient use of the PON resource. For an ATM-PON the TC layer must have cell rate decoupling and support HEC calculation error correction (both are described in I.432.1).

The downstream signal is broadcast to all ONUs on the PON. Each upstream transmission from each ONU is controlled by OLT and governed by grant sent in the downstream effecting aTime Division Multiple Access (TDMA) technique. The transfer capability for ATM cells includes information cells, signaling cells, OAM cells, and unassigned cells used for cell rate decoupling.

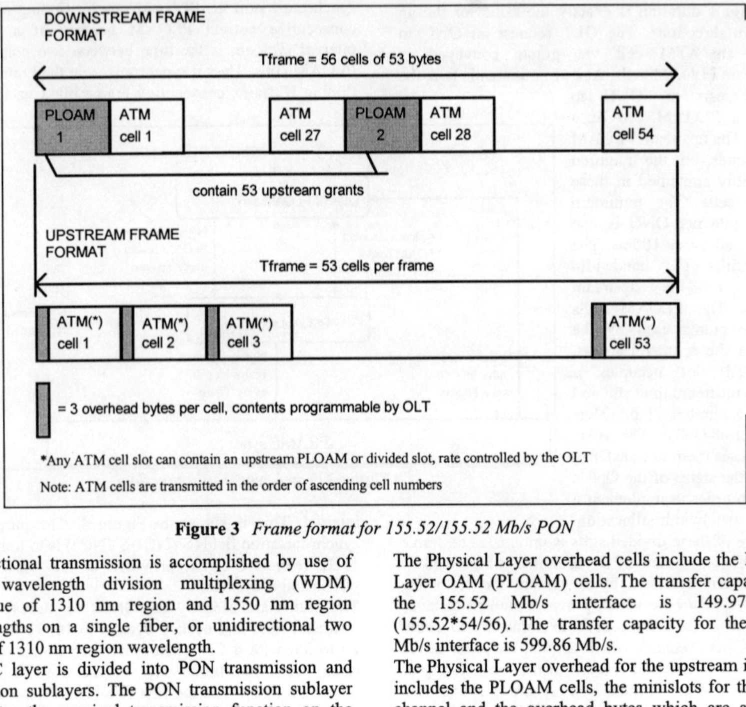

Figure 3 *Frame format for 155.52/155.52 Mb/s PON*

Bi-directional transmission is accomplished by use of either wavelength division multiplexing (WDM) technique of 1310 nm region and 1550 nm region wavelengths on a single fiber, or unidirectional two fibers of 1310 nm region wavelength.

The TC layer is divided into PON transmission and adaptation sublayers. The PON transmission sublayer terminates the required transmission function on the ODN. The PON specific functions are terminated by the PON transmission sublayer, and it is not seen from the adaptation sublayer. The two layers considered are based on G.958 layering principles.

PON addressing can use the full 12 bit VP field of the ATM cell header, as it is used across the VB5 reference point [7]. The VPI values on the PON do not have to be equal to the VPI values across the VB5 reference point, because the OLT will have a VP cross-connect function. The limit of up to 4096 VPs avoids costly

The Physical Layer overhead cells include the Physical Layer OAM (PLOAM) cells. The transfer capacity for the 155.52 Mb/s interface is 149.97 Mb/s (155.52*54/56). The transfer capacity for the 622.08 Mb/s interface is 599.86 Mb/s.

The Physical Layer overhead for the upstream interface includes the PLOAM cells, the minislots for the MAC channel and the overhead bytes which are added in front of each upstream ATM cell, PLOAM cell or minislot. The transfer capacity for the 155.52 Mb/s interface has an upper limit of 147.2Mb/s (155.52*53/56Mb/s). Some extra bandwidth is allocated by the OLT for the upstream PLOAM channel and MAC channel. The upstream transfer capacity is shared amongst the ONUs based on their allocated upstream bandwidth.

Further, we will see in more detail the functions that take place inside the TC layer.

Transport specific TC functions

Frame structure

The downstream interface structure consists of a continuous stream of timeslots for both 155.52Mb/s and 622.08Mb/s, with each timeslot containing 53 octets of an ATM cell or a PLOAM cell. Every 28 timeslots a PLOAM cell is inserted. A downstream frame contains 2 such PLOAM cells and is 56 slots long for the 155Mb/s downstream case. For the 622Mb/s case, it contains 8 PLOAM cells and is 224 slots long.

The upstream frame contains 53 time slots of 56 bytes, i.e. the frame duration is exactly the same for the up and down directions. The OLT request an ONU to transmit an ATM cell via grants conveyed in downstream PLOAM cells. At a programmable rate, the OLT requests an ONU to transmit a PLOAM cell or a minislot. The upstream PLOAM rate depends on the required functionality contained in these PLOAM cells. The minimum PLOAM rate per ONU is one PLOAM cell every 100ms. The OLT defines the bandwidth allocated to the upstream minislots. The PLOAM cells carry the grants used by the ONUs for the upstream access. A divided slot occupies a complete upstream time slot and contains a number of minislots from a set of ONUs. The MAC protocol uses them to transfer to the OLT the status of the ONUs queues, in order to implement a dynamic bandwidth allocation.

The usage of these divided slots is optional. The frame structure for a symmetric PON is shown in Figure 33

The upstream overhead bytes contain the following fields: (i) *Guard time* which provides enough distance between two consecutive cells or minislots to avoid collisions, (ii) *Preamble* which extracts the phase of the arriving cell or minislot relative to the local timing of the OLT, and/or acquires bit synchronization and amplitude recovery, and (iii) *Delimiter* which is a unique pattern indicating the start of the ATM cell or minislot, which can be used to perform byte synchronization. The minimum guard time length is 4 bits. The total overhead length is 24 bits. The guard time length, preamble pattern and delimiter pattern are programmable under the OLT's control. The content of these fields is defined by the Upstream_overhead message in the downstream PLOAM cells.

Downstream PLOAM cells

PLOAM cells are terminated at the Transport Specific TC layer of the ONU. The payload of the PLOAM cell is processed as long as the ONU is frame synchronized and did not detect any alarm. Any cell, numbered 'ATM cell 1' up to 'ATM cell 54' in Figure 3 or numbered 'ATM cell 1' up to 'ATM cell 216', in the case of a 622 downstream rate, that has a header equal to the specified header of a PLOAM cell, is discarded at the ONU in the ATM specific TC layer.

The contents of the IDENT, the first byte in the PLOAM cell payload are: bits 1..7 all '0' for future use and bit 8 '1' for the first PLOAM cell of a downstream frame and '0' for the others.

Bytes two and three are used by the ONU to be synchronized on the downstream frame, based on the Frame bit in the downstream PLOAM cells, before it can access the upstream link. Once the downstream ATM cell delineation is completed, the ONU synchronizes on the PLOAM rate by finding N_ploam consecutive correct PLOAM headers at a Tploam interval. Tploam is the time between two consecutive PLOAM cells. Then it synchronizes on the Frame bit by finding N_frame consecutive Frame bit=1 at a Tframe

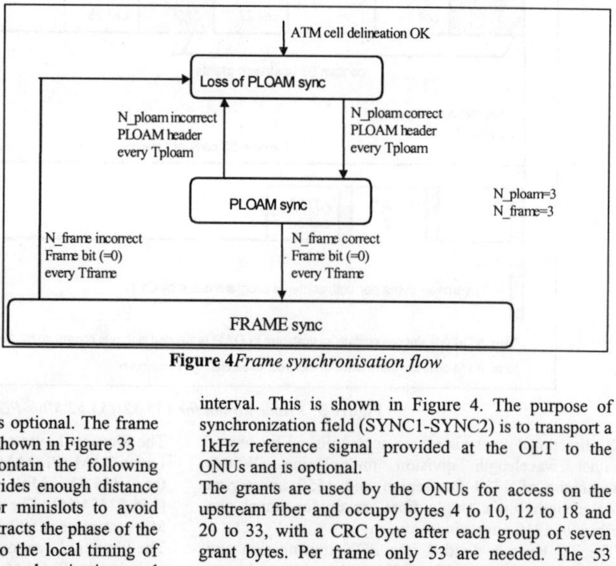

Figure 4*Frame synchronisation flow*

interval. This is shown in Figure 4. The purpose of synchronization field (SYNC1-SYNC2) is to transport a 1kHz reference signal provided at the OLT to the ONUs and is optional.

The grants are used by the ONUs for access on the upstream fiber and occupy bytes 4 to 10, 12 to 18 and 20 to 33, with a CRC byte after each group of seven grant bytes. Per frame only 53 are needed. The 53 grants are mapped in the first two PLOAM cells of the downstream frame. All 53 grants are non-idle grants. The last grant of the second PLOAM cell is filled with an idle grant. The grant fields of the six remaining PLOAM cells for the asymmetrical case are all filled with idle grants and hence will not be used by the ONU. The length of a grant is 8 bits and has the following types: Data grant, PLOAM grant, Divided_slot grant, Reserved grants, Ranging grant, Unassigned grant, and Idle grant. The OLT can address 32 ONUs at the same time and optionally it may address up to 64 ONUs. A Cyclic Redundancy Check (CRC) protects a group of 7 grants. The generating CRC polynomial for the grants is: $g(x) = x^8 + x^2 + x + 1$. It can protect up to 15 bytes and has a Hamming distance of 4. It is able to detect up to 3 bit errors. No error correction is done. Once the ONU is in frame sync and as long as there is no loss of cell delineation, the grant groups are processed independent of the correctness of the PLOAM cell header.

All OAM related alarms or threshold-crossing alerts triggered by events, are transported via messages in the PLOAM cells. These messages cover bytes 35 to 46 followed from a CRC byte. Also all ranging related messages are mapped in the message field of the PLOAM cell. The processing of a message received at the ONU relating to the ranging procedure should be completed within the time of 6 frame periods (6*Tframe). This includes the eventual preparation of an upstream message corresponding to this downstream message. The messages are protected by the same polynomial as the grants. Once the ONU is in frame sync, the message field is processed independent of the correctness of the PLOAM cell header. No error correction is applied to this received message field. The message will be discarded at reception when the CRC is incorrect. This message field has the following field types: MESSAGE_PON_ID which addresses a particular ONU, MESSAGE_ID which indicates the type of the message, and MESSAGE_FIELD which contains the message.

The Bit Interleaved Parity (BIP8) field is used for monitoring the BER on the downstream link is the last byte of the PLOAM cell, the 48th. A one byte BIP8 in each PLOAM cell covers 28*53-1=1483 bytes. Each of the bits of the BIP8 byte is the XOR of all the same-position bits in all the covered bytes before scrambling. The ONU compares the received BIP8 with the BIP8 it calculated on the received byte stream. Each differing bit is counted. The BIP is a good estimate for the real BER when the BER is smaller than 10^{-4}.

Upstream PLOAM structure

The contents of the payload of the upstream PLOAM cell are relevant with those of the downstream but not the same. The IDENT field is all '0', message fields now occupy bytes 2 to13, byte 14 is CRC. Bytes 15 to 31 are LCF1 to LCF17 (Laser Control Field), which are used to maintain the nominal specified mean optical output power and to control the extinction ratio when the ONU is allowed to send a cell. Also bytes 32 to 47 are RXCF1 to RXCF16 (Receiver Control Field), which are used in the upstream OLT receiver to recover the correct threshold level for regenerating the data from the incoming analog signal. Finally, byte 48 is the BIP. PLOAM cells are terminated at the Transport Specific TC layer of the OLT.

Divided_slots

An upstream slot can contain a Divided_Slot. It fits in one upstream slot and contains a number of minislots coming from a set of ONUs. The OLT assigns one divided_slot grant to this set of ONUs for sending their minislot. The format of the divided_slot is shown in Figure 5. The start of a minislot is at byte boundaries. The length of the minislot is a multiple number of bytes. The end of the last minislot must be before or coincident with the end of the upstream slot. The three overhead bytes have the same definition.

Churning

Due to the multicast nature of the PON, downstream cells are churned at the TC layer with a churning key sent upstream by the ONU. The churning is performed for point to point downstream connections and churning can be enabled or disabled per VP. The churning key update rate is at least 1 update per second per ONU. If churning is not enough for a security requirement of a provided service, a suitable encryption mechanism should be employed at a higher layer than the TC layer to provide data scrambling.

ATM specific TC functions

The normal ATM delineation method is used in the downstream direction. However, in the upstream a special method is needed since a different transmitter is sending each slot

Initially, cell delineation is achieved by the ranging method. The ONU equalizes the round trip delay to make its cell arrive at the correct time for the OLT. The ranging process can be seen as the HUNT state as defined in ITU-T Recommendation I.432.1. After one correct delimiter and HEC, the ONU is declared in sync. For 8 consecutive incorrect delimiters or HECs, the ONU is declared out of sync (LCDi, loss of cell delineation) and it will be deactivated and reranged. Still pending grants for this ONU will be discarded.

The upstream cells are scrambled with a generating polynomial $x^9 + x^4 + 1$.

OAM functions

The general principles as defined in I.610 can be applied to the PON. However, due to the point to multipoint nature of the physical medium, some notifications from OLT to ONU are obsolete because principally the ONU slaves to the OLT and the ONU cannot do anything with these notifications.

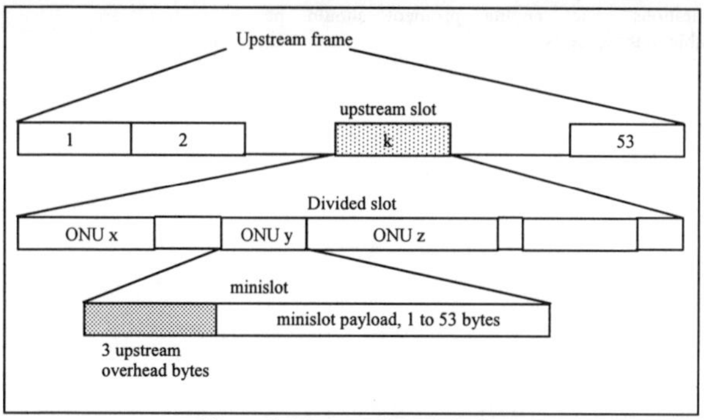

Figure 5 *Format of Divided_slot*

Ranging Method

A full digital in-band based ranging method should be used by the PON system to measure the logical reach distances between each ONU and the OLT. The maximum range of the PON is at least 20 km. The transmission delay measurement for each ONU should be capable of being performed while the PON is in-service without disrupting service to other ONUs. The window size for the delay measurement signal can be minimised by using some information about the position of the ONU, for example an a priori minimum and maximum OLT - ONU distance, which can be provisioned with a granularity as defined by the network operator. The ranging protocol is specified and applicable for several types of installation methods of ONUs and several types of ranging processes, if necessary, with additional or optional functions.

Different situations as described below are possible where the ranging process may occur. There are four categories under which the ranging process would occur:

(i) Cold PON, cold ONU: This situation is characterized when no upstream traffic is running on the PON and the ONUs have not yet received PON-IDs from the OLT.

(ii) Warm PON, cold ONU: This situation is characterized by the addition of new ONU(s) which have not been previously ranged or by the addition of previously active ONU(s) having power restored and coming back to the PON while traffic is running on the PON.

(iii) Warm PON, warm ONU: This situation is characterized by a previously active ONU which remains powered-on and connected to an active PON but prohibited from sending upstream cells due to loss of downstream signal or deactivation order from the OLT etc. And also, this situation includes an active ONU connected to an active PON with running traffic.

(iv) Switch over: There can be several types of possible duplex and/or partially duplexed ATM-PON configurations. The ranging protocol should be applicable in these cases.

Acknowledgement. This work was funded by the Greek General Secretariat for Research, PENED 426/95: "Protocols for Access to PONs"

References

[1] ITU-TS Rec. G.983, "High speed optical access systems based on PON techniques" question 2/15 offered for resolution to SG-15, Feb. 1998.

[2] U. Killat, editor, "Access to B-ISDN via PONs", John Wiley /Teubner 1st Edition, 1996.

[3] W.Verbiest, G.Van der Plas, D.Mestdagh, "FITL and BISDN: A Marriage with a Future", IEEE Communications Mag., Vol 31, No. 6, June 1993.

[4] L.F. Wojnaroski, "Baseline text for the Residential Broadband Sub-working group," ATM Forum Doc. No. ATMF95-0458R1, Aug.1995.

[5] J.D.Angelopoulos, I.S.Venieris, E.N. Protonotarios, "A Transparent MAC Method for Bandwidth Sharing and CDV Control at the ATM layer of Passive Optical Networks", *IEEE/OSA Journal of Lightwave Technology,* Vol., 14, No. 12, December 1996.

[6] J. D. Angelopoulos, G.C. Boukis, I.S.Venieris, "Delay priorities enhance utilization of ATM PON Access Systems", *Computer Communications Journal*. 20 (1997), pp 937-949.

[7] ETSI, "V interfaces at the digital Service Node, Identification of the applicability of existing specifications for a VB5 reference point in an access arrangement with access networks". ver. 1.4, 05/9/95.

[8] Ingrid Van de Voorde, Gert Van der Plaas, "Full Services Optical Networks: ATM Transport on Passive Optical Networks", *IEEE Comm. Magazine,* Vol. 35, No. 4, April 1997.

AN ALTERNATIVE METHOD FOR SECURING PRIVACY IN PON AND HFC NETWORKS

JOHN KOULOURIS, ANDREAS KOULOURIS

National Technical University of Athens
Electrical and Computer Science Dptm.
157 73 Polytechniopolis Zographou, Greece
Tel. (+301) 2615800, Fax: (+301) 6118455, 7722534
e-mail: johnkoul@cs.ntua.gr

ABSTRACT

In Some kind of networks like PON (Passive Optical Networks) and HFC (Hybrid Fiber Coaxial) networks, the information from the central station (headend) to the terminals is broadcast to all of them. So each station besides its own data gets also the data destined to the others. Under these conditions privacy and confidentiality do not exist. The usual way to overcome this drawback is conventional encryption of the data between headend and terminals. Even with this procedure however, some basic characteristics of the ongoing connections, like traffic data, cannot be protected, as encryption of the connection identifiers is not possible. Here an alternative method is presented, which, although not encryption in the conventional meaning of the term, secures a high degree of individuality and confidentiality and has also some other advantages over conventional encryption. The basic idea is to use different multiplexing patterns for each connection so that each terminal can demultiplex only its own data. The method is suited for the high data speed of the PON networks and maybe preferable to conventional encryption.

I. INTRODUCTION

Modern high capacity services like video on demand, teleworking, high data transfer, e.t.a. require fiber optic or coaxial cables. In order to reduce the high costs of laying individual cables for each user and install costly optical terminals to both ends of them, Passive Optical Networks (PON) are being developed in the recent years, in which the larger part of the network is common and shared by many terminals and only the last section (usually tens or hundreds of meters) is exclusively for one terminal. In other cases existing cable TV coaxial networks are used in combination with new fiber optic cables constituting Hybrid Fiber Coaxial (HFC) networks. All these networks work in ATM mode and the data going from the central station (headend) to the terminals (downstream data) are time multiplexed and broadcast to all of them, each terminal selecting and processing the data destined to it. The data from the terminals to the headend (upstream data) are also time multiplexed and driven through the common medium. The downstream capacity is much larger (usually 8fold) than the upstream capacity, which is in accordance with the needs of most of the services provided. This do not excludes of course services, like POTS, which demand an equal upstream and downstream capacity. The whole communication is controlled by the Medium Access Controller (MAC) through a sophisticated Protocol.

Because of this topology individuality and confidentiality do not practically exist in the downstream direction, since every user can receive and process all data. For operational reasons the identity of the terminal to which every packet is destined is stated in the overhead of the cells so that eavesdropping in the data of others is easy and cannot be avoided. The usual method to overcome this drawback is encryption of the data in the MAC Layer [2,4]. The encryption could be avoided for the payload of the cells if end to end encryption of ATM cells was generally applied, but this seems not to be the general case for the next years [1]. Even in that case however encryption should be necessary for the PLOAM and signaling cells as well as for some fields of the overhead, in order to avoid access to the traffic and other data of a terminal by another terminal. Encryption of these data is not an easy task though and it may prove impossible.

In the upstream direction confidentiality is secured, at least in networks like the above, because the reflections of the signals in the splitting positions, are detectable by the other users but not readable. In upstream direction other security problems arise, like authentication, data integrity e.t.a. which are not the main subject of this paper, although a brief reference to them will be made.

2 CONVENTIONAL ENCRYPTION

Conventional encryption is generally carried out by using some ciphering code according to which every bit of the original text is replaced by another bit, so that the resulting text has no meaning to any one except for the user to whom it is destined, who has the proper code to decrypt it and recover the original text.

Several methods for encryption have been developed and proposed using both block cipher (like DES) [4] and stream cipher principles [5]. In networks like PON it is very easy to have both the plaintext and its corresponding ciphertext of a message and, much worst, it is easy to have a chosen plaintext and its ciphertext. This is possible since every user who wishes

to attack the encryption system of another user simply sends him a chosen plaintext and then receives the corresponding ciphertext
which is broadcast to all terminals. As it is well known, having both a chosen plaintext and its corresponding ciphertext gives an attacker the best opportunity to break a cryptosystem. Following this the encryption methods used should be resistant to such attacks, which leads to sophisticated and hence slow encryption algorithms. This contradicts with the need of very fast encryption algorithms to deal with the high speed of downstream data.
Most problems in the conventional encryption arise exactly from the above contradiction. The use of parallel processing in order to increase the speed could perhaps solve this problem, but besides the rising cost and the complexity, it is not always sure that the desired results can be reached.
More problems arise when we wish to encrypt also the headers of the downstream cells in order to avoid speculations on ones traffic parameters. If we encrypt for example the destination field of each cell which contains the identification number (ID Number) of the addressed terminal, then all terminals should have to decrypt this field in all received cells in order to see if the cell is addressed to them. This poses a very heavy and time consuming work on the terminals which, even if it will be possible to be executed in the necessary speed, leads to expensive terminals.
Still worst is the case when the decryption of a field by two terminals gives to both of them their correct ID number, following that the one of them who will try to decrypt the wrong payload, will get confused and most probably lose encryption synchronization. This cannot be avoided because in the encryption procedure we do not
control the resulting ciphertext, and so it can be that the encipherment of two different plaintexts (in our case two different ID numbers) using different ciphercodes for each of them will lead to the same ciphertext, and hence the decipherment of this ciphertext by the corresponding deciphering codes will lead both to their original ID numbers. This happening has the same probability as randomly selecting two numbers out of a collection of them. If we consider that usually the ID field of the downstream cells is 14 bit long and that a super PON network can have 2000 terminals, we will have a probability of 50%, that this will happen every 5 cells! In order to minimize this probability we should use very long ID fields, which, besides other disadvantages leads to bad efficiency.

3. THE PROPOSED METHOD

Our method utilizes the same characteristic of the network architecture that causes the problem, that is the broadcasting nature of the downstream data, in order to restore the lost privacy and individuality.
The basic idea is quite simple: Since we use multiplexing in order to make a single large bit stream out of the several incoming individual streams, and since every terminal demultiplex it in order to get its own stream, why we should do multiplexing in the same way for all terminals (so that every terminal can demultiplex not only its own but also every other's stream) and don't do it differently for each terminal, so that every one of them can demultiplex only its own stream?
Multiplexing is usually done in cell level, that is each ATM cell contains data of one connection and, by means of the VCI Number contained in the corresponding field of the header, is destined to the terminal serving that connection. Sometimes however for reason of maintaining low delay or delay variation it is necessary that multiplexing is done in byte level, in which case composite cells are formed with bytes from more than one connection destined to more than one users. In the later case the terminal understands which bytes of the cell are destined to it either by information contained in front of the bytes, or by the fix places within the ATM cells in which the bytes destined to it are placed. The corresponding information is given to all terminals, so that also in the case of the composite cells every terminal can eavesdrop in the data of the other terminals.
Our method uses always composite cells for the connections to be encrypted, but the bits in the cells are multiplexed in a different random way for every user, which we call *multiplexing pattern*, and this pattern is known only to the central station and to him This pattern plays the role of the session key of the conventional encryption and is changed in every new connection.
The exact procedure is as follows:
All downstream cells, which have usually 54 bytes, have a characteristic bit in their header. If the bit is 1 then the cell is a composite («encrypted») cell. If the bit is 0 the cell is not encrypted. Practically only some OAM cells and general information cells will be unencrypted. In the field where the unencrypted cells have their 14 bit ID Number the encrypted cells have an identification number ranging from 0 to $\mathbf{T_n}$. The number $\mathbf{T_n}$ is the period of the downstream module for encrypted cells and is depended on the capacity of the downstream data flow and the desired granularity of the services offered.
Here we will describe the case of a super PON with a downstream capacity of 2.54 Gbps. For reasons which will be understood later T_n has been chosen to be $(2^{11}-1)$. So in case that no unencrypted cells intervene the same identification number of a cell will appear every 2^{11} cells. Given that every downstream cell has 400 payload bits (the ATM payload plus the VCI field), the basic module contains about $400 \times 2^{11} = 819200$ bits (The "about" is because the payload of the downstream cell can contain more fields than the two referred above).
Every bit place of the cell is enumerated from 0 to 400. So with 9 bits we can enumerate all the places of a cell, while with 20 bits we can enumerate uniquely all the places in the basic module, where the first 11 bits refer to the cell and the last 9 to the place inside the cell

The basic module will be used for connections of 16 Kbps . Finer granularity is not considered since it is very unlikely that such networks will support slower rates. A 16kbps connection needs 8 bits in the basic period.
When a new 16 Kbps connection is to be established the central station selects randomly 8 out of the 819200 possible places for that connection, taking care that they are free from other connections. This constrain do not influence the randomness of the choice because the occupied places have also been chosen randomly. These places, ordered in a random and fixed way, are the multiplexing pattern of the connection. For the description of the pattern we need 8x20=160 bits. We need also 4 extra bits to indicate that this pattern refers to the basic module. The above pattern, which play the role of the session key of the conventional encryption, is communicated to the corresponding terminal through one of the OAM (operation and maintenance) cells interchanged between headend and terminal station during the establishment of the connection. The payload of the OAM cell is encrypted by one of the public key encryption methods (such as RSA). We do not clarify more this point, because key exchange is done in all encryption methods and the procedure is well known [2,4,6,7].
All the bits of the connection are placed in the places of the downstream spectrum which correspond to the multiplexing pattern in the same order that they arrive at the head end. The only thing that the corresponding terminal has to do in order to reassemble the bits of the connection is to select and place one after the other the bits contained in the places indicated by the multiplexing pattern.
When a connection is terminated the places are free again and together with the other free places can be used for the formation of other multiplexing patterns.
An attacker who has not the corresponding multiplexing pattern has no way of knowing which 8 out of the 819200 possible places are destined for the target terminal. So in order to get the data destined for it, he should analyze all possible combinations (with their permutations) of 8 out of 819200 bits for some basic modules to see if the resulting bit sequence has any meaning. Given that there are about 10^{47} such possible combinations in a basic module, trying each combination for some number of modules requires a non realistic time even for the fastest computer. So even in the case that the attacker knows that the data are asci characters it doesn't help him.
Here some points should be discussed about the difficulty of breaking this system but this will be done at chapter 4 of the paper.
If we have a 64Kbps connection, which corresponds to 32 bits per basic module, it is not necessary to use a pattern extended in the whole period of the module. Instead of it we use a subperiod consisting of the first 2^9 bits (that is the ¼) of the basic module in which we choose a pattern of 8 bits. This pattern is repeated 4 times to cover the basic module. For the description of each place of this subperiod we need 18 bits (9 for the cells and 9 for the places inside the cells). So for the description of the whole pattern we need 8x18=144 bits, plus the 4 bits for the indication that this pattern refers to an ¼ period. The corresponding terminal will know this fact and will accordingly collect the correct bits. In this case the number of possible combinations is something lower, that is about 10^{43}, but it is still large enough to be safe.
For a 128 Kbps connection, the same ¼ subperiod is used. In this case we need a 16 bit pattern, which requires 292 bits for description and has about 10^{84} possible combinations.
For a 256 Kbps connection we use a 1/8 subperiod and a 16 bit pattern. The number o possible combinations is about 10^{80}.
For the 512, 1024, 2048 Kbps we use correspondingly 1/16, 1/32 and 1/64 sub periods, always with a 16 bit pattern, and about 10^{75}, 10^{70}, and 10^{65} possible combinations.

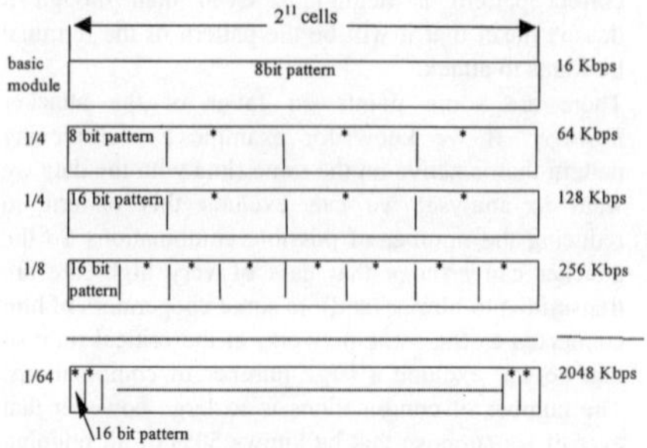

Fig. 1 Overview of the different multiplexing patterns according to the required capacity
* Repetition of the same pattern

For intermediate values of bitrate we use either the longer subperiod with more bits per pattern, or the shorter subperiod with fewer bits per pattern.
The scope is always to have the more possible combinations, while for the description of the pattern and the rest information which will be communicated in the Key Exchange we won't need more than 512 bits. This number is usual in the public Key Exchange procedures.
According to the above the general view of the different cases of multiplexing patterns is as shown in fig.1

4.SECURITY ASPECTS

In order to find out how secure the above method is, one should try to see how the situation can be analysed by an attacker. The attacker doesn't know the multiplexing pattern so he doesn't know also which of the above period is used. So he has to try all kinds of

patterns. Since he cannot do the analysis on line he has to save all data. This is not easy, because as he doesn't know which data are destined for the target terminal , he has to save all downstream data. For a downstream rate of 2.5 Gbits/s this means that even if he wants to analyse a connection that lasts for 10 minutes he has to save 1500 Gbits of data. This is already an enormous quantity.
Since all data are randomly perplexed he should try each of the many possible combinations for a number of periods to see if the resulting data have any meaning. The usual parameters that help him in conventional cryptanalysis do not help in this case, because here we have not to do with the data of a connection but with the data of more connections that can be of entirely different kind (voice, text, data, video e.t.c.). So each time he should check the possibility that the data are of a particular kind, say text, and see if they make any meaning. With all possible combinations been more than 10^{42} the probability that he will find in realistic time some correct pattern is negligible. Even then though it doesn't mean that it will be the pattern of the terminal he wants to attack.
There are some points on favor of the attacker however. If we know for example a multiplexing pattern that is active on the same time with the data we want to analyse, we can exclude this pattern so reducing the number of possible combinations So the attacker can arrange that data of very high rate are transmitted to him or (and) to some cooperators of him connected to the same network, at the critical time so that he can exclude a large number of combinations. The number of combinations is so large however that even if we suppose that he knows 50% of all ongoing connections he has still to analyse a number of combinations of the order of 10^{35} or more. So far we know of no way of attacking such a situation and we believe that it is very secure.

5. FUNCTIONALITY APECTS

The use of multiplexing patterns fits very well if we have CBR services. In that case we calculate the necessary bitrate and give the connection a multiplexing pattern with a rate slightly higher than the nominal constant rate. In case of non CBR services the pattern needs to be continually modified during the connection in order to be adapted to the changes of the rate. This is done, in general terms, as follows:

a. Initial rate

The initial rate is set about 10% higher than the expected mean rate, if we can have an estimation of that rate. Otherwise we give a relatively high initial rate, considering also the overall load of the network, and afterwards we follow the procedure described in the following paragraphs.

b. Increase of rate

The on board controller supervizes constantly the condition of the buffers of each connection and if some buffer is going to overflow, gives the terminal a pattern with more bandwidth till the buffer is normalised. In order to be able to react as fast as possible to the changes, the controller should have ready patterns for substitution of the working patterns. For this reason it continually groups the free cells in patterns of different kinds. Here a very important remark should be made. That is, a multiplexing pattern of low rate actually reserves much more places than the places it actually occupies In a pattern on the basic period, for example, which consist of 8 bits and services a connection of 16Kbps, each one of its bits can block the formation of a 16 bit pattern in the 1/64 period. So in the extreme case, from each bit of the 8 bit pattern, 63 other bit places can be blocked which corresponds to a capacity 63 times that of 16 Kbps, that is about 1 Mbps. In order to avoid these side effects the selection of the bit pattern is not absolutely random, but is done according to some rules. A general rule that can be followed is that we select a pattern of higher rate, and then from its places we form several patterns of lower capacity. If for example we select a 2 Mbps pattern, we can construct 128 16 Kbps pattern from that. This of course greatly reduces the number of possible patterns for the 16 Kbps connections, and hence the security of the method. As can be shown, however, the security of the method is so high that it can tolerate such reductions.
As soon as the controller sees that the buffer of a connection is going to overflow, because the rate of incoming data is higher than the rate of the transmitted data , it selects a multiplexing pattern of higher rate and through the established secure communication, notifies the new pattern to the corresponding terminal. For that reason it transmits a special cell to the terminal, called adaptation cell .

These special cells should be distinguished from the normal ATM cells of the connection. Remark that the ATM cells of the connection are not the same with the downstream cells of the network. The ATM cells are reassembled by the terminal serving the connection, after collecting the individual bits according to the multiplexing pattern and they are identical, except from some fields, with the ATM cells of the connection coming to the headend. In order to distinguish between the normal ATM cells of a connection and the adaptation cells for that connection a two bit field is added to the overhead of the ATM cell . The different combination of these two bits have the following meanings: "00", indicate a normal cell. "01", indicates an adaptation cell for changing the multiplexing pattern (and hence the rate). "10" indicates a cell with empty payload (actually there are not empty payload places, but in absence of data these places are padded with a random bit sequence), "11" indicates an OAM cell addressed individually to the terminal, not necessarily having to do with the connection.

OLT writes the new multiplexing pattern in the payload of the adaptation cell. Immediately after the adaptation cell the bits of the connection are put in the places of the new multiplexing pattern. No return information is necessary from the terminal. The terminal knows that after receiving an adaptation cell the bits of the connection concerned are to be found in the places indicated by the new multiplexing pattern and collects them accordingly.

In order to specify the new multiplexing pattern OLT follows some rules. The rules are elastic and depend on the overall load of the network. If the overall load is very low for example and we don't mind about the efficiency, we can give a multiplexing pattern of high rate, so that we are sure that the buffer is not going to overflow again. On the contrary if the overall load is high, we will try to increase the rate gradually. We should distinguish also among connections tolerating cell loses (TCP/IP connections for example), and those which do not. From simulations we have done, it follows that for a load less than the 70% of the maximum capacity of the network, we can follow simple rules without any problem. For a load around 80% more sophisticated rules should be followed, while for loads around 90% no absolutely satisfactory rules have been found till now.

c. Decrease of rate

In the case the incoming rate is less than the rate of the working multiplexing pattern, cases will come where there are no bits to be put in the corresponding places of the multiplexing pattern. In order to preserve robustness, no bit is placed in the multiplexing pattern if there are not enough bits in the butter to complete a full ATM cell. In the case that the bits waiting for transmission are less than the payload of an ATM cell, an empty ATM cell is transmitted to the terminal. The empty cell is padded with random bits, and is distinguished from the normal cells as it is described above.
Immediately after the transmission of an empty cell, bits of the normal cell are sent, if there are enough to fill an ATM cell. If many empty cells are sent continuously it is an indication that the multiplexing pattern is too "rich" for that connection and a pattern for lower rate should be given, through the transmission of an adaptation cell. Here similar rules as in the case of the increased rate are followed, but in this case, thanks to the possibility of sending empty cells, the situation can be handled more easily. It should be also remarked that it is very easy to go from a multiplexing pattern of high rate to one of lower rate. The only thing to be done is to omit randomly some bit-places from the pattern, if we want to keep the same sub-period, or to use the double sub-period and omit randomly half of the places.

6.IMPLEMENTATION ASPECTS

In order to implement the above method we need to follow a special multiplexing procedure, different from what is followed in the conventional praxis. Such a procedure, based on existing equipment is shown in fig.2 below.

Referring to the figure the most important thing is the way incoming cells are buffered , before they are transmitted. The buffer has the virtual form of a rectangular with vertical columns. The first columns to the right are registers which upon receiving a proper pulse from the controller transfer their contain to the corresponding place of the register to the right. The first right most register transfers its bits directly to the transmission bus. Between this registers and the transmission bus , however, there are control units which permit the transfer of a bit only under certain conditions. The condition is that the bit string set at the imputes of the control unit matches that coming from the central controller. The bit string at each control unit is set at the beginning of the connection and is the number of the place inside the module in which the corresponding bit should be put. This number, as already described above, consist of the 9 bits indicating the place inside the ATM cell, plus the bits indicating the number of cell inside the corresponding module (11 bits for the basic module, 9 for the 1/4 module, 8 for the 1/8 module , 7 for the 1/16 module, 6 for the 1/32 module and 5 for the 1/64 module). This number is called the *multiplexing mask* in the rest of this paper. From the central controller a string of 20 bits is generated at each clock pulse , each bit going to the corresponding impute of all control units. The generation of string begins with the string 00000000001000000001, and is increased by 1 at each clock pulse, till the first nine bits reach the value 110010000 which corresponds to the 400th place of the ATM cell. In the next pulse the first 9 bits take again the value 000000001 while the first 11 bits are increased by 1, taking the value 00000000010 and so on. So the string in the 401 clock pulse has the form 00000000010000000001. In the rest of the paper we will call this string as the *control string*. Although the control string has always 20 bits, the multiplexing masks may have fewer bits. A matching happens if all the bits of a mask are the same with the corresponding bits of the control string.
As it is obvious from the above consideration, only the mask of one control unit will match each time with the control string, and so only one bit will be transmitted. When all bits of the last register have been transmitted, all bits of the register to its left are transferred to it.

Hardware implementation of the method is not difficult and can be incorporated in the whole process of the routing of ATM cells. The software implementation, which seems a bit sophisticated, poses no problem because it is done not on line but only once at the beginning of each connection and eventually sometimes during the connection. The MAC controller has all the time to analyse the resulting situation after the establishment or the end of a connection

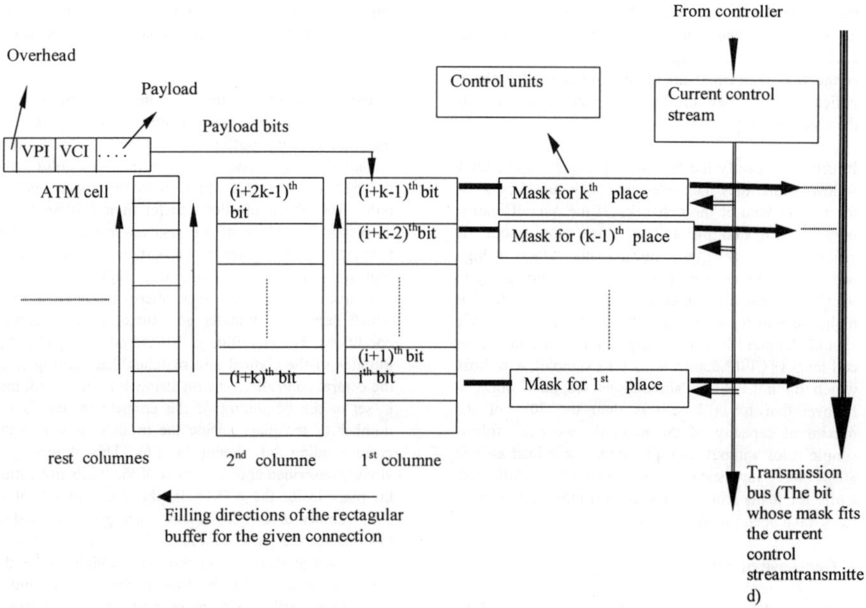

Fig.2

and to calculate and have ready patterns for the next connection or the changes in established connections. The method can be implemented in the desired high speed, has no need of extra synchronization, and specially from the side of the terminals is extremely simple, and hence cheap. Furthermore with this method the traffic parameters of the terminals are kept secret what is not possible with normal encryption. Generally it restores very well the lost individuality of PON and HFC Networks which arises from their tree topology. The main disadvantage that seems to exist is the need of often change of the multiplexing patterns in case of connections with variable bit rate, which leads to reduced efficiency. For loads of the network less than 70% however it seems this effect is negligible. On the other hand we have not similar data of the conventional encryption to compare with.

CONCLUSION

The suggested method may prove the best way to overcome the privacy and security problem which arises in PON and HFC networks because of their topology, and furthermore may be implemented also in other kind of communications that have broadcasting characteristics, like cellular telephony

REFERENCES

[1] ATM Forum/BTD-SECURITY-01.02. *Phase I ATM Security Specification (draft), Feb1997*

[2]U.Heister, U.Killat, A.Profumo, I.S. Venieris Privacy and Security Aspects of a Passive Optical Network Based Access System, *International Conf. on Advances in Telecommunications, Rhodes, June 1993*

[3] Mohammad Peyravian, Asynchronous Transfer Mode Security, *IEEE Network, May/June 1997*.

[4] IEEE Project 802.14/a Draft 2 Revision2 1997 *.Cable-TV access method and physical layer specification,(A.1.9 Security, M.8 MAC Layer Security)*

[5] D.Polemi, J.Koulouris, J.Angelopoulos. Safeguarding privacy and efficiency in Passive Optical Networks, *The Fourth IEEE Workshop on High-Performance Communication Systems (HPFC'97). June 23-25 1997*

[6] Walter Fumy, Peter Landrock. Principles of Key Management, *IEEE Journal, Vol.11, No 5, June 1993.*

[7] R.Rivest, A.Shamir, L.Adleman. A Method for obtaining digital signatures and public key cryptosystems. *Communications of the ACM,21: 120-126, 1978*

ON HIERARCHICALLY ORGANISED NETWORKS - AN ALGEBRAIC APPROACH

A. ANDREATOS
Hellenic Air Force Academy
Dekeleia Air Force Base
Attica, TGA-1010
email: aandre@tee.gr

P. STEFANEAS
Network Operating Centre
National Technical Univ. of Athens
Zografou 15773
email: petros@noc.ntua.gr

ABSTRACT

In this paper we attempt to define some fundamental concepts of network theory mathematically, employing categorical General Systems Theory; next we focus on hierarchical networks and we attempt to provide a mathematical definition of hierarchical networks, and we present some relational operators of hierarchy. Finally we present two case studies as applications of the above: TEN-34, the European Internet of the National Research Networks and the global Internet. To address the specific needs of network theory we hereby introduce the concept of many-sorted categories.

1. BRIEF INTRODUCTION TO GENERAL SYSTEMS THEORY

Mathematical background in computing varies from area to area. Some of them have a strong background, such as programming languages, automata and finite state machines, computer vision, digital design, algorithms and complexity. There are other areas with limited but growing mathematical background, such as Data Base theory, etc. Finally there are other areas with no holistic formalisation, where only some sub-areas may have a mathematical formalisation. We believe that Network Theory falls in this latter case.

In this paper we therefore attempt to establish a formal background for network theory. For this purpose we employ the General Systems Theory (GST) of J. Goguen [goguen69, goguen73]. After a brief introduction to GST and Network Theory, we show how basic concepts (such as network architecture, protocol stac0ks, network hierarchy, internetworking and temporal network evolution) can be formally described using GST. To address the specific needs of Network Theory we have introduced the concept of **many-sorted categories** and the accompanying categorical definitions.

The concept of **system** is considered fundamental in modern science. The ancient Greek word *system means something composed of or consisting of many things together, a compound (composite) whole, an organic whole.* According to the Shorter Oxford English Dictionary, *system is a complex whole, set of connected things or parts, or organised body of material or immaterial things.*

Many attempts have been made towards a general mathematical definition of systems. **Category Theory** [maclane, pierce] has offered the most abstract definition so far. This is based on Goguen's mathematical representation of hierarchically organised systems [goguen69]. In contrast to the traditional system theories, this approach focuses on the concepts of *object, interconnection, level* and *behaviour*. In particular:

- ***Objects*** (composing a system) are ***presheaves.***
- ***Objects*** may be organised in a category, say, ***category* O of *objects*.**
- A ***system*** is a diagram in the ***category O*** **of *objects*.**
- The ***behaviour*** of a system is its ***inverse limit***.
- ***Two systems*** are said to be ***equivalent*** if they have ***isomorphic behaviour***.
- ***System interconnection*** is a ***direct limit*** in the category of diagrams.

Applications of this theory can be found in software engineering, automata theory, specification languages, concurrent systems and object oriented development environments like SLP (Systems Limit Programming) [paine].

2. CATEGORICAL REPRESENTATION OF SYSTEMS

2.1. Previous work

Networks have already been defined as sheaves of attributes (T-objects) by Andreatos and Stefaneas [andr-stef]. Here, an alternative approach is presented for the definition of fundamental networking concepts, based on General Systems Theory (GST). To cope with all different building components of a network, we introduce the concepts of *many sorted categories and functors.* Many sorted (MS) categories contain the usual notion of (plain) categories as a special case, that of a single sort.

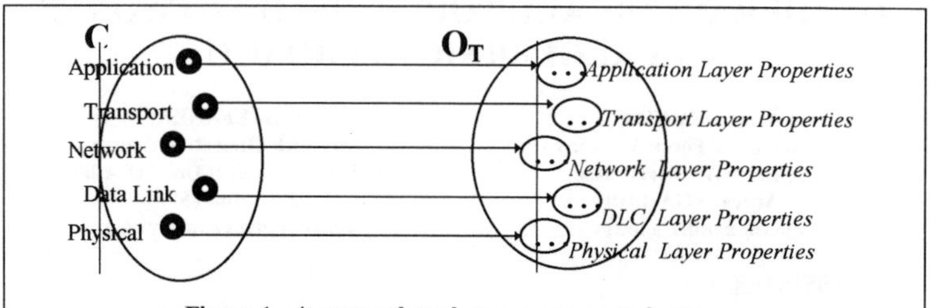

Figure 1 - A protocol stack as a many- sorted category

2.2. *Introducing many sorted categories and systems*

This section generalises Goguen's work on systems theory [goguen69, goguen73], providing a many-sorted version. Goguen's results correspond to the trivial case of single-sorted systems. In order to describe networks better, we hereby introduce Many Sorted categories and related issues. The concept of sort corresponds to a *type* of object, here considered merely as an element of a set S.

An *S-indexed* or *S-sorted* set is defined as follows: let S be a set of sorts, then an S-indexed (or S-sorted) set A is just a family of component sets A_s for each index s in S.

Examples of sorts are: **bool**, **int** and **real** corresponding to the sets of booleans, integers, and real numbers. Hence sorts are interpreted as sets (classes) of entities which share one or more common properties.

Definition: An S-sorted category *A* consists of:

1. A family $<|A_S \mid s \in S>$ of S-sorted sets of objects.
2. A set $A_{S,U}(A_1,A_2)$ defined for any pair A_1,A_2 of objects of A_S and A_U respectively. The elements $f_{s,u} \in A_{S,U}(A_1,A_2)$ are called *(s, u)* morphisms and are written as $f_{s,u}$: $A_1 \rightarrow A_2$, or $A_1 \xrightarrow{f_{s,u}} A_2$;
3. A composition law which to morphisms $A_1 \xrightarrow{f_{s,u}} A_2$ and $A_2 \xrightarrow{g_{u,v}} A_3$ assigns a morphism $A_1 \xrightarrow{(f;g)_{s,v}} A_3$. The following axioms are postulated:
   3.1. *Associativity*: Given morphisms $A_1 \xrightarrow{f_{s,u}} A_2$, $A_2 \xrightarrow{g_{u,v}} A_3$ and $A_3 \xrightarrow{h_{v,w}} A_4$ we have $(f_{s,u};g_{u,v});h_{v,w} = f_{s,u};(g_{u,v};h_{v,w})$.

   3.2. *Identity*: For every object A_S of sort *s* there exists a morphism $I_S : A \rightarrow A$ such that in $A_S \xrightarrow{I_s} A_S \xrightarrow{f_{s,u}} A_u \xrightarrow{I_u} A_u$, we have $I_u;f_{u,s} = f_{u,s} = f_{u,s};I_s$.

Examples of MS categories

1. A network consisting of routers and hosts is a two-sorted category.
2. A token-ring network is a *2-sort* category; there are two sorts of nodes: hosts and taps (T-connections). Its *topology* is a *circular graph.*

2.3. *Definition of MS system*

Given an MS category O, an **MS system** can be defined **as a diagram** in O, i.e., a functor S:D→O, where D is called the MS index category.

2.4. *Examples of MS systems*

1. Any network with a server station and printers, scanners, mass storage devices, transceivers, repeaters, terminators, etc. is an MS system.
2. A **star** network is a 2-sorted system; there are two sorts of nodes: the **hub** node, which is a special routing processor, and all other (user) nodes.

2.5. *Network architecture - protocol stacks*

Network layer N communicates with its two neighbour layers: upper layer N+1 and lower layer N-1. There are two different automata in layer N. The first automaton (located on the N+1 - N layer interface) is receiving data (i.e. frames and service requests) from the upper layer from layer N+1 and is giving data (i.e. frames of layer N) to the lower layer; the flow is downwards. The flow in the second automaton is upwards; it receives frames from layer N-1 and it delivers frames of layer N to layer N+1. The **interfaces** may be considered as the input and output functions of these automata.

During a communication session between two users of a network, all layers of user nodes are functioning *concurrently*. There is a virtual communication

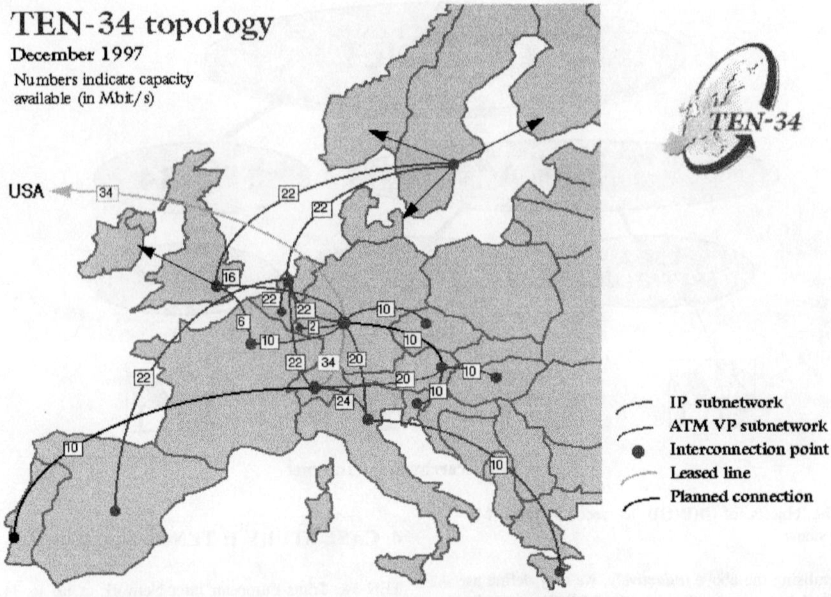

Figure 2 - TEN-34 topology

between peer processes at each layer of the two communicating nodes. As stated earlier, this communication is governed by the protocol of each layer.

2.6. Algebraic description of the protocol stack

A protocol stack is an MS ordered category where its sorts are the various layers (see Fig. 1). The order of the layers is strictly defined.

The elements of C are the protocols of the stack. The attributes of each component of C are the functions performed by this protocol which by defined by the corresponding reference model.

It is usual for a layer to support multiple protocols. For this reason, network layers are meta-sorts. As an example consider the Novell Netware stack [tanen]. Each such meta-sort layer can be described as a set of sorts; for example, the Transport layer of Novell Netware supports the following protocols: TCP, NCP, SPX. This is denoted as Transport={TCP, NCP, SPX}.

Example: An upgrade of the offered bit rate at a network can be shown as a morphism between the two different snapshots of the same network: before and after the upgrade.

3. HIERARCHY

3.1. Hierarchy in GST

In order to define a hierarchical system employing GST, it is first necessary to define morphisms among systems.

Definition: A morphism G from MS system G: K $\rightarrow$ O to G': K' $\rightarrow$ O is a pair <F, n>, where F: K $\rightarrow$ K' is a functor and F : G $\rightarrow$ G' is a natural transformation.

Let **O** be a category. Then the class **D(O)** of all diagrams (MS systems) in **O** may get organised into a category with morphisms the corresponding morphisms among MS systems.

Let a category O. Then the class **D(O)** of all diagrams (MS systems) in O may be organised in a category with morphisms, the morphisms among MS systems.

By proper use of the above definition, a hierarchical structure for MS systems may be defined. Thus, given a category O, we may define:

1. The objects of **D(O)** as first- level MS systems;

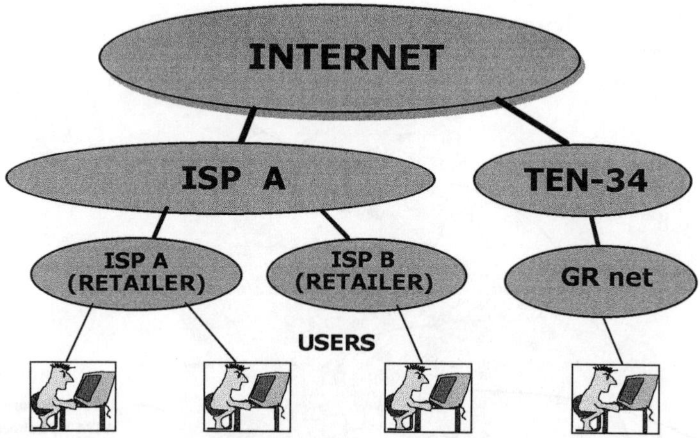

Figure 3 - Hierarchy in the Internet

2. The objects of **D(D(O))** as second- level MS systems;

Generalising the above ***inductively***, we may define as nth-level MS systems the objects of $\mathbf{D^n(O) = D(D^{n-1}(O))}$, **where** $\mathbf{D^0(O) = O}$.

That is, we observe that transition from one layer to its subsequent layer may be defined using MS system interconnection concepts.

The interconnection of two n-level MS systems produces a new (n+1)-level MS system.

It can be proven that $\mathbf{D^n(O)^{op} \subseteq D^{n+1}(O)}\ \forall\ \mathbf{n}$. Since the category of categories is co-complete, the sequence $\mathbf{O^{op} \subseteq D(O) \subseteq D^2(O)^{op} \subseteq \ldots}$ has a direct limit which is the category of all the MS systems of finite level, $\mathbf{D^\infty(O)}$.

3.2. Hierarchy operators

Let us consider a hierarchical network H with m nodes: $n_1, n_2, \ldots, n_m$.

1. Depth of a node n_l is its distance $D(n_l)$ (in links) from the root. Example: $D(n_1)=4$.
2. Depth Operator D(H): returns the depth of a hierarchical network H: D(H)=6 for instance, an integer representing the maximum distance of a node n_i from the root R: $D(H) = Max\ \{D(n_1), D(n_2), \ldots, D(n_m)\}$.
3. Depth relational operators ("<", ">"). $D(n_1)>D(n_2) \Leftrightarrow L_1 > L_2$.

   Associativity of this operator: if $D(n_1)>D(n_2)$ and $D(n_2)>D(n_3) \Rightarrow D(n_1)>D(n_3)$.

4. CASE STUDY 1: TEN-34

TEN-34, Trans-European inter-Network at up to 34 Mb/s is a European continental high speed network, offering high quality of Internet facilities to the European academic and research community [maglaris]. The TEN-34 high speed backbone interconnects European NRNs offering multimedia and real-time applications such as vide-oconferencing across Europe, promoting international collaboration of European researchers. TEN-34 is a major partner in the network of networks, the global Internet. TEN-34 is based on the TCP/IP protocol stack. As per transmission media, TEN-34 uses high speed leased lines and ATM virtual paths, which are used as dedicated lines.

TEN-34 is a perfect example of an MS system. It consists of two subnetworks: the first is based on leased lines offering IP service among the NRNs of: NORDUnet, (Scandinavia), SURFnet (NL), SWITCH (Swiss), RedIRIS (Spain) and BELNET (B). The second subnetwork, provided by a joint initiative of the PNOs of France (F), UK (U), Germany (D) and Italy (I), referred to as FUDI, provides ATM-based data transmission services among the NRNs of France (RENATER), Germany (DFN), Italy (INFN), the UK (UKERNA), Greece (GRnet), Austria (ACOnet), Luxemburg (RESTENA) and Hungary (HUNGARnet).

The two subnetworks are interconnected at three points: London, Geneva and Frankfurt. These nodes support both ATM and TCP/IP and are therefore two sorted.

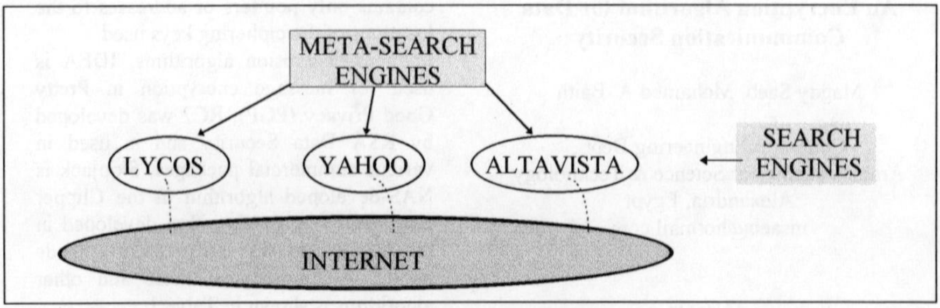

Figure 4 - Internet Search Engines hierarchy

TEN-34 uses the following transmission media: IP subnet, ATM VP subnet, leased line. This is another many sorted category. Also the capacities of the links vary from 2 to 34 Mb/s; hence the links form an MS category. Some nodes use pure TCP/IP while others have a hybrid protocol stack consisting of some TCP/IP layers on top of some ATM layers.

5. CASE STUDY 2: THE GLOBAL INTERNET

5.1. Internet as the current limit of all interconnected networks

The Global Internet is a system of layer n (it has the largest hierarchy of any other known internet), and n tends to increase. Theoretically there is no upper limit for n, i.e. $n \rightarrow \infty$. Based on this formalism we may mathematically define Internet as the current limit $\mathbf{D^{\infty}(O)}$.

Given the trend towards global internetworking in order to reach a global internetworking infrastructure, we may see **GII (Global Information Infrastructure)** as the future limit $\mathbf{D^{\infty}(O)}$.

5.2. Internet Search Engines

Search Engines are specialised Web sites which maintain databases of the available WWW servers and their contents, allowing the user to search for his subject of interest quickly and efficiently. Due to the rapid growth of WWW, indexing and searching has become a difficult task for a search engine. **Meta-Search engines** are search engines which search directly the contents of selected popular search engines instead of searching the Web (Fig. 4). This is a hierarchical model which can be described easily with our GST tools.

6. REFERENCES

[andr-stef] A. Andreatos and P. Stefaneas, "Applying Category Theory to Computer Networks", in Proc. of 1st CSC '96 Confe-rence, Hellenic Naval Academy, July 1996.

[goguen69] J. A. Goguen, "Mathematical representation of hierarchically organised systems", Proceedings of the Global Systems Dynamics Int'l symposium, Charlottesville 1969, pp. 112-128.

[goguen73] J. A. Goguen, "Categorical foundations for general systems theory", Proceedings of the European meeting, Vienna 1973.

[koomen] C. J. Koomen, "The design of communicating systems - A system engineering approach", Kluwer Academic Publishers, 1991.

[maclane] Sauders Mac Lane, "Categories for the Working Mathematician", Springer-Verlag, 1971.

[maglaris] V. Maglaris et al., "Recent trends in European Research Networking - the role of Greece as a regional node", Net-Med'98, Nicosia, Cyprus, March 1998.

[paine] J. Paine, "Web-O-Matic: using System Limit Programming in a declarative object-oriented language for building complex interactive Web applications", presented at Document Processing and SGML, Workshop of project DAVID - Algebraic Document Processing BRAGA - Portugal 2-4 September 1996.

[pierce] B. C. Pierce, "Basic Category Theory for Computer Scientists", MIT Press 1991.

[tanen] A. Tanenbaum, "Computer Networks", 3rd Ed., Prentice-Hall International. 1996. ■

An Encryption Algorithm for Data Communication Security

Magdy Saeb, Mohamed A. Baith

Computer Engineering Dept.,
Arab Academy for Science & Technology
Alexandria, Egypt
msaeb@hotmail.com

Abstract

Yet another encryption algorithm for secure computer communications, nevertheless this algorithm is hardware-dependent. It can be only deciphered either by using a series of stored keys or equivalently a hardware implementation of these stored keys.

The method depends on storing a series of files either on a diskette or using an EPROM and a Field Programmable Gate Array (FPGA) chip. The algorithm selects randomly a file and searches this file for an octet that represents the character to be encrypted. Using this octet as a key for the original character to be encrypted, we guarantee that without the original binary file there is hardly any way to decrypt the code. The same technique can be also implemented as part of the system BIOS, if so required by the user. The technique could prove its importance in the Internet communications environment.

Overview

One motivation behind the focus on encryption algorithms these days is the recent developments such as differential attacks on block ciphers and correlation attacks on stream ciphers. In the following few lines we provide a run through existing algorithms with some comparative evaluation. We then turn to describe our proposal that, we will show, is hardware-dependent and can be hardly deciphered since the transmitted file contains only pointers or addresses to the locations of the ciphering keys used.

In block-encryption algorithms, IDEA is used for message encryption in Pretty Good Privacy (PGP), RC2 was developed by RSA Data Security and is used in various commercial packages, Skipjack is NAS-developed algorithm in the Clipper chip, GOST is an algorithm developed in the USSR and was only recently made public. A summary of these and other algorithms is shown in Table 1.

These were discussed in references [1, 2, 3, 4, & 6].

Table 1.
Summary of Block-encryption algorithms

	Key Length	Block Length	Problem
DES	56 bits	64 bits	key too small
Triple-DES	112 bits	64 bits	slow
Khufu	64 bits	64 bits	key too small
FEAL 32	64 bits	64 bits	key too small
REDCO 11	160 bits	80 bits	Patented
IDEA	128 bits	64 bits	Patented
Skipjack	80 bits	64 bits	Secret
GOST	256 bits	64 bits	Not Totally specified
MMB	128 bits	128 bits	Insecure

In this work, we propose, and provide an implementation of an algorithm capable of encrypting data at " a reasonable number of clock cycles per byte" for the emerging class of high data-rate applications.

We call this method Yet Another Encryption Algorithm (YAEA).

Methodology

On designing this algorithm, we have considered the following situations:

-The cryptoanalyst knows all details of the algorithm, has some ciphered text, and his job is to deduce the plaintext. This case is called "ciphertext-only attack.."
-The cryptoanalyst has the algorithm, some encrypted ciphered text and also the unencrypted plaintext. His or her job is to deduce the key known as "plaintext attack."
-Not only does the cryptoanalyst have some ciphered text, and the unencrypted plaintext, but also he or she gets to choose what it is. If there is a particular plaintext sequence that is to be encrypted, it will easily yield the key. This is the case called "chosen-plaintext attack."

In all of the above cases, we proclaim, that our method is hardly decryptable since the encrypted text is not related directly to the plaintext but rather it contains only pointers to the locations of the used keys. This can be demonstrated as follows:

The method is basically quite simple. We start with a random access binary file *known only to the sender and receiver*. Starting from a random location, we search through the bit stream of this file for an octet representing the character to be ciphered, we then store a pointer to the location of this octet in a file. We, rather incorrectly, call this file the encrypted text. However, this file contains only pointers to the locations of the keys used to encrypt the original plaintext as mentioned before.

The procedure is then repeated for all other characters of the original plaintext and all corresponding pointers are then recorded. The resulting file is then sent to the receiver who, as stated before, knows and has beforehand the binary file containing the searched octets. To decrypt the file, the procedure is then reversed to get the original plaintext file. A summary of this procedure is shown in Figure 1.

Refinements

We propose, and have implemented the following refinements:

1. Use of a convolutional encoder, implemented using Xilinx workstation for Field Programmable Gate Arrays (FPGA.) This encoder is used to generate a number that seeds the random number generator. This random number is used to start the search for the required octet in the given binary file.
2. Different types of random events that normally occur in the window environment are trapped and then serially communicated to the convolutional encoder to generate the above number.
3. Different "Robust" algorithms of random number generators are used.
4. The resulting file containing the above-mentioned pointers is compressed before transmitting it, if so required by the user.
5. Using an EPROM to store a series of binary files used as the key files to speed up the process.
6. The sender and receiver agree beforehand on two different points:
The first point is the sequence of binary files to be used depending on the day of the week, where they need in this case seven different files, or the week of the year, and in this case 52 files or the day of the year and in this case 366 different files.
The second point is the number of times to repeat the above reverse procedure, since the file containing the pointers can be encrypted itself using the same binary file.

Implementation

A window C^{++} program was developed to implement the above algorithm. A default 32-bit pointer was used to store the locations of the various octets. This puts a maximum on the size of the plaintext file of about 4 GB. However, a 16-bit can be also used with a relatively large saving in the resulting transmitted file but with a maximum plaintext file size of about
64 KB. As shown in Figure 2, the user is asked to enter the names of the plaintext file (The Message), the name of the file that will contain the resulting pointers (The Encrypted Message), and the name

of the binary file (The Key) containing the octets to be searched.

Figure 1.
A summary of the method used.

The user clicks the button with the "Lock" icon to encrypt the plaintext file. Other user options, as mentioned before, are:
-Generating a key or a random binary file.
-Different window events to be trapped to seed the convolutional encoder that, in turn, seeds the random number generator.
-Different random number engine settings.
-Choice of either 32 or 16-bit pointers.
For maximum security, the key files can be exchanged manually. However, any existing binary files can be used, if so agreed upon by the two parts. For other applications, these files can be saved on a ROM on a specially designed add-on card.
To quantitatively compare between our method and other algorithms, would be comparing a search algorithm to direct encryption algorithms. Nevertheless, our testing of the method showed that a file of about 4MB was processed in less than 20 seconds on a Pentium, 100 MHz, and 16 MB RAM machine.
We believe that this method, though quite simple, yet it is thoroughly sturdy against any type of cipher attacks.

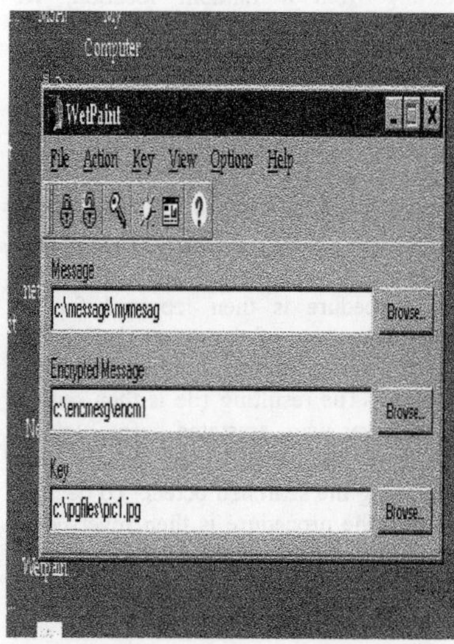

Figure 2
A view of the C^{++} window program implementation of the algorithm.

Summary & Conclusions

We have implemented a codebook digital version for data encryption. The method has refined an idea into a hardware-dependent hardly decryptable method. These refinements are:

-Use of a convolutional encoder to seed different random generator engines,

-Use of Multiple random number generator engines,

-Use of an EPROM to store the key binary files, and

-Secondary encryption of the file containing the pointers, if so required by the user.

The method is based on transmitting files containing sets of pointers to the locations of the stored keys rather than transmitting encrypted text. Therefore, we believe it can withstand any type of cipher attacks.

References

1. Douglas R. Stinson, Cryptography, Theory and Practice, CRC Press, 1995.

2. E. Biham & A. Shamir, Differential Cryptoanalysis of the Data Encryption Standard, Springer-Verlag, 1993.

3. P. Beauchemin & G. Brassard, "The generation of random numbers that are probably prime," Journal of Cryptology, 1(1988), 53-64.

4. E.F. Brickell (Ed.), Advances in Cryptology-Crypto '92 Proceedings. Lecture Notes in Computing Science, vol. 740, Springer-Verlag, 1993

5. Information Theory, Richard Hamming, Wiley & Sons, 1989.

6. Bruce Schneir, Applied Cryptology, John Wiley & Sons, 1994.

Acknowledgment

The authors thank the reviewers for their helpful comments and encouraging remarks.

Thanks are also due to M. A. Ibrahim for his help regarding the computer program implementation.

Bearing estimation and Blind source separation

M. Frikel [†], *V. Barroso* [†], *J. Gomes* [†] *and S. Bourennane* [‡]
[†] IST - ISR, Torre Norte, Piso 7
1096 Lisboa Codex, Portugal
Ph: (351) 1 841 8 286, Fax: (351) 1 841 8 291

[‡] SDEM URA 2053 CNRS, 20250 Corte - France
e-mail: `frikel@isr.ist.utl.pt`

Abstract

This paper deals with the estimation of the direction of arrival of radiating sources using classical array processing methods such as Music, minimum norm, Capon's methods and source separation using blind techniques. Indeed, algorithms for the separation of independent sources are often referred to as blind methods. Blind technique refers to lack of knowledge about the mixing system. It also often refers to very limited assumptions about the sources themselves. Some numerical results for bearing estimation are presented.

Keywords: "Blind" array processing, source separation.

1 Introduction

The received data can be modeled as a superposition of finite number of elementary source signals and an additive noise, in many problems in signal processing. Generally, in a multi-sensor environement application, such as sonar, underwater acoustics and seismology, the principal objectives are estimating the number and bearing estimation, of the radiating sources. Over, the last decade, eigenstructure based methods yield resolution have been proposed to the problem of source bearing estimation. In recent years, there hase been, the growing interest in the problem of improving high-resolution eigenstructure techniques with the object of lowering the SNR resolution threshold or of exploiting the modeling of the background noise. The high-resolution modelling methods are better compared to the classical methods. However, these method need the model of sources. In many case, this model is not available, indeed, the appearance, last decade, of the blind methods. It assumes very weak assumptions either on signals or mixtures. The key assumption is that sources are assumed statistically independent.
Blind source separation consists in identifying the sensors/sources transfer matrix and retrieving the source signals without resorting a priori information about the above matrix, it exploits only the information carried by the received signals themselves. The potential benefit of such a blind approach is that source separation is essentially unaffacted by errors in the propagation model or in array calibration. Whereas the classical array processing methods assume that the array geometry is known and the sources are in the far field of the array.
The organization of this paper is as follows. Problem formulation is given in section II. In section III, we present the classical methods of bearing estimation. In setion IV, the blind source separation is formulated.

2 Problem Formulation

2.1 Notations

Let the following notations: $\mathbf{A}^T$, $\mathbf{A}^+$, $\mathbf{A}^*$ are, respectively, the transpose, the transpose conjuguate and the conjugate of the matrix $\mathbf{A}$.
$diag(.)$ is the diagonal matrix.
$\mathbf{I}$: is the identity matrix.
$E[.]$ is the statistical expectation.
In the mathematical formulas: matrices (capital) "$\mathbf{A}$" and vectors "$\mathbf{a}$" are in boldface type. The scalars are represented by normal character "a".
N, P and T are the number of sensors, number of sources and the number of realisations, respectively.

2.2 Propagation model

Consider an array of N sensors which received the wavefield generated by P narrow-band sources in the presence of an additive noise. The received signal vector, in the frequency domain, is given by:

$$\mathbf{r}(f) = \mathbf{A}(f)\mathbf{s}(f) + \mathbf{b}(f),$$

where $\mathbf{r}(f)$ is the Fourier transform of the array ouput vector, $\mathbf{s}(f)$ is the $(P \times 1)$ vector of complex signals of P

wavefronts: $\mathbf{s}(f) = [s_1(f), s_2(f), ..., s_P(f)]^T$.
$\mathbf{n}(f)$ is the $(P \times 1)$ vector of additive noise in sensors, $\mathbf{n}(f) = [n_1(f), n_2(f), ..., n_N(f)]^T$
and $\mathbf{A}(f)$ is the $(N \times P)$ transfer matrix of the source-sensor array systems with respect to some chosen reference point, $\mathbf{A}(f, \theta) = [\mathbf{a}(\theta_1), \mathbf{a}(\theta_2), ..., \mathbf{a}(\theta_P)]$.
$\mathbf{a}(\theta_i)$ is the steering vector of the array toward the direction θ_i. For example, the steering vector of a linear uniform array with N sensors is given by:
$\mathbf{a}(\theta_i) = \frac{1}{\sqrt{N}} \left[1,\ e^{j\varphi_i},\ e^{2j\varphi_i}, ...\ , e^{(N-1)j\varphi_i}\right]^T$.
where $\varphi_i = 2\pi f \frac{d}{c} \sin(\theta_i)$;
d denotes the inter-element distance;
θ_i is the direction of arrival (DOA) of the *ith* source as measured from the array broadside;
c is the velocity wave propagation and f is the center frequency of the narrow-band source.
Assume that the signals and the additive noises are stationary and ergodic zero mean complex valued random processes. In addition, the noises are assumed to be uncorrelated between sensors, and to have identical variance σ^2 in each sensor. It follows from these assumptions that the spatial $(N \times N)$ cross-spectral matrix of the observation vector at frequency f is given by:
$\mathbf{\Gamma}(f) = E\left[\mathbf{r}(f)\mathbf{r}^+(f)\right] = \mathbf{A}(f)\mathbf{\Gamma}_s(f)\mathbf{A}^+(f) + \sigma^2\mathbf{I}$
where $E[.]$ denotes the expectation operator, the superscript $^+$ represents conjugate transpose,
$\mathbf{\Gamma}_s(f) = E\left[\mathbf{s}(f)\mathbf{s}^+(f)\right]$ is the $(P \times P)$ sources cross-spectral matrix, and $\mathbf{I}$ is the identity matrix.
The eigendecomposition of the cross-spectral matrix $\mathbf{\Gamma}(f)$ yields:

$\mathbf{\Gamma}(f) = \sum_{i=1}^{N} \lambda_i(f)\mathbf{v}_i(f)\mathbf{v}_i^+(f)$, where $\lambda_i(f)$, $i = 1,..,N$ $(\lambda_1 \geq \lambda_2 \geq .. \geq \lambda_N)$, and $\mathbf{v}_i(f)$ are the *ith* eigenvalue and *ith* corresponding eigenvector, respectively. It is well known that the following properties hold [1-4]:
1) The minimum eigenvalue of $\mathbf{\Gamma}(f)$ is equal to σ^2 with multiplicity $N - P$. Then, we have:
$\lambda_1 \geq \lambda_2 \geq ... \geq \lambda_P > \lambda_{P+1} = \lambda_{P+2} = ... = \lambda_N = \sigma^2$
2) The eigenvectors corresponding to the minimum eigenvalue are orthogonal to the columns of the matrix $\mathbf{A}(f, \theta)$. Namely, they are orthogonal to the steering vectors of the signals:
$\{\mathbf{v}_{P+1}(f), ..., \mathbf{v}_N(f)\} \perp \{\mathbf{a}(\theta_1), ..., \mathbf{a}(\theta_P)\}$
$\mathbf{\Gamma} = \mathbf{V}_s\mathbf{\Lambda}_s\mathbf{V}_s^+ + \mathbf{V}_n\mathbf{\Lambda}_n\mathbf{V}_n^+$
Let $\mathbf{V}_n(f) = [\mathbf{v}_{P+1}(f), \mathbf{v}_{P+2}(f), ..., \mathbf{v}_N(f)]$ be the $(N \times (N-P))$ matrix constructed with the $N-P$ last eigenvectors, which is the well-known noise subspace, corresponding to the smallest $(N-P)$ eigenvalues of the cross-spectral matrix $\mathbf{\Gamma}(f)$.
The classical array processing problem is:

From the received signals and some a priori knowledge of the propagation model and on the statistical proprieties of noises, the goal is to identify the sources: to estimate their number, their azimuths and their powers.

The blind source separation problem can be posed below:

Without any a priori knowledge of the array manifold, the goal is first to identify the transfer matrix, then to recover the source signals from the array output. The potential benefit of such a blind approach is that source separation is essentially unaffected by errors in the propagation model or in array calibration

---

For estimating the direction-of-arrival of sources, the vector source model must be known. This model can be derived analiticaly, from the received wavefronts, indeed, the uniform linear array is used, and the sources are supposed in far-field; the received wavefronts are, then, planes. The azimuths $\theta_1, ..., \theta_P$ are estimated using the relationship between the delays τ_p $(p = 1, ..., P)$ of propagation inter-sensors and the source azimuth: $\sin(\theta_p) = \frac{c\tau_p}{d}$. The source vector model, with the first sensor is the reference, is:
$\mathbf{a}(f, \theta) = \frac{1}{\sqrt{N}} \left[1, \ldots, \exp(-i\frac{2\pi(N-1)fd\sin\theta}{c})\right]^T$, with $i^2 = -1$.

3 Bearing estimation

The first attempt to automaticaly localize signal sources using antenna arrays was through beamforming techniques. The idea is to turn the array in one direction at a time and measure the output power. The steering locations which result in maximum power yield the direction-of-arrival estimates. The array response is steered by forming a linear combination of the sensor outputs.
We recall, in the following, the classical methods for DOA estimation. We assume that the additve noise is white, and the wavefronts are planes:
$\mathbf{a}(f, \theta) = \frac{1}{\sqrt{N}}([1, \exp(-i\varphi(\theta, f)), \ldots, \exp(-i(N-1)\varphi(\theta, f))]^T$
with $\varphi(\theta, f) = \frac{2\pi fd}{c}\sin\theta$.

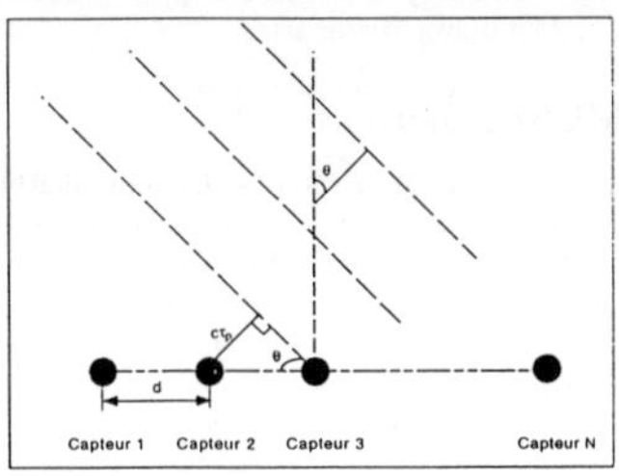

Figure 1: Propagation model

Below, a class of direction-of-arrival estimators are briefly recalled. A relationship between the different estimators is established.

3.1 Beamforming method

Among the several methods of spatial analysis to estimate the directions of arrival of the sources at a frequeny analysis, we quote beamforming method. for DOA θ corresponding to the incremental phase φ, it consist to multiply the vector elements of $\mathbf{r}(f)$ by the phase gradient $d\varphi$ and make the sum. The phase gradient $d\varphi$ corresponding to the model of plane wavefront of incremental phase φ is: $d\varphi = \mathbf{a}(f, \varphi)$. The value of the beamforming at analysis frequency and for a desired incremental phase, is equal to scalar product of the received signal and the phase gradient $d\varphi$. In other term, the conventional beamformer is a natural extension of classical Fourier-based spectral analysis to sensor array data. For an array of arbitrary geometry, this algorithm maximises the power of the beamforming output for given input signal. The corresponding localization function is given by [4]:

$$F_{fv}(f,\theta) = \left[\mathbf{a}^{+}(f,\theta)\mathbf{\Gamma}(f)\mathbf{a}(f,\theta)\right], \quad \theta \in [-\pi/2, \pi/2]$$

This method need little of calculation in comparison with matricial and algebra methods e.g. eigedecomposition.

3.2 Capon's method

Capon's method [3] is derived from classic beamforming techniques. The array output power contains the contributions from both the signal and noise. To minimize the contribution of the noise, the array output power is minimized while maintaining the gain along the DOA of the signal sources. The optimal obtained solution, the so-called Capon spectrum is:
$F_{capon}(\theta) = \left[\mathbf{a}^{+}(\theta)\mathbf{\Gamma}^{-1}(f)\mathbf{a}(\theta)\right]^{-1}$
The directions of arrival of signal sources are found by taking θ which minimizes $F_{capon}(\theta)$. It is noteworthy that the number of signal sources is not required for this method. In the next section we will consider a DOA estimation method without eigendecomposition of the spectral matrix. This method is based upon an approximation of the eigenvector noise subspace by the subspace spanned by the spectral matrix power vector basis.

3.3 MUSIC method

Many spectral methods in the past have implicitly called upon the spectral decomposition of a cross-spectral matrix to carry out the analysis. One of the most significant contributions came about when the eigenstructure of the covariance matrix was explicitely invoked, and its intrinsic properties were directely used to provide a solution to an underlying estimation problem for a given observed process.
It is one of high-resolution methods developed in array processing, it is based to eigendecomposition of the received cross-specral matrix. The MUSIC (MUltiple SIgnal Classification) [2] null-spectrum $F_{Music}(\theta)$ is defined by:

$$F_{Music}(f,\theta) = \left[\mathbf{a}^{+}(f,\theta)\mathbf{V}_B(f)\mathbf{V}_B^{+}(f)\mathbf{a}(f,\theta)\right]^{-1}.$$

and it has been shown that $F_{Music}(\theta)$ has maximum points at round $\theta \in \{\theta_1, ..., \theta_P\}$. Therefore we can estimate the DOA by taking the local maximum points of $F_{Music}(\theta)$.

3.4 Minimum norm method

It was shown in [1] that the minimum-norm estimator can be represented as the noise-subspace version of the linear prediction method of spectral estimation:

$$F_{NM}(f,\theta) = \left[\mathbf{a}^{+}(f,\theta)\mathbf{V}_B(f)\mathbf{V}_B^{+}(f)\mathbf{e}_1\right]^{-1},$$

where $\mathbf{e}_1$ denotes a $(N \times 1)$ vector with all zero elements except the first one, equal to unity: $\mathbf{e}_1 = [1, \;\; 0, ..., 0]^T$.
The minimum-norm algorithm estimates the DOA's as the location of the P highest peaks of $F_{MN}(\theta)$.

3.5 General estimator

The eigenstructure method spawned a significnt increase in research activity which led to a multitude of proposed modification. These were attempts to improve/overcome some of its shortcomings in various specific scenarios. The most notable was the unifying theme of weighted music which, for different $\mathbf{W}$, particularized to various algorithms:
Let the orthogonal projector onto the nois subspace defined as: $\mathbf{\Pi}(f) = \mathbf{V}_B(f)\mathbf{V}_B^{+}(f)$

$$F_W(f,\theta) = \left[\mathbf{a}^{+}(f,\theta)\mathbf{\Pi}(f)\mathbf{W}\mathbf{\Pi}(f)\mathbf{a}(f,\theta)\right]^{-1},$$

The weighting matrix $\mathbf{W}$ is introduced to take into account the influence of each of the eigenvectors. It is clear that a uniform weighting of the eigenvectors, $\mathbf{W} = \mathbf{I}$ results in the original Music method. if $\mathbf{W} = \mathbf{e}_1\mathbf{e}_1^T$, where $\mathbf{e}_1$ is defined above, the bearing estimator corresponds to the minimum-norm.

Numerical example

We assumed an uniformly spaced linear array of 10 sensors with half-wave length spacing and also assumed that the noise was spatially uncorrelated and also uncorrelated with the signal. When $N = 10$, $P = 3$, and the DOAs of three uncorrelated signal sources of equal power are $10°, 15°, and\ 20°$, the results obtained are shown in Figures 1 to 10, which are drawn for 1000 snapshots and the number of sources is taken exact ($P = 3$). The SNR ($SNR = 3dB$) is defined as the ratio of the signal source power to the noise power at the receiver.

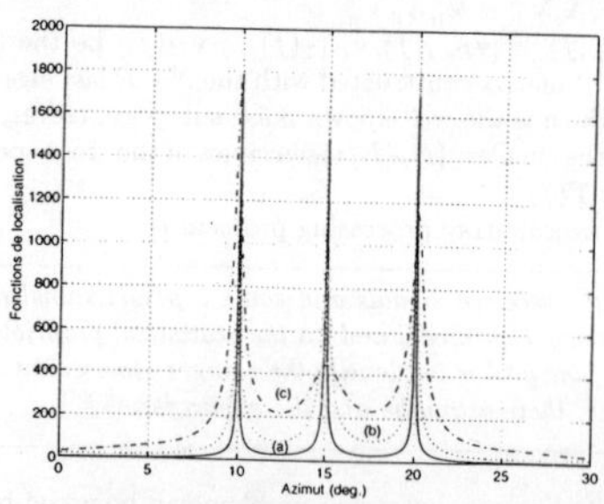

Figure 2: Bearing estimation
MUSIC (a), minimum-norm (b) and Capon's method (c)

Above, we have presented the classical array processing which assume that the transfer matrix **A** has a certain structure. This information may be provided either by physical modeling, e.g. when the array geometry is known and when the sources are in the far field of the array or by direct array calibration. In many cases, this information is not available or not reliable. Below, we present blind source separation without a priori knowledge of the transfer matrix **A**.

4 Blind source separation

Most standard approaches to array signal processing make no use of any available information about the signal structure. However, many man-made signals have a rich structure that can be used to improve the estimator performance. In digital communication applications, the transmitted signals are often cyclostationary, which implies that their autocorrelation functions are periodic. A different approach utilizing signal structure is based on high-order statistics. As is well-known, all information about a Gaussian signal is conveyed in the first and second order moments. Communication signals have a rich structure that can be exploited for source separation using antenna arrays. Indeed, the DOAs need not be estimated. Instead, signal structure methods such as the constant-modulus beamformer have been described for directly estimating the steering vectors of the signals. Techniques based on combining beamforming and demodulation of digitally modulated signals have also recently been proposed [5-8].
Recently, several methods are presented to blind source separation using second order statistics. Among the existing second-order statistics based methods, the subspace method shown in [5] appears to be very robust to noise. The concept behind the subspace method is also versatile, whih not only has proved to be useful for many array processing problems. It has already been shown that blind identificaton is feasible based on spatial covariance matrices. These matrices show a simple structure that allows straightforward blind identification procedures based on eigendecomposition. When the source signals are temporally correlated but still mutually independent, it is possible to base source separation on this property. Also, if the source signals have different spectra, then the transfer marix **A** is easy to identify. If sources are temporally correlated with different spectra, then separation can be achieved using only second-order statistics. We can quote the algorithm developed in [6] based on correlation matrices.
The goal of the subspace blind separation is to identify the transfer matrix **A** *and to recover the original signals* **s** *(or to separate the source signals) from the array output* **r**.

5 Conclusion

This paper describes some methods for bearing estimation using the "standard" array processing techniques with the model of sources is supposed known. However, "blind" source separation can be used without a priori knowledge about the transfer system. This paper is a short recall of the evolution of the array processing in the last decade.

6 Bibliography

[1] R. O. Kumaresan and D. W. Tufts, "Estimating the angle of arrival of multiple plane waves", IEEE Trans. Aerosp. Electron. Syst., vol. AES-19, pp. 134-139, Jan.1983.

[2] R. O. Schmidt, "Multiple emitter location and signal parameters estimation, IEEE Trans. Antennas and propagation", vol. AP-34, pp.276-280, March 1986.

[3] J. Capon, "High-resolution frequency-wavenumber spectrum analysis", Proc. IEEE, vol. 57, no. 8, Aug. 1969, pp. 2408-2418.

[4] M. S. Bartlett, "Smoothing periodograms from time seriess with continuous spectra", Nature, vol. 161, pp. 686-687, 1948.

[5] E. Moulines, P. Duhamel, J.F. Carodoso and S. Mayrargue, "Subspace methods for the blind identification of multichannel FIR filters", IEEE Trans. on Signal Processing, vol. 43, no. 2, February 1995, pp. 516-525.

[6] A. Belouchrani, K. Abed-Meraim, J.F. Carodoso and E. Moulines, "A blind source separation technique using second-order statistics", IEEE Trans. on Signal Processing, vol. 45, no. 2, February 1997, pp. 434-444.

[7] J. Xavier, V.A.N. Barroso, J.M.F. Moura, "Closed-form blind channel identification and source separation in SDMA systems through correlative coding", submitted for IEEE Journal on Selected Areas on Communication, Special Issue on Signal Proessing for Wireless Communications, September 1997.

[8] L. Tong, G. Xu and T. Kailath, "Blind identification and equalization based on second-order statistics: A time domain approach", IEEE Trans. on information Theory, vol. 40, no. 2, pp. 340-349, March 1994.

NEW HORIZONS IN NETWORK MANAGEMENT

Gábor Bányász, Géza Lucz, Hassan Charaf and István Vajk

Department of Automation Technical University of Budapest
H-1521 Budapest, Hungary
Fax: (+36) 14632871, Tel.: (+36) 14632870

hassan @ aut.bme.hu
vajk@ aut.bme.hu

Abstract:
This paper is about design and development of a system for the management of small (small companies, schools, departmental) networks. The goal of this paper is to introduce a new concept for the small network management systems. The developed system is distributed, platform-independent and the client software can be any one of the well known Web browsers.

1 INTRODUCTION

The appearance of new technologies and the spreading of WWW, Java and Intranet technologies drive the evolution of network management tools forward. With these new tools network administrators can develop solutions that better conform their specific administration needs. As a first step we designed and developed a system for the management of small (small companies, schools, departmental) networks. These organisations do not have the resources to buy the high-end network management products and thus have to choose lower cost solutions (tkined for UNIX, NetGuard for Microsoft Windows). The services offered by these products are however below expectations. Most importantly they do not have the capacity to monitor, record and store the ever-changing parameters of a local network. This inability to handle large amount of data makes the product impossible to adapt to local hardware and software configurations. All these factors create a vacuum in low cost, network management software today. With our software we tried to conquer this vacuum and to show that the new emerging technologies mentioned above are beginning to fulfil their promise. In the following sections we will describe the design and the development of SNMS (Small Network Management system) our network management tool.

2 PRIMARY REQUIREMENTS

The most important expectation toward a network management tool is the ability to monitor and log the traffic on a subnet and continuously store and analyse the parameters of network equipment. Also important factors are the ability to query system information of network equipment and warning in case of unexpected or strange events.

A few products on the market had already fulfilled some or all of these primary requirements. We however set fort a few other points that make our tool capable of being used in a wide variety of environments. These points include platform independence and a graphical administration interface available via a simple, third generation network browser.

Other, mostly natural requirements toward SNMS are robustness and affordability. Robustness is achieved via modularity and distributed processing. Affordability means the unnecessary of purchasing new hardware and software.

3 SNMP (SIMPLE NETWORK MANAGEMENT PROTOCOL)

SNMP had been developed in the middle '80's. It was meant to prepare the grounds for a new more general management protocol, but turned out to be far more popular to be simply replaced by something else. By today it is the primary protocol in network management. Part of its fame is due to simplicity and ease of implementation. Also important that most brand name vendors started to build it into their networking products including server packages. The availability of free SNMP development tools cannot be underestimated and served as a further reason for us to choose this protocol [1].

The solutions offered by SNMP are simple. Network equipment answers in the form of PDU's (Protocol data UNIT) to client queries. All we have to implement is a network transport (datagram) mechanism, which can be done on any network and transport protocol [2].

SNMP consists of three distinct parts: Manager, Agent and a management information base - MIB. The Agent is built into the management ready network equipment. It's main objective is to answer the queries received from the manager. The manager runs on the client machine and transmits SNMP command words and parameters to the agents [2]. The management information base – MIB – is a virtual database that contains information about its host device, the managed network equipment [3]. This is the database that a given agent can access.

Our system is a distributed manager that uses the communication opportunities offered by the managed network.

4 STRUCTURE

Our system fulfils the primary requirements set forth above by using SNMP with which it

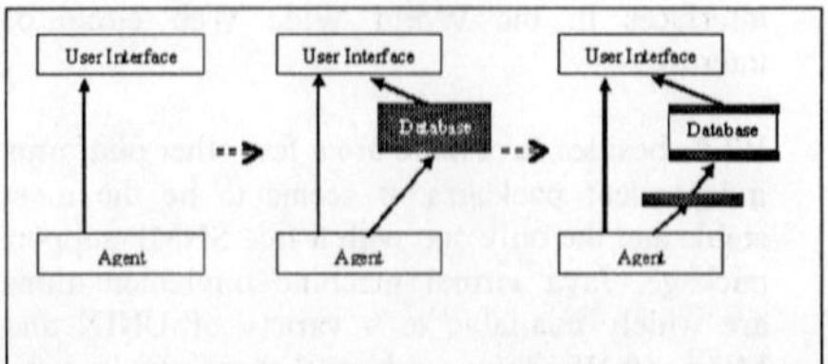

Figure 1. Evolution of the structure

accesses dynamic and static information stored in network devices.

As we mentioned previously there are two main groups of information that can be queried from the managed equipment. One is static the other is dynamic information. Storing dynamic information is crucial in our quest in building statistics and analysis that reflect the changes in the state of the managed network over a longer period of time. This brings up the question of a database module *(Fig. 1.)*. This database module stores the information collected by the collection daemons and forwarded via data translation interfaces. These interfaces are noted as dark grey layers over the collection programs and the database. The former makes communication possible between the distributed system, while the later layer maintains database product independence. For platform independence, all modules had been implemented in Java or Perl.

Our user interface is the component where deviations between our system and other tools are most apparent. For the sake of platform independence we had to rely on the practice developed by the WWW community. Our interface is purely made up of HTML, CGI and Java components. This makes our tool accessible from anywhere on the Internet. Also, no installation of new software but only a browser is needed to perform the tasks of network administration.

4.1 JAVA

Java developed by Sun Microsystems is an object oriented, C, C++ like language but more simple and uniform. According to the description provided by Sun, it is simple, distributed, interpreted, secure, architecturally neutral, portable, high-performance, multithreaded, and dynamic language [4]. Most importantly however it is the only tool for more advanced user interfaces in the World Wide Web circle of interest.

While besides Java there are a few other platforms independent packages, it seems to be the most stable and the only one with a free SNMP support package. Java virtual machine implementations are widely available to a variety of UNIX and Microsoft Windows products that are usually used in servers of smaller networks.

4.2 PERL

For server programming, network communication and database access layers we had to use a platform independent product that besides being industrial strength is freely redistributable and had been around for enough time to be implemented to all major operating systems.

Perl in many ways is a simple language. It needs no compilation and executes like a shell script. Perl borrows syntax and semantics from other widely used languages (C, English, awk) and that makes it a natural choice for busy programmers. Perl started out as a data processing language designed to scan text and files and to create reports. Today there are packages for all kinds of web development, database access and even secure programming. While becoming information management- and object-oriented Perl still functions as glue between a wide variety of components mostly UNIX in origin. [5]

5 SNMS STRUCTURE BASICS

On the lowest level work components, those communicate directly with the managed network components. These collect dynamic data and monitor unexpected events.

Our core component is an arbitrary web server that has the capability to run CGI scripts. We need this web server for the Java security model only allows applets to reconnect back to only to that server where they were downloaded. On this we server machine runs the database with all its communication layers and the archiving module. Also on this machine we have the daemon that redirects SNMP request. The database service could be exported to a different server, solving the communication between the web and the database with a further redirection component.
The Web component is rather advanced. It unifies applets that query static information from the network devices and the applets that retrieve dynamic information via the redirection components directly from the network equipment. Also it solves the user management, allowing users to access tools only for which the administrator has previously cleared them.

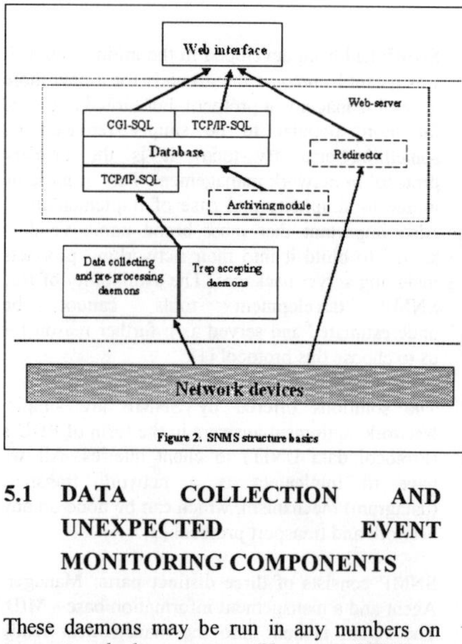

Figure 2. SNMS structure basics

5.1 DATA COLLECTION AND UNEXPECTED EVENT MONITORING COMPONENTS

These daemons may be run in any numbers on any networked computers. They use SNMP to access the managed network devices, but use TCP/IP in reaching the database gateway.

5.1.1 Data collection and pre processing daemon

These components query the dynamic information from network equipment and send them off, after pre-processing to the database gateway. They don't access data that is irrelevant in the building of time based statistics. Static information may be directly accessed using the modules on the Web interface.

These daemons can work both from command line and off a graphical interface, depending on our preferences or options available. The only parameters they require are the route (IP address) to the server running the TCP/IP - SQL bridge, (database gateway) and the IP address of devices to be monitored. If no parameters are supplied, we are presented with a graphical setup window.

When using the graphical setup interface the daemons automatically query the database about the devices monitored up to date and offer them as a possible choice for further monitoring. In our system, devices are distinguished by the IP addresses. This is useful for networks without or with but none working name servers. If name service is available network names are automatically converted to IP addresses.
The structure of the module is shown on *Figure 3*.

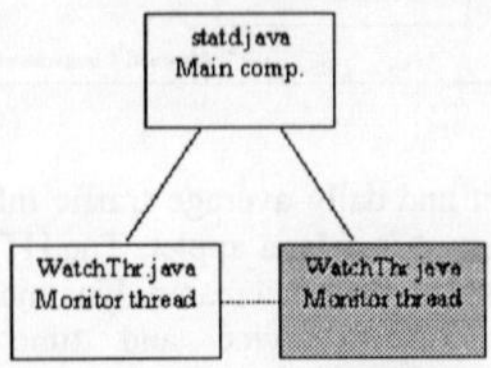

Figure 3. Structure of the data collection daemon

Taking advantage of the options offered by Java, the module had been implemented as a multi-thread application. The main thread manages the watcher treads and communicates with the user. For all monitored devices a new watcher thread is started. They all operate in parallel and query their target devices every 5 minutes. If needed, they also calculate the average change of the monitored property. All data are reported to the database via a TCP/IP – SQL bridge.

5.1.2 Unexpected events monitoring daemon

This daemon assembles error reporting tickets based on the messages it receives and forwards the tickets into the database. The daemon accepts the SNMP Traps that the monitored devices send (after the necessary configuration). To process SNMP Traps, the daemon loads and processes ASN.1 coded MIB files at startup time. The daemon can receive messages from multiple devices, but can only file error messages that network devices actually report.

5.2 DATABASE INTERFACES

Clients and CGI scripts access the database via a network socket server. To achieve maximum portability this is a standalone (rather than Inetd type) server written purely in standard Perl. It monitors the port 2345 on the host machine. Clients send actual SQL statements to the server with community encryption. SQL statements are then forwarded to the database interface layers.
The database interface layer's main purpose is to have the SQL command executed by the database server and bring the output into a form that may easily be processed by a non text processing oriented language application. This is the point that guarantees database independence, as specific SQL accents can here be brought to a common denominator and different kinds database outputs can also be brought to a common form.

5.3 ARCHIVING MODULE

Our system cannot store the large number of time variable information, as we cannot be sure that the database product used can handle the required load. This means that from time to time certain information must be deleted from the database. We clean out network traffic information that is older than 24 hour, but do a daily average before the actual deletion. We have two different version of this archiving module, the two being different in only the method they may be started. One was created to be started from the UNIX crontab or some scheduler, typically once every day. It determines the current date automatically. The other version is a command line application that receives the date as an input parameter. In this way we can archive and delete dates where for some reason automatic archiving was not on.

5.4 REDIRECTOR

The redirector is the component that replays SNMP transmissions received from Java applets started from the web interface to the actual network devices and vice versa. It is needed for the Java security issues mentioned above. This component uses an asynchronous communication model.

5.5 WEB INTERFACE

The web component is the main administration and display interface of our product. It shows all the marks of usual network management software but is dynamic, very flexible and is easy to configure. Using function components and the supplied examples anyone can build the representation of the needed networking architecture and rename the network devices shown in the examples.

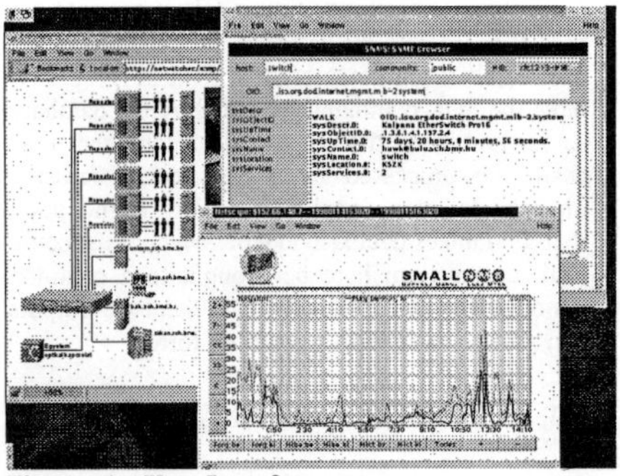

Figure. 4a. User Interface

The components of the visual interface may be grouped into 3 different categories:

5.5.1 Direct data access applets

These applets query the network devices directly via the redirection modules. They read tables and tree structures besides actual values. Reading trees and tables and finally values implement a walk method that displays all stored information in a network equipment database. This is the only way to receive first hand up to date information about the state of our small network. Since these modules are in the network administration section of the web interface, they do not create a heavy network traffic load. They load the necessary MIB files, to know what to ask from a network device from the web server.

The attached table query applet uses the property of the SNMP MIB tree that tables containing related information are indexed via a separate table. Based on this index file, all related information may be accessed simultaneously. This allows for better organised and easier to interpret information.

The SNMP browser applet has a more advanced user interface. With it's help we can easily find new information in the MIB database of the managed network equipment. If the new information proves useful we can post it to be monitored in the dynamic or static section.

5.5.2 Statistical display applets

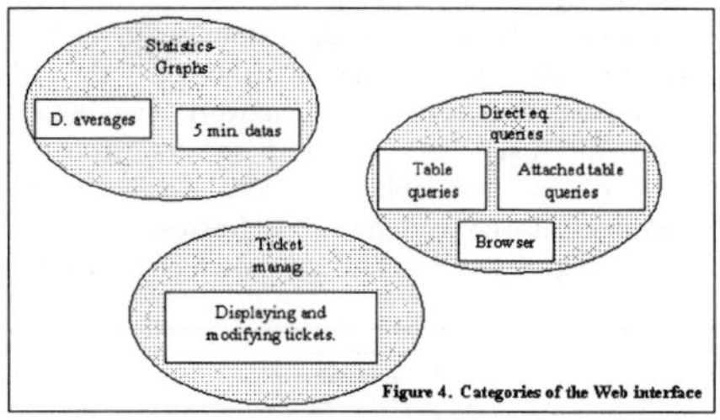

Figure 4. Categories of the Web interface

The current and daily average traffic information may be viewed in a Java applet. The HTML page that houses the applet is created dynamically as to pass the correct device and time interval parameters to the applet. It's usage is intuitive. To see the data, error or multicast packages, in- and outbound components, we have to push the appropriate button on the bottom. There is the ability to do x and y scaling and to also move the display window along the x axis. The applet presents the option of showing data next to each other or superimposed on each other.

5.5.3 CGI

On many occasions dynamic HTML pages are generated via a CGI script, like the parameterisation of Java applets. CGI scripts reach the database using an on-board server that executes all network connections and community encoding if necessary.

5.5.4 Authentication level on the WWW interface

Our interface is divided into a public and a private part. We placed all information that may be relevant to people in general to the public section. All administrative and ticket management functions received their place in the private half that is password protected. The system can handle an infinite amount of access levels, so a network that is managed by many people or institutions will all be able to have their special private quarters in our system. We also have a user tracking session management built into our product. This logs who did what and when, so potential intrusions may be noticed and necessary measures or precautions can be taken.

5.6 CONCLUSION

Comparing our system to the commercial packages we have the advantage of distributed processing and data collection and the manageability from any Internet capable computer. Although SNMS is a complete package and is successfully used at our department, we continue its development for further enhancing its ease of use with friendlier user interfaces and configuration schemes.

ACKNOWLEDGMENTS

The Hungarian Academy of Sciences supported this research for control research.

REFERENCES

[1] TYLER, SNMP & CMIP an introduction to network management, http://www.concentric.net/~tkvallil/snmp.html

[2] J. CASE, M. FEDOR, M. SCHOFFSTALL, J. DAVIN, A Simple Network Management Protocol, RFC 1157

[3] K. MCCLOGHRIE, M. ROSE, Management Information Base for Network Management of TCP/IP-based Internets, RFC 1156

[4] KARANJIT S. SIYAN, Ph D., Inside Visual J++, New Riders, 1996

[5] L. WALL, T. CHRISTIANSEN, R. SCHWARZ, Programming Perl, O'Reilly, 1997

Part 5

MODERN NUMERICAL TECHNIQUES AND RELATED TOPICS

Explicit A-Stable Runge-Kutta Methods for Some Linear Stiff-Equations

By Masaharu Nakashima
Department of Mathematics, Faculty of Science, Kagoshima University Korimoto cho 21-35, Kagoshima city 890, Japan
e-mail; naka @sci.kagoshima-u.ac.jp

Key word: Runge-Kutta methods
Subject Classification 65L06,65L07

Abstract

Some Runge-Kutta type methods of order 1 for solving Stiff-Differential Equations are present. Stability analyze of the methods for 2-dim differential equations are given. It is shown that the methods presented are suitable for solving some kind linear stiff-equations. Some numerical test justifying the results are presented.

1 Introduction

During the last years, there has been a considerable amount of research on the numerical integration of stiff systems of ODE's. A basic difficulty in the numerical solution of stiff systems is the satisfying of the requirement of stability. J.C Butcher [2] provided Implicit Runge-Kutta methods(abb;R-K methods) to overcome the stability problem. However for solving the stiff equations by using explicit methods, Lambert [3,4], Shaw[4], and many scholars have studied and proposed explicit type methods imposing stability conditions. In previous paper [6], the author proposes the variable coefficients explicit R-K methods for solving system of stiff equations, and some numerical results for stiff equations are presents. The idea of the method is that,taking the parameters suitably , A-stable methods are derived. However, stability analysis in general differential systems equations was not given.The discussion of stability analysis of variable coefficients formulas for system equations is quite difficult. In this paper, using the technique for deriving variable coefficients methods which was proposed in [6] , the author propose variable coefficients algorithms of order 1 and studies the stability analysis for 2-dim system differential equation;

$$\dot{Y} = AY,$$

$$with \quad A = \begin{pmatrix} a & b \\ c & d \end{pmatrix}, \quad (a, b, c, d \in R) \tag{1.1}$$

whose eigenvalues have negative real parts. We impose the conditions on the matrix A,

$$a + d < 0, \tag{1.2}$$

$$ad - bc > 0, \tag{1.3}$$

to sure that the eigen values of A have negative real part. The outline of this paper is as follows; In § 2, we consider first order three stage variable coefficients and study stability for (1.1), in § 3, some numerical tests justifying the results are present.

2 Derivation of Methods for a single equation of the first order

Firstly we consider the case,

Case (I). $\quad a < 0,\ d < 0.$ (2.1)

and the condition,in addition to (2,1),

Case (I.1). $\quad b < 0,\ c < 0.$ (2.2)

With the condition (2.1) and (2.2), we study the following first order formulas;

$$^1y_{n+1} = {}^1y_n + h\,{}^1k_1 + h^2 \sum_{i=1}^{2} {}^1d_i,$$

$$^2y_{n+1} = {}^2y_n + h\,{}^2k_1 + h^2 \sum_{i=1}^{2} {}^2d_i,$$

$$^1k_1 = {}^1f(x_n, {}^1y_n, {}^2y_n),$$

$$^2k_1 = {}^2f(x_n, {}^1y_n, {}^2y_n), \tag{2.3}$$

where

$$^1d_1 = \frac{a^2}{1-ha}{}^1y_n, \quad {}^1d_2 = \frac{b^2}{1-hb}{}^2y_n,$$

$$^2d_1 = \frac{c^2}{1-hc}{}^1y_n, \quad {}^2d_2 = \frac{d^2}{1-hd}{}^2y_n, \tag{2.4}$$

which may be written in the form;

$$Y_{n+1} = AY_n, \qquad (2.5)$$

where

$$A = \begin{pmatrix} r_1 & r_2 \\ r_3 & r_4 \end{pmatrix},$$

$$r_1 = \frac{1}{1-ha},\ r_2 = \frac{hb}{1-hb},$$

$$r_3 = \frac{hc}{1-hc},\ r_4 = \frac{1}{1-hd}. \qquad (2.6)$$

We now study the conditions under which the error of numerical processes (2,5) will grow with n or not. Thus we define the following definition.

Definition; The numerical processes (2.3) is stable if

$$lim_{n\to\infty}\|Y_n\| = 0.$$

where $\|.\|$ denotes an euclidean norm in R^n.

Clearly we know that,as n increases,the numerical processes Y_n is stable if and only if the absolute value of the spectral radius of matrix A of (2.5) is less than one. To study the spectral radius of matrix A, we use the Routh-Hurwitz criterion. The characteristic polynomial of the matrix A of (2.5) is

$$\rho(\lambda) = \lambda^2 - (r_1 + r_4)\lambda + r_1r_4 - r_2r_3. \qquad (2.7)$$

An applying the transformation, which maps the interior of the unit circle into the left-hand half-plan,

$$\lambda = (1 + z)/(1 - z),$$

(2.7) becomes

$$(1-z)^2\rho(\lambda) = a_0z^2 + 2a_1z + a_2,$$

where

$$a_0 = (r_1 + 1)(r_4 + 1) - r_2r_3,$$

$$a_1 = \{1 - (r_1r_4 - r_2r_3)\},$$

$$a_2 = (r_1 - 1)(r_4 - 1) - r_2r_3. \qquad (2.8)$$

and the conditions for stability of the numerical processes (2.5) are given by

$$a_1 > 0,\ a_1 > 0,\ a_2 > 0. \qquad (2.9)$$

Using the stability condition (2.9), we have the following result.

Theorem [1]. The numerical processes (2.5) with (2.1) and (2.2) is stable if and only if, in addition to (1.3),

$$ad(b+c) - bc(a+d) \le 0. \qquad (2.10)$$

Proof

Putting (2.6) into (2.8), we have

$$a_0 = \{1+\frac{1}{(1-ha)}\}\{1+\frac{1}{(1-hd)}\} - \frac{h^2bc}{(1-hb)(1-hc)},$$

$$a_1 = 1 - \frac{1}{(1-ha)(1-hd)} + \frac{h^2bc}{(1-hc)(1-hb)},$$

and

$$a_2 = \frac{\{(ad - bc) - h\{ad(b+c) - bc(a+d)\}\}h^2}{(1-ha)(1-hd)(1-hb)(1-hc)}.$$

We know clearly that the conditions (1.3) and (2.10) are necessary and sufficient conditions so that the stability conditions (2,9) are satisfied

Q.E.D

If we set the constants ρ_1, ρ_2 by

$$b = \rho_1 a,$$

$$c = \rho_2 d,$$

then

$$ad - bc = (1-\rho_1\rho_2)ad,$$

$$ad(b+c) - bc(a+d) = \rho_1(1-\rho_2)a^2d + \rho_2(1-\rho_1)ad^2,$$

which leads to the following result.

Corollary [1]. The numerical process (2.5) with (2.1) and (2.2) is stable if

$$max\{-a,-d\} > max\{-c,-d\},$$

$$min\{-a,-d\} > min\{-c,-d\}.$$

Next we consider the case, in addition to (2.1).

Case (I.II). $\quad b > 0,\ c < 0. \qquad (2.11)$

We define the formula (2.3) with

$$^1d_1 = \frac{a^2}{1-ha}{}^1y_n,\ {}^1d_2 = \frac{-b^2}{1+hb}{}^2y_n,$$

$$^2d_1 = \frac{c^2}{1-hc}{}^1y_n,\ {}^2d_2 = \frac{d^2}{1-hd}{}^2y_n,$$

which may be written in the form;

$$Y_{n+1} = AY_n, \qquad (2.12)$$

where

$$A = \begin{pmatrix} r_1 & r_2 \\ r_3 & r_4 \end{pmatrix},$$

$$r_1 = \frac{1}{1-ha},\ r_2 = \frac{hb}{1+hb},$$

$$r_3 = \frac{hc}{1-hc},\ r_4 = \frac{1}{1-hd}. \qquad (2.13)$$

Proceeding in a same way as Theorem [1], we have the following theorem.

Theorem [2]. The numerical process (2.12) with (2.1) and (2.11) is stable if and only if

$$ad + bc - (a+d)(b-c) \ge 0. \qquad (2.14)$$

Proof

Proceeding in the same way in the proof of the previous result, we prove the theorem.

Putting r_1, r_2, r_3 and r_4 of (2.13) into (2.8), we have

$$a_0 = \{1+\frac{1}{(1-ha)}\}\{1+\frac{1}{(1-hd)}\} - \frac{bch^2}{(1-hc)(1+hb)},$$

$$a_1 = \frac{[-(a+d) + \{ad+bc-(a+d)(b-c)\}h]h}{(1-ha)(1-hd)(1-hc)(1+hb)} + \frac{ad(b-c)h^3}{(1-ha)(1-hd)(1-hc)(1+hb)},$$

$$a_2 = \frac{adh^2}{(1-ha)(1-hd)} - \frac{bch^2}{(1-hc)(1+hb)}.$$

We know clearly that the conditions (1.2) and (2.14) are necessary and sufficient conditions so that the stability condition (2.9) are satisfied.

Q.E.D

The stability condition (2.14) may write in the form;

$$\begin{aligned} ad + bc - (a+d)(b-c) &= b(c - a - d) + ad + ac + cd \\ &= c(b + a + d) + ad - ab - bd. \end{aligned}$$

and we have the following result.

Corollary [2]. The numerical process (2.12) with (2.1) and (2.11) is stable if,

$$c - (a + d) \geq 0,$$

or

$$b + (a + d) \leq 0.$$

Next we consider the case, in addition to (2.1).
Case (I.III). $b < 0,\ c > 0.$ (2.15)
We define the algorithm (2.3) with

$$^1d_1 = \frac{a^2}{1-ha}{}^1y_n,\ {}^1d_2 = \frac{b^2}{1-hb}{}^2y_n,$$

$$^2d_1 = \frac{-c^2}{1+hc}{}^1y_n,\ {}^2d_2 = \frac{d^2}{1-hd}{}^2y_n,$$

which leads to

$$Y_{n+1} = AY_n, \tag{2.16}$$

where

$$A = \begin{pmatrix} r_1 & r_2 \\ r_3 & r_4 \end{pmatrix},$$

$$r_2 = \frac{hb}{1-hb},\ r_3 = \frac{hc}{1+hc}, \tag{2.17}$$

the other r_1 and r_4 are same to that of (2.13).

Replacing b by c in (2.13), we have the formula (2.17), then the result of Theorem [2] leads to the following theorem.

Theorem [3]. The numerical process (2.16) with (2.1) and (2.15) is stable if and only if

$$ad + bc - (a+d)(c-b) \geq 0. \tag{2.18}$$

Next we consider the case, in addition to (2.1).
Case (I.IV). $b > 0,\ c > 0.$ (2.19)
We define the algorithm in (2.3) with

$$^1d_1 = \frac{a^2}{1-ha}{}^1y_n,\ {}^1d_2 = \frac{-b^2}{1+hb}{}^2y_n,$$

$$^2d_1 = \frac{-c^2}{1+hc}{}^1y_n,\ {}^2d_2 = \frac{d^2}{1-hd}{}^2y_n,$$

which leads to

$$Y_{n+1} = AY_n, \tag{2.20}$$

where

$$A = \begin{pmatrix} r_1 & r_2 \\ r_3 & r_4 \end{pmatrix},$$

$$r_1 = \frac{1}{1-ha},\ r_2 = \frac{hb}{1+hb},$$

$$r_3 = \frac{hc}{1+hc},\ r_4 = \frac{1}{1-hd}. \tag{2.21}$$

Proceeding in the same way as the previous theorems, we have the following result.

Theorem [4]. The numerical process (2.20) with (2.1) and (2.19) is stable if and only if in addition to (1.3),

$$ad(b+c) + bc(a+d) \geq 0.$$

Proof

Putting (2.21) into (2.8), we have

$$a_0 = \{1+\frac{1}{(1-ha)}\}\{1+\frac{1}{(1-hd)}\} - \frac{h^2bc}{(1+hb)(1+hc)},$$

$$\begin{aligned} a_1 &= [1 - \frac{1}{(1-ha)(1-hd)} + \frac{h^2bc}{(1+hc)(1+hb)}], \\ &= \frac{[-(a+d) + \{ad+bc-(b+c)(a+d))\}h+]h}{(1-ha)(1+hb)(1+hc)(1-hd)}, \\ &+ \frac{[\{ad(b+c) - 2bc(a+d)\}h^2 + 2abcdh^3]h}{(1-ha)(1+hb)(1+hc)(1-hd)}, \end{aligned}$$

$$\begin{aligned} a_2 &= \{1-\frac{1}{(1-ha)}\}\{1-\frac{1}{(1-hd)}\} - \frac{h^2bc}{(1+hb)(1+hc)} \\ &= \frac{[(ad - bc) + h\{ad(b+c) + bc(a+d)\}]h^2}{(1-ha)(1+hb)(1+hc)(1-hd)}. \end{aligned}$$

We know clearly that the conditions (2.1) and (1.3) are necessary and sufficient conditions so that the stability conditions (2.9) are satisfied.

Q.E.D

Secondly we consider the case,
Case II. $a > 0,\ d < 0.$ (2.22)
and we consider the cases, in addition to (2.22).
Case (II.I). $b > 0,\ c < 0.$ (2.23)
We consider the scheme (2.3) with

$$^1d_1 = \frac{-a^2}{1+ha}{}^1y_n,\ {}^1d_2 = \frac{-b^2}{1+hb}{}^2y_n,$$

$$ {}^2d_1 = \frac{c^2}{1-hc}{}^1y_n,\ {}^2d_2 = \frac{d^2}{1-hd}{}^2y_n, $$

which may be written in the form;

$$ Y_{n+1} = AY_n, \tag{2.24} $$

where

$$ A = \begin{pmatrix} r_1 & r_2 \\ r_3 & r_4 \end{pmatrix}, $$

$$ r_1 = \frac{1+2ha}{1+ha},\ r_2 = \frac{hb}{1+hb}, $$

$$ r_3 = \frac{hc}{1-hc},\ r_4 = \frac{1}{1-hd}. \tag{2.25} $$

Analyzing the numerical process (2.24) in a same way as the previous methods, we have the following result.

Theorem [5] The numerical process (2.24) with (2.22) and (2.23) is stable if and only if, in addition to (1.2) and (1.3) ,

$$ -(b-c)(a+d) - ad + bc \geq 0, $$

$$ ad(b-c) - bc(a-d) > 0, $$

$$ 2abc - ad(b-c) > 0 $$

or

$$ -(b-c)(a+d) - ad + bc \leq 0, $$

$$ 2abc - ad(b-c) > 0, $$

$$ \{-(b-c)(a+d) - ad + bc\}^2 + $$

$$ 4\{a+d\}\{2abc - ad(b-c)\} \leq 0. \tag{2.26} $$

Proof

Proceeding in a same way as before, we prove the theorem.

Putting r_1, r_2, r_3 and r_4 of (2.25) into (2.8), we have

$$ a_0 = (2+\frac{ha}{(1+ha)})(1+\frac{1}{(1-hd)}) - \frac{h^2bc}{(1+hb)(1-hc)}, $$

$$ a_1 = \frac{[-(a+d)+h\{-(b-c)(a+d)-ad+bc)\}+]h}{(1+hb)(1+ha)(1-hc)(1-hd)} + \frac{[h^2\{-ad(b-c)+2abc\}]h}{(1+hb)(1+ha)(1-hc)(1-hd)}, $$

$$ a_2 = \frac{[ad-bc + h\{ad(b-c)-bc(a-d)\}]h^2}{(1+hb)(1+ha)(1-hc)(1-hd)}. $$

From the the stability conditions (2.9), clearly, we know that the conditions (1.2),(1.3) and (2.26) are necessary. It is also true that if (1.2), (1.3) and (2.26) are satisfied, the stability condition (2.9) are satisfied.

Q.E.D

Next we consider the case, in addition to (2.22).

Case (II.II). $b < 0,\ c > 0.$ (2.27)

We consider the algorithm (2,3) with

$$ {}^1d_1 = \frac{-a^2}{1+ha}{}^1y_n,\ {}^1d_2 = \frac{b^2}{1-hb}{}^2y_n, $$

$$ {}^2d_1 = \frac{-c^2}{1+hc}{}^1y_n,\ {}^2d_2 = \frac{d^2}{1-hd}{}^2y_n, $$

which may be written in the form;

$$ Y_{n+1} = AY_n, \tag{2.28} $$

where

$$ A = \begin{pmatrix} r_1 & r_2 \\ r_3 & r_4 \end{pmatrix}, $$

and

$$ r_1 = \frac{1+2ha}{1+ha},\ r_2 = \frac{hb}{1-hb}, $$

$$ r_3 = \frac{hc}{1+hc}\ r_4 = \frac{1}{1-hd}. \tag{2.29} $$

Replacing b by c in (2.25), we have the formula (2.29), then the result of Theorem [5] leads to the following theorem.

Theorem [6] The numerical process (2.28) with (2.22) and (2.27) is stable if and only if, in addition to (1.2) and (1.3),

$$ -(c-b)(a+d) - ad + bc \geq 0, $$

$$ ad(c-b) - bc(a-d) > 0, $$

$$ 2abc - ad(c-b) > 0 $$

or

$$ -(c-b)(a+d) - ad + bc > 0, $$

$$ 2abc - ad(c-b) > 0, $$

$$ \{-(c-b)(a+d) - ad + bc\}^2 + $$

$$ 4\{a+d\}\{2abc - ad(c-b)\} \leq 0. \tag{2.30} $$

Thirdly we consider the case,

Case (III). $a < 0,\ d > 0.$ (2.31)

and we consider the cases, in addition to (2.31).

Case (III.I). $b > 0,\ c < 0.$ (2.32)

Setting

$$ {}^1d_1 = \frac{a^2}{1-ha}{}^1y_n,\ {}^1d_2 = \frac{-b^2}{1+hb}{}^2y_n, $$

$$ {}^2d_1 = \frac{c^2}{1-hc}{}^1y_n,\ {}^2d_2 = \frac{-d^2}{1+hd}{}^2y_n, $$

we have the following result, replaced a by d in Thorem [5].

Theorem [7] The numerical process (2.29) with (2.31) and (2.32) is stable if and only if, in addition to (1.2) and (1.3) ,

$$ -(b-c)(a+d) - ad + bc \geq 0, $$

$$ ad(b-c) - bc(d-a) > 0, $$

$$ 2bcd - ad(b-c) > 0 $$

or

$$ -(b-c)(a+d) - ad + bc \leq 0, $$

$$2bcd - ad(b-c) > 0,$$

$$\{-(b-c)(a+d) - ad + bc\}^2 +$$

$$4\{a+d\}\{2bcd - ad(b-c)\} \le 0.$$

Next we consider the case, in addition to (2.31).

Case (III.II). $\quad b < 0,\ c > 0.$ (2.34)

Setting

$$^1d_1 = \frac{a^2}{1-ha}\,{}^1y_n,\ {}^1d_2 = \frac{b^2}{1-hb}\,{}^2y_n,$$

$$^2d_1 = \frac{-c^2}{1+hc}\,{}^1y_n,\ {}^2d_2 = \frac{-d^2}{1+hd}\,{}^2y_n,$$

we have the following result, replaced a by d in Thorem [6].

Theorem [8] The numerical process (2.35) with (2.31) and (2.34) is stable if and only if, in addition to (1.2) and (1.3),

$$-(c-b)(a+d) - ad + bc \ge 0,$$

$$ad(c-b) - bc(d-a) > 0,$$

$$2bcd - ad(c-b) > 0$$

or

$$-(c-b)(a+d) - ad + bc > 0,$$

$$2bcd - ad(c-b) > 0,$$

$$\{-(c-b)(a+d) - ad + bc\}^2 +$$

$$4\{a+d\}\{2bcd - ad(c-b)\} \le 0.$$

Lastly we consider the case.

Case (VI). $\quad a > 0,\ d > 0.$ (2.36)

In this case, the condition (2.36) contrdicts to the assumption (1.2).

We define the algorithm (2.3) in the same way as before,

$$^1d_1 = \frac{-a^2}{1+ha}\,{}^1y_n,\ {}^1d_2 = \frac{\alpha_2 b^2}{1+h\alpha_1 b}\,{}^2y_n,$$

$$^2d_1 = \frac{\beta_2 c^2}{1+\beta_1 hc}\,{}^1y_n,\ {}^2d_2 = \frac{-d^2}{1+hd}\,{}^2y_n,$$

which leads to

$$Y_{n+1} = AY_n, \tag{2.37}$$

$$A = \begin{pmatrix} r_1 & r_2 \\ r_3 & r_4 \end{pmatrix},$$

$$r_1 = \frac{1+2ha}{1+ha},\ r_2 = \{b + \frac{h\alpha_2 b^2)}{1+h\alpha_1}\}h,$$

$$r_3 = \{c + \frac{h\beta_2 c^2}{1+h\beta_1 c}\}h,$$

$$r_4 = \frac{1+2hd}{1+hd}. \tag{2.38}$$

We study the stability of the numerical processes in a similar way as before. (2.28),computing the eigenvalues of A leads to the following equation,

Putting (2.38) into (2.8), we have,

$$a_1 = 1 - \frac{(1+2ha)}{(1+ha)}\frac{(1+2hd)}{(1+hd)}$$

$$+h^2\{b + \frac{\alpha_2 h}{1+h\alpha_1}\}\{c + \frac{\beta_2 h}{1+h\beta_1}\}$$

$$= [\frac{-(a+d)+3had}{(1+ha)(1+hd)} + h\{b + \frac{\alpha_2 h}{(1+h\alpha_1)}\}\{c + \frac{\beta_2 h}{(1+h\beta_1)}\}]h.$$

We know that, from the stability condition $a_1 > 0$, even if we take any real values of $\alpha_1, \alpha_2, \beta_1$ and β_2 in a_1, the following condition is necessary.

$$a + d \le 0. \tag{2.39}$$

Clearly (2.39) contradicts to the assumption (2.36). Consequently, we have the following Theorem.

Theorem [9] The numerical process (2.37) with $a,\ d > 0$ is instable.

The algorithms derived from the case (I.I),(I.II), (I,III),(I,IV) , (II,I) , (II,II) ,(III,I) and (III,II) are then given by

$$^ly_{n+1} = {}^ly_n + h^l k_1 + h^2 \sum_{i=1}^{2} {}^l d_i,$$

$$^2y_{n+1} = {}^2y_n + h^2 k_1 + h^2 \sum_{i=1}^{2} {}^2 d_i,$$

$$^lk_1 = {}^lf(x_n, {}^1y_n, {}^2y_n), \quad (l = 1,2)$$

where

$$^1d_1 = -\frac{sgn(a)a^2}{1+sgn(a)ha}\,{}^1y_n,$$

$$^2d_1 = -\frac{sgn(b)b^2}{1+sgn(b)hb}\,{}^2y_n,$$

$$^1d_2 = -\frac{sgn(c)c^2}{1+sgn(c)hc}\,{}^1y_n,$$

$$^2d_2 = -\frac{sgn(d)d^2}{1+sgn(d)hd}\,{}^2y_n,$$

$$a = {}^1f_1(0,1,0),\ b = {}^2f_1(0,0,1),$$

$$c = {}^1f_2(0,1,0),\ d = {}^2f_2(0,0,1), \tag{2.40}$$

or

$$^1d_i = -\{sgn({}^1f_i(x_n, {}^1y_n, 0))\}\{{}^1f_i(x_n, {}^1y_n, 0)\}^2$$

$$\star \frac{1}{{}^1y_n + h\,\{sgn({}^1f_i(x_n, {}^1y_n, 0)\}\{{}^1f_i(x_n, {}^1y_n, 0)\}},$$

$$^2d_i = -\{sgn(^2f_i(x_n,0,^2y_n))\}\{^2f_i(x_n,0,^2y_n)\}^2$$
$$\star\frac{1}{^2y_n + h\,\{sgn(^2f_i(x_n,0,^2y_n))\}\{^2f_i(x_n,0,^2y_n)\}}.$$
$$(i = 1,2) \qquad (2.41)$$

We have proposed some numerical algorithms for solving initial value problem (1.1). It is desirable that if the numerical solution is stable, then the analytic solution of (1.1) is also stable. However We know that if the numerical solution is stable, then the algorithm (2.40) or (2.41) satisfies the conditions (1.2) and (1.3), we have the following theorem.

Theorem [10]. If the numerical algorithms defined by (2.38) or (2.41) are stable, then the analytic solution of (1.1) is also stable.

Remark. Under the conditions, which are weaker than condition (2.1)

$$a \leq 0, d \leq 0, a + d > 0,$$

the theorems [2] and [3] are also true.

3 Numerical Example

Using the numerical process (2.39), we present some numerical tests to sure the stability of the methods proposed in this paper. By some numerical comparison the methods described in the preceding section with Implicit Euler's method, it is also shown that our methods are much more useful. The numerical example are taken from the paper of A.I. Johnoson and J.B. Barney [1] and Hull, Enright and Sedgwick [5].

We set the heading

Fev; number of function evaluations necessary to integrate the given integration interval.

SDJ; The absolute error of the j-th component with respect to a given reference solution.

Problems

(1) A stiff with real eigenvalues:

$$\dot{Y} = AY, \quad A = \begin{pmatrix} -1 & 0 \\ 0 & -100 \end{pmatrix}, Y(0) = \begin{pmatrix} 1 \\ 1 \end{pmatrix}.$$

Its theoretical solution is

$$y_1 = exp(-x)\,,$$
$$y_2 = exp(-100x)\,.$$

(2) A linear, modestly stiff with real eigenvalues:

$$\dot{Y} = AY, \quad A = \begin{pmatrix} -500.5 & 499.5 \\ 499.5 & -500,5 \end{pmatrix}, Y(0) = \begin{pmatrix} 0 \\ 2 \end{pmatrix}.$$

Its theoretical solution is

$$y_1 = exp(-x) - exp(-1000x),$$
$$y_2 = exp(-x) + exp(-1000x).$$

(3) A linear, highly stiff system with complex eigenvalues:

$$\dot{Y} = AY, \quad A = \begin{pmatrix} -10^4 & 10^3 \\ -10^3 & -10^4 \end{pmatrix},$$
$$Y(0) = \begin{pmatrix} 1 \\ 1 \end{pmatrix}.$$

Its theoretical solution is

$$Y(x) = (u(x), v(x)),$$

where

$$u(x) = exp(-10^4x)(cos(10^3x) + sin(10^3x)),$$
$$v(x) = exp(-10^4x)(cos(10^3x) - sin(10^3x)),$$

The data are the absolute error of numerical solution with constant step size

TABLE I

Problem 1.

Implicit Euler's Methods

h $=1/2^8$

x	$1/2^8$	$2/2^8$	$49/2^8$	Fev
$SD1$	0.759E-5	0.518E-4	0.307E-3	460
$SD2$	0.424E-1	0.344E-1	0.976E-7	460

Remark; Implicit Euler's Methods diverges for the step size $h \geq 1/2^n, (n \leq 7)$.

Variable Coefficient Methods (2.40)

h $=1/2^8$

x	$1/2^8$	$2/2^8$	$49/2^8$	Fev
$SD1$	0.759E-5	0.518E-4	0.307E-3	49
$SD2$	0,424E-1	0.344E-1	0.912E-7	49

h $=1/2^3$

x	$1/2^3$	$7/2^3$	$49/2^3$	Fev
$SD1$	0.639E-2	0.216E-1	0.927E-3	49
$SD2$	0.740E-1	0.122E-7	0.00E-30	49

h =1

x	1	2	10	Fev
$SD1$	0.132E+0	0.114E+0	0.931E-3	10
$SD2$	0.990E-2	0.980E-4	0.905E-20	10

TABLE II

Problem 2.

Implicit Euler's Methods

h =1/2^12

x	$1/2^{12}$	$2/2^{12}$	$49/2^{12}$	Fev
$SD1$	0.203E-1	0.356E-1	0.498E-6	554
$SD2$	0.203E-1	0.356E-1	0.308E-5	554

Remark;Implicit Euler's Methods diverge for the step size $h \geq 1/2^n, (n \leq 11)$.

Variable Coefficient Methods (2.40)

h =1/2^12

x	$1/2^{12}$	$2/2^{12}$	$49/2^{12}$	Fev
$SD1$	0.100E-2	0.189E-2	0.243E-2	49
$SD2$	0.907E-3	0.119E-2	0.243E-2	49

h =1/2^5

x	$1/2^5$	$7/2^5$	$97/2^5$	Fev
$SD1$	0.910E+0	0.603E+0	0.940E+0	97
$SD2$	0.910E+0	0.212E+0	0.940E+0	97

h =1

x	1	2	10	Fev
$SD1$	0.163E+1	0.135E+0	0.540E-5	10
$SD2$	0.367E+0	0.186E+1	0.199E+1	10

TABLE III

Problem 3.

Implicit Euler's Methods

h =1/2^15

x	$1/2^{15}$	$2/2^{15}$	$97/2^{15}$	Fev
$SD1$	0.245E-1	0.373E-1	0.124E-11	813
$SD2$	0.336E-1	0.370E-1	0.868E-11	813

Remark;Implicit Euler's Methods diverges for the step size $h \geq 1/2^n, (n \leq 14)$.

Variable Coefficient Methods (2.40)

h =1/2^15

x	$1/2^{15}$	$2/2^{15}$	$97/2^{15}$	Fev
$SD1$	0.366E-1	0.513E-1	0.890E-11	97
$SD2$	0.224E-1	0.181E-1	0.147E-11	97

h =1/2^8

x	$1/2^8$	$7/2^8$	$49/2^8$	Fev
$SD1$	0.821E+0	0.242E+0	0.149E-4	49
$SD2$	0.771E+0	0.154E+0	139E-4	49

h =1

x	1	2	10	Fev
$SD1$	0.999E+0	0.997E+0	0.989E+0	10
$SD2$	0.998E+0	0.998E+0	0.991E+0	10

Conclusion. As we have said in the abstract, various explicit R-K type methods for solving stiff equations have been presented,unfortunately, the methods which have been already proposed are useful for scalar differential equations, however, inappropriate for system equations.

In this paper, the author have proposed order one R-K methods, giving the stability analysis for two-system differential equation, we have showed the usefulness of our methods for solving stiff equations, we also present some numerical tests which are often encounters in stiff problems.

We have developed the algorithms (2.3) only for 2-dim differential equation, it remain the problem to develop the algorithm (2.2) for general differential equation and for getting high order R-K methods of type (2.3) .

In deriving the formula (2.3) , we confine our consideration ${}^id_j(i,j=1,2)$ in the form (2.40) , then by setting ${}^id_j(i,j=1,2)$ in the other form, we may expect to have more useful methods for solving system stiff equation. It remain to study what is probably the most useful formula in determining ${}^id_j(i,j=1,2)$ of the formula (2.3) .

References

[1] A.I. Johnson and J.R. Barney, Numerical solution of large systems of stiff ordinary differential equations in a modular framework. Numerical Methods for Differential Systems(eds.L.Lapidus and W.E.Schiesser), Academic Press INC(1976).

[2] J. C. Butcher, Coefficients for the study of Runge-Kutta integration process, J. Austral. Math. Soc,3(1963),185-201.

[3] J.D. Lambert, Two unconditional classes of methods for stiff systems, in Stiff Differential Systems (Ed. R. A. Willoughby), Plenum Press, New York(1974a),171-186.

[4] J.D. Lambert and B. Shaw, Hull, On the numerical solution of $y^{0} = f(x,y)$ by a class of formulae based onrational approximation. Math. Comp.19(1965),456-462.

[5] T.E Hull, W.H. Enright ,B.M. Fellen and A.E. Sedgwick,Comparing numerical methods for ordinary differential equations, SIAM J. Numer. Anal,9(1972),603-637.

[6] M. Nakashima, Variable Coefficients A-stable Explicit Runge-Kutta Methd, J,I,A,M,12(1995),285-308.

[7] A. Wambecq, Rational Runge Kutta methods for solving systems of ordinary differential equations, Computing, 20(1978),333-342.

A Linear Matrix Inequality Approach to VSCS Design for Linear Systems with Mismatched Uncertainties

Han Ho Choi

Dept. of Elec. Edu., Andong National Univ.

388 Songchon-dong, Andong, Kyungbuk 760-749, SEOUL KOREA

TEL:+82-571-50-5430, FAX:+82-571-841-1624

E-mail : hhchoi@phoenix.dwe.co.kr

Abstract

In this paper, the problem of designing sliding mode controllers for a class of uncertain systems with mismatched unstructured uncertainties is considered. Based on the linear matrix inequality (LMI) approach we develop a new design method of linear sliding surfaces that are linear to the state. We give existence conditions of linear sliding surfaces in terms of LMIs, which define a convex solution set, and we give explicit characterizations of linear sliding surfaces in terms of positive-definite solution matrices to the LMI existence conditions. Additionally, in terms of LMIs we give sufficient conditions for the existence of linear sliding surfaces guaranteeing regional pole clustering constraints of reduced-order equivalent dynamics, together with an example.

Key Words- Variable structure control system(VSCS), linear matrix inequality (LMI), uncertain system, sliding surface

1. Introduction

Over the year, many researchers have considered the problem of stabilizing uncertain linear systems using state feedback control. And many researchers have recently developed control algorithms using the VSCS theory. The VSCS theory has been successfully applied to robotic manipulators, underwater vehicles, high-performance electric motors, and power systems or so. In the VSCS the controller structure around the plant is intentionally changed by using a viable high speed switching feedback control to obtain a desired plant behavior or response, from which the term VSCS arises. Using the switching feedback control law the VSCS drives the trajectory of the system onto a specified and user-chosen surface, which is termed the sliding surface or the switching surface, and maintain the trajectory on this sliding surface for all subsequent time. The VSCS has various attractive features such as fast response, good transient performance, order reduction, insensitivity to internal parameter variations, and invariance to external disturbances. The central feature of the VSCS is the so-called sliding mode on the sliding surface within which the system remains insensitive to internal parameter variations and extraneous disturbance satisfying the matching condition. Thus, the design of the proper switching surface as well as the existence of a sliding mode on the switching surface is key problems in VSCS design and much attention has been paid to the problems. And, several approaches for designing the proper switching surface have been proposed based on the fact that, if the pair (A,B) is controllable where $A \in R^{n \times n}$ is the nominal system characteristic matrix and $B \in R^{n \times m}$ is the nominal input matrix then in the sliding mode m state variables of the linear system can be expressed in terms of the remaining $(n-m)$ state variables and the poles of the reduced $(n-m)$ order equivalent system restricted to the sliding surface can be freely assigned [1-6]. However, the traditional VSCS design methods do not yet give us a clear solution to the problem of designing sliding mode control laws for uncertain multivariable systems where the uncertainty does not satisfy the matching condition, and the problem is rarely been considered.

On the other hand, various linear control design problems have been recently formulated by using linear matrix inequalities (LMIs). Since LMIs can be solved very efficiently via various powerful convex optimization algorithms with a polynomial-time worst-case complexity, LMI-based formulations offer a numerically tractable means of attacking robust control system design problems and therefore reducing a control design problem to an LMI can be considered as a practical solution to this problem [7][9].

In this paper, we consider the problem of designing a VSCS for a class of linear systems with mismatched unstructured uncertainties. We give an LMI-based formulation for designing a sliding mode control law and we derive sufficient conditions for the existence of a linear sliding surface. In terms of LMIs we give an explicit parameterization of linear sliding surfaces guaranteeing robust stability of the reduced-order equivalent dynamics. The main advantage of our formulation is in the computational aspect. Since LMI problems can be easily determined whether they are feasible or not, and if it is, they can be solved very efficiently by using powerful convex optimization algorithms such as the LMI Control Toolbox [8], thus our method enables one to easily compute sliding surfaces for even large scale systems. Additionally, our LMI-based formulation offers some design flexibility which can be used to improve design, thus using our LMI-based formulation one may design sliding mode controllers satisfying additional convex constraints because LMIs can be used to represent a wide class of constraints. We also give sufficient conditions for the existence of a linear sliding surface guaranteeing general pole clustering constraints of the reduced-order equivalent system dynamics restricted to the sliding surface. This paper is based on [3]. Similar work on VSCS design for uncertain systems with structured uncertainties in the state space model is also reported in [6].

2. System Description and Preliminary Results

Let the system to be controlled be represented by the following differential equation

$$\dot{x} = Ax + Bu + D\rho(t) \qquad (1)$$

where $x \in R^n$ is the state, $u \in R^m$ is the control input, and $\rho(t): R^+ \to R^q$ is the lumped uncertainty, and A, B, D are constant matrices with appropriate dimensions. Without loss of generality, we will assume that the input matrix B has full rank. Suppose that the pair (A,B) is stabilizable, and $\|\rho(t)\|$ is cone-bounded, i.e. there exist positive constants ρ_0, ρ_1 such that

$$\|\rho(t)\| < \rho_0 + \rho_1 \|x(t)\|$$

Before proceeding further, we will give some useful results.

Definition [8]: A subset Ω of the complex plane is called *an LMI region* if there exist a symmetric matrix $\Delta \in R^{(n-m)\times(n-m)}$ and a matrix $\Gamma \in R^{(n-m)\times(n-m)}$ such that

$$\Omega = \left\{z \in C : \Delta + z\Gamma + \bar{z}\Gamma^T < 0\right\}$$

Lemma 2.1[8] : All eigenvalues of a matrix $F \in R^{(n-m)\times(n-m)}$ lie in the LMI region Ω if and only if there exists a positive-definite matrix P_0 such that

$$\left[\Delta_{ij}P_0 + \Gamma_{ij}FP_0 + \Gamma_{ji}P_0F^T\right]_{1\le i,j\le(n-m)} < 0$$

where the notation $\Delta = [\Delta]_{1\le i,j\le(n-m)}$ means that Δ is an $(n-m)\times(n-m)$ matrix with generic entry Δ_{ij}.

Lemma 2.2[7]: The following linear matrix inequality

$$\begin{bmatrix} Q(x) & S(x) \\ S(x)^T & R(x) \end{bmatrix} > 0$$

where $Q(x) = Q(x)^T, R(x) = R(x)^T$, and $S(x)$ depend affinely on x, is equivalent to

$$R(x) > 0, Q(x) - S(x)R(x)^{-1}S(x)^T > 0$$

3. Main Results

A. Robust Stability Condition

Consider the following LMI:

$$\Pi^T \begin{bmatrix} -Q^{-1} + \frac{1}{2\delta}X & X + \frac{1}{2\delta}XA^T \\ X + \frac{1}{2\delta}AX & AX + XA^T \frac{1}{2\delta}AXA^T \end{bmatrix} \Pi < 0 \quad (2)$$

where δ is a positive constant, Q is a positive-definite matrix,

$$\Pi = \begin{bmatrix} I & 0 \\ 0 & \widetilde{B} \end{bmatrix}$$

and $\widetilde{B}$ is any matrix whose columns form the basis of the null space of B^T, i.e. $\widetilde{B}$ is an orthogonal complement of B. Note that $\widetilde{B}$ is not unique for given B but any choice is acceptable. Assume that the sliding surface σ, which is linear to the state x, is given by

$$\sigma(x) = Sx = B^T X^{-1} x = 0 \quad (3)$$

Now, let the control strategy be given as follows:

$$u(t) = -G[\delta I + A]x(t) - \hat{\rho}(t)\frac{\sigma}{\|\sigma\|} \quad (4)$$

where $\hat{\rho} = \|(B^T B)^{-1} B^T D\| [\rho_0 + \rho_1 \|x(t)\|]$ and $G = (SB)^{-1} S = (B^T X^{-1} B)^{-1} B^T X^{-1}$. Then we can establish the followings:

Lemma 3.1: For given positive constant δ, if there exist positive-definite matrices Q, X satisfying the LMI (2), then the solution matrices Q, X also satisfy the following matrix inequality

$$\begin{aligned} A^T P + PA - PBG(\delta I + A) \\ -(\delta I + A)^T G^T B^T P + Q < 0 \quad (5) \end{aligned}$$

where $P = X^{-1}$

Proof: By using congruence transformation with $T^T = [X\widetilde{B}, B]$ one can easily show that (5) is equivalent to

$$\begin{bmatrix} \widetilde{B}^T (AX + XA^T)\widetilde{B} & \widetilde{B}^T AB \\ B^T A^T \widetilde{B} & -2\delta B^T X^{-1} B \end{bmatrix} + \begin{bmatrix} \widetilde{B}^T X \\ B^T \end{bmatrix} Q \begin{bmatrix} \widetilde{B}^T X \\ B^T \end{bmatrix}^T < 0$$

By the Lemma 2.2, we can easily see that the above is equivalent to

$$\begin{bmatrix} -Q^{-1} & X\widetilde{B} & B \\ \widetilde{B}^T X & \widetilde{B}^T (AX + XA^T)\widetilde{B} & \widetilde{B}^T AB \\ B^T & B^T A^T \widetilde{B} & -2\delta B^T XB \end{bmatrix} < 0$$

which is equivalent to

$$\begin{bmatrix} -Q^{-1} & X\widetilde{B} \\ \widetilde{B}^T X & \widetilde{B}^T (AX + XA^T)\widetilde{B} \end{bmatrix} + \frac{1}{2\delta}\begin{bmatrix} I \\ \widetilde{B}^T A \end{bmatrix} B(B^T X^{-1} B)^{-1} B^T \begin{bmatrix} I \\ \widetilde{B}^T A \end{bmatrix}^T < 0$$

Since $B(B^T X^{-1} B)^{-1} B^T \le X$ the above matrix inequality is always satisfied for any positive-definite solution matrices Q, X satisfying

$$\begin{bmatrix} -Q^{-1} & X\widetilde{B} \\ \widetilde{B}^T X & \widetilde{B}^T (AX + XA^T)\widetilde{B} \end{bmatrix} + \frac{1}{2\delta}\begin{bmatrix} I \\ \widetilde{B}^T A \end{bmatrix} X \begin{bmatrix} I \\ \widetilde{B}^T A \end{bmatrix}^T < 0$$

After all, by resorting to the Lemma 2.2 again we can see that (5) is satisfied if (2) holds. ∇∇∇

Remark 1: The LMI (2) defines a convex set of solution pairs (Q, X) for given δ and therefore one can easily test whether the LMI (2) is solvable, and if so, on can get solutions by using an efficient convex optimization algorithm such as the LMI Control Toolbox and the LMI Lab[7-8].

Now, let's define a Lyapunov function candidate as $V(x) = x^T Px = x^T X^{-1} x$ where X is a positive-definite solution matrix to the LMI (2). Then the time derivative of the Lyapunov function candidate along the solution trajectory of the system (1) with the control (4) is given by

$$\dot{V} = 2x^T X^{-1}[Ax + Bu + D\rho(t)]$$

Using $\widetilde{B}(\widetilde{B}^T \widetilde{B})^{-1} \widetilde{B}^T + B(B^T B)^{-1} B^T = I$ one can obtain

$$\begin{aligned} \dot{V} = 2x^T X^{-1}[Ax + Bu + \widetilde{B}(\widetilde{B}^T \widetilde{B})^{-1} \widetilde{B} D\rho(t)] \\ + 2x^T X^{-1} B(B^T B)^{-1} BD\rho(t) \end{aligned}$$

By using the Lemma 3.1, the above equation can be reduced to

$$\dot{V} \le -x^T Qx + 2x^T X^{-1} \widetilde{B}(\widetilde{B}^T \widetilde{B})^{-1} \widetilde{B}^T D\rho(t)$$

Since the uncertain term $\rho(t)$ is bounded as

$$\|\rho(t)\| < \rho_0 + \rho_1 \|x(t)\|$$

one can get

$$\dot{V} \le -[\lambda_{\min}(Q) - 2k\rho_1]\|x\|^2 + 2k\rho_0 \|x\|$$

where $k = \|X^{-1} \widetilde{B}(\widetilde{B}^T \widetilde{B})^{-1} \widetilde{B}^T D\|$. Therefore, if $\lambda_{\min}(Q) > 2k\rho_1$ then by resorting to the notion of uniform ultimate boundedness of Corless and Leitmann[10] one can establish the following:

Theorem 3.2: Consider the uncertain system (1). Suppose that for some positive constant δ there exists a positive-definite solution matrix pair (Q, X) satisfying the LMI (2) and $\lambda_{\min}(Q) > 2k\rho_1$. Let the control strategy be given by (4). Then every system response of the closed –loop system is uniformly bounded and uniformly ultimately bounded within a neighborhood of zero state.

Remark 2: For fixed ρ_1, the following is a convex functional on the convex set $\{(\mu, X) : \mu > 0, X > 0\}$

$$2\|X^{-1}\widetilde{B}(\widetilde{B}^T \widetilde{B})^{-1} \widetilde{B}^T D\| \rho_1 . - \mu \quad (6)$$

therefore, for given ρ_1 one can design a sliding

mode surface as well as sliding mode control law by finding a feasible solution satisfying the following system of LMIs (7) below via a convex optimization technique

$$(2), \quad X>0, \quad Q \geq \mu I > 0, \quad (6)<0 \quad (7)$$

Remark 3: By using the following procedure one can obtain an estimate of the maximum bound of ρ_1 which can be tolerated by the control law (4) with the sliding surface.

1) Set initial estimate $\rho_1 > 0$
2) Test feasibility of the matrix inequality (7) via a convex optimization technique. If yes go to Step 3, otherwise go to Step 4.
3) Test whether ρ_1 converges. If yes terminate, otherwise increase ρ_1 and go to Step 2.
4) Decrease ρ_1 and go to Step 2.

Remark 4: Assume that there exists a constant matrix E with an appropriate dimension such that $D = BE$, i.e. the uncertain term $\rho(t)$ is matched, then one can easily show that the following sliding mode control law also guarantees sliding motion

$$u(t) = -G[\delta I + A]x(t) - \|E\|(\rho_0 + \rho_1 \|x\|)\frac{\sigma}{\|\sigma\|} \quad (4')$$

and the resulting reduced-order dynamics of the closed-loop system restricted to the sliding surface is stable and given by

$$\widetilde{B}^T \dot{x} = \widetilde{B}^T A X \widetilde{B} (\widetilde{B}^T X \widetilde{B})^{-1} \widetilde{B}^T x$$

Remark 5: We have considered only the case that the input matrix B has full rank m, i.e. there exists no redundant actuator. However, some systems may have redundant actuators, which implies that the rank of B is less than m. Even though a system has redundant actuators, i.e. the rank of input matrix B is less than m, one may design a sliding surface for the system by using our method. If a system has redundant actuators, the control input values of the redundant actuators can be set as zero for all time and the control input values of the other actuators can be designed by using the proposed method with a new input matrix B which is formed from the original input matrix by eliminating the columns corresponding to the redundant actuators.

B. Pole-Clustering Constraint

Many properties of system dynamics such as the minimum decay rate, the maximum overshoot, the frequency of oscillatory modes, the rise time and the settling time or so can be defined by specifying regions in the complex plane in which eigenvalues of the system lie. Especially, the notion of the LMI region is a very useful tool to assign poles in convex regions of the complex plane. The LMI regions are dense in the set of convex regions, which are symmetric with respect to the real axis, and include a wide class of typical clustering regions such as ellipses, conic sectors, vertical strips, and horizontal strips or so. Moreover, simultaneous pole clustering constraints can be expressed as a system of LMIs without introducing any conservatism.

The given explicit parameterization of linear sliding surfaces provides some degrees of freedom that can be used to improve the design. In this section, we will give a method for exploiting the degrees of freedom and specifying regions in the complex plane where eigenvalues of reduced-order equivalent system dynamics lie.

Now, consider the following nominal dynamics of the uncertain system (1)

$$\dot{x} = Ax + Bu \quad (1')$$

Let the control strategy be given by (4) with the sliding surface (3). From the Remark 4, one can see that the $(n-m)$ reduced-order equivalent dynamics of the closed-loop system of the nominal system (1') and the control (4) with (3) is given by

$$\widetilde{B}^T \dot{x} = \widetilde{B}^T A X \widetilde{B} (\widetilde{B}^T X \widetilde{B})^{-1} \widetilde{B}^T x \quad (8)$$

Now, assume that all poles of the above $(n-m)$ reduced-order equivalent dynamics of the closed-loop system of the nominal system (1') and the control (4) are required to lie in some LMI region Ω. Then by resorting to the Lemma 2.1 one can obtain the following LMI conditions

$$P_0 > 0$$

$$\left[\Delta_{ij} P_0 + \Gamma_{ij} \widetilde{B}^T A X \widetilde{B} (\widetilde{B}^T X \widetilde{B})^{-1} P_0 + \Gamma_{ji} P_0 (\widetilde{B}^T X \widetilde{B})^{-1} \widetilde{B}^T X A^T \widetilde{B}\right]_{1 \leq i,j \leq (n-m)} < 0$$

If we set $P_0 = \widetilde{B}^T X \widetilde{B}$, the above condition is reduced to

$$\widetilde{B}^T X \widetilde{B} > 0 \quad (9a)$$

$$\left[\widetilde{B}^T (\Delta_{ij} X + \Gamma_{ij} A X + \Gamma_{ji} X A^T) \widetilde{B}\right]_{1 \leq i,j \leq (n-m)} < 0 \quad (9b)$$

After all, one can conclude that

Theorem 3.3: Consider the uncertain system (1). Suppose that for some positive constant δ there exists a positive-definite solution matrix pair (Q, X) satisfying the LMIs (7) and (9). Let the control strategy be given by (4) with the sliding surface (3). Then every system response of the closed-loop system (1) and (4) with (3) is uniformly bounded and uniformly ultimately bounded within a neighborhood of zero state. And the $(n-m)$ reduced-order equivalent dynamics of the closed-loop system of the nominal system (1') and the control (4) with (3) is given by (8), whose poles are lie in the LMI region Ω.

Remark 6: Let the LMI region Ω be a vertical strip given by as follows:

$$\Omega = \{z \in C : -\alpha < \mathrm{Re}(z) < -\beta < 0\} \quad (10)$$

then the above theorem is still valid even though the LMI condition (9) is replaced by

$$X > 0, \widetilde{B}^T(AX + XA^T + 2\alpha X)\widetilde{B} < 0 \quad (11a)$$

$$\widetilde{B}^T(AX + XA^T + 2\beta X)\widetilde{B} > 0 \quad (11b)$$

Remark 7: Let the LMI region Ω be a disk of radius r and center $(-p,0)$ where r, p are positive constants. Then the LMI region Ω is given by

$$\Omega = \left\{ z \in C : \begin{bmatrix} -r & p \\ p & -r \end{bmatrix} + z\begin{bmatrix} 0 & 1 \\ 0 & 0 \end{bmatrix} + \bar{z}\begin{bmatrix} 0 & 1 \\ 0 & 0 \end{bmatrix}^T < 0 \right\}$$

and the LMI condition (9) can be rewritten as

$$X > 0, \begin{bmatrix} \widetilde{B} & 0 \\ 0 & \widetilde{B} \end{bmatrix}^T \begin{bmatrix} -rX & pX + AX \\ pX + XA^T & -rX \end{bmatrix} \begin{bmatrix} \widetilde{B} & 0 \\ 0 & \widetilde{B} \end{bmatrix} < 0$$

4. Example

Consider the system (1) with the data

$$A = \begin{bmatrix} 0 & 1 \\ 1 & 0 \end{bmatrix}, \; B = \begin{bmatrix} 0 \\ 2 \end{bmatrix}, \; D = \begin{bmatrix} \zeta \\ 2 \end{bmatrix} \quad (12a)$$

$$\rho(t) = 0.5\cos(120\pi t) + 0.1\sin(x_1)x_2 \quad (12b)$$

where ζ is an uncertain but bounded variable such that $|\xi| \le 0.3$ for all time. Assume that all poles of the reduced-order equivalent dynamics of the closed-loop system of the nominal system (1') and a sliding mode control are required to lie in the LMI region Ω of (10) with $\alpha = 1, \beta = 3$. Since the basis of the null space of B^T can be given as $[1 \;\; 0]^T$, one can set $\widetilde{B}$ as $\widetilde{B} = [1 \;\; 0]^T$. And $\rho(t)$ can be bounded as $\|\rho(t)\| \le 0.5 + 0.1\|x\|$, thus one can set $\rho_0 = 0.5, \rho_1 = 0.1$. Using the Theorem 3.3 one can get the following LMI conditions

$$\left\| X^{-1}\begin{bmatrix} 0.06 & 0 \\ 0 & 0 \end{bmatrix} \right\| - \mu < 0$$

$$(2), \quad \mu > 0, \quad Q \ge \mu I$$

$$[1 \;\; 0](AX + XA^T + 2X)[1 \;\; 0]^T < 0$$

$$X > 0, \quad [1 \;\; 0](AX + XA^T + 6X)[1 \;\; 0]^T > 0$$

With $\delta = 5$ one can obtain a solution matrix X to the above LMIs as follows:

$$X = \begin{bmatrix} 1 & -2 \\ -2 & 6 \end{bmatrix}$$

Using the explicit formula (3) one can obtain the following linear sliding surface

$$\sigma(x) = Sx = B^T X^{-1} x = [2 \;\; 1]x = 0 \quad (13)$$

And using (4) one can obtain the following control strategy

$$u(t) = -[5.5 \;\; 3.5]x(t) - (0.5 + 0.1\|x\|)\frac{\sigma}{\|\sigma\|} \quad (14)$$

The Theorem 3.3 implies that, in case of $\rho(t) = 0$, the reduced-order equivalent dynamics of the closed-loop system of the nominal system (1') and the control (14) is given by

$$\dot{z} = -2z, \qquad z = \widetilde{B}^T x = [1 \;\; 0]x$$

One can easily see that the pole of the above reduced-order dynamics lies in the LMI region Ω of (10) with $\alpha = 1, \beta = 3$. The Theorem 3.3 also implies that every system response of the closed-loop VSCS of the uncertain system (1) with the data (12) and the control law (14) with (3) is uniformly bounded and uniformly ultimately bounded within a neighborhood of zero state.

5. Conclusion

In this paper, based on the LMI approach a new VSCS design method for a class of uncertain systems with mismatched unstructured uncertainties was developed. We derived a sufficient condition for the existence of linear sliding surfaces in terms of LMIs. And linear sliding surfaces were parameterized in terms of positive-definite solution matrices to the LMI existence conditions. Additionally, in terms of LMIs we derived sufficient conditions for the existence of linear sliding surfaces guaranteeing regional pole clustering constraints of reduced-order equivalent dynamics. Finally, we gave an example.

Our LMI-based formulation has advantages over the traditional method. First, our formulation enables one to easily attack analyzing the stability as well as synthesizing a sliding mode control law for uncertain systems with mismatched uncertainties. Second, because the stability conditions are LMIs, which can be solved very efficiently via various powerful convex optimization algorithms with a polynomial-time worst-case complexity, our formulation has advantages in the computational aspect and therefore for even large scale systems one can easily design sliding surfaces as well as sliding mode control laws. Additionally, our LMI-based formulation offers some design flexibility which can be used to improve design, thus using our LMI-based formulation one may design sliding mode controllers satisfying additional convex constraints in order to improve the design.

6. References

[1] O.M.E. El-Ghezawi, A.S.I. Zinober, and S.A. Billings, "Analysis and design of variable structure systems using a geometric approach," *Int. J. Contr.*, vol. 38, pp.657-671, 1983

[2] V.I. Utkin, Variable structure systems with sliding modes," *IEEE Trans. Automat. Contr.*, vol. AC-22, pp. 212-222, 1977

[3] H.H. Choi, "A new method for variable structure control system design: A linear matrix inequality approach," *Automatica*, vol. 33, pp. 2089-2092, 1997

[4] H.H. Choi and M.J. Chung, "Estimation of the asymptotic stability region of uncertain systems with bounded sliding mode controllers," *IEEE Trans. Automat. Contr.*, vol. AC-39, pp. 2275-2278, 1994

[5] R.A. Decarlo, S.H. Zak, and G.P. Mathews, "Variable structure control of nonlinear multivariable systems: A tutorial," *IEEE Proceedings*, vol. 76, pp. 212-232,1988

[6] H.H. Choi, "An explicit formula of linear sliding surfaces for a class of uncertain dynamic systems with mismatched uncertainties," to be published in the *Automatica*, 1998

[7] S. Boyd, L.E. Ghaoui, E. Feron, and V. Balakrishnan, *Linear matrix inequalities in system and control theory*, SIAM, Philadelphia, 1994

[8] M. Chilali and P. Gahinet, H_∞ design with pole placement constraint: An LMI approach, *IEEE Trans. Automat. Contr.*, Vol. AC-41, pp. 358-367, 1996

[9] A. Packard, K. Zhou, P. Pandey and G. Becker, "A collection of robust control problems leading to LMIs," *Proceeding of IEEE Conf. On Decision and Control*, pp. 1245-1250, 1991

[10] M.J. Corless, and G. Leitmann, "Continuous state feedback guaranteeing uniform ultimate boundedness for uncertain dynamic systems," *IEEE Trans. Automat. Contr.*, vol. AC-26, pp. 1139-1144, 1981

Solving Block-Structured Matrix Problems on RISC-Based Supercomputers

M. Paprzycki
Department of Computer Science and Statistics
University of Southern Mississippi
Hattiesburg, MS 39406, USA

P. Yalamov
Center of Applied Mathematics and Informatics
University of Rousse
7017 Rousse, Bulgaria

N.E. Mastorakis
Military Institutions of University Education
Chair of Computer Science
Hellenic Naval Academy
18539 Piraeus, Greece

ABSTRACT

Block-structured matrices appear in computational practice as results of discretizations of a number of mathematical problems. Usually, operations on these matrices become the most expensive part of the solution of the original problem. To provide an efficient tool to operate on such matrices, a level 3 BLAS based library of subroutines is proposed and its performance studied on the RISC-based SGI Power Challenge 8000 and Power Challenge 10000 supercomputers.

1. INTRODUCTION

A number of mathematical problems give rise to block bidiagonal (*BBD*), block tridiagonal (*BTD*), almost block diagonal *(ABD)* and other block-structured matrices [1,4,6,8,9,11]. In computational practice there exist a number of situations when efficiency of operations on such matrices becomes particularly important: first, when the matrix size is very large and thus operating on it is very time consuming; second, when a block-structured matrix appears in a non-linear problem which is solved using an iterative scheme and thus it has to be factorized in almost every step of the algorithm; third, when operations on a very large block-structured matrix are performed on a parallel computer. In the last case a tearing-type strategy is typically applied to achieve parallelization [1,2,5]. In all three cases the efficiency of the matrix operations becomes the bottleneck of the solution process.

In this note, we study the efficiency of a level 3 BLAS based [3] library of subroutines designed to perform three basic operations on block structured matrices: matrix multiplication, LU factorization with partial pivoting and back substitution. Obviously, when the solution process calls for operating on block structured matrices (of the three types described above) there are at least two possibilities of representing them. First, they can be represented directly in the blocked form. For instance, in Fortran they would be represented as a sequence of block-rows stored consecutively in a long vector. Each row-block would be stored as a sequence of columns. Second, they can be represented as a banded matrix encompassing the blocked structure. In this case the main diagonal, as well as each super- and sub-diagonal will be stored as a vector. In this case a penalty of storing a number of zeroes (residing outside of the block structure) is paid. At the same time, it can be argued that some simplicity of programming can be gained. In addition, the results gathered earlier on the Cray J-9x suggest that (on a vector computer) when the block size (n) is relatively small the banded approach based on long vectors has a significant advantage over the blocked representation [10]. Here we concentrate our attention on the RISC-based supercomputers reporting results collected on the SGI Power Challenge 8000 (PC 8000) and Power Challenge 10000 (PC 10000) supercomputers. For these two computers we will try to answer a basic question: should the block-structured matrices be represented in the blocked form, or should they be represented as banded matrices. We will also use the collected benchmarking data to compare the performance of the two machines.

2. MATRIX-VECTOR MULTIPLICATION

Multiplication of a block-structured matrix by a vector or by a square dense matrix of any size can be easily realized by a sequence of calls to the level 3 BLAS matrix multiplication routine *_GEMM*. In each step of the algorithm a complete block-row is multiplied by an appropriate part of the vector (matrix). Following the design principles of the *LAPACK* library, both the straightforward matrix multiplication and the multiplication by the transposed block-matrix are available in the same driver subroutine. The latter is achieved by appropriately applying the *transpose* option of the *_GEMM* subroutine.

Let us assume that A is a *BTD* matrix consisting of k row-blocks of size n. Here, the first and last row-block are of size $n\times 2n$ while the remaining row blocks are of size $n\times 3n$. When this matrix is stored as a banded matrix it is stored as a collection of vectors representing the main diagonal, the $2n-1$ sub-diagonals

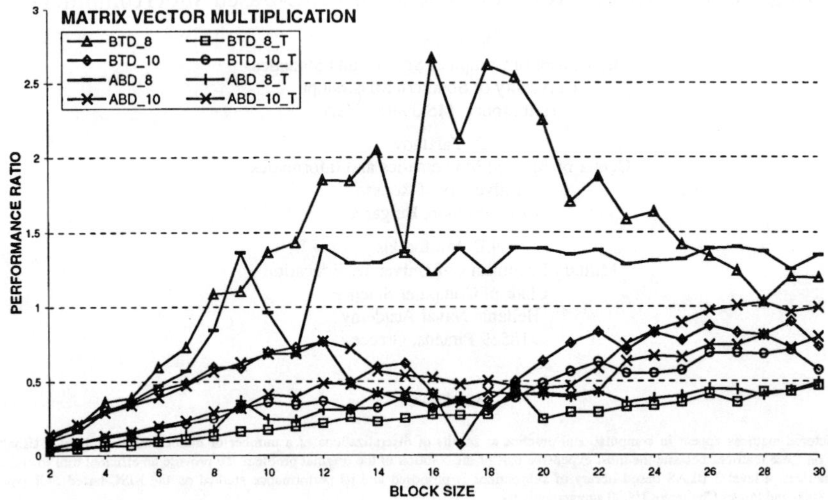

Figure 1. Matrix-vector multiplication banded vs. blocked approach; 'BTD' denotes block tridiagonal matrix; 'ABD' denotes almost block diagonal matrix; '8' denotes PC 8000; '10' denotes PC 10000; 'T' denotes transpose.

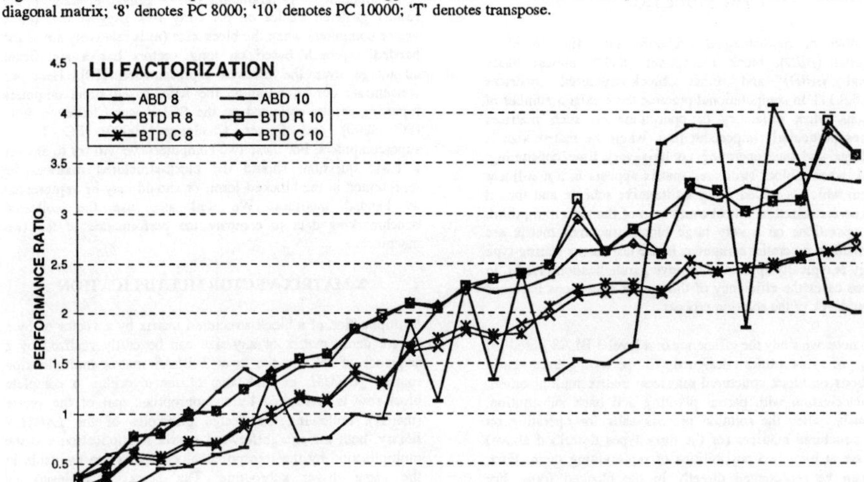

Figure 2. Matrix factorization banded vs. blocked approach; 'ABD' denotes almost block diagonal matrix; 'BTD' denotes block tridiagonal matrix; '8' denotes PC 8000; '10' denotes PC 10000; 'R' denotes row pivoting, 'C' denotes column pivoting.

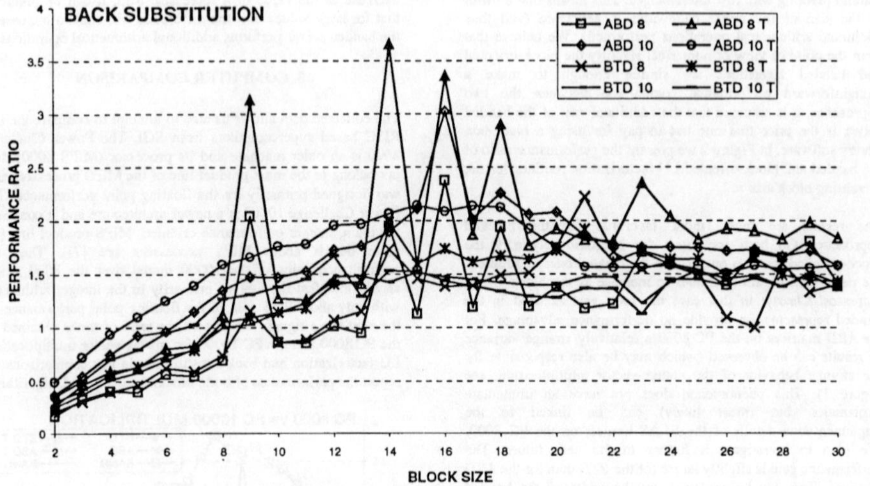

Figure 3. Back substitution; banded vs. blocked approach; 'ABD' denotes almost block diagonal matrix; 'BTD' denotes block tridiagonal matrix; '8' denotes PC 8000; '10' denotes PC 10000; 'T' denotes transpose.

and the *2n-1* super-diagonals. In case when A is an almost block diagonal matrix, the situation is slightly more complicated. Such matrices arise typically when boundary value problems for ordinary differential equations are discretized. The sizes of particular blocks (and especially the top and the bottom block) depend on the choice of the discretization scheme and the distribution of boundary conditions. For the purpose of this paper we restrict our attention to the simplest case of matrices that arise when a system of n first order differential equations with separated boundary conditions is discretized using a finite difference approach. In this case each internal row-block is of size $n \times 2n$. To further simplify the picture let us assume that the boundary conditions are equally distributed on both sides of the interval ($q = \lfloor n/2 \rfloor$). In this case the first block is of size $q \times n$ and the last block is of size $(n-q) \times n$. This *ABD* matrix can be represented as a banded matrix with $2n$-q-1 super-diagonals and as many sub-diagonals.

In the first series of experiments the performance of the block-oriented matrix-vector multiplication was compared with the performance of the level 2 BLAS routine *_GBMV* from the *LAPACK* library. This routine performs a matrix-vector multiplication for a banded matrix stored as described above. In Figure 1 we present the ratio of time of the banded and block-oriented routines for the increasing block size n for *BTD* and *ABD* matrices and their transposes (denoted by T) on both PC 8000 and PC 10000. The results for the *BBD* matrices have been omitted to preserve the readability of the figure, but they were similar to the *BTD* matrices. In all experiments the CPU times have been collected using the *dtime* Unix timer and each result represents an average of multiple runs. In this, and the remaining figures, the results are reported for k = 400 blocks.

We have also performed experiments varying the number of blocks and have found not effects on performance.

The results are rather discouraging. Only for the straightforward matrix-vector multiplication of the *BTD* matrices on the PC 8000 the blocked approach becomes a feasible alternative to the banded one. This result is similar to what was detected on the Cray and shows a high level of optimization of the *LAPACK* routines. In can be noticed that, as the size of the blocks increases, the performance of the blocked routine slowly reaches the level of the banded one. This suggests that for very large blocks the blocked approach would become a viable alternative.

3. MATRIX FACTORZATION

The second series of experiments was designed to compare the performance of the LU factorization routines. Here the question of fairness of comparison needs to be addressed. The block oriented algorithms perform the LU factorization utilizing special pivoting strategies designed to avoid fill-in. In case of *ABD* matrices, an alternate row and column pivoting strategy is used (for more details see Varah [12]). The numerical stability of this approach has been proven to be equivalent to the stability of LU factorization with partial pivoting [12]. For the *BTD* and *BBD* matrices a restricted pivoting is applied (for more details see Varah [11]). The pivot element is sought only in the diagonal block. (In this case, restricted row or column pivoting can be applied so both methods have been implemented for both *BBD* and *BTD* matrices.) In [11] Varah has proven that this approach is stable if the matrices are block diagonally dominant. In the *LAPACK* library the LU factorization for banded matrices is performed by the *_GBTRF* routine which uses standard column pivoting with row interchanges. This means that a fill-in of the size of the upper bandwidth is generated (and thus additional arithmetical operations performed). We believe that from the point of view of numerical stability the block-oriented and banded algorithms are similar enough to make a straightforward performance comparison between the two approaches. It is assumed that the additional cost of the banded solver is the price that one has to pay for using a black-box library software. In Figure 2 we present the performance ratio of the banded and block-oriented LU factorization routines for the increasing block size *n*.

The results are much more favorable for the blocked approaches. On both computers for approximately $n>9$ the block-oriented routines outperform the banded one. In addition, the performance gain continues to increase as the block size *n* increases. Clearly, in this case the long vectors used in the banded representation provide no performance advantage. For the *ABD* matrices on the PC 8000 a relatively strange variance of results can be observed (which may be also responsible for the strange behavior of the matrix-vector multiplication, see Figure 1). This phenomenon does not have an immediate explanation but (most likely) can be linked to the implementation details of the BLAS kernels on the PC 8000. We plan to investigate it further in the near future. The performance gain is slightly larger for the *BTD* than for the *ABD* matrices. This can be explained by the width of the banded matrix that encompasses both block structures. In case of the *BTD* matrices the banded system is wider and while larger fill-in is generated also a more substantial number of arithmetical operations is performed. In case of *BTD* (and, as our other experiments show, also *BBD* matrices) there is almost no performance difference between the column and row pivoting strategies. Additionally, no numerical difference between these strategies has been observed.

4. BACK SUBSTITUTION

The third series of experiments compared the performance of the block oriented and banded back solvers applied to the problem with a single right hand side. In Figure 3 we present the ratio of times used by the level 2 BLAS based banded solver *_GBTRS* from the *LAPACK* library and the block-oriented back-solvers, for the increasing block size *n*. Since, for the *BTD* matrices, both the row and column pivoting based factorizations have been implemented the library contains four back solvers: row pivoting, row pivoting for a transposed original matrix, and similar two versions of column pivoting oriented solvers. However, since there was no particular difference in performance between them, only the row pivoting based back solvers are reported. They are compared with the banded and banded transposed solvers as appropriate.

As in the case of LU factorization, starting from a relatively small block size ($n>13$) the block-oriented solvers outperform the banded approach (similar results were observed for the *BBD* matrices). Again, a significant variance in performance occurs on the PC 8000 for the *ABD* matrices. No substantial difference between the transposed and the non-transposed solvers can be observed. It should be noted that the behavior of the back solvers differs from that of the matrix-vector multiplication and the LU factorization. In the earlier cases, as the block size *n* increased the performance gains from using the blocked approach increased. For the back solvers, the performance ratio is relatively flat (centered around 1.5 times faster) and seems to decrease as the value of *n* increases. Still, it can be predicted that for large values of *n* the difference will start to increase as the banded solver performs additional arithmetical operations.

5. COMPUTER COMPARISON

The collected data allows us also to attempt to compare the two RISC based supercomputers from SGI. The Power Challenge 8000 is an older machine and its processor (MIPS 8000) does not belong to the main product line of the MIPS processors as it was designed primarily for the floating point performance. The Power Challenge 10000 is a newer architecture and it continues the main, integer performance oriented, MIPS product line (for more details about MIPS processors see [7]). Thus the performance gains of the 10000 model over the 8000 model should manifest themselves primarily in the integer arithmetic, with only about 25% gain in the floating point performance. In the next three figures we present the ratio of times obtained on the PC 8000 and the PC 10000 for matrix vector multiplication, LU factorization and back substitution. In our comparisons we report the performance of both, blocked and banded, algorithms.

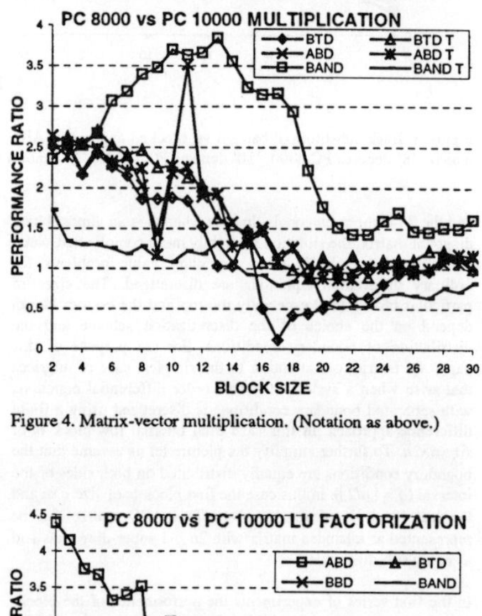

Figure 4. Matrix-vector multiplication. (Notation as above.)

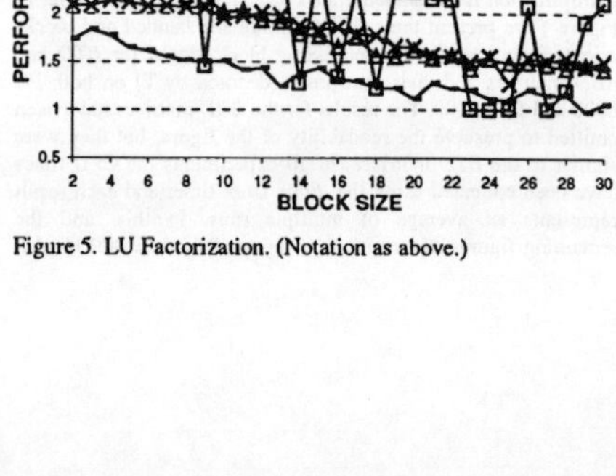

Figure 5. LU Factorization. (Notation as above.)

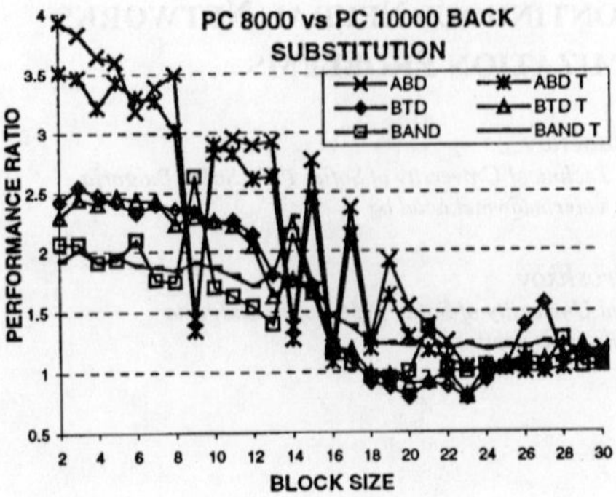

Figure 6. Back substitution. (Notation as above.)

We can observe that in all cases the performance advantage of the PC 10000 decreases as the problem size increases. This result holds for both the proposed *BLAS* based blocked codes and the *LAPACK* library based banded matrix oriented routines. The performance difference is particularly small for the matrix-vector multiplication and back substitution. Again, the performance jumps of the ABD routines can be observed, but the general pattern remains unchanged. These results are rather surprising as they indicate that already for blocks of size approximately $n = 15$ the floating point arithmetic dominates the solution and acts as the performance equalizer.

6. CONCLUDING REMARKS

We have compared the performance of banded and block-oriented approaches to the basic operations (multiplication, factorization and back-substitution) on block-structured matrices. We have found that on the SGI Power Challenge 8000 and Power Challenge 10000 RISC-based supercomputers the block-oriented approach outperforms the banded method for the LU factorization and back substitution for matrices with blocks of size $n>10$. In case of matrix vector multiplication the banded approach is a clear winner for all block sizes studied. These results resemble quite closely those observed on the Cray vector computer [10]. The results present an interesting challenge to the designers of codes similar to COLNEW [4] that rely heavily on block structured linear algebra. Finally, the results also show that for floating point arithmetic based applications there is almost no difference in performance between the PC 8000 and the PC 10000 RISC based supercomputers.

7. ACKNOWLEDGEMENTS

Computer time grant from NCSA at Urbana is kindly acknowledged. The research has been initiated by a COBASE grant from the National Research Council. The second author was supported by Grant I-702/97 from the National Research Fund of the Bulgarian Ministry of Education and Science.

REFERENCES

[1] P. Amodio, T. Politi, M. Paprzycki, "Survey of Parallel Algorithms for Block Bidiagonal Linear Systems," *Journal of Computers in Mathematics Applications*, Vol. 31, No. 7, 1996, pp. 111-127

[2] P. Amodio, T. Politi, M. Paprzycki, "Solving Block Bidiagonal Linear Systems on Distributed Memory Compters," *Proceedings of the Seventh International Conference on Parallel and Distributed Computing Systems*, ISCA, Raleigh, NC, 1994, pp. 812-815

[3] E. Anderson, Z. Bai, C. Bischof, J. Demmel, J. Dongarra, J. Du Croz, A. Greenbaum, S. Hammarling, A. McKenney, S. Ostrouchov and D. Sorensen, *LAPACK Users' Guide*, SIAM, Philadelphia, 1993

[4] U. Ascher, J. Christiansen, R. D. Russell, "*Numerical Solution of Boundary Value Problems for Ordinary Differential Equations*," Prentice-Hall, New York, 1988

[5] M. Berry, A. Sameh, "Multiprocessor Schemes for Solving Block Tridigonal Linear Systems," *The International Journal of Supercomputing Applications*, Vol. 2, 1988, pp. 37-57

[6] C. Cyphers, M. Paprzycki, A. Karageorghis, "High Performance Solution of Partial Differential Equations Discretized Using a Chebyshev Spectral Collocation Method," *Journal of Computational and Applied Mathematics*, Vol. 66, No. 1, 1996, pp. 71-80

[7] J. Foster, "Evolution of MIPS RISC Microprocessor Architecture," *Journal of Computing in Small Colleges*, Vol. 12, No. 4, 1997, pp. 215-229

[8] M. Paprzycki, C. Cyphers, "Level 3 BLAS Based Library for Block Tridiagonal Matrices," in: S. Elaydi, et. al. (eds.), *Advances in Difference Equations*, Gordon and Breach, Amsterdam, 1997, pp. 491-498

[9] M. Paprzycki, I. Gladwell, "Solving Almost Block Diagonal Systems Using Level 3 BLAS," *Proceedings of The Fifth SIAM Conference on Parallel Processing for Scientific Computing*, SIAM, Philadelphia, 1992, pp. 52-62

[10] M. Paprzycki, A. Karageorghis, C. Cyphers, "Solving Structured Matrix Problems on a Cray Vector-Computer," Technical Report, University of Cyprus, *Mathematica Balcanica*, to appear.

[11] J. Varah, "On the Solution of Block-Tridiagonal Systems Arising from Certain Finite-Difference Equations," *Mathematics of Computation*, Vol. 26, 1972, pp. 859-868

[12] J. Varah, "Alternate row and column elimination for solving certain linear systems," SIAM J. Numer. Anal. Vol. 13, 1976, pp. 71-75

MODELLING AND SIMULATION OF CONTINUOUS NEURAL NETWORKS FOR CONSTRAINED OPTIMIZATION PROBLEMS

Valeri M. Mladenov
Dept. Theoretical Electrotechnics, Faculty of Automation, Technical University of Sofia, 1756 Sofia, Bulgaria
telx. +359 2 636 2388, e-mail: valerim@vmei.acad.bg

Proshko N. Proshkov
Faculty of Automation, graduate student, Technical University of Sofia, 1756 Sofia, Bulgaria
tel +359 2 666 991, e-mail: pnpr@cblink.net

ABSTRACT

In this paper we consider the modelling and the simulation of continuous Neural Networks for constrained optimization problems. The idea of using analogue circuits and Neural Networks to solve constrained optimization problems is used by many authors. For proper work of the network many of the parameters of the circuit should be adjusted and hence the simulation of the network behavior before the VLSI realization is recommended. In the paper we present a systematic approach for modelling of this kind of networks. We use SIMULINK™ and give a generalized structure for modelling and simulation of Neural Networks and analogue circuits for constrained optimization problems.

I. Introduction

Analogue circuits to solve mathematical programming problems are used by many authors and various types of Neural Networks are proposed to obtain the solutions of constrained optimization problems. In 1984 Chua and Lin [1] developed the canonical non-linear programming circuit, using the Kuhn-Tucker conditions from the mathematical programming theory. Later, Tank and Hopfield [2] developed an optimization network for solving linear programming problems. Some practical design problems of their network along with its stability properties are discussed in [3].

An extension of the results of Tank and Hopfield to more general non-linear programming problems is presented in [4]. The authors noted that the network introduced by Tank and Hopfield could be considered to be a special case of the canonical non-linear programming network proposed in [1], with capacitors added to account for the dynamic behavior of the circuit. In [7] the Kennedy and Chua approach [4] is used and Forty and Tesi proved that the network in [4] is globally asymptotically stable also when the constraint amplifiers are dynamic for both symmetric and nonsymmetric interconnection matrices. As a consequence their convergence can be exploited to the fullest extent for on-line optimization. The above discussed approaches implicitly utilize the penalty function method [5] where a constrained optimization problem is approximated by an unconstrained optimization problem. In [6] the authors use the penalty function method approach and synthesize a new neural optimization network capable of solving a general class of constrained optimization problems. The proposed architecture can be viewed as a continuous Neural Network model.

A simplified approach to neural optimization in the presence of linear equality constraints is presented in [8]. In contrast to the standard Lagrangian approach, the constraints simplify the final neural circuit instead of complicate it. The advantage of the above approach (when only equality constraints exist) is the fact that it doesn't implement penalty function strategy and thus is not dependent on the choice of the penalty parameters or the Lagrange multiplier generation strategy. In [9] the authors deal with a quadratic assignment problem. The suggested weighted intrazonal connection method improves the dynamics of the presented optimization network by weighting and controlling the convergence speed of the quadratic assignment problem and works most effectively with up-to-date techniques.

The advantage of using Neural Networks for solving a constrained optimization problem is in the rapid action of the network (VLSI scheme), where the solution is obtained in real time. Before the realization of the network the users usually simulate its behavior and during the simulation the necessary circuit parameters could be adjusted properly. We present a simple and effective

approach for modelling and simulation of the behavior of this type of networks.
The paper is outlined as follows. In the next section we describe the neural network for constrained optimization problems. In section III we present a "SIMULINK" model of the network. In section IV we consider some simulation results of our model and we end up with some conclusion remarks in section V.

II. Continuous Neural Network for Constrained Optimization Problems

The following general form of a constrained optimization problem is considered

$$\text{minimize } f(x)$$
$$\text{subject to} \qquad \mathbf{g(x)\geq 0}, \quad \mathbf{h(x)=0} \qquad (1)$$

where $x \in R^n$, $f: R^n \to R$ and $\mathbf{g} = [g_1, g_2, \dots g_q]^T$: $R^n \to R^q$ and $\mathbf{h} = [h_1, h_2, \dots h_m]^T : R^n \to R^m$ are vector valued functions of n variables with dimensions q and m respectively. Due to dealing with physical devices, the functions f, $\mathbf{g}$ and $\mathbf{h}$ are restricted to be continuously differentiable.
The canonical non-linear programming circuits for modelling and simulating the above constrained optimization problem proposed in [1] and [4] are shown in Figure 1. The circuits are based on the Kuhn-Tucker conditions from mathematical programming theory.

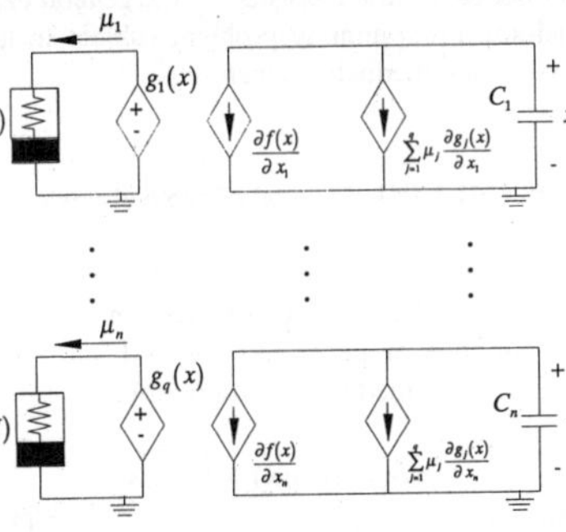

Figure 1

The authors analyzed the case when only inequality constraints are presented. The functions Φ_j, j=1,2, … , q are defined as

$$V = \Phi_j(I) = \begin{cases} -cI, & I \geq 0 \\ 0, & I < 0 \end{cases}$$

and after applying Kirchhoff's current law and solving for dx_k/dt the system of state equations became

$$\frac{dx_k}{dt} = -\frac{1}{C_k}\left(\frac{\partial f(x)}{\partial x_k} + \sum_{j=1}^{q}\mu_j\frac{\partial g_j(x)}{\partial x_k}\right), \quad k = 1, \dots, n$$

It should be noted that in the steady state the Kuhn-Tucker conditions are satisfied and the state trajectories will sattle down after the transient at the solution of the problem (1).
When the general case (1) is considered an equality constraint $h_j(x)$ can be represented in terms of inequality constraint(s) in one of the following ways

$$g_j(x) = -[h_j(x)]^2 \geq 0$$

or

$$g_{j_1}(x) = h_j(x) \geq 0, \quad g_{j_2}(x) = -h_j(x) \geq 0$$

In [6] the penalty function approach is used to synthesize a neural optimization network capable of solving a general class of constrained optimization problems (with both equality and inequality constraints). The penalty function approach allows better control of the constraint effects of the network building blocks than the previously proposed approaches do. This is the reason to focus the modelling of the suggested circuit in [6] where constrained optimization problem (1) is approximated by the unconstrained problem

$$\text{minimize } (f(x)+cP(x)) \qquad (2)$$

where c>0 is a constant, referred to as a weight, and P(x) is a penalty function. A penalty function is a continuous non-negative function which is zero at a point if and only if all constraints are satisfied at that point and the authors use the function

$$P(x) = \sum_{j=1}^{q} g_{\bar{j}}(x) + \sum_{j=1}^{m}\left[g_{\bar{j}_1}(x) + g_{\bar{j}_2}(x)\right] \qquad (3)$$

where

$$g_j^-(x) = -\min[0, g_j(x)]$$

and

$$g_{j_1}(x) = h_j(x),\; g_{j_2}(x) = -h_j(x)$$

On this base they suggest the network on Figure 2, where

$$\widetilde{S}_{\alpha,\beta}(x) = \begin{cases} -\alpha & for\ \ x < -\beta \\ (\alpha/\beta)x & for\ \ -\beta \le x \le \beta \\ \alpha & for\ \ x > \beta \end{cases} \quad (4)$$

$$\widetilde{S}_\alpha = \widetilde{S}_{\alpha,\alpha}$$

$$\widetilde{\mu}_j = -\widetilde{S}_{c,\zeta}[g_j(x)] = \min[0, \widetilde{S}_{c,\zeta}[g_j(x)]] \quad (5)$$

$$\widetilde{\lambda}_j = \widetilde{S}_{c,\zeta}[h_j(x)] \quad (6)$$

Since regularly ζ is approximately zero, $\widetilde{\mu}_j$ and $\widetilde{\lambda}_j$ terms are approximated by

$$\widetilde{\mu}_j = \frac{c}{2}\operatorname{sgn}[g_j(x)] - \frac{c}{2} \quad (7)$$

$$\widetilde{\lambda}_j = c\operatorname{sgn}[h_j(x)] \quad (8)$$

and it is assumed that $\alpha > \gamma$.

In this application $\widetilde{\mu}_j$ and $\widetilde{\lambda}_j$ terms are bounded (in contrast to the canonical dynamical circuit from Figure 1) in order to accommodate the saturation limits of op amps used in implementing the functions.

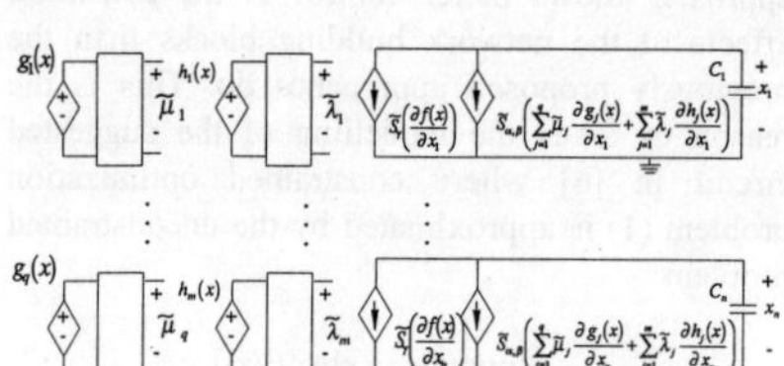

Figure 2

Applying Kirchhoff's current law to the circuits of Figure 2 yields

$$\frac{dx_k}{dt} = -\frac{1}{C_k}[\widetilde{S}_{\alpha,\beta}(\sum_{j=1}^{q}\widetilde{\mu}_j \frac{\partial g_j(x)}{\partial x_k} + \sum_{j=1}^{m}\widetilde{\lambda}_j \frac{\partial h_j(x)}{\partial x_k}) + \widetilde{S}_\gamma(\frac{\partial f(x)}{\partial x_k})] \;, k = 1,\dots,n \quad (9)$$

Substituting $\widetilde{\mu}_j$ and $\widetilde{\lambda}_j$ from (7) and (8) we get

$$\frac{dx_k}{dt} = -\frac{1}{C_k}[\widetilde{S}_{\alpha,\beta}(-c\sum_{j\in J}\frac{\partial g_j(x)}{\partial x_k} + c\sum_{j=1}^{m}\operatorname{sgn}(h_j(x))\frac{\partial h_j(x)}{\partial x_k}) + \widetilde{S}_\gamma(\frac{\partial f(x)}{\partial x_k})] \;,\; k = 1,\dots,n \quad (10)$$

where J is the index set of violated inequality constraints.

In the region where the gradient of P(x) is defined, equation (10) can be rewritten as

$$\frac{dx_k}{dt} = \left(-\frac{1}{C_k}\right)\left[\widetilde{S}_{\alpha,\beta}\left(c\frac{\partial P(x)}{\partial x_k}\right) + \widetilde{S}_\gamma\left(\frac{\partial f(x)}{\partial x_k}\right)\right],\; k = 1,\dots,n \quad (11)$$

It is proved simply [6] that whenever $\widetilde{S}_{\alpha,\beta}$ saturates and the state trajectory is in the region where P(x) is differentiable, then P(x) is decreasing along that trajectory and thus the penalty function P(x) would decrease along the trajectories outside the feasible region.

For the case of quadratic programming problems subject to linear equality and inequality constraints the circuit shown in Figure 2 is implemented [6] using a continuous Neural Network given in Figure 3.

Furthermore the authors give a possible implementation of the different nodes ($\widetilde{\mu}_j, \widetilde{\lambda}_j, x_k$) which represents the inequality constraints, equality constraints and state variables.

The above implementation can be realized on silicon and one can have VLSI chip performing the continuous Neural Network for the general case of quadratic programming problem subject to linear equality and inequality constraints.

III. "SIMULINK" Model of the Network

In the paper we present a "SIMULINK" model of the Neural Network considered in section II. Without loss of generality we will start with a simple constrained optimization problem

$$minimize\;\; f(x) = 2x_1^2 + x_2^2$$

subject to (12)

$$g_1(x) = -x_1 + x_2 - 2 \ge 0$$

$$h_1(x) = x_1 + x_2 - 7 = 0$$

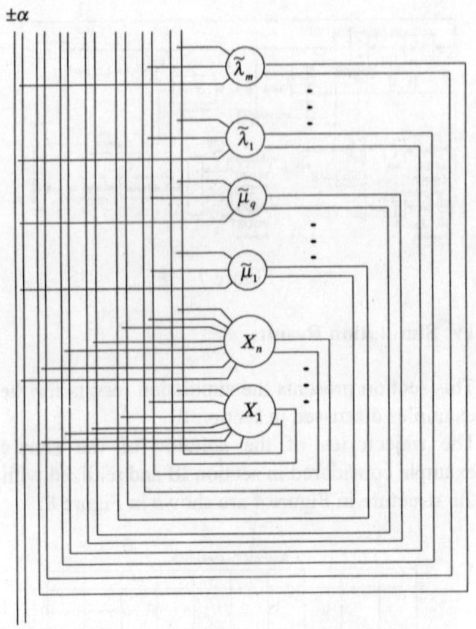

Figure 3

In this case

$$\frac{\partial f(x)}{\partial x_1}=4x_1\ ;\ \frac{\partial f(x)}{\partial x_2}=2x_2$$

$$\frac{\partial g_1(x)}{\partial x_1}=-1\ ,\ \frac{\partial h_1(x)}{\partial x_1}=1$$

$$\frac{\partial g_1(x)}{\partial x_2}=1\ ,\ \frac{\partial h_1(x)}{\partial x_2}=1$$

and the corresponding model is given in Figure 4.

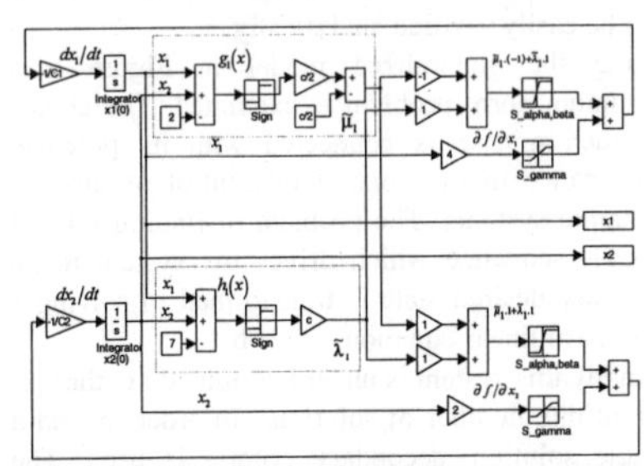

Figure 4

The outputs of the integrators are the state variables x_1 and x_2. As input of each of the integrators are used the right parts of the corresponding system (9), where the weighted sums $\tilde{\mu}_1.\frac{\partial g_1(x)}{\partial x_1}+\tilde{\lambda}_1.\frac{\partial h_1(x)}{\partial x_1}=\tilde{\mu}_1.(-1)+\tilde{\lambda}_1.1$ and $\tilde{\mu}_1.\frac{\partial g_1(x)}{\partial x_2}+\tilde{\lambda}_1.\frac{\partial h_1(x)}{\partial x_2}=\tilde{\mu}_1.1+\tilde{\lambda}_1.1$ are input signals for the two non-linear blocks $\tilde{S}_{\alpha,\beta}$ /see (4)/, and $\frac{\partial f(x)}{\partial x_1}=4x_1$, $\frac{\partial f(x)}{\partial x_2}=2x_2$ are input signals for the non-linear blocks $\tilde{S}_{\gamma}$ /see (4)/ . The terms $\tilde{\mu}_1$ and $\tilde{\lambda}_1$ are realized with non-linear blocks according to (7) and (8) respectively. It should be stressed that in the circuit implementation the clipping of the op amps is used to perform saturations.

Using SIMULINK's capability of working with vector variables the above model is generalized for the most common case (1) with the restriction - $g_j(x)$ and $h_j(x)$ to be linear functions in order to use the continuous Neural Network implementation in Figure 3. Otherwise if an arbitrary functions are considered for the constraints a generalization in the above sense is hard to be made and the reasonable approach is a different structure to be built according to (9) for every particular problem. Thus in agreement with the assumption of solving quadratic programming problems with objective function

$$f(x)=\frac{1}{2}\sum_{k=1}^{n}a_k x_k^2 \tag{13}$$

subject to linear constraints we construct a generalized "SIMULINK" model of the continuous Neural Network given in Figure 5. The attractiveness of this paradigm is the comparatively simple implementation of the $\tilde{\mu}_j, \tilde{\lambda}_j, x_k$ nodes in the Neural Network in Figure 3.

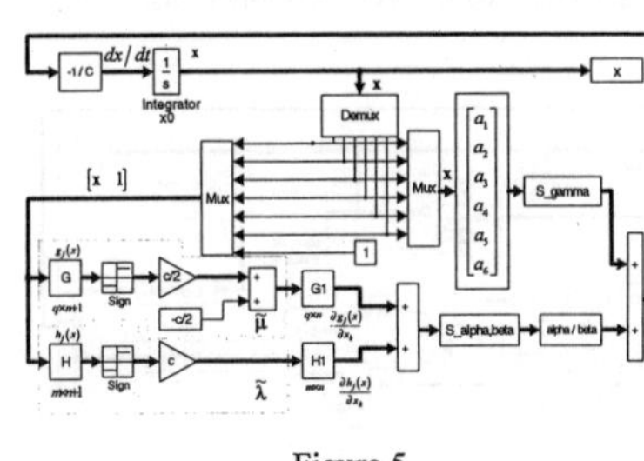

Figure 5

In our case an argument vector x of six elements is denoted. The argument vector is expanded with an element of value "1" in order to accommodate the eventual presence of coefficients before the 0-th order of x in (in)equalities. The matrices $\mathbf{G} \in R^{q \times n+1}$ and $\mathbf{H} \in R^{m \times n+1}$ contain the coefficients in inequality and equality constraints. The elements of matrices $\mathbf{G}_1 \in R^{q \times n}$ and $\mathbf{H}_1 \in R^{m \times n}$ represent the partial derivatives $\frac{\partial g_j(x)}{\partial x_k}$, $j = 1,...,q; k = 1,...,n$ and $\frac{\partial h_j(x)}{\partial x_k}$, $j = 1,...,m; k = 1,...,n$ respectively (note that $g_j(x)$ and $h_j(x)$ are linear functions). The saturation blocks "*S_gamma*" and "*S_alpha,beta*" have linear characteristic of the type $f(u) = u$. Therefore in order to acquire output value α of the block "*S_alpha,beta*" when the input is equal β, a scaling gain α/β ("*alpha/beta*") has to be incorporated (see Figure 5, 6, 7).

The gain vector $[a_1 \ a_2 \ a_3 \ a_4 \ a_5 \ a_6]^T$ contains the coefficients in the objective function (13) and represents its partial derivatives over the elements of x (which are linear functions of the type $\frac{\partial f(x)}{\partial x_k} = a_k x_k$, $k = 1,...,n$).

We also offer an expansion of the network in Figure 5 in which the partial derivatives $\frac{\partial f(x)}{\partial x_k}$, $k = 1,...,n$ of the objective function over the elements of x are described with a MATLAB function. It is shown in Figure 6 and allows an arbitrary type of $f(x)$ to be minimized. Finally, the most general problem of minimizing arbitrary objective function subject to arbitrary type of constraints can be solved by the modified network presented in Figure 7. Here the constraints as well as their derivatives over the elements of x are also described with MATLAB functions.

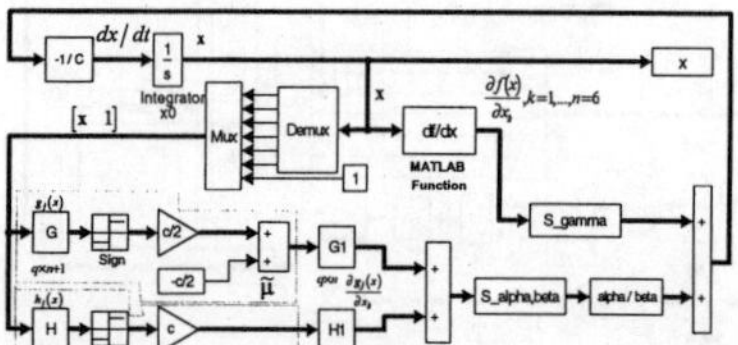

Figure 6

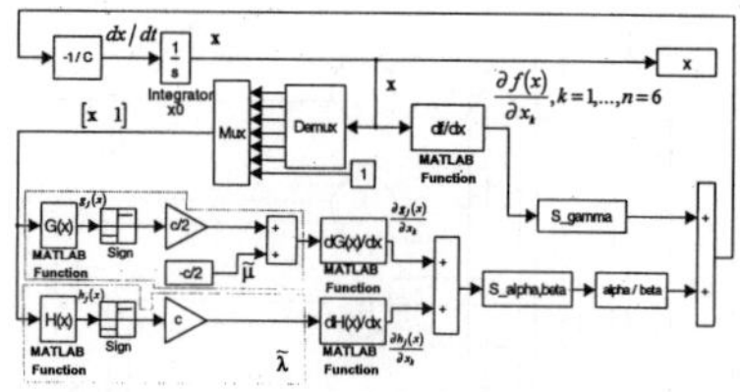

Figure 7

IV. Simulation Results

This section presents the simulation results for the examples discussed in section III.

The trajectories of the solution of the simple example considered in section III and realized with the structure in Figure 4 are shown in Figure 8:

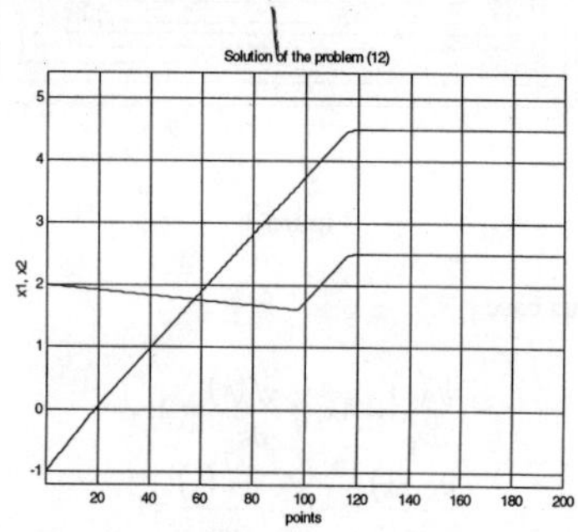

Figure 8

The trajectories converge to the point

$$x = [\ 2.495 \quad 4.501\ ]$$

which corresponds to $f(x) = 32.70$ and the result can be easily verified analytically.

Using the generalized model in Figure 6 a minimum norm problem is examined. The choice of such a case is connected with its practical importance in the context of control of discrete dynamic systems. The problem of finding a input signals sequence which drives the system to an arbitrary desired state is transformed to solving a system of linear equations $\mathbf{A}x = \mathbf{b}$.

Usually this system is underdetermined i.e. there is an infinite number of solutions. In order to find a single solution, secondary criteria is used. The solution is required to minimize in some sense the input signal $\boldsymbol{x}$.

As a second example we consider the following minimum norm problem [6]

The problem chosen for simulation is similar to the one explored in [6] and has the form:

$$\text{minimize } \|x\|_p$$

subject to

$$\mathbf{A}x = \mathbf{b}$$

where $p = 1, 2, \infty$ and

$$\mathbf{A} = \begin{bmatrix} 2 & 1 & 4 & 0 & 3 & 1 \\ 5 & 1 & -3 & 1 & 2 & 0 \\ 1 & -2 & 1 & -5 & -1 & 4 \end{bmatrix}, \quad \mathbf{b} = \begin{bmatrix} 2 \\ 1 \\ -4 \end{bmatrix}$$

The variables x_j, $j = 1, \ldots, 6$, are constrained to be in the interval [-12, 12].

According to the recommendations in [6] the values for the parameters of the non-linear blocks were set $\alpha = 12, \beta = 0.5, \gamma = 6$. The term c used in defining the variables $\tilde{\mu}_j$ and $\tilde{\lambda}_j$ was set $c = 1000$. In addition the following remarks should be mentioned:

- for the case *p=1*, $\dfrac{\partial f(x)}{\partial x_k} = \operatorname{sgn}(x_k)$ and the function *sgn* was approximated as

$$\operatorname{sgn}(x) = \begin{cases} 1 & x \geq 0.001 \\ 1000x & 0.001 > x > -0.001 \\ -1 & x \leq -0.001 \end{cases}$$

- for the case $p = \infty$ the components of the gradient of the objective function are

$$\frac{\partial f(x)}{\partial x_k} = \begin{cases} \operatorname{sgn}(x_k) & |x_k| = \max_i(|x_i|) \\ 0 & \text{elsewhere} \end{cases}, \; k = 1, \ldots, n.$$

The next three figures show the trajectories of the solution of the minimum norm problem for the cases - $p = 1, 2, \infty$. The transient of the solution is shown separately by the vector elements for clarification.

p=1

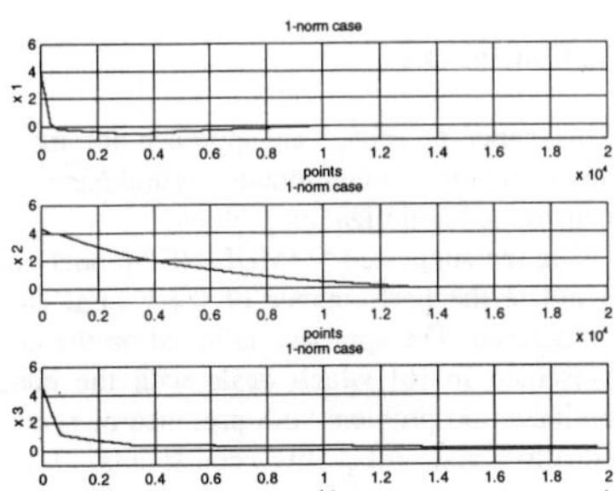

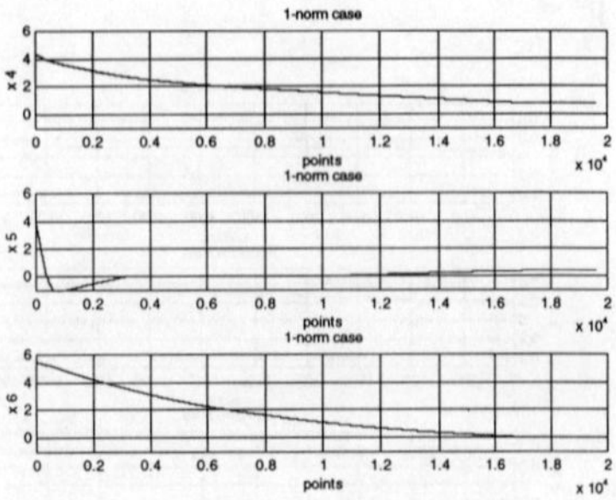

Figure 9

The trajectories converge to the point
x=[-0.008 0.000 0.185 0.741 0.429 -0.009]
which corresponds to $\|x\|_1 = 1.372$.

p=2

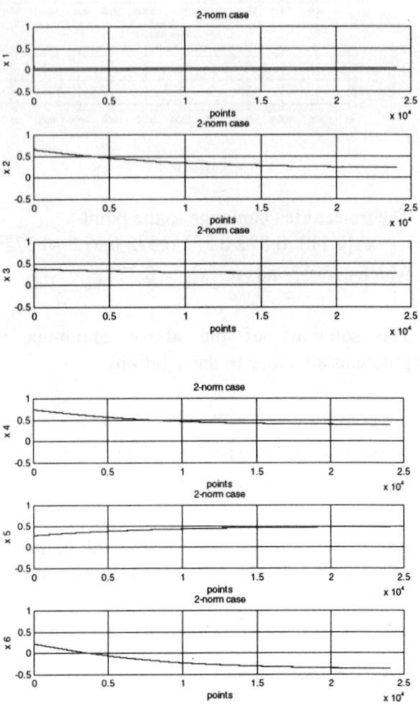

Figure 10

The trajectories converge to the point
x=[0.048 0.242 0.271 0.385 0.474 -0.359]
which corresponds to $\|x\|_2 = 0.797$.

p=∞

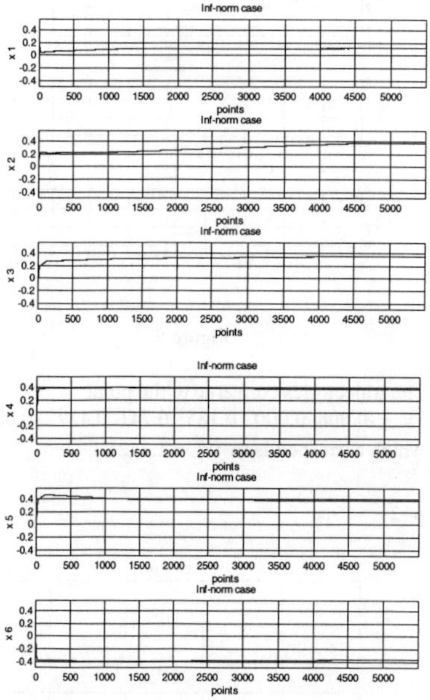

Figure 11

The trajectories converge to the point

x=[0.113 0.372 0.351 0.372 0.372 -0.372]

which corresponds to $\|x\|_\infty = 0.372$.

The solutions of the above minimum norm problems are close to the solutions

$$\begin{array}{l} x = [0.000\ 0.000\ 0.192\ 0.756\ 0.410\ 0.001]\ /for\ p = 1/ \\ x = [0.088\ 0.112\ 0.273\ 0.503\ 0.383\ -0.310]\ /for\ p = 2/ \\ x = [0.113\ 0.372\ 0.351\ 0.372\ 0.372\ -0.372]\ /for\ p = \infty / \end{array} \quad (14)$$

which were found via constrained optimization procedures of the Optimization Toolbox for MATLAB.

Notes on the results:

The speed of simulation and the precision of the solution are contradictable demands. The compromise in favour of one or the other is made by varying the values of the capacitors $C_k, k = 1,...,n$ as well as the thresholds of the non-linear blocks. The results acquired by simulation are close to (14) within the tolerance of the numerical method which was set to 10^{-3} (otherwise a more rigorous demand leads to considerable slowdown of the simulation). The existing offset between the solution derived with a MATLAB optimization toolbox procedure and the simulation results is also explained with the penalty method approximation used. This kind of approximation yields the same global minimizers as the constrained problem only when $c \to \infty$ (note that c is weight for the penalty function (3) in the unconstrained objective function (2)). Otherwise as long as c has a finite value (the maximal reachable value depends on the op amps used) an unbiased estimate of the solution cannot be acquired. In order to improve the accuracy of the results one may reduce the thresholds of the non-linear blocks at the cost of significant decrease of simulation speed.

The choice of numerical method and step of integration are also critical for the precision of the obtained solution. The simulation of the dynamic behavior of the Neural Network considered is most appropriately performed by using *Runge-Kutta* with fourth order step-size control or *Gear*.

An obvious drawback of the neural network based on the penalty method approach is its inability to escape local minima. When the network reaches a steady state it is guaranteed that the solution satisfies the constraints but it is not necessarily the global minima of the function. The successful solving depends much on the initial conditions (which is typical for every optimization procedure). The choice of initial conditions should be "reasonable", according to the considerations for the particular problems. It is recommended to solve the constrained optimization problem with various sets of initial conditions. Furthermore after the VLSI realization, the Neural Network is able to find the solution in real time.

V. Conclusions

This paper presented an approach for modelling and simulation of continuous Neural Networks for constrained optimization problems.

Using the suggested "SIMULINK" model one can simulate the performance of the Neural Network considered. The approach is based on the network presented in [6] which deals with the quadratic optimization problem with presence of both linear equality and inequality constraints. We also generalize the model for the case of constrained optimization problem with an arbitrary objective function and constraints.

The obtained results show that the proposed network in [6] is on average effective for the general case, even though its performance depends on the problem itself.

ACKNOWLEDGEMENTS

The authors acknowledge any constructive remarks of the reviewers.

References

[1]. L. O. Chua and G. N. Lin. “Non-linear programming without computation”, *IEEE Trans. Circuits and Systems*, CAS-31, 182-186 (1984).

[2]. D. W. Tank and J. J. Hopfield. “Simple “neural” optimization networks: an A/D converter, signal decision circuit, and a linear programming circuit”, *IEEE Trans. Circuits and Systems*, CAS-33, 533-541 (1986).

[3]. M. J. Smith and C. L. Portmann. “Practical design and analysis of a simple “neural” optimization circuit”, *IEEE Trans. Circuit and Systems*, CAS-36, 42-50 (1989).

[4]. M. P. Kennedy and L. O. Chua. “Neural networks for non-linear programming”, *IEEE Trans. Circuit and Systems*, CAS-35, 554-562 (1988).

[5]. W. E. Lillo, M. H. Loh, S. Hui and S. H. Żak. “On solving constrained optimization problems with neural networks a penalty method approach”, *Technical Report TR EE 91-43*, School of EE, Purdue University, West Lafayette, IN, 1991.

[6]. W. E. Lillo, S. Hui, S. Hui and S. H. Żak. “Neural network for constrained optimization problems”, *International Journal of Circuit Theory and Applications*, vol. 21, 385-399 (1993).

[7]. M. Forty, A. Tesi. “New Conditions for Global Stability of Neural Networks with Application to Linear and Quadratic Programming Problems”, *IEEE Trans. On CAS*, part I, vol. 41, pp. 354-366, 1995.

[8]. S. Osowski. “Neural Network for Non-Linear Programming with Linear Equality Constraints”, *Int. journal cir. Theor. Applic.*, vol. 20, pp. 93-98, 1992.

[9]. Y. Obuchi, H. Masui and M. Ohki. “Weighted Parallel Problem Solving by Optimization Networks”, *Neural Networks*, vol. 9, N2, pp. 357-366, 1996.

MODELLING AND ESTIMATION OF SYNTHETIC APERTURE SONAR PLATFORM MOTION

D. Kraus, F. Mello Petey and J. Kalwa

STN ATLAS Elektronik GmbH
Sebaldsbrücker Heerstraße 235
D-28305 Bremen
Tel. : 0421/457-3788
Fax.: 0421/457-2020,
e-mail: kraus.d@stn-atlas.de

Abstract - High resolution sonars for minehunting, particular synthetic aperture sonars (SAS), require an accurate sensing of platform motion. Since the precision of customary inertial systems will be seldom sufficient an additional model based path estimation procedure should be employed. In this paper a path estimator based on the prediction process of an conventional identification algorithm for linear, rational and multidimensional systems is proposed and first promising numerical investigations are carried out and partially presented.

1 INTRODUCTION

Synthetic aperture techniques are of growing interest in recent minehunting sonar concepts. The German's MJ2000 minehunting program includes a synthetic aperture sonar (SAS) for the detection of buried mines. This so-called sediment SAS (SSAS) is mounted on a towfish which is towed by an unmanned surface vessel via a tow cable, cf. left part of Fig. 1.

To achieve a satisfactory SAS performance the towfish motion has to be known over the extent of the synthetic aperture up to an accuracy of $\lambda/16$, where λ denotes the acoustical wavelength. For instance, an SAS operating at 20KHz requires a path accuracy of approx. 5mm. Since usual inertial systems (INS) do not provide this precision due to measurement noise, a model based path estimation procedure for smoothing the INS data is mandatory.

The paper is organized as follows. In section 2 and 3 a motion model for the surface ship, cable and towfish including the essential non-linearities is developed, cf. right part of Fig. 1. Using this model as reference, system identification techniques for linear and rational multidimensional systems are applied for path estimation in section 4. Finally, the accuracy of this path estimation technique is empirically demonstrated.

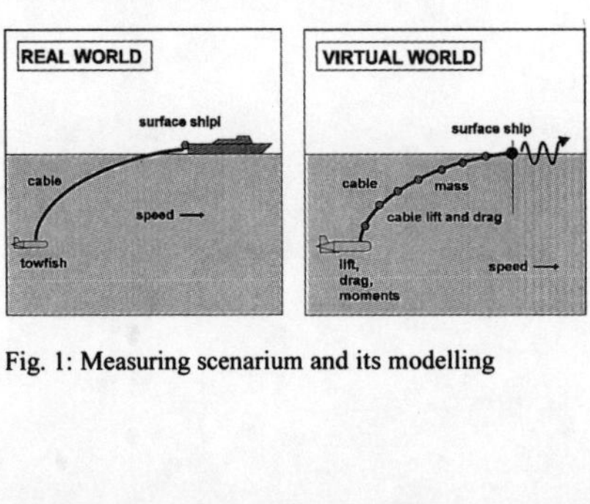

Fig. 1: Measuring scenarium and its modelling

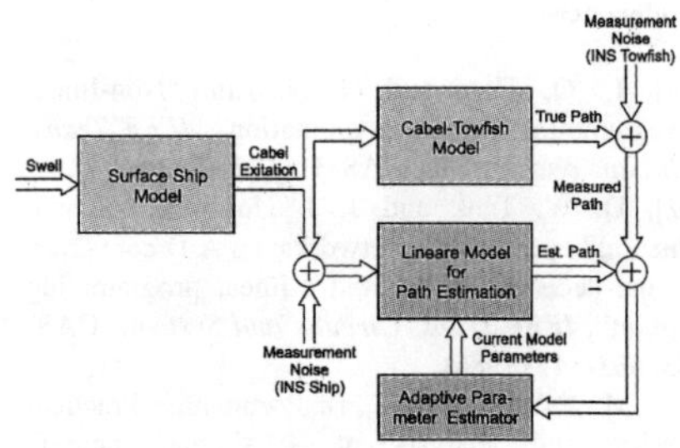

Fig. 2: Adaptive path estimator concept

2 SURFACE SHIP

The motion of the ship travelling in a swell can severely disturb that of the tow fish attached to the stern of the ship by a tow-cable.

In this paper the ship is considered as a six degrees of freedom system travelling at a constant course relative to the dominant direction of swell. The stationary swell (automatically generated from a Pierson-Moskowitz spectrum) is represented as the sum of a large number of regular waves, each having a particular frequency, amplitude, direction (i.e. short-crested swell) and random phase angle.

The numerical method combines the simulation of the surge motion of the ship in the time domain with a linear treatment of the other five motions by the strip theory for the following reasons:

- The surge motion of the vessel is highly nonlinear and greatly affects the motion of the towfish. A nonlinear time domain simulation is therefore mandatory in this case.
- Though rolling is a notoriously nonlinear phenomenon it hardly affects the motion of the winch (and therefore the motion of the towfish) set up in the centre line of the vessel.
- The classical strip theory (response amplitude operator) is a very efficient tool for handling the heave, pitch, sway and yaw motions of a ship even in heavy seas.

In the surge simulation the equation of motion is solved by using the familiar Runge-Kutta's integration scheme. The longitudinal forces considered in the equation of motion are the disturbances due to the waves, the propeller thrust assumed to be constant (i.e. no speed controller), the ship's resistance and the hydrodynamic force associated with the ship's longitudinal added mass. The program considers particularly the elevation of the sea surface along the ship's hull. In each time step the contribution of each individual wave to the surge force is considered by taking into account the horizontal component of the wave buoyancy (determined assuming an undisturbed wave pressure field) [2] and [5]. The resultant wave force is obtained by superposing the individual contributions of all waves.

Figs. 3 and 4 present simulation results for a ship with a length of 25m (approximately 100t displacement) travelling at a ("still water") speed of 11kn in a swell defined by a significant wave height of 1.2m and a dominant wave period of 4s. The wave period of 4s corresponds to a dominant wave velocity of about 12kn and a wave length of approximately 25m.

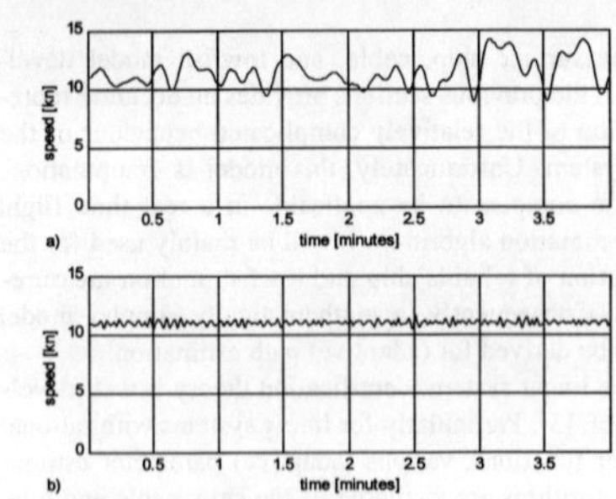

Fig. 3: Ship speed travelling
a) in following seas,
b) in head seas

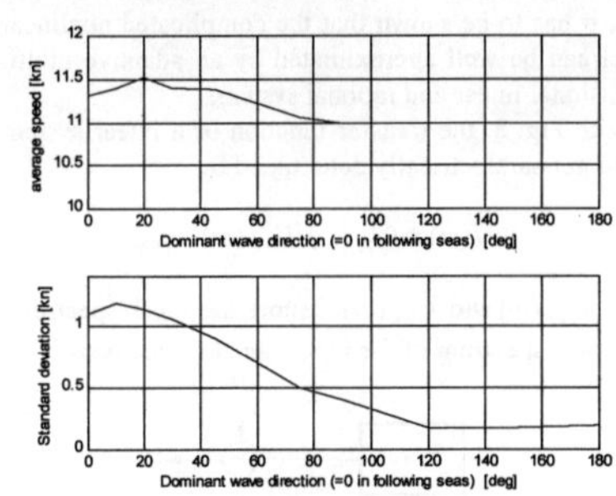

Fig. 4: Ship speed fluctuation at 11kn

The longitudinal wave disturbance plays an important role only in following and quartering seas because in these situations the encounter period between ship and waves can be very long, so that the ship is acted upon by a slowly oscillating force (causing a more or less severe fluctuation of ship speed). Conversely, in head seas the above mentioned encounter period is so short, that the inert ship is hardly affected by the high frequency wave excitation, cf. Fig. 3.

When in following seas the ship's speed and the dominant wave velocity have the same order of magnitude (resulting in very long encounter periods) there is additionally the danger of the ship being carried along by the waves. In this case the average ship speed in the seaway differs from that achieved with same propeller thrust in still water. Results (statistics of the ship speed fluctuation, i.e., the deviation of the actual speed from the corresponding constant "still water speed") are summarised in Fig. 4.

3 CABLE TOWFISH SYSTEM

As depicted in Fig. 5 the cable is represented by a chain of mass-points which are linked by a rigid cable element. This cable element and its position relative to the environmental current situation determines the hydrodynamic forces lift and drag. Weight, buoyancy, and mass are concentrated in the mass points, which are located at the end of each cable element.

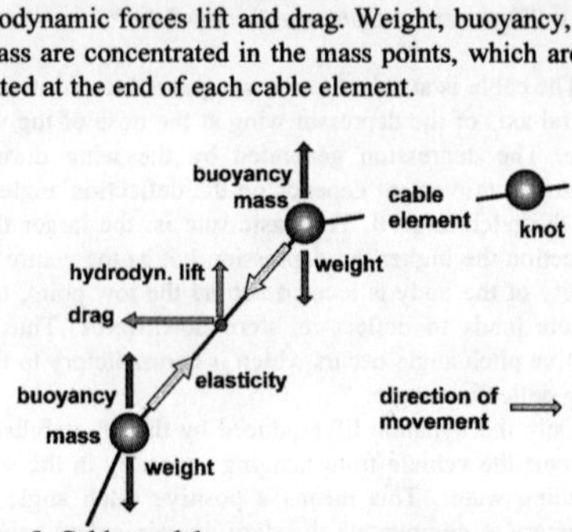

Fig. 5: Cable model

The resulting equations of motion are solved by a time discrete integration. The typical drawback of this method is the requirement of very small time steps (e. g. 1ms) due to a small element length, elasticity and the speed of pressure waves within the material. By incorporation of the following assumptions the computional load could be significantly reduced.

- Elasticity of the cable is neglected (the cable length is less than 100 m).
- Rotational degrees of freedom are neglected (rotational movements are very slow).

With these simplifications a cable motion simulation tool has been achieved that provides real time capabilities.

The cable is coupled to the motion of the surface ship and towfish as follows:

The first node of the system (at surface) receives a prescribed displacement which is defined by the movement of the surface ship. The mass of the towing ship exceeds by far the mass of the cable towfish system so that this assumption is applicable.

On the other side of the cable the static and dynamic forces of the towfish are added to the forces of the last mass point. Based on the sum of forces, the translation (displacement) of the node can be calculated. This translation, superimposed with a rotational movement of the towfish describes the complete motion.

The towfish itself is modelled in all 6 degrees of freedom. Therefore three force and three momentum equations have to be solved. The hydrodynamic forces and moments are estimated by a formulation based on derivatives - a common and proved method. A side view of a generic towfish and the forces acting in the symmetric plane is given in Fig. 6.

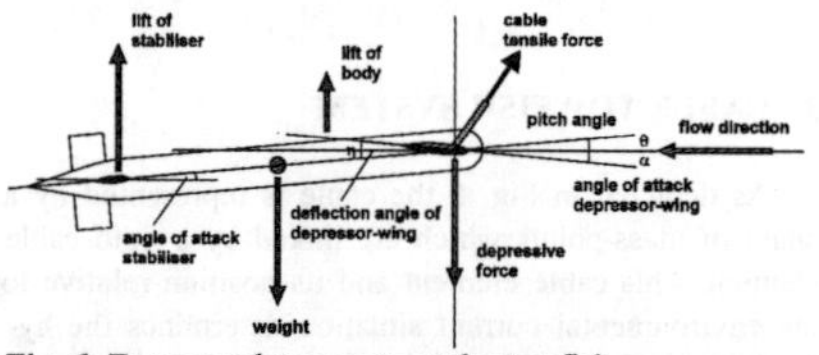

Fig. 6: Forces and momenta at the towfish

The cable is attached to a towinglever located in the neutral axis of the depressor wing at the nose of the vehicle. The depression generated by the wing during horizontal movement depends on the deflection angle η and the pitch angle θ. The basic rule is: the larger the deflection the higher the depression but as the centre of gravity of the body is located behind the tow point, the vehicle tends to deflect its stern downwards. Thus a positive pitch angle occurs which is contradictory to the wing deflection angle.

Only the dynamic lift produced by the aft stabiliser prevents the vehicle from hanging vertically in the surrounding water. This means a positive pitch angle is necessary to compensate the stern down moment generated by the gravity and the mass of the vehicle. Further the effective angle of attack of the depressor-wing ($\alpha=\theta-\eta$) and thus the depression or lift coefficient C_l depends on the speed of the vehicle.

An interesting - but expected - fact is, that a greater depth can also be achieved by moving the centre of gravity to the front of the vehicle. The new balance of moments requires a smaller pitch angle θ (while η=const.) which leads to a higher effective angle of attack, producing a higher depression.

Fig. 7 presents a typical dynamic behaviour of such a system excited by an sine wave of±2.5m. The cable length is approx. 80m, the diving depth of the vehicle approx. 22m. At the start of a typical excitation period the surface ship moves upwards. The tensile force generated by this motion is transfered to the towfish via the cable. In this configuration the cable is attached to the towfish at an angle of approx. 80°. Thus the towfish is pulled upwards (negative z-direction). The dynamic stability of the towfish generates a nose up movement (positive pitch angle). During the next step - the surface ship has passed the wave maximum - the tension in the cable decreases rapidly, so that the towfish moves downwards, driven by gravity only. This more or less free motion of the vehicle exhibits an oscillation which is typical for towed bodies fitted with depressors.

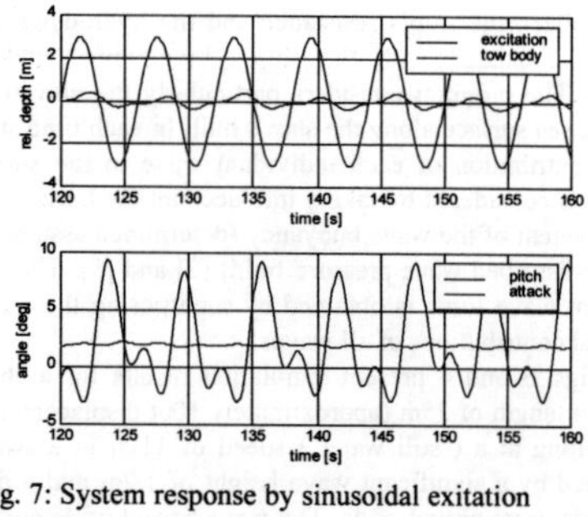

Fig. 7: System response by sinusoidal exitation

4 PATH ESTIMATOR

The surface ship, cable, and towfish model developed in the previous sections provides an accurate representation of the relatively complicated behaviour of the real system. Unfortunately, this model is computationally too complex to be applicable in a real time flight path estimation algorithm. It will be mainly used for the generation of reliable ship and towfish motion measurements. Consequently, a mathematically simpler model has to be derived for (adaptive) path estimation.

The linear system identification theory is well developed, cf. [3]. Particularly for linear systems with rational transfer functions, various (adaptive) parameter estimation algorithms are available. If the ship, cable and towfish system can be satisfactorily modelled by rational transfer functions, the aforementioned parameter estimation algorithms can be directly employed, cf. [4]. Thus, it has to be shown that the complicated nonlinear model can be well approximated by an adaptive multi-dimensional linear and rational system.

With Fig. 8, the transfer function of a linear system can be nonparametrically determined by

$$H(\omega) = C_{XY}(\omega)/C_{XX}(\omega),$$

where $C_{XY}(\omega)$ and $C_{XX}(\omega)$ denote the cross spectrum and power spectrum of the input signal respectively.

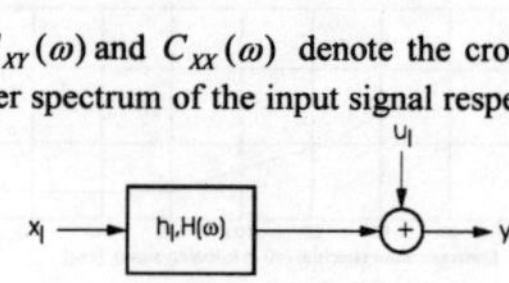

Fig. 8: Output error model for a linear SISO system

The power spectrum of the output signal can be expressed by

$$C_{YY}(\omega) = |H(\omega)|^2 C_{XX}(\omega) + C_{UU}(\omega)$$

The linearity of a system can be investigated by measuring the coherence of the input and ouput signals, cf. [1]. The coherence (magnitude squared coherence) is defined by

$$R_{XY}(\omega)=\frac{|C_{XY}(\omega)|^2}{C_{XX}(\omega)\,C_{YY}(\omega)}=\frac{|H(\omega)|^2\,C_{XX}(\omega)}{|H(\omega)|^2\,C_{XX}(\omega)+C_{UU}(\omega)}.$$

Using the complicated ship, cable and towfish model as measurement generator the power spectra, cross spectra and the magnitude squared coherences have been calculated for all motion components. Interpretation of these results lead to the following qualitative conlusions.

- The cable greatly attenuates the transmission of the cross track motion down to the towfish and acts as a low pass filter for the other motion components.
- A rather perfect coherence (>0.9) between the various motion components could be observed within the low pass band.

Therefore, the towfish motion components of interest can be model arround the working point by linear and rational systems.

To estimate the unknown system parameters (polynom coefficients), a prediction error approach based upon an equation error model for multiple input single output data is used, cf. Fig. 9.

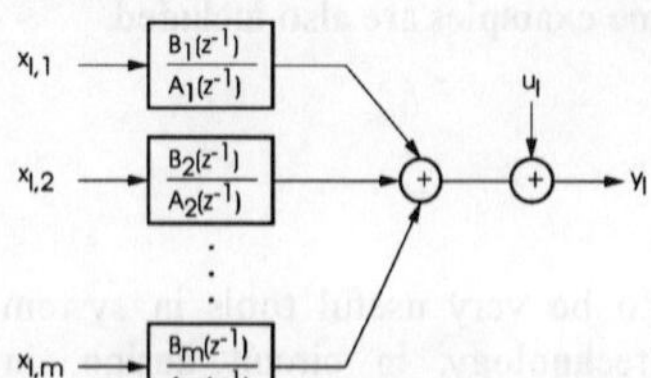

Fig. 9: Output error model for a rational MISO system

The model parameters are determined by minimising the squared prediction error using Gauss-Newton iterations The path estimates are simultaneously provided by the inherent prediction process. The capabilities of the proposed predictor (path estimator) have been analysed under various swell and system conditions (cable length, ship speed, etc.). The motion components are assumed to be accurate generated by using the complicated nonlinear model. Space limitations only allow the presentation of an particular example. A short sequence of towfish depth motion is depicted in the upper diagram of Fig. 10. The motion data are then corrupted by white noise for simulating noisy INS measurements. The simulated INS depth measurements of the towfish are shown in the middle of Fig. 10. On these simulated INS measurements the supposed predictor has been applied. The predictor output for the towfish depth motion is presented in the lower diagram of Fig. 10. The difference between the true and predicted depth motion is visualized in the upper part of Fig. 11. Since synthetic aperture processing requires a certain position accuracy within a predefined time intervall, e.g. T=4s, only relative deviations are of interest. The relative depth error is depicted in the lower part of Fig. 11.

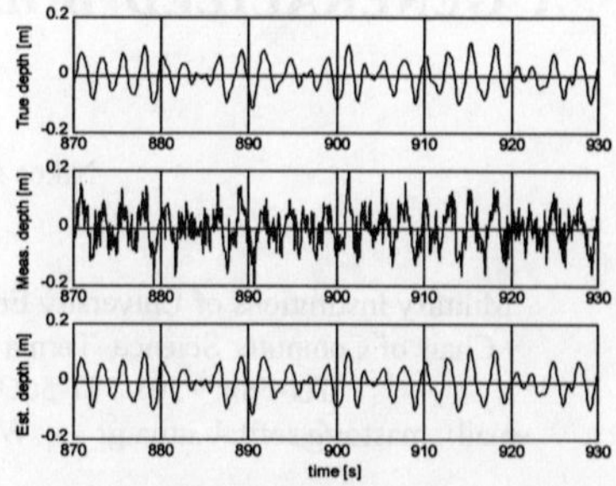

Fig. 10: True, measured and estimated depth motion

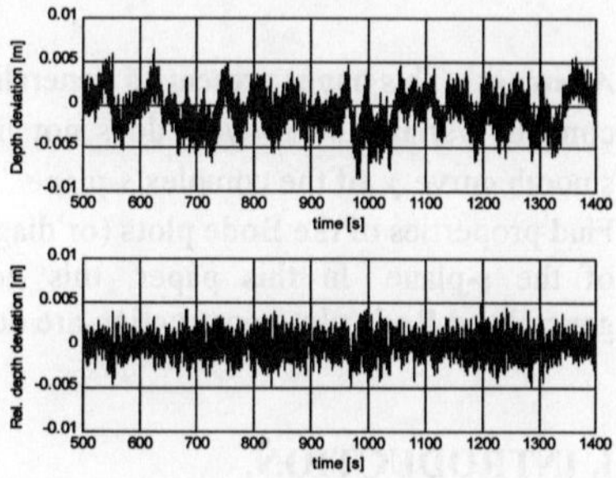

Fig. 11: Depth deviation and relative depth deviation

5 CONCLUSION

A sophisticated surface ship, cable and towfish motion model has been developed. Since the computational complexity prevents the application of this model in an online path estimation procedure (therefore essentially used as reference model) a simpler approach has been derived by exploiting linear system identification techniques. This approach is then investigated by several numerical experiments. The results demonstrate that the path estimation accuracy required for SAS processing can be achieved by the prediction process inherent in the system identification algorithm.

6 REFERENCES

[1] J.S. Bendat and A.G.Piersol: Random Data, Analysis and Measurement Procedures, Wiley, 1971

[2] P. Blume and H.G. Hattendorf: Stability and safety against capsizing of modern ships (in German), Report Nr. S165/83 of the Hamburg Ship Model Basin, 1983.

[3] L. Ljung: System Identification, Theory for the User Prentice Hall, 1987

[4] MATLAB: Identification Toolbox User's Guide, MathWorks Inc, 1997

[5] H. Söding: Sea loads for the ship design (in German), 22. Fortbildungskurs, Institut für Schiffbau der Universität Hamburg, 1986.

A GENERALIZED BODE PLOT CONSTRUCTION

Nikos E. Mastorakis

Military Institutions of University Education (MIUE), Hellenic Naval Academy,
Chair of Computer Science, Terma Hatzikyriakou, 18539, Piraeus, GREECE
Tel-Fax: +301 777-5660 or FAX: +301 4181768
email: mastor@softlab.ntua.gr Web Page: http://www.softlab.ntua.gr/~mastor

Abstract. This paper presents a generalization of the Bode plot in the case where the complex variable s ($s = j\omega$) does not lie on the imaginary axis but in general on a smooth curve γ of the complex s-plane. This gives the idea to make the generalization: Find properties of the Bode plots (or diagrams) when s does lie on such smooth curves of the s-plane. In this paper, this generalization is attempted. Some rules for generalized Bode plot construction are derived. Some examples are also included.

I. INTRODUCTION.

Bode plots (or diagrams) have been proved to be very useful tools in system analysis and synthesis, in control theory and technology, in circuit design, in communication and electronics engineering, in analogue and digital filtering, in distributed parameter systems theory, in stability analysis, in electro-mechanical systems, etc. Bode plots construction rules have been developed for rational transfer function $H(s)$ having the form

$$H(s) = \frac{\prod_{i=1}^{m}(s - z_i)}{\prod_{i=1}^{n}(s - p_i)} \tag{1}$$

where z_i, $p_i \in \mathbf{C}$. Since z_i, $p_i \in \mathbf{C}$, the numerator and denominator of $H(s)$ are factored into products of first-degree factors. z_i, p_i are called zeros and poles respectively. In real systems, z_i, as well as p_i are appeared as complex conjugate pairs if z_i, $p_i \in \mathbf{C} - \mathbf{R}$. It is well known that the amplitude (in dB) and the phase (in degrees) are defined as follows

$$|H(s)|_{db} = 20\,log_{10}\frac{\prod_{i=1}^{m}|(s-z_i)|}{\prod_{i=1}^{n}|(s-p_i)|} = \sum_{i=1}^{m} 20\,log_{10}|s-z_i| - \sum_{i=1}^{n} 20\,log_{10}|s-p_i| \tag{2}$$

$$arg(H(s)) = \sum_{i=1}^{m} arg(s-z_i) - \sum_{i=1}^{n} arg(s-p_i) \tag{3}$$

The functions $|H(s)|_{db}$ and $\arg H(s)$ have the important property to convert a product form into a summation form. This property is used in the construction of a Bode diagram by adding Bode diagrams of the elementary terms $(s-z_i)$ and $(s-p_i)$.

Classical Bode plots refer in the case that $s=j\omega$ and they are the plots of $|H(s)|_{db}$ and $arg(H(s))$ versus $log_{10}\,\omega$. However, in practice, there exists some interesting cases where s lies on a smooth curve γ of the s-plane.

A first interesting case is: Suppose that a linear (time invariant) system is described by the transfer function $H(s)$ or equivalently by the impulse response $h(t)$. If we desire to modify some properties of the system, we define the system $H(s+a)$ or equivalently $e^{-at}\cdot h(t)$. In a sinus steady state $s=j\omega$ and therefore we obtain $H(a+j\omega)$. So starting from the original transfer function $H(s)$ a substitution $s\to\sigma+j\omega$ seems to take place (where $\sigma=a$). If some relation exists between σ and ω, then, for the Bode plot, s lies on a curve of the s-plane

A second very interesting case arises from the discrete time linear systems analysis. In these systems, the transfer function $H(z)$ is used (z is the complex variable of the utilised z-transform). In a sinus steady state $z=e^{j\omega}$. Therefore z lies on the unit circle.

Other special cases can be obtained in multidimensional systems theory. See for example the excellent books [1÷3].

In a recent paper, [4], C.S.Lindguist examined the Bode plots in the case that $s=\sigma\in R$. This very interesting case is applied in several cases in networks, electronics, control, communications and distributed systems. In [4], some important remarks are made and several examples are given.

In this paper, the Bode plots are investigated in the case that s lies on a smooth curve γ of the complex plane. $20\,log_{10}|H(s)|$ and $arg(H(s))$ are plotted versus $log_{10}\,\theta$ where θ is the parameter of the smooth curve γ on which s lies. These Bode plots are a generalization of the classical Bode plots as well as of the plots of [4].

We focus our analysis on the study of the factor $(s-p_i)$. It is not difficult to modify it for the factors $(s-z_i)$. In reality, the amplitude or the phase Bode diagram of a factor $(s-a)$ is the mirror diagram of the diagram of $1/(s-a)$.

Suppose that $p_i = a + jb$ and the complex variable s lies on the smooth curve γ having the parameter equations: $\sigma_1 = \sigma_1(\theta)$ and $\omega_1 = \omega_1(\theta)$ where $\sigma_1(\theta)$ and $\omega_1(\theta)$ are differentiable functions and $\left(\frac{d\sigma_1(\theta)}{d\theta}\right)^2 + \left(\frac{d\omega_1(\theta)}{d\theta}\right)^2 \neq 0 \ \forall \ \theta$. Since

$$(s - p_i) = \sigma_1(\theta) + j\omega_1(\theta) - a - jb = \sigma(\theta) + j\omega(\theta) - k - jl$$

where

$$\sigma(\theta) = \sigma_1(\theta) - \sigma_1(0)\ , \quad \omega(\theta) = \omega_1(\theta) - \omega_1(0)$$

and

$$k + jl = a + jb - \sigma_1(0) - j\omega_1(0)$$

we can say that the curve starts from the origin of the axes, i.e. $\sigma(0) = 0$ and $\omega(0) = 0$. The new pole, after this displacement in the complex plane, is $k + jl$. So, $s = \sigma(\theta) + j\omega(\theta)$ where $\theta \in R_+$ and $\sigma(0) = 0$, $\omega(0) = 0$.

In the next section, we refer to the behaviour of the Bode plot a) when $\theta << 1$, b) when $\theta \to \infty$.c-d) when $|s - p_i|$ is minimum or maximum.

2. RESULTS.

Suppose that $\theta = 10^u$. Therefore $u = \log_{10}\theta$.

It is repeated that the Bode plot of the factor $(s - p_i)$ is examined. It should be noted that our analysis has the advantage to be restricted only on first order factors.

a). Obviously, $\theta \to 0 \Leftrightarrow u \to -\infty$. However $\theta \to 0 \Rightarrow \sigma(\theta) \to 0$ and $\omega(\theta) \to 0$

For this reason one can write $-20\log_{10}|s - p_i| \cong -20\log_{10}|-p_i| \cong -20\log_{10}|p_i|$ as well as $-arg(s - p_i) \cong -arg(-p_i) = 180^0 - arg(p_i)$. The conclusion is that the amplitude plot for $\theta \to 0$ is approximated by the asymptote (straight line) $|H(s)|_{db} = -20\log_{10}|p_j|$ having 0 *db/dec* slope and the phase plot for $\theta \to 0$ is approximated by the asymptote (straight line) $arg(H(s)) = -arg(-p_i) = 180^0 - arg(p_i)$ having *0 degrees/dec* slope.

b). If $\theta \to \infty \Leftrightarrow u \to \infty$. We distinguish two cases:

b1). Our curve on which s lies is a closed curve. In this case $\theta \to \infty \Rightarrow \sigma(\theta) \xrightarrow{not} \infty$ and $\omega(\theta) \xrightarrow{not} \infty$. If $\sigma(\theta)$ and $\omega(\theta)$ are considered periodical functions, then the amplitude and the phase plot appeared to be periodical plots too. If $\sigma(\theta)$ and $\omega(\theta)$ are considered bounded functions, then the amplitude and the phase plot appeared to be bounded plots too. The proof is trivial.

b2). Our curve on which s lies is such that $\sigma(\theta)\xrightarrow{\theta\to\infty}\infty$ or $\omega(\theta)\xrightarrow{\theta\to\infty}\infty$. In this case, one can write $-20\log_{10}|s-p_i|\cong -20\log_{10}|s|$ and $-arg(s-p_i)\cong -arg(s)$. Various cases can be obtained if $|s|=\sqrt{\sigma^2(\theta)+\omega^2(\theta)}$ is approximated, for example, by a polynomial of θ or by an exponential function of θ or by a logarithmic function of θ in big θ. So if $\sigma(\theta)$ behaves as a d_1-th degree polynomial, and $\omega(\theta)$ behaves as a d_2-th degree polynomial, then $|s|=\sqrt{\sigma^2(\theta)+\omega^2(\theta)}$ behaves as a d-th degree polynomial where $d=max(d_1,d_2)$. Therefore the asymptote is the straight line $y(\theta)=20\log_{10}\dfrac{1}{c\theta^d}=-20\cdot d\cdot\log_{10}\theta-20\log_{10}c$ where c is a positive constant. More analytically $c=\begin{cases}|c_1| & \text{if } d_1>d_2\\ |c_2| & \text{if } d_1<d_2\\ \sqrt{c_1^2+c_2^2} & \text{if } d_1=d_2 \text{ and } |d_1|+|d_2|\neq 0\end{cases}$ where c_1 is the coefficient of the maximum power of the polynomial that approximates $\sigma(\theta)$ in big θ and c_2 is the coefficient of the maximum power of the polynomial that approximates $\omega(\theta)$ in big θ too. So an asymptote with a slope *-20d* db/decade is obtained. The phase plot asymptote is $y(\theta)=-arg(s)$

$$=\begin{cases}-arg(c_1) & \text{if } d_1>d_2\\ -90^0-arg(c_2) & \text{if } d_1<d_2\\ -arg(c_1+jc_2) & \text{if } d_1=d_2 \text{ and } |d_1|+|d_2|\neq 0\end{cases}$$

It is reminded that *arg(c)* =0 if c>0 and *arg(c)=180* if c<0.

Remark: If $\sigma(\theta)$ is bounded (for $\theta\to\infty$) or $\omega(\theta)$ is bounded (for $\theta\to\infty$) (or is *exclusive* or), we define $d_1=0$ when $\sigma(\theta)$ is bounded (for $\theta\to\infty$) as well as we define $d_2=0$ when $\omega(\theta)$ is bounded (for $\theta\to\infty$).

If a more sensible approximation in big θ is $\sigma(\theta)\approx c_1\cdot Exp(\varepsilon_1\cdot\theta)$ or $\omega(\theta)\approx c_2\cdot Exp(\varepsilon_2\cdot\theta)$ where ε_1 and ε_2 are positive constants , then we have the asymptote (no-straight line) $y(\theta) = 20\log_{10}\frac{1}{ce^{\varepsilon\theta}}$ $= -20\cdot\varepsilon\cdot\theta\cdot\log_{10}e - 20\log_{10}c = -20\cdot\varepsilon\cdot\log_{10}e\cdot 10^{\log_{10}\theta} - 20\log_{10}c$ where

$$c = \begin{cases} |c_1| & \text{if}\,\varepsilon_1 > \varepsilon_2 \\ |c_2| & \text{if}\,\varepsilon_1 < \varepsilon_2 \\ \sqrt{c_1^2 + c_2^2} & \text{if } \varepsilon_1 = \varepsilon_2 \text{ and } |\varepsilon_1| + |\varepsilon_2| \neq 0 \end{cases}$$

and $\varepsilon = max(\varepsilon_1, \varepsilon_2)$. Therefore the amplitude plot asymptote is an exponential curve (no-straight line). Furthermore, the phase plot asymptote is

$$y(\theta) = -arg(s) = \begin{cases} -arg(c_1) & \text{if}\,\varepsilon_1 > \varepsilon_2 \\ -90^0 - arg(c_2) & \text{if}\,\varepsilon_1 < \varepsilon_2 \\ -arg(c_1 + jc_2) & \text{if } \varepsilon_1 = \varepsilon_2 \text{ and } |\varepsilon_1| + |\varepsilon_2| \neq 0 \end{cases}$$

. Therefore, the phase plot asymptote is a straight line.

Remark: If $\sigma(\theta)$ is bounded (for $\theta \to \infty$) <u>or</u> $\omega(\theta)$ is bounded (for $\theta \to \infty$) (<u>or</u> is *exclusive* or), we define $\varepsilon_1 = 0$ when $\sigma(\theta)$ is bounded (for $\theta \to \infty$) as well as we define $\varepsilon_2 = 0$ when $\omega(\theta)$ is bounded (for $\theta \to \infty$) .

If the approximation in big θ, is $\sigma(\theta) \approx c_1 \cdot \log_{10}(\lambda_1 \cdot \theta)$ and $\omega(\theta) \approx c_2 \cdot \log_{10}(\lambda_2 \cdot \theta)$ where λ_1 and λ_2 are positive constants, then we have the asymptote $y(\theta) = 20\log_{10}\frac{1}{c\log_{10}(\lambda\theta)} = -20\log_{10}[c(\log_{10}\theta) + c\log_{10}\lambda]$ where

$$c = \begin{cases} |c_1| & \text{if}\,\lambda_1 > \lambda_2 \\ |c_2| & \text{if}\,\lambda_1 < \lambda_2 \\ \sqrt{c_1^2 + c_2^2} & \text{if } \lambda_1 = \lambda_2 \text{ and } |\lambda_1| + |\lambda_2| \neq 0 \end{cases}$$

and $\lambda = max(\lambda_1, \lambda_2)$. Thus the asymptote is also a "logarithmic" curve. Furthermore the phase plot asymptote is

$$y(\theta) = -arg(s) = \begin{cases} -arg(c_1) & \text{if}\,\lambda_1 > \lambda_2 \\ -90^0 - arg(c_2) & \text{if}\,\lambda_1 < \lambda_2 \\ -arg(c_1 + jc_2) & \text{if } \lambda_1 = \lambda_2 \text{ and } |\lambda_1| + |\lambda_2| \neq 0 \end{cases}$$

, thus this asymptote is a straight line.

Remark: If $\sigma(\theta)$ is bounded (for $\theta \to \infty$) or $\omega(\theta)$ is bounded (for $\theta \to \infty$) (or is *exclusive* or), we define $\lambda_1 = 0$ when $\sigma(\theta)$ is bounded (for $\theta \to \infty$) as well as we define $\lambda_2 = 0$ when $\omega(\theta)$ is bounded (for $\theta \to \infty$).

c). Suppose that a local minimum of the distance $|\sigma(\theta) + j\omega(\theta) - k - jl|$ is obtained at the point θ^*. This can be obtained simply by a geometric inspection on our work chart. In order to avoid problems with respect to differentiability of the quantity $|\sigma(\theta) + j\omega(\theta) - k - jl|$, the square of this quantity, i.e. $|\sigma(\theta) + j\omega(\theta) - k - jl|^2$, is considered. Henceforth, we denote $f(\theta) = |\sigma(\theta) + j\omega(\theta) - k - jl|^2$. So θ^* is a (local) minimum of $f(\theta)$. A Taylor expansion of $f(\theta)$ yields

$$f(\theta) \cong f(\theta^*) + f''(\theta^*)(\theta - \theta^*)^2 / 2 \tag{4}$$

since $f'(\theta^*) = 0$. It can been shown that after simple algebraic manipulation

$$f(\theta) = a\left[1 - 2\zeta\left(\frac{\theta}{\theta^*}\right) + \zeta\left(\frac{\theta}{\theta^*}\right)^2\right] \quad \text{where} \quad a = \frac{f''(\theta^*)\theta^{*2}}{2} + f(\theta^*) \quad \text{and}$$

$$\zeta = \frac{f''(\theta^*)\theta^{*2} / 2}{f''(\theta^*)\theta^{*2} / 2 + f(\theta^*)}.$$ Obviously $20\log_{10}|\sigma(\theta) + j\omega(\theta) - k - jl| = 10\log_{10} f(\theta)$.

Thus $10\log_{10} f(\theta) = 10\log_{10} a + 10\log_{10}\left[1 - 2\zeta\left(\frac{\theta}{\theta^*}\right) + \zeta\left(\frac{\theta}{\theta^*}\right)^2\right]$, therefore a standardisation can be made, since the usual second-order Bode plot factor is locally obtained. See Example 3. The same is also true for the Bode phase plot.

d). In the case which a local maximum of the distance $|\sigma(\theta) + j\omega(\theta) - k - jl|$ is obtained at the θ^* point, a similar analysis can be followed. This maximum is also obtained simply by a geometric inspection on our work chart. The square of this distance is also considered: $f(\theta) = |\sigma(\theta) + j\omega(\theta) - k - jl|^2$. The same Taylor expansion of $f(\theta)$ is also true, since $f'(\theta^*) = 0$ too. The analysis follows the same steps as in the case of the local minimum. As a conclusion one can also say that in both (amplitude and phase) plots, a standardisation can be made based on ζ and θ.

3. EXAMPLES

Some numerical examples are now presented. Here, the exact plots were derived by using the *Mathematica* software package. However one can see that an important part of the information of these plots can also be extracted by using the rules discussed above.

Example 1. Plot the amplitude and phase Bode plot for the transfer function $H(s)=\dfrac{1}{s+3}$ **when** $s=\theta+j\theta$.

Amplitude Bode Plot (dB versus $log_{10}\,\theta$):

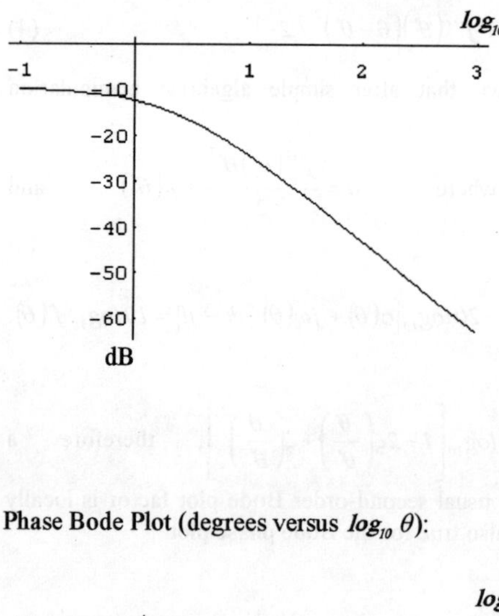

Phase Bode Plot (degrees versus $log_{10}\,\theta$):

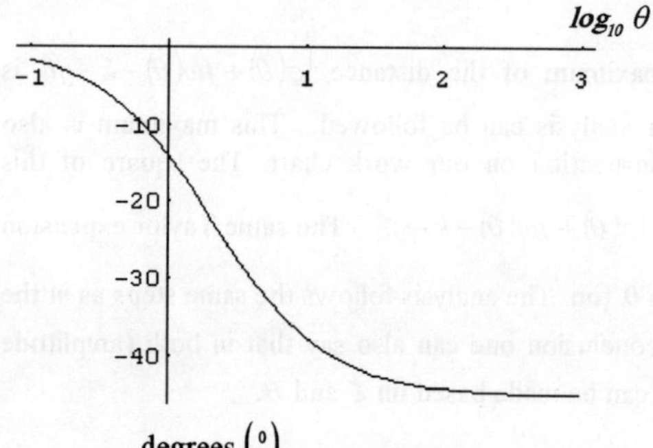

Example 2. Plot the amplitude and phase Bode plot for the transfer function

$H(s) = \dfrac{1}{s+3}$ when $s = Exp(3\theta) + jExp(5\theta)$.

Amplitude Bode Plot (dB versus $log_{10}\ \theta$):

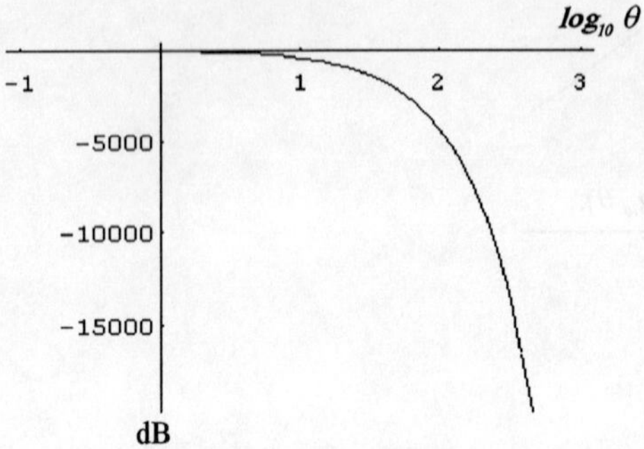

Phase Bode Plot (degrees versus $log_{10}\ \theta$):

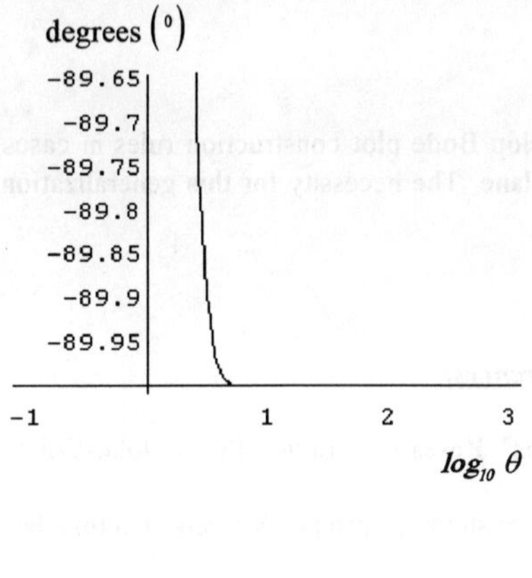

Example 3. Plot the amplitude and phase Bode plot for the transfer function

$H(s) = \dfrac{1}{s-3-2j}$ when $s = \theta + j\theta$

Amplitude Bode Plot (dB versus $log_{10}\,\theta$):

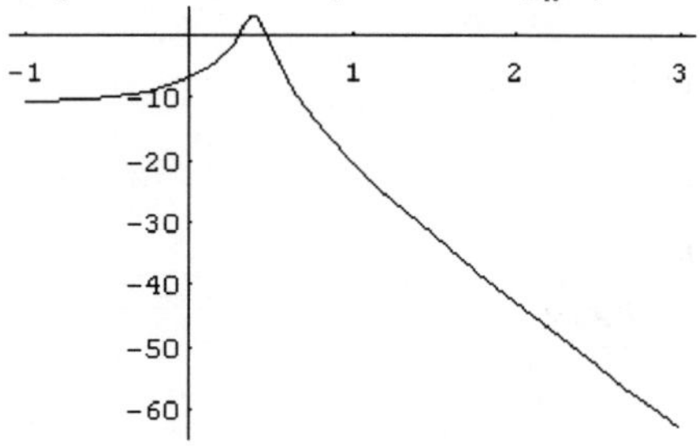

Phase Bode Plot (degrees versus $log_{10}\,\theta$):

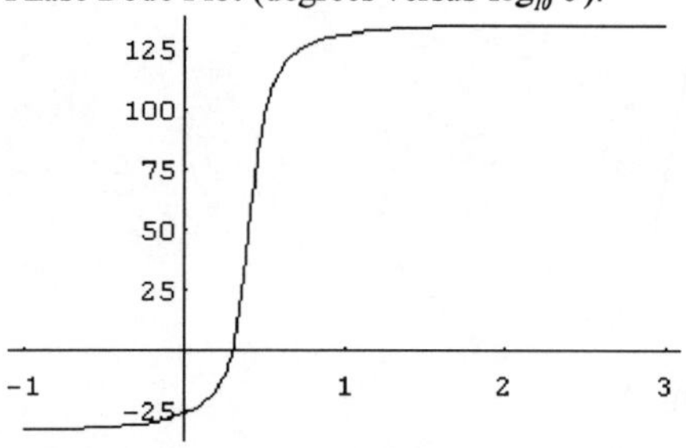

4. CONCLUSION:

In this note, an attempt is made to develop Bode plot construction rules in cases in which s lies on a smooth curve of the s-plane. The necessity for this generalization is presented. Some examples are included.

References:

[1] T.Kaczorek, "Linear Control Systems" Research Studies Press, John-Wiley & Sons, Vol.1 & 2.1993.

[2] T.Kaczorek, "Two-dimensional Linear Systems", Springer-Verlang, Lecture Notes in Control and Information Science, 1985.

[3] S.G.Tzafestas (editor), "Multidimensional Systems. Techniques and Applications", Marcel Dekker, Electrical Engineering and Electronics / 29, 1986.

[4] C.S.Lindquist, "Bode Plot Constructions for Real-valued Rational Functions", Journal of the Franklin Institute, Vol. 330, No.2, pp.315-331, 1993.